Meta-Ethics

The International Research Library of Philosophy
Series Editor: John Skorupski

Metaphysics and Epistemology

Identity *Harold Noonan*
Personal Identity *Harold Noonan*
Scepticism *Michael Williams*
Infinity *A.W. Moore*

Theories of Truth *Paul Horwich*
Knowledge and Justification, Vols I & II
Ernest Sosa
Space and Time *Jeremy Butterfield,*
Mark Hogarth, Gordon Belot

Future Volumes: Substance and Causation; Necessity; The Existence and Knowability of God; Faith, Reason and Religious Language.

The Philosophy of Mathematics and Science

The Ontology of Science *John Worrall*
Mathematical Objects and Mathematical Knowledge *Michael D. Resnik*
Theory, Evidence and Explanation *Peter Lipton*
Future Volumes: Proof and its Limits; Probability; The Philosophy of the Life Sciences; The Philosophy of History and the Social Sciences; Rational Choice.

The Philosophy of Logic, Language and Mind

Understanding and Sense, Vols I and II *Christopher Peacocke*
Metaphysics of Mind *Peter Smith*
Relativity in Logic *Stewart Shapiro*
Events *Achille C. Varzi, Roberto Casati*
Future Volumes: Truth and Consequence; Modality, Quantification, High-order Logic; Reference and Logical Form; The Nature of Meaning; Functionalism; Interpretation; Intentionality and Representation; Reason, Action and Free Will.

The Philosophy of Value

Consequentialism *Philip Pettit*
Punishment *Antony Duff*
Meta-ethics *Michael Smith*

Duty and Virtue *Onora O'Neill*
The Ethics of the Environment *Andrew Brennan*
Medical Ethics *Robin Downie*

Future Volumes: Aesthetics; The Foundations of the State; Justice; Liberty and Community.

Meta-Ethics

Edited by

Michael Smith
The Australian National University, Canberra

Dartmouth
Aldershot · Brookfield USA · Singapore · Sydney

Published by
Dartmouth Publishing Company Limited
Gower House
Croft Road
Aldershot
Hants GU11 3HR
England

Dartmouth Publishing Company
Old Post Road
Brookfield
Vermont 05036
USA

British Library Cataloguing in Publication Data
Meta-ethics. – (International Research
Library of Philosophy)
  I. Smith, Michael II. Series
  170

Library of Congress Cataloging-in-Publication Data
Meta-ethics / edited by Michael Smith.
        p. cm. — (The international research library of philosophy.
  The philosophy of value)
    Includes bibliographical references.
    ISBN 1-85521-502-0
    1. Ethics. I. Smith, Michael (Michael A.) II. Series:
  International research library of philosophy. Philosophy of value.
  BJ1031.M48 1995
  170′.42—dc20   95–5686
                                                                      CIP

ISBN 1 85521 502 0

Printed in Great Britain at the University Press, Cambridge

Contents

PART VIII   AN OVERVIEW OF META-ETHICS

Acknowledgements

The editor and publishers wish to thank the following for permission to use copyright material.

The Aristotelian Society for the essays: John McDowell (1978), 'Are Moral Requirements Hypothetical Imperatives?', *Proceedings of the Aristotelian Society*, pp. 13–29. Reprinted by courtesy of the Editor of the Aristotelian Society: © 1978. David Lewis (1989), 'Dispositional Theories of Value', *Proceedings of the Aristotelian Society*, pp. 113–37. Reprinted by courtesy of the Editor of the Aristotelian Society: © 1989. Mark Johnston (1989), 'Dispositional Theories of Value', *Proceedings of the Aristotelian Society*, pp. 139–74. Reprinted by courtesy of the Editor of the Aristotelian Society: © 1989.

The Australasian Association of Philosophy for the essay: Frank Jackson (1992), 'Critical Notice of S.L. Hurley *Natural Reasons: Personality and Polity*', *Australasian Journal of Philosophy*, **70**, pp. 475–88.

Blackwell Publishers for the essay: Bob Hale (1986), 'The Compleat Projectivist', *Philosophical Quarterly*, **36**, pp. 65–84.

Columbia University Press for the essays: John Rawls (1993), 'Kantian Constructivism in Moral Theory: Rational and Full Autonomy' and 'Construction and Objectivity', *Journal of Philosophy*, **LXXVII**, pp. 513–35 and pp. 554–72. Copyright © Columbia University 1993.

The Journal of Philosophy for the essays: Christine M. Korsgaard (1986), 'Skepticism about Practical Reason', *Journal of Philosophy*, **LXXXIII**, pp. 5–25; Norman Daniels (1979), 'Wide Reflective Equilibrium and Theory Acceptance in Ethics', *Journal of Philosophy*, **LXXVI**, pp. 256–82.

Midwest Studies in Philosophy Inc. for the essay: Geoffrey Sayre-McCord (1988), 'Moral Theory and Explanatory Impotence', *Midwest Studies in Philosophy*, **XII**, pp. 433–57. Copyright © 1988 by the University of Minnesota. Reprinted by permission of Midwest Studies in Philosophy Inc.

The Monist for the essay: Peter Singer (1974), 'Sidgwick and Reflective Equilibrium', *The Monist*, pp. 490–517. Copyright © 1974 The Monist. Reprinted by permission.

Oxford University Press for the essays: Simon Blackburn (1984), 'Evaluations, Projections, and Quasi-Realism', in *Spreading the Word*, pp. 181–202, 210–23. © Simon Blackburn 1984. Reprinted from *Spreading the Word* by Simon Blackburn (1984) by permission of Oxford University Press. James C. Klagge (1984), 'An Alleged Difficulty Concerning Moral Properties', *Mind*, **XCIII**, pp. 370–80.

The Philosophical Review for the essays: Philippa Foot (1972), 'Morality as a System of Hypothetical Imperatives', *Philosophical Review*, pp. 305–16 (in public domain); Gilbert Harman (1975), 'Moral Relativism Defended', *Philosophical Review*, pp. 3–22 (in public domain); Peter Railton (1986), 'Moral Realism', *Philosophical Review*, **XCV**, pp. 163–207. Copyright 1986 Cornell University. Reprinted by permission of the publisher and author. Stephen Darwall, Allan Gibbard and Peter Railton (1992), 'Toward *Fin de siècle* Ethics: Some Trends', *Philosophical Review*, **101**, pp. 115–89. Copyright 1992 Cornell University. Reprinted by permission of the publisher and authors.

Ridgeview Publishing Company for the essay: Simon Blackburn (1993), 'Circles, Finks, Smells and Biconditionals', in James E. Tomberlin (ed.), *Philosophical Perspectives, Language and Logic*, **7**, pp. 259–79. Reprinted by permission of Ridgeview Publishing Company.

The Southern Journal of Philosophy for the essays: David O. Brink (1986), 'Externalist Moral Realism', *Southern Journal of Philosophy*, **XXIV**, pp. 23–41; Gilbert Harman (1986), 'Moral Explanations of Natural Facts – Can Moral Claims be Tested Against Moral Reality?', *Southern Journal of Philosophy*, **XXIV**, pp. 57–68.

The University of Calgary Press for the essay: David Gauthier (1975), 'Reason and Maximization', *Canadian Journal of Philosophy*, **IV**, pp. 411–33.

The University of Kansas for the essay: Gilbert Harman (1986), 'Moral Agent and Impartial Spectator', *Lindley Lecture*, University of Kansas, pp. 1–15.

Every effort has been made to trace all the copyright holders, but if any have been inadvertently overlooked the publishers will be pleased to make the necessary arrangements at the first opportunity.

Series Preface

The International Research Library of Philosophy collects in book form a wide range of important and influential essays in philosophy, drawn predominantly from English-language journals. Each volume in the Library deals with a field of inquiry which has received significant attention in philosophy in the last 25 years, and is edited by a philosopher noted in that field.

No particular philosophical method or approach is favoured or excluded. The Library will constitute a representative sampling of the best work in contemporary English-language philosophy, providing researchers and scholars throughout the world with comprehensive coverage of currently important topics and approaches.

The Library is divided into four series of volumes which reflect the broad divisions of contemporary philosophical inquiry:

- Metaphysics and Epistemology
- The Philosophy of Mathematics and Science
- The Philosophy of Logic, Language and Mind
- The Philosophy of Value

I am most grateful to all the volume editors, who have unstintingly contributed scarce time and effort to this project. The authority and usefulness of the series rests firmly on their hard work and scholarly judgement. I must also express my thanks to John Irwin of the Dartmouth Publishing Company, from whom the idea of the Library originally came, and who brought it to fruition; and also to his colleagues in the Editorial Office, whose care and attention to detail are so vital in ensuring that the Library provides a handsome and reliable aid to philosophical inquirers.

John Skorupski
General Editor
University of St. Andrews
Scotland

Introduction

In everyday life we think and talk about morality all the time. This reflects not just the importance we attach to doing the right thing as opposed to the wrong, but also the extent to which questions about which acts are right and wrong are themselves controversial. Thus, for example, we teach our children to be honest because we think that they, like all of us, should be honest; but we are well aware of the fact that, on occasion, it would be better if people were dishonest instead. We resent friends who are disloyal because we think that friends shouldn't be disloyal to each other, but we realize all too well that there is a limit to the loyalty friends can legitimately demand. We praise those who give large amounts of money to charitable causes, but we know that no one is required to give all that they have to charity and that there is therefore a real question as to how much is enough.

Issues like these are not just the subject matter of thought and talk in everyday life, they are also the subject matter of normative ethics, that part of philosophy in which systematic theories detailing the different views that can be taken on issues like these are constructed and their relative merits debated. I mention this in part to make it clear what this book is not about: it is not about normative ethics, not about issues like those just mentioned. But I also mention it in part so that I can more easily explain what this book is about: meta-ethics, that part of philosophy in which we step back and ask questions about the claims we make when we engage in normative ethics. Let me explain this idea.

Consider the claim that we should all be honest. In meta-ethics we ask what the 'should' in this claim really means or signifies. Are there facts about what we should and shouldn't do, and if so, what sorts of facts are they? Can we argue that the claim that we should all be honest is true or false in the same way that we argue for the truth or falsehood of other factual claims; claims in science, for example? And if the meaning of the 'should' implies that claims about what we should and shouldn't do are not factual, then we might instead pursue a different line of questioning. If the point or function of claiming that we should all be honest is not to state what the facts are, then what is the point or function of making such claims? By what standard are we to judge whether such claims are to be accepted or rejected? If there is no fact of the matter, then are we free to accept or reject them as we please?

Though such meta-ethical questions are no doubt more abstract than normative ethical questions, they are also in a certain sense more urgent. For how could we decide whether to affirm or deny the claim that, say, we should all be honest, without first being in a position to say what the claim really means? My hope is that by reading through the essays in this collection readers will come to have a sense of what is involved in giving one answer rather than another to this question about the meaning of moral terms. More than that, I hope that readers will be able to decide for themselves where they stand.[1]

The papers collected together here have all been written over the last 20 years or so. This has been a time of profound interest and progress in meta-ethics, coinciding as it does with the decline of the influence of logical positivism on philosophy generally and on meta-ethics in particular, and the consequent rise in the influence of philosophy of mind and language. The volume divides into eight parts. The first seven deal with different questions that arise in the course of debates in meta-ethics. The eighth and final part contains a recent overview of meta-ethics in the 20th century (Chapter 22). It not only locates the questions dealt with here in a larger, even if still recent, historical context, but also has something useful to say about nearly all of the topics covered.

The book begins by asking whether moral claims purport to be about a matter of fact. It is here that we see the influence of the logical positivists, for they famously thought that moral claims had no factual content at all (see especially Ayer 1936). Their reason for thinking this is simple enough to state. According to the positivists, claims which purport to have factual content divide into two sorts. There are claims that are made true or false by the very meanings of the words used; that is, analytic truths. And there are claims that are made true or false by the way the world around us happens to be: that is, synthetic truths. In these terms, the positivists argued that claims like 'We should all be honest' are neither made true or false by the very meanings of the words used, and so are not analytic truths; nor are they made true or false by the way the world around us happens to be, and so are not synthetic truths either. They therefore concluded that such claims have no factual content at all, that we do not use moral language to express our beliefs about the way things are morally.

This led the positivists to speculate about the function of moral language in our lives. If we do not make moral claims in order to express our beliefs about the way things are morally, then why do we make such claims at all? The conclusion they came to was that we make moral claims in order to express our emotions – our feelings of approval and disapproval – and to get others to share in these emotions too. Their view was thus dubbed 'emotivism' or, more disparagingly, the 'Boo!-Hooray!' theory of ethics. For according to the emotivists, moral judgements lack factual content altogether and have emotive content instead, in much the same way that the exclamations 'Boo!' and 'Hooray!' lack factual content altogether while having emotive content instead. When someone says 'We should all be honest' what she is really saying is something much like 'Hooray for our all being honest!' Or so say the emotivists.

At this point it might be helpful to introduce some terminology. There are three basic issues on which we must take a stand when we answer meta-ethical questions: a semantic, a psychological and a metaphysical issue. The semantic issue concerns the linguistic function typically served by moral claims. Are these claims descriptions or do they belong to some other category of non-descriptive claim: exclamations, imperatives or whatever? The psychological issue concerns the nature of the state that is typically expressed by someone who makes moral claims. Are these states cognitive (that is beliefs) or non-cognitive (that is desires, where 'desire' is used to include approval, disapproval and the like)? Finally, the metaphysical issue concerns the nature of reality. Does reality include any moral facts or are there no moral facts at all? In terms of these three basic issues, emotivists are non-descriptivists rather than descriptivists, for they think that moral claims fall within the category of non-descriptive exclamations; they are non-cognitivists rather than cognitivists, for they think those who make moral claims express their desires rather than their beliefs; and they are irrealists rather than realists, for they deny that there are any moral facts.

Though, as I said, the global influence of logical positivism on philosophy has pretty much disappeared, emotivism retains its influence in meta-ethics. In this collection that influence is represented in Chapter 1 by Simon Blackburn's classic statement and defence of projectivism, his own modern variation on emotivism. However, putting to one side for a moment the more positive arguments Blackburn gives in support of this theory, it must be said that projectivism is not without its problems. Such problems plague any variation on the emotivist theme.

In the 1960s, P.T. Geach pointed out that the central emotivist idea that the function of moral language is to express the speaker's feelings of approval and disapproval will seem plausible only if we restrict our attention to a sub-class of occasions on which moral language is used: specifically, to those cases in which moral claims are *asserted* (Geach 1965). But, as he went on to remind us, there are other occasions on which moral language is used in *non-asserted* contexts – in the antecedents of conditionals, to give just one example – and it is altogether unclear how this could be so if the projectivist's explanation of moral language in asserted contexts were correct. For how are we to explain the behaviour of 'We should all be honest' in the conditional 'If we should all be honest then we shouldn't tell lies', if all we are told about the former is that it is an expression of an attitude of approval on behalf of the speaker, roughly equivalent to 'Hooray for honesty!'? For one thing, whereas the claim 'If we should all be honest then we shouldn't tell lies' is both perfectly grammatical and plausibly true, the claim 'If hooray for honesty! then boo for telling lies!' is not even grammatical, let alone true. Worse still, someone who accepts the conditional need have no such attitudes of approval. This objection is spelled out in some detail by Simon Blackburn.

Geach's objection is potentially very troubling for the projectivist. For it counters the contention that moral claims do not serve the linguistic function of describing by citing semantic evidence – the behaviour of moral claims in non-asserted contexts like conditionals – which seems to provide us with good reasons for supposing that moral claims are descriptions. Whether the reasons are compelling is a matter about which theorists disagree; in part this depends on the success of Blackburn's other independent arguments for projectivism.[2] But in any event, if Geach is right that moral claims are descriptions then, when we make moral claims, we must be expressing our beliefs that things are as we are describing them to be. The projectivist's distinctive psychological thesis, non-cognitivism, is left behind along with his distinctive semantic thesis, non-descriptivism. And if this is right, then the only question left to ask is the metaphysical one. Is the world really the way that moral claims describe it to be or is it not? Blackburn confronts this problem fairly and squarely. Bob Hale shows the limitations of Blackburn's reply in Chapter 2. Darwall, Gibbard and Railton consider the issue in Chapter 22 (pp. 528–36).

In the remaining parts of the collection it is pretty much taken for granted that, semantically, moral claims are descriptions and that, psychologically, they express our beliefs about the way things are morally. However the influence of emotivism, or projectivism, remains. For even those who reject projectivism agree that there are real obstacles in the way of a descriptivist, cognitivist, realist view of morality. These obstacles are well summed up in Blackburn's three arguments for projectivism. Indeed, they can be seen as giving structure to the issues that must be confronted by those who seek a descriptivist, cognitivist, realist construal of moral claims when they come to defend their own views.

One of these arguments is similar to the original argument given by the logical positivists, outlined above. It begins from the truism that if someone makes a particular moral judgement about a state of affairs with certain ordinary, everyday, non-moral features (or 'naturalistic' features as they are called) – suppose she judges a particular act of inflicting pain on a cat, simply for the sake of amusement, to be wrong – but refuses to make the same judgement about another act identical in all natural respects – another act of inflicting the same amount of pain on a similar cat for similar amusement-related reasons – then she thereby displays a lack of understanding of moral language. As the point is usually put, it is a conceptual truth that the moral supervenes on the natural; there can be no moral difference without a difference in naturalistic features.

The argument then proceeds by adding to this truism a second claim, argued for at great length by G.E. Moore (1903). This claim is that no matter how much naturalistic information we have about an act, we can never *deduce* a moral conclusion from that information. Suppose, for example, that someone inflicts pain on a cat simply for the sake of amusement. The claim 'It is wrong to inflict pain on a cat simply for the sake of amusement is wrong' is then, presumably, true. But even if it is, the claim is not true in virtue of the meanings of the words. It is a substantial moral truth, not an analytic truth, and no amount of extra information of a naturalistic kind about the act in question would turn it into an analytic truth either. That this is so is made plain – or so the argument goes – by the fact that any claim to the effect that an act with certain naturalistic features has some moral feature can coherently be denied. Thus, someone who says 'Inflicting pain on a cat simply for the sake of amusement is not wrong' is not contradicting himself. Even if he is saying something false, he does not betray a failure to understand the moral words he is using. His is a substantial moral failure, not a failure to grasp the meanings of words.

Blackburn thinks that this combination of claims – that the moral supervenes on the natural, but that no combination of natural facts entails any moral facts – is bad news for those who think that our moral judgements are expressions of our beliefs about the way things are morally. For he thinks that they cannot explain why this pair of claims should be true, while those who deny that our moral judgements express our beliefs can easily do so. I leave the details of the argument to Blackburn. Another slightly different and fuller presentation of Blackburn's argument (from Blackburn 1971) is summarized in the first section of the first essay in Part II.

In Chapters 3 and 4, James Klagge and Frank Jackson give quite different responses to this argument. Klagge argues that, contrary to Blackburn, we can deduce moral facts from natural facts, but he insists that it does not follow from this that moral claims can be analysed or defined in natural terms. Klagge's argument depends on the distinction between entailment claims that hold in virtue of the laws of logic and the meanings of words – entailment claims that are analytic – and entailment claims that do not hold in virtue of the laws of logic and the meanings of words – entailment claims that are synthetic. Jackson's response is quite different. He argues for the stronger claim that the supervenience of the moral on the natural shows that we can analyse or define moral claims in natural terms. He then attempts to show how this can be done, drawing on work by David Lewis on the definition of theoretical terms.

Another of the arguments Blackburn gives for projectivism begins from the truism that moral judgement is essentially connected with the will. If someone judges an act to be right then, absent weakness of will or some similar form of practical irrationality, she is motivated to act accordingly. But, Blackburn asks, how could this be so if moral judgements were expressions of the judge's beliefs? For what someone does depends on what she desires on the one hand, and her beliefs about how to get what she desires on the other. So if moral judgements were expressions of the judge's beliefs, then whether or not she is motivated to act accordingly would have to depend on whether or not she happens to have a desire to act in the way she judges to be right. This would in turn make the connection between moral judgement and the will wholly contingent, dependent on the presence of a desire that the judge may or may not have. The only way we can preserve the essential connection between moral judgement and the will, Blackburn tells us, is by seeing the judgement as itself the expression of the desire that motivates the agent, or perhaps as an expression of a complicated disposition to have such a desire.

This argument is taken up in Part III. Philippa Foot and David Brink (Chapters 5 and 8) both argue against the claim that there is an essential connection between moral judgement and the will. In their view, whether or not someone who judges an act to be right is motivated accordingly does indeed depend on whether or not she happens to have a desire to do what she judges right. An agent who acknowledges moral requirements may quite rationally opt out of morality and have no desire at all to act in accordance with moral requirements, much as someone may acknowledge that she is required by etiquette to act in all sorts of ways, while having no desire at all to act in accordance with the requirements of etiquette.

The authors of the remaining papers in Part III all agree that there is an essential connection between moral judgement and the will, but deny that conceding this essential connection gives us reason to favour projectivism. However there are some quite striking differences in the views these authors take about the relationship between morality and reasons for action.

Blackburn's argument is premised on assumption that (a) is true:

(a) If an agent judges that it is right that she ϕs then, absent some form of practical irrationality, she is motivated to ϕ.

But equally, it is premised on the assumption that (a) is not true because (b) is true:

(b) An agent's believing that it is right that she ϕs *is identical with* her desiring to ϕ.

Indeed, it is premised on the assumption that (b) is false. This emerges in his claim that, if moral judgements were expressions of beliefs, then it would have to be a contingent matter of fact whether or not the judge happened to have a corresponding desire. For there would be nothing contingent about the presence of the desire if moral beliefs were themselves identical with desires. This assumption is therefore crucial to Blackburn's argument. For if belief and desire were necessarily connected in the manner of (b), then there could hardly be an argument from (a) to the effect that moral claims are not descriptive, that they express our desires rather than our beliefs.

More positively, then, what Blackburn assumes is that belief and desire are *distinct existences*; that for any belief and desire pair, we can always imagine an agent who has the belief, but who lacks the desire. This is why he assumes that if a moral judgement were the expression of a belief, we could always imagine an agent having that belief while lacking a desire to act accordingly. The assumption that belief and desire are distinct existences is certainly widespread and attractive. It is shared by the authors of virtually all of the other papers in the collection. But it is precisely this assumption that John McDowell challenges in Chapter 6.

Blackburn's argument from (a) to the claim that moral claims are not descriptive is also premised on the assumption that (a) is not true because (c) is true:

(c) If it is right that an agent ϕs then it is rationally required that she ϕs.

Indeed, the argument must once again be premised on the assumption that (c) is false. For if (a) were true because (c) were true, then we would have a quite straightforward way of representing the descriptive content of a moral claim. The claim that an act is right would be equivalent to the claim that it is rationally required for people to act in that way.[3] More-over note that (c) might be true while (b) is false. An agent's belief that she is rationally required to ϕ may be a 'distinct existence' from her desiring to ϕ even though, if she has the belief, she would have to exhibit some form of practical irrationality if she did not have the desire. Again, the assumption that (c) is false is widespread. Yet it is precisely this assumption – that (c) is false – that Christine Korsgaard questions in Chapter 9. The assumption is also explicitly discussed in the preceding contributions by Foot, Harman and Brink, and by Darwall, Gibbard and Railton in Chapter 22 (see especially pp. 515–21, 558–64).

The connection between morality and our reasons for action is once again at issue in Part IV. If we assume that there is a connection between moral requirements and requirements of rationality or reason – that is, if we assume that something like (c) is true – then the question arises whether we can give a more precise content to this idea. One standard way of doing so has been by thinking of moral facts as facts about the ways in which people would agree to behave in some hypothetical situation of choice, a hypothetical situation in which people are constrained to choose the reasonable or rational course of action. David Gauthier in Chapter 10 and John Rawls in Chapters 11 and 12 offer two quite different interpretations of this idea. This difference between their approaches is commented on by Darwall, Gibbard and Railton in Chapter 22 (pp. 515–28). Gilbert Harman gives a rather different inter-pretation of the idea in Chapter 7.

The essays in Part V each ask whether the connection between moral judgement and the will can be turned to the advantage of those who favour a descriptivist, cognitivist, realist view of morality. For whereas the projectivist thinks that the connection supports the idea that a moral judgement is an expression of the judge's desires, the papers in this part ask whether we mightn't suppose instead that her judgement is, in some sense, an expression of the judge's beliefs about her own desires. In Chapters 13 and 14, Harman and Lewis discuss sophisticated versions of this idea. Johnston criticizes Lewis, but goes on to offer an even more sophisticated variation on the theme. In Chapter 16, Simon Blackburn explains why he thinks no variation on the theme will work. He tells us why we should prefer instead the projectivist's view that our moral judgements are expressions of our desires, or complicated dispositions to have desires, not expressions of our beliefs about our desires. Darwall, Gibbard and Railton comment on the issue in Chapter 22 (pp. 536–48).

Blackburn's simplest argument for the claim that moral judgements are not descriptions of the way things are morally is that, if they were, then our beliefs about the moral features possessed by acts would have to be capable of explanation by reference to those moral features. Suppose, for example, that I come to believe that a particular agent's act of inflicting pain on a cat simply for the sake of his own amusement is wrong. If his act really had the moral feature of being wrong then, Blackburn argues, it would have to be possible to explain my belief that his act is wrong by reference to the fact that his act actually has the feature of being wrong. But, he urges, all such explanations are bogus. There is no room for the wrongness of an agent's act in an explanation of my coming to judge that his act is wrong. The best explanation is the two-stage projectivist one. First, I acquire the belief that the act has the natural features it has in virtue of which I judge it to be wrong: that is, I acquire the belief that, by acting, the agent causes a cat to suffer pain merely for his own amusement. And then, second, I express my feelings of disapproval towards such acts by making the judgement that the act is wrong.

The claim that there are no distinctive moral explanations is discussed in the essays by Peter Railton, Gilbert Harman and Geoffrey Sayre-McCord in Part VI (Chapters 17 to 19). Railton argues for the strongest thesis. In his view we identify moral features in part by their capacity to explain certain sorts of social phenomena. Harman disagrees. Sayre-McCord shows the relevance to this debate of the important distinction between explanation and justification.

Part VII takes up a question that has been in the background in nearly every other part. How do we come by moral knowledge? The standard answer is that we acquire moral knowledge via a procedure of finding a reflective equilibrium between our moral judgements about particular cases and our general principles. This procedure, which was first described in great detail by John Rawls (1951), is sketched and endorsed in many of the essays in the collection. But not everyone thinks that the reflective equilibrium procedure is a plausible characterization of how we come by moral knowledge. Peter Singer explains in Chapter 20 why he finds the procedure a misdescription. Norman Daniels defends reflective equilibrium, *inter alia* against Singer's attack, and in the process makes the idea more precise (Chapter 21).

One idea very influential in the meta-ethics literature over the last 20 years has not been highlighted thus far. Let me close by mentioning it and explaining where those interested in the issue can find it discussed in this collection.

At the very beginning of his influential 1977 book *Ethics: Inventing Right and Wrong*, John Mackie took a stand against the projectivists. He argued that, semantically, moral claims are descriptions of the way things are morally and that, psychologically, they are therefore expressions of our beliefs. However Mackie also took a stand against the realists, for he was convinced that when we give a clear statement of the descriptive content of these claims, what we discover is that they describe nothing in reality. In his view, what we believe when we believe that an act is right is that the act in question has an objectively prescriptive feature, a feature whose recognition is capable of motivating us to act independently of our contingent desires and interests. But, says Mackie, there are no such features. We do what we do simply because we happen to desire to do so, not because the acts we perform demand or elicit our performance of them. Mackie is thus led to combine his descriptivism and cognitivism with irrealism rather than realism. This led him to endorse an error theory in meta-ethics, the view that moral practice is based on an error of presupposition – that acts have objectively prescriptive features when in fact they do not.

Though, as I said, the error theory is not placed on centre-stage in this collection, it is explicitly discussed by David Lewis in Chapter 14. Readers will get a good sense of what is at stake in deciding whether to combine descriptivism and cognitivism with realism or irrealism by reading Lewis' paper. In different ways the error theory is also touched on by Brink and in the essays by Foot, and McDowell (Chapters 8, 5 and 6). Foot, in particular, shares Mackie's feeling that there is something bogus about morality – that morality may seem to be founded on a false presupposition about the inescapability of moral motivation – but, unlike Mackie, she tries to rescue our commitment to morality from these destructive thoughts. And of course, in contrast to Mackie, John McDowell in effect argues that the presupposition that both Mackie and Foot think false is in fact true. Reality does indeed include acts with the feature of being objectively prescriptive. Or so he argues.

Debate in meta-ethics will no doubt go on. But those who read through this collection will, I hope, come away with the feeling that real progress has been made. The essays reprinted here not only bring into sharper focus the issues on which we have to take a stand in forming our meta-ethical views, but they also help us to decide what our own views should be by stating the alternatives in such stark relief.[4]

Notes

1. For a statement of my own views, see Smith 1994b.
2. Some theorists of truth have recently argued that, if a sentence figures in certain grammatical constructions – conditional contexts, propositional attitude contexts, and the like – then it follows that the sentence is apt for assessment in terms of truth and falsehood; that to deny this is to have a false view of the nature of truth. According to Wright (1992) and Horwich (1993), for example, Geach's observations are tantamount to a disproof of the emotivist's contention that moral claims are not apt for assessment in terms of truth and falsehood. But this is surely wrong. A necessary condition for a sentence to be assessable in terms of truth and falsehood – putting to one side sentences that are too long to be entertained, obvious contradictions and the like – is presumably that we can use the sentence to express our beliefs. And yet Blackburn's more positive arguments for projectivism purport to show that *there can be no moral beliefs*; thus, whatever their linguistic potential, moral sentences do not meet a necessary condition for their being apt for appraisal in terms of truth and falsehood. This issue is discussed in Smith 1994a and in Jackson, Oppy and Smith 1994.
3. I here assume that we are not going to be sceptical about the existence of facts about what people are rationally required to do; but see Gibbard 1990.
4. I would like to thank John Skorupski, Frank Jackson and Philip Pettit for their help and advice. Thanks also to the publishers of the Dartmouth International Research Library of Philosophy Series for allowing me to include Chapter 6 of Simon Blackburn's *Spreading the Word* in this collection, thereby making an exception to their policy of including only journal and periodical articles. Blackburn's chapter has become the standard reference point for the idea that moral claims do not purport to be descriptions of the way things are morally. More than that, however, as is I hope clear from the Introduction, it also has the great virtue of spelling out nearly all of the problems that have to be addressed by those who think that moral claims are descriptions of such a moral reality.

References

Ayer, A.J. (1936), *Language, Truth and Logic*, Gollancz.
Blackburn, Simon (1971), 'Moral Realism' in John Casey (ed.), *Morality and Moral Reasoning*, Methuen, 101–24.
Geach, P.T. (1965), 'Assertion', *Philosophical Review*, **74**, 449–65.
Gibbard, Alan (1990), *Wise Choices, Apt Feelings*, Oxford University Press.
Horwich, Paul (1993), 'Gibbard's Theory of Norms', *Philosophy and Public Affairs*, **22**, 67–78.
Jackson, Frank, Graham Oppy and Michael Smith (1994), 'Minimalism and Truth-Aptness', *Mind*, **103**, 287–302.

Mackie, John (1977), *Ethics: Inventing Right and Wrong*, Penguin.

Moore, G.E. (1903), *Principia Ethica*, Cambridge University Press.

Rawls, John (1951), 'Outline of a Decision Procedure for Ethics', *Philosophical Review*, **60**, 177–97.

Smith, Michael (1994a), 'Why Expressivists about Value Should Love Minimalism about Truth', *Analysis*, **54**, 1–12.

Smith, Michael (1994b), *The Moral Problem*, Blackwell.

Wright, Crispin (1992), *Truth and Objectivity*, Harvard University Press.

Part I
Are the Moral Judgements
We Make Judgements About
a Matter of Fact?

[1]

CHAPTER 6

Evaluations, Projections, and Quasi-Realism

What then is truth? A movable host of metaphors, metonymies, anthropomorphisms: in short, a sum of human relations which have been poetically and rhetorically tempered by, transferred, and embellished, and which, after long usage, seem to be fixed, canonical and binding. Truths are illusions which we have forgotten are illusions; they are metaphors that have become worn out and have been drained of sensuous force, coins which have lost their embossings, and are now considered as metal and no longer as coins.

Nietzsche, 'On Truth and Lies in a Normal Sense'.

1. *More Detailed Motivations*

A projective account of some commitments puts them at the top of the following picture:

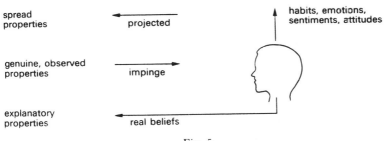

Fig. 5

This is contrasted with the two other places for them. In the middle one, the features talked about (e.g. the possession of value by things, or the existence of rights, duties, and so on) are themselves part of the genesis of our beliefs. It would be *because* values, etc. are distributed in some way around the world, and because we are capable of reacting to them, of knowing them by some acquaintance or intuition, that we moralize as we do. In the other lower place there would be no cognizance of these features, nothing to be compared with a more ordinary mode of perception. All the information about the world which we take in would be describable in natural terms. But just as we can use that information to construct theories involving higher-order concepts, such as those of physics, so we can use it to construct the moral concepts. But when we have done so, we have a further description of the world, and are regarding it as containing further, moral, states of affairs.

To ensure that a projective theory starts at reasonable odds, I shall briefly mention three motives for preferring it to either of its rivals. The first of these is economy. The projective theory intends to ask no more from the world than what we know is there – the ordinary features of things on the basis of which we make decisions about them, like or dislike them, fear them and avoid them, desire them and seek them out. It asks no more than this: a natural world, and patterns of reaction to it. By contrast a theory assimilating moral understanding to perception demands more of the world. Perception is a causal process: we perceive those features of things which are responsible for our experiences. It is uneconomical to postulate both a feature of things (the values they have) *and* a mechanism (intuition) by which we are happily aware of it.

The second argument for preferring projective theories is metaphysical. It concerns the relation between the values we find in the world, and the other properties of things of value.[1] The argument arises from the common claim in philosophy that one kind of state *supervenes* upon another. The idea is that some properties, the A-properties, are consequential upon some other base properties, the underlying B-properties. This claim is supposed to mean that in some sense of *necessary*, it is necessary that if an A-truth changes, some B-truth changes; or if two situations are identical in their B-properties they are identical

---

[1] The argument of the next few pages is quite hard, and self-contained. It can quite easily be skipped, especially if the reader already sympathizes with projectivism. The main thread is resumed in 6.2.

in their A-properties. A-properties *cannot* (in this same sense) vary regardless of B-properties. Now there are very different strengths of 'necessity' and of 'cannot'. Most people would say that colour properties cannot vary independently of underlying physical properties, such as those of surfaces, the kind of wavelength of light reflected, and so on. This is a physical, empirical, claim. It is easy to *imagine* finding that the colours of things have started to vary independently of their physical properties, so that two things which are reflecting the same wavelengths nevertheless have different colours. No doubt scientists would either disbelieve this, or start to search for other, more obscure physical differences which cause this variation. But there is no conceptual inevitability that they succeed: the supervenience of colour on other (primary) properties is a matter of physical rather than conceptual necessity. By contrast moral properties seem to have to supervene upon natural ones in some much stronger sense. It seems conceptually impossible to suppose that if two things are identical in every other respect, one is better than the other. Such a difference *could* only arise if there were other differences between them. So suppose that we have a complete, base description of a thing, B*, telling us everything that *could* be relevant to determining its A-state. The supervenience claim is that necessarily *if* there is a thing which is B* and A, then anything else which is like it in being B* is like it in being A as well. There is no possible world in which one thing is B* and A, but other things are B* and not A (in this it is important to remember that B* is some complete specification of the B-states of a thing, whereas A is some particular A-property – being good to a certain degree, being of a certain colour, or whatever). Call this *B*/A supervenience*.

This property now needs contrasting with a stronger property, that necessarily, if a thing is B*, it is A. This links B* to A *rigidly* – in all possible worlds, if a thing is B*, it is A. It is a stronger property, for B*/A supervenience does not rule out possible worlds in which there are things which are B* but not A. It merely rules out any in which there are both things which are B* and A, and things which are B* and not A. Thus even if the supervenience claim holds, it does not enable you to infer that a thing is A from the fact that it is B*. It just means that once you know of something which is A and has this underlying state, you can be sure that anything else just like it is A as well. Call the stronger property *B*/A necessity*.[2]

The point of introducing these two properties is that philosophers sometimes find it plausible to claim B*/A supervenience without going so far as B*/A necessity. In particular in the moral case it seems conceptually or logically necessary that if two things share a total basis of natural properties, then they have the same moral qualities. But it does not seem a matter of conceptual or logical necessity that any given total natural state of a thing gives it some particular moral quality. For to tell which moral quality results from a given natural state means using standards whose correctness cannot be shown by conceptual means alone. It means moralizing, and bad people moralize badly, but need not be confused.

How does the argument proceed that this point favours projectivism? The argument is best thought of by imagining possible worlds – complete states of affairs corresponding to the various possibilities involved. If a truth is necessary, then it obtains in all possible worlds. Otherwise there is one in which it does not. A contingent proposition, which merely happens to be so, is true in some possible worlds and not in others. Then the structure is that possible worlds divide into *two* sorts. There are those in which *something* B* is A, and in those everything else B* is A also. But there are those in which things are B* *without* being A. Now this distribution of possible worlds needs explanation. For at first sight there should be a further mixed kind allowed – in which some things are B* and A; but in which some things are like those whose possibility is already allowed – B* and not A. So we need to explain the *ban on mixed worlds*, and the argument goes that anti-realism does this better than realism.

Consider a different example from the moral one. It has been influentially argued that there can be no 'psychophysical laws', meaning no necessity that a given physical state B* produces a given mental state, A'. The reason why there cannot be such laws is, in Davidson's view, that mental predicates, expressing

---

[2] The contrast is neatly expressed formally:

$N(\ (\exists x)\ (B^*x\ \&\ A'x) \rightarrow (\forall y)\ (B^*y \rightarrow A'y)\ )$, as opposed to:
$N(\forall y)(B^*y \rightarrow A'y)$,

the latter being the necessitation of the consequent, when the former only necessitates the conditional.

as they do a different set of concepts from the physical, answer to different constraints, so that we would never be in a position to insist upon the existence of a given mental state, on the basis of a given physical state.[3] We can leave on one side whether this argument is forceful (at first sight the same thought rules out e.g. laws connecting wave length of light and colour, or forces and motions, or indeed any interesting laws). But Davidson also believes in the supervenience of the mental upon the physical. So we have the same structure: we should allow the possibility of B* which might be, for instance, a given pattern of neurones or brain stuff without A', but given that *one* B* thing is A', the others in any particular world *must* also be. It is as though God had it in his power to make a given physical state underlie one mental state – e.g. thinking of my aunt – or underlie another – e.g. thinking of my dog. But once he had decided to let it underlie the one state in *me*, say, then he has to do the same for *you*. Whereas at first sight if we allow that he could associate the states as he likes, we would expect him to be able to associate the one state with B* in me, and the other one in you, breaking supervenience. So why is God thus constrained? The whole point of talking of possible worlds is to allow as many as we can conceive of. Equally, if it could be true, as far as conceptual constraints go, that Fred has some set of dispositions and is vicious, but also that he has the very same set, and differs in no other way except that he is not vicious, then why could it not also be true that Fred has the set, and is vicious, whereas Bill has the set and is not? The matter is especially obvious with physical necessity. If there is no necessity that a given wavelength underlies a given colour, how could there be a necessity that if it does in one case, then it does in all the others? Why the ban on mixed possible worlds?

These questions are especially hard for a realist. For he has the conception of an actual A-state of affairs, which might or might not distribute in a particular way across the B-states. Supervenience then becomes a mysterious fact, and one which he will have no explanation of (or no right to rely upon). It would be as though some people are B* and thinking of dogs, and others are B* and thinking of their aunts, but there is a

---

[3] Davidson, 'Mental Events'.

ban on them travelling to inhabit the same place: completely
inexplicable. From the anti-realist point of view things are a
little easier. When we announce the A-commitments we are
projecting, we are neither reacting to a given distribution of
A-properties, nor speculating about one. So the supervenience
can be explained in terms of the constraints upon proper projection. Our purpose in projecting value predicates may demand
that we respect supervenience. If we allowed ourselves a system
(shmoralizing) which was like ordinary evaluative practice, but
subject to no such constraint, then it would allow us to treat
naturally identical cases in morally different ways. This could
be good shmoralizing. But that would unfit shmoralizing from
being any kind of guide to practical decision-making (a thing
could be properly deemed shbetter than another although it
shared with it all the features relevant to choice or desirability).

Supervenience claims are very popular in philosophy, because
they promise some of the advantages of reduction without the
cost of defending B*/A necessity claims. But the promise is
slightly hollow: supervenience is usually quite uninteresting by
itself. What is interesting is the reason why it holds. Thus in the
philosophy of mind, although many writers claim the
supervenience of the mental upon the physical, not so many are
clear about why we ought to accept it, nor about the strength of
the necessity involved. From a Cartesian perspective, according
to which mental properties are logically quite distinct from any
physical ones, and as it were are only accidentally found in
conjunction with any given physical set-up (brains rather than
wood fibres) there would be no right to rely upon supervenience. So when we rely upon it we are in effect promising an
alternative to the Cartesian picture of mind and body. But the
supervenience claim does not by itself fulfil that promise, and
the pair of properties, supervenience and lack of necessity are
awkward bedfellows in the theory of mind just as they are in
moral theory. If there is no necessity that a given physical
set-up generates a particular mental property, it is hard to force
the ban on mixed worlds, in which it sometimes does and
sometimes does not. And it is not nearly so plausible to take the
anti-realist way out, thinking of our attribution of mental states
to one another in other terms than descriptions (although
Wittgenstein was tempted to an expressive theory, at some

points in the later philosophy).[4] All in all, then, philosophers of mind who want to oppose Cartesianism are better off trying to defend the stronger necessity claims. Merely relying upon supervenience, and disowning the stronger thesis, seems likely to leave an unstable position.

It should also be noticed that the relation between theoretical facts in a science, and the empirical facts which afford evidence for them, is not like that in the moral case. Suppose we imagine a total phenomenal description of a world, giving an answer to every possible question about what is observed or would be observed under any circumstances. Suppose that this B* description does not as a matter of conceptual necessity entail the truth of any particular scientific theory, A: it merely affords evidence for it, whilst leaving open the possibility of other and perhaps conflicting theoretical truths, A'. Just because of this there is no conceptual pressure to suppose that wherever we have B* we must have the same truth A. Nor is there any reason to suppose that if one part of a world is phenomenally just like another, there must be the same underlying A-truths. At least for a scientific realist, the real underlying A-facts, the theoretical states of affairs which explain the appearances, might be different in one case from another. It would be only considerations of simplicity and economy which would make it natural to *hope* that they are the same from case to case. Whereas in the moral case it is not just simpler and more economical to believe that naturally identical states of affairs compel the same moral description. It is absurd, contradictory, a failure to understand the nature of evaluation, to believe otherwise. This damages the approach to moral language according to which we infer the existence of moral states of affairs in the same kind of way that we infer the nature of scientific truths.

This argument for a projective moral theory is in effect a development of the simple thought that moral properties must be given an intelligible connection to the natural ones upon which they somehow depend. It generates a metaphysical motive for projectivism. The third and last motive I shall mention comes from the philosophy of action. Evaluative commitments are being contrasted with other, truth-conditional judgements or beliefs. This contrast means that to have a commitment of

---

[4] *Philosophical Investigations*, p. 178.

this sort is to hold an attitude, not a belief, and that in
turn should have implications for the explanation of people's
behaviour. The standard model of explanation of why someone
does something attributes both a belief and a desire to the
agent. The belief that a bottle contains poison does not by itself
explain why someone avoids it; the belief coupled with the
normal desire to avoid harm does. So if moral commitments
express *attitudes*, they should function to supplement *beliefs* in
the explanation of action. If they express *beliefs*, they should
themselves need supplementing by mention of *desires* in a fully
displayed explanation of action (fully displayed because, of
course, we often do not bother to mention obvious desires and
beliefs, which people will presume each other to have). It can
then be urged that moral commitments fall in the right way of
the active, desire, side of this fence. If someone feels moral
distaste or indignation at cruelty to animals, he only needs to
believe that he is faced with a case of it to act or be pulled
towards acting. It seems to be a conceptual truth that to regard
something as good is to feel a pull towards promoting or choosing it, or towards wanting other people to feel the pull towards
promoting or choosing it. Whereas if moral commitments
express beliefs that certain truth-conditions are met, then they
could apparently co-exist with any kind of attitude to things
meeting the truth-conditions. Someone might be indifferent to
things which he regards as good, or actively hostile to them.
Being moral would need two stages: firstly discerning whether
the truth-conditions are met, and secondly forming desires to
which those truth-conditions matter. But if that were the right
account, morality could be short-circuited. You could hope to
obtain the *same* actual dispositions, the same choices for or
against things possessing given natural properties, the same
behaviour, the same indignations and passions, by reacting to
the natural features of things. It is an unnecessary loop to use
those *natural* features to determine a belief in further *moral*
features, and then to hope for a particular attitude to the
revealed moral features.

Unfortunately this argument is not quite as compelling as it
looks. The relationship between evaluative commitment and
action is subtle. For there is undoubtedly an attitude of "not
caring about morality". As Philippa Foot has persistently

argued, there is no straight inference from moral commitment to desire. People often care more about etiquette, or reputations, or selfish advantage, than they do about morality. So the moral attitude, if it is an attitude, cannot be distinguished from belief through an inevitable connection with choice and action. Its influence on these things is indirect. But in turn this does not completely block this third argument. For other attitudes also have indirect and variable influences on action. If I find it wryly amusing that a colleague is drunk I may channel my sentiment into a variety of actions or inaction. But finding it amusing is surely a matter of having an attitude rather than a further belief, true or false, about my colleague.

To establish projectivism would need a close exploration of the nature of the attitude which is spread on the world. This involves locating what it is about an attitude which makes it a moral one, whether we would be better off without having such attitudes, what their best replacement might be, and so on. It would involve discussing whether moralizing is a relatively parochial habit of people with particular cultural and theological traditions, or whether any society whatsoever can be regarded as holding distinctively moral attitudes. But the philosophy of language can remain relatively quiet about these juicy issues. Our concern is whether one range of argument, starting from the theory of the meaning of moral remarks, blocks projectivism. The issue is whether quasi-realism (see 5.6 above) is successful in explaining why we can permit ourselves the linguistic expressions, and the thoughts they enable us to express, if projectivism is true. For my part I would say that the success of quasi-realism, as I shall try to present it, leaves a projective account of morality far the most attractive, on grounds of economy, of metaphysics, and of the theory of desire and action. It is, in fact, the only progressive research programme in moral philosophy. But why does the philosophy of language provide any kind of obstacle to it?

2. *Frege's Argument*

In a very influential article, P. T. Geach used a point of Frege's to block expressive theories.[5] The "Frege point" is very simple.

[5] 'Assertion', *Philosophical Review* (1964).

Sentences containing given predicates may occur in utterances by which we are claiming the predicates to apply, as when I call something good, true, probable, a cause of something else, and so on. But such sentences may also occur unasserted, inside the context provided by other words, making up larger sentences. I may assert: 'It is wrong to tell lies.' But I may also assert: 'If *it is wrong to tell lies*, then it is wrong to get your little brother to tell lies.' In this latter occurrence the italicized sentence is not asserted. It is the antecedent of a conditional – in other words, it is put forward to introduce an hypothesis or supposition. The Frege point is that nevertheless the sentence *means the same* on each occurrence. The proof of this is simple and decisive. The two sentences mate together to make up the premises of a valid argument:

> It is wrong to tell lies.
> If it is wrong to tell lies, it is wrong to get your little
>   brother to tell lies.
>
> *So*   It is wrong to get your little brother to tell lies.

This is a valid argument, illustrating the general form: *P*; if *P* then *Q*; *so Q*. But the argument is only of this form because the sentence 'It is wrong to tell lies' means the same on each occurrence. If it did not there would be a fallacy of equivocation, as in: 'He is working at the bank; if he is working at the bank he must have his feet in the river; *so* he must have his feet in the river.' Here the second premise is true only if 'bank' is taken in a different sense from that in which, we might imagine, it makes the first premise true, and if so the argument does not illustrate the valid form. The question now is: how does an expressive theory explain the identity of meaning? For anyone asserting the second, hypothetical premise is *not* expressing an attitude of condemnation towards telling lies. He commits himself to no attitude towards it at all. He just says: 'If telling lies is wrong . . .' without offering any indication of whether he thinks it is. Let is call contexts in which a sentence occurs like this, an *unasserted* context. Then the question is whether expressive theories can cope with unasserted contexts in such a way as to allow sentences the same meaning within them, as they have when they are asserted.

It is a nice sharp problem. It might seem to provide a swift refutation of expressive theories. In unasserted contexts no attitude, etc. is evinced when the sentence is uttered; the meaning is the same as in direct contexts when such an attitude is evinced; therefore this (variable) feature does not give the (constant) meaning. But before quasi-realism surrenders it needs to see whether expressive theories can give any account at all of these contexts.

There are in fact two distinct aspects to this problem. Firstly, can we explain what we are up to when we make these remarks? Unasserted contexts show us treating moral predicates like others, *as though* by their means we can introduce objects of doubt, belief, knowledge, things which can be supposed, queried, pondered. Can the projectivist say why we do this?

Here he faces two questions. Consider the fact that we can conjoin evaluations and ordinary expressions of belief: 'It is wrong to tell lies and your mother is going to be annoyed'. Now it is surely not surprising that we might link together two commitments, even if one expresses an attitude, and the other a belief. The one sentence conjoins the two disparate commitments, and since we often want to communicate that we have both, it is hardly surprising that we have a way of doing it. That gives us an idea of *what we are up to* in offering the conjunction. But it does not fully answer the second question: why do we have this *particular* sentence to serve that purpose. For we might want to say other things about 'and', which make it difficult to see why it is serving this function. For instance, we might explain the semantic function of 'and' like this: it stands between two sentences to make one large sentence out of them; the large sentence is true if and only if each smaller one is true. Otherwise it is false. Now this little semantic theory fits badly, initially at any rate, with the occurrence of the evaluation as a conjunct. For suppose, according to the expressive theory, the evaluation is not susceptible of truth or falsity. Then it should not mingle with an operator which needs truths and falsities to work on. But there are ways of easing around this obstacle. One is to expand the way we think of 'and'. We have to do this anyway, for it can link utterances when they certainly do not express beliefs which are genuinely susceptible of truth-value – e.g. commands: 'hump that barge and tote that bale.' We would instead say something like this: 'and' links commitments to give an overall commitment which is accepted only if each component is accepted. The notion of a commitment is then capacious enough to include both ordinary beliefs, and these other attitudes, habits, and prescriptions.

So to tackle Frege's problem the first thing we need is a view of what we are up to in putting commitments into conditionals. Working out their implications, naturally. But how can attitudes as opposed to beliefs have implications? At this point we must turn again to the projective picture. A moral *sensibility*, on that picture, is defined by a function from *input* of belief to *output* of attitude.[6] Now not all such sensibilities are admirable. Some are coarse, insensitive, some are plain horrendous, some are conservative and inflexible, others fickle and unreliable; some are too quick to form strict and passionately held attitudes, some too sluggish to care about anything. But it is extremely important to us to rank sensibilities, and to endorse some and to reject others. For one of the main features affecting the desirability of the world we live in is the way other people behave, and the way other people behave is largely a function of their sensibility. So much is obvious enough. And amongst the features of sensibilities which matter are, of course, not only the actual attitudes which are the output, but the interactions between them. For instance, a sensibility which *pairs* an attitude of disapproval towards telling lies, and an attitude of calm or approval towards getting your little brother to tell lies, would not meet my endorsement. I can only admire people who would reject the second action as strongly as they reject the first. It matters to me that people should have only this pairing because its absence opens a dangerous weakness in a sensibility. Its owner would have the wrong attitude to indirect ways of getting lies told (and for that matter the wrong attitude to his little brother).

The conditional form shows me expressing this endorsement. Of course, it is an endorsement which is itself the expression of a moral point of view. Some casuistry might lead people to the other commitment, that there is a great difference between telling lies and getting your little brother to do so (am I my

---

[6] Or, more generally, an input of *awareness* rather than belief. A man may respond to perceived features without realizing that they are the ones responsible for his reactions. For example, we often do not know what we find funny in a situation.

brother's keeper?).[7] Such people would reject the conditional. But it is quite satisfactory that the conditional expresses a moral point of view. The task was not to show that it does not, but to explain what it does at all. Other conditionals have the same general role:

> If lying makes you feel good, then it's all right.
> If you ought to give him £10, then you ought to give him something.

The latter is held on logical grounds. I can only endorse a sensibility which, in the presence of the antecedent attitude, also has the consequent one, because it is logically impossible that the action specified in the antecedent can be done without giving the man something. I could not endorse at all an illogical sensibility, which itself paired approval of an action with disapproval of a logical implication of the performance of the action. The former conditional is the expression of a repulsive *standard*: it endorses a function from an input of knowledge that a lie has made you feel good to an output of satisfaction with it. Finding better descriptions of admirable input/output functions is the task of moral philosophy.

This account of what we are up to when we use the conditional form with evaluative components now needs supplementing by a semantic theory. We can put the need this way. Imagine a language unlike English in containing no evaluative predicates. It wears the expressive nature of value-judgements on its sleeve. Call it E_{ex}. It might contain a 'hooray!' operator and a 'boo!' operator (H!, B!) which attach to descriptions of things to result in expressions of attitude. H!(the playing of Tottenham Hotspur) would express the attitude towards the playing. B!(lying) would express the contrary attitude towards lying, and so on. For the reasons I have developed, we would expect the speakers of E_{ex} to want another device, enabling them to express views on the structure of sensibilities. They would need a notation with which to endorse or reject various couplings of attitudes, or couplings of beliefs and attitudes. Suppose

---

[7] Examples of genuinely controversial commitments of the form may help: 'if something ought to be done, any means to it ought to be allowed'; 'if a group has been discriminated against, it is now right to give it better treatment.'

we talk *about* an attitude or belief by putting its expression inside bars: |H! (X)| refers to approval of (X). And suppose we use the semi-colon to denote the view that one attitude or belief involves or is coupled with another. Then the speakers of E_{ex} will need to express themselves thus:

> H! (|H! (Tottenham)|;|H! (Arsenal)|)
> H! (|B! (lying)|;|B! (getting little brother to lie)|)

The first endorses only sensibilities which, if they endorse Tottenham, also endorse Arsenal, and this is what we express by saying that if Tottenham is a good team, so is Arsenal. The second is our old friend.

E_{ex} will naturally want further constructions. We want to say things like 'X used to be a good thing, but now it is not', in which evaluations connect with tenses. Notice that this does not mean the same as 'I used to approve of X but now I do not': it implies that X has changed, not that I have. The favourable evaluation attaches to X as it was, so E_{ex} will need a device to express this: perhaps an index indicating that the past state is the object of evaluation. Again, consider our different attitudes to our own attitudes. Since I have the concept of improvement and deterioration in a sensibility, I know that I am vulnerable to argument that in forming a particular attitude I am myself falling victim to a flawed input/output function. I may be exhibiting dispositions which I do not endorse, or committing myself to pairings of attitude and attitude, or attitude and belief, which I also cannot endorse. So in some cases I can be uncertain not only of the facts of the case, but of how to react to them. I will need to explore the other aspects of my moral commitments, and see whether, when they are brought to bear, one attitude or another begins to settle itself. And when I have taken up an attitude, I might be uncomfortably aware that it may turn out to be vulnerable to criticism. So E_{ex} will need a way of signalling different degrees of robustness in our attitudes: different ways in which they can be regarded as likely or unlikely to succumb to an improved perspective. H!(X) can co-exist with something like ? H! (|H! (X)|): uncertainty that one's own attitude of approval can itself be endorsed.

E_{ex} will be spoken by people who need to signal and respect consistencies and inconsistencies. Consider:

B! (lying)
H! (|B! (lying)|;|B! (getting little brother to lie)|)

Disapproval of lying, and approval of making (disapproval of getting little brother to lie), follow upon (disapproval of lying). Anyone holding this pair must hold the consequential disapproval: he is committed to disapproving of getting little brother to lie, for if he does not his attitudes clash. He has a fractured sensibility which cannot itself be an object of approval. The 'cannot' here follows not (as a realist explanation would have it) because such a sensibility must be out of line with the moral facts it is trying to describe, but because such a sensibility cannot fulfil the practical purposes for which we evaluate things. E_{ex} will want to signal this. It will want a way of expressing the thought that it is a logical mistake that is made, if someone holds the first two commitments, and not the commitment to disapproval of getting your little brother to lie.

In short, E_{ex} needs to become an instrument of serious, reflective, evaluative practice, able to express concern for improvements, clashes, implications, and coherence of attitudes. Now one way of doing this is to become like ordinary English. That is, it would invent a predicate answering to the attitude, and treat commitments as if they were judgements, and then use all the natural devices for debating truth. If this is right, then our use of indirect contexts does not prove that an expressive theory of morality is wrong; it merely proves us to have adopted a form of expression adequate to our needs. *This is what is meant by 'projecting' attitudes onto the world.*

What I have done here is to explain how conditionals can be regarded as ways of following out implications, although it is not imperative that the commitments whose implications they trace have 'truth-conditions'. Now you might say: even if this can be done, hasn't the quasi-realist a very dreary task in front of him? For remember that the Frege point was entirely general: it could cite any unasserted context. So mightn't others arise which require separate and ingenious explanations, and is the quasi-realist faced with an endless task? Isn't he like Ptolemaic astronomers, having to bolster his theory with ever more complex or *ad hoc* epicycles, whereas by comparison there is a simple, common-sense view that moral predicates are just the

196   LANGUAGE AND THE WORLD

same as more ordinary ones, so that there is nothing to explain about the way they function in unasserted contexts?[8]

Questions of what does or does not require explanation involve delicate matters of philosophical judgement, but the objection here is surely overdrawn. For what plays the role of Copernicus to the allegedly Ptolemaic complexities? What was wrong with Ptolemaic astronomy (by the end of its reign) was that there was a better way of explaining the same things. But this better way did not just take those things for granted. It was not the stultifying position that everything is just in order without our bothering to explain it. We have seen enough of why projectivism is a plausible moral philosophy. And this being so it is extremely important to tell whether it is blocked by arguments from the philosophy of language. Nobody denies that the surface phenomena of language – the fact that we use moral predicates, and apply truth or falsity to the judgements we make when we use them – pose a problem for projectivism. This is why they tempt people into realism. But by overcoming the problem projectivism also steals a march on its rivals. For it removes the temptation to think that our surface forms of expression embody a mistake, that they are "fraudulent" or "diseased": it *protects* our ordinary thinking, in a way that mere reminders of the way we do actually proceed cannot do. It solves Kant's question of the *right* to our concepts, as well as the question of what they are actually like.

But now a new and rather surprising vista is opened. For if this is right, might 'it is true that . . .' also be given this quasi-realist explanation? Initially an expressive theory stands in stark contrast to one giving moral remarks truth-conditions. But if we sympathize with the pressures I have described, we come to appreciate why it should be natural to treat expressions of attitude as if they were similar to ordinary judgements. We come to need a predicate, whose behaviour is like that of others. Why not regard ourselves as having *constructed* a notion of moral truth? If we have done so, then we can happily say that moral judgements are true or false, only not think that we have sold out to realism when we do so.

---

[8] This response was made to me by Professor Geach.

3. *Constructing Truth*

The arguments of the last section may give us a right to a notion of an *improved* set of attitudes; they give us some right to a notion of the *coherence* and *consistency* of such a set. But do they suffice to build all that we need from a conception of truth, applicable to moral judgements?

The root disquiet here runs very deep. In effect, quasi-realism is trying to earn our right to talk of moral truth, while recognizing fully the subjective sources of our judgements, inside our own attitudes, needs, desires, and natures. The sense of subjectivity triggers all kinds of wild reactions. Can the projectivist take such things as obligations, duties, the "stern daughter of the voice of God", seriously? How can he if he denies that these represent external, independent, authoritative requirements? Mustn't he in some sense have a schizoid attitude to his own moral commitments – holding them, but also holding that they are ungrounded? And when the tension comes out, shouldn't he become frivolous, amoral? A recent influential book even believes that an emotivist should approve of manipulating people, bullying and lying and brainwashing as we please, rather than respecting their independence.[9] Words like 'relativism' and 'subjective' focus these fears; books and sermons alike pronounce that the projectivist should, if consistent, end up with the morals of a French gangster.

Fortunately, all this is ridiculously beside the point. Just as the senses constrain what we can believe about the empirical world, so our natures and desires, needs and pleasures, constrain much of what we can admire and commend, tolerate and work for. There are not so many livable, unfragmented, developed, consistent, and coherent systems of attitude. A projectivist, like anyone else, may be sensitive to the features which make our lives go well or badly; to the need for order, contracts, sources of stability. If his reflection on these things leads him to endorse a high Victorian love of promises, rectitude, contracts, conventional sexual behaviour, well and good: there is nothing in his meta-ethic to suggest otherwise. For instance, a proper respect for promises, the kind of respect which sees them as

---

[9] A. MacIntyre, *After Virtue*, p. 22, and throughout.

making requirements, as bounds on conduct, is certainly a good
attitude to foster. But it may, for all that, be just that: an
attitude.

The problem is not with a subjective source for value in itself,
but with people's inability to come to terms with it, and their
consequent need for a picture in which values imprint
themselves on a pure passive, receptive witness, who has no
responsibility in the matter. To show that these fears have no
intellectual justification means developing a concept of moral
truth out of the materials to hand: seeing how, given attitudes,
given constraints upon them, given a notion of improvement
and of possible fault in any sensibility including our own, we
can construct a notion of truth. The exercise is important. For
one moral of the brush with Goodman's paradox and the rule-
following considerations (chapter 3) is that judgement never
involves quite the pure passivity which is supposed to be an
untainted source of objectivity and truth. We have to see our
concepts as the product of our own intellectual stances: how
then are they suitable means for framing objectively correct,
true, judgement, describing the mind-independent world as it
in fact is? It is not only moral truth which starts to quake. But
we can learn how to approach the general problems of truth by
starting with it.

The simplest suggestion is that we define a 'best possible set
of attitudes', thought of as the limiting set which would result
from taking all possible opportunities for improvement of attitude. Saying that an evaluative remark is true would be saying
that it is a member of such a set, or is implied by such a set.[10]
Call the set M^*. Then if m is a particular commitment,
expressing an attitude U;

   m is true $=$ U is a member of M^*

To test this suggestion we must find conditions which truth
obeys, and see whether they square with it. In particular, does
the definition justify the constraint of *consistency* (m cannot be
true and false)? The first hurdle is to define the idea of a unique
best possible sensibility. Certainly there is improvement and
deterioration. But why should not improving sensibilities

[10] Although this is the simplest projectivist account of truth, and is one used by many
anti-realists, I do not myself think it is the best. It is only a first approximation, but
serves to make the immediate points. See below (7.7).

diverge in various ways? An imperfect sensibility might take any of several different trajectories as it evolves into something better. We might imagine a tree (see Fig. 6). Here each node (point at which there is branching) marks a place where equally admirable but diverging opinion is possible. And there is no unique $M*$ on which the progress of opinion is sighted. So there is no truth, since the definition lapses. More precisely, truth would shrink to only those commitments which are shared by all the diverging systems: truth belongs to the trunk.

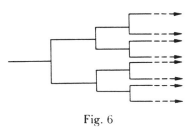

Fig. 6

This is the deep problem of *relativism*. It is not the vague and unfounded disquiet that I have no right to judge unfavourably people with any other opinion – those who practice human sacrifice, or murder Jews, for instance. Of course I have. My attitudes, and those involved in any system I could conceive of which might be superior to mine, alike condemn them. The deep problem is the suspicion that other, equally admirable sensibilities, over which I can claim no superiority of my own, lead to divergent judgements. This does take away my right to think of mine as true, which is equivalent to unsettling my commitments.

The classic introduction of the problem is Hume's superb and neglected essay 'Of the Standard of Taste'. He introduces "such diversity in the internal frame or external situation as is entirely blameless on both sides". He illustrates it with the difference between "a young man, whose passions are warm" and "a man more advanced in years, who takes pleasure in wise, philosophical reflections concerning the conduct of life and the moderation of the passions". The former prefers the amorous and tender images of Ovid, the latter the wisdom of

200   LANGUAGE AND THE WORLD

Tacitus; in the twentieth century no doubt the one reads *Playboy*
and the other *The Economist*. Now we imagine the young man's
literary sensibility improved and refined into a system M^*_o and
the old man's into a system M^*_t, and one containing the commitment that Ovid is a better writer than Tacitus, whilst the
other contains the reverse. How can we recover a notion of truth
for either judgement? Hume's answer is subtle: it consists in
expanding the difference between a (mere) matter of predilec-
tion, and a fit object of literary comparison: "it is plainly an
error in a critic, to confine his approbation to one species or style
of writing, and condemn all the rest." The point of this emerges
if we ask the question: who is to adopt the following three views:

(1) $M^*_o \rightarrow$ it is true that Ovid is better than Tacitus
(2) $M^*_t \rightarrow$ it is true that Tacitus is better than Ovid
(3) There is no possible improvement on either M^*_o or M^*_t

(where '$M^* \rightarrow$ it is true that m' means that M^* contains an
attitude which is expressed by the sentence m).

How can you have each of these? Think of the detail. Is
someone who has either of the two sensibilities aware of the
other? If not, it would surely be an improvement if he were. But
if so, then quite what is the combination of attitudes required?
It surely begins to seem wrong to hold, straight out, that Ovid
is better than Tacitus, or vice versa. If we admit a really
developed rival way of looking at it, are we not required to
soften the opposition – to say, for instance, that Ovid and
Tacitus are of equal merit, although each has features which
appeal to different people? In short, as soon as *I* hold that a case
begins to look as though the tree structure applies, *I* also hold
that there is a truth about the subject on which the divergent
attitudes are held, and, holding that, *I* would also judge that
one or both of the rival sensibilities is capable of improvement,
until it yields my own attitude. Hume's case depends upon the
audience accepting that Ovid and Tacitus actually are of equal
merit – otherwise it would not be just the different tastes of
different ages which result in the different rankings. But if we
think this, then each of the two systems is flawed. The young
but able literary critic is insensitive to the virtues which appear
to the older man, and which in truth result in the two writers
coming out equally; similarly for the older literary critic.

What does this mean? It means that an evaluative system should contain the resources to *transcend the tree structure*: evidence that there is a node *itself* implies that it is wrong to maintain either of the conflicting commitments. It is itself a signal that the right attitude – the truth about the relative merits of Ovid and Tacitus – is not that expressed by either of these partial perspectives. The better perspective may judge the merits equal, or it may award the prize to just one view, or it may regret and change the terms of the discussion, by losing interest in the simplistic question of whether Ovid is a better writer than Tacitus, and concentrating upon different merits of each, with no intention of finding a summary comparison. In that case the system of *each* of these literary critics is defective, by containing too many crude comparisons. So in practice evidence that there is a node is just treated as a signal that the truth is not yet finally argued, and it goes into discussions as part of the evidence. We are constrained to argue and practise as though the truth is single, and this constraint is defensible in spite of the apparent possibility of the tree-structure.

It is as though the trunk – the core of opinion to which there is no admirable alternative – contains the power to grow through any of the choices of opinion which lead to branching: the choices become themselves part of the knowledge which the progress of attitude must use to form its course.[11] In so far as acquaintance with another value-system makes me respect it, then it properly makes me rethink both systems, transcending the tree-structure.

One common element of "relativism" is the thought that if we can conceive of different, equally admirable systems, then that must weaken our own in favour of *toleration*. It seems to be particularly the attitudes associated with *obligation* which are vulnerable to worries about rival systems. The explanation of this is quite pleasant, although perhaps slightly peripheral to language.

Suppose we symbolize 'it is obligatory to do A' by OA, and 'it is permissible to avoid A' by '$P\neg A$'. $P\neg A$ contradicts OA. Now imagine:

---

[11] Readers may be reminded of the Hegelian three-step (look left, look right, and then cross over) of thesis, antithesis, synthesis, by which we lurch towards the Absolute.

202   LANGUAGE AND THE WORLD

   (1) $M^*_1 \rightarrow OA$
   (2) $M^*_2 \rightarrow P\neg A$
   (3) There is no possible improvement on either M^*_1 or M^*_2.

This is the tree structure. One way of transcending it goes:

   (4) (3) implies that it is permissible to hold M^*_2; this implies
        that it is permissible to hold that $\neg A$ is permissible,
        which in turn implies that $\neg A$ is permissible;
   (5) So any view, such as M^*_1 which implies the reverse, is
        wrong, and *ipso facto* capable of improvement.

This transcends the tree by showing that if we suppose that the
choice leading to M^*_2 is permissible, then we must dislike the
other. We cannot maintain the even-handed, Olympian stance
which finds them each blameless. But now notice that if we have
a *prima facie* case of (1), (2), and (3), it is *likely to be the obligation*
which is the more threatened. Suppose we try to transcend the
tree by the reverse argument:

   (4') (3) implies that it is permissible to hold M^*_1; this
         implies that it is permissible to hold that A is obligatory,
         which in turn implies that A is obligatory;

we need the different reduction principle that if it is permissible
to hold that A is obligatory, then A *is* obligatory, and that is not
nearly so intuitive.[12] Evidence of a permissible system which
permits $\neg A$ is evidence that $\neg A$ is permissible; evidence of a
permissible system which obligates A is not so plausibly
thought of as evidence that A is obligatory. So here, once we
have an initial inclination to each of the three propositions, we
are more likely to escape the inconsistency by seeing M^*_1 as
capable of improvement.

   So on this account it is correct, as well as natural, to find faith
in particular obligations shaken, if what seems to be admirable
sensibilities do not recognize them. This is why travel
broadens the mind.

[12] Formally the reduction principles differ in a way analogous to the difference
between the modal system S4 and the stronger system S5. If 'it is permitted to permit A'
implies 'A is permitted', we have $PPx \rightarrow Px$, which corresponds to S4. This does not
demand that 'it is permitted to obligate x' implies 'x is obligatory', for which S5 is
needed. The comparison is suggestive, and indicates a respectable side of worries about
relativism.

210   LANGUAGE AND THE WORLD

5. *Other Anti-Realisms: Causes, Counterfactuals, Idealism*

Let us get back to projectivism.

Apart from its own interest as an account of moralizing, there is one supremely important point about a projective theory. Suppose the quasi-realist earns us the right to put our commitments in the terms we do. It is just that the explanation of this right starts from the subjective source, in attitude and sentiment. It follows that the issue of whether projectivism is correct is *not readily decidable.* That is, you cannot rely upon first thoughts, or immediate armchair reactions, or your unprocessed knowledge of what you mean by some commitments, to determine whether the theory is true. This alters the terms in which anti-realism needs discussing: in particular it alters it from those in which the analytic tradition has usually tried to discuss it. That tradition has persistently tried to make the anti-realist a reductionist, bent upon giving an account of all we mean by various commitments; from the armchair we can announce that we really mean more (and this can be supplemented by arguments that we do), and then this is seen as a victory for realism. Whereas now there need be no attempt to deny the distinctive nature of the commitments, and the unique meaning of the various vocabularies, and this still leaves open a projective theory of what is true of us when we use them. This implies that the pure philosophy of language has less to offer to such problems than most recent discussions assume. Nevertheless such a return to an *explanatory* mode, away from an *analytic* mode, is essential, especially if we are to understand the history of philosophy rightly.

Consider for instance Hume's treatment of causal necessity, perhaps the classic projective theory in philosophy. The central thought is that dignifying a relationship between events as casual is spreading or projecting a reaction which we have to something else we are aware of about the events – Hume

EVALUATIONS, PROJECTIONS   211

thought of this input in terms of the regular succession of similar
such events, one upon the other. Exposed to such regularity,
our minds (cannot help but) form habits of expectation, which
they then project by describing the one event as causing the
other. We are more subtle than Hume suggests: we take more
into account than regular succession of similar events.[15] But
this does not matter to the overall nature of the theory. The
essential anti-realist core is quite missed by counterexamples
where we think that *A* causes *B*, although *B*'s do not regularly
follow *A*'s (e.g. because of countervailing circumstances), or
where *B*'s do but we do not think that *A*'s cause them (e.g.
because some third thing causes them both). We may both be
subtle and active in choosing to dignify various relations as
causal: it is still possible than when we do we give expression to
a habit of reliance, a habit which we depend upon in inference
and in other practice, and which we project when we insist upon
the existence of causal connection. Again, since we have a
purpose in so projecting we will have standards by which to
assess the evidence we use for the existence of causal connections, and the quasi-realist can again earn a right to the notion
of truth, and a notion of the true causal structure of things.
  Since this is the basic structure of Hume's theory, it follows
that he has been shamefully abused by many commentators
and their victims. He is not denying that there exist causes; he is
not inconsistent when he says that there are unknown causes of
things; he is not concerned to say that causal propositions can
be analysed into ones about the regular successions of events,
which then capture their entire content. He is merely explaining our normal sayings, our normal operations with the concept, in terms of the reactions we have, after exposure to a
reality which exhibits no such feature. The explanation may be
defective; even in principle it may not work, but at least it needs
tackling for what it is. We fail to do this if we insist on seeing it as
a meaning equation (consider again my strictures against
naturalism in ethics). We also fail to do it if we merely insist, as
many thinkers do, that we properly describe the *perceived* states
of affairs in causal terms — *see* bricks splashing in water, balls

[15] Although Hume is more careful than often realized: *Treatise*, Bk. I, pt. III, sect.
XV.

breaking windows, things pushing and pulling. Certainly we do: but what is the best explanation of our so seeing them?

Amongst the questions which genuinely arise the most prominent will be the kind of conception of a non-causal reality whose features explain our reactions. Hume thought in terms of a regular succession of events, describable in purely phenomenal terms. But is this even a possible conception of the world? Perhaps we have to use the concept of a causal connection to describe the world at all (ordinary descriptions involve *things* with all their *powers*). In that case there is no way to explain our causal sayings as projections generated by something else, for there will be no stripped, B-vocabulary in which to identify the something else.

These questions loom still larger when we get to Kant, and the whole description of the world as spatially extended and temporally ordered is seen as the work of the mind, whose only exposure is to a noumenal, inaccessible reality of things-we-know-not-what. For the picture at the beginning of this chapter defines one of the central problems of philosophy. How far does the projected reality extend: what is our creation and what is given? When the spread world drips down entirely over the real world, whose nature is blotted out and left completely "noumenal", we have idealism. Before rushing to embrace it, there are two points to remember. One is that respectable projectivism is an explanatory theory. But in so far as we lack a conception of the noumenal reality on which our reactions depend, we also fail to explain how its features are responsible for our reactions. A particularly gross instance of this general problem is Kant's removal of the noumenal reality from space and time. For there is no prospect at all of an explanatory account of how our reactions depend on the features (events? changes?) of such a reality: *depends* is a causal notion, and at home only within the familiar world.[16] Secondly, in my development, projectivism needs a sense of the role of a saying contrasted with simple expression of belief – in the case of evaluations, a role of expressions of attitude, or in the case of cause, a role as dignifying a regularity for some theoretical or practical purpose – and this is the foundation for the belief-

---

[16] Kant is well aware that this is only a form of explanation and that we can, on his own grounds, do nothing to fill it out: *Critique of Pure Reason*, B146, B166, footnote.

EVALUATIONS, PROJECTIONS   213

expressing appearance. But describing a world in spatial and
temporal terms is just that – describing. These two points
suggest that each class of commitments faces the decision on its
own: quasi-realism needs detail, not pictures.

Amongst commitments which seem particularly likely to
benefit from such treatment are those involving modal idioms –
possibility and necessity. As already noticed, these come in
different strengths. We talk of physical possibility and necessity; metaphysical possibility (is it metaphysically possible that
there should be minds without body, experience without time,
etc.?); logical possibility (the bare possibility that persons
should fly or horses talk is not ruled out by logical considerations); sometimes epistemic possibility – situations left open by
some body of knowledge. How are we to understand claims of
necessity and possibility? Naturally, the sources of these judgements, in our connections of logic, or of metaphysics, or of
natural laws, attract detailed philosophical treatment, and
have their own problems. But as far as the realist/anti-realist
debate goes, there are some general points to be made. Consider
this famous passage from the chapter on 'Foundations', in
David Lewis's book, *Counterfactuals*:

I believe that there are possible worlds other than the one we happen
to inhabit. If an argument is wanted, it is this. It is uncontroversially
true that things might be otherwise than they are. I believe, and so do
you, that things could have been different in countless ways. But what
does this mean? Ordinary language permits the paraphrase: there are
many ways things could have been besides the way they actually are.
On the face of it, this sentence is an existential quantification. It says
that there exist many entities of a certain description, to wit 'ways
things could have been'. I believe that things could have been different in countless ways; I believe permissible paraphrases of what I
believe; taking the paraphrase at its face value I therefore believe in
the existence of entities that might be called 'ways things could have
been'. I prefer to call them 'possible worlds'. (p. 84)

Lewis goes on to make two further comments: that talking
about possible worlds leads to no decisive problems, and that
the modal idioms are irreducible. You cannot express things
that we say using 'necessary', 'possible', and closely connected
notions, such as 'ways things might have been', in other terms.
Given this, he wants to take the idioms "at face value", which

means, in his view, having a realistic theory of possible worlds. There really are such things, and we really describe them, and can know what they contain and what they do not. Now it will be evident that this ignores the resources of anti-realism, and in particular the possibility of a projective view. For does the fact that we have commitments expressed in modal terms, and that those commitments are irreducible, support realism? Only if rejecting an idiom or reducing it are the only anti-realist options, and they are not. (Of course, an identical mistake is made by those who dislike realism about possible worlds, and conclude that we *must* either reject or reduce the idiom.)

Thinking about necessities and possibilities in terms of related possible worlds is helpful for many purposes. It provides a picture or image which aids thinking; it enables logicians to approach modal arguments by mapping them onto more familiar arguments. For instance, the inference from 'necessarily *p*' to '*p*', is mapped into 'in all possible worlds *p*' to 'in this possible world *p*', and becomes just the instantiation of a generalization. This is a familiar inference form of basic 'first order' logic. But *realism*? In present terms the issue must be one about how we explain our making of modal commitments. We certainly do not explain it by thinking that we are made sensitive to possibilities because of some quasi-sensory capacity which responds to the presence or absence of possible worlds. Firstly, since the only possible world that is actual is the actual world, others cannot *actually* influence us: we cannot receive information about them, because there is nothing to actually influence any receptors. Ways things might have been cannot be seen or heard. Secondly, the position that we are simply describing different aspects of reality needs a supplementation which it finds hard to give. If the possible worlds, like moral properties, represent a new realm of fact, why should we be interested in it? Talking of possibilities would be as optional to us, interested in the actual world, as talk of neighbouring countries or different times would be to us, if we are interested in the here and now. But it is not. We want to know whether to *allow* possibilities or *insist upon* necessities because we want to know how to conduct our thinking about the actual world. The possibilities we allow or which we rule out, determine how we conduct our inferences, and eventually our practices in the actual world. It is quite inexplic-

able how they should do that, if we relied upon the image of
different spheres of real facts or states of affairs. Why should it
interest me if in such spheres something holds, or in some it does
not, or if in ones quite similar to the actual world things do or do
not hold, if I want to discover and use truths about the ways
things actually are?

Thus consider the claim that if you had fallen off the edge of
some cliff, you would have hurt yourself. Think of this as Lewis
wishes: it means that in any possible world as closely similar to
ours as may be, but in which you have fallen off the cliff, you
have hurt yourself.[17] But then there is debate over what makes
for *similarity*. After all, a world just like ours, except that your fall
off the cliff was followed by a minor miracle restoring you to the
top (perhaps with amnesia), continues just like our world – isn't
that similarity for you? There has been considerable debate
over how to select the *right* similarity ranking, for otherwise we
would endorse the wrong counterfactuals (on this occasion: if
you had fallen over the cliff, you would have been quite unharmed). There is then a question over whether rightness can
be defined without circularity.[18] But suppose it can be. There is
still something crucial to explain. Why are we interested in just
that "right" kind of similarity? If our interest lay exclusively
in possible worlds, it would seem legitimate to roam around
describing the various dimensions of similarity and difference
with equal concern and respect. We only select one kind of
similarity as the "right" one because we *use* counterfactuals in
the real world – for the purpose of arguing, modifying practice,
avoiding falling over cliffs, and so on. In other words, the person
who thinks that if you had fallen over the cliff you would have
been unharmed is not just someone who describes possible
worlds with idiosyncratic standards of similarity. He is not just
like a tourist who makes odd judgements of similarity between
two places bcause he is more concerned with the botany than
with the food. He is a menace. Lewis's realism leaves this use
unexplained. It would need supplementing by a theory of why

[17] I abstract here from the complications of counterpart theory, which do not affect
the present point.
[18] The kind of circularity which threatens is this. Perhaps a minor miracle makes a
world *very* dissimilar from ours because it involves breaking a law of nature, but perhaps
laws of nature are identified by thinking of which counterfactuals we hold true. Myself,
I doubt whether this problem is decisive against Lewis.

one kind of similarity between possible worlds should be the one which *matters*. But then the whole package becomes extravagent, like the moral theory which sees us as responding to a real world of duties, obligations, and so forth, and *then* has to add an explanation of why we bother about these things, as well as the pains, pleasures, harms, and desires which make up the actual world.

By contrast the quasi-realist will start by seeing the remark (whether formulated in terms of possible worlds or not) as expressing a commitment – one which endorses the structuring of our beliefs about the world in a certain way. Notably, it endorses an inference from supposing that someone has fallen off a cliff, to supposing that they have got hurt. It dignifies this connection, allowing it to be a reliable guide to the conduct of affairs. The quasi-realist must then pursue the way we can come to treat such a commitment as if it represented a judgement with genuine truth-conditions. Similar problems arise as in the moral case. Consider a simple example. We can regard even our most reasonable counterfactual commitments as potentially false. We know Henry's habits: we know that the best bet is that if he had come to the party he would have got drunk. But for all that it may be true if he had come he would have stayed sober. Once again, this contrast must be explained, essentially with the same materials as in the case of evaluations. We have a sense of the potential for improvement in any argument: our reliable estimate of Henry's behaviour might be supplemented by information unknown to us (he had a cold, has just got a girl-friend in the Salvation Army, etc.). We need a proper notion of the *improvement or deterioration in the bases* for argument, and proceed to construct a notion of truth. The eventual theory (counterfactuals are intricate, and this is not the place to pursue all the detail) would be one which maintains the benefits of possible-world imagery, but disallows the metaphysical extravagance.[19]

Projectivism is also a promising option in the theory of logical necessity. We not only believe it to be true that $7 + 5 = 12$, but we also find the truth inexorable: it could not have been

---

[19] The treatment of counterfactuals as condensed arguments was begun by John Mackie, 'Counterfactuals and Causal Law', in Butler, ed., *Analytical Philosophy, 1st Series*.

otherwise. We cannot imagine it otherwise; we could make nothing of a way of thought which denied it. But this may be just a fact about us and the limitations of our present imaginations, and it is natural to complain that this fact cannot justify us in saying that the proposition *has* to be true, or is true in all logically possible worlds. One reaction would be to avoid saying this, and eschew the category of logically necessary truth: this is Quine's position. But another is to face the fact that such truths do occupy a special category, for we can easily imagine otherwise many of our most cherished beliefs, and to say that when we dignify a truth as necessary we are expressing our own mental attitude – in this case our own inability to make anything of a possible way of thinking which denies it. It is this blank unimaginability which we voice when we use the modal vocabulary. It is then natural to fear that this has nothing to do with the *real* modal status of propositions. (Compare: what have our sentiments to do with the *real* moral truths about things?) But the quasi-realist will fight this contrast: he will deny that anything more can be meant by the real modal status of a proposition, than can be understood by seeing it as a projection of our (best) attitude of comprehension or imagination towards it. Once again, the advantage of such a theory is that it avoids the mystery of a necessity-detecting faculty and it avoids the strained scepticism which tries to avoid admitting that any truths are necessary at all.

6. *Mind-Dependence*

There is one more aspect of such theories I need to mention. It is tempting to think that a projective theory must leave the truth of commitments on which it works "mind-dependent". And this prompts hostility. It is not because of the way we think that if kangaroos had no tails they would topple over. We discover such facts, we do not invent them. It is not because of the way we form sentiments that kicking dogs is wrong. It would be wrong whatever we thought about it. Fluctuations in our sentiments only make us better or worse able to appreciate how wrong it is. It is not because of the way we conduct our arguments that trees cause shade. The "mind-independence" of such facts is part of our ordinary way of looking at things. Must a projectivist deny it? On his construction is truth mind-dependent?

Fortunately the quasi-realist treatment of indirect contexts shows that it is not. Suppose someone said 'if we had different sentiments, it would be right to kick dogs', what could he be up to? Apparently, he endorses a certain sensibility: one which lets information about what people feel dictate its attitude to kicking dogs. But nice people do not endorse such a sensibility. What makes it wrong to kick dogs is the cruelty or pain to the animal. *That* input should yield disapproval and indignation as the output. Similarly, if someone so organizes his beliefs and the way he makes inferences that he cannot let the presence of a tree in suitable sunshine suffice to give him confidence that there is a shadow, but needs information about whether people think one way or another, he is in a mess. He will fail to be confident in truths about the actual world when he should be.

Of course there *are* moral truths and counterfactuals which are "mind-dependent". Behaviour which we call rude is often wrong only because people think that it is wrong; sermons cause people to switch off because people have those kinds of minds. The point is that when a commitment is unlike these in being independent of our minds and their properties, the projectivist can conform to ordinary claims that it is. He does not need to deny any of the common-sense commitments or views about the way in which their truth arises. This is extremely important. Idealists always face the problem of finding an acceptable way of putting what they want to say about the involvement of the mind in the world. Some fudge it: it is quite common to find people writing that 'objects' do not exist outside our conceptual schemes, or that we 'create' objects (values, numbers) rather than discover them.[20] This is not a good way to put anything. With the inverted commas off, such remarks are false. (We do not create trees and galaxies, nor the wrongness of cruelty, nor the evenness of the number 2. Nor can we destroy them either, except perhaps for the trees.) But what can they mean otherwise: what is meant by saying that 'trees' are mind-dependent, if trees are not? Perhaps just the platitude that if we did not have minds of a certain kind, we could not possess the concept of a tree. The problem for the idealist, or the anti-realist

[20] e.g. Putnam, *Reason, Truth and History*, p. 52.

EVALUATIONS, PROJECTIONS   219

in general, is to steer a course between the platitude and the paradox.

The quasi-realist way of approaching indirect contexts offers a better approach. The utterance 'whatever I or we or anyone else ever thought about it, there would still have been (causes, counterfactual truths, numbers, duties)' can be endorsed even if we accept the projective picture, and work in terms of an explanation of the sayings which gives them a subjective source. The correct opinion about these things is not necessarily the one we happen to have, nor is our having an opinion or not the kind of thing which makes for correctness. The standards governing projection make it irrelevant, in the way that opinion is irrelevant to the wrongness of kicking dogs. The temptation to think otherwise arises only if a projective theory is mistaken for a reductionist one, giving the propositions involved a content, but one which makes them about us or our minds. They are not – they have a quite different role, and one which gives them no such truth-condition. When I say that Hitler was evil or that trees cause shade I am not talking about myself.[21]

It may now appear that a projective approach is too good to be true. Initially, the contrast between expressive theories and ones giving the same commitments genuine truth-conditions seemed reliable enough. But the subtleties, the earning power of quasi-realist devices, have tended to blur it. We can hear the philosopher who gives a projective explanation say highly realistic-sounding things. Why not regard him as giving the

---

[21] Wittgenstein may have come close to the kind of theory here explained. He certainly seems to want an anti-realist theory of arithmetical necessity without in any way regarding truths of arithmetic as truths about *us* or as truths of natural history. And my projective way with mind-dependence offers a model for doing this.

It should be noticed that because of the twist in construing these counterfactuals this way, it comes out *false* that if we had thought or felt otherwise, it would have been permissible to kick dogs. This means that the metaphor of 'projection' needs a little care. Values are the children of our sentiments in the sense that the full explanation of what we do when we moralize cites only the natural properties of things and natural reactions to them. But they are not the children of our sentiments in the sense that were our sentiments to vanish, moral truths would alter as well. The *way* in which we gild or stain the world with the colours borrowed from internal sentiment gives our creation its own life, and its own dependence on facts. So we should not say or think that were our sentiments to alter or disappear, moral facts would do so as well. This would be endorsing the defective counterfactuals, i.e. endorsing the wrong kinds of sensibility, and it will be part of good moralizing not to do that. Similarly, it would have been true that $7 + 5 = 12$, whatever we had thought about it.

commitments in question genuine (mind-independent) truth-
conditions? He practises soberly and responsibly, as though
there were one truth which it is his business to find. So perhaps
the right thing to say is that the commitments are true or false,
in a straightforward way, after all. Perhaps expressive theories,
properly developed, pull themselves into truth-conditional ones
by their own resources. It is just that by disavowing the direction of explanation associated with the idea of a truth-
condition, they do this without entering troubles of metaphysics
and epistemology, and the resulting scepticism which plagues
other approaches. To assess whether this is right, we need to
turn to more general considerations about truth.

Notes to Chapter 6

6.1 Supervenience, in the sense of this section, should not be confused with the stronger requirement often called 'universalizability',
following the usage of R. M. Hare. There are actually three importantly
different notions:

Consistency: the requirement that you do not contradict yourself, both judging that something is the case and that it is not.
Supervenience: the requirement that moral judgements supervene,
or are consequential upon natural facts.
Universalizability: the requirement that moral judgements are
somehow dependent only upon universal facts; facts specified
without reference to particular individuals or groups.

The last of these is an attempt to build into the very definition of
morality a requirement of impartiality, or of treating like cases alike,
or of abstracting from any personal position or interest in achieving a
moral point of view. Little is gained by building this into the definition
of morality, or into the "logic" of the term moral and its dependent
vocabulary: this just invites the question: why be moral? why not be
"shmoral" – something a degree or two less strenuous than being
moral, allowing one to pay some attention to other people's interests,
but discounting for their distance from oneself? A clearer approach is
to admit that it is a substantive question whether we conduct our
practical reasoning by abstracting away from particular interests,
and to stress the advantages (to themselves or to the community) of
bringing up people to do so. This would be a variety of what is called
'motive utilitarianism': universalizing is defended as being a good

EVALUATIONS, PROJECTIONS   221

thing to do, because if we can get people to respect the results of doing
so, things go better. The relevant literature is, in my view, rather
muddy on this. It includes:

> R. M. Hare, *Moral Thinking*, esp. ch. 6.
> J. Mackie, *Ethics: Inventing Right and Wrong*.

and specifically on supervenience:

> J. Kim, 'Supervenience and Nomological Incommensurables',
> *American Philosophical Quarterly* (1978).
> J. Dancy, 'On Moral Properties', *Mind* (1981).

The argument from the modal relations between moral and natural
judgements, to anti-realism, can be challenged. If we pay careful
attention to the different possible ways of taking the necessity
involved, there is a possible counter. This would involve distinguishing metaphysical necessity from logical or conceptual necessity. The
realist might say that if we are talking of metaphysical necessity, then
once a total natural grounding for a moral judgement is located, it will
be metaphysically necessary, i.e. true in all possible worlds, that when
that grounding is present, the relevant judgement is also true. In
short, he would accept $B*/A$ necessity. If we are talking of conceptual
or logical necessity, then he does better to deny this, although he must
still accept the conceptual necessity of supervenience. But then he
could try accepting the conclusion: saying that it is a conceptual or
logical constraint on the moral vocabulary that it supervenes on the
natural, whereas no particular $B*/A$ connection is logically forced
upon us. The request for explanation still arises, however. Where
does the logical constraint come from if realism is true? Logic is
interested in what can be true, and as far as realism can show us, it
could be true that the moral floats quite free of the natural.

6.2   The theory of conditionals with evaluative components, which I
develop in this section, is just part of the larger programme of quasi-
realism, the attempt to show how an economical, anti-realist, and
expressive theory of such things as ethics can account for the
phenomena which lead people to realism. Papers in which I pursue
the same theme include:

> 'Truth, Realism and The Regulation of Theory', in French *et al.*
> (1980).
> 'Opinions and Chances' in Mellor (1980).
> 'Rule Following and Moral Realism', in Holtzman and Leich
> (1981).

6.3 '. . . a schizoid attitude to his own moral commitments . . .'
Why is it that people want more than the projectivist gives them?
Thomas Nagel talks (*The Possibility of Altruism*) of philosophers such as
Kant, "driven by the demand for an ethical system whose motivational grip is not dependent on desires which must simply be taken for
granted" (p. 11). This is the permanent chimaera, the holy grail of
moral philosophy, the knock-down argument that people who are
nasty and unpleasant and motivated by the wrong things are above
all *unreasonable*: then they can be proved to be wrong by the pure sword
of reason. They aren't just selfish or thoughtless or malignant or
imprudent, but are reasoning badly, or out of touch with the facts. It
must be an occupational hazard of professional thinkers to want to
reduce all the vices to this one. In reality the motivational grip of
moral considerations is bound to depend upon desires which must
simply be taken for granted, although they can also be encouraged
and fostered. Notice that this is consistent with saying that there are
values which we come to recognize or discover, just as there are
rewards and satisfactions which we come to recognize and discover.

'. . . we are constrained to argue and practise as though the truth is
   single . . .'
This needs some care. People may be wrongly tempted to relativism
by this thought. There are obligations which we feel although we are
also aware that other equally admirable systems do not recognize
them. The best examples are those of ceremonies and rituals which
arise, we suppose, because there is some deep need in us which they
serve, although how this need is served can then be highly variable.
For example, I might feel the strictest obligation to dispose of the
body of a relative in some prescribed way, even when I know that
other societies would do it differently. In this case I do not assent to
'all human beings ought to bury (say) their dead'; I do assent to 'I
ought to bury my dead'. But this is not relativism in the sense of the
text, for I would also regard each judgement (that I ought to bury my
dead, that not everyone ought to bury their dead) as true, and there is
no equally admirable conflicting alternative to either of them. It is
just that what creates such obligations are parochial facts about
people and their societies and their customs.

EVALUATIONS, PROJECTIONS   223

6.5 '. . . Hume's treatment . . .'
The two classic places are:

Treatise of Human Nature, Bk. 1, Pt. III, sect. XIV.
Enquiry Concerning Human Understanding, sect. VII.

For possible worlds, and some of the disputes over their standing, see:

A. Plantinga, *The Nature of Necessity*, chs. VI–VIII.
S. Kripke, *Naming and Necessity*, *passim*.

6.6 The relationship between post-Wittgensteinian attempts to avoid realism and the actual work of Wittgenstein is hard to unravel. Two modern metaphysicians tempted towards recognizably idealist positions include Hilary Putnam and Richard Rorty (see Rorty, *Philosophy and the Mirror of Nature* and more recently, *The Consequences of Pragmatism*). I discuss some of these things further in the next chapter. An excellent paper is 'Wittgenstein and Idealism' by Bernard Williams, reprinted in his collection *Moral Luck*.

In this chapter I have not discussed directly the 'anti-realism' about science which allows theoretical sentences to have an intelligible truth-condition, and allows us to accept them and to use them when they are empirically adequate, but counsels us not to *believe* them. This is the position of van Fraassen, and perhaps Popper. It needs faith in some distinction between accepting a statement with a truth-condition, and believing it, and I see no such distinction. I would urge that the right path for instrumentalism is to deny that the commitments have a truth-condition, at least until the quasi-realist does his work.

[2]

The Philosophical Quarterly Vol. 36 No. 142
ISSN 0031–8094 $2.00

CRITICAL STUDY

THE COMPLEAT PROJECTIVIST

BY BOB HALE

SIMON BLACKBURN, *Spreading the Word. Groundings in the Philosophy of Language.*
Oxford, Clarendon Press; 1984, pp. xi + 368. Price £16.00, pb. £6.95.

The temptation to comment on this book's title is scarcely resistable. Spread the word it surely does. It is indeed quite long, and covers much ground. It has also a missionary aim. Blackburn set himself to produce a book which would make modern philosophy of language accessible to the ordinary student and even, perhaps, to the layman. A third, and perhaps the most interesting sense in which the book lives up to its delightfully ambiguous title will be noticed later.

The book has two parts. The first – *Our Language and Ourselves* – is largely concerned with current problems about meaning: the second – *Language and the World* – deals mainly with matters of truth and reference. Apart from a few cheques drawn in Part 1 against arguments delivered in Part 2, and a handful of cross-references, the two parts are, I think, pretty well independent. Part 1 probably has to be read as a whole. Part 2 is divisible – its first three chapters need to be read together, but the remaining two ("Truth & Semantics" and "Reference") can be taken separately.

Space does not permit full discussion. I shall briefly review Part 1, largely confining myself to summary comment, thereby saving most of my words for Part 2.

I. MEANING

For many recent philosophers of language, the dominant question has been: What form should a theory of meaning for a natural language assume? Impressed by the competent speaker's ability to understand any of a potential infinitude of new sentences, they have sought an account of the semantic structure of language which is at least consistent with this and, better still, helps to explain it. Such a theory would show how knowledge of finitely many primitives – words and constructions – can suffice for understanding new sentences. The favoured model has, of course, been Tarski's work on truth. If we had a theory of this sort which also observed Tarski's self-imposed restriction to extensional vocabulary, we could claim to have shed light on the troublesome, intentional concept of meaning. Much impressive work has gone into the task of removing apparent obstacles to the construction.

Blackburn, whilst granting the need for some account of semantic structure, rejects this general approach to meaning and argues the limitations of "compositional semantics" (pp. 10–18, 293–300). The leading questions concern the inter-relations between language, mind and the world, and the interaction between the corresponding departments of philosophy – questions like: Given that a language can be described by a set of syntactic and semantic rules, in what sense, if any, can competent speakers be said to *know* them? What sorts of fact about a linguistic community make it true that they speak and understand the language as described? (The first question, concerning the 'psychological reality' of linguistic rules, receives some lively discussion in ch 1.5: the second dominates the whole of Part 1). The compositional approach leaves such questions untouched. The point is illustratively argued via the example of arabic numerals. We can easily supply a compositional theory which tells us, for an arbitrary numeral *n*, what number *n* refers to. But this does nothing to settle the issues that might trouble a philosopher who wants to know whether numbers exist or are genuine objects of reference.

Chapters 2 and 3 confront the questions: What kind of fact is it that we can use words to mean something? How can any world – "a natural world of things in space and time, and made of flesh and blood" – make room for a fact of this sort? Despite the words last quoted, Blackburn is far from committing himself to an austerely physicalist or extensionalist explanation of representation and communication. Indeed, a later chapter (ch 8.4, 5) argues that the prospects for any such programme, essentially that of the "bleak radical interpreter", are themselves quite bleak.

Chapter 2 is mainly concerned to argue for "the negative point". This is that no thing, and, in particular, no mental item is such that its representational powers can be taken for granted, because any candidate must itself be capable of different interpretations. First victims of this negative point are "dog-legged" theories, which seek to explain how words mean by regarding them as proxies for items of some other sort (Lockean Ideas, images, or the like) whose representational powers are assumed unproblematic. Unless these items are "essentially representative", i.e. carry their own interpretation with them, the theory is hopelessly regressive. The negative point ensures that there are no such items. This horse, one might have supposed, is well and truly dead. But Blackburn has some reasons for administering another flogging. First, some quite recent writers are still trying to ride it – e.g. Fodor in his *Language of Thought*. Second, and more interestingly, Blackburn argues that lessons to be learned from the failure of dog-legged theories can be deployed against some less obvious contemporary targets. One such is Quine's use of the figure of the radical translator (others are Davidson's doctrine that we can make no sense of fundamentally divergent conceptual schemes, and Dummett's claim that meaning must be capable of manifestation in use). The lesson is that *understanding* what someone says cannot be properly equated with *translating* his words into some other medium (the home language). The argument against Quine is that drawing the distinction allows us to agree that different radical translators may properly come up with rival schemes, whilst resisting his sceptical conclusion that there is therefore no determinate fact of the matter about what the native means. To get at what he means, we may have to give up trying to translate him and understand him by going native, by "learning to appreciate things his way" (p. 60).

As stated, the argument seems to be that Quine can't pass from indeterminacy of translation to indeterminacy of meaning. If so, it is puzzling. For suppose there is determinate native meaning. Either there is *no* meaning-preserving mapping from native sentences to those of the translator's language, or there is one. Suppose there is. Then the problem is this. By hypothesis, the native expresses determinate meanings by his sentences and the translator can learn his language and thus come to grasp them. But he cannot, even in principle, determinately translate him, not because there is no determinate meaning-preserving mapping, but because any translation scheme, including the right one, is radically underdetermined by any evidence he could get. Yet whatever the native makes available to him by way of instruction in his tongue can, it seems, contain nothing that is not in principle available to him as translator. How then can it enable him to learn determinate native meanings whilst being insufficient, in principle, to identify a determinate translation scheme? Retreating into the first alternative – no mapping – is not an attractive escape route. It will not, I think, be enough to insist that as a matter of contingent fact, no meaning-preserving mapping exists. For then there *could* be one. So we have no solid ground for refusing to attempt an explanation of the kind demanded on the second alternative. The claim that there is necessarily no such mapping, even though native meaning is determinate, is scarcely plausible. Blackburn would, I suspect, claim that he has provided the needed explanation – it is not that there is helpful material available to the learner but not the translator, but that the latter's alien conceptual scheme gets in the way. He must "[drop] his own preconceptions, and then [learn] to appreciate things their way". But this mislocates Quine's argument (from below). The translator needs his "analytical hypotheses" because he can't progress beyond translation up to truth-functions without them. Certainly the learner has no need of them, simply because he is not in the translation business. But it remains to be explained how it is that the material which, we are supposing, radically underdetermines choice of analytical hypotheses, nonetheless ensures that the learner acquires determinate native quantifiers, etc., and the right ones. How can he be sure he's come away from his lessons with that much?

With dog-legged theories demolished and the negative point established, Blackburn turns to the idea that meaning something is a matter of following rules. and its associated problems. What kind of fact about a speaker makes it the case that he is following a particular rule, rather than some other rule – perhaps a "bent" rule, involving a transition point, such as one that requires you to call something 'round' before a certain date if it is round, but to apply the term after that date only to square things, or even no rule at all? Is the crucial fact one about the speaker's mind (e.g. that he has a determinate intention of some sort), or is it one which essentially involves other speakers (e.g. that he participates in some communal practice in which criticism by his fellow practitioners plays an indispensable part)? These are the central questions of Chapter 3. On the former, Blackburn argues that whilst there is nothing intrinsically wrong with bent rules, a bent rule follower's application of his term must be guided by his belief about where he stands with respect to the transition point. This gives us, he infers, a genuine difference in dispositions between him and us, and one which is in principle detectable in advance of his passage round the bend. On the latter, he argues that the negative point does not force us to deny that the crucial facts are ones about the speaker's mind – it rather puts constraints on the kind of fact it could be, and on the kind of knowledge he can have of it. Participation in public practice, he tries to show, is neither necessary nor sufficient for genuine rule-following. A born Crusoe, who follows self-imposed rules in (contingent) isolation is an undeniable possibility. And "if the practice of an individual in isolation is not enough to create the fact that his words have meaning, how is the practice of a lot of us together to create the fact that *our* words have meaning?" (p. 85). If public practice is not needed, if isolated practice or determinate individual intentions can sustain genuine rule-following, what becomes of the arguments against private language, and more specifically the denial that private objects (sensations, etc) can play any part in fixing meanings? The closing sections of this chapter try to show that they are inconclusive at best.

Chapter 4 seeks to provide an account of what it is to have a language – this Blackburn takes to be a matter of making clear what kinds of conventions are basic to language. Grice, he argues, has given us a good account of how communication can be accomplished in the "one-off predicament" (in which no linguistic or other conventional means are available), and, moreover, an account which can be rendered much simpler than others have supposed, but the project of building a general account of language on this basis ("linguistic nominalism", in Bennett's phrase) is unpromising. Blackburn favours a "convention-belief" account, which allows the Gricean mechanism a role in getting communication under way, but sees working language as relying on conventions of a kind quite different from ones which would make regular linguistic meaning a matter of "fossilized" Gricean meaning$_{nn}$.

II. QUASI-REALISM

The central chapters (5–7) of Blackburn's book elaborate and defend a position he calls *quasi-realism*. The q-realist case is most fully developed in the area of ethical judgments, where it involves defending an expressive account of our use of moral predicates, reminiscent of, but more sophisticated than, the notorious Boo! Hooray! or emotivist theory. Q-realism seems to be intended to be a version of anti-realism. So the best way to understand it is to see how it differs both from Realism and from the various other anti-realist positions considered.

Realism. The reader may regret that Blackburn offers no clean, sharp and explicit account of what he takes Realism to be – the more so, because q-realism appears eventually to approach so closely to what one might take to be the realist position under discussion that one begins to wonder whether it is not just Realism under a new title. But perhaps this complaint mistakes Blackburn's strategy, which is to argue that there is nothing clear, or clearly true, that the would-be realist can say which the q-realist cannot accommodate. In any case, a rough and ready account, based on some remarks early in 5.1, will serve well enough for our purposes. On this account, a Realist with respect to a certain class of statements is one who holds that there is, in the world, a distinctive range of facts in virtue of which statements in that class are true or false. Thus a moral realist is one who holds there to be a class of distinctively moral facts in virtue of which some moral judgments are true, others false. The realist, thus characterized, is not committed to bivalence, though he may of course subscribe to it (Blackburn argues, in 6.4, that the q-realist can explain commitment to bivalence).

Kinds of anti-realism. The realist about a class of statements A incurs commitments which others may be unwilling to share: ontological commitments, obviously, to there being A-facts (and thereby, probably, to A-objects, A-properties, etc.) and also, unless his position is to be quite mysterious, epistemological commitments – he will at least need to have some account of how we come to know about A-facts, and this may lead him to espouse the view that there is some distinctive manner of coming to know them (ethical intuition, say, or some Gödelian quasi-perceptual acquaintance with mathematical states of affairs).

Blackburn discerns three options for one who lacks stomach for the realist feast: rejection, reduction and non-cognitivism. *Rejection* is just to give up A-talk altogether (cf. Quine's attitude to beliefs, dispositions; or Wittgenstein's denial, in the *Tractatus*, of the causal nexus). Suppose A-statements to be the problematic class. The familiar *reductionist* move is to find a class of unproblematic B-statements such that any given A-statement can be held to have the same content as some suitably constructed B-statement. There is then no need to desist from making A-statements – we can continue to make them, secure in the knowledge that we incur thereby no extra commitments (i.e. additional to those already involved in B-statements). There are facts that make A-statements true, but no distinctively A-facts. The third possibility, *non-cognitivism*, is to retain A-statements but deny that they have the informational function suggested by their outward form – to hold that their function is not, as it appears, to convey *truths* (about the A-realm [realism] or any other [reductionism]) but to express attitudes, emotions or some other sort of non-cognitive state. The best-known example of this position is the emotivist account of ethical judgments.

Q-realism is, as I understand it, a species of non-cognitivism. Its *differentia* is that it promises to secure the advantages which reduction would bring without its well-known problems. Blackburn comes at it from two directions – from consideration of the reasons why reductionism is likely to fail, at least in interesting cases, and by developing and extending the expressive account of evaluative statements. He presses several familiar objections to reduction. Except perhaps in isolated and rather trivial cases, credible reductive analyses of the required sort (meaning equivalences between ostensibly problematic A-statements and unproblematic B-statements) are not, it seems, to be had. To the extent that Quine's holistic picture of the "interanimation of sentences" with its consequence that no individual sentence has a "fund of implications to call its own" is right, reductionist hopes are bound to be frustrated.

The (likely) failure of reductionism does not however, according to Blackburn, mean that the underlying anti-realist aim may not be achieved. For the anti-realist:

> ... A-states of affairs have to be brought down to the B-earth, and the natural way to set about this is to equate A-statements with particular B-statements. But is it the only way? (p. 158)

It is not:

> ... there is another option. What philosophers certainly want is a way of *explaining* our propensity to use and understand the problematic vocabulary given only that we live in a world in which we are sensitive to no more than the *underlying* truths (p. 159).

The reductionist gambit can be seen to be *one* way of winning such an explanation, but it is not the only way. It may be possible to provide an explanation which is faithful to the anti-realist distaste for additional types of fact and ways of coming to know them, because it invokes no more than the underlying (B-) facts and our capacity to discern them, and which yet avoids appeal to any sort of would-be reductive analysis (*vide* pp. 162–3).

Expressive theories, projection and q-realism. A simple expressive theory of a given class of A-statements secures the anti-realist aim (doing without A-facts, etc.) without appeal to reductive analysis. Making or endorsing A-statements commits us to no extra facts, not because such statements are really B-statements in disguise (and so are true, when true, in virtue of B-facts) but because we are playing an altogether different game – expressing some attitude rather than stating something true or false.
Here Blackburn introduces the idea of *projection*:

> ... we *project* an attitude or habit or other commitment which is not descriptive onto the world, when we speak and think as though there were a property of things which our sayings describe which we can reason about, know about, be wrong about, and so on (p 170–1).

He notes the tendency of philosophers attracted to the idea that such a projection underlies our use of evaluative or causal language to hold that a projective explanation of our talk of values or causes shows it to involve an *error* – we mistake ourselves for stating facts when we are not and thereby embrace a false and inflated view of the underlying reality. The thought is that once we become aware of the projective origin of our talk, we must give up our practice of talking as if e.g. evaluative remarks had truth-conditions. Q-realism is:

> ... the enterprise of showing that there is [no error] – that even on anti-realist grounds, there is nothing improper, nothing "diseased" in projected predicates ... [q-realism] tries to earn, on the slender basis, the features of moral language (or of the other commitments to which a projective theory might apply) which tempt people to realism (p. 171).

Suppose we focus, as Blackburn himself does, on the q-realist position with respect to moral talk. Then the line of thought is, I take it, broadly as follows: (1) We talk as if there were moral facts, as if there are, in addition to natural properties, moral properties which actions, or agents, may have or lack. (2) But there are, in reality, no such moral facts or moral properties, only actions and agents with natural properties, together with our attitudes of (dis)approval, etc. directed upon them. Thus in so talking, we are projecting – spreading the word in the last sense alluded to in my opening paragraph. The distinctive meaning of moral talk is expressive, not descriptive. Because this is so, both realism and anti-realist reductionism (here, ethical naturalism) are to be rejected. The former because there are no distinctively moral facts, etc., the latter because moral utterances, properly understood, are not utterances with genuine truth-conditions and are thus not equivalent in meaning to statements of any other (non-moral) kind, with genuine truth-conditions. (3) Whilst it may appear that, having its roots in such a projection, our practice of presenting our attitudes as if they were genuine candidates for truth must be in error, this is not so.

For we can, so the q-realist holds, explain our practice in a way which does not oblige us to abandon it as misguided once we appreciate the correctness of his explanation.

There is much that is obscure in this. In particular, we have as yet no sharp conception of the *kind* of explanation that is being proposed, nor of what constraints it must respect. It is clear, I think, that the "no error" claim cannot be the claim that when we project, we are not in error if we *think that* there are moral facts, properties, etc. – it must be the claim that we are not in error if we *thing as if*, as well as talk as if, there were moral facts, etc., even though there are none. [There is a small problem here which I shall not pursue – whilst there is no difficulty in separating talking as if p from thinking that p, it is not so clear that we can cleanly separate thinking as if p from thinking that p in the way that seems to be required. We can of course make a distinction – we think as if p, without necessarily thinking that p, when we reason on the supposition that p. But this does not seem to be quite the distinction that is called for here.] The q-realist's explanation must exhibit our practice as one we have adequate reason to maintain even though there are no facts of the kind that practice suggests. Obviously enough, the explanation must make no appeal to facts of the forbidden variety. Still, we may wonder not just how the trick is to be pulled off, but what the conditions for successful conjuring are. I shall come back to this in a more literal fashion later. For now, we had better see how Blackburn tries to do it. Although he offers some interesting arguments for q-realism in morals, its explanatory strategy emerges most clearly in his attempt to meet what he sees as, perhaps, the main obstacle to it – namely Professor Geach's well-known objection to expressive theories, based on what he calls the Frege point. This, as Geach first formulates it, is that

> a thought may have just the same content whether you assent to its truth or not; a proposition may occur in discourse now asserted, now unasserted, and yet be recognizably the same proposition. [*Philosophical Review* Vol. LXXIV No. 4, pp. 449]

There may be room for dispute about what precisely the Frege point amounts to. But at the very least, it constrains us not to propose an analysis of the meaning or use of a type of sentence A which fails to allow sentences of that type to figure, without shift of meaning, as unasserted or, more neutrally, unendorsed components of disjunctions or conditionals. For if we do, we shall be at a loss to explain how it is that we commit no fallacy of equivocation when we argue: *If A then B, but A. Hence B or A or B, but not-A. Hence B.*

The Frege point certainly poses a problem for the Expressive theorist who would have it that the whole meaning of e.g. 'Lying is wrong' is captured by saying that its function is not to state any fact but to express an attitude. For he may then be confronted with the fact that we can, apparently, argue validly:

(1) If lying is wrong then getting little brother to lie is also wrong.
(2) Lying is wrong.
Hence
(3) getting little brother to lie is wrong.

Plainly, 'lying is wrong', as it occurs in (1), does not serve to express disapproval for lying. Hence if the whole meaning of (2) consists in its doing just that, the sentence has different meanings in its two occurences and the argument equivocates.

72   BOB HALE

It might appear that the argument just rehearsed is a knock-down – that it shows, at a stroke, that no expressive theory of evaluative predications is tenable. But that is fairly clearly an overestimate of what it achieves. It does unquestionably reveal a gap in the simple expressive theory, which concentrates on the simplest ("asserted") uses of evaluative predication and supplies no account of their use in compounds such as conditionals. Until it fills this gap it lacks credibility – particularly so, since the prospects of filling out the theory do not seem too bright.

Blackburn's theory comprises: (1) a general account of the function of conditionals, etc., incorporating evaluative predications which accords with a projectivist view of them:

> . . . can we explain what we are up to when we make these remarks? Unasserted contexts show us treating moral predicates like others, *as though* by their means we can introduce objects of doubt, belief, knowledge, things which can be supposed, queried, pondered. Can the projectivist say why we do this? (p. 191)

and (2) a semantic theory to supplement this general account.

(1) It is easy enough for the projectivist to explain why we should be found asserting evaluative *conjunctions* like: 'Lying is wrong and so is stealing'. Given that we may hold both of a pair of attitudes, it is only to be expected that we should avail ourselves of the conjunctive form to register our double commitment. This is the easy case of course – because one who asserts a conjunction is committed to both conjuncts. All that is needed to bring this into line with the expressive theory is a simple broadening of the notion of commitment to cover not only beliefs but also attitudes. Such broadening is further eased, as Blackburn observes, by the fact that we have an accepted practice of conjoining components not susceptible of truth-value (*viz.* imperatives).

What of the seemingly harder case of conditionals? We are not, when we assert (1), registering disapproval of lying. But this does not mean that we are not to be understood as registering a commitment at all. If we are doing so, what commitment is it, and why should we choose the conditional form to express it? Blackburn's answer is that we put our commitments conditionally because we are "working out their implications". But what is it to work out the implications of something which is itself not a candidate for truth?

> At this point we must turn again to the projective picture. A moral *sensibility* . . . is defined by a function from *input* of belief to *output* of attitude. Now not all such sensibilities are admirable . . . it is extremely important for us to rank sensibilities, and to endorse some and reject others . . . amongst the features of sensibilities which matter are, of course, not only the actual attitudes which are the output, but the interactions between them. For instance, a sensibility which *pairs* an attitude of disapproval towards telling lies, and an attitude of calm or approval towards getting your little brother to tell lies, would not meet my endorsement. I can only admire people who would reject the second action as strongly as they would reject the first . . . The conditional form shows me expressing this endorsement (p. 192).

So the projectivist account of (2) is that what we are doing is voicing approval for combining the attitude of disapproval of lying with a similar attitude towards getting little brother to lie.

(2) *Blackburn's semantic theory.* Blackburn invites us to consider a variant on actual English, E_{ex}, in which value-judgments wear their expressive nature on their sleeves. This contains a pair of operators 'H!' (Hooray!) and 'B!' (Boo!) which attach to descriptions of things to yield expressions of attitude. Thus 'H! (giving money to the miners)' would express approval for giving etc., and 'B! (lying)' would express disapproval of lying. Speakers of this language will also need a notation for endorsing or rejecting various couplings of attitude, or couplings of belief and attitude. He introduces the notation '[H!(x)]', '[B!(x)]' to denote respectively the attitudes of approval and disapproval of x, and the notation: 'A;B' to "denote the view that one attitude or belief involves or is coupled with another".

With this apparatus we can, Blackburn proposes, form a compound "expressive" corresponding to the conditional (2); it is:

H!([B!(lying)]; [B!(getting little brother to lie)])

This language will be spoken, he suggests, by people who need to signal and respect consistencies and inconsistencies. One who combines the foregoing complex attitude with the simple one expressible by: 'B!(lying)' is involved in such an inconsistency if he condones getting little brother to lie: for anyone who combines

> disapproval of lying, and approval of making (disapproval of getting little brother to lie) follow upon (disapproval of lying) . . . must hold the conse-quential disapproval . . . if he does not his attitudes clash (p. 195).

Since speakers of E_{ex} have this need, what more natural than that they should fall into using predicates (e.g. '. . . is wrong') corresponding to attitudes (e.g. disapproval) and treat commitments as if they were genuine judgments, thereby making available to themselves the argumentative apparatus associated with genuine truths and false-hoods? *"This is what is meant by 'projecting' attitudes onto the world"* (p. 195).

This is Blackburn's semantic theory. The proposal, I take it, is that beneath evaluative inferences, ostensibly involving evaluative *propositions*, there is always an underlying or "deep" structure representable in E_{ex}, or something like it. What makes for the validity of our sample inference, and others like it, is not that it would be logically inconsistent to assent to the premises but reject the conclusion, in the sense that it is *impossible* for the premises to be true without the conclusion being true as well. This account is available to the realist and the reductionist, but not to the projectivist. Rather, what underpins the inference is inconsistency of another, evalua-tive or attitudinal sort – accepting the premises but rejecting the conclusion involves one in a "clash of attitudes".

It is an ingenious theory. But will it work? It is clearly crucial that we should be able to understand attitudinal inconsistency independently, without falling back on "descriptive" inconsistency (impossibility of joint truth). Can we? Blackburn's infor-mal reading of 'H!([B!(lying)];[B!(getting little brother to lie)])' as "approval of making (disapproval of getting little brother to lie) *follow upon* (disapproval of lying)" makes it look straightforward enough, perhaps. But it involves reading 'A;B' as 'making B follow upon A', and it seems to me that the projectivist is not entitled to this gloss, at least not without further explanation. The obvious one is that making B follow upon A is ensuring that if you have the attitude described by A, you also have that described by B. But this is surely unavailable; the problem was, *inter alia*, to *explain* how we come to speak conditionally of our commitments – the theory loses all interest if it merely sneaks in conditionality in unfamiliar guise. So we had better stick to the more austere reading of 'A;B' as 'combining A with B'. The trouble now is that it is unclear in what way precisely the combination of attitudes in question is supposed to be inconsistent. Certainly an inconsistency could be located if we could appeal to a principle of inference such as: from 'B!(x), H!([B!(x)];[B!(y)])' *infer* 'B!(y)'. But to appeal to any such principle at this stage would be to assume clear precisely what was to be explained, i.e. how principles of inference get a grip on expressives.

This problem can be solved by adopting a different "deep structure" for conditionals like (1). The important thing about accepting it is that it commits you to *disapproving* of anyone who disapproves of lying but does not disapprove of getting little brother to lie. To bring this out in E_{ex} we need to supplement it with a kind of negation – we need to represent lack of attitude. So let '–[H!(x)]', '–[B!(x)]' denote lacking the attitudes of (dis)approval for x. (It is worth stressing that this is not ordinary sentential negation.) Then (1) becomes:

B!([B!(lying)];–[B!(getting little brother to lie)])

Now put this disapproval together with 'B!(lying)' and '–B!(getting little brother to lie)' and you have a simple inconsistency. Someone with this pattern of attitudes combines disapproval of lying with condonation of getting little brother to lie – a compound "action" of which he himself disapproves. This solution locates the inconsistency, not in a clash of attitudes but in failure to make one's actions (including the actions of adopting/adhering to attitudes) cohere with one's other attitudes. It suggests a general principle of attitudinal inconsistency which we could put:

B!([B!(x)];x)

Don't do what you Boo! More seriously, this proposal appeals to a notion of moral inconsistency which is plausible independently of projectivist leanings – one is guilty of a morally important kind of failing (we might as well call it inconsistency) to the extent that one fails to make one's actions accord with one's principles. There are, to be sure, other kinds of inconsistency which may be indulged in this area. In particular, we have yet to provide for inconsistency between principles (Blackburn's clashes of attitude). But we might, I think, say that attitudes clash if they consist of approval and disapproval towards the same action-type, or if they are attitudes of approval towards x-ing and not-x-ing.

We have, then, the beginnings of a projectivist theory of moral judgment. Clearly they are no more than that – moral judgments may take other forms, and we have yet to be told how to extend the theory to them. This may occasion the worry, noted by Blackburn, that the q-realist faces the "endless task" of constructing "separate and ingenious explanations" for each new context. The best way to answer this worry would be to develop this sketch into a full-blooded general (probably recursive) theory. This is no place for that. But I shall comment briefly on one kind of unasserted context which will clearly have to be handled. How should we deal with "mixed" conditionals, in which the consequent is a sentence which the projectivist would take as expressing an attitude (at least when separately "asserted") but the antecedent is a candidate for truth? For example:

If Edward stole the money, he should be punished

It will not do to render this as:

If Edward stole the money, H! (punishing Edward)

This is of doubtful syntactic propriety, but that is the least of its troubles. How are we to understand the conditional as a whole? Is it a candidate for truth? Apparently not. But if we say instead that it is a conditional expression of attitude, we surely have not got the form right. For although one who asserts the original is not voicing approval for punishing Edward, he is voicing some attitude. So it will not do to have the expressive operator buried within the scope of the conditional.

What is wanted, I suggest, is not a mixture of English and E_{ex}, but a purely E_{ex} form for which our conditional can be seen as a natural substitute. We have already seen reason to take "action" broadly enough to cover having or adopting attitudes, as well as more exhausting activities such as digging and whistling. This allows us complex terms of E_{ex} like '[B!(lying)];lying', denoting the complex action of combining disapproval of lying with lying. Why not allow cognitive attitudes to count, alongside evaluative ones, as actions in this broad sense? If we do, we shall have a place for compound expressives like: 'H!(believing that snails are about to overrun the world; treading on them)'. Our conditional about Edward might then be seen as the surface form of something like:

B!(believing that Edward stole the money; –[H! (punishing Edward)])

The theory just outlined might be called *modest q-realism* – it aims to explain how, in the absence of a realm of distinctively moral facts and any notion of truth properly applicable to moral judgments, we are nonetheless engaged in a respectable enterprise when we talk as if there were. Whilst it requires further elaboration and defence, the theory is clearly one to be reckoned with. Blackburn's q-realism is more ambitious, in two ways. First, he tries to show that, whilst there are no distinctively moral facts, there is a decent notion of moral truth available to the q-realist. Second, he carries the q-realist flag into other areas – e.g. counterfactuals, the theory of modality [6.5], and ultimately truth in general [7.5–7.8].

Moral Truth. The applicability of truth-words to moral utterances ('It is true that eating people is wrong, . . .', etc.) poses no serious threat to the modest q-realist enterprise, and certainly seems to require no projectivist explanation additional to that already offered for our propensity to use evaluative predicates. The attempt to build a projectivist notion of moral truth may thus be found puzzling. Wasn't the point of the preceding account to explain how we can avail ourselves of the machinery for "debating truth" in moral contexts *without* regarding moral remarks as genuine candidates for truth? So why now try to develop a notion of truth for them? Supposing that a projectivist account of moral truth can be upheld, wouldn't that make the preceding explanation simply redundant? The answer, I think, is that it wouldn't, because the notion of moral truth is to be constructed out of materials provided by the earlier account, in particular, the notion of an improvement on a set of attitudes.

Blackburn's proposed account of moral truth is that

76   BOB HALE

m is true if m belongs to M*

where m is any sentence expressing an attitude and M* is the "best possible set of attitudes", this being understood as "the limiting set which would result from taking all possible opportunities for improvement of attitude".

The obvious difficulty is: what right have we to suppose that there is a single limit on which any series of improvements on any imperfect set converges? Blackburn seeks to meet it with some help from Hume's essay "Of the standard of taste", from which he draws the example of the two literary critics – one "a young man whose passions are warm", who prefers the amorous and tender images of Ovid, the other "a man more advanced in years, who takes pleasure in wise, philosophical reflections ..." and prefers the work of Tacitus. We are to imagine the young man's literary sensibility improved and refined into a system M^*_O and the other's into a different system M^*_r. The former still holds Ovid to be the better writer, the latter Tacitus. The question is: how can we recover a notion of truth for either judgment? Elaborating on Hume's claim ("it is plainly an error in a critic, to confine his approbation to one species or style of writing, and condemn all the rest"), B argues that one cannot coherently hold that there is no possible improvement on either M^*_O or M^*_r, whilst accepting that they involve conflicting attitudes:

> How can you have each of these? . . . We are constrained to argue and practise as though the truth is single, and this constraint is defensible in spite of the apparent possibility of [divergent attitudes] (pp. 200–01).

Blackburn's argument here moves rather mysteriously. The idea seems to be that anyone who is intelligently aware of two conflicting sets of attitudes enjoys thereby a better perspective on both, from which he is bound to see at least one of them as open to improvement. But even if his claim that I cannot hold that neither of the two sets of attitudes is open to improvement is true (and I suspect it is), some crucial questions remain. Why, exactly, is this so? And if it is, what good reason does it afford for thinking that "truth is single", i.e. that there is a unique best set of attitudes? To these questions, it seems to me, he provides no (clear) answer. A possible answer to the first is quite simply that (evaluative) consistency constrains me to avoid so thinking – if I really think that a set of attitudes is without fault, I have no good reason not to endorse it, and if I think this about two conflicting such sets, that leaves me endorsing inconsistent attitudes. But this answer will not suit Blackburn, since there is plainly no sound move from this to the conclusion that truth is single. The argument seems to draw a conclusion about what cannot be the case from a premiss about what cannot coherently be asserted. But such moves are apt to be unreliable – no-one can coherently assert both that he believes that p and that p is false, but this does not of course warrant the supposition that he is infallible.

Extending q-realism – counterfactuals and *modality*. Projectivism is, of course, not new. Hume's projective account of causation – the doctrine that our experience of regularities leads to the formation of habits of expectation which we then project onto the observed world – is, as Blackburn notes, perhaps the classic example from the history of philosophy. He neither endorses nor rejects it, but is content to insist that Hume's theory be tackled for what it is, not irrelevantly slated as a flawed attempt at reduction with grotesque psychological accretions. Still, as Blackburn observes, it may fail for want of a way of describing the underlying facts in wholly non-causal terms.

In the area of counterfactuals and modality, Blackburn is less neutral on the prospects for q-realist reconstructions. Lewis's notorious argument for Realism, he argues, simply ignores the possibility of a q-realist alternative, which will accept and explain such talk without invoking any realm of specifically modal facts (facts about merely possible worlds), and assumes the only rival options are rejecting modal talk altogether (Quine) or reducing it.

Why should we prefer a q-realist account of these matters? The arguments offered are, disappointingly, familiar and, indeed, just plain disappointing:

(a) since the only possible world that is actual is the actual world, others cannot *actually* influence us: we cannot receive information about them, because there is nothing to actually influence any receptors (p. 214).

(b) If the possible worlds, like moral properties, represent a new realm of fact, why should we be interested in it? Talking of possibilities would be as optional to us, interested in the actual world, as talk of neighbouring countries or different times would be to us, if we are interested in the here and now ... Why should it interest me if in such spheres something holds, or in some it does not, or if in ones quite similar to the actual world things do or do not hold, if I want to discover and use truths about the ways things actually are? (pp. 214–15)

Argument (a) seems to rely on one or both of two disputable assumptions – that the realist with respect to a class of statements is *bound* to hold that there is some mysterious, quasi-perceptual mode of acquaintance with the facts they report, or admit that we can have no epistemological basis for making them, and that nothing exists but what can causally interact with us.

Argument (b) comes from the same box as Kripke's notorious Humphrey argument against counterpart theory, well criticised by Allen Hazen, but Blackburn has apparently not taken the point. Briefly, it is this: there is no problem about why we should be interested in the truth-value of propositions like 'That uninsulated wire may be live'. [It is, incidentally, amazing that Blackburn should be so confident that someone interested in the here and now could have no interest in the there and then.] These are modal truths or falsehoods about the actual world. No-one in his right mind will argue, if it turns out that the wire wasn't live, that we had no good reason to treat it so gingerly. What makes such modal propositions true or false, on a possible worlds account, is how things are in other possible worlds. If there is a world (perhaps one like ours in relevant respects) in which this wire (or a counterpart of it, in Lewis's theory) is live, then it is true in the actual world that that wire might be live. Since that is so, we have every reason in the world (the actual world!) to be interested in whether there is some such possible world.

What positive account will the q-realist offer? Blackburn gestures at a projectivist treatment of counterfactuals, taking Mackie's view that they are condensed arguments (rather than true or false) as its starting point:

We have a sense of the potential for improvement in any argument. . . . We

> need a proper notion of the *improvement or deterioration in the bases* for
> argument, and proceed to construct a notion of truth. The eventual theory
> . . . would be one which maintains the benefits of possible world imagery,
> but disallows the metaphysical extravagance (p. 216).

This is too programmatic for serious criticism. I await the eventual theory with
interest, noting in the meanwhile that whilst we do certainly possess a sense of the
potential for improvement in arguments, it is far from clear that the kinds of
improvements we would normally think of lend themselves to a projectivist treatment.
As regards logical necessity, he is more forthcoming:

> Projectivism . . . avoids the mystery of a necessity–detecting faculty [real-
> ism] and it avoids the strained scepticism [e.g. Quine's] which tries to avoid
> admitting that any truths are necessary at all . . . [the projectivist option is]
> to face the fact that such truths [as e.g. that $7 + 5 = 12$] do occupy a special
> category, for we can easily imagine otherwise most of our most cherished
> beliefs, and to say that when we dignify a truth as necessary we are
> expressing our own mental attitude – in this case our own inability to make
> anything of a possible way of thinking which denies it. It is this blank
> unimaginability which we voice when we use the modal vocabulary (pp.
> 216–17).

This proposal, like the projective account of evaluative predication on which it is
modelled, avoids crude subjectivism and can thus sidestep some familiar objections.
But it confronts others, including the standard ones to Hume's apparent equation of
the logically possible with the imaginable, to which, of course, it bears a striking
resemblance. These Blackburn does not discuss, save to remark that the projectivist
will respond to the charge that he confuses psychological facts about our sentiments
with the "real modal status of propositions" by denying that anything more can be
meant by the latter "than can be understood by seeing it as a projection of our (best)
attitude of comprehension or imagination towards [them]". The crucial question
here is what, in detail, the projectivist can tell us to explain the parenthetical best,
which promises to give his theory the edge over earlier and cruder accounts of this
ilk. If he can give a good account of this, it may help him to deal with the difficulty
posed by the fact that remarks of the form:

> I cannot imagine how it could be the case that p, but it may be possible that
> p all the same

and even ones of the simpler form:

> I cannot imagine its being the case that p, but it could be

are seemingly well-formed and possibly true.

Two other difficulties are worth mentioning, though neither can be discussed here
at any length. What, if anything, can be made of iterated modalities on a projective
account? On that account, 'Lp' *asserts* nothing (or nothing over and above plain 'p')
but serves rather to express inability to imagine 'p's not being true. Presumably the
same will go for 'LLp' – but what is it that I profess an inability to imagine in this
case? The difficulty is, or appears to be that 'Lp' is explained as a device for
expressing an attitude towards a *proposition*; this seems to require that we understand

'Lp' as introducing a proposition towards which we express that attitude when we assert 'LLp', but we are debarred from so regarding it by the theory. Suppose, in pursuit of the parallel with the treatment of evaluative predication, we introduce 'L!' as an operator which when attached to a (declarative) sentence, yields a sentence expressing inability to imagine the falsehood of that sentence, and use ' L!(p)]' to denote the inability thus expressed. The difficulty is then: how are we to understand such things as 'L!([L!(2+2=4)])'? 'L!' demands a sentence as operand, so the embedded 'L!' is all right, but '[L!(2+2=4)]' is not a sentence (it is a term denoting a certain inability), so the whole thing should be simply ill-formed.

The second difficulty concerns the attitude to which, according to the theory, we give expression in saying 'Lp'. It is, and probably has to be, specified in modal terms (can/can't imagine . . .). If the possibility referred to here is *logical*, the theory is circular. If not, of what sort is it? Declaring it to be psychological would avoid direct circularity but threatens to square ill with the hinted normativeness ("our *best* attitude of comprehension or imagination"). This difficulty is further aggravated if a projectivist account of non-logical modalities is to be given. Indeed, one wonders whether the projectivist will be able to preserve the distinctions many of us think we discern between logical and natural or physical necessity, etc.

Truth. What general account of truth should a q-realist favour? Blackburn argues – unsurprisingly, given the character of his attempted construction of moral truth – that he should embrace a form of Coherence theory.

Against its traditional rival – some form of Correspondence, more congenial to the Realist – Blackburn rehearses some familiar objections. If he is to be seen as *explaining* truth, he must get beyond the platitudinous equation of 'true' with 'corresponds to the facts' – he needs to be able to appeal to independently workable notions of *fact* and *correspondence*, in terms of which truth can be explained. The fatal weakness, Blackburn contends, is that urged by traditional critics – no such independent conceptions are to be had. Correspondence collapses with exposure of the myth of the given: "Experience cannot be regarded as an independent source of a conception of fact – independent, that is, of the operation of judgement" because judgement is inextricably involved in all experience. This objection appears to depend on the assumption that the only way we could come by a conception of facts (as states of affairs obtaining independently of our or anyone's thought or belief) is by experience presenting us with undressed samples on a plate – surely some argument is needed here.

It is important for Blackburn that Correspondence falls to specific objections of this sort rather than to Frege's "blockbuster" – that any definition in terms of correspondence generates an infinite regress. For this argument (see "The Thought") is, as Frege observed, independent of any peculiarities of correspondence and thus seems to block *any* definition of truth, be it in terms of correspondence or something else, such as coherence. Thus Blackburn, far from being able to enlist the support of Frege's argument against correspondence, needs to find a way round it. The difficulty, as he sees it, is that any correct definition of truth must share with 'is true' what may be called the "transparency" property (to think, wonder, etc., whether it is true that p is the same thing as thinking, wondering, etc., whether p) but that any elucidation which does more than offer a trivial synonym must apparently lack this

80   BOB HALE

property, since it will introduce some property which makes for the truth of p, and of this further property p itself (and hence, via transparency, the statement that it is true that p) says nothing. Blackburn's preferred way round the difficulty is to broaden the notion of elucidation. So long as what is sought is a definition or analysis, the *analysans* will indeed have to share transparency with the *analysandum*. But just as the best route for the moral anti-realist is not naturalistic reduction but a q-realist explanation of "what we are up to" in applying truth idioms in the moral sphere, so:

> There is no principled reason why a conception of what truth is might not play the same role, although it provides no analysing phrase with the same repetitive powers as 'it is true that . . .'. It would explain what we are doing when we make judgements, display a conception of success or correctness which governs judgement and make it unsurprising that we have a notion of truth, and the consequent behaviour of predicates announcing it (p. 232).

His claim is that some useful account of truth (as what we aim at in judgment, etc.) can be given, in terms of coherence, without pretending to offer a definition or meaning-equivalence.

Despite its initial unattractiveness and widespread unpopularity, a coherence approach has, Blackburn claims, some advantages to commend it. It dismisses the "barely given facts" as "the imaginary creatures of false theory" (Bradley's phrase). Anticipating Quine and Wittgenstein, its British Idealist defenders embraced a holistic view of meaning scarcely congenial to the correspondence conception. And it is well placed to explain why generally accepted merits of scientific theories – simplicity, strength, fertility, etc. – are indeed merits. The connection of these virtues with truth – opaque on rival approaches – is transparent enough for the coherence theorist, for whom truth is no more than membership of a system of beliefs which is the ideal possessor of these and related virtues. "*The root idea is that the virtue of truth is constructed from the virtues of method*" (p. 237).

Earlier defenders of coherence saw that simple *consistency* of a system of beliefs is insufficient for truth – all too obviously, there can be mutually incompatible but internally consistent belief systems – and added a requirement of *comprehensiveness*. Critics, most notably Russell, have argued that this is still not good enough: you can satisfy the demands of consistency and increase comprehensiveness by making entirely fanciful additions to the system of beliefs, conveniently plugging the gaps left open by other, more respectable sources of information. Blackburn interprets Bradley's response to Russell's objection as arguing for a third requirement – *control*. Exactly what this comes to is less fully explained than one might wish, but it seems to involve at least this much: if a belief is to be added, perhaps in the interests of increasing comprehensiveness, we must add along with it what Blackburn calls its "pedigree" (roughly, our epistemological backing for it) and be prepared to add too any further beliefs which enjoy the same or a relevantly similar pedigree. The hope is that, with this extra requirement in force, the coherence theorist has a principled reason to resist fanciful augmentations – any such addition will now require the admission of many other fanciful beliefs, all with an equally good pedigree, and inconsistency will swiftly result.

Will this defence work? It will only do so, Blackburn argues, if the coherence

THE COMPLEAT PROJECTIVIST   81

theorist can single out the *right* kinds of control and, moreover, explain why they are the right kinds without appealing to the idea that conformity to them leads to truth, or at least increases our chances of attaining to it. For if he cannot do so, it is hard to see what cogent objection he could make to the proposal that we should follow a policy of "admitting fancies-tailored-for-consistency", that is, of making fanciful additions to our set of beliefs just when doing so preserves consistency. So can the coherence theorist "describe the virtues of proper control, comprehension and coherence" and can he "say what is *good* about systems with these features, without mentioning the idea that they deliver the truth"? (p. 240–1) Blackburn notes the temptation to appeal here to Pragmatic considerations – "it is hard to see how it could generally be *useful* to form beliefs without respecting the judgements delivered by the senses, by memory, or by sober processes of enquiry" as opposed to mere fancy – but properly resists it, because the notion of utility seems to presuppose that of truth, and thus to be unavailable to help construct it. He hopes to find a better way out of the difficulty in the idea that our beliefs are subject to *natural controls* – nature does not leave us free to believe just what we fancy, and we cannot help but believe some things rather than others when we open our eyes or prick up our ears.

This suggestion is, on the face of it, puzzling. What we wanted to be told was what is good about consistency, comprehensiveness and the favoured kinds of control, and in particular, respect for the judgements delivered by the senses, memory, etc. What we are told is that we just do form beliefs in some ways and not others, like it or not. The proposed solution seems not to match the agreed problem. I can see, certainly, how the appeal to "what nature commands us (not) to believe" might figure in an answer to the question "What stops us forming beliefs according to a policy of admitting fancies-tailored-for-consistency?" But if there really is needed an account of what is *good* about having one's beliefs shaped by sense experience, this does not seem to be it. Perhaps the thought is that to the extent that nature controls our formation of beliefs, there is after all no need for such an explanation. But even if that is granted – and it is not clear that it should be – there remains the problem of explaining why comprehension and consistency, etc. are virtues, and that of saying just what these virtues *are*. Nature manifestly does not make us consistent believers, even if She encourages us to be comprehensive ones. And consistency needs characterizing independently, if it is to figure in an explanation of truth; the natural account in semantic terms is thus unavailable, but syntactic characterization requires specification of the assumed means of deduction – it is far from clear that this can be provided.

Perhaps Blackburn would not wish to claim that these somewhat undeveloped thoughts about natural controls on belief are enough to resolve the difficulty. Certainly he allows that a correspondence approach seems better placed to do justice to the idea, which cannot be simply dismissed as false metaphysics but is just common sense, that some of our beliefs are acquired in response to mind-independent facts. This much, he concedes, is right about correspondence – "whether or not true beliefs *correspond with* the facts, true believers must certainly *respond* to the facts" (p. 246). The concession is, roughly, that any credible account of truth and knowledge must make room for some at least of our beliefs (e.g. homely perceptually grounded ones, such as that there is a cat in the garden, acquired by looking in the

82   BOB HALE

appropriate place) to be got in response to, have their causal origin in mind-independent states of affairs (e.g. there being a cat loose in the garden). Can the CCC[1] theorist make room for as much? The question is pressing, as Blackburn sees, because if he cannot do so, he may be unable to disentangle himself from an unwelcome liaison with Idealism:

> The loss of the 'barely given fact', and the difficulty of describing the control of a system of beliefs by experience, seems to leave an image of such a system as entirely self-absorbed ... disconnected from the world (p. 243).

The difficulty can, he suggests, be put like this. We are "good instruments for detecting [such things as] cats", i.e. provided we take reasonable precautions, our perceptually grounded beliefs on such matters tend to be true or reliable. Thus any decent theory needs to make sure that we can assert what he calls "correspondence conditionals", such as:

> (1) If I form only beliefs with a proper pedigree, and end up believing that there is a cat in the garden, then there is a cat in the garden.

Such conditionals are intended to express substantive claims, broadly to the effect that our trusted procedures of observation are generally reliable. They are meant to "represent a general truth, not an unbreakable one" (p. 244). It is, of course, easy to ensure their truth by so interpreting "proper pedigree" that nothing that ever issues in a false belief counts as one. But this is to trivialize them. The CCC theorist is in danger of trivializing them in a different way. For by transparency, we can prefix 'it is true that' to the consequent of (1), which then reduces, by substitution of the CCC gloss on the truth idiom, to

> (1**) If I form only beliefs with a proper pedigree, and end up believing that there is a cat in the garden, then the belief that there is a cat in the garden is a member of some best CCC system of beliefs.

This not only looks tautological (interdefinability of 'proper pedigree' and 'best CCC system') but makes us out to be good at discerning members of best CCC systems, whereas (1) was meant to record the fact that we are generally reliable detectors of cats. Blackburn's rescue attempt is unconvincing. The coherence theorist must, he says,

> try to respect the real content of conditionals like (1). He must recognize the causal element underlying them. He must avoid the mistaken equation giving (1**). But he must still maintain that he has a distinct conception of success in judgment, and that it sees success in terms of membership of a CCC system (p. 247).

Certainly he must. As Blackburn agrees, the hard question is whether he *can*.

> The idea would have to be that *internally* we talk of states of affairs, or of correspondence, and of the causal theory allowing (1); but that this permits an *external* reflection that all this is part of our own system of beliefs, and

---

[1] "Controlled, comprehensive, coherent" (p. 240)

that truth accrues to any such system in virtue of its coherence, comprehensiveness, and control (p. 247).

This seems, and surely is, too easy. If our "causal theory of the world" and of perception in particular is just part of the system of beliefs we develop in conformity to the virtues of coherence, comprehensiveness and control, how can we regard our perceptual encounters with the world as central to a natural control mechanism which helps to block perverse epistemological policies such as admitting fancies-tailored-for-consistency? If the virtues, including proper sorts of control, are to shape our system of beliefs in a way that warrants talk of improvements in the direction of a best system (and if that is not warranted, the prospects for a coherentist construction of truth seem to disappear), then they must be recognizable as such independently of the contents of this or that less-than-best system. The comfortable-sounding contrast between internal talk and external thought may cover up a bit of wishful double-think – dangerous double-think too, for if the q-realist is allowed this external reflection, he can surely manage a similar one that will ruin Blackburn's defence against the charge that q-realism makes morals, etc., mind-dependent in some obnoxious sense (cf 6.6).

Space permits for no more than summary comment on the last two chapters. Chapter 8 is deflationary – the philosophical significance claimed for Tarski's work on truth is, he argues, largely illusory. The main theses are: (1) that Tarski's method of defining truth sheds no light on the semantic concepts of truth, reference and satisfaction, (2) that Davidson's programme of constructing extensional theories of meaning for natural languages after Tarski's model, with T-sentences as theorems, is misconceived and doomed to failure, (3) that "bleak" (as opposed to "homely") radical interpretation – which confines its evidence to purely natural, non-psychological features of the situations in which native utterances are produced – is hopeless, and (4) that a compositional theory of meaning is not guaranteed to be logically illuminating, and may fail to address troublesome logical issues relating to the constructions which it recognizes.

Chapter 9 on the topic of reference opens with a lively defence of Russell's Theory of Descriptions, exploiting the Gricean distinction between what's *said* and what's conversationally *implicated* to fend off some familiar objections. Its central sections address an issue brought into prominence by Gareth Evans' work on reference – is there a kind of thought ("singular" or, as Evans called them "information-based" thoughts) the individuation of which involves essential reference to objects outside the mind of the thinker? To the view that there is, Blackburn opposes what he labels the "universalist" view, according to which *all* thoughts are to be individuated *via* universal features (which he identifies with Fregean "modes of presentation"). He tries to show that singular thought theories, at least in the strong form advocated by Evans, are ill-motivated and that the universalist view fares as well, if not better than, weaker, and allegedly more plausible, singular thought theories in saving the relevant appearances. In particular, he argues, the universalist is better placed to do justice to the phenomena of referential opacity. The chapter nicely focusses some key issues and deserves a detailed response. I believe that Blackburn underestimates the arguments, including Evans' own, which support a strong singular thought theory,

84   BOB HALE

and overplays the apparent advantages of the universalist view: but I must reserve
defence of those claims for another occasion.

   Blackburn has given us a fine book, clearly and refreshingly argued, which should
be widely read and discussed. It is hard to imagine, much less write, a book which
really lives up to the golden words of Quintilian of which he reminds us ("do not
write so that you can be understood, but so that you cannot be misunderstood") –
Spreading the Word comes closer to doing so than a good many. It provides a useful
and readable introduction to many of the most important and least accessible areas of
contemporary philosophy of language and metaphysics. And, as I hope to have made
clear, it is a good deal more than a beginner's guide.

University of Lancaster.

Part II
Is the Way Things are Morally Entailed by the Way Things are Non-Morally?

[3]

Mind (1984) Vol. XCIII, 370 380

An Alleged Difficulty Concerning Moral Properties

JAMES C. KLAGGE

I would like to consider a logical difficulty that has been thought to embarrass the moral realist. The difficulty is pressed by Simon Blackburn in his intriguing paper 'Moral Realism'.[1] Blackburn's argument raises substantial issues for the moral realist, and raises them in an intuitive and perspicuous way.

I

There are two conditions for the truth of moral judgements that seem to preclude the view that such truth consists in a correspondence with states of affairs involving moral properties. Loosely, the conditions are these: (1) Moral properties cannot vary over time for a given object or action, nor can they differ between distinct objects or actions, unless the natural properties of the objects or actions in question also vary or differ. But (2) the natural properties of an object or action do not necessarily determine the moral properties of that object or action. Blackburn sharpens these conditions considerably and defends them, but the difficulty they give rise to is this: Since the natural properties of an object do not necessarily determine its moral properties, it is puzzling that their persistence should guarantee the persistence of the moral properties, and that their duplication should guarantee the duplication of the moral properties. There seems to be no explanation of the guaranteed persistence or duplication available to the realist. And, indeed, the second condition seems to suggest that the persistence or duplication would not be guaranteed.

According to Blackburn's own emotivist view of the truth of moral judgements, the conjunction of these conditions seems not to be problematic. People hold moral attitudes towards objects and actions in virtue of the natural properties of the objects and actions. Since different people may have different standards of evaluation,

1   In *Morality and Moral Reasoning*, ed. John Casey (Methuen, 1971).

DIFFICULTY CONCERNING MORAL PROPERTIES   371

the natural properties of an object or action do not constrain all
people to have the same moral attitude toward that object or action.
Thus the natural properties do not necessarily determine the moral
attitude. Nevertheless, once a person has taken up a moral attitude
toward an object or action in virtue of its natural properties,
consistency requires the person to hold the same attitude toward
the same object at another time or toward any other object if it has
the same natural properties. Failure to do so would show that the
attitude was not taken up in virtue of the natural properties in the
first case.

   This sort of explanation is not available to the realist. According
to the realist, moral beliefs are true or false in virtue of their
correspondence or non-correspondence with facts involving moral
properties. While it might seem natural to impose a requirement of
consistency on moral beliefs similar to the one Blackburn imposes
on moral attitudes, the primary requirement for moral beliefs must
be that they should correspond to moral truth. Thus, moral beliefs
can be required to be consistent over naturalistic similarities only if
moral truth must be consistent over naturalistic similarities. Yet,
this latter condition is precisely what is being called into question.
According to Blackburn there is no reason, in the realist's view, to
expect that it would hold, and some reason, namely condition (z), to
expect that it would not.

   Having set out the difficulty in an informal way, I will now turn to
Blackburn's formulation and defence of the two conditions. The
first condition is that moral properties are supervenient upon
naturalistic properties. Blackburn distinguishes two senses of
supervenience according to whether the requirement applies to the
same object through time or to different objects. He formulates the
two senses as follows:

   (S)   A property M is supervenient upon properties $N_1 \ldots N_n$ if
         M is not identical with any of $N_1 \ldots N_n$ nor with any truth
         function of them, and it is logically impossible that a thing
         should become M, or cease to be M, or become more or less
         M than before, without changing in respect of some
         member of $N_1 \ldots N_n$.

   (S_2) A property M is supervenient$_2$ upon properties $N_1 \ldots N_n$ if
         M is not identical with any of $N_1 \ldots N_n$, nor with any truth
         function of them, and it is logically impossible that two
         things should each possess the same properties from the set

$N_1 \ldots N_n$ to the same degree, without both failing to
possess M, or both possessing M, to the same degree.

Blackburn takes the supervenience of moral properties to be
virtually self-evident. The consequence of rejecting supervenience,
according to Blackburn, would be that moral properties would be
quite unconnected with what we had taken to be their grounds. For
example, moral properties might be divorced from human desires
and interests. We could have no reason for concern with moral truth
that was so remote.

The second condition for the truth of moral judgements might be
called the autonomy of moral properties in relation to naturalistic
properties. Blackburn first states the condition in the following way:

(E)   There is no moral proposition whose truth is entailed by
      any proposition ascribing naturalistic properties to its
      subject.

His defence of this condition consists primarily in distinguishing it
from other claims with which he does not wish it to be confused. For
instance, he does not mean to be denying that certain natural
properties may necessarily be reasons for the ascription of a moral
property. He is only denying that they may be conclusive reasons. It
seems clear that Blackburn is here relying on the widely discussed
view that an 'ought' cannot be derived from an 'is'.

Given the controversy that has raged over the is-ought question,
one could hardly except (E) to be universally accepted. Foot and
Searle have offered persuasive counterexamples to (E). What has
not been established, however, in Blackburn's view, is that *all* moral
propositions are entailed by propositions ascribing only naturalistic
properties. Thus, he weakens (E) to the more defensible claim:

(E') There are some moral propositions which are true, but
      whose truth is not entailed by any naturalistic facts about
      their subject.

This claim, he thinks, is both unobjectionable and sufficient to
generate the difficulty for realism. The supervenience of the moral
properties governed by (E') will continue to be puzzling.

The puzzle can now be restated in more precise terms which help
to clarify the modality of the constraints imposed on the truth of
moral judgements by the two conditions. There are some moral
properties with instantiations that are not entailed by the existence

DIFFICULTY CONCERNING MORAL PROPERTIES   373

of the naturalistic properties with which they are co-instantiated. Yet the persistence of those co-instantiated natural properties, or their duplication in another object, entails the persistence or duplication of the moral property. This is puzzling because whatever accounts for the truth of (E') would seem to count against the truth of (S) and (S$_2$). According to Blackburn, 'supervenience becomes, for the realist, an opaque, isolated, logical fact, for which no explanation can be proffered'.

II

A proper evaluation of Blackburn's claims depends on the interpretation of his terminology. Blackburn tends to use the terminology of 'entailment', 'strict implication' and 'logical impossibility' interchangeably. Although the official formulation of (S$_2$) is in terms of logical impossibility, Blackburn sometimes paraphrases (S$_2$) in terms of strict implication (pp. 105–106), and sometimes in terms of entailment (p. 110). Various paraphrases are also given for (E) (p. 110).

There is a subtle difference between entailment and strict implication. A proposition that is necessarily true is strictly implied by any proposition whatever, however unrelated it may otherwise seem. This is one of the so-called paradoxes of strict implication. Entailment is sometimes taken to be a relationship that avoids these paradoxes. It involves the further condition that there be some connection of 'content' or 'meaning' between two propositions if one is to entail the other. This distinction, however, is not crucial for the topic under consideration. Propositions attributing moral properties to a thing are not themselves necessarily true. At best they are necessarily true relative to some naturalistic description of the thing to which the moral property is attributed. Thus, the paradoxes will not arise for moral properties. Presumably, then, strict implication, like entailment, would involve some connection of content or meaning. According to the usual understanding the connection could be derived solely by means of the laws of logic and the meanings of words.

I do not think the terminology of strict implication and logical impossibility is meant to signal any differences. One proposition strictly implies another just in case it is logically impossible for the first to be true and the second to be false.

By the autonomy condition (E'), therefore, Blackburn should be

understood to be making the following claim: There are some moral
propositions that are true, but whose truth cannot be derived, by
the laws of logic and the meanings of words, from any propositions
ascribing naturalistic properties to their subject. This, indeed, is
just what is being claimed in the usual rejection of naturalism or
neo-naturalism in ethics. Although the supervenience condition has
two aspects—diachronic and synchronic—I will mainly be concerned with the second—(S_2). From what has been said so far,
Blackburn should be understood to be making the following claim
by (S_2): If two things possess the same naturalistic properties to the
same degree, then from this fact we can infer, by the laws of logic
and the meanings of words, that they possess the same moral
properties to the same degree.

Here is where the difficulties for Blackburn begin. In his defence
of supervenience, Blackburn seems to be defending something
rather different from what he claims. He argues that if we were to
give up supervenience, then 'it is possible that the worth, say, of a
feature of human life, such as courage, should alter although its
intrinsic nature . . . remain[s] the same . . . nothing hangs upon the
worth of courage changing if its relation to everything perceptible
remains the same, and no reason could possibly be given for being
interested in this fact' (pp. 115 and 116). Thus, according to
Blackburn, one who rejects (S_2) must allow that naturalistically
indiscernible objects might be morally discernible.

However unacceptable this consequence may be, one can avoid it
without accepting Blackburn's interpretation of supervenience.
One might hold that naturalistically indiscernible objects were
necessarily morally indiscernible without also holding that this
connection could be derived by the laws of logic and the meanings
of words. Of course the connection, then, would not be *logically*
necessary. Blackburn's defence of supervenience, in that case,
would be satisfied by something weaker than (S_2).

Blackburn makes a point of insisting (pp. 106–107) that no
weaker sort of impossibility, such as physical or moral impossibility, makes sense of the principles of supervenience. I agree that
physical or moral impossibility will not do. But, as a general point,
his insistence on logical impossibility does not fit well with his
defence of supervenience. Furthermore, I do not see any reason to
suppose that moral indiscernibility can be inferred from naturalistic indiscernibility solely by appeal to the laws of logic and the
meaning of moral terms. It does not seem, for example, that a

divine-command theory, according to which moral properties supervene upon God's commands rather than upon natural properties, involves a logical contradiction or a misuse of moral language. What does seem important to hold on to is the condition that naturalistically indiscernible objects cannot be morally discernible. This would satisfy the intuitions on which Blackburn relies just as well as his own formulation of supervenience.

It is tempting to hold that the impossibility employed here is just simple impossibility and not to characterize it in other terms. Perhaps it could be called metaphysical impossibility, but in any event the important point is that the connection involved is synthetic rather than analytic.[1]

The moral realist should reject (S) and (S_2) in favour of the following diachronic and synchronic supervenience conditions on the truth of moral judgements:

(DS)   It is impossible that a thing should change in some moral respect without changing in some naturalistic respect.

(WSS) It is impossible that two things should differ in some moral respect without differing in some naturalistic respect.

Adoption of (DS) and (WSS) in place of (S) and (S_2) removes Blackburn's difficulty for the realist. Since naturalistic indiscernibility does not entail moral indiscernibility, there is no longer any reason to be puzzled by the fact that propositions about a thing's natural properties do not entail propositions about its moral properties.

Nevertheless, it would seem easy to reinstate the difficulty in the following way. Blackburn could adjust the autonomy condition in the same way I have proposed to adjust the supervenience conditions. Instead of (E′) we would then have:

(A′)   A thing could have had different moral properties from those it actually has even if all its natural properties had been the same.

This would make it puzzling why those moral properties could not change if the natural properties persisted through time or were duplicated by another thing.

---

1   The best-known advocates of synthetic necessity have, of course, been Kripke and Putnam.

Not only would (A') reinstate the puzzle, but it might appear to create an outright contradiction with (WSS). Yet Blackburn is at pains to point out (pp. 110–111) that the difficulty the realist is in is not an inconsistency, but is only mysterious and not very inviting philosophically. Whether (WSS) and (A') result in contradiction depends on how we understand synchronic supervenience.

To clarify this matter, it will help to use the terminology of possible worlds. If synchronic supervenience only puts constraints on how things are for objects in any given possible world, then no contradiction results, for (A') only rules out such a constraint on how things are for an object in different possible worlds. This form of synchronic supervenience has been called 'weak supervenience' and it seems to be what Blackburn intended. My condition (WSS) is a statement of weak supervenience. (Thus the label (W̲SS).)

Weak supervenience stands in contrast with strong super-venience. Intuitively, strong supervenience puts constraints on how things are for objects whether they are in different possible worlds or the same possible world:

>   (SSS) If a thing of a certain naturalistic description has certain moral properties, then it is impossible that anything should differ from it in some moral respect without differing from it in some naturalistic respect.

(SSS) straight-forwardly contradicts (A'). For the moment, however, I wish to put (SSS) aside.

The conjunction of (WSS) and (A') would be puzzling for the realist, but, as far as I can see, there is no compelling reason to suppose that (A') is true. While the evidence against naturalism and neo-naturalism in ethics tends to support (E'), it does not support (A') unless the only sort of necessity is analytic necessity. While the rejection of synthetic necessity is not transparently mistaken, that rejection has been strongly disputed in recent years. If (A') cannot be established, then the puzzle for the moral realist cannot be reinstated. The realist should reject (A') in favour of a 'necessary connection' condition for the truth of moral judgements:

>   (NC) If a thing of a certain naturalistic description has certain moral properties, then it is impossible that it should have been different in some moral respect without being different in some naturalistic respect.

Having endorsed (NC), the realist is free to accept or reject (E').

DIFFICULTY CONCERNING MORAL PROPERTIES   377

III

The conjunction of (WSS) and (NC) as conditions for the truth of moral judgements is neither inconsistent nor puzzling. The naturalistic properties of an object or action necessarily determine its moral properties: In any possible world in which that object or action exists and has the same naturalistic properties as it has in a given possible world, it will have the same moral properties as it has in the given possible world. And the persistence of the naturalistic properties of an object or action, or their duplication by another object or action in the same possible world, necessarily guarantees the persistence or duplication of the moral properties of the object or action.

Not only is the conjunction of these conditions not puzzling, it is quite natural. One reason for the affinity of these conditions is this. It is natural (though in certain respects misleading) to think of possible worlds on the model of times. The actual world is one world among many in something like the way that the present moment is one time among many. Thus (NC) would seem plausible if the condition (DS) were plausible. Also, (NC) and (WSS) naturally go together. If naturalistically indiscernible objects in the same possible world must have the same moral properties, this suggests that naturalistic indiscernibility of the same object in different possible worlds is no different. If the bare identity of the object makes no moral difference in the first case, the bare identity of the possible world should make none in the second. (WSS) establishes the universality of moral judgements: They are (potentially) applicable to all objects (in a given possible world). (NC) establishes the necessity of moral judgements: They are true in all possible worlds. (DS) establishes the eternality or timelessness of moral judgements.

It is natural to wonder whether strong supervenience is just the conjunction of necessary connection and weak synchronic supervenience. In fact it is not, though it does imply both of them.

Consider two possible worlds, W_1 and W_2. Let each world contain two objects and let all the objects be naturalistically indiscernible from each other. Then weak synchronic supervenience requires that both the objects in W_1 have the same moral properties, and that both the objects in W_2 have the same moral properties. If one of the objects in W_1 were identical with one of the objects in W_2, then the necessary-connection condition would

378   JAMES C. KLAGGE:

require that it have the same moral properties in both worlds. So strong supervenience would not be violated. But if there do not happen to be any trans-world identities, then necessary connection will not be able to operate to block a violation of strong supervenience. (The condition of necessary connection is trivially satisfied in this case.)

I do not see that there is any other condition, weaker than strong supervenience, which together with (WSS) and (NC) would imply strong supervenience. Although (WSS) ensures that the bare identity of an object is not a morally relevant difference in a given possible world, and (NC) ensures that the bare identity of the possible world is not a morally relevant difference for a given object, (WSS) and (NC) together allow that the bare identity of the object *along with* the bare identity of the possible world might together constitute a morally relevant difference. Thus strong supervenience is ultimately what the moral realist should want to defend.

                                            IV

Confronted with the proposal that the conditions for the truth of moral judgements be interpreted as involving synthetic or metaphysical necessities, Blackburn could preserve his objection in either of two ways. He could reject the very idea of synthetic necessity. Or he could concede the plausibility of synthetic necessity in general, but reject its use in the moral context.

On the basis of his other writings,[1] I expect that Blackburn would choose the first option. He seems to be basically Humean in tendency. While synthetic necessity has gained a good deal of popularity, its existence has not been demonstrated. Followers of Quine and Wittgenstein will attest to this. Even if I had the arguments, I could not hope to establish the legitimacy of synthetic necessity in this discussion.

But supposing the legitimacy of synthetic necessity were granted, its use in moral philosophy would still need to be justified. Interpreting the conditions for the truth of moral judgements as synthetic necessities does have the merit of resolving Blackburn's difficulty while doing justice to the intuitions he marshals. Perhaps there are special features of morality that make synthetic necessity

1   See, especially, 'Truth, Realism, and the Regulation of Theory', *Midwest Studies in Philosophy, Volume 5: Studies in Epistemology,* 1980.

unsuitable there. I regard this as an important open problem in moral philosophy.

Appendix

For connoisseurs of logical detail I offer the following formalizations of what I have taken to be the appropriate conditions for the truth of moral judgements.

Let the necessity operator indicate metaphysical, rather than logical, necessity. Let the variables $\underline{x}$ and $\underline{y}$ range over objects, actions and states of affairs. Let the variables $\underline{s}$ and $\underline{t}$ range over times. Let the variable $\underline{M}$ range over moral properties. Finally, let the variable $\underline{\bar{N}}$ range over maximally consistent, i.e., complete, sets of natural properties. (I have overscored the 'N' so that it is not confused with a variable that ranges over single properties, as the 'M' does.) Then the diachronic supervenience condition is represented as:

(DS) $\quad \Box \, \forall x \, \forall s \, \forall t \, [\forall \bar{N}(\bar{N}x_s \equiv \bar{N}x_t) \rightarrow \forall M \, (Mx_s \equiv Mx_t)]$

and weak synchronic supervenience is represented as:

(WSS) $\quad \Box \, \forall x \, \forall y \, [\forall \bar{N} \, (\bar{N}x \equiv \bar{N}y) \rightarrow \forall M \, (Mx \equiv My)]$

There is no logically simple way to convert the symbolization of weak synchronic supervenience into a symbolization of strong synchronic supervenience. We cannot simply allow the variables $\underline{x}$ and $\underline{y}$ to range over objects in different possible worlds, for this would result in logical gibberish. Instead, the strong supervenience condition can be represented by a symbolization that contains two occurrences of the necessity operator:

(SSS) $\quad \Box \, \forall x \, \forall M \, \forall \bar{N} \, [Mx \,\&\, \bar{N}x \rightarrow \Box \, \forall y \, (\bar{N}y \rightarrow My)]$

Note that there is no distinction between strong and weak for the diachronic supervenience condition.

Finally, the necessary-connection condition is represented as:

(NC) $\quad \Box \, \forall x \, \forall M \, \forall \bar{N} \, [Mx \,\&\, \bar{N}x \rightarrow \Box(\bar{N}x \rightarrow Mx)].$

As I have formalized the strong supervenience condition and the necessary-connection condition, we must first fix on the complete naturalistic description of an object. Thus I have required the variable $\underline{\bar{N}}$ to range over maximally consistent sets of naturalistic properties. A variable ranging over single naturalistic properties

380   JAMES C. KLAGGE: MORAL PROPERTIES

would have sufficed for representing diachronic and weak synchronic supervenience, but the overscored variable also suffices, so
I have used it for the sake of uniformity.

From the formalizations it is easy to show that strong supervenience implies, but is not implied by, the conjunction of weak
synchronic   supervenience   and   the   necessary-connection
condition.[1]

DEPARTMENT OF PHILOSOPHY,
B-002,
UNIVERSITY OF CALIFORNIA AT SAN DIEGO,
LA JOLLA,
CALIFORNIA, 92093,
U.S.A.

1   In writing this paper I have benefitted from suggestions of Colin McGinn,
     Rogers Albritton, and especially Warren Quinn.

[4]

Australasian Journal of Philosophy
Vol. 70, No. 4; December 1992

CRITICAL NOTICE

Hurley, S.L., *Natural Reasons: Personality and Polity*. (Oxford: Oxford University Press, 1989) pp. xii, 462. A$140.00 (cloth)

This rich, long and complex book discusses and interconnects issues in ethics, decision theory, philosophy of mind, philosophy of law, and political theory. I am going to concentrate on the substantial and interesting things Susan Hurley has to say in ethics. After describing her position and making some passing comments, I will argue that there is a problem with her treatment of ethical scepticism. I will conclude by taking the liberty of suggesting what in my view she should, and consistently with her overall position could, have said about scepticism.

I. Hurley's Ethical Theory

Hurley espouses cognitivism, non-centralism, coherentism and realism. What does all this amount to in words rather than labels?

She is a cognitivist in the usual sense. For her, to assert that slavery is wrong is to make a claim about how things are (and a true one we take it). The statement 'Slavery is wrong' is truth-valued in the substantial sense that the statement purports to represent how things are, and counts as true precisely when it gets the way things are right, that is, when slavery does indeed have the property of being wrong.

She is a non-centralist in the sense that she denies the conceptual priority of the central ethical concepts of good, bad, right, and wrong — those sometimes called the 'thin' ethical concepts — by contrast with the 'thick', specific ethical concepts like courageous, inequitable, just, dishonest, and so on. Her concern is not so much to deny that, say, being inequitable is equivalent to the conjunction of (a) being a certain purely-naturalistically- describable skewed way with (b) being wrong, but to deny that such an analysis would reveal that being wrong was the conceptually prior notion: '*Non-centralism* about reasons for action rejects the view that the general concepts such as *right* and *ought* are conceptually prior to and independent of specific reason-giving concepts such as *just* and *unkind* '(11).

She holds a coherence theory of the right: 'to say that a certain act ought to be done is to say that it is favoured by the theory, whichever it may be, which gives the best account of the relationships among the specific values that apply to the alternatives in question . . . '(11). This coherence theory of the right is developed at length as the book proceeds, but I take it that the central idea can be put briefly but not too misleadingly as follows. Coherentism about the right is an approach to ethics akin to the commonsense functionalist approach to the mind.[1] In the case of the mind we have folk psychology, a body of folk opinion about the mind encapsu-

See Lewis [15] and Shoemaker [26].

lated in: input clauses telling us what sorts of situations typically cause what sorts of mental states; internal role clauses telling us how various mental states typically inter-connect; and output clauses telling us what sort of behaviour various combinations of mental states typically give rise to. In the case of ethics we have what we might call 'folk morality', a body of folk opinion encapsulated in: input clauses telling us what sorts of situations naturalistically described typically warrant what sorts of moral descriptions ('If an action increases suffering and has no other effects, it is wrong', for example); internal role clauses telling us about the internal connections between matters ethically described ('Rights generate duties of respect'; 'One ought to promote what is good', for example); and output clauses telling us about the actions and motivations associated with moral judgements ('If someone believes that they ought to do something, then they will typically be motivated to some extent to do it', for example). According to the coherentist, the task of one who seeks an ethical theory is to construct from the folk beginnings the best theory which makes sense of it all. In particular, as Hurley emphasises, we have a pre-analytic apprehension that acts which are friendly, just, deserved, benevolent, the honouring of a promise, and the like typically ought to be done; and acts which are cowardly, insensitive, reckless, and the like ought not to be done. As she plausibly sees it, we move from the various specific values displayed by the actions we may be contemplating to verdicts in terms of the general values of rightness and wrongness. But in tricky cases we have to weigh up competing claims. Perhaps the choice is between courageously telling the truth at the cost of losing a friend, or keeping a friend by prevarication. And the principal theoretical business of ethics on her conception, as I read it, is the development of a theory that articulates the inter-relations between potentially competing specific values in a way that enables us to arbitrate between them, and so arrive at all-things-considered judgements of rightness and wrongness. The right action then is by definition the action recommended by the theory with the best credentials to be the arbitrator; and the theory with the best credentials to be the arbitrator is the theory that best articulates the inter-relations between the various specific values. Hurley has a lot to say (mainly in chapter 11: 'Deliberation') about how theories which articulate the inter-connections and adjudicate between the claims of specific values may be arrived at. The general idea, though, is familiar from, for instance, John Rawls and Henry Sidgwick. We consider various actual and possible cases together with intuitively appealing general moral principles and their underlying rationales, and seek 'considered judgement in reflective equilibrium'[2] or a 'harmonious system'.[3] Hurley works out the idea in very much her own way and gives interesting discussions of some detailed case histories.

It is, incidentally, no part of her theory that the best theory — the theory whose verdicts settle what is right and wrong — must be *irreducibly* pluralistic. Her coherentism leaves open the possibility that it might turn out as Sidgwick held (hoped?) that the theory which best articulates and makes sense of the inter-connec-

[2]   Rawls [25, p. 46], though, as Philip Pettit reminded me, the best parallel for the cognitivist would be the role of reflective equilibrium in discussions of rationality.
[3]   Sidgwick [27, p. 13].

tions between the various specific values and the naturalistically described facts sees them as having a common underlying utilitarian vindication. It is however clear that she does not think that it is at all likely that this will turn out to be the case. She has her money on pluralism about values. Also, although Hurley talks (as we will) of the best theory, I take it that she would allow that it might turn out that we should talk of the best *theories*, that a number of similar but not identical theories might turn out to have equal claims to be the arbitrator, in which case to be *definitely* obligatory would presumably be to come out obligatory on *all* the best theories.

Hurley's non-centralism is a more or less immediate consequence of her coherentism about the right. If what is right is settled by what is the best theory, and the best theory is the one we would end up with in the limit of inquiry if we took folk morality and refined it into a harmonious system *à la* Rawls, Sidgwick or Hurley, the various ethical concepts, specific and general, are all interconnected. None forms the conceptual bedrock. No ethical concept gets its sense in isolation from the other ethical concepts and the relevant naturalistic ones. We have a great big package deal of inter-related concepts, and mastery of any one concept requires mastery of the system to some significant extent. 'Non-centralism' on this reading is importantly distinct from the doctrine that the specific or thick concepts cannot be analysed out into a purely naturalistic component combined with a general or thin component. Being a wife and being a husband are logically inter-connected and neither concept is prior to the other; nevertheless, being a wife is analysable as having a husband, and being a husband is analysable as having a wife.

I agree with Hurley that coherentism and non-centralism are very attractive doctrines, and that the general coherentist picture which I have described in terms of what we might call 'matured folk morality' is a very appealing one. Indeed, it is hard from the cognitivist perspective to see how else the various ethical concepts could get their sense other than through their positions in a network. The only alternative would seem to be a kind of platonism about the values which Hurley rightly dismisses briskly (14-15). In any case I will be following Hurley in accepting the coherentist picture, and will be addressing the issue of realism and scepticism from this vantage point.

II. Hurley's Treatment of Scepticism

Hurley is well aware that cognitivism and realism are distinct doctrines in ethics (see especially 185-186). The cognitivist holds that ethical statements make claims about how things are. Realism holds in addition that the claims so made are on the appropriate occasions true: things really are the way they are claimed to be. A pressing question thus becomes how to justify moving from a cognitivist position to a realist one; or to put the matter in terms of personalities, how to show that J.L. Mackie was wrong to move from cognitivism to scepticism.[4] Mackie could have agreed with the coherentist's way of articulating cognitivism, namely, that the right

4   In his error theory, Mackie [16].

or obligatory is identified by a position in the network of matured folk morality; he could simply add that nothing falls under the concept so identified.

Hurley identifies three principal challenges to moral realism as she sees it from her coherentist perspective. One is the claim that there is no coherent theory to be had. Her model is Kenneth Arrow's impossibility proof in social choice theory.[5] Arrow proved that no social choice function could simultaneously satisfy a set of individually appealing principles. This was a surprising result. Perhaps a similar surprise awaits us in ethics. We cannot award the role of arbitrator of the right to the best theory inter-connecting the specific values because there is no such theory. Every theory which captures enough to be a contender captures enough to be inconsistent. She argues against this possibility in chapters 12 ('Coherence') and 13 ('Commensurability').

A second challenge is the position on moral conflict most particularly associated with Bernard Williams. If, as the realist maintains, there is a property of being obligatory, and an action is right precisely if it possesses that property, no action can be simultaneously what ought to be done and what ought not to be done. A property cannot be both had and not had. But Williams has argued that a proper respect for the reality of moral conflict shows that an action can be both what ought to be done and what ought not to be done.[6] If I am under an obligation to do A and an obligation to do B, and learn that I cannot fulfil both obligations, both obligations typically survive the discovery that they cannot both be honoured. Otherwise there would be no such phenomenon as being unable to honour all one's obligations. (If only that were true!) According to Williams there is only one way to accommodate this insight about the reality of moral conflict, namely, by allowing that sometimes it is simultaneously the case that one ought to do A, and ought not to do A.

Hurley's interesting reply to this threat to moral realism is to distinguish *prima facie* from *pro tanto* reasons for performing some action. *Pro tanto* reasons are like forces. (As I see it. Do not hold Hurley responsible for the illustration.) A force F_1 acting on a particle can be such that by itself it would accelerate the particle towards North. At the same time there may be another force F_2 which by itself would accelerate the particle towards South. Perhaps F_1 is greater than F_2 so that there is a resultant force towards North. Nevertheless, F_2 still exists; it explains why the particle does not accelerate more briskly towards North. The overwhelmed force is still there. Similarly, when *pro tanto* reasons clash, the overwhelmed reason survives. When justice requires giving the money to Smith, whereas benevolence requires giving the money to Jones, and benevolence has (let us suppose) the greater claim in the particular case, the *single* answer to what ought to be done all things considered is that Jones ought to get the money. But it is still the case that an injustice has been committed; an injustice that ought to be committed but an injustice nevertheless. The injustice done survives as a morally relevant feature of the situation and as an appropriate object of regret. The detailed, and to my mind very appealing, case for this treatment of moral conflict is developed in chapter 7 ('Conflict').

---

5   Arrow [1].
6   Williams [30].

It is the third challenge to moral realism that I want to discuss in a little detail. This is the challenge of finding a plausible place for the moral properties in our picture of the world. It is mentioned a number of times through the book but takes centre stage in chapter 14 ('Skepticism'), which is the longest chapter in the book.

For the moral realist, ethics and metaphysics are not separate areas of philosophical inquiry. To be a moral realist is to take a position on what the world is like. Thus, among the objections to Moore's claim[7] that goodness is a non-natural, unanalysable, sometimes instantiated property, there is the objection from metaphysical plausibility. We have no reason to think that there is any such property instantiated by anything. Moorean goodness is like the redness of naive commonsense, that putative property of surfaces that is quite distinct from their disposition to look red, and quite distinct from any complex of their primary properties.

Hurley's question in chapter 14 is whether something we know about how the world is and works rules out the existence, in the sense of instantiation, of moral properties. The chapter is devoted to stating various ways you might seek, and many have sought, to argue from such information to the falsity of moral realism, and rebutting them in turn. I think that her rebuttals succeed, or at the worst leave the issue stalemated. Thus Hurley (279-287) considers the following style of argument: i) we know enough about the world to know that all the causal-explanatory work is done by the kinds of properties that figure in the scientific picture of the world; ii) moral properties are not among the kinds of properties that figure in the scientific picture of the world; iii) we should only believe in properties that earn their causal-explanatory keep. Hence, we should not believe in moral properties. Her reply, reasonably enough, is to deny the premise that we should only believe in properties that earn their causal-explanatory keep. There are other ways of paying the bill — for instance, by supervening on properties that earn their causal-explanatory keep.[8]

The fact remains, though, that in the course of giving her various replies she never specifies precisely the relationship she thinks holds between moral properties and natural properties, and between statements about how things are naturalistically and how things are ethically. My impression is that she regards this as a hard question she does not need to address for the purposes at hand. I think that this is a mistake. How natural properties and ethical properties inter-connect, how the way things are naturalistically and the way things are ethically relate one to another, is it seems to me a compulsory question for the realist. Without an answer to it, the question of scepticism cannot be addressed adequately.

The reason is not to do with what science tells us about the causal-explanatory character of our world. Our justification for believing in goodness, rightness, justice and so on is quite different from our justification for believing in redness. They are not posited as what explains our sensory responses to the world, or as the occupiers of some causal-explanatory role. The analogy we bruited above between folk psychology and matured folk morality was that both theories specified their key con-

---

⁻   Moore [18, ch. 1].

ˣ   Her overall position seems closest to that of McDowell [17] and opposed to those of
     Blackburn [2] and Harman [9].

cepts by locating them in a complex network. Only in the folk psychology case is
that network largely composed of causal principles. The reason the moral realist
should be explicit about how moral and naturalistic properties inter-connect is that
there is a strong case for saying (a) that moral properties are one and all natural
properties, and (b) that total naturalistic information about how things are includes
inter alia all there is to know about the way things are morally, that is, about moral
properties.[9] It follows that to be a moral realist is to take a position about the naturalistic way our world is, and until we know what that position is, or is in broad outline, we cannot identify what it is that we are committing ourselves to when we
espouse moral realism. We are without a handle with which to grasp the issue
between realist and sceptic.

Although Hurley does not describe the kind of position the moral realist is taking
about the naturalistic nature of our world, she could have. Her book contains the
essential ideas that enable an explicit account of moral properties, and of moral discourse in general, in purely naturalistic terms.[10] But first I should outline the case
for (a) and (b), and here too the essential idea is to be found in her book.

III. Hurley's Treatment of Supervenience

At a number of points Hurley addresses the supervenience of the moral on the natural. Here is a typical passage:

> Consistent with the denial that ethical truths are conceptually necessary is the
> conceptual doctrine that the evaluative characteristics of alternatives supervene
> on, or are some function of, their non-evaluative characteristics. It is not a con-
> ceptually necessary truth that slavery, as identified by its non-evaluative charac-
> teristics, is wrong, all things considered (though it may be necessary in some
> other sense), but supervenience requires that if it weren't wrong there would be
> some further difference between slavery in our world and slavery in the close
> conceptually possible world we've imagined. (296)

This passage, and her discussions of supervenience elsewhere in the book, commit
Hurley to what is sometimes called the *inter-world* as opposed to the *intra-world*
supervenience of the ethical on the natural. The intra-world supervenience of the
ethical on the natural is: in every possible world, if x and y are naturalistically
exactly alike, they are ethically exactly alike. The inter-world (global) supervenience of the ethical on the natural is: any two possible worlds which are naturalistically exactly alike are ethically exactly alike.[11] In both cases the relevant notion of

---

9   In discussions of moral realism, moral properties are moral 'ways to be'. To adopt moral real-
    ism is not of course to repudiate nominalism *per se* .
10 Or so I will argue: her remarks on pp. 196-200 suggest that she would resist this conclusion.
11 For a recent discussion of the various forms of supervenience and their implications, see
    Oddie [19]. It is compatible with inter-world supervenience that x in w_1 and y in w_2 be natu-
    ralistically exactly alike in all the properties and relations people typically have in mind when
    they talk of the 'right making' properties of actions and yet x be right in w_1 and y wrong in w_2,
    provided w_1 and w_2 differ appropriately in naturalistic nature elsewhere.

a possible world should be thought of in the wide sense Hurley indicates by her use of the prefix 'conceptually'.[12] Both theses are put forward as conceptual truths graspable by anyone who has the relevant concepts.

In the quoted passage Hurley is committing herself to the inter-world version (though I have no doubt that she holds the intra-world version also). Intra-world supervenience tells us that anything in our world naturalistically exactly like slavery is wrong, but says nothing about the naturalistic nature of worlds where slavery is *not* wrong. Hence, in order to insist that such worlds must differ naturalistically from ours she must be interpreting the supervenience doctrine in the inter-world way. And fair enough. The doctrine is very plausible when understood in either way. I will understand it in the inter-world way from now on.

To avoid possible misunderstanding I should emphasise the difference between the inter-world supervenience of the ethical on the natural and the inter-world supervenience of the psychological on the physical. The inter-world supervenience of the psychological on the physical is *false*. Let w_1 be a world containing one electron and nothing else. Let w_2 be a world containing one electron and many thoughtful 'angels' — thinkers realised entirely in non-physical stuff — and nothing else. Materialist and dualist agree that both worlds are possible, and that they are physically exactly alike. They are physically exactly alike because in each the one electron exhausts their physical nature (though it does not exhaust their naturalistic nature, for in the sense relevant here the angels have naturalistic natures). Nevertheless, w_1 and w_2 differ psychologically.[13]

The inter-world supervenience of the ethical on the natural provides a strong reason for thinking that moral properties are a species of naturalistic properties, that the moral way of being is some one or another, more or less complex, natural way of being. Think of the vast mosaic of instantiated naturalistic properties and relations which constitutes the total naturalistic nature of our world. If there is another possible world, exactly alike with respect to this vast mosaic but differing ethically, we would have clear reason to hold that moral properties are distinct from natural properties. As we go from one world to the other the ethical properties, or some of them, vary, whereas the naturalistic properties do not. But inter-world supervenience tells us that this never happens. Hence, the only way we can hold that ethical properties are distinct from natural properties is by holding that they are distinct but necessarily connected. This anti-Humean stance is possible but unattractive.[14] A way to bring out its unattractiveness is to consider the task of the interpreter of our language required to justify assigning these mysteriously distinct-but-necessarily-con-

---

[12] The remark in parentheses suggests that Hurley thinks that 'Slavery is wrong all things considered' might be necessary though not conceptually necessary. However, it seems to be straightforwardly contingent. Slavery in a world where perpetual torment is the only alternative, is right all things considered. The status of 'Slavery is *pro tanto* wrong' is, of course, another matter.

[13] Of course some more or less complicated and more or less substantial modification of the claim that the psychological supervenes on the physical may be true, or at least may express what materialists believe. See, e.g., Horgan [10] and Lewis [14]. The point is that the modifications are not called for in the ethics-natural properties case.

[14] One way to pay the price is to hold that the moral properties are properties of properties, see Forrest [7].

nected-to naturalistic properties as being the properties our moral predicates really attach to. Corresponding to any such assignment there will be a more mundane assignment of the purely naturalistic to the very same predicates; and because moral nature makes no distinctions among the possibilities that are not made by naturalistic nature, this more mundane assignment will obey the canons of good interpretation to the very same extent. Or rather, it will obey, in addition to all the canons obeyed by the exotic assignment to the moral predicates of the allegedly distinct but necessarily connected moral properties, the canon that counsels assigning to that whose instantiation is most beyond question.

It might be objected that I have overlooked the distinction between the metaphysically possible worlds and the conceptually or analytically possible worlds. Every metaphysically possible world is conceptually or analytically possible but not conversely. Consider one who holds that God exists necessarily.[15] Such a person typically does not think that God exists as a matter of analytic or conceptual necessity, that the necessity that God exists is deducible from reflection on concepts alone. She thinks that it is synthetic *a priori* (as it used to be said) or that it is synthetic necessary (as it is better said, particularly post *Naming and Necessity*[16]) that God exists. The view of such a person might be captured by saying that they hold that 'God exists' is true at every metaphysically possible world, but not at every conceptually possible world. Similarly, it might be (has been) held that 'Water = H_2O' is true at every metaphysically possible world, but not at every conceptually possible world. It might then be claimed, though not I think by Hurley, that inter-world supervenience is only plausible when the worlds in question are understood as metaphysically possible worlds. Among the *conceptually* possible worlds, there are naturalistic duplicates which are not ethical duplicates, and hence moral properties are distinct from naturalistic ones.

I think that it is a mistake to hold that the analytically or conceptually necessary on the one hand, and the synthetically necessary and the necessary *a posteriori* on the other, differ in the kind of necessity they possess. To think that they differ in the kind of necessity they possess is to make the same kind of mistake that Quine famously identified over existence.[17] The difference between the existence of numbers (if indeed they do exist) and the existence of tables is in the nature of what exists, not in the kind of existence possessed. Similarly, the necessity possessed by 'Water = H_2O' is the same kind of necessity as that possessed by 'Water = water'.[18] The difference is in how we ascertain that they are necessary, not in what we ascertain when we ascertain that they are necessary. Indeed, to suppose that there is a

---

[15]   I take the example and the possibility of the objection from Forrest [8]. The objection is also considered by Blackburn [4, p. 221].

[16]   Kripke [11].

[17]   See Quine [24, sec. 27].

[18]   I am taking for granted here the view, widely accepted as a result of Kripke [11] and Putnam [23] that, modulo worlds where there is no water, 'Water = H_2O' is necessary *a posteriori*. I am in fact agnostic on the question of whether 'water' as used by the person in the street is a rigid designator. But clearly it is a rigid designator in the mouths and from the pens of many philosophers alive today, and for the purposes of the discussion here and below we will give it that meaning.

conceptually possible world C where water is not H_2O but instead is, say, XYZ, would commit one to holding that being water is a different property from being H_2O; for being water and being H_2O would differ in that the first would have, and the second would not have, XYZ in its extension in C. But what we are supposed to have learned from Kripke and Putnam is precisely that being water and being H_2O is one and the same property, despite the fact that it took empirical work to show it.

Moreover, the inter-world supervenience of the ethical on the natural is, as we noted following Hurley, a conceptual truth.[19] Someone who includes in their list of all the possibilities two or more naturalistically identical but ethically distinct ones reveals an inadequate grasp of the relevant concepts. Similarly, it is part of our concept of water that it is the very same stuff in every possible world, and so it is a conceptual mistake to think that it is both possible that water is H_2O, and possible that water is XYZ. What is true is that our concept of water does not reveal which of water's being H_2O and water's being XYZ is possible (and if possible necessary), and which is not a possibility at all.[20]

There is therefore a good case from inter-world supervenience for holding that moral properties are natural properties. But it is one thing to use inter-world supervenience to show that ethical properties are naturalistic properties, and quite another to show that enough knowledge of naturalistic facts yields in itself knowledge of moral properties, or to show that, in the limit, total information about how things are naturalistically includes all there is to know about how things are morally. Facts about water fix or logically determine facts about H_2O. For instance, the way water is distributed fixes or logically determines the way H_2O is distributed in the following sense: any possible world where water is distributed thus and so is a possible world where H_2O is distributed thus and so. However, knowing water facts is not enough for knowing H_2O facts. Information about how things are as far as water is concerned is not *per se* information about how things are as far as H_2O is concerned. This is of course a reflection of the *a posteriori*, albeit necessary, nature of 'Water is H_2O'. Accordingly, it might be suggested that although inter-world supervenience shows that the total naturalistic picture fixes the ethical way our world is down to the last detail, and so makes it plausible that ethical properties (and relations) are naturalistic, we cannot move *a priori* from the total way things are naturalistically to the total way they are ethically, and so information, total or otherwise, about naturalistic facts does not constitute information about the ethical facts.

I think, however, that the water-H_2O example is very different from the ethics-natural properties case. Exactly how to explain the necessary *a posteriori* is controversial. But the general picture is reasonably non-controversial. The necessary *a posteriori* truths are ones where in order to know that they are necessary you need to know something about the actual world which is itself contingent and *a posteriori*. The concept of water is not that of that which falls from the sky, is essential to life, is odourless and colourless, and so on; it is the concept of that which *actually* falls

[19] A point emphasised in this connection by Blackburn [3].
[20] For one way of making this way of looking at the issue formally precise see Stalnaker [28]. In this treatment, and in general in treatments in the style of two-dimensional modal logic, there is a *single* set of possible worlds.

from the sky, is essential to life, is odourless and colourless, and so on.[21] Water in any given possible world is the stuff which does the falling and so on in the *actual* world regardless of whether it does the falling and so on in the given world. It is this fact which simultaneously makes it necessary that water is H_2O, and makes the fact that it is necessary an *a posteriori* matter. For in order to know that it is necessary, you have to know which stuff it is which falls from the sky and so on in the actual world. This means that whenever we have a case where some contingent body of information *I* fixes some body of information *I**, but we cannot move *a priori* from *I* to *I** — a case, that is, where every *I*-world is an *I**-world, but it is necessary *a posteriori* that if *I* then *I** — there will be some additional, contingent bit of information which if conjoined to *I* would enable us to move *a priori* from the conjunction of that information with *I* to *I**. The additional information will be precisely the relevant facts about the actual world which reveal the necessary status of 'if *I* then *I**'. The reason we cannot move *a priori* from the way water is distributed to the way H_2O is distributed relates to the *partial* nature of the information that water is distributed thus and so. Supplement the information suitably and all will be well. For instance, although you cannot move *a priori* from the fact that water is distributed thus and so hereabouts, to the fact that H_2O is distributed thus and so hereabouts; you can move *a priori* from the fact that water is distributed thus and so hereabouts conjoined with the fact that it is H_2O which falls from the sky, is essential to life, is odourless and colourless, and so on, to the fact that H_2O is distributed thus and so hereabouts.

The crucial point about the ethics-natural properties case is that enough information about the naturalistic nature of a world fixes the position of the world uniquely in logical space. It is not just that it fixes the ethical nature of the world. It fixes all there is to fix. It is not partial information. Any two naturalistically exactly alike worlds are exactly alike *simpliciter*. (This would not of course be true if 'naturalistic' meant 'physicalistic' as it sometimes does in the philosophy of mind.) This means that full information about the naturalistic nature of our world will constitute full information about the ethical nature of our world. It won't just fix the ethical nature; it will reveal it. Of course there may well be necessary *a posteriori* truths of the form 'If *N* then *E*', in which case knowing that *N* will fix that *E* but not in itself enable the deduction of *E*. But the contingent fact about the actual world needed to reveal the necessary nature of 'If *N* then *E*' will itself be capturable naturalistically — if it couldn't be, naturalistic nature would not fix position in logical space without remainder — and from the additional piece of information together with *N*, it will be possible to deduce *E*.

There are, that is, two distinguishable things the inter-world supervenience of the ethical on the natural tells us. One is that the total naturalistic story fixes the *ethical* position of a world in logical space. This is the result which supports ontological naturalism in ethics. The other and stronger message is that the total naturalistic story fixes the position of a world in logical space *simpliciter*. It is this result which supports informational naturalism in ethics — the doctrine that all there is to tell

---

21   To put the matter in the terms of Davies and Humberstone [6].

about moral nature can be told in naturalistic terms.

IV. From Coherentism to Analytic Naturalism

If informational naturalism is true, there should be a way to give the meanings of ethical expressions in purely naturalistic terms. Our language is a remarkably powerful instrument for describing how things are, for giving information about the way our world is. If all the information about the ways things are ethically can be given naturalistically, it should be possible to do this, or to sketch the general way it might be done, in our language in a way which makes it explicit that it is naturalistic information that is being given.[22] Hurley's coherentism spelt out in the way we have suggested combined with David Lewis's method of defining theoretical terms via Ramsey sentences gives us a way of doing exactly this, and so a way of stating a species of *analytic naturalism*.

We noted at the beginning that we can think of coherentism in ethics as holding that the various ethical concepts, specific and general, are identified by their place in the complex network which constitutes matured folk morality. If this is right, naturalistic definitions of the ethical terms drop out in the way made familiar by Lewis for theoretical terms in general, and for mental state terms in particular.[23] Here is the story in outline.

Let **M** be matured folk morality written out as a long conjunction, with the moral predicates written in property-name style. For example, 'Killing someone is typically morally wrong' becomes 'Killing typically has the property of being morally wrong'. Replace each distinct moral property term by a distinct variable to give '$M(x_1, \ldots, x_n)$'. Then '$(Ex_1)(Ex_2) \ldots M(x_1, x_2, \ldots)$' is the Ramsey sentence of **M**, and

$$(Ex_1)(Ex_2) \ldots (y_1)(y_2) \ldots [M(y_1, y_2, \ldots) \text{ iff } x_1 = y_1 \,\&\, x_2 = y_2 \ldots$$

is the modified Ramsey sentence of **M** which says that there is a unique realisation of **M**. If coherentism is true, **M** and the modified Ramsey sentence of **M** say the same thing. For that is what holding that the ethical concepts are fixed by their place in the network comes to (of course, the elements in a unique realisation may themselves be disjunctive). Justice is what plays the justice role. Now we can spec-

[22]   Some recent expositions of naturalism in ethics have emphasised that though they hold the ontological doctrine that moral properties and facts are one and all natural properties and facts, they do not hold that moral terms can be analysed naturalistically: see Boyd [5, p. 199], and Sturgeon [29, p. 240]. It would be easy to see how moral properties could be natural properties without ethical terms being analysable naturalistically if those natural properties which are moral properties had themselves non-natural features which we used to secure reference to those natural properties when we used ethical terminology. But according to ontological naturalists themselves, *all*, or at least all contingent, properties are natural. How ethical terms pick out those natural properties which are moral properties cannot depend on non-natural properties simply because there are none such to depend on. (A similar point is made by Charles Pigden in [21], [22].)

[23]   See Lewis [13] and [15]. I am grateful to Ian Ravenscroft and David Lewis for help in spotting two (!) blunders in an earlier presentation of what follows..

ify what it is for some action *a* to be, say, right, thus:

a is right iff $(Ex_1)(Ex_2) \ldots \{a$ has x_r & $(y_1)(y_2) \ldots [M(y_1, y_2, \ldots) $ iff $x_1 = y_1$ & $x_2 = y_2 \ldots]\}$

where 'x_r' replaced 'being right' in **M**. The right hand side will be framed entirely in naturalistic terms because each and every moral term in **M** was replaced by an existentially bound variable. Hence we have derived from the coherentist picture a specification of the meaning of 'right' in the sense of a specification of the truth conditions of 'a is right' in naturalistic terms as required by analytic naturalism.[24] The same could of course be done for 'good', 'just', 'courageous' and so on.

There is much that might be said about the story I have just outlined, but I will restrict myself to our topic set from Hurley: its bearing on the debate between moral realism and scepticism. I said earlier that we need to be explicit about the naturalistic nature of the ethical in order to get a handle on that debate. We now have the needed handle. Rightness will be instantiated, some actions will indeed be right and scepticism will be false, just if '$(Ex_1)(Ex_2) \ldots \{ -$ has x_r & $(y_1)(y_2) \ldots [M(y_1, y_2, \ldots)$ iff $x_1 = y_1$ & $x_2 = y_2 \ldots]\}$' is true of some actions. And that in turn will depend both on the nature of **M**, and on the naturalistic nature of our world. **M** specifies the naturalistic conditions that need to be met for an action to be right, and whether or not they are in fact satisfied will depend on how things actually are.

This specifies the question that needs to be addressed but not the answer. We have not said enough about **M** to give the answer. If Mackie is right, if it is an essential part of **M** that there be properties which of *necessity* attract anyone who contemplates them, no doubt nothing is right. But more moderate views about **M** are possible.[25] The answer Hurley should give is, I think, clear from her remarks (24-25, 50-52 and 86-88, for example) about the importance of the principle of charity in interpretation. Any account of **M** which makes it all but impossible for any actions in the world as it is actually constituted, to be right must be mistaken. It is a constraint on interpreting our moral discourse that some actions have the moral properties our discourse putatively ascribes to them.

So that is the story about how Hurley's interesting, and to my mind plausible, account of ethical theory could provide an answer to moral scepticism.

V. Postscript: The Open Question

Analytic naturalism is often taken to be refuted by the open question argument. If analytic naturalism is true, then if I know all there is to know about the naturalistic

---

[24] We can think of the meaning specification in two different ways. We can think of it as giving the meaning of 'right' in the traditional sense. An action is right in a possible world iff it has the property, if any, which occupies the 'x_r' position in that world. Or we can (less plausibly, it seems to me) think of it as fixing the reference of 'right' in the sense of Kripke [11]. An action is right in a possible world iff it has the property which occupies the 'x_r' position in the actual world, whether or not the action has that property in the world in question.

[25] See Lewis [12, p. 137].

facts and have *per impossibile* properly got my mind around this enormous body of information, any given moral judgement is analytically determined. The only sense in which the matter can still be open is semantic — I might for example waver about what judgement to make in the way I might waver about what to say about an object on the borderline between red and pink, or whether someone has lost enough hair to count as bald. But, runs the objection, it is intuitively evident that the matter might still be open in a substantial sense.

There is (notoriously) much to say about this objection but I think that Hurley tells us the most important thing to say. In many places in the book, but most particularly in chapters 3 and 5, she forcefully attacks the idea of 'mythically intrinsically self-interpreting entities' (84) and the idea that 'there could be a residual content to our concepts which transcends all the uses to which we put them' (51). To find it *evident* in the face of supervenience that any given moral matter might remain open in a substantial sense despite total naturalistic information, is to be a captive of the idea that somehow we internally fix on the senses of the moral terms. It is a kind of platonism but without the dubious ontology.[26]

Frank Jackson *Australian National University*

[26] Some of the ideas in this notice were presented at a conference at Monash·University in 1991. I am greatly indebted to discussion on that occasion. I am also very much indebted to many discussions before and after that conference with Peter Railton, David Lewis, Lloyd Humberstone, Michael Smith (who pointed out a serious confusion in an earlier version of the final section), Charles Pigden and Philip Pettit, and to reading Pargetter and Campbell [20].

REFERENCES

1. Arrow, Kenneth J., *Social Choice and Individual Values* (New Haven: Yale University Press, 1963).

2. Blackburn, Simon, 'Errors and the Phenomenology of Value' in Ted Honderich (ed.), *Morality and Objectivity* (London: Routledge & Kegan Paul, 1985).

3. Blackburn, Simon, 'Supervenience Revisited' in Ian Hacking (ed.), *Exercises in Analysis* (Cambridge: Cambridge University Press, 1985).

4. Blackburn, Simon, *Spreading the Word* (Oxford: Oxford University Press, 1984).

5. Boyd, Richard, 'How to be a Moral Realist' in Geoffrey Sayre-McCord (ed.), *Essays on Moral Realism* (Ithaca: Cornell University Press, 1988) pp. 181-228.

6. Davies M.K. and I.L. Humberstone, 'Two Notions of Necessity', *Philosophical Studies* 38 (1980) pp. 1-30.

7. Forrest, Peter, 'Supervenience: The Grand Property Hypothesis', *Australasian Journal of Philosophy* 66 (1988) pp. 1-12.

8. Forrest, Peter, 'Universals and Universalisability', *Australasian Journal of Philosophy* 70 (1992) pp. 93-98.

9. Harman, Gilbert, *The Nature of Morality* (New York: Oxford University Press, 1977).

10. Horgan, Terence, 'Supervenience and Microphysics', *Pacific Philosophical Quarterly* 63 (1982) pp. 29-43.

11. Kripke, Saul, *Naming and Necessity* (Oxford: Blackwell, 1980).

12. Lewis, David, 'Dispositional Theories of Value', *Proceedings of the Aristotelian Society*, Supp. Vol. LXIII (1989) pp. 113-137.

13. Lewis, David, 'How to Define Theoretical Terms', *The Journal of Philosophy* 67 (1970) pp. 427-446

14. Lewis, David, 'New Work for a Theory of Universals', *Australasian Journal of Philosophy* 61 (1983) pp. 343-377.

15. Lewis, David, 'Psychophysical and Theoretical Identifications', *Australasian Journal of Philosophy* 50 (1972) pp. 291-315.

16. Mackie, J.L., *Ethics: Inventing Right and Wrong* (Harmondsworth: Penguin, 1977).

17. McDowell, John, 'Values and the Secondary Qualities' in Ted Honderich (ed.), *Morality and Objectivity* (London: Routledge & Kegan Paul, 1985).

18. Moore, G.E., *Principia Ethica* (Cambridge: Cambridge University Press, 1903).

19. Oddie, Graham, 'Supervenience and Higher-Order Universals', *Australasian Journal of Philosophy* 69 (1991) pp. 20-47.

20. Pargetter, Robert and John Campbell, 'Goodness and Fragility', *American Philosophical Quarterly* 23 (1986) pp. 155-166.

21. Pigden, Charles R., *The Reluctant Nihilist* (manuscript, 1991).

22. Pigden, Charles R., 'Naturalism' in Peter Singer (ed.), *A Companion to Ethics* (Oxford: Blackwell, 1991).

23. Putnam, Hilary, 'The meaning of "Meaning" ' in his *Mind, Language and Reality* (Cambridge: Cambridge University Press, 1975).

24. Quine, W.V.O., *Word and Object* (Cambridge, MA: MIT Press, 1960).

25. Rawls, John, *A Theory of Justice* (Oxford: Oxford University Press, 1972).

26. Shoemaker, Sydney, 'Some Varieties of Functionalism', *Philosophical Topics* 12 (1981) pp. 83-118.

27. Sidgwick, Henry, *Methods of Ethics* (London: Macmillan, 1907) p. 13.

28. Stalnaker, Robert C., 'Assertion' in P. Cole (ed.), *Syntax and Semantics*, Vol. 9 (New York: Academic Press, 1978) pp. 315-332.

29. Sturgeon, Nicholas L., 'Moral Explanations' in Geoffrey Sayre-McCord (ed.), *Essays on Moral Realism* (Ithaca: Cornell University Press, 1988), pp. 229-255.

30. Williams, Bernard, 'Ethical Consistency' in his *Problems of the Self* (Cambridge: Cambridge University Press, 1981).

Part III
Are Moral Claims Made True or False by Facts About our Reasons for Action?

[5]

MORALITY AS A SYSTEM OF HYPOTHETICAL IMPERATIVES

THERE are many difficulties and obscurities in Kant's moral philosophy, and few contemporary moralists will try to defend it all; many, for instance, agree in rejecting Kant's derivation of duties from the mere form of law expressed in terms of a universally legislative will. Nevertheless, it is generally supposed, even by those who would not dream of calling themselves his followers, that Kant established one thing beyond doubt—namely, the necessity of distinguishing moral judgments from hypothetical imperatives. That moral judgments cannot be hypothetical imperatives has come to seem an unquestionable truth. It will be argued here that it is not.

In discussing so thoroughly Kantian a notion as that of the hypothetical imperative, one naturally begins by asking what Kant himself meant by a hypothetical imperative, and it may be useful to say a little about the idea of an imperative as this appears in Kant's works. In writing about imperatives Kant seems to be thinking at least as much of statements about what ought to be or should be done, as of injunctions expressed in the imperative mood. He even describes as an imperative the assertion that it would be "good to do or refrain from doing something"[1] and explains that for a will that "does not always do something simply because it is presented to it as a good thing to do" this has the force of a command of reason. We may therefore think of Kant's imperatives as statements to the effect that something ought to be done or that it would be good to do it.

The distinction between hypothetical imperatives and categorical imperatives, which plays so important a part in Kant's ethics, appears in characteristic form in the following passages from the *Foundations of the Metaphysics of Morals:*

All imperatives command either hypothetically or categorically. The former present the practical necessity of a possible action as a means

---

[1] *Foundations of the Metaphysics of Morals*, Sec. II, trans. by L. W. Beck.

PHILIPPA FOOT

to achieving something else which one desires (or which one may possibly desire). The categorical imperative would be one which presented an action as of itself objectively necessary, without regard to any other end.[2]

If the action is good only as a means to something else, the imperative is hypothetical; but if it is thought of as good in itself, and hence as necessary in a will which of itself conforms to reason as the principle of this will, the imperative is categorical.[3]

The hypothetical imperative, as Kant defines it, "says only that the action is good to some purpose" and the purpose, he explains, may be possible or actual. Among imperatives related to actual purposes Kant mentions rules of prudence, since he believes that all men necessarily desire their own happiness. Without committing ourselves to this view it will be useful to follow Kant in classing together as "hypothetical imperatives" those telling a man what he ought to do because (or if) he wants something and those telling him what he ought to do on grounds of self-interest. Common opinion agrees with Kant in insisting that a moral man must accept a rule of duty whatever his interests or desires.[4]

Having given a rough description of the class of Kantian hypothetical imperatives it may be useful to point to the heterogeneity within it. Sometimes what a man should do depends on his passing inclination, as when he wants his coffee hot and should warm the jug. Sometimes it depends on some long-term project, when the feelings and inclinations of the moment are irrelevant. If one wants to be a respectable philosopher one should get up in the mornings and do some work, though just at that moment when one should do it the thought of being a respectable philosopher leaves one cold. It is true nevertheless to say of one, at that moment, that one wants to be a respectable philosopher,[5]

---

[2] *Ibid.*

[3] *Ibid.*

[4] According to the position sketched here we have three forms of the hypothetical imperative: "If you want *x* you should do *y*," "Because you want *x* you should do *y*," and "Because *x* is in your interest you should do *y*." For Kant the third would automatically be covered by the second.

[5] To say that at that moment one wants to be a respectable philosopher would be another matter. Such a statement requires a special connection between the desire and the moment.

HYPOTHETICAL IMPERATIVES

and this can be the foundation of a desire-dependent hypothetical imperative. The term "desire" as used in the original account of the hypothetical imperative was meant as a grammatically convenient substitute for "want," and was not meant to carry any implication of inclination rather than long-term aim or project. Even the word "project," taken strictly, introduces undesirable restrictions. If someone is devoted to his family or his country or to any cause, there are certain things he wants, which may then be the basis of hypothetical imperatives, without either inclinations or projects being quite what is in question. Hypothetical imperatives should already be appearing as extremely diverse; a further important distinction is between those that concern an individual and those that concern a group. The desires on which a hypothetical imperative is dependent may be those of one man, or may be taken for granted as belonging to a number of people, engaged in some common project or sharing common aims.

Is Kant right to say that moral judgments are categorical, not hypothetical, imperatives? It may seem that he is, for we find in our language two different uses of words such as "should" and "ought," apparently corresponding to Kant's hypothetical and categorical imperatives, and we find moral judgments on the "categorical" side. Suppose, for instance, we have advised a traveler that he should take a certain train, believing him to be journeying to his home. If we find that he has decided to go elsewhere, we will most likely have to take back what we said: the "should" will now be unsupported and in need of support. Similarly, we must be prepared to withdraw our statement about what he should do if we find that the right relation does not hold between the action and the end—that it is either no way of getting what he wants (or doing what he wants to do) or not the most eligible among possible means. The use of "should" and "ought" in moral contexts is, however, quite different. When we say that a man should do something and intend a moral judgment we do not have to back up what we say by considerations about his interests or his desires; if no such connection can be found the "should" need not be withdrawn. It follows that the agent cannot rebut an assertion about what, morally speaking, he should do by

PHILIPPA FOOT

showing that the action is not ancillary to his interests or desires. Without such a connection the "should" does not stand unsupported and in need of support; the support that *it* requires is of another kind.[6]

There is, then, one clear difference between moral judgments and the class of "hypothetical imperatives" so far discussed. In the latter "should" is used "hypothetically," in the sense defined, and if Kant were merely drawing attention to this piece of linguistic usage his point would be easily proved. But obviously Kant meant more than this; in describing moral judgments as non-hypothetical—that is, categorical imperatives—he is ascribing to them a special dignity and necessity which this usage cannot give. Modern philosophers follow Kant in talking, for example, about the "unconditional requirement" expressed in moral judgments. These tell us what we have to do whatever our interests or desires, and by their inescapability they are distinguished from hypothetical imperatives.

The problem is to find proof for this further feature of moral judgments. If anyone fails to see the gap that has to be filled it will be useful to point out to him that we find "should" used non-hypothetically in some non-moral statements to which no one attributes the special dignity and necessity conveyed by the description "categorical imperative." For instance, we find this non-hypothetical use of "should" in sentences enunciating rules of etiquette, as, for example, that an invitation in the third person should be answered in the third person, where the rule does not *fail to apply* to someone who has his own good reasons for ignoring this piece of nonsense, or who simply does not care about what, from the point of view of etiquette, he should do. Similarly, there is a non-hypothetical use of "should" in contexts where something like a club rule is in question. The club secretary who has told a member that he should not bring ladies into the smoking room does not say, "Sorry, I was mistaken" when informed that this member is resigning tomorrow and cares nothing about his

---

[6] I am here going back on something I said in an earlier article ("Moral Beliefs," *Proceedings of the Aristotelian Society, 1958-1959*) where I thought it necessary to show that virtue must benefit the agent. I believe the rest of the article can stand.

HYPOTHETICAL IMPERATIVES

reputation in the club. Lacking a connection with the agent's desires or interests, this "should" does not stand "unsupported and in need of support"; it requires only the backing of the rule. The use of "should" is therefore "non-hypothetical" in the sense defined.

It follows that if a hypothetical use of "should" gives a hypothetical imperative, and a non-hypothetical use of "should" a categorical imperative, then "should" statements based on rules of etiquette, or rules of a club, are categorical imperatives. Since this would not be accepted by defenders of the categorical imperative in ethics, who would insist that these other "should" statements give hypothetical imperatives, they must be using this expression in some other sense. We must therefore ask what they mean when they say that "You should answer . . . in the third person" is a hypothetical imperative. Very roughly the idea seems to be that one may reasonably ask why anyone should bother about what should$_e$ (should from the point of view of etiquette) be done, and that such considerations deserve no notice unless reason is shown. So although people give as their reason for doing something the fact that it is required by etiquette, we do not take this consideration as *in itself giving us reason to act*. Considerations of etiquette do not have any automatic reason-giving force, and a man might be right if he denied that he had reason to do "what's done."

This seems to take us to the heart of the matter, for, by contrast, it is supposed that moral considerations necessarily give reasons for acting to any man. The difficulty is, of course, to defend this proposition which is more often repeated than explained. Unless it is said, implausibly, that all "should" or "ought" statements give reasons for acting, which leaves the old problem of assigning a special categorical status to moral judgment, we must be told what it is that makes the moral "should" relevantly different from the "shoulds" appearing in normative statements of other kinds.[7] Attempts have sometimes been made to show that some kind of irrationality is involved in ignoring the "should" of

---

[7] To say that moral considerations are *called* reasons is blatantly to ignore the problem.

PHILIPPA FOOT

morality: in saying "Immoral—so what?" as one says "Not *comme il faut*—so what?" But as far as I can see these have all rested on some illegitimate assumption, as, for instance, of thinking that the amoral man, who agrees that some piece of conduct is immoral but takes no notice of that, is inconsistently disregarding a rule of conduct that he has accepted; or again of thinking it inconsistent to desire that others will not do to one what one proposes to do to them. The fact is that the man who rejects morality because he sees no reason to obey its rules can be convicted of villainy but not of inconsistency. Nor will his action necessarily be irrational. Irrational actions are those in which a man in some way defeats his own purposes, doing what is calculated to be disadvantageous or to frustrate his ends. Immorality does not *necessarily* involve any such thing.

It is obvious that the normative character of moral judgment does not guarantee its reason-giving force. Moral judgments are normative, but so are judgments of manners, statements of club rules, and many others. Why should the first provide reasons for acting as the others do not? In every case it is because there is a background of teaching that the non-hypothetical "should" can be used. The behavior is required, not simply recommended, but the question remains as to why we should do what we are required to do. It is true that moral rules are often enforced much more strictly than the rules of etiquette, and our reluctance to press the non-hypothetical "should" of etiquette may be one reason why we think of the rules of etiquette as hypothetical imperatives. But are we then to say that there is nothing behind the idea that moral judgments are categorical imperatives but the relative stringency of our moral teaching? I believe that this may have more to do with the matter than the defenders of the categorical imperative would like to admit. For if we look at the kind of thing that is said in its defense we may find ourselves puzzled about what the words can even mean unless we connect them with the feelings that this stringent teaching implants. People talk, for instance, about the "binding force" of morality, but it is not clear what this means if not that we *feel* ourselves unable to escape. Indeed the "inescapability" of moral requirements is often cited when they are being contrasted with hypothetical imperatives. No one, it is said,

HYPOTHETICAL IMPERATIVES

escapes the requirements of ethics by having or not having particular interests or desires. Taken in one way this only reiterates the contrast between the "should" of morality and the hypothetical "should," and once more places morality alongside of etiquette. Both are inescapable in that behavior does not cease to offend against either morality or etiquette because the agent is indifferent to their purposes and to the disapproval he will incur by flouting them. But morality is supposed to be inescapable in some special way and this may turn out to be merely the reflection of the way morality is taught. Of course, we must try other ways of expressing the fugitive thought. It may be said, for instance, that moral judgments have a kind of necessity since they tell us what we "must do" or "have to do" whatever our interests and desires. The sense of this is, again, obscure. Sometimes when we use such expressions we are referring to physical or mental compulsion. (A man has to go along if he is pulled by strong men, and he has to give in if tortured beyond endurance.) But it is only in the absence of such conditions that moral judgments apply. Another and more common sense of the words is found in sentences such as "I caught a bad cold and had to stay in bed" where a penalty for acting otherwise is in the offing. The necessity of acting morally is not, however, supposed to depend on such penalties. Another range of examples, not necessarily having to do with penalties, is found where there is an unquestioned acceptance of some project or role, as when a nurse tells us that she has to make her rounds at a certain time, or we say that we have to run for a certain train.[8] But these too are irrelevant in the present context, since the acceptance condition can always be revoked.

No doubt it will be suggested that it is in some other sense of the words "have to" or "must" that one has to or must do what morality demands. But why should one insist that there must be such a sense when it proves so difficult to say what it is? Suppose that what we take for a puzzling thought were really no thought at all but only the reflection of our *feelings* about morality? Perhaps it makes no sense to say that we "have to" submit to the

---

[8] I am grateful to Rogers Albritton for drawing my attention to this interesting use of expressions such as "have to" or "must."

PHILIPPA FOOT

moral law, or that morality is "inescapable" in some special way.
For just as one may feel as if one is falling without believing that
one is moving downward, so one may feel as if one has to do what
is morally required without believing oneself to be under physical
or psychological compulsion, or about to incur a penalty if one
does not comply. No one thinks that if the word "falling" is used
in a statement reporting one's sensations it must be used in a
special sense. But this kind of mistake may be involved in looking
for the special sense in which one "has to" do what morality
demands. There is no difficulty about the idea that we feel we
have to behave morally, and given the psychological conditions
of the learning of moral behavior it is natural that we should have
such feelings. What we cannot do is quote them in support of the
doctrine of the categorical imperative. It seems, then, that in so
far as it is backed up by statements to the effect that the moral
is inescapable, or that we *do* have to do what is morally required of
us, it is uncertain whether the doctrine of the categorical imperative even makes sense.

The conclusion we should draw is that moral judgments have no
better claim to be categorical imperatives than do statements about
matters of etiquette. People may indeed follow either morality or
etiquette without asking why they should do so, but equally well
they may not. They may ask for reasons and may reasonably
refuse to follow either if reasons are not to be found.

It will be said that this way of viewing moral considerations
must be totally destructive of morality, because no one could ever
act morally unless he accepted such considerations as in themselves
sufficient reason for action. Actions that are truly moral must be
done "for their own sake," "because they are right," and not for
some ulterior purpose. This argument we must examine with care,
for the doctrine of the categorical imperative has owed much to its
persuasion.

Is there anything to be said for the thesis that a truly moral
man acts "out of respect for the moral law" or that he does what is
morally right because it is morally right? That such propositions
are not prima facie absurd depends on the fact that moral
judgment concerns itself with a man's reasons for acting as well
as with what he does. Law and etiquette require only that certain

HYPOTHETICAL IMPERATIVES

things are done or left undone, but no one is counted as charitable if he gives alms "for the praise of men," and one who is honest only because it pays him to be honest does not have the virtue of honesty. This kind of consideration was crucial in shaping Kant's moral philosophy. He many times contrasts acting out of respect for the moral law with acting from an ulterior motive, and what is more from one that is self-interested. In the early *Lectures on Ethics* he gave the principle of truth-telling under a system of hypothetical imperatives as that of not lying *if it harms one* to lie. In the *Metaphysics of Morals* he says that ethics cannot start from the ends which a man may propose to himself, since these are all "selfish."[9] In the *Critique of Practical Reason* he argues explicitly that when acting not out of respect for the moral law but "on a material maxim" men do what they do for the sake of pleasure or happiness.

All material practical principles are, as such, of one and the same kind and belong under the general principle of self love or one's own happiness.[10]

Kant, in fact, was a psychological hedonist in respect of all actions except those done for the sake of the moral law, and this faulty theory of human nature was one of the things preventing him from seeing that moral virtue might be compatible with the rejection of the categorical imperative.

If we put this theory of human action aside, and allow as ends the things that seem to be ends, the picture changes. It will surely be allowed that quite apart from thoughts of duty a man may care about the suffering of others, having a sense of identification with them, and wanting to help if he can. Of course he must want not the reputation of charity, nor even a gratifying role helping others, but, quite simply, their good. If this is what he does care about, then he will be attached to the end proper to the virtue of charity and a comparison with someone acting from an ulterior motive (even a respectable ulterior motive) is out of place. Nor will the conformity of his action to the rule of charity be merely contingent.

---

[9] Pt. II, Introduction, sec. II.
[10] Immanuel Kant, *Critique of Practical Reason*, trans. by L. W. Beck, p. 133.

PHILIPPA FOOT

Honest action may happen to further a man's career; charitable actions do not *happen* to further the good of others.

Can a man accepting only hypothetical imperatives possess other virtues besides that of charity? Could he be just or honest? This problem is more complex because there is no one end related to such virtues as the good of others is related to charity. But what reason could there be for refusing to call a man a just man if he acted justly because he loved truth and liberty, and wanted every man to be treated with a certain minimum respect? And why should the truly honest man not follow honesty for the sake of the good that honest dealing brings to men? Of course, the usual difficulties can be raised about the rare case in which no good is foreseen from an individual act of honesty. But it is not evident that a man's desires could not give him reason to act honestly even here. He wants to live openly and in good faith with his neighbors; it is not all the same to him to lie and conceal.

If one wants to know whether there could be a truly moral man who accepted moral principles as hypothetical rules of conduct, as many people accept rules of etiquette as hypothetical rules of conduct, one must consider the right kind of example. A man who demanded that morality should be brought under the heading of self-interest would not be a good candidate, nor would anyone who was ready to be charitable or honest only so long as he felt inclined. A cause such as justice makes strenuous demands, but this is not peculiar to morality, and men are prepared to toil to achieve many ends not endorsed by morality. That they are prepared to fight so hard for moral ends—for example, for liberty and justice—depends on the fact that these are the kinds of ends that arouse devotion. To sacrifice a great deal for the sake of etiquette one would need to be under the spell of the emphatic "ought$_e$." One could hardly be devoted to behaving *comme il faut*.

In spite of all that has been urged in favor of the hypothetical imperative in ethics, I am sure that many people will be unconvinced and will argue that one element essential to moral virtue is still missing. This missing feature is the recognition of a *duty* to adopt those ends which we have attributed to the moral man. We have said that he *does* care about others, and about causes such as liberty and justice; that it is on this account that he will accept

HYPOTHETICAL IMPERATIVES

a system of morality. But what if he never cared about such things, or what if he ceased to care? Is it not the case that he *ought* to care? This is exactly what Kant would say, for though at times he sounds as if he thought that morality is not concerned with ends, at others he insists that the adoption of ends such as the happiness of others is itself dictated by morality.[11] How is this proposition to be regarded by one who rejects all talk about the binding force of the moral law? He will agree that a moral man has moral ends and cannot be indifferent to matters such as suffering and injustice. Further, he will recognize in the statement that one *ought* to care about these things a correct application of the non-hypothetical moral "ought" by which society is apt to voice its demands. He will not, however, take the fact that he ought$_m$ to have certain ends as in itself reason to adopt them. If he himself is a moral man then he cares about such things, but not "because he ought." If he is an amoral man he may deny that he has any reason to trouble his head over this or any other moral demand. Of course he may be mistaken, and his life as well as others' lives may be most sadly spoiled by his selfishness. But this is not what is urged by those who think they can close the matter by an emphatic use of "ought." My argument is that they are relying on an illusion, as if trying to give the moral "ought" a magic force.[12]

This conclusion may, as I said, appear dangerous and subversive of morality. We are apt to panic at the thought that we ourselves, or other people, might stop caring about the things we do care about, and we feel that the categorical imperative gives us some control over the situation. But it is interesting that the people of Leningrad were not similarly struck by the thought that only the *contingent* fact that other citizens shared their loyalty and devotion to the city stood between them and the Germans during the terrible years of the siege. Perhaps we should be less troubled than we are by fear of defection from the moral cause; perhaps we should even have less reason to fear it if people thought of themselves as volunteers banded together to fight for liberty and justice and against inhumanity and oppres-

[11] See, e.g., *The Metaphysics of Morals*, pt. II, sec. 30.
[12] See G. E. M. Anscombe, "Modern Moral Philosophy," *Philosophy* (1958). My view is different from Miss Anscombe's, but I have learned from her.

PHILIPPA FOOT

sion. It is often felt, even if obscurely, that there is an element of deception in the official line about morality. And while some have been persuaded by talk about the authority of the moral law, others have turned away with a sense of distrust.[13]

PHILIPPA FOOT

Somerville College, Oxford

Recantation 1994

The idea that morality is a system of hypothetical imperatives is so alien to my present views that I no longer want to reprint this paper without explaining that I have long thought the positive part of it misconceived. It is true that the challenge that the paper started with was good, and that it has not, perhaps, to this day been satisfactorily answered. I pointed out that if we say that it is rational to follow moral injunctions but not rational to follow just any old rule, as e.g. a rule of etiquette or of the proper procedure for fighting a duel, it will not do to invoke usage to show that moral imperatives are categorical and the rest hypothetical. If we have reason, quite apart from our desires, to keep promises or tell the truth but not to bother about etiquette or duelling rules, then it must be shown that and why this is so.

At the time that I was writing the article I was unable to see how this could be done, because I was still under the influence of Humean theories of reasons for action. To be sure I had elsewhere (rather inconsistently) allowed self interest an independent reason giving force; but I nevertheless insisted e.g. that only one who could be described as a lover of justice would have reason to be just. What I was doing, in my own mind, was to contrast rational action with the unthinking, perhaps habitual, following of rules one had been trained to follow; and I simply assumed that I had to find the difference within the mentality of the agent. I therefore dismissed as irrelevant the obvious difference between, say, morality and etiquette which would be the first to strike anyone innocent of philosophy:

---

[13] So many people have made useful comments on drafts of this article that I despair of thanking them all. Derek Parfit's help has been sustained and invaluable, and special thanks are also due to Barry Stroud.

An earlier version of this paper was read at the Center for Philosophical Exchange, Brockport, N.Y., and published in *Philosophical Exchange* (Summer 1971).

I mean the fact that much good for human beings hangs on such things as promise-keeping and truth-telling, whereas rules of etiquette may have to do with unimportant matters, and often seem designed to produce anxiety rather than to safeguard the good things of human life.

In my present view, facts about human life are the ones we should call on to develop an account of practical rationality: that is an account of goodness in respect of the recognising and following of reasons for action as it is for creatures situated as human beings are. Moral virtues are needed for this practical rationality, as is a modicum of self love, and the rightful pursuit of more desire-dependent ends. Someone acts well in all these respects only if he recognises what he has reason to do in each area, and allows this to influence his conduct. Wherever exactly we want to use the word 'irrationality', we must admit that someone is *deficient in practical rationality* if he fails to recognise moral considerations as reasons for acting; as also if he thinks he has no reason to look after himself, or to take trouble to attain his more particular ends. But of course he can also be defective if, in spite of knowing what he should do, he does not do it. 'Hypothetical imperatives' having to do with the pursuit of ends that are not mandatory belongs only to part of this story, and definitely not to the part that concerns morality.

For an exposition of the later view of the practical rationality I must refer readers to a lecture of mine called 'Does Moral Subjectivism Rest on a Mistake?' printed in the *Oxford Journal of Legal Studies,* vol. 15, No. 1. (January 1995). The present note will not stand on its own, except as a statement of my firm opposition to the thesis of the earlier piece.

For an excellent criticism of 'Morality as a System of Hypothetical Imperatives' see G. Lawrence 'The Rationality of Morality' in R. Hursthouse et al. (eds.) *Virtues and Reasons,* Oxford University Press, 1995.

[6]

ARE MORAL REQUIREMENTS HYPOTHETICAL IMPERATIVES?

John McDowell and I. G. McFetridge

I—John McDowell

1. In "Morality as a System of Hypothetical Imperatives" (*Philosophical Review* lxxxi, 1972, 305), Philippa Foot argues against the Kantian doctrine, and prevailing orthodoxy, that the requirements of morality are categorical imperatives. She notes that there is a distinction between a use of "should" in which a "should" statement needs withdrawing if the action in question cannot be shown to be ancillary to the agent's desires or interests, and one in which that is not so; and that moral uses of "should" are of the latter sort. She argues, however, that this latter use of "should" does not mark a categorical imperative in the sense intended in the orthodox doctrine; for it is found equally in expressions of the requirements of etiquette. Defenders of the orthodoxy, she assumes, would deny that the requirements of etiquette are categorical imperatives, and would ground the denial on the thesis that it is possible, without irrationality, to question whether one has reason to conform to them. On this assumption, the orthodoxy amounts to the claim that such questioning is not possible with morality. But Mrs Foot insists that the claim is false: there is no irrationality in questioning whether one has reason to act as morality is alleged to require. On this construal of the orthodoxy, then, a categorical imperative is something which must, on pain of irrationality, be recognized as a reason for acting; and Mrs Foot's thesis is that moral requirements are not categorical imperatives in that sense. She concludes that the requirements of morality exert a rational influence on the will only hypothetically; their influence is conditional on the presence of desires which are lacked by those who question whether they have reason to conform.

I want to agree that one need not manifest irrationality in failing to see that one has reason to act as morality requires, but to query whether it follows that moral requirements are only hypothetical imperatives.

2. The terminology calls for some preliminary comment. As Mrs Foot notes, Kant's concern was not with imperatives on a strict grammatical construal of the classification. She concentrates on judgments expressible with the words "should" or "ought"; but I prefer to shift attention away from explicitly prescriptive or normative language altogether.

It seems plausible that if one accepts that one should do something, one accepts that one has a reason to do it. But the reason is not expressed by the "should" statement itself. The reason must involve some appropriate specific consideration which could in principle be cited in support of the "should" statement. Thus, if one does something because one thinks one should, then unless the thought that one should is merely accepted on authority, a more illuminating account of one's reason will be available, citing the appropriate specific consideration which one takes to justify the view that one should act in that way. A formulation of the specific consideration will at least include a mention of what one takes to be relevant features of the circumstances in which the action is to be performed.

Now the fundamental difference at which I think Kant was aiming is one between different ways in which conceptions of circumstances influence the will; that is, between different ways in which they function in the explanation of behaviour in terms of the agent's reasons. To a virtuous person, certain actions are presented as practically necessary—as Kant might have put it—by his view of certain situations in which he finds himself. The question is whether his conceptions of the relevant facts weigh with him only conditionally upon his possession of a desire.

If we think of the requirements of morality as imposed by the circumstances of action, as they are viewed by agents, rather than by the associated "should" thoughts, we make it possible to defend the thesis that virtuous actions are dictated by non-hypothetical imperatives without committing ourselves to the insane thesis that simply to say "You should . . ." to someone is enough to give him a reason for acting; as if, when he protested "But why should I?", it was sufficient to reply "You just should, that's all".

3. When we explain an action in terms of the agent's reasons, we credit him with psychological states given which we can see how doing what he did, or attempted, would have appeared to him in some favourable light. A full specification of a reason must

ARE MORAL REQUIREMENTS HYPOTHETICAL IMPERATIVES? 15

make clear how the reason was capable of motivating; it must contain enough to reveal the favourable light in which the agent saw his projected action. We tend to assume that this is effected, quite generally, by the inclusion of a desire. (Of course a reason which includes a desire can be specified elliptically, when the desire is obvious enough not to need mentioning; as when we explain someone's taking an umbrella in terms of his belief that it is likely to rain.) However, it seems to be false that the motivating power of all reasons derives from their including desires.

Suppose, for instance, that we explain a person's performance of a certain action by crediting him with awareness of some fact which makes it likely (in his view) that acting in that way will be conducive to his interest. Adverting to his view of the facts may suffice, on its own, to show us the favourable light in which his action appeared to him. No doubt we credit him with an appropriate desire, perhaps for his own future happiness. But the commitment to ascribe such a desire is simply consequential on our taking him to act as he does for the reason we cite; the desire does not function as an independent extra component in a full specification of his reason, hitherto omitted by an understandable ellipsis of the obvious, but strictly necessary in order to show how it is that the reason can motivate him. Properly understood, his belief does that on its own. Thomas Nagel (in *The Possibility of Altruism*, Clarendon Press, Oxford, 1970, pp. 29-30) puts the point like this:

> That I have the appropriate desire simply *follows* from the fact that these considerations motivate me; if the likelihood that an act will promote my future happiness motivates me to perform it now, then it is appropriate to ascribe to me a desire for my own future happiness. But nothing follows about the role of the desire as a condition contributing to the motivational efficacy of those considerations.

This passage is quoted in part, and its thesis endorsed, by Mrs Foot at p.204 of her contribution to the symposium "Reasons for Action and Desires", *Aristotelian Society Supplementary Volume* xlvi, 1972, 189.

Why should the reasons which move people to virtuous behaviour not be similar to the reasons which move them to prudent behaviour? To explain an action we regard as virtuous, we typically formulate a more or less complex characterization of the

action's circumstances as we take the agent to have conceived
them. Why should it not be the case, here too, that the agent's
conception of the situation, properly understood, suffices to show
us the favourable light in which his action appeared to him? If
we credit him with a suitable desire, then, as before, that need be
no more than a consequence of the fact that we take his conception of the circumstances to have been his reason for acting as he
did; the desire need not function as an independent component
in the explanation, needed in order to account for the capacity of
the cited reason to influence the agent's will.

4. There may seem to be a difficulty: might not another person have exactly the same conception of the circumstances, but
see no reason to act as the virtuous person does? If so, adverting
to that conception of the situation cannot, after all, suffice to
show us the favourable light in which the virtuous person saw his
action. Our specification of his reason must, after all, have been
elliptical; a full specification would need to add an extra psychological state to account for the action's attractiveness to him in
particular—namely, surely, a desire.

We can evade this argument by denying its premiss: that is,
by taking a special view of the virtuous person's conception of the
circumstances, according to which it cannot be shared by
someone who sees no reason to act as the virtuous person does.

This may seem problematic. But if one concedes that a conception of the facts can constitute the whole of a reason for prudent
behaviour, one is not at liberty to object to the very idea that a
view of how things are might not need supplementing with a desire in order to reveal the favourable light in which someone saw
some action; and a view with that property surely cannot be
shared by someone who sees no reason to act in the way in question. If this is allowed for prudence, why should it not be allowed
for morality too?

Suppose someone was incapable of seeing how a fact about the
likely effect of an action on his own future could, on its own, constitute a reason for the action. On some suitable occasion, he
might be unmoved by such a fact. It would not be wrong to say
that an ordinarily prudent person, in parallel circumstances,
would differ from him in having a certain desire. But according
to the concession, the desire is not a further component, over and
above the prudent person's conception of the likely effects of his
action on his own future, in the explanation of his prudent be-

haviour. It is not that the two people share a certain neutral conception of the facts, but differ in that one, but not the other, has an independent desire as well, which combines with that neutral conception of the facts to cast a favourable light on his acting in a certain way. The desire is ascribable to the prudent person simply in recognition of the fact that his conception of the likely effects of his action on his own future by itself casts a favourable light on his acting as he does. So the admitted difference in respect of desire should be explicable, like the difference in respect of action, in terms of a more fundamental difference in respect of how they conceive the facts.

It is not clear that we really can make sense of the idea of someone who is otherwise rational but cannot see how facts about his future can, by themselves, constitute reasons for him to act in various ways. But to the extent to which the idea does make sense, it seems to be on just the lines we should expect: we picture him as someone with an idiosyncratic view of what it is for a fact to concern his own future. Perhaps he thinks of the person involved in such a fact as some future person, connected with the one who is currently deliberating by links of continuity and resemblance which are too tenuous, in his view, for it to be anything but arbitrary for the current deliberator to pay special attention to that future person's welfare. What is special about a prudent version is a different understanding of what it is for a fact to concern his own future. He sees things otherwise in the relevant area; and we comprehend his prudent behaviour by comprehending the relevant fragment of his world view, not by appealing to the desire which is admittedly ascribable to him. That is to be understood, no less than the behaviour is, in terms of the world view.

Why should it not be similar with explanations of virtuous behaviour in terms of the virtuous person's conceptions of situations in which he acts?

5. So far I have responded only *ad hominem* to qualms about the idea that a conception of how things are might constitute, on its own, a reason for virtuous action. That is how it was conceded to be with prudential reasons, and there is no obvious argument that the possibility, once granted, should be restricted to prudential considerations. But presumably someone with sufficiently strong doubts about the case of morality will be encouraged to doubt the whole idea, and suppose that it cannot be so

even with prudential reasons; he will not be impressed by the thought that, if granted there, the possibility cannot be dismissed out of hand for the case of morality.

I suppose the general doubt is on these lines. A view of how things are is a state or disposition of one's cognitive equipment. But the psychological states we are considering are to suffice, on their own, to show how certain actions appeared in a favourable light. That requires that their possession entails a disposition of the possessor's will. And will and belief—the appetitive and the cognitive—are distinct existences; so a state which presents itself as cognitive but entails an appetitive state must be, after all, only impurely cognitive, and contain the appetitive state as a part. If such a state strikes its possessor as cognitive, that is because he is projecting his states of will on to the world (a case of the mind's propensity to spread itself upon objects). The appetitive state should be capable in principle of being analysed out, leaving a neutrally cognitive residue. Thus where it appears that a conception of how things are exhausts an agent's reason for acting in a certain way, an analysed and less misleading formulation of the reason will be bipartite: it will specify, first, a neutral conception of the facts, available equally to someone who sees no reason to act in the way in question, and, secondly, a desire, which combines with that conception of the facts to make the action attractive to its possessor.

This paper is primarily addressed to those who are vulnerable to the *ad hominem* argument. In their view, since the line of thought I have just sketched falsifies the workings of prudential explanations of behaviour, it simply cannot be generally right. In the rest of this section I shall make some remarks, not *ad hominem*, about the general issue; but a proper discussion is impossible here.

There is room for scepticism about the acceptability of discounting the appearances in the way the objection urges. Explanation of behaviour by reasons purports to show the favourable light in which an agent saw his action. If it strikes an agent that his reason for acting as he does consists entirely in his conception of the circumstances in which he acts, then an explanation which insists on analysing that seemingly cognitive state into a less problematically cognitive state combined with a separate desire, while it will show the action as attractive from

ARE MORAL REQUIREMENTS HYPOTHETICAL IMPERATIVES? 19

the standpoint of the psychological states it cites, is not obviously guaranteed to get the favourable light right. If one accepts an explanation of the analysing sort, one will not be baffled by inability to find any point one can take the agent to have seen in behaving as he did; but what leaves one unpuzzled is not thereby shown to be a *correct* explanation.

The analysis will nevertheless seem compulsory, if the objection seems irresistible. If the world is, in itself, motivationally inert, and is also the proper province of cognitive equipment, it is inescapable that a strictly cognitive state—a conception of how things are, properly so called—cannot constitute the whole of a reason for acting. But the idea of the world as motivationally inert is not an independent hard datum. It is simply the metaphysical counterpart of the thesis that states of will and cognitive states are distinct existences; which is exactly what is in question.

If a conception of a set of circumstances can suffice on its own to explain an action, then the world view it exemplifies is certainly not the kind of thing that could be established by the methods of the natural sciences. But the notion of the world, or how things are, which is appropriate in this context is a metaphysical notion, not a scientific one: world views richer than that of science are not scientific, but not on that account unscientific (a term of opprobrium for answers other than those of science to science's questions). To query their status as world views on the ground of their not being scientific is to be motivated not by science but by scientism.

6. It is not to be denied that behaviour which is in fact virtuous can in some cases be found unsurprising through being what one would expect anyway, given an acceptably ascribed desire which is independently intelligible. That is why sheer bafflement at virtuous behaviour in general is very difficult to imagine. At some points even the rankest outsider would be able to attain a measure of comprehension of virtuous actions in terms of desires which people just naturally have: for instance the desire that people related to them in various ways should not suffer. Such coincidences constitute possible points of entry for an outsider trying to work his way into appreciation of a moral outlook. Similarly, they perhaps partly explain how it is possible to acquire a moral outlook of one's own (not the same topic, since one can understand a moral outlook without sharing it).

20   I—JOHN MCDOWELL

What is questionable is whether there need *always* be an independently intelligible desire to whose fulfilment a virtuous action,
if rational at all, can be seen as conducive.

Charitable behaviour aims at an end, namely the good of
others. (See "Morality as a System of Hypothetical Imperatives",
pp. 313–4.) It does not follow that a full specification of the
agent's reason for a charitable act would need to add a desire to
his conception of the circumstances in which he acted. For prudent behaviour equally aims at an end, namely one's own future
happiness. The desire for the good of others is related to charity
as the desire for one's own future happiness is related to prudence; not, then, as a needed extra ingredient in formulations of
reasons for acting. Rather, the desire is ascribed, as in the prudential case, simply in recognition of the fact that a charitable person's special way of conceiving situations by itself casts a
favourable light on charitable actions. Of course a desire ascribed
in this purely consequential way is not independently intelligible.

It does not seem plausible that any purely natural fellow-feel-
ing or benevolence, unmediated by the special ways of seeing
situations which are characteristic of charity as it is thought of
above, would issue in behaviour which exactly matched that of a
charitable person; the objects of a purely natural benevolence
could not be guaranteed to coincide in all cases with the good of
others as a possessor of the virtue would conceive it. It seems still
less plausible that virtuous behaviour in general could be duplicated by means of the outcomes of independently intelligible desires.

Mrs Foot sometimes seems to suggest that if someone acts in a
way he takes to be morally required, and his behaviour cannot be
shown to be rational as a case of conformity to an hypothetical
imperative, then he must be blindly obeying an inculcated code.
(See "Reasons for Action and Desires", p. 210: "Perhaps we
have been bewitched by the idea that we *just do* have reason to
obey this part of our moral code". This thought, about honesty, is
not endorsed; but it seems to be put forward as the sole alternative to the thought that we should explain honest behaviour in
terms of desires.) But if we deny that virtuous behaviour can
always be explained as the outcome of independently intelligible
desires, we do not thereby commit ourselves to its being mere obedience to a code. There need be no possibility of reducing

virtuous behaviour to rules. In moral upbringing what one learns is not to behave on conformity with rules of conduct, but to see situations in a special light, as constituting reasons for acting; this perceptual capacity, once acquired, can be exercised in complex novel circumstances, not necessarily capable of being foreseen and legislated for by a codifier of the conduct required by virtue, however wise and thoughtful he might be.

On this view, independently intelligible desires will take an outsider only some of the distance towards full understanding of virtuous behaviour. In the first place, there will be some actions which simply cannot be explained as the outcomes of such desires. Second, if one sticks with explanations in terms of independently intelligible desires at the points of entry, where such explanations do make actions unpuzzling, one will not have the full picture even of those actions: if they manifest a virtuous person's distinctive way of seeing things, they must be explicable also in terms of exercises of that perceptual capacity, which need no supplementing with desires to yield full specifications of reasons. (This need not imply that the initial explanations, at the points of entry, were wrong. Someone can have two separate reasons for what he does; perhaps he can do it for both of them. If so, we need not suppose—as Kant perhaps did—that an action's being the outcome of a natural desire disqualifies it as a manifestation of virtue.)

§ 4 suggests that if someone could not see the force of prudential considerations, one might appropriately protest: "You don't know what it means for a fact to concern your future." Rather similarly, in urging behaviour one takes to be morally required, one finds oneself saying things like this: "You don't know what it means that someone is shy and sensitive." Conveying what a circumstance means, in this loaded sense, is getting someone to see it in the special way in which a virtuous person would see it. In the attempt to do so, one exploits contrivances similar to those one exploits in other areas where the task is to back up the injunction "See it like this": helpful juxtapositions of cases, descriptions with carefully chosen terms and carefully placed emphasis, and the like. (Compare, for instance, what one might do and say to someone who says "Jazz sounds to me like a mess, a mere welter of uncoordinated noise".) No such contrivances can be guaranteed success, in the sense that failure would show irrationality on the part of the audience. That, together with the importance of rhetorical skills to their successful deployment, sets them apart from the sorts of thing we typically regard as paradigms of argument. But these seem insufficient grounds for concluding that they are appeals to passion as opposed to reason: for concluding that "See it like this" is really a covert invitation to feel, quite over and above one's view of the facts, a desire which will combine with one's belief to recommend acting in the appropriate way.

Failure to see what a circumstance means, in the loaded sense, is of course compatible with competence, by all ordinary tests, with the language used to describe the circumstance; that brings out how loaded the notion of meaning involved in the protest is. Notice that, as the example of "shy and sensitive" illustrates, the language used to express a special reason-constituting conception of a situation need not be explicitly evaluative.

The question "Why should I conform to the dictates of morality?" is most naturally understood as asking for an extra-moral motivation which will be gratified by virtuous behaviour. So understood, the question has no answer. What may happen is that someone is brought to see things as a virtuous person does, and so stops feeling the need to ask it. Situation by situation, he knows why he should behave in the relevant ways; but what he now has is a set of answers to a different interpretation of the question. (See pp. 152–3 of D. Z. Phillips, "In Search of the Moral 'Must': Mrs Foot's Fugitive Thought", *Philosophical Quarterly* xxvii, 1977, 140—an article from which I have profited in writing this.)

7. We have, then, an apparent contrast between two ways in which an agent's view of how things are can function in explaining his actions. In one, exemplified by the case of taking one's umbrella (§ 3), the agent's belief about how things are combines with an independently intelligible desire to represent the action as a good thing from the agent's point of view. In the other, a conception of how things are suffices on its own to show us the favourable light in which the action appeared. Beliefs about one's future well-being standardly operate in the second way, according to the concession of § 3; so, according to the suggestion of this paper, do moral reasons.

With reasons which function in the second way, it is not false that they weigh with people only if they have a certain desire. But that is just because the ascription of the desire in question follows from the fact that the reasons weigh as they do. It would be wrong to infer that the conceptions of situations which constitute the reasons are available equally to people who are not swayed by them, and weigh with those who are swayed only contingently upon their possession of an independent desire. That would be to assimilate the second kind of reason to the first. To preserve the distinction, we should say that the relevant conceptions are not so much as possessed except by those whose wills are influenced appropriately. Their status as reasons is hypothetical only in this truistic sense: they sway only those who *have* them.

When we envisaged a person immune to the force of prudential considerations, we supposed that he might have an idiosyncratic understanding of what it was for a fact to concern his own future (§ 4). Particular facts about his own future, by themselves, would leave him cold. Now we might imagine equipping him with a separate desire, for the welfare of the future person he takes to be involved in the relevant facts. Then his conception of those facts might move him to action, with their influence conditional upon his possession of that extra desire. But the resulting behaviour, only hypothetically called for by his conception of the facts, would match ordinary prudent behaviour only externally. It would be wrong to conclude that ordinary prudent behaviour is likewise only hypothetically commanded.

Similarly, someone who lacks a virtuous person's distinctive view of a situation might perhaps be artificially induced into a simulacrum of a virtuous action by equipping him with an independent desire. His conception of the situation would then be influencing his will hypothetically. But it would be wrong to conclude that a virtuous person's actions are likewise only hypothetically commanded by his conceptions of such situations. (§ 6 suggests, anyway, a special difficulty about the idea that virtuous behaviour might be thus artificially duplicated across the board.)

According to this position, then, a failure to see reason to act virtuously stems, not from the lack of a desire on which the rational influence of moral requirements is conditional, but from the lack of a distinctive way of seeing situations. If that perceptual capacity is possessed and exercised, it yields non-hypothetical reasons for acting. Now the lack of a perceptual capacity, or failure to exercise it, need show no irrationality. (It might be argued that not to have the relevant conception of one's own future, in

the prudential case, would be irrational; but a parallel argument
in the moral case would lack plausibility.) Thus we can grant
Mrs Foot's premiss—that it is possible without irrationality to
fail to see reason to act as morality requires—without granting
her conclusion—that moral requirements exert a rational influence on the will only hypothetically. The gap opens because
we have undermined the assumption that a consideration can
exert a rational influence on a will other than hypothetically only
if it is recognizable as a requirement by all rational men.

Mrs Foot thought her opponents would differentiate moral
requirements from those of etiquette by claiming that moral requirements, unlike those of etiquette, are recognizable as requirements by all rational men; that is, that they are categorical
imperatives in the sense stipulated by the assumption we have
undermined. Obviously this paper does not conform to that
expectation. In respect of not necessarily impressing any rational
man, moral requirements and the requirements of etiquette are
alike, and it is not my intention here to discuss in detail what
makes them different. (Many actions performed for reasons of etiquette can be explained in terms of bewitchment by a code.
There may be a residue of actions not explicable in that way. It
does not seem to me to be obviously absurd, or destructive of the
point of any distinction between categorical and hypothetical imperatives, to suppose that such residual actions might be most
revealingly explained in terms of non-hypothetically reason-constituting conceptions of circumstances. One can attribute such
conceptions to others without being compelled oneself; for one
can appreciate how someone might see things a certain way without seeing them that way oneself.)

I have said nothing about where the line is to be drawn
between hypothetical and non-hypothetical reasons for action.
For purposes of exposition, I have assumed that when one explains taking an umbrella in terms of the agent's belief that it will
probably rain, the reason specified needs supplementing with
a desire. But it would not matter if someone insisted that what
appears as a desire, in the most natural filling out of the reason, is
actually better regarded as a cognitive state, a colouring of the
agent's view of the world. If it is admitted that we can make
sense of the idea of a reason of the second sort distinguished
above, then there is content to the thesis that moral reasons are of

that sort, even if it turns out that there are no reasons of the first sort.

Note that consequentially ascribed desires are indeed desires. Construing obedience to a categorical imperative as acting for a certain sort of reason, we can see the obedience as a case of doing what one wants. So subjection to categorical imperatives, even without the coincidences with natural desires mentioned in § 6, need not be pictured as a grim servitude.

8. The strategy of this paper must raise the question whether I am treating prudential considerations as categorical imperatives. (It would be pleasant if Mrs Foot could be represented as holding that prudential imperatives are categorical and moral imperatives hypothetical.) The answer depends on which of Kant's characterizations of hypothetical imperatives we have in mind.

On the one hand, I interpret the concession of § 3 as implying this: a prudent person's conception of facts about his own future exerts an influence on his will in its own right, not contingently upon his possession of an independent desire.

On the other hand, Kant's hypothetical imperatives are supposed to "declare a possible action to be practically necessary as a means to the attainment of something else that one wills (or that one may will)" (translation by H. J. Paton, *The Moral Law*, Hutchinson, London, 1948, p. 82). And it is certainly true that prudential considerations typically recommend actions as means to ends distinct from themselves.

Are not moral imperatives sometimes equally hypothetical in the second sense? Kant was committed to denying that moral considerations can recommend an action as a means to an end distinct from itself, but the denial seems desperately implausible. Perhaps the idea that one has to exclude means-end reasons from the sphere of virtue can be explained on the following lines. From the concession of § 3, we can see that if an action's rationality consists in its conduciveness to an end distinct from itself (the agent's future happiness, say), it does not follow that the willing of the distinct end is a desire intelligible independently of understanding the reason-constituting character of facts about such conduciveness. But though it does not follow, it would be natural to suppose that it does. Kant's fundamental aim was to deny that the motivating capacity of moral considerations needs explaining from outside, in terms of desires which are not intrinsically moral

26   I—JOHN MCDOWELL

– that is, to deny that moral requirements are hypothetical imperatives in the first sense. Given the natural error, he would
think he had to deny that virtuous behaviour is ever rational as a
means to a distinct end—that is, to deny that moral requirements
are ever hypothetical imperatives in the second sense.

9. The suggestion, so far, has been this: one cannot share a
virtuous person's view of a situation in which it seems to him that
virtue requires some action, but see no reason to act in that way.
The following possibility is still open: one sees reason to act in
that way, but takes the reason to be outweighed by a reason for
acting in some other way. But part of the point of claiming that
the requirements of virtue are categorical imperatives may lie in a
rejection of that possibility.

The rejection might stem from the idea that the dictates of virtue always outweigh reasons for acting otherwise. But I believe a
more interesting ground for it is the idea that the dictates of virtue, if properly appreciated, are not weighed with other reasons
at all, not even on a scale which always tips on their side. If a
situation in which virtue imposes a requirement is genuinely conceived as such, according to this view, then considerations which,
in the absence of the requirement, would have constituted reasons
for acting otherwise are silenced altogether—not overridden—by
the requirement.

"What shall it profit a man, if he shall gain the whole world,
and lose his soul?" Obviously we are not meant to answer "The
profits are outweighed by counterbalancing losses". The intended
answer is "Nothing". At that price, whatever one might achieve
does not count as profit. Or, in the terminology of reasons: the
attractions of whatever wickedness might bring do not constitute
some reason for wickedness, which is, however, overridden by
the reasons against it; rather, given that they are achieved by
wickedness, those attractive outcomes do not count as reasons at
all.

10. Aristotle's thoughts about continence, incontinence, and
virtue involve such a view of the status of the requirements of virtue. Perhaps the requirements are not exactly moral requirements, since Aristotle's notion of virtue is perhaps not exactly a
moral notion. But his view may nevertheless usefully illustrate the
structure of the position described in § 9, and help to explain the
distinction between silencing and overriding.

ARE MORAL REQUIREMENTS HYPOTHETICAL IMPERATIVES? 27

For Aristotle, if one needs to overcome an inclination to act otherwise, in getting oneself to act temperately, then one's action manifests continence rather than the virtue of temperance. Readers are apt to be puzzled about how they are meant to think of the virtue. Is the temperate person's libido somehow peculiarly undemanding? Does his inclination to sleep with someone he ought not to sleep with evaporate under the impact of the thought that he would not enjoy it at all (why ever not, unless he is not quite human?); or under the impact of the thought that his enjoyment would be counterbalanced by pangs of remorse?

In fact the idea is on these lines. The temperate person need be no less prone to enjoy physical pleasure than the next man. In suitable circumstances it will be true that he would enjoy some intemperate action which is available to him. In the absence of a requirement, the prospective enjoyment would constitute a reason for going ahead. But his clear perception of the requirement insulates the prospective enjoyment—of which, for a satisfying conception of the virtue, we should want him to have a vivid appreciation—from engaging his inclinations at all. Here and now, it does not count for him as any reason for acting in that way.

Virtues like temperance and courage involve steadfastness in face of characteristic sorts of temptation, and it can seem impossible to register that fact without regarding them as cases of continence. Insisting nevertheless on the distinction between virtue and continence yields a view of these virtues which has a certain sublimity. Their proper manifestation is a renunciation, without struggle, of something which in the abstract one would value highly (physical pleasure, security of life and limb). The lack of struggle is ensured by keeping the attention firmly fixed on what Aristotle calls "the noble"; not by a weighing of attractions which leads to the conclusion that on balance the virtuous course is more desirable. (It is true that the competing course could not really satisfy a virtuous person. But that is not to say that he judges it on balance less desirable; it records a consequence of his conviction that in these circumstances the attractions of the competing course count for nothing.) Genuinely courageous behaviour, on this view, combines a lively awareness of risk, and a normal valuation of life and health (see *Nicomachean Ethics* III. 9), with a sort of serenity; taking harm to be, by definition, what one has reason to avoid, we can see the serenity as based on the belief, paradoxical in juxtaposition with the valuing of life and health, that no harm can come to one by acting thus.

This view of virtue obviously involves a high degree of idealization; the best we usually encounter is to some degree tainted with continence. But in a view of what genuine virtue is, idealization is not something to be avoided or apologized for.

It is evident that this view of virtue makes incontinence problematic. The weak incontinent person must conceive the circumstances of his action in a way which, in some sense, matches the way a virtuous person would conceive them, since he knows he is not acting as virtue demands. But the virtuous person conceives the relevant sorts of situation in such a way that considerations which would otherwise be reasons for acting differently are silenced by the recognized requirement. If the incontinent person has such a conception, how can those considerations make themselves heard by his will, as they do? Obviously continence poses a parallel difficulty.

The way out is to attenuate the degree to which the continent or incontinent person's conception of a situation matches that of a virtuous person. Their inclinations are aroused, as the virtuous person's are not, by their awareness of competing attractions: a lively desire clouds or blurs the focus of their attention on "the noble".

Curiously enough, if we approach incontinence on these lines, we entirely disarm one difficulty which threatens it on other approaches. (I owe this thought to David Wiggins.) Suppose we think of the incontinent person as failing to act on a judgment "all things considered", in which the motivating potential of alternative actions is registered by his counting their attractions, suitably weighted, as reasons for acting in those ways. The judgment will have to be that those reasons are outweighed by the force of the reason for the virtuous action. But now it seems mysterious how one of those alternative motivations can take charge. Why is its ability to move one not exhausted by the weight it is pictured as bringing to the scale? On the view I am describing, by contrast, the motivating potential of the competing attractions has not exerted any influence in forming the judgment which the person should have acted on—so that, as above, it might be expected to have used itself up there, and it is mysterious how it can still have energy to inject after it has been outweighed. The virtuous view of what should be done does not so much as take those attractions into account. So we can think of them as a potential source of motivating energy, not used up in the formation of the judgment. There can be a risk that the potential will be actualized, if the attractions are not insulated, by the clear perception of a silencing requirement, from engaging the inclinations.

A *caveat*: notice that the position is not that clear perception of any moral reason, however weak, silences any reasons of other sorts, however strong. The reasons which silence are those which mark out actions as required by virtue. There can be less exigent moral reasons, and as far as this position goes, they may be overridden.

11. In § 8 I left moral and prudential considerations not sharply distinguished in the manner of their influence on the will. But the view that those moral reasons which count as imposing requirements are special, in the way described in § 9 and illustrated in § 10, restores a distinction. On this view, to conceive some relevant fact about one's future as an ordinarily prudent person would is not, after all, *eo ipso* to take oneself to have a reason for the prudent behaviour which would normally be recommended by such a fact. If one is clearly aware of a moral requirement to behave differently, one will not take the prudential consideration as the reason it would otherwise be. (It is not plausible to suppose that perception of the moral requirement effects this by tampering with one's understanding of what it is for a fact to concern one's own future.) So prudential considerations, on this view, are hypothetical imperatives in a new sense: their rational influence on the will is conditional, not upon a desire, but upon the absence of a clearly grasped moral requirement to do something else. Moral requirements, by contrast, are not conditional at all: neither upon desires nor upon the absence of other reasons.

[7]

MORAL RELATIVISM DEFENDED

MY thesis is that morality arises when a group of people reach an implicit agreement or come to a tacit understanding about their relations with one another. Part of what I mean by this is that moral judgments—or, rather, an important class of them—make sense only in relation to and with reference to one or another such agreement or understanding. This is vague, and I shall try to make it more precise in what follows. But it should be clear that I intend to argue for a version of what has been called moral relativism.

In doing so, I am taking sides in an ancient controversy. Many people have supposed that the sort of view which I am going to defend is obviously correct—indeed, that it is the only sort of account that could make sense of the phenomenon of morality. At the same time there have also been many who have supposed that moral relativism is confused, incoherent, and even immoral, at the very least obviously wrong.

Most arguments against relativism make use of a strategy of dissuasive definition; they define moral relativism as an inconsistent thesis. For example, they define it as the assertion that (a) there are no universal moral principles and (b) one ought to act in accordance with the principles of one's own group, where this latter principle, (b), is supposed to be a universal moral principle.[1] It is easy enough to show that this version of moral relativism will not do, but that is no reason to think that a defender of moral relativism cannot find a better definition.

My moral relativism is a soberly logical thesis—a thesis about logical form, if you like. Just as the judgment that something is large makes sense only in relation to one or another comparison class, so too, I will argue, the judgment that it is wrong of someone to do something makes sense only in relation to an agreement or understanding. A dog may be large in relation to chihuahuas

---

[1] Bernard Williams, *Morality: An Introduction to Ethics* (New York, 1972), pp. 20-21; Marcus Singer, *Generalization in Ethics* (New York, 1961), p. 332.

3

GILBERT HARMAN

but not large in relation to dogs in general. Similarly, I will argue, an action may be wrong in relation to one agreement but not in relation to another. Just as it makes no sense to ask whether a dog is large, period, apart from any relation to a comparison class, so too, I will argue, it makes no sense to ask whether an action is wrong, period, apart from any relation to an agreement.

There is an agreement, in the relevant sense, if each of a number of people intends to adhere to some schedule, plan, or set of principles, intending to do this on the understanding that the others similarly intend. The agreement or understanding need not be conscious or explicit; and I will not here try to say what distinguishes moral agreements from, for example, conventions of the road or conventions of etiquette, since these distinctions will not be important as regards the purely logical thesis that I will be defending.

Although I want to say that certain moral judgments are made in relation to an agreement, I do not want to say this about all moral judgments. Perhaps it is true that all moral judgments are made in relation to an agreement; nevertheless, that is not what I will be arguing. For I want to say that there is a way in which certain moral judgments are relative to an agreement but other moral judgments are not. My relativism is a thesis only about what I will call "inner judgments," such as the judgment that someone ought or ought not to have acted in a certain way or the judgment that it was right or wrong of him to have done so. My relativism is not meant to apply, for example, to the judgment that someone is evil or the judgment that a given institution is unjust.

In particular, I am not denying (nor am I asserting) that some moralities are "objectively" better than others or that there are objective standards for assessing moralities. My thesis is a soberly logical thesis about logical form.

I. INNER JUDGMENTS

We make inner judgments about a person only if we suppose that he is capable of being motivated by the relevant moral considerations. We make other sorts of judgment about those

4

MORAL RELATIVISM DEFENDED

who we suppose are not susceptible of such motivation. Inner judgments include judgments in which we say that someone should or ought to have done something or that someone was right or wrong to have done something. Inner judgments do not include judgments in which we call someone (literally) a savage or say that someone is (literally) inhuman, evil, a betrayer, a traitor, or an enemy.

Consider this example. Intelligent beings from outer space land on Earth, beings without the slightest concern for human life and happiness. That a certain course of action on their part might injure one of us means nothing to them; that fact by itself gives them no reason to avoid the action. In such a case it would be odd to say that nevertheless the beings ought to avoid injuring us or that it would be wrong for them to attack us. Of course we will want to resist them if they do such things and we will make negative judgments about them; but we will judge that they are dreadful enemies to be repelled and even destroyed, not that they should not act as they do.

Similarly, if we learn that a band of cannibals has captured and eaten the sole survivor of a shipwreck, we will speak of the primitive morality of the cannibals and may call them savages, but we will not say that they ought not to have eaten their captive.

Again, suppose that a contented employee of Murder, Incorporated was raised as a child to honor and respect members of the "family" but to have nothing but contempt for the rest of society. His current assignment, let us suppose, is to kill a certain bank manager, Bernard J. Ortcutt. Since Ortcutt is not a member of the "family," the employee in question has no compunction about carrying out his assignment. In particular, if we were to try to convince him that he should not kill Ortcutt, our argument would merely amuse him. We would not provide him with the slightest reason to desist unless we were to point to practical difficulties, such as the likelihood of his getting caught. Now, in this case it would be a misuse of language to say of him that he ought not to kill Ortcutt or that it would be wrong of him to do so, since that would imply that our own moral considerations carry some weight with him, which they do not. Instead we can

GILBERT HARMAN

only judge that he is a criminal, someone to be hunted down by the police, an enemy of peace-loving citizens, and so forth.

It is true that we can make certain judgments about him using the word "ought." For example, investigators who have been tipped off by an informer and who are waiting for the assassin to appear at the bank can use the "ought" of expectation to say, "He ought to arrive soon," meaning that on the basis of their information one would expect him to arrive soon. And, in thinking over how the assassin might carry out his assignment, we can use the "ought" of rationality to say that he ought to go in by the rear door, meaning that it would be more rational for him to do that than to go in by the front door. In neither of these cases is the moral "ought" in question.

There is another use of "ought" which is normative and in a sense moral but which is distinct from what I am calling the moral "ought." This is the use which occurs when we say that something ought or ought not to be the case. It ought not to be the case that members of Murder, Incorporated go around killing people; in other words, it is a terrible thing that they do so.[2] The same thought can perhaps be expressed as "They ought not to go around killing people," meaning that it ought not to be the case that they do, not that they are wrong to do what they do. The normative "ought to be" is used to assess a situation; the moral "ought to do" is used to describe a relation between an agent and a type of act that he might perform or has performed.

The sentence "They ought not to go around killing people" is therefore multiply ambiguous. It can mean that one would not expect them to do so (the "ought" of expectation), that it is not in their interest to do so (the "ought" of rationality), that it is a bad thing that they do so (the normative "ought to be"), or that they are wrong to do so (the moral "ought to do"). For the most

---

[2] Thomas Nagel has observed that often, when we use the evaluative "ought to be" to say that something ought to be the case, we imply that someone ought to do something or ought to have done something about it. To take his example, we would not say that a certain hurricane ought not to have killed fifty people just on the ground that it was a terrible thing that the hurricane did so; but we might say this if we had in mind that the deaths from the hurricane would not have occurred except for the absence of safety or evacuation procedures which the authorities ought to have provided.

6

MORAL RELATIVISM DEFENDED

part I am here concerned only with the last of these interpretations.

The word "should" behaves very much like "ought to." There is a "should" of expectation ("They should be here soon"), a "should" of rationality ("He should go in by the back door"), a normative "should be" ("They shouldn't go around killing people like that"), and the moral "should do" ("You should keep that promise"). I am of course concerned mainly with the last sense of "should."

"Right" and "wrong" also have multiple uses; I will not try to say what all of them are. But I do want to distinguish using the word "wrong" to say that a particular situation or action is wrong from using the word to say that it is wrong *of someone* to do something. In the former case, the word "wrong" is used to assess an act or situation. In the latter case it is used to describe a relation between an agent and an act. Only the latter sort of judgment is an inner judgment. Although we would not say concerning the contented employee of Murder, Incorporated mentioned earlier that it was wrong *of him* to kill Ortcutt, we could say that *his action* was wrong and we could say that it is wrong that there is so much killing.

To take another example, it sounds odd to say that Hitler should not have ordered the extermination of the Jews, that it was wrong of him to have done so. That sounds somehow "too weak" a thing to say. Instead we want to say that Hitler was an evil man. Yet we can properly say, "Hitler ought not to have ordered the extermination of the Jews," if what we mean is that it ought never to have happened; and we can say without oddity that what Hitler did was wrong. Oddity attends only the inner judgment that Hitler was wrong to have acted in that way. That is what sounds "too weak."

It is worth noting that the inner judgments sound too weak not because of the enormity of what Hitler did but because we suppose that in acting as he did he shows that he could not have been susceptible to the moral considerations on the basis of which we make our judgment. He is in the relevant sense beyond the pale and we therefore cannot make inner judgments about him. To see that this is so, consider, say, Stalin, another mass-murderer.

7

GILBERT HARMAN

We can perhaps imagine someone taking a sympathetic view of Stalin. In such a view, Stalin realized that the course he was going to pursue would mean the murder of millions of people and he dreaded such a prospect; however, the alternative seemed to offer an even greater disaster—so, reluctantly and with great anguish, he went ahead. In relation to such a view of Stalin, inner judgments about Stalin are not as odd as similar judgments about Hitler. For we might easily continue the story by saying that, despite what he hoped to gain, Stalin should not have undertaken the course he did, that it was wrong of him to have done so. What makes inner judgments about Hitler odd, "too weak," is not that the acts judged seem too terrible for the words used but rather that the agent judged seems beyond the pale— in other words beyond the motivational reach of the relevant moral considerations.

Of course, I do not want to deny that for various reasons a speaker might pretend that an agent is or is not susceptible to certain moral considerations. For example, a speaker may for rhetorical or political reasons wish to suggest that someone is beyond the pale, that he should not be listened to, that he can be treated as an enemy. On the other hand, a speaker may pretend that someone is susceptible to certain moral considerations in an effort to make that person or others susceptible to those considerations. Inner judgments about one's children sometimes have this function. So do inner judgments made in political speeches that aim at restoring a lapsed sense of morality in government.

II. The Logical Form of Inner Judgments

Inner judgments have two important characteristics. First, they imply that the agent has reasons to do something. Second, the speaker in some sense endorses these reasons and supposes that the audience also endorses them. Other moral judgments about an agent, on the other hand, do not have such implications; they do not imply that the agent has reasons for acting that are endorsed by the speaker.

If someone S says that A (morally) ought to do D, S implies that A has reasons to do D and S endorses those reasons—whereas

MORAL RELATIVISM DEFENDED

if S says that B was evil in what B did, S does not imply that the reasons S would endorse for not doing what B did were reasons for B not to do that thing; in fact, S implies that they were not reasons for B.

Let us examine this more closely. If S says that (morally) A ought to do D, S implies that A has reasons to do D which S endorses. I shall assume that such reasons would have to have their source in goals, desires, or intentions that S takes A to have and that S approves of A's having because S shares those goals, desires, or intentions. So, if S says that (morally) A ought to do D, there are certain motivational attitudes M which S assumes are shared by S, A, and S's audience.

Now, in supposing that reasons for action must have their source in goals, desires, or intentions, I am assuming something like an Aristotelian or Humean account of these matters, as opposed, for example, to a Kantian approach which sees a possible source of motivation in reason itself.[3] I must defer a full-scale discussion of the issue to another occasion. Here I simply assume that the Kantian approach is wrong. In particular, I assume that there might be no reasons at all for a being from outer space to avoid harm to us; that, for Hitler, there might have been no reason at all not to order the extermination of the Jews; that the contented employee of Murder, Incorporated might have no reason at all not to kill Ortcutt; that the cannibals might have no reason not to eat their captive. In other words, I assume that the possession of rationality is not sufficient to provide a source for relevant reasons, that certain desires, goals, or intentions are also necessary. Those who accept this assumption will, I think, find that they distinguish inner moral judgments from other moral judgments in the way that I have indicated.

Ultimately, I want to argue that the shared motivational attitudes M are intentions to keep an agreement (supposing that others similarly intend). For I want to argue that inner moral judgments are made relative to such an agreement. That is, I want to argue that, when S makes the inner judgment that A

---

[3] For the latter approach, see Thomas Nagel, *The Possibility of Altruism* (Oxford, 1970).

9

GILBERT HARMAN

ought to do *D*, *S* assumes that *A* intends to act in accordance
with an agreement which *S* and *S*'s audience also intend to
observe. In other words, I want to argue that the source of the
reasons for doing *D* which *S* ascribes to *A* is *A*'s sincere intention
to observe a certain agreement. I have not yet argued for the
stronger thesis, however. I have argued only that *S* makes his
judgment relative to *some* motivational attitudes *M* which *S*
assumes are shared by *S*, *A*, and *S*'s audience.

Formulating this as a logical thesis, I want to treat the moral
"ought" as a four-place predicate (or "operator"), "Ought (*A*,
D, *C*, *M*)," which relates an agent *A*, a type of act *D*, considerations *C*, and motivating attitudes *M*. The relativity to considerations *C* can be brought out by considering what are sometimes
called statements of prima–facie obligation, "Considering that
you promised, you ought to go to the board meeting, but considering that you are the sole surviving relative, you ought to go to
the funeral; all things considered, it is not clear what you ought
to do."[4] The claim that there is *this* relativity, to considerations,
is not, of course, what makes my thesis a version of moral relativism, since any theory must acknowledge relativity to considerations. The relativity to considerations does, however, provide
a model for a coherent interpretation of moral relativism as a
similar kind of relativity.

It is not as easy to exhibit the relativity to motivating attitudes
as it is to exhibit the relativity to considerations, since normally
a speaker who makes a moral "ought" judgment intends the
relevant motivating attitudes to be ones that the speaker shares
with the agent and the audience, and normally it will be obvious
what attitudes these are. But sometimes a speaker does invoke
different attitudes by invoking a morality the speaker does not
share. Someone may say, for example, "As a Christian, you
ought to turn the other cheek; I, however, propose to strike
back." A spy who has been found out by a friend might say, "As
a citizen, you ought to turn me in, but I hope that you will not."
In these and similar cases a speaker makes a moral "ought"

---

[4] See Donald Davidson, "Weakness of Will," in Joel Feinberg (ed.), *Moral
Concepts* (Oxford, 1969).

MORAL RELATIVISM DEFENDED

judgment that is explicitly relative to motivating attitudes that the speaker does not share.

In order to be somewhat more precise, then, my thesis is this. "Ought (A, D, C, M)" means roughly that, given that A has motivating attitudes M and given C, D is the course of action for A that is supported by the best reasons. In judgments using this sense of "ought," C and M are often not explicity mentioned by are indicated by the context of utterance. Normally, when that happens, C will be "all things considered" and M will be attitudes that are shared by the speaker and audience.

I mentioned that inner judgments have two characteristics. First, they imply that the agent has reasons to do something that are capable of motivating the agent. Second, the speaker endorses those reasons and supposes that the audience does too. Now, any "Ought (A, D, C, M)" judgment has the first of these characteristics, but as we have just seen a judgment of this sort will not necessarily have the second characteristic if made with explicit reference to motivating attitudes not shared by the speaker. If reference is made either implicitly or explicitly (for example, through the use of the adverb "morally") to attitudes that are shared by the speaker and audience, the resulting judgment has both characteristics and is an inner judgment. If reference is made to attitudes that are not shared by the speaker, the resulting judgment is not an inner judgment and does not represent a full-fledged moral judgment on the part of the speaker. In such a case we have an example of what has been called an inverted-commas use of "ought."[5]

III. MORAL BARGAINING

I have argued that moral "ought" judgments are relational, "Ought (A, D, C, M)," where M represents certain motivating attitudes. I now want to argue that the attitudes M derive from an agreement. That is, they are intentions to adhere to a particular agreement on the understanding that others also intend to

---

[5] R. M. Hare, *The Language of Morals* (Oxford, 1952), pp. 164-168.

GILBERT HARMAN

do so. Really, it might be better for me to say that I put this forward as a hypothesis, since I cannot pretend to be able to prove that it is true. I will argue, however, that this hypothesis accounts for an otherwise puzzling aspect of our moral views that, as far as I know, there is no other way to account for.

I will use the word "intention" in a somewhat extended sense to cover certain dispositions or habits. Someone may habitually act in accordance with the relevant understanding and therefore may be disposed to act in that way without having any more or less conscious intention. In such a case it may sound odd to say that he *intends* to act in accordance with the moral understanding. Nevertheless, for present purposes I will count that as his having the relevant intention in a dispositional sense.

I now want to consider the following puzzle about our moral views, a puzzle that has figured in recent philosophical discussion of issues such as abortion. It has been observed that most of us assign greater weight to the duty not to harm others than to the duty to help others. For example, most of us believe that a doctor ought not to save five of his patients who would otherwise die by cutting up a sixth patient and distributing his healthy organs where needed to the others, even though we do think that the doctor has a duty to try to help as many of his patients as he can. For we also think that he has a stronger duty to try not to harm any of his patients (or anyone else) even if by so doing he could help five others.[6]

This aspect of our moral views can seem very puzzling, especially if one supposes that moral feelings derive from sympathy and concern for others. But the hypothesis that morality derives from an agreement among people of varying powers and resources provides a plausible explanation. The rich, the poor, the strong, and the weak would all benefit if all were to try to avoid harming one another. So everyone could agree to that arrangement. But the rich and the strong would not benefit from an arrangement whereby everyone would try to do as much as possible to help those in need. The poor and weak would get all of the benefit of

---

[6] Philippa Foot, "Abortion and the Doctrine of Double Effect," in James Rachels (ed.), *Moral Problems* (New York, 1971).

MORAL RELATIVISM DEFENDED

this latter arrangement. Since the rich and the strong could foresee that they would be required to do most of the helping and that they would receive little in return, they would be reluctant to agree to a strong principle of mutual aid. A compromise would be likely and a weaker principle would probably be accepted. In other words, although everyone could agree to a strong principle concerning the avoidance of harm, it would not be true that everyone would favor an equally strong principle of mutual aid. It is likely that only a weaker principle of the latter sort would gain general acceptance. So the hypothesis that morality derives from an understanding among people of different powers and resources can explain (and, according to me, does explain) why in our morality avoiding harm to others is taken to be more important than helping those who need help.

By the way, I am here only trying to *explain* an aspect of our moral views. I am not therefore *endorsing* that aspect. And I defer until later a relativistic account of the way in which aspects of our moral view can be criticized "from within."

Now we need not suppose that the agreement or understanding in question is explicit. It is enough if various members of society knowingly reach an agreement in intentions—each intending to act in certain ways on the understanding that the others have similar intentions. Such an implicit agreement is reached through a process of mutual adjustment and implicit bargaining.

Indeed, it is essential to the proposed explanation of this aspect of our moral views to suppose that the relevant moral understanding is thus the result of *bargaining*. It is necessary to suppose that, in order to further our interests, we form certain conditional intentions, hoping that others will do the same. The others, who have different interests, will form somewhat different conditional intentions. After implicit bargaining, some sort of compromise is reached.

Seeing morality in this way as a compromise based on implicit bargaining helps to explain why our morality takes it to be worse to harm someone than to refuse to help someone. The explanation requires that we view our morality as an implicit agreement about what to do. This sort of explanation could not be given if we were to suppose, say, that our morality represented an agree-

13

GILBERT HARMAN

ment only about the facts (naturálism). Nor is it enough simply
to suppose that our morality represents an agreement in attitude,
if we forget that such agreement can be reached, not only by way
of such principles as are mentioned, for example, in Hare's
"logic of imperatives,"[7] but also through bargaining. According
to Hare, to accept a general moral principle is to intend to do
something.[8] If we add to his theory that the relevant intentions
can be reached through implicit bargaining, the resulting theory
begins to look like the one that I am defending.

Many aspects of our moral views can be given a utilitarian
explanation. We could account for these aspects, using the logical
analysis I presented in the previous section of this paper, by
supposing that the relevant "ought" judgments presuppose
shared attitudes of sympathy and benevolence. We can equally
well explain them by supposing that considerations of utility
have influenced our implicit agreements, so that the appeal is to
a shared intention to adhere to those agreements. Any aspect of
morality that is susceptible of a utilitarian explanation can also
be explained by an implicit agreement, but not conversely.
There are aspects of our moral views that seem to be explicable
only in the second way, on the assumption that morality derives
from an agreement. One example, already cited, is the distinction
we make between harming and not helping. Another is our
feeling that each person has an inalienable right of self-defense
and self-preservation. Philosophers have not been able to come
up with a really satisfactory utilitarian justification of such a
right, but it is easily intelligible on our present hypothesis, as
Hobbes observed many years ago. You cannot, except in very
special circumstances, rationally form the intention not to try to
preserve your life if it should ever be threatened, say, by society
or the state, since you know that you cannot now control what
you would do in such a situation. No matter what you now
decided to do, when the time came, you would ignore your prior
decision and try to save your life. Since you cannot now intend
to do something later which you now know that you would not

---

[7] R. M. Hare, *op. cit.* and *Freedom and Reason* (Oxford, 1963).
[8] *The Language of Morals*, pp. 18-20, 168-169.

MORAL RELATIVISM DEFENDED

do, you cannot now intend to keep an agreement not to preserve your life if it is threatened by others in your society.[9]

This concludes the positive side of my argument that what I have called inner moral judgments are made in relation to an implicit agreement. I now want to argue that this theory avoids difficulties traditionally associated with implicit agreement theories of morality.

IV. Objections and Replies

One traditional difficulty for implicit agreement theories concerns what motivates us to do what we have agreed to do. It will, obviously, not be enough to say that we have implicitly agreed to keep agreements, since the issue would then be why we keep *that* agreement. And this suggests an objection to implicit agreement theories. But the apparent force of the objection derives entirely from taking an agreement to be a kind of ritual. To agree in the relevant sense is not just to say something; it is to intend to do something—namely, to intend to carry out one's part of the agreement on the condition that others do their parts. If we agree in this sense to do something, we intend to do it and intending to do it is already to be motivated to do it. So there is no problem as to why we are motivated to keep our agreements in this sense.

We do believe that in general you ought not to pretend to agree in this sense in order to trick someone else into agreeing. But that suggests no objection to the present view. All that it indicates is that *our* moral understanding contains or implies an agreement to be open and honest with others. If it is supposed that this leaves a problem about someone who has not accepted our agreement—"What reason does *he* have not to pretend to accept our agreement so that he can then trick others into agreeing to various things?"—the answer is that such a person may or may not have such a reason. If someone does not already accept something of our morality it may or may not be possible to find reasons why he should.

---

[9] Cf. Thomas Hobbes, *Leviathan* (Oxford, 1957, *inter alia*), Pt. I, Ch. 14, "Of the First and Second Natural Laws, And of Contracts."

GILBERT HARMAN

A second traditional objection to implicit agreement theories is that there is not a perfect correlation between what is generally believed to be morally right and what actually is morally right. Not everything generally agreed on is right and sometimes courses of action are right that would not be generally agreed to be right. But this is no objection to my thesis. My thesis is not that the implicit agreement from which a morality derives is an agreement in moral judgment; the thesis is rather that moral judgments make reference to and are made in relation to an agreement in intentions. Given that a group of people have agreed in this sense, there can still be disputes as to what the agreement implies for various situations. In my view, many moral disputes are of this sort. They presuppose a basic agreement and they concern what implications that agreement has for particular cases.

There can also be various things wrong with the agreement that a group of people reach, even from the point of view of that agreement, just as there can be defects in an individual's plan of action even from the point of view of that plan. Given what is known about the situation, a plan or agreement can in various ways be inconsistent, incoherent, or self-defeating. In my view, certain moral disputes are concerned with internal defects of the basic moral understanding of a group, and what changes should be made from the perspective of that understanding itself. This is another way in which moral disputes make sense with reference to and in relation to an underlying agreement.

Another objection to implicit agreement theories is that not all agreements are morally binding—for example, those made under compulsion or from a position of unfair disadvantage, which may seem to indicate that there are moral principles prior to those that derive from an implicit agreement. But, again, the force of the objection derives from an equivocation concerning what an agreement is. The principle that compelled agreements do not obligate concerns agreement in the sense of a certain sort of ritual indicating that one agrees. My thesis concerns a kind of agreement in intentions. The principle about compelled agreements is part of, or is implied by, our agreement in intentions.

MORAL RELATIVISM DEFENDED

According to me it is only with reference to some such agreement in intentions that a principle of this sort makes sense.

Now it may be true our moral agreement in intentions also implies that it is wrong to compel people who are in a greatly inferior position to accept an agreement in intentions that they would not otherwise accept, and it may even be true that there is in our society at least one class of people in an inferior position who have been compelled thus to settle for accepting a basic moral understanding, aspects of which they would not have accepted had they not been in such an inferior position. In that case there would be an incoherence in our basic moral understanding and various suggestions might be made concerning the ways in which this understanding should be modified. But this moral critique of the understanding can proceed from that understanding itself rather than from "prior" moral principles.

In order to fix ideas, let us consider a society in which there is a well-established and long-standing tradition of hereditary slavery. Let us suppose that everyone accepts this institution, including the slaves. Everyone treats it as in the nature of things that there should be such slavery. Furthermore, let us suppose that there are also aspects of the basic moral agreement which speak against slavery. That is, these aspects together with certain facts about the situation imply that people should not own slaves and that slaves have no obligation to acquiesce in their condition. In such a case, the moral understanding would be defective, although its defectiveness would presumably be hidden in one or another manner, perhaps by means of a myth that slaves are physically and mentally subhuman in a way that makes appropriate the sort of treatment elsewhere reserved for beasts of burden. If this myth were to be exposed, the members of the society would then be faced with an obvious incoherence in their basic moral agreement and might come eventually to modify their agreement so as to eliminate its acceptance of slavery.

In such a case, even relative to the old agreement it might be true that slave owners ought to free their slaves, that slaves need not obey their masters, and that people ought to work to eliminate slavery. For the course supported by the best reasons, given that one starts out with the intention of adhering to a particular

GILBERT HARMAN

agreement, may be that one should stop intending to adhere to certain aspects of that agreement and should try to get others to do the same.

We can also (perhaps—but see below) envision a second society with hereditary slavery whose agreement has no aspects that speak against slavery. In that case, even if the facts of the situation were fully appreciated, no incoherence would appear in the basic moral understanding of the society and it would not be true in relation to that understanding that slave owners ought to free their slaves, that slaves need not obey their masters, and so forth. There might nevertheless come a time when there were reasons of a different sort to modify the basic understanding, either because of an external threat from societies opposed to slavery or because of an internal threat of rebellion by the slaves.

Now it is easier for us to make what I have called inner moral judgments about slave owners in the first society than in the second. For we can with reference to members of the first society invoke principles that they share with us and, with reference to those principles, we can say of them that they ought not to have kept slaves and that they were immoral to have done so. This sort of inner judgment becomes increasingly inappropriate, however, the more distant they are from us and the less easy it is for us to think of our moral understanding as continuous with and perhaps a later development of theirs. Furthermore, it seems appropriate to make only non-inner judgments of the slave owners in the second society. We can say that the second society is unfair and unjust, that the slavery that exists is wrong, that it ought not to exist. But it would be inappropriate in this case to say that it was morally wrong of the slave owners to own slaves. The relevant aspects of our moral understanding, which we would invoke in moral judgments about them, are not aspects of the moral understanding that exists in the second society. (I will come back to the question of slavery below.)

Let me turn now to another objection to implicit agreement theories, an objection which challenges the idea that there is an agreement of the relevant sort. For, if we have agreed, when did we do it? Does anyone really remember having agreed? How did we indicate our agreement? What about those who do not

MORAL RELATIVISM DEFENDED

want to agree? How do they indicate that they do not agree and what are the consequences of their not agreeing? Reflection on these and similar questions can make the hypothesis of implicit agreement seem too weak a basis on which to found morality.

But once again there is equivocation about agreements. The objection treats the thesis as the claim that morality is based on some sort of ritual rather than an agreement in intentions. But, as I have said, there is an agreement in the relevant sense when each of a number of people has an intention on the assumption that others have the same intention. In this sense of "agreement," there is no given moment at which one agrees, since one continues to agree in this sense as long as one continues to have the relevant intentions. Someone refuses to agree to the extent that he or she does not share these intentions. Those who do not agree are outside the agreement; in extreme cases they are outlaws or enemies. It does not follow, however, that there are no constraints on how those who agree may act toward those who do not, since for various reasons the agreement itself may contain provisions for dealing with outlaws and enemies.

This brings me to one last objection, which derives from the difficulty people have in trying to give an explicit and systematic account of their moral views. If one actually agrees to something, why is it so hard to say what one has agreed? In response I can say only that many understandings appear to be of this sort. It is often possible to recognize what is in accordance with the understanding and what would violate it without being able to specify the understanding in any general way. Consider, for example, the understanding that exists among the members of a team of acrobats or a symphony orchestra.

Another reason why it is so difficult to give a precise and systematic specification of any actual moral understanding is that such an understanding will not in general be constituted by absolute rules but will take a vaguer form, specifying goals and areas of responsibility. For example, the agreement may indicate that one is to show respect for others by trying where possible to avoid actions that will harm them or interfere with what they are doing; it may indicate the duties and responsibilities of various members of the family, who is to be responsible for bringing up the

GILBERT HARMAN

children, and so forth. Often what will be important will be not so
much exactly what actions are done as how willing participants
are to do their parts and what attitudes they have—for example,
whether they give sufficient weight to the interests of others.

The vague nature of moral understandings is to some extent
alleviated in practice. One learns what can and cannot be done
in various situations. Expectations are adjusted to other expectations. But moral disputes arise nonetheless. Such disputes may
concern what the basic moral agreement implies for particular
situations; and, if so, that can happen either because of disputes
over the facts or because of a difference in basic understanding.
Moral disputes may also arise concerning whether or not changes
should be made in the basic agreement. Racial and sexual issues
seem often to be of this second sort; but there is no clear line
between the two kinds of dispute. When the implications of an
agreement for a particular situation are considered, one possible
outcome is that it becomes clear that the agreement should be
modified.

Moral reasoning is a form of practical reasoning. One begins
with certain beliefs and intentions, including intentions that are
part of one's acceptance of the moral understanding in a given
group. In reasoning, one modifies one's intentions, often by
forming new intentions, sometimes by giving up old ones, so
that one's plans become more rational and coherent—or, rather,
one seeks to make all of one's attitudes coherent with each other.

The relevant sort of coherence is not simply consistency. It is
something very like the explanatory coherence which is so important in theoretical reasoning. Coherence involves generality
and lack of arbitrariness. Consider our feelings about cruelty to
animals. Obviously these do not derive from an agreement that
has been reached with animals. Instead it is a matter of coherence.
There is a prima-facie arbitrariness and lack of generality in a
plan that involves avoiding cruelty to people but not to animals.

On the other hand, coherence in this sense is not the only
relevant factor in practical reasoning. Another is conservatism
or inertia. A third is an interest in satisfying basic desires or needs.
One tries to make the least change that will best satisfy one's
desires while maximizing the overall coherence of one's atti-

20

MORAL RELATIVISM DEFENDED

tudes. Coherence by itself is not an overwhelming force. That is why our attitudes towards animals are weak and wavering, allowing us to use them in ways we would not use people.

Considerer again the second hereditary slave society mentioned above. This society was to be one in which no aspects of the moral understanding shared by the masters spoke against slavery. In fact that is unlikely, since there is *some* arbitrariness in the idea that people are to be treated in different ways depending on whether they are born slave or free. Coherence of attitude will no doubt speak at least a little against the system of slavery. The point is that the factors of conservatism and desire might speak more strongly in favor of the *status quo*, so that, all things considered, the slave owners might have no reason to change their understanding.

One thing that distinguishes slaves from animals is that slaves can organize and threaten revolt, whereas animals cannot. Slaves can see to it that both coherence and desire oppose conservatism, so that it becomes rational for the slave owners to arrive at a new, broader, more coherent understanding, one which includes the slaves.

It should be noted that coherence of attitude provides a constant pressure to widen the consensus and eliminate arbitrary distinctions. In this connection it is useful to recall ancient attitudes toward foreigners, and the ways people used to think about "savages," "natives," and "Indians." Also, recall that infanticide used to be considered as acceptable as we consider abortion to be. There has been a change here in our moral attitudes, prompted, I suggest, largely by considerations of coherence of attitude.

Finally, I would like to say a few brief words about the limiting case of group morality, when the group has only one member; then, as it were, a person comes to an understanding with himself. In my view, a person can make inner judgments in relation to such an individual morality only about himself. A familiar form of pacifism is of this sort. Certain pacifists judge that it would be wrong of them to participate in killing, although they are not willing to make a similar judgment about others. Observe that such a pacifist is unwilling only to make *inner* moral judgments about others. Although he is unwilling to judge that those who do participate are wrong to do so, he is perfectly willing to say that it is a bad thing that they participate. There are of course many other examples of individual morality in this sense, when a person imposes standards on himself that he does not apply to others. The existence of such examples is further confirmation of the relativist thesis that I have presented.

My conclusion is that relativism can be formulated as an intelligible thesis, the thesis that morality derives from an implicit agreement and that moral judgments are in a logical sense made in relation to such an agreement. Such a theory helps to explain otherwise puzzling aspects of our own moral views, in particular why we think that it is more important to avoid harm to others than to help others. The theory is also partially confirmed by what is, as far as I can tell, a previously unnoticed distinction between inner and non-inner moral judgments. Furthermore, traditional objections to implicit agreement theories can be met.[10]

GILBERT HARMAN

Princeton University

---

[10] Many people have given me good advice about the subjects discussed in this paper, which derives from a larger study of practical reasoning and morality. I am particularly indebted to Donald Davidson, Stephen Schiffer, William Alston, Frederick Schick, Thomas Nagel, Walter Kaufmann, Peter Singer, Robert Audi, and the editors of the *Philosophical Review*.

[8]

The Southern Journal of Philosophy (1986) Vol. XXIV, Supplement

EXTERNALIST MORAL REALISM

David O. Brink
Case Western Reserve University

1. *Introduction*

I believe that reflection on the nature of moral inquiry and practice supports a realistic construal of moral claims. Considerations about moral inquiry as well as considerations about the nature of inquiry in general show that our moral inquiries are directed at discovering moral facts whose existence and nature are independent of our moral theorizing. Thomas Nagel summarizes the kind of considerations I have in mind when he writes, concerning practical reasoning in general:

> The ordinary process of deliberation, aimed at finding out what I have reason to do, assumes that the question has an answer. And in difficult cases especially, deliberation is often accompanied by the belief that I may not *arrive* at that answer. I do not assume that the correct answer is just whatever will result or has resulted from consistent application of deliberative methods—even assuming perfect information about the facts. In deliberation we are trying to arrive at conclusions that are correct in virtue of something *independent* of our arriving at them.[1]

Our moral inquiries aim at true moral beliefs, and the truth of our moral beliefs appears to be independent of their justification. We may not be able to doubt that beliefs which are justified are reasonable to hold, but we can sensibly ask whether such beliefs are true. There may be no answer for us to make short of rehearsing our justification for holding these beliefs, but the question of their correctness is coherent.[2]

We might, perhaps misleadingly, represent this kind of argument for moral realism by saying that moral realism is presupposed or supported by certain features of common sense moral thinking. Now both those who accept this kind of argument for moral realism and those who do not often identify another important feature in common sense moral thinking, namely, the practical or action guiding character of morality. The practical character or morality is often thought to call for an anti-realist construal of moral claims. If moral judgments merely purported to state facts, it is claimed, they could not fulfill the action guiding function which they do. It is this sort of anti-realist argument which I wish to consider here. I will argue that, properly understood, the practical or action guiding character or morality not only fails to undermine the case for moral realism but actually strengthens it.

2. *Moral Realism*

It is worth explaining how I shall understand moral realism and its metaethical rivals. Even if there should be problems in giving a single account of moral realism which is adequate for all purposes, I think we can formulate a version which will serve present (and many other) purposes. According to this formulation, moral realism claims that there are moral facts and true moral propositions whose existence and nature are independent of our beliefs about what is right and wrong. Moral realism's metaphysical claim suggests the semantic claim that moral judgments and terms typically refer to moral facts and properties and the epistemological claim that we have some at least approximate moral knowledge. It makes little sense to believe in moral realism, I think, without believing these semantic and epistemological claims as well. These claims must surely be part of any adequate formulation of moral realism.

So construed, moral realism is a special case of common formulations of metaphysical realism. Realist theories about a subject matter x · usually claim that (a) there are facts or truths of kind x, and (b) these facts or truths are metaphysically or conceptually independent of our evidence (beliefs) and our methods of verification. Anti-realist theories about a subject matter typically deny (a) or (b).

So construed, moral realism also contrasts with familiar metaethical views which are typically viewed as anti-realist. The traditional opponent of moral realism is the nihilist or noncognitivist who denies that there are moral facts or true moral propositions or, as a result, any moral knowledge. Noncognitivism is the most familiar form of anti-realism, and, for reasons we shall see, it is the form I shall focus on here. Traditional forms of noncognitivism claim not only that moral terms and phrases are non-referring[3] but also that their meaning is primarily expressive or prescriptive rather than descriptive. Emotivists such as Stevenson claim that moral judgments are not primarily fact stating but rather express approval and invite others to join in the appraiser's attitudes.[4] Prescriptivists such as Hare claim that moral judgments are not primarily fact stating but rather express universal prescriptions or recommendations.[5]

Constructivism in ethics is in some ways the less traditional opponent of moral realism. Constructivism agrees with moral realism that there are moral facts and true moral propositions but disagrees with realism about the nature or status of these moral facts and truths. A constructivist in ethics claims that moral facts or truths are *constituted by* some function of those beliefs which are our evidence in ethics (e.g. our moral beliefs in reflective equilibrium).[6]

This way of characterizing moral realism helps explain the sense in which a realist thinks that ethics is objective and helps distinguish moral realism from rival metaethical views. A moral realist thinks that moral claims should be construed literally; there are moral facts and true moral propositions, and moral judgments purport to state these facts and express these propositions. Ethics is objective, then, insofar as it concerns matters of fact. But moral realism claims that ethics is objective in a further sense which is not always distinguished from this first kind of objectivity. Not only does ethics concern matters of fact; it concerns facts which hold independently of anyone's beliefs about what is right or wrong. This first kind of objectivity distinguishes moral realism and other cognitivist theories from noncognitivism; the second kind of objectivity distinguishes moral realism from constructivist versions of cognitivism.

If there are moral facts, as realism claims there are, what are they like? My characterization of moral realism is in important respects still metaphysically neutral; it does not itself place any constraints upon the nature of these evidence-independent moral facts. In particular, moral realism is compatible with a wide variety of views about the relationship between moral and nonmoral facts and properties. Familiar views include naturalism, supernaturalism, and nonnaturalism. Whatever the merits of these alternatives, they are all equally realist theories. I believe that there are reasons to prefer ethical naturalism, but, for present purposes, we can remain neutral among these alternatives.

3. *Moral Realism and the Action Guiding Character of Morality*

It has seemed to many people that moral considerations are practical in some very important sense. Agents engage in moral deliberation in order to decide what to do and give moral advice with the aim of influencing others' conduct in certain ways. We regard moral considerations as important practical considerations. We expect people who accept moral claims or make moral judgments to act in certain ways. We would regard it as odd for people who accepted moral claims about some issue to be completely indifferent about that issue. For these reasons, we expect moral considerations to motivate people to act in certain ways or at least to provide them with reason to act in those ways. As a result, we would be surprised by, and rightly suspicious of, any metaethical or normative theory according to which moral considerations are considerations to which well informed, reasonable people might always be completely indifferent.

3.1 *Internalism, Externalism, and Realism. Internalism* is one way of representing these beliefs about the nature of morality. Internalism has often been formulated as a thesis about the connection between morality and motivation; it builds motivation into moral considerations themselves. As Richard Price puts it,

When we are conscious that an action is *fit* to be done, or that it *ought* to be done, it is not conceivable that we can remain *uninfluenced*, or want a *motive* to action.[7]

In part because internalists have not always distinguished clearly between having a motive or desire to do something and having a reason to do that thing, they have not always distinguished their thesis about the connection between morality and motivation from what seems,

25

upon reflection, to be a different, if related, thesis about the connection
between morality and reasons for action. W.D. Falk, who often
formulates internalism as the thesis about motivation, here formulates
it as a thesis about reasons for action.

But, in fact, we believe that morality needs no external sanction: the very thought that we
morally ought to do some act is sufficient without reference to any ulterior motive to
provide us with a reason for doing it . . . .[8]

Bearing these two possibilities in mind, we can, for our purposes,
formulate internalism as the claim that the concept of a moral
consideration itself (read: 'concept itself') necessarily motivates the
agent to perform the moral action or necessarily provides the agent with
reason to perform the moral action.[9]

What is the bearing of this upon moral realism? If we must recognize
the practical character of morality and if internalism is the appropriate
way to represent this practical character, then moral realism must be
compatible with internalism. In particular, the moral realist must claim
that it is in virtue of the concept of a moral fact that moral facts or their
recognition necessarily motivate or provide reasons for action. On this
view, it must be inconceivable for someone to recognize a moral fact
and remain unmoved or fail to have reason to act. Some moral realists
accept these claims; they combine moral realism and internalism.[10] But
many others regard realism and internalism as uneasy, indeed,
incompatible bed fellows. Internalism is a premise in many arguments
for noncognitivism. To some, it seems inconceivable that any set of facts
or any beliefs should necessitate an attitude or a reason for action.[11] To
any set of facts it seems possible to be indifferent, but this cannot be true
of moral facts if internalism is true. To others, it is conceivable that
there are moral facts which, in virtue of the concept of morality alone,
necessarily motivate or provide reasons for action. But these moral facts
would be "metaphysically queer" and, hence, internalism gives us
reason to deny the existence of moral facts.[12] If reflection on common
moral beliefs and practices supports internalism and these philosophers
are right about the incompatibility of realism and internalism, then
some general features of common moral beliefs and practices provide
an argument against moral realism.

These considerations are thought not only to undermine moral
realism but also to support noncognitivist anti-realism. For, while
realism and internalism are thought to be incompatible, traditional
noncognitivist theories are internalist. Though there are differences
between emotivism and prescriptivism, both claim that it is an essential
part of the meaning of moral judgments to express the appraiser's
attitudes or commitments. Emotivists claim that moral judgments
express the appraiser's approval of something and invite others to join
in the appraiser's attitudes; prescriptivists claim that moral judgments
express (universal) prescriptions or recommendations. On both forms

of noncognitivism, therefore, it is part of the meaning of moral judgments, and so a conceptual truth, that the appraiser holds a pro-attitude to things judged moral and a negative attitude to things judged immoral. This builds motivation into the concept of a moral judgment and so commits noncognitivism to a form of internalism.

I think that we can agree with part of this anti-realist argument, there is reason to doubt the existence of moral facts which, in virtue of the concept of morality alone, necessarily motivate or provide reasons for action. But the implausibility of conjoining realism and internalism in this way derives from internalism and not from moral realism. Morality is practical, as our moral beliefs and practices assume, and so we should expect to find important connections between morality and both motivation and reasons for action. But internalism is not the correct way to represent these connections.

In assessing internalism, it is important to distinguish a number of different theses. The claim that it is in virtue of the concept of morality that moral considerations necessarily motivate or provide reasons for action is ambiguous in a number of ways. First, we might distinguish among agent, appraiser, and hybrid internalism. *Agent internalism* claims that it is in virtue of the concept of morality that *moral obligations* motivate, or provide reason for, the agent to do the moral thing. Thus, it is a conceptual truth about morality, according to agent internalism, that agents have reason or motive to comply with their moral obligations. *Appraiser internalism* claims that it is in virtue of the concept of morality that *moral belief* or *moral judgment* provides the appraiser with motivation or reason for action. Thus, it is a conceptual truth about morality, according to appraiser internalism, that someone who holds a moral belief or makes a moral judgment is motivated to, or has reason to, perform the action judged favorably. (Of course, the person who is the appraiser is very often the person who is the moral agent.) Agent internalism is objective in the sense that it ties motivation or reasons for action to moral obligations, independently of anyone's recognition of these obligations. By contrast, appraiser internalism is subjective in the sense that it ties the appraiser's motivation or reasons for action to the appraiser's beliefs or judgments, independently of whether these beliefs or judgments are correct or justifiable. These features of agent and appraiser internalism allow us to construct a hybrid version of internalism which is both objective and subjective. *Hybrid internalism* claims that it is a conceptual truth about morality that the *recognition of a moral obligation* motivates or provides the agent (the person who recognizes his obligation) with reason for action.

The distinctions among agent, appraiser, and hybrid internalism are not usually made. For many purposes, these distinctions are not important. In these situations, I will not distinguish among them; I will speak merely about the motivational force or rationality of moral considerations. However, in some situations, the distinctions are important. Here, I will distinguish among them or allow context to do so.

These distinctions within internalism cut across a very important distinction, which we have already noticed: that between internalism about *motives* and internalism about *reasons*. Vera's actual motivation to do x is neither a necessary nor a sufficient condition for there being a reason for her to do x; she can be motivated to do x without her doing x being justified or rational, and she can have reason to do x without being motivated to do it.[13] Internalism about motives holds that the concept of morality itself shows that moral considerations necessarily motivate, while internalism about reasons claims that the concept of morality itself reveals that moral considerations necessarily provide the agent with reason for action.

Internalism (of any form) has at least three distinguishable components. The first claim is that moral considerations *necessarily* motivate or provide reasons for action. The second and third claims come out of the internalist thesis that it is the concept of morality which establishes this. Since it is the *concept* of morality which shows that moral considerations necessarily motivate or provide reasons for action, this claim about the motivational power or rationality of morality must be *a priori*. Since it is the concept of morality *itself* which determines this fact, the rationality or motivational power of moral considerations cannot depend upon what the content of morality turns out to be, facts about agents, or a substantive theory of rationality.[14]

Externalism is the denial of internalism; externalism claims that the motivational force and rationality of moral considerations depend upon factors which are external to the moral considerations themselves. One can be an externalist by denying any one of the three claims internalism involves. The externalist can claim, first, that moral considerations only *contingently* motivate or justify, second, that the motivational power or rationality of morality, whether necessary or contingent, can be known only *a posteriori*, or third, that the motivational power or rationality of morality, whether necessary or contingent, *a priori* or *a posteriori*, depends upon things other than the concept of morality such as what the content of morality turns out to be, a substantive theory of reasons for action, or facts about agents such as their interests or desires.[15] (For many, these last two externalist strategies will coincide.)

Like internalism, externalism admits of many possible versions. We can distinguish externalism about motives and externalism about reasons for action, and we can distinguish agent, appraiser, and hybrid versions of either. Again, I will observe or mark these distinctions only where this affects the course of the argument.

It seems clear from reflection on our beliefs about the nature and role of morality that there are important connections between morality and both motivation and rationality. We expect moral considerations to

28

motivate people to act in certain ways or at least to provide them with reasons to act in those ways. In assessing internalism and externalism, we must compare their accounts of these connections. It is perhaps best to start this assessment by considering their accounts of the connection between morality and motivation.

3.2 *Morality and Motivation.* Internalists often assume that externalism threatens morality's importance. If the motivational force of moral considerations depends upon factors external to those considerations, don't we lose our assurance that moral considerations will motivate? Internalism provides this assurance, because it makes it part of the very concept of morality that moral considerations motivate. According to the internalist about motives, it is inconceivable that moral considerations should fail to motivate.

Now agent internalism may itself threaten morality. We have some initial idea about what people's moral obligations are; call the actions which we think we are morally obligated to perform x, y, and z. We also believe that, even if most people have a desire to perform x, y, and z, some people do not have this desire. If this second belief is correct, then agent internalism forces us to revise our first belief about the moral obligations of those who are indifferent to x, y, and z. If agent internalism is true, it would seem that our views about people's moral obligations would have to be restricted or tailored to actions which people already have a desire to perform.[16] Though our initial moral beliefs are revisable, it does not seem that they should be revised for this reason. It is no vindication of the importance of moral demands if, in order to insure their motivational force, we must compromise the moral demands themselves.

At this point, the internalist about motives may insist upon representing internalism as appraiser or hybrid internalism. Motivation follows, the internalist might insist, only from recognition of a moral obligation (hybrid internalism) or moral belief or judgment (appraiser internalism); there must be motivation to perform x, y, and z if *and only if* x, y, and z are *regarded as moral obligations.* And this is just what appraiser and hybrid internalism claim.

But internalism, so construed, seems just false to the psychological facts. Though indifference to what are regarded as moral considerations may be fairly rare, it does seem to exist. Some people (e.g. certain sociopaths) do not care about moral considerations. The internalist may reply that his position is vindicated if it is only sociopaths and other psychologically disordered people who are indifferent to moral considerations. But, even then, the internalist must give up his claim that recognition of moral considerations implies actual motivation.

Moreover, the internalist cannot rest content with the extensional claim that everyone is in fact motivated by moral considerations. Any externalist could claim this. The internalist about motives claims that it is true in virtue of the concept of morality that moral considerations necessarily motivate. According to the internalist, then, it must be conceptually impossible for someone to recognize a moral consideration or assert a moral judgment and remain unmoved. This fact raises a problem for internalism: internalism makes the amoralist conceptually impossible.

Even if everyone is, as a matter of fact, motivated by moral considerations, we still regard it as possible to ask for a justification for this concern. Much moral skepticism is skepticism about the objectivity of morality, that is, skepticism about the existence of moral facts. But another traditional kind of skepticism accepts the existence of moral facts and asks why we should care about these facts. Amoralists are the traditional way of representing this second kind of skepticism; the amoralist is someone who recognizes the existence of moral considerations and remains unmoved.

The internalist must dismiss the amoralist challenge as incoherent; the amoralist is inconceivable. We may think that the amoralist challenge is coherent, but this can only be because we confuse moral senses of terms and "inverted commas" senses of those same terms.[17] People can be unmoved by considerations which are only *conventionally regarded* as moral, but a genuine amoralist is inconceivable. Thus, according to the internalist, apparent amoralists, such as Plato's Thrasymachus and Dickens' Uriah Heep, remain unmoved, not by what they regard as moral considerations, but only by what *others* regard as moral considerations.

The problem for internalism is that it does not take the amoralist's challenge seriously enough. Whatever the merits of this internalist gambit as an interpretation of Thrasymachus or Uriah Heep, the amoralist challenge need not depend upon a failure to recognize inverted commas usage of terms. We can imagine someone who regards certain demands as moral demands—and not simply as conventional moral demands—and yet remains unmoved. We may think that such a person is being irrational and that he can be shown to be irrational. We may even think that such a person is merely possible and has never and will never exist (though I think this thought is wrong). But we do think that such a person is possible, and, if we are to take the amoralist challenge seriously, we must attempt to explain why the amoralist should care about morality.

These are reasons for rejecting internalism about motives as the correct account of the connection between morality and motivation. Internalism overstates the connection between morality and motivation; agent internalism holds our moral theories hostage to agents' desires, and appraiser and hybrid internalism prevent us from taking the amoralist seriously.[18]

Externalism provides a more plausible account of the connection between morality and motivation; it makes the motivational force of

30

moral considerations a matter of contingent psychological fact. Because it does not make the motivational force of moral obligations a conceptual feature of morality, externalism does not hold the scope and stringency of moral obligations hostage to people's actual desires.

Though it makes the motivational force of moral considerations a matter of contingent psychological fact, externalism can base this motivation on "deep" or widely shared psychological facts. If, for example, sympathy is, as Hume held, a deeply seated and widely shared psychological trait, then, as a matter of contingent psychological fact, the vast majority of people will have at least *a* desire to comply (even) with other-regarding moral demands. Moral motivation, on such a view, can be widespread and predictable, even if it is neither necessary, nor universal, nor overriding. These are limitations in the actual motivational force of moral considerations which, I think, reflection on common sense morality recognizes.

Finally, externalism allows us to take amoralism and the amoralist challenge seriously. Because externalism does not build motivational force into the concept of a moral consideration, it recognizes that we can imagine someone who recognizes moral considerations and remains unmoved. The fact that externalism about motives allows us to formulate the amoralist challenge does not make the amoralist challenge unanswerable. There is nothing about externalism about motives which prevents us from showing that an amoralist is irrational not to care about moral considerations. Whether the amoralist is irrational depends upon the rationality, not the motivational force, of moral considerations.

Since externalism provides a better account of the connection between morality and motivation than internalism does, the connection between morality and motivation which reflection on common sense morality recognizes does not support anti-realist arguments. The externalist could concede that no statement of fact entails an attitude or that intrinsically motivational facts are queer; neither of these claims, if true, would undermine a realistic construal of moral claims.

3.3 *Morality and Reasons for Action.* What about the debate between internalism and externalism about the connection between morality and rationality? As we saw, this is a distinct debate from the previous one, because we can have reasons for action without having the corresponding desires or motives. So, even if internalism about motives is false, internalism about reasons might be true. Since we think that moral considerations not only do but should guide conduct, we expect moral considerations to provide agents with reasons for action. Are internalists right to think that internalism alone respects this expectation?[19] Does our ability to justify the rationality of moral considerations depend upon internalism about reasons?

Here, it is agent or hybrid internalism about reasons which is important. The claim that one has reason to do x is the claim that one has good reason to do x or is justified in doing x. But no one thinks that merely believing or judging that one has a moral obligation to do x gives one reason to do x; one's moral belief or judgment may be wrong. And bad moral beliefs or judgments do not provide good reasons to act. Internalism about reasons, therefore, must be construed as claiming that moral obligation provides reason for action (agent internalism) or as claiming that recognition of a moral obligation provides reason for action (hybrid internalism).

Internalist arguments against moral realism typically fail to discuss or assess alternative substantive theories of rationality or reasons for action. Given the way noncognitivists have relied upon internalism to argue against moral realism, therefore, it is clear that internalism finds the rationality of moral considerations in the concept of morality itself. According to the internalist, the rationality of morality cannot depend upon anything external to moral considerations themselves, such as a substantive theory of reasons for action or facts about agents and the world. Internalism claims that it is true in virtue of the concept of morality that moral considerations necessarily provide agents with reasons for action.

Internalism succeeds in guaranteeing the rationality of morality, but too easily and at too high a price. The internalist about reasons, like the internalist about motives, cannot represent the amoralist's skepticism and so cannot take this form of skepticism seriously. Unlike the internalist about motives, the internalist about reasons can conceive of the amoralist—someone who is not motivated by moral considerations. But he cannot regard as coherent the amoralist challenge 'Why should I care about moral demands?'. The figure of the amoralist is someone who is unmoved by moral considerations, but the point of his challenge is to ask for a justification of the rationality of concern with moral demands. The internalist must regard the amoralist challenge as conceptually confused. It is "simply part of the concept of a moral consideration" that moral considerations provide reasons for action. Anyone who asks for a reason for doing a good deed must be using the words 'good deed' in inverted commas.

But surely we can ask whether we have reason to be moral without using 'moral' in inverted commas. No doubt, it can be odd to say 'I ought to do x, but do I have reason to do x?'.[20] But this does not show that the claim is conceptually confused or that it is part of the meaning of 'ought' that moral obligations provide reasons for action. This claim could be odd, though not conceptually confused, because we believe, on grounds independent of the concept of morality, that there is always reason to be moral. The claim is not conceptually confused, if we distinguish two senses of 'ought': a moral ought and an ought of rationality. We might admit that it is part of the meaning of the ought of rationality that if we ought (in this sense) to do something, then we have reason to do that thing, and still deny that it is part of the meaning of a moral ought that if we ought (in this sense) to do something, we thereby have a reason to do that thing. We could then claim that it is only by failing to distinguish these two senses of 'ought' that the claim in question could be conceptually confused. This diagnosis of the oddity in the claim 'I ought to do x, but do I have reason to do x?' is supported by the fact that what should be an equivalent claim, however odd, does not seem conceptually confused. 'I have a moral obligation to do x, but do I have reason to do x?' does not seem conceptually confused. Philosophical reflection and common sense thinking about the stringency of many moral demands can make us wonder whether there is in fact good reason to act on moral considerations. For this reason, the amoralist challenge not only seems intelligible but deserves to be taken seriously.

Taking the amoralist challenge seriously, however, does not require giving in to it. We can attempt to answer this challenge by theorizing about the exact nature of morality, the correct theory of rationality, and, in all probability, facts about people's interests or desires. Taking the amoralist challenge seriously in this way commits us to externalism: if the rationality of moral considerations can be justified, it is not merely in virtue of the concept of morality. Externalism, therefore, does not of itself undermine the rationality of morality.

It is assumed by some internalists that externalism cannot account for the Kantian idea that the justification of morality should not depend upon the inclinations or desires of agents.[21] We cannot beg off our moral obligations simply by pointing out that we are not inclined to do our duty. Nagel reflects this motivation when he writes:

> It will in any case not do to rest the motivational influence [rationality] of ethical considerations on fortuitous or escapable inclinations. Their hold on us must be deep, and it must be essentially tied to the ethical principles themselves, and to the conditions of their truth. The alternative is to abandon the objectivity of ethics.[22]

Nagel frequently fails to distinguish between the motivational influence of moral considerations and their rationality. I think that this argument is best construed as concerning the rationality and not the motivational force of moral considerations. If so, this internalist argument assumes two things. First, it assumes, what internalism about motives denies, that moral considerations do not necessarily motivate. Only if moral motivation is contingent might we jeopardize the authority of moral considerations by basing it upon an agent's inclinations. As my discussion of internalism about motives should make clear, this seems to be a plausible assumption. Second, this argument assumes that an externalist must accept a purely *desire-based* theory of rationality or reasons for action. How is this assumption justified?

We should distinguish between at least three different theories of reasons for action. *Desire-based theories* of reasons for action claim that one has reason to do x just in case doing x would satisfy one's

33

desires. On desire-based theories, whether recognition of a moral fact
provides an agent with reason for action depends not only upon what
the moral facts are but also upon contingent (even if deep) facts about
what the agent's desires are.[23] It is not entirely clear how the truth of
desire-based theories of reasons for action would undermine the
objectivity of ethics. For even if the existence of reasons to be moral
required the agent to have some desire to be moral, this would at most
prevent us from giving a reason to callous people to comply with moral
requirements; it would not show that there were no moral requirements.
Nagel must assume that the action guiding character of morality
requires that moral considerations give everyone reason for action.[24]

Rational egoism claims that one has reason to do x just in case doing
x would be in one's own interest.[25] Different versions of rational egoism
correspond to different conceptions of welfare or interest. Desire-based
theories of reasons for action can be represented as one kind of egoist
theory; they represent subjective versions of egoism, because they make
an individual's interest depend upon his preferences or desires.
Objective versions of rational egoism make an agent's interest largely
independent of his preferences or desires; they construe an agent's
interest as consisting in such things as having a certain sort of character,
engaging in certain kinds of activities, and exercising certain capacities.[26] According to rational egoism, whether moral considerations
provide reasons for action depends not only upon the content of
morality but also upon facts about the interests of agents. According to
objective versions of rational egoism, the rationality of moral considerations does not depend upon "fortuitous and escapable inclinations;" it depends upon the demands of morality and the objective
constituents of an agent's good. If, as seems plausible, an agent's good
contains significant social or other-regarding components (perhaps a
certain kind of moral character), an egoist can explain why moral
considerations provide an agent with reason for action, whatever his
inclinations are.

Rational altruism, by contrast, holds that one has reason to do x just
in case it is in someone's interest that x be done. This is the theory of
rationality which Nagel defends.[27] But even rational altruism makes the
rationality of morality depend upon the content of morality and facts
about agents. We can paraphrase Nagel as claiming that morality, in
particular, other-regarding considerations provide an agent with reason
for action just in case solipsism is false and the agent is merely one
person among others.[28] Of course, Nagel's claim, even if true, does not
fall out of the concept of morality; it requires and he provides (via an
analogy with prudence) substantive argument about reasons for action.
I won't here try to reconstruct and assess Nagel's argument for this
claim.[29] But it should be clear that even if Nagel's claim is correct, the
rationality of moral requirements depends upon the content of
morality, a substantive defense of rational altruism, and the further and
contingent fact that solipsism is false.

34

So, the Kantian intuition about the authority of morality, even if well founded, fails to support internalism or undermine externalism. Externalism is not committed to desire-based theories of rationality.[30] An externalist can defend the authority of morality by appeal to a different theory of rationality; in particular, he can appeal to objective versions of rational egoism or to rational altruism. So we can concede that the existence of reasons to be moral does not depend upon the inclination of agents without conceding that internalism is true. In fact, *only* an externalist can provide such a defense of the authority of morality. As Nagel's defense of the authority of morality illustrates, any such defense depends upon the content of morality, facts about agents or the world, and a substantive theory of reasons for action and so does not fall out of the concept of morality itself.

If this is right, internalism is not needed to establish an important connection between morality and reasons for action; indeed, internalism establishes this connection too easily and so fails to take amoralist skepticism seriously. Since a defense of the rationality of moral considerations can and should be attempted on externalist assumptions, the action guiding character of moral considerations does not undermine moral realism. Moral facts can, as the externalist claims, combine with facts about rationality, agents, and the world to provide us with reason to be moral.

3.4 *Moral Realism and Amoralism.* As we have seen, externalism can, and internalism cannot, take amoralist skepticism seriously. This virtue of externalism, it should be clear, is available to the moral realist but not to the anti-realist (at least not to the traditional noncognitivist). While some realists have been internalists, we have seen that realists can and should be externalists. Noncognitivists, we saw, however, must be internalists. Whatever the differences between emotivism and prescriptivism, both claim that it is an essential part of the meaning of moral judgments to express the appraiser's attitudes or commitments. On both forms of noncognitivism, therefore, it is part of the meaning of moral judgments, and so a conceptual truth, that the appraiser holds a pro-attitude to things judged moral and a negative attitude to things judged immoral. This builds motivation into the concept of a moral judgment and so commits noncognitivism to internalism about motives.

Because of its commitment to internalism about motives, noncognitivists must dismiss the possibility of a genuine amoralist—one who is indifferent to moral considerations—as incoherent. The noncognitivist must insist that these putative amoralists are only using the terms with which they express moral judgments in an inverted commas sense; sincere moral judgments reflect motivation in the appraiser.

The noncognitivist's strategy is to dismiss what seems to be a genuine philosophical challenge by accusing the amoralist of conceptual or semantic confusion. Indeed, the noncognitivist reply to the amoralist resembles other skeptical solutions to skeptical problems.[31] A "straight solution" to a skeptical problem recognizes the skeptic's challenge and attempts to answer it; a "skeptical solution" attempts to dissolve the skeptical problem as misconceived.[32] Phenomenalism offers a skeptical solution to epistemological skepticism about our knowledge of an external world. According to the phenomenalist, "material-object language" expresses only claims about actual or possible sensory experience. As a result, the skeptic's problem about how sensory experience could be evidence about an external world of material objects is, according to the phenomenalist, really incoherent. Similarly, since the very meaning of moral judgments ensures motivation, the skeptical problem posed by the amoralist is, according to the noncognitivist, really misconceived.

But skeptical solutions are in general not very satisfying responses to skeptical problems. Skeptical solutions dispose of disturbing challenges too easily. The noncognitivist's victory over the amoralist also seems to be won too easily. We can imagine someone who sincerely thinks that some action, say, is wrong—and not simply that it is conventionally regarded as wrong—and yet remains unmoved. If so, the amoralist is conceivable and we cannot simply dismiss amoral skepticism as incoherent. At the very least, we should accept a skeptical solution to this or other skeptical problems only when all straight solutions have failed.

The moral realist can attempt a straight solution to amoral skepticism. The realist can and should be an externalist. As an externalist, the realist can recognize the amoralist as intelligible and so can take the amoralist challenge seriously. The realist can attempt to show that an amoralist is irrational not to care about moral considerations. A defense of the rationality of morality will depend upon a conception of the nature of moral demands, a substantive theory of rationality (such as an objective version of rational egoism or some version of rational altruism), and facts about agents and the world. Of course, I cannot conduct such a defense here, but we could begin our research with a close reading of Plato, Aristotle, Butler, Kant, and Nagel.

3.5 A Realist Explanation of the Action Guiding Character of Morality.
Indeed, not only does the practical character of morality not undermine moral realism; moral realism is able to *explain* the action guiding character of morality in a way that most anti-realist theories cannot. As we have seen, it is noncognitivists who like to stress the practical or dynamic character of morality. It is a fundamental feature of moral judgments, on their view, that they have emotive or prescriptive force. But, interestingly, it seems that we can explain the emotive or prescriptive force which moral judgments have only on the assumption that our moral judgments are, or at least purport to be, true.[33]

36

The emotive force of a moral judgment consists in part in an invitation to others to share the appraiser's attitude; the prescriptive force of a moral judgment consists in recommending to others things the appraiser judges favorably and recommending against things he judges unfavorably. The noncognitivist seems unable to explain not only the possibility of making moral judgments with no emotive or prescriptive force (in contexts in which we have no intention to express attitudes or influence others' conduct) but also such emotive or prescriptive force as moral judgments have. For it is hard to see *why* anyone should be so keen on getting others to share his attitude or on recommending a course of action unless he thought that the attitude he was expressing or the course of action he was recommending was correct or valuable. We typically invite others to share our attitudes and prescribe courses of action *only because* we believe these attitudes and courses of action to be correct or valuable. Nor would an appraiser's audience have much reason to share his attitude or heed his recommendation if they had no reason to regard the attitude he was expressing or the course of action he was recommending as correct or valuable. But people do seek and heed moral advice.

Perhaps the anti-realist will tell us that we can invite others to share our attitudes or prescribe courses of action without believing those attitudes or courses of action are objectively valuable so long as we share enough closely related attitudes and preferences with our audience. But this reply makes our moral practices look too much like the practices of some exclusive club. The fact is that we address our moral judgments to audiences whose psychology we are not familiar with or whom we fear hold preferences and attitudes different from our own. Moreover, people seek and sometimes even heed moral advice from others with unknown or even quite different psychological make-up. The natural explanation of why we bother to invite others to share our moral attitudes or prescribe to them some course of action and the natural explanation of why they have reason to listen to us is that, on various grounds, we purport to hold correct (or nearly correct) attitudes or to prescribe right (or nearly right) actions. If we reject moral realism, there seems to be no ground or explanation for the emotive or prescriptive force which our moral judgments carry.

4. *Conclusion*

Because some think that internalism is the correct way to represent the practical character of morality, they think that the practical character of morality tells against moral realism. But moral realism is perfectly compatible with the practical character of morality. This is because externalism, rather than internalism, is the appropriate way to represent the practical or action guiding character of morality. The rationality and motivational force of moral considerations depend, as the externalist claims, not simply upon the concept of morality but

37

(also) upon the content of morality, facts about agents. and a
substantive theory of reasons for action. Not only can moral realism
accommodate the action guiding character of morality, properly
understood; it can do so better than its traditional opponents can. The
realist, but not the noncognitivist, can take amoralist skepticism
seriously, and the realist, but not the noncognitivist, can explain the
action guiding character of morality.[34] Consideration of the action
guiding character of morality, therefore, supports, rather than under-
mines, moral realism.[35]

NOTES

[1] Thomas Nagel "The Limits of Objectivity" in S. McMurrin (ed), *The Tanner Lectures
on Human Values I* (Salt Lake City: University of Utah Press, 1980), p. 100.

[2] See my *Moral Realism and the Foundations of Ethics* (manuscript), chapter 2.

[3] This is a bit oversimplified. Noncognitivists typically claim that moral terms or
phrases have a primary emotive or prescriptive sense and a secondary descriptive sense. It
is in this primary sense which the noncognitivist claims that moral language is non-
referring. In its secondary, descriptive sense, however, moral language can refer in a
certain way. Moral language can, secondarily, refer to those nonmoral facts upon the
basis of which individual speakers express their attitudes or make their prescriptions. Not
only is the reference of moral language secondary, on this view; the referent of a moral
term or phrase is a matter of brute psychological fact which can vary from speaker to
speaker and from utterance to utterance. Though perhaps noncognitivists can claim that
moral langauge refers, their claim should be distinguished from the way in which moral
realists think moral terms refer and the way in which most people (moral realists or not)
think that natural and social scientific terms refer (i.e. independently of people's beliefs or
attitudes).

[4] See C.L. Stevenson, *Ethics and Language* (New Haven: Yale, 1944), especially pp.
206f. and "The Emotive Meaning of Ethical Terms" reprinted in his *Facts and Values*
(New Haven: Yale, 1963).

[5] See R.M. Hare, *The Language of Morals* (New York: Oxford University Press, 1952).

[6] Cf. C.S. Peirce *Collected Works*, vol. 5 (Cambridge, MA: Harvard University Press,
1934), p. 395; Ronald Dworkin, "The Original Position" reprinted in N. Daniels (ed),
Reading Rawls (New York: Basic Books, 1975); and John Rawls "Kantian Constructivism in Moral Theory" *Journal of Philosophy* 77 (1980), pp. 515-72 (see my
"Rawlsian Constructivism in Moral Theory" *Canadian Journal of Philosophy*,
forthcoming). We can distinguish between relativist and nonrelativist forms of
constructivism. Relativist constructivism (relativism) is true just in case there are a
plurality of sets of moral facts each constituted by different moral beliefs or different
bodies of moral beliefs. According to moral relativism, x is a moral fact for S (x is true for
S) just in case S believes x, S would believe x upon reflection, S is part of a social group the
majority of whom believe x, or some such thing. Nonrelativist constructivism
(constructivism) holds that there is a single set of moral facts which are constituted by
some function of our beliefs, e.g., by our moral beliefs in reflective equilibrium.

[7] Richard Price, *A Review of the Principal Questions in Morals* reprinted in D. Raphael
(ed), *British Moralists* (New York: Oxford University Press, 1969), p. 194. Compare:
". . . somehow the very fact of a duty entails all the motive required for doing the
act . . . ." (W.D. Falk, "'Ought' and Motivation" reprinted in W. Sellars and J. Hospers
(eds), *Readings in Ethical Theory* (New York: Appleton-Century Crofts, 1947), p. 499);
"To think that you ought to do something is to be motivated to do it. To think that it
would be wrong to do something is to be motivated not to do it." (Gilbert Harman, *The
Nature of Morality* (New York: Oxford University Press, 1977), p. 33); "It seems to be a
conceptual truth that to regard something as good is to feel a pull towards promoting or

choosing it, or towards wanting other people to feel the pull towards promoting or choosing it." (Simon Blackburn. *Spreading the Word* (New York: Oxford University Press, 1984), p. 188).

[5] Falk, p. 494. Compare: "Objective wrongness, if there is such a thing, is intrinsically prescriptive or action-guiding, it in itself gives or constitutes a reason for not doing the wrong action . . . ."(J.L. Mackie, *The Miracle of Theism* (New York: Oxford University Press, 1982), p. 115).

[9] Cf. Price, pp. 167-8, 194; Harold Prichard. "Does Moral Philosophy Rest on a Mistake?" reprinted in his *Moral Obligation* (New York: Oxford University Press, 1949) (but see Falk); Falk, pp. 494-5, 499-501; P.H. Nowell-Smith. *Ethics* (New York: Philosophical Library, 1957), pp. 88-9, 174; R.M. Hare. *Moral Thinking* (New York: Oxford University Press, 1981), pp. 21, 23-4, 83-6 and *The Language of Morals*. pp. 20, 31, 169, 197; Philippa Foot. "Moral Arguments," p. 101, and "Moral Beliefs," pp. 111, 125, 128, both reprinted in her *Virtues and Vices* (Los Angeles: University of California Press, 1978); Russell Grice. *The Grounds of Moral Judgment* (New York: Cambridge University Press, 1967), pp. 3-4, 27, 29; Harman, pp. 33, 66, 91; J.L. Mackie. *Ethics: Inventing Right and Wrong* (New York: Penguin Books, 1977), pp. 23, 26-7, 29, 40, 42, 49, *Hume's Moral Theory* (Boston: Routledge and Kegan Paul, 1980), pp. 22, 52, 55, 134, 146, *The Miracle of Theism*. pp. 102, 104, 115-6; John McDowell, "Are Moral Requirements Hypothetical Imperatives?" *Proceedings of the Aristotilean Society*. supp. vol. (1978), p. 26, and "Virtue and Reason" *The Monist* 62 (1979), p. 335; Blackburn, pp. 187-8.

This kind of internalism about morality should be distinguished from internalism as a thesis about the nature of rationality. Internalism about rationality assumes that all reasons for action depend upon actual or counterfactual desires of the agent. see, e.g., Stephen Darwell. *Impartial Reason* (Ithaca, NY: Cornell University Press, 1983), pp. 51f.

[10] I suppose that Price; Falk; Foot, "Moral Arguments" and "Moral Beliefs;" and McDowell, "Are Moral Requirements Hypothetical Imperatives?" and "Virtue and Reason" qualify as both realists and internalists.

[11] See, e.g., Hare, *The Language of Morals*. pp. 79f. and Nowell-Smith. pp. 36-43.

[12] Mackie. *Ethics: Inventing Right and Wrong*, pp. 38-42 and *The Miracle of Theism*. pp. 115f.

[13] Cf. Kurt Baier. *The Moral Point of View* (Ithaca, NY: Cornell University Press, 1958). pp. 100, 149; Kai Nielsen, "Why Should I Be Moral?" reprinted in P. Taylor (ed), *Problems of Moral Philosophy* (Belmont, CA: Wadsworth, 1978), p. 539; William Frankena, *Ethics*, second edition (Englewood Cliffs, NJ: Prentice-Hall, 1973), p. 114. Of course, it might be that there is some deeper, counterfactual connection between motivated and having a reason. For instance, it might turn out that one has reason to do x just in case a perfectly rational being under suitably idealized conditions would desire x and so be motivated to do x. Cf. Darwall, pp. 20, 41-2, 79-80, 86. My distinction between having a reason and having a motive is not meant to rule out this kind of connection between desires or motives and reasons; thus, this distinction does not rule out internalism about rationality (see note 9).

[14] Traditional defenders of internalism (see note 9) are, I believe, committed, explicitly or implicitly, to all three of these claims. It might be that some of those who subscribe to 'internalism' accept only the first or second component of what I call 'internalism'. I have no immediate quarrel with such people; my present concern is only to explain why a realist should resist all three claims.

[15] Thus, I take the following to be externalists or provide externalist arguments: Plato, *Republic* and Aristotle, *Nicomachean Ethics* (cf. T.H. Irwin, *Plato's Moral Theory* (New York: Oxford University Press, 1977), chapter 8 and "Aristotle's Methods of Ethics" in D. O'Mera (ed), *Studies in Aristotle* (Washington, DC: Catholic University of America Press, 1981)); Henry Sidgwick, *The Methods of Ethics*, seventh edition (Chicago: University of Chicago Press, 1907), pp. 498-503; William Frankena, "Obligation and Motivation in Recent Moral Philosophy" reprinted in his *Perspectives on Morality*, ed. K. Goodpaster (Notre Dame: University of Notre Dame Press, 1976) and *Ethics*, pp.

114-5; Nielsen; David Gauthier, "Morality and Advantage" reprinted in D. Gauthier (ed), *Morality and Rational Self-Interest* (Englewood Cliffs, NJ: Prentice-Hall, 1970); Philippa Foot, "Morality as a System of Hypothetical Imperatives" and "Reasons for Action and Desire" both reprinted in *Virtues and Vices*.

[16] Cf. Frankena, "Obligation and Motivation in Recent Moral Philosophy," p. 73.

[17] See Hare, *The Language of Morals*, pp. 124-6, 163f.

[18] The real or fictional figure of the amoralist—one who is indifferent to what he concedes are moral considerations—is the traditional way of raising what I have called amoralist skepticism—skepticism about the justification or rationality of moral demands. I suppose, however, that it is possible to formulate amoralist skepticism without assuming the actual or possible existence of the amoralist. Even if it is a conceptual truth about morality that recognition of moral considerations motivates, we may still ask whether such motivation or concern is justified. Thus, someone might claim, internalism about motives is not committed to dismissing amoralist skepticism, only the amoralist. Even so, it seems a defect in internalism about motives that it must dismiss as inconceivable, something which surely seems conceivable, namely, the amoralist.

[19] Cf. Falk, p. 493.

[20] Cf. Winston Nesbitt, "Categorical Imperatives: A Defense" *Philosophical Review* 86 (1977), pp. 217-25. David Wong and Philip Gasper both brought this worry to my attention.

[21] Immanuel Kant, *Foundations of the Metaphysic of Morals* (London: Hutchinson, 1956) (Prussian Academy pagination), p. 389.

[22] Thomas Nagel, *The Possibility of Altruism* (New York: Oxford University Press, 1970), p. 6. Cf. Nagel, *The Possibility of Altruism*, pp. 15-6, 22, 144; Mackie, *Ethics: Inventing Right and Wrong*, pp. 29-30 and *The Miracle of Theism*, p. 115.

[23] For criticisms of desire-based theories of reasons for action, see Grice, pp. 10-12, 15-6; Nagel, *The Possibility of Altruism*; McDowell, "Are Moral Requirements Hypothetical Imperatives?"; E.J. Bond, *Reason and Value* (New York: Cambridge University Press, 1983), pp. 27, 33, 40-1, 57; Darwall, p. 25.

[24] Foot, "Morality as a System of Hypothetical Imperatives" rejects this assumption. She accepts something like a desire-based theory of reasons for action (though, see note 30 for some necessary qualifications) and claims that it is no discredit to morality that we cannot show a callous amoralist to be irrational.

[25] I regard Plato and Aristotle as defenders of rational egoism; see Irwin, *Plato's Moral Theory*, chapter 8 and "Aristotle's Methods of Ethics". Rational egoism is not, as some writers seem to think (e.g. Baier, "Moral Reasons and Reasons to Be Moral" in J. Kim and A. Goldman (eds), *Values and Morals* (Boston: Reidel, 1978), p. 241 and Darwall, p. 136), committtted to psychological egoism.

[26] Cf. Richard Kraut, "Two Conceptions of Happiness" *Philosophical Review* 88 (1979), pp. 167-196 and my *Moral Realism and the Foundations of Ethics*, chapter 9.

[27] Cf. Nagel, *The Possibility of Altruism* (Nagel, "The Limits of Objectivity" qualifies this commitment to rational altruism in certain ways).

[28] Nagel, *The Possibility of Altruism*, pp. 3, 19, 83-4, 99-100. As far as I can see, Nagel is wrong to think that his justification of morality depends only upon our *rejection* of solipsism (p. 106). In order for there to *be* reasons for an agent to comply with moral demands, solipsism must be *false*. Bond, pp. 82, 92 also accepts this Nagelian justification of morality.

[29] See my "Rational Egoism, Self, and Others" (manuscript).

[30] McDowell is another who appears to infer the truth of internalism from the falsity of certain desire-based accounts of reasons for action. He seems to argue that since we can have prudential reason to do x without any occurrent desire for x or x's consequences, moral reasons need not depend upon any facts about the agent ("Are Moral Requirements Hypothetical Imperatives," pp. 14-7). But occurrent desires are not the only facts about agents which might underwrite reasons for action. Indeed, the prudential case shows this. Prudential reasons are reasons for action grounded in an agent's interests, independently of what he might desire or want. An analogy with prudence, therefore,

40

hardly demonstrates that an agent can have reason to do as morality requires independently of any facts about him or his welfare. Moreover, in criticizing Foot, McDowell appears to attribute to her, mistakenly, a purely desire-based account of reasons for action (ibid., p. 13); Foot explicitly denies that all reasons for action are desire-dependent ("Reasons for Action and Desire," pp. 148, 156).

[31] Cf. Nicholas Sturgeon, "What Difference Does it Make Whether Moral Realism is True?" (this volume).

[32] Cf. Saul Kripke, *Wittgenstein on Rules and Private Language* (Oxford: Blackwell, 1982), pp. 66f.

[33] Cf. Thomas Carson, *The Status of Morality* (Boston: Reidel, 1984), pp. 21-4.

[34] Moral realism will have these advantages over certain forms of constructivism in ethics as well. Some forms of constructivism (see section 2 and note 6) rely heavily on a publicity constraint, according to which a "true" moral principle must be a standard which is taught and which serves as a public justification of actions, policies, institutions, etc. Cf. John Rawls, *A Theory of Justice* (Cambridge, MA: Harvard University Press, 1971), pp. 133, 177-82, 582 and "Kantian Constructivism in Moral Theory," pp. 517, 537-8, 555. This publicity constraint is often defended on internalist grounds; cf. Brian Medlin, "Ethical Egoism and Ultimate Moral Principles" reprinted in D. Gauthier (ed), *Morality and Rational Self-Interest*. If the argument of this paper is correct, externalist moral realism is preferable to internalist constructivism as well as to internalist noncognitivism.

[35] This paper grew out of my work on *Moral Realism and the Foundations of Ethics*. It also provides a more adequate reply to Mackie's association of realism with internalism than I had space to offer in my "Moral Realism and the Sceptical Arguments from Disagreement and Queerness" *Australasian Journal of Philosophy* 62 (1984), pp. 111-25. I would like to thank participants at the 1985 Spindel Conference—especially Gilbert Harman, John Post, Geoffrey Sayre-McCord, and David Wong—and Philip Gasper, Terry Irwin, and Nicholas Sturgeon for helpful discussion of this material.

THE JOURNAL OF PHILOSOPHY

VOLUME LXXXIII, NO. 1, JANUARY 1986

SKEPTICISM ABOUT PRACTICAL REASON*

THE Kantian approach to moral philosophy is to try to show that ethics is based on practical reason: that is, that our ethical judgments can be explained in terms of rational standards that apply directly to conduct or to deliberation. Part of the appeal of this approach lies in the way that it avoids certain sources of skepticism that some other approaches meet with inevitably. If ethically good action is simply rational action, we do not need to postulate special ethical properties in the world or faculties in the mind, in order to provide ethics with a foundation. But the Kantian approach gives rise to its own specific form of skepticism, skepticism about practical reason.

By *skepticism about practical reason*, I mean doubts about the extent to which human action is or could possibly be directed by reason. One form that such skepticism takes is doubt about the bearing of rational considerations on the activities of deliberation and choice; doubts, that is to say, about whether "formal" principles have any content and can give substantive guidance to choice and action. An example of this would be the common doubt about whether the contradiction tests associated with the first formulation of the categorical imperative succeed in ruling out anything. I will refer to this as *content skepticism*. A second form taken by skepticism about practical reason is doubt about the scope of reason as a motive. I will call this *motivational skepticism*. In this paper my main concern is with motivational skepticism and with the question whether it is justified. Some people think that motivational considerations alone provide grounds for skepticism about the project of founding ethics on practical reason. I

* I would like to thank Timothy Gould, Charlotte Brown, and audiences of an earlier version of this paper at Columbia and the University of Chicago, for comments on and discussions of the issues of this paper, from which I have learned a great deal.

will argue, against this view, that motivational skepticism must always be based on content skepticism. I will not address the question of whether or not content skepticism is justified. I want only to establish the fact that motivational skepticism has no independent force.

I

Skepticism about practical reason gets its classical formulation in the well-known passages in the *Treatise of Human Nature* that lead Hume to the conclusion that

> Reason is, and ought only to be the slave of the passions, and can never pretend to any other office than to serve and obey them.[1]

According to these passages, as they are usually understood, the role of reason in action is limited to the discernment of the means to our ends. Reason can teach us how to satisfy our desires or passions, but it cannot tell us whether those desires or passions are themselves "rational"; that is, there is no sense in which desires or passions are rational or irrational. Our ends are picked out, so to speak, by our desires, and these ultimately determine what we do. Normative standards applying to conduct may come from other sources (such as a moral sense), but the only standard that comes from reason is that of effectiveness in the choice of means.

The limitation of practical reason to an instrumental role does not only prevent reason from determining ends; it even prevents reason from ranking them, except with respect to their conduciveness to some other end. Even the view that those choices and actions which are conducive to our over-all self-interest are rationally to be preferred to self-destructive ones is undermined by the instrumental limitation. Self-interest itself has no rational *authority* over even the most whimsical desires. As Hume says:

> 'Tis not contrary to reason to prefer the destruction of the whole world to the scratching of my finger. 'Tis not contrary to reason for me to chuse my total ruin, to prevent the least uneasiness of an *Indian* or person wholly unknown to me. 'Tis as little contrary to reason to prefer even my own acknowledg'd lesser good to my greater, and have a more ardent affection for the former than the latter (*Treatise* 416).

Under the influence of self-interest [or of "a general appetite to good, and aversion to evil, consider'd merely as such" (417)] we may rank our ends, according to the amount of good that each represents for us, and determine which are, as Hume puts it, our "greatest and most valuable enjoyments" (416). But the self-interest that would

---

[1] David Hume, *Treatise of Human Nature*, L. A. Selby-Bigge, ed. (London: Oxford, 1888), p. 415. Page references to the *Treatise* will be to this edition.

make us favor the greater good need not itself be a stronger desire, or
a stronger reason, than the desire for the lesser good, or than any of
our more particular desires. Reason by itself neither selects nor ranks
our ends.

Hume poses his argument as an argument against "the greatest
part of moral philosophy, ancient and modern" (413). Moral philosophers, Hume says, have claimed that we ought to regulate our conduct by reason, and either suppress our passions or bring them into
conformity with it; but he is going to show the fallacy of all this by
showing, first, that reason alone can never provide a motive to any
action, and, second, that reason can never oppose passion in the
direction of the will. His argument for the first point goes this way: all
reasoning is concerned either with abstract relations of ideas or with
relations of objects, especially causal relations, which we learn about
from experience. Abstract relations of ideas are the subject of logic
and mathematics, and no one supposes that those by themselves give
rise to any motives. They yield no conclusions about action. We are
sometimes moved by the perception of causal relations, but only
when there is a pre-existing motive in the case. As Hume puts it, if
there is "the prospect of pleasure or pain from some object," we are
concerned with its causes and effects. The argument that reason
cannot oppose a passion in the direction of the will depends on, and
in fact springs directly from, the argument that reason by itself cannot give rise to a motive. It is simply that reason *could* oppose a
passion only if it could give rise to an *opposing motive*.

What is important to notice in this discussion is the relation between Hume's views about the possible content of principles of reason bearing on action and the scope of its motivational efficacy. The
answer to the question what sorts of operation, procedure, or judgment of reason exist is presupposed in these passages. In the first part
of the argument Hume goes through what by this point in the *Treatise*
is a *settled* list of the types of rational judgment. The argument is a sort
of process of elimination: there are rational judgments concerning
logical and mathematical relations; there are empirical connections
such as cause and effect: Hume looks at each of these in turn in order
to see under what circumstances it might be thought to have a bearing
on decision and action. In other words, Hume's arguments against a
more extensive practical employment of reason depend upon
Hume's own views about what reason is—that is, about what sorts of
operation and judgment are "rational." His motivational skepticism
(skepticism about the scope of reason as a motive) is entirely dependent upon his content skepticism (skepticism about what
reason has to *say* about choice and action).

Yet Hume's arguments may give the impression of doing something much stronger: of placing independent constraints, based solely on motivational considerations, on what might count as a principle of practical reason. Hume seems to say simply that all reasoning that has a motivational influence must start from a passion, that being the only possible source of motivation, and must proceed to the means to satisfy that passion, that being the only operation of reason that transmits motivational force. Yet these are separate points: they can be doubted, and challenged, separately. One could disagree with Hume about his list of the types of rational judgment, operation, or possible deliberation, and yet still agree with the basic point about the source of motivation: that all rational motivation must ultimately spring from some nonrational source, such as passion. At least one contemporary philosopher, Bernard Williams, has taken something like Hume's argument to have this kind of independent force, and has so argued in his essay "Internal and External Reason,"[2] which I will take up later in this paper.

The Kantian must go further, and disagree with Hume on both counts, since the Kantian supposes that there are operations of practical reason which yield conclusions about actions and which do not involve discerning relations between passions (or any pre-existing sources of motivation) and those actions. What gives rise to the difficulty about this further possibility is the question of how such operations could yield conclusions that can motivate us.

II

The problem can best be stated in some terms provided by certain recent discussions in moral philosophy. W. D. Falk, William Frankena, and Thomas Nagel, among others, have distinguished between two kinds of moral theories, which are called "internalist" and "externalist."[3] An *internalist* theory is a theory according to which the knowledge (or the truth or the acceptance) of a moral judgment implies the existence of a motive (not necessarily overriding) for acting on that judgment. If I judge that some action is right, it is

---

[2] This paper was originally published in Ross Harrison, ed., *Rational Action* (New York: Cambridge, 1980), and is reprinted in Williams, *Moral Luck* (New York: Cambridge, 1981), pp. 101–113. Page references to Williams are to this article, as it appears in *Moral Luck*.

[3] Actually, Falk and Frankena speak of internalist and externalist senses of 'ought'. See Falk, " 'Ought' and Motivation," *Proceedings of the Aristotelian Society*, 1947/1948. Frankena's discussion, "Obligation and Motivation in Recent Moral Philosophy," was originally published in A. I. Melden, ed., *Essays in Moral Philosophy* (Seattle: University of Washington Press, 1958) and is reprinted in *Perspectives on Morality: Essays of William K. Frankena*, Kenneth E. Goodpaster, ed. (Notre Dame, Ind.: University Press, 1976), pp. 49–73 (page references are to this volume). Nagel's discussion is in *The Possibility of Altruism* (New York: Oxford, 1970), Part I.

implied that I have, and acknowledge, some motive or reason for performing that action. It is part of the sense of the judgment that a motive is present: if someone agrees that an action is right, but cannot see any motive or reason for doing it, we must suppose, according to these views, that she does not quite know what she means when she agrees that the action is right. On an *externalist* theory, by contrast, such a conjunction of moral comprehension and total unmotivatedness is perfectly possible: knowledge is one thing and motivation another.

Examples of unquestionably external theories are not easy to find. As Falk points out (125/6), the simplest example would be a view according to which the motives for moral action come from something wholly separate from a grasp of the correctness of the judgments—say, an interest in obeying divine commands. In philosophical ethics the best example is John Stuart Mill (see Nagel 8/9), who firmly separates the question of the proof of the principle of utility from the question of its "sanctions." The reason why the principle of utility is true and the motive we might have for acting on it are not the same: the theoretical proof of its truth is contained in chapter IV of *Utilitarianism*, but the motives must be acquired in a utilitarian upbringing. It is Mill's view that *any* moral principle would have to be motivated by education and training and that "there is hardly anything so absurd or so mischievous" that it cannot be so motivated.[4] The "ultimate sanction" of the principle of utility is *not* that it can be proved, but that it is in accordance with our natural social feelings. Even to some who, like Mill himself, realize that the motives are acquired, "It does not present itself . . . as a superstition of education, or a law despotically imposed by the power of society, but as an attribute which it would not be well for them to be without" (Mill 36). The modern intuitionists, such as W. D. Ross and H. A. Prichard, seem also to have been externalists, but of a rather minimal kind. They believed that there was a distinctively moral motive, a sense of right or desire to do one's duty. This motive is triggered by the news that something is your duty, and only by that news, but it is still separate from the rational intuition that constitutes the understanding of your duty. It would be possible to have that intuition and not be motivated by it.[5] The reason why the act is right and the motive you have for doing it are separate items, although it is nevertheless the

[4] *Utilitarianism*, in Samuel Gorovitz, ed., *Utilitarianism with Critical Essays* (Indianapolis: Bobbs-Merrill, 1971), p. 34.
[5] See Prichard, "Duty and Interest," in *Duty and Interest* (London: Oxford 1928). Falk's original use of the distinction between internal and external senses of ought in " 'Ought' and Motivation" is in an argument responding to Prichard's paper.

case that the motive for doing it is "because it is right." This falls just short of the internalist position, which is that the reason why the act is right is the reason, and the motive, for doing it: it is a practical reason. Intuitionism is a form of rationalist ethics, but intuitionists do not believe in practical reason, properly speaking. They believe there is a branch of theoretical reason that is specifically concerned with morals, by which human beings can be motivated because of a special psychological mechanism: a desire to do one's duty. One can see the oddity of this if one considers what the analogue would be in the case of theoretical reasoning. It is as if human beings could not be convinced by arguments acknowledged to be sound without the intervention of a special psychological mechanism: a belief that the conclusions of sound arguments are true.

By contrast, an internalist believes that the reasons why an action is right and the reasons why you do it are the same. The reason that the action is right is both the reason and the motive for doing it. Nagel gives as one example of this the theory of Hobbes: the reason for the action's rightness and your motive for doing it are both that it is in your interest. The literature on this subject splits, however, on the question of whether the Kantian position is internalist or not. Falk, for instance, characterizes the difference between internalism and externalism as one of whether the moral command arises from a source outside the agent (like God or society) or from within. If the difference is described this way, Kant's attempt to derive morality from autonomy makes him a paradigmatic internalist (see Falk 125, 129). On the other hand, some have believed that Kant's view that the moral command is indifferent to our desires, needs, and interests— that it is categorical—makes him a paradigmatic externalist.[6] Since Kant himself took the categorical character of the imperative and autonomy of the moral motive to be necessarily connected, this is a surprising difference of opinion. I will come back to Kant in section VII.

This kind of reflection about the motivational force of ethical judgments has been brought to bear by Bernard Williams on the motivational force of reason claims generally. In "Internal and External Reasons" Williams argues that there are two kinds of reason claims, or two ways of making reason claims. Suppose I say that some person *P* has a reason to do action *A*. If I intend this to imply that the person *P* has a motive to do the action *A*, the claim is of an internal reason; if not, the claim is of an external reason. Williams is concerned to argue that only internal reasons really exist. He points out

---

[6] See Frankena, *op. cit.*, p. 63, for a discussion of this surprising view.

SKEPTICISM ABOUT PRACTICAL REASON   11

(106/7) that, since an external-reason claim does not imply the existence of a motive, it cannot be used to explain anyone's action: that is, we cannot say that the person *P* did the action *A* because of reason *R;* for *R* does not provide *P* with a motive for doing *A,* and *that* is what we need to explain *P*'s doing *A:* a motive. Nagel points out that if acknowledgment of a reason claim did not include acknowledgment of a motive, someone presented with a reason for action could ask: Why do what I have a reason to do? (9; see also Falk 121/2). Nagel's argument makes from the agent's perspective the same point that Williams makes from the explainer's perspective, namely, that unless reasons are motives, they cannot prompt or explain actions. And, unless reasons are motives, we cannot be said to be practically rational.

Thus, it seems to be a requirement on practical reasons, that they be capable of motivating us. This is where the difficulty arises about reasons that do not, like means/end reasons, draw on an obvious motivational source. So long as there is doubt about whether a given consideration is able to motivate a rational person, there is doubt about whether that consideration has the force of a practical *reason.* The consideration that such and such action is a means to getting what you want has a clear motivational source; so no one doubts that this is a reason. Practical-reason claims, if they are really to present us with reasons for action, must be capable of motivating rational persons. I will call this the *internalism requirement.*

                                        III
In this section I want to talk about how the internalism requirement functions—or, more precisely, malfunctions—in skeptical arguments. Hume winds up his argument by putting the whole thing in a quite general form. Reason is the faculty that judges of truth and falsehood, and it can judge our ideas to be true or false because they represent other things. But a passion is an original existence or modification of existence, not a copy of anything: it cannot be true or false, and therefore it cannot in itself be reasonable or unreasonable. Passions can be unreasonable, then, only if they are accompanied by judgments, and there are two cases of this kind. One is when the passion is founded on the supposition of the existence of objects that do not exist. You are outraged at the mocking things you heard me say about you, but I was talking about somebody else. You are terrified by the burglars you hear whispering in the living room, but in fact you left the radio on. It is of course only in an extended sense that Hume can think of these as cases where a passion is irrational. Judgments of irrationality, whether of belief or action, are, strictly speaking, relative to the subject's beliefs. Conclusions drawn from

mistaken premises are not *irrational*.[7] The case of passions based on false beliefs seems to be of this sort.

The second kind of case in which Hume says that the passion might be called unreasonable is

> . . . when, in exerting any passion in action, we chuse means insufficient for the design'd end, and deceive ourselves in our judgment of causes and effects (*Treatise* 416).

This is in itself an ambiguous remark. Hume might, and in fact does, mean simply that we base our action on a false belief about causal relations. So this is no more genuinely a case of irrationality than the other. Relative to the (false) causal belief, the action is not irrational. But it is important that there is something else one might mean in this case, which is that, knowing the truth about the relevant causal relations in the case, we might nevertheless choose means insufficient to our end or fail to choose obviously sufficient and readily available means to the end. This would be what I will call *true irrationality*, by which I mean a failure to respond appropriately to an available reason.

If the only possibility Hume means to be putting forward here is the possibility of action based on false belief about causes and effects, we get a curious result. Neither of the cases that Hume considers is a case of true irrationality: relative to their beliefs, people *never* act irrationally. Hume indeed says this:

> . . . the moment we perceive the falsehood of any supposition, or the insufficiency of any means, our passions yield to our reason without any opposition (*Treatise* 416).

But it looks as if a theory of means/end rationality ought to allow for at least one form of true irrationality, namely, failure to be motivated by the consideration that the action is the means to your end. Even the skeptic about practical reason admits that human beings can be motivated by the consideration that a given action is a means to a desired end. But it is not enough, to explain this fact, that human beings can engage in causal reasoning. It is perfectly possible to

---

[7] I am ignoring here the more complicated case in which the passion in question is parent to the false beliefs. In my examples, for instance, there might be cases such as these: irritation at me predisposes you to think my insults are aimed at you; terror of being alone in the house makes you more likely to mistake the radio for a burglar. Hume does discuss this phenomenon (*Treatise* 120). Here, we might say that the judgment is irrational, not merely false, and that its irrationality infects the passions and actions based on the judgment. If Hume's theory allows him to say that the judgment is irrational, he will be able to say that some passions and actions are truly irrational, and not merely mistaken, although he does not do this.

imagine a sort of being who could engage in causal reasoning and who could, therefore, engage in reasoning that would point out the means to her ends, but who was not motivated by it.

Kant, in a passage early in the *Foundations,* imagines a human being in just such a condition of being able to reason, so to speak, theoretically but not practically. He is talking about what the world would have been like if nature had had our happiness as her end. Our actions would have been controlled entirely by instincts designed to secure our happiness, and:

> . . . if, over and above this, reason should have been granted to the favored creature, it would have served only to let it contemplate the happy constitution of its nature.[8]

The favored creature is portrayed as able to see that his actions are rational in the sense that they promote the means to his end (happiness); but he is not motivated by their reasonableness; he acts from instinct. Reason allows him to admire the rational appropriateness of what he does, but this is not what gets him to do it—he has the sort of attitude toward all his behavior that we in fact might have toward the involuntary well-functioning of our bodies.

Being motivated by the consideration that an action is a means to a desirable end is something beyond merely reflecting on that fact. The motive force attached to the end must be transmitted to the means in order for this to be a consideration that sets the human body in motion—and only if this is a consideration that sets the human body in motion can we say that reason has an influence on action. A practically rational person is not merely capable of performing certain rational mental operations, but capable also of transmitting motive force, so to speak, along the paths laid out by those operations. Otherwise even means/end reasoning will not meet the internalism requirement.

But the internalism requirement does not imply that nothing can interfere with this motivational transmission. And generally, this is something there seems to be no reason to believe: there seem to be plenty of things that could interfere with the motivational influence of a given rational consideration. Rage, passion, depression, distraction, grief, physical or mental illness: all these things could cause us to act irrationally, that is, to fail to be motivationally responsive to the rational considerations available to us.[9] The necessity, or the compel-

---

[8] Immanuel Kant, *Foundations of the Metaphysics of Morals,* Lewis White Beck, trans. (New York: Library of Liberal Arts, 1959), p. 11. Prussian Academy Edition, p. 395.

[9] "Available to us" is vague, for there is a range of cases in which one might be uncertain whether or not to say that a reason was available to us. For instance there are

lingness, of rational considerations lies in those considerations themselves, not in us: that is, we will not necessarily be motivated by them.
Or rather, to put the point more properly and not to foreclose any
metaphysical possibilities, their necessity may lie in the fact that, when
they do move us—either in the realm of conviction or in that of
motivation—they move us with the force of necessity. But it will still
not be the case that they necessarily move us. So a person may be
irrational, not merely by failing to observe rational connections—say,
failing to see that the sufficient means are at hand—but also by being
"willfully" blind to them, or even by being indifferent to them when
they are pointed out.[10]

In this respect practical reason is no different from theoretical
reason. Many things might cause me to fail to be convinced by a good
argument. For me to be a theoretically rational person is not merely
for me to be capable of performing logical and inductive operations,
but for me to be appropriately *convinced* by them: my conviction in
the premises must carry through, so to speak, to a conviction in the
conclusion. Thus, the internalism requirement for theoretical reasons is that they be capable of convincing us—insofar as we are

---

(1) cases in which we don't know about the reason, (2) cases in which we couldn't
possibly know about the reason, (3) cases in which we deceive ourselves about the
reason, (4) cases in which some physical or psychological condition makes us unable to
see the reason; and (5) cases in which some physical or psychological condition makes
us fail to respond to the reason, even though in some sense we look it right in the eye.
Now no one will want to say that reason claims involving reasons people do not know
about are therefore external, but as we move down the list there will be a progressive
uneasiness about whether the claim is becoming external. For toward the end of the list
we will come to claim that someone is psychologically incapable of responding to the
reason, and yet that it is internal: capable of motivating a rational person. I do not
think there is a problem about any of these cases; for all that is necessary for the reason
claim to be internal is that we can say that, if a person did know and *if nothing were
interfering with her rationality,* she would respond accordingly. This does not trivialize
the limitation to internal reasons as long as the notion of a psychological condition that
interferes with rationality is not trivially defined.

[10] I have in mind such phenomena as self-deception, rationalization, and the various
forms of weakness of will. Some of these apply to theoretical as well as practical reason,
and for the former we can add the various forms of intellectual resistance or ideology
(though "willful" is not a good way to characterize these). For some reason, people
find the second thing that I mention—being indifferent to a reason that is pointed out
to you—harder to imagine in a theoretical than in a practical case. To simply shrug in
the face of the acknowledged reason seems to some to be possible in practice in a way
that it is not in theory. I think part of the problem is that we can push what the
practically paralyzed person accepts over into the realm of theory: he *believes* "that he
ought to do such-and-such," although he is not moved to; whereas there seems to be
nowhere further back (except maybe to a suspense of judgment) to push what the
theoretically paralyzed person accepts. It may also be that the problem arises because
we do not give enough weight to the difference between being convinced by an
argument and being left without anything to say by it, or it may be just that what
paralysis *is* is less visible in the case of belief than in the case of action.

rational. It is quite possible for me to be able to perform these operations without generating any conviction, as a sort of game, say, and then I would not be a rational person.

Aristotle describes the novice in scientific studies as being able to repeat the argument, but without the sort of conviction that it will have for him later, when he fully understands it. In order for a theoretical argument or a practical deliberation to have the status of reason, it must of course be capable of motivating or convincing a rational person, but it does not follow that it must at all times be capable of motivating or convincing any given individual. It may follow from the supposition that we are rational persons and the supposition that a given argument or deliberation is rational that, if we are not convinced or motivated, there must be some explanation of that failure. But there is no reason at all to believe that such an explanation will always show that we had mistaken reasons, which, if true, would have been good reasons. Many things can interfere with the functioning of the rational operations in a human body. Thus there is no reason to deny that human beings might be practically irrational in the sense that Hume considers impossible: that, even with the truth at our disposal, we might from one cause or another fail to be interested in the means to our ends.

IV

My speculation is that skepticism about practical reason is sometimes based on a false impression of what the internalism requirement requires. It does not require that rational considerations always succeed in motivating us. All it requires is that rational considerations succeed in motivating us insofar as we are rational. One can admit the possibility of true irrationality and yet still believe that all practical reasoning is instrumental. But once this kind of irrationality is allowed in the means/end case, some of the grounds for skepticism about more ambitious forms of practical reasoning will seem less compelling. The case of prudence or self-interest will show what I have in mind. I have already mentioned Hume's account of this matter: he thinks that there is "a general appetite to good, and aversion to evil" and that a person will act prudently insofar as this calm and general passion remains dominant over particular passions. It is under the influence of this end that we weigh one possible satisfaction against another, trying to determine which conduces to our greater good. But if this general desire for the good does not remain predominant, not only the motive, but the reason, for doing what will conduce to one's greater good, disappears. For Hume says it is not contrary to reason to prefer an acknowledged lesser good to a greater.

Suppose, then, that you are confronted with a choice and, though informed that one option will lead to your greater good, you take the other. If true irrationality is excluded, and you fail to take the means to some end, this is evidence either that you don't really have this end or that it is not the most important thing to you. Thus, in this imagined case, where you do not choose your greater good, this is evidence either that you do not care about your greater good or that you do not care about it as much as you do about this particular lesser good. On the other hand, if you do respond to the news that one option leads to your greater good, then we have evidence that you do care about your greater good. This makes it seem as if your greater good is an end you might care about or not, and rationality is relative to what you care about. But, once we admit that one might from some other cause fail to be responsive to a rational consideration, there is no special reason to accept this analysis of the case. I do not mean that there is a reason to reject it, either, of course; my point is that whether you accept it depends on whether you *already* accept the limitation to means/end rationality. If you do, you will say that the case where the lesser good was chosen was a case where there was a stronger desire for it, and so a stronger reason; if you do not, and you think it *is* reasonable to choose the greater good (because prudence has rational authority), you will say that this is a case of true irrationality. The point is that the motivational analysis of the case *depends* upon your views of the content of rational principles of action, not the reverse. The fact that one might or might not be motivated to choose a certain course of action by the consideration that it leads to the greater good does not by itself show that the greater good is just one end among others, without special rational authority, something that some people care about and some people do not. Take the parallel case. The fact that one might or might not be motivated to choose a certain course of action by the consideration that it is the best available means to one's end does not show that taking the means to one's ends is just one end among others, an end some people care about and some people do not. In both cases, what we have is the fact that people are sometimes motivated by considerations of this sort, and that we all think in the latter case and some think in the former case that it is rational to be so motivated.

The argument about whether prudence or the greater good has any special rational authority—about whether it is a rational consideration—will have to be carried out on another plane: it will have to be made in terms of a more metaphysical argument about just what reason does, what its scope is, and what sorts of operation, procedure, and judgment are rational. This argument will usually consist in an attempt to arrive at a general notion of reason by discovering features or characteristics that theoretical and practical reason share; such characteristic features as universality, sufficiency, timelessness, impersonality, or authority will be appealed to.[11] What the argument in favor of prudence would be will vary from theory to theory; here, the point is this: the fact that someone might fail to be motivated by the consideration that something will serve her greater good cannot by itself throw any doubt on the argument, whatever it is, that preferring the greater good is rational. If someone were not convinced by the logical operation of conjunction, and so could not reason with conviction from "*A*" and from "*B*" to "*A* and *B*", we would not be eager to conclude that conjunction was just a theory that some people believe and some people do not. Conjunction is not a theory to believe or disbelieve, but a principle of reasoning. Not everything that drives us to conclusions is a theory. Not everything that drives us to action need be a desired end (see Nagel 20–22).

V

An interesting result of admitting the possibility of true irrationality is that it follows that it will not always be possible to argue someone into rational behavior. If people are acting irrationally only because they do not know about the relevant means/end connection, they may respond properly to argument: point the connection out to them, and their behavior will be modified accordingly. In such a person the motivational path, so to speak, from end to means is open. A person in whom this path is, from some cause, blocked or nonfunctioning may not respond to argument, even if this person understands the argument in a theoretical way. Aristotle thinks of the incontinent person as being in a condition of this sort: this happens to people in fits of passion or rage, and the condition is actually physiological.[12] Now this is important; for it is sometimes thought, on the basis of the internalism requirement, that if there is a reason to do something it must be possible to argue someone into doing it: anyone who understands the argument will straightaway act. (The conclusion of a practical syllogism is an action.) Frankena, for example, argues against an internalist construal of the moral "ought" on the grounds that even after full reflection we do not always do what is right (71). But if there is a gap between understanding a reason and being motivated by it, then internalism does not imply that people can always be argued into reasonable conduct. The reason motivates someone who is capable of

---

[11] Universality and sufficiency are appealed to by Kant; timelessness and impersonality by Nagel, and authority by Joseph Butler.
[12] *Nicomachean Ethics*, VII.3, 1147b 5–10.

being motivated by the perception of a rational connection. Rationality is a condition that human beings are capable of, but it is not a condition that we are always in.

It is for this reason that some ethical theories centered on the idea of practical reason are best thought of as establishing ideals of character. A person with a good character will be, on such a view, one who responds to the available reasons in an appropriate way, one whose motivational structure is organized for rational receptivity, so that reasons motivate in accord with their proper force and necessity. It is not an accident that the two major philosophers in our tradition who thought of ethics in terms of practical reason—Aristotle and Kant—were also the two most concerned with the methods of moral education. Human beings must be taught, or habituated, to listen to reason: we are, as Kant says, imperfectly rational.

In fact, the argument of the last section can be recast in terms of virtues. Suppose that it *is* irrational not to prefer the greater good: this need have nothing at all to do with having the greater good *among* your desired ends. It is of course true that some people are more steadily motivated by considerations of what conduces to their greater good than others: call such a person *the prudent person.* The fact that the prudent is more strongly motivated by reasons of greater good need not be taken to show that he has stronger reasons for attending to his greater good. (People have varying theoretical virtues too.[13]) We may indeed say that the prudent person "cares more" about his greater good, but that is just another way of saying that he responds more strongly to these kinds of consideration, that he has the virtue of prudence. It need not be taken to imply that his greater good is a more heavily weighted end with him and that, therefore, it really does matter more to him that he achieve his greater good than it does to another person, an imprudent person, that he achieve his. It makes more sense to say that this other person ignores reasons that he has. Again, take the parallel: some people respond much more readily and definitely to the consideration that something is an effective means to their end. We might call such a person a *determined* or *resolute* person. Presumably no one feels like saying that the determined or resolute person has a stronger reason for taking the means to her ends than anyone else does. We all have just the same reason for taking the means to our ends. The fact that people are motivated

[13] The comparisons I have been drawing between theoretical and practical reason now suggest that there should also be something like an ideal of good theoretical character: a receptivity to theoretical reasons. The vision of someone free of all ideology and intellectual resistance might be such an ideal.

differently by the reasons they have does not show that they have different reasons. It may show that some have virtues that others lack. On a practical-reason theory, the possibility of rationality sets a standard for character; but that standard will not always be met. But this is not by itself a reason for skepticism about the scope of the deliberative guidance that reason *can* provide. This is a reason for skepticism only about the extent to which that guidance will ever be taken advantage of.

VI

Nevertheless, the fact that a practical reason must be capable of motivating us might still seem to put a limitation on the scope of practical reason: it might be thought that it is a subjective matter which considerations can motivate a given individual and that, therefore, all judgments of practical reason must be conditional in form. In Hume's argument, this kind of limitation is captured in the claim that motivation must originate in a passion. In the means/end case, we are able to be motivated by the consideration that action *A* will promote purpose *P* because, and only if, we have a pre-existing motivational impulse (a passion) attached to purpose *P*. As Hume says, a relation between two things will not have any motivational impact on us unless one of the two things has such impact. This does not limit practical reason to the means/end variety, but it might seem to impose a limitation of this sort: practical-reason claims must be reached by something that is recognizably a rational deliberative process from interests and motives one already has. This position is advocated by Bernard Williams in "Internal and External Reasons." Williams, as I have mentioned, argues that only internal reasons exist; but he takes this to have a strong Humean implication. Williams takes it that internal reasons are by definition relative to something that he calls the agent's "subjective motivational set": this follows from the fact that they can motivate. The contents of this set are left open, but one kind of thing it will obviously contain is the agent's desires and passions. Internal reasons are reasons reached by deliberation from the subjective motivational set: they can motivate us because of their connection to that set. Means/end deliberation, where the end is in the set and the means are what we arrive at by the motivating deliberation, is the most characteristic, but not the only, source of reasons for action. Williams calls the means/end view the "sub-Humean model", and he says this:

> The sub-Humean model supposes that φ-ing [where φ-ing is some action we have a reason for doing] has to be related to some element in [the subjective motivational set] as causal means to end (unless perhaps it is straightforwardly the carrying out of a desire which is itself that element

in [the subjective motivational set].) But this is only one case. . . . there are much wider possibilities for deliberation, such as: thinking how the satisfaction of elements in [the subjective motivational set] can be combined, e.g. by time ordering; where there is some irresoluble conflict among the elements of [the subjective motivational set] considering which one attaches most weight to . . . or again, finding constitutive solutions, such as deciding what would make for an entertaining evening, granted that one wants entertainment (104/5).[14]

Anything reached by a process of deliberation from the subjective motivational set may be something for which there is an internal reason, one that can motivate. External reasons, by contrast, exist regardless of what is in one's subjective motivational set. In this case, Williams points out, there must be some rational process, not springing from the subjective motivational set and therefore not relative to it, which could bring you to acknowledge something to be a reason and at the same time to be motivated by it. Reason must be able to produce an entirely new motive, the thing that Hume said could not be done.

Thus, Williams takes up one part of the skeptic's argument: that a piece of practical reasoning must start from something that is capable of motivating you; and drops the other, that the only kind of reasoning is means/end. One might suppose that this limits the operations or judgments of practical reason to those functions which are natural extensions or expansions of the means/end variety, and the things Williams mentions in this passage, such as making a plan to satisfy the various elements in the set, or constitutive reasoning, are generally thought to be of that sort. But in fact this is not Williams' view, nor is it necessitated by his argument, as he points out.

> The processes of deliberation can have all sorts of effect on [the subjective motivational set], and this is a fact which a theory of internal reasons should be very happy to accommodate. So also it should be more liberal than some theorists have been about the possible elements in the [subjective motivational set]. I have discussed [the subjective motivational set] primarily in terms of desires, and this term can be used, formally, for all elements in [the subjective motivational set]. But this terminology may make one forget that [the subjective motivational set] can contain such things as dispositions of evaluation, patterns of emotional reaction, personal loyalties, and various projects, as they may abstractly be called, embodying commitments of the agent (105).

Williams can accommodate the case of someone's acting for reasons

---

[14] Williams uses the designation 'S' for 'subjective motivational set', but I have put back the original phrase wherever it occurs; hence the brackets.

of principle, and in this case the form the deliberation will take is that of applying the principle or of seeing that the principle applies to the case at hand. The advocate of the view that all deliberation is strictly of the means/end variety may claim to assimilate this case by the formal device of saying that the agent must have a desire to act on this principle, but this will not change the important fact, which is that the reasoning in this case will involve the application of the principle, which is not the same as means/end reasoning.[15]

In this kind of case, Williams' point will be that in order for the principle to provide reasons for a given agent, acceptance of the principle must constitute part of the agent's subjective motivational set. If the principle is not accepted by the agent, its dictates are not reasons for her. Reasons are relativized to the set. If this is true, it looks at first as if all practical reasons will be relative to the individual, because they are conditioned by what is in the subjective motivational set. Reasons that apply to you regardless of what is in your subjective motivational set will not exist.

This argument, however, having been cut loose from Hume's very definite ideas about what sort of rational operations and processes exist, has a very unclear bearing on claims about pure practical reason. If one accepts the internalism requirement, it follows that pure practical reason will exist if and only if we are capable of being motivated by the conclusions of the operations of pure practical reason as such. Something in us must make us capable of being motivated by them, and this something will be part of the subjective motivational set. Williams seems to think that this is a reason for doubting that pure practical reasons exist, whereas what seems to follow from the internalism requirement is this: if we can be motivated by considerations stemming from pure practical reason, then that capacity belongs to the subjective motivational set of every rational being. One cannot argue that the subjective motivational set contains only ends or desires; for that would be true only if all reasoning were of the means/end variety or its natural extensions. What sorts of items can be found in the set does not limit, but rather depends on, what kinds of reasoning are possible. Nor can one as-

---

[15] It is true that the application of a principle may be so simple or immediate that it will be a matter of judgment or perception rather than deliberation. In such a case there will be some who want to deny that practical reason has been used. On the other hand, the reasoning involved in applying a principle may be quite complicated (as in the case of the contradiction tests under the categorical imperative), and so be such that anyone should be willing to call it reasoning. If the fact that you hold the principle gives motivational force to either the insight or the deliberative argument to the effect that this case falls under the principle, then the result is a practical reason.

sume that the subjective motivational set consists only of individual or idiosyncratic elements; for that is to close off without argument the possibility that reason could yield conclusions that every rational being must acknowledge and be capable of being motivated by. As long as it is left open what kinds of rational operations yield conclusions about what to do and what to pursue, it must be left open whether we are capable of being motivated by them.

Consider the question of how an agent comes to accept a principle: to have it in her subjective motivational set. If we say that the agent comes to accept the principle through reasoning—through having been convinced that the principle admits of some ultimate justification—then there are grounds for saying that this principle is in the subjective motivational set of every rational person: for all rational persons could be brought to see that they have reason to act in the way required by the principle, and this is all that the internalism requirement requires. Now this is of course not Williams' view: he believes that the principles are acquired by education, training, and so forth, and that they do not admit of any ultimate justification.[16] There are two important points to make about this.

First, consider the case of the reflective agent who, after being raised to live by a certain principle, comes to question it. Some doubt, temptation, or argument has made her consider eliminating the principle from her subjective motivational set. Now what will she think? The principle does not, we are supposing, admit of an ultimate justification, so she will not find that. But this does not necessarily mean that she will reject the principle. She may, on reflection, find that she thinks it better (where this will be relative to what other things are in her motivational set) that people should have and act on such a principle, that it is in some rough way a good idea—perhaps not the only but an excellent basis for community living, etc.—and so she may retain it and even proceed to educate those under her influence to adopt it. The odd thing to notice is that this is almost exactly the sort of description Mill gives of the reflective utilitarian who, on realizing that his capacity to be motivated by the principle of utility is an acquirement of education, is not sorry. But Mill's position, as I mentioned earlier, is often taken to be the best example of an *externalist* ethical position.

---

[16] Williams himself remarks that the "onus of proof about what is to count as a 'purely rational process' . . . properly belongs with the critic who wants to oppose Hume's general conclusion and to make a lot out of external reason statements" (108). Although I think he is quite right in saying that the burden of proof about what is to count as a purely rational process—about *content*—belongs to Hume's opponents, I am arguing that there is no reason to suppose that if this burden is successfully picked up the reasons will be external.

SKEPTICISM ABOUT PRACTICAL REASON 23

More immediately to the point, what this kind of case shows is that for Williams, as for Hume, the motivational skepticism depends on what I have called the "content skepticism." Williams' argument does not show that if there were unconditional principles of reason applying to action we could not be motivated by them. He only thinks that there are none. But Williams' argument, like Hume's, gives the appearance of going the other way around: it looks as if the motivational point—the internalism requirement—is supposed to have some force in limiting what might count as a principle of practical reason. Whereas in fact, the real source of the skepticism is a doubt about the existence of principles of action whose content shows them to be ultimately justified.

VII

The internalism requirement is correct, but there is probably no moral theory that it excludes. I do not think that it even excludes utilitarianism or intuitionism, although it calls for a reformulation of the associated views about the influence of ethical reasoning or motivation. The force of the internalism requirement is psychological: what it does is not to refute ethical theories, but to make a psychological demand on them.

This is in fact how philosophers advocating a connection between morality and practical reason have thought of the matter. From considerations concerning the necessity that reasons be internal and capable of motivating us which are almost identical to Williams', Nagel, in the opening sections of *The Possibility of Altruism,* argues that investigations into practical reason will yield discoveries about our motivational capacities. Granting that reasons must be capable of motivating us, he thinks that if we then are able to show the existence of reasons, we will have shown something capable of motivating us. In Nagel's eyes, the internalism requirement leads not to a limitation on practical reason, but to a rather surprising increase in the power of moral philosophy: it can teach us about human motivational capacities; it can teach us psychology.[17]

As Nagel points out, this approach also characterizes the moral philosophy of Kant. By the end of the Second Section of the *Foundations,* there is in *one* sense no doubt that Kant has done what he set out to do: he has shown us what sort of demand pure reason would make

---

[17] *Op. cit.,* p. 13. Nagel calls this a "rebellion against the priority of psychology" (11) and accordingly distinguishes two kinds of internalism: one that takes the psychological facts as given and supposes that we must somehow derive ethics from them in order to achieve an internalist theory, and one that supposes that metaphysical investigations —investigations into what it is to be a rational person—will have psychological conclusions. Hobbes would be an example of the first kind and Kant of the second.

on action. Working from the ideas that reasons in general (either theoretical or practical) must be universal, that reason seeks the unconditioned, and that its binding force must derive from autonomy, he has shown us what a law of pure reason applying to action would look like. But until it has been shown that we can be motivated to act according to the categorical imperative, it has not been completely shown that the categorical imperative really exists—that there really is a law of pure practical reason. And this is because of the internalism requirement. The question how the imperative is possible is equated to that of "how the constraint of the will, which the imperative expresses in the problem, can be conceived" (Beck 34; Acad. 417). Thus, what remains for proof by a "deduction" is that we are capable of being motivated by this law of reason: that we have an autonomous will. In the Third Section of the *Foundations,* Kant does try to argue that we can be motivated by the categorical imperative, appealing to the pure spontaneity of reason as evidence for our intelligible nature and so for an autonomous will (Beck 70/1; Acad. 452). In the *Critique of Practical Reason,*[18] however, Kant turns his strategy around. He argues that we know that we are capable of being motivated by the categorical imperative and therefore that we know (in a practical sense) that we have an autonomous will. Again, explorations into practical reason reveal our nature. It is important, however, that although in the *Critique of Practical Reason* Kant does not try to argue *that* pure reason can be a motive, he has detailed things to say about *how* it can be a motive—about how it functions as an incentive in combatting other incentives.[19] Something is still owed to the internalism requirement: namely, to show what psychological conclusions the moral theory implies.

It may be that we are immune to motivation by pure practical reason. But, for that matter, it may be that we are immune to motivation by means/ends connections. Perhaps our awareness of these in cases where we seem to act on them is epiphenomenal. In fact we are quite sure that we are not immune to the reasons springing from means/ends connections; and Kant maintained that, if we thought about it, we would see that we are not immune to the laws of pure practical reason: that we know we can do what we ought. But there is

[18] See especially pp. 30 and 43–51 in the translation by Lewis White Beck (New York: Library of Liberal Arts, 1956) and pp. 30 and 41–50 in the Prussian Academy Edition.

[19] In Chapter III of the Analytic of the *Critique of Practical Reason,* where Kant's project is "not . . . to show a priori why the moral law supplies an incentive but rather what it effects (or better, must effect) in the mind, in so far as it is an incentive" (Beck 17; Acad. 72).

no guarantee of this; for our knowledge of our motives is limited. The conclusion is that, if we are rational, we will act as the categorical imperative directs. But we are not necessarily rational.

VIII

I have not attempted to show in this paper that there is such a thing as pure practical reason, or that reason has in any way a more extensive bearing on conduct than empiricism has standardly credited it with. What I have attempted to show is that this question is open in a particular way: that motivational considerations do not provide any reason, in advance of specific proposals, for skepticism about practical reason. If a philosopher can show us that something that is recognizably a law of reason has bearing on conduct, there is no special reason to doubt that human beings might be motivated by that consideration. The fact that the law might not govern conduct, even when someone understood it, is no reason for skepticism: the necessity is in the law, and not in us.

To the extent that skepticism about pure practical reason is based on the strange idea that an acknowledged reason can never fail to motivate, there is no reason to accept it. It is based on some sort of a misunderstanding, and I have suggested a misunderstanding of the internalism requirement as a possible account. To the extent that skepticism about pure practical reason is based on the idea that no process or operation of reason yielding unconditional conclusions about action can be found, it depends on—and is not a reason for believing—the thesis that no process or operation of reason yielding unconditional conclusions about action can be found. To the extent that skepticism about pure practical reason is based on the requirement that reasons be capable of motivating us, the correct response is that if someone discovers what are recognizably reasons bearing on conduct and those reasons fail to motivate us, that only shows the limits of our rationality. Motivational skepticism about practical reason depends on, and cannot be the basis for, skepticism about the possible content of rational requirements. The extent to which people are actually moved by rational considerations, either in their conduct or in their credence, is beyond the purview of philosophy. Philosophy can at most tell us what it would be like to be rational.

CHRISTINE M. KORSGAARD

University of Chicago

Part IV
What is the Relationship between Morality and Facts about Agreements?

[10]

CANADIAN JOURNAL OF PHILOSOPHY
Volume IV, Number 3, March 1975

*Reason and Maximization**

DAVID GAUTHIER, University of Toronto

I

Economic man seeks to maximize utility. The rationality of economic man is assumed, and is identified with the aim of utility-maximization.[1] But may rational activity correctly be identified with maximizing activity? The object of this essay is to explore, and in part to answer, this question.

This is not an issue solely, or perhaps even primarily, about the presuppositions of economics. The two great modern schools of moral and political thought in the English-speaking world, the contractarian and the utilitarian, identify rationality with maximization, and bring morality into their equations as well. To the contractarian, rational man enters civil society to maximize his expectation of well-being, and morality is that system of principles of action which rational men collectively adopt to maximize their well-being.[2] To the utilitarian, the rational and moral individual seeks the maximum happiness of mankind, with which he identifies his own maximum happiness.[3]

---

* I am grateful to the Canada Council for research support during part of the period in which the ideas in this paper were developed. Earlier versions were discussed in my graduate seminar, and at the Institute on Contractarian Philosophy of the Canadian Philosophical Association. I am grateful for comments received on those occasions; I am especially grateful to David Braybrooke, Steven de Haven, Aaron Sloman, and Howard Sobel for their ideas.

1 Cf. D. M. Winch, *Analytical Welfare Economics* (Harmondsworth, Middlesex, 1971): "we assume that individuals behave rationally and endeavour to maximize utility" (p. 25). Also cf. Kenneth J. Arrow, *Social Choice and Individual Values* (2nd ed.; New York, 1963), pp. 3, 21.

2 Cf. Thomas Hobbes, *Leviathan*, Chaps. 14, 15, 17, for the classic statement of contractarian theory. Also cf. Kurt Baier, *The Moral Point of View* (Ithaca, New York, 1958), pp. 308-315.

3 Cf. J. S. Mill, *Utilitarianism*, Chap. 3.

David Gauthier

Neither school identifies rationality with the straightforward aim of individual utility-maximization; this is the position of egoism, which each criticizes. But the criticism is that egoism is self-defeating; if the result of unrestrained individual utility-maximizing activities were the greatest utility for each, then neither the contractarian nor the utilitarian would find any need for morality or civil society. It is rational to maximize one's utilities, but it is not rational to do this by a straightforward policy of individual utility-maximization. In examining the connection of rational activity with maximizing activity, this paradox must be elucidated.[4]

But this is not all. For although I shall show that we can define a quite precise conception of maximizing activity, which resolves this paradox, and which should satisfy the conception of rationality which the economist, the contractarian, the utilitarian, and even the egoist, actually share (although perhaps only the contractarian correctly understands it), this conception of reason, and its associated conception of man, remain problematic. My concern is to show precisely what is involved in identifying rational activity with maximizing activity, indeed to develop the best possible case for this identification, so that it will be easier to see on the one hand its real practical consequences, and on the other hand its ideological underpinning. But I can only point to these further matters in this present essay.

I shall take for granted that the primary subject of action, or activity, is the individual human person. And I shall presuppose that it is primarily to the individual that we ascribe rationality. To speak of a rational action, or rational activity, or a rational morality, or a rational society, is to speak of rationality in a way which must be derived from our conception of a rational individual or person. This is a very important presupposition, but one which I shall leave unexamined here, save to remark that it does not, in itself, imply that our conception of a rational person is of an atomic individual, capable of existing independently of other persons or of society.

Since our concern is with rational activity, our first task is to connect this activity to the rational person. What must a person do, *in virtue of being rational*? The first point to note is that rationality is not an individuating characteristic of persons. It is the individual who is rational, but *qua* rational, one individual is the same as another. Hence any answer to this question must be the same for all persons: what one person must do, in virtue of being rational, is to be characterized in the same way as what any other person must do, in virtue of being rational.

The second point is another presupposition, perhaps *the* presupposition of what I shall call the modern Western view of man. To characterize a person as rational is not to relate him to any order, or system, or framework, which would

---

4 Cf. my paper, "Morality and Advantage," *Philosophical Review*, LXXVI (1967), 460-475.

constrain his activities. It is not, as Plato thought, to relate man to the Good. It is not, as St. Thomas thought, to relate man to God. It is not, as Kant thought, to relate man to the Kingdom of Ends. To characterize a person as rational is not then to determine his ends either positively, in terms of a goal or goals to be sought, or negatively, in terms of beings (such as other persons) to be respected.

In calling this the modern Western view of man, I do not intend to claim that it has been embraced by all Western thinkers; Kant, and Hegel, would be obvious counterexamples. What I am claiming is that this presupposition underlies our scientific theories and our social practices. It is part of the way in which each of us understands, unreflectively, in practice, what it is to be human. To demonstrate this would require an historical and social enquiry falling quite outside the scope of this essay. What I wish to do is to develop some of the implications of this presupposition—implications which are relevant to an assessment of our understanding of what it is to be human. For it is this understanding which ultimately is called into question by an enquiry into rationality and maximization.

Given this supposition, the strict answer to the question, What must a person do, solely in virtue of being rational? is: Nothing. Reason of itself determines no actions. The modern Western view of man implies at least part of the Humean view of reason, that it is the slave of the passions.[5] Reason takes the ends of our activities as given, and determines the means to those ends.

On this instrumental view of reason, to characterize a man as rational is to characterize the way in which he goes about his activities. And so our first question about rational activity is replaced by the question, How must a man act, in virtue of being rational? What, in other words, is the *rational manner* of acting?

II

The immediate consequence of the instrumental view of reason is that rationality is, or at least involves, efficiency. The rational man endeavours to select those actions which achieve his ends, and which achieve them with the minimum expenditure of time and effort. He does what is necessary to secure what he wants, and no more than is necessary.

But efficiency is not the whole of the rational manner of acting. The interesting problems of practical reason arise because we can not secure all of what we want. We have incompatible ends, so that the means which bring about one exclude another. We have ends to which there are no available sufficient means, and which therefore are at least partially unattainable. We have open ends, such as happiness, to which no set of means can be complete.

---

5 David Hume, *A Treatise of Human Nature*, Bk. II, Pt. III, Sec. III.

David Gauthier

The identification of rationality with maximizing activity requires the reduction of problems about incompatible or unattainable ends to problems about a single open end, characterized in a purely formal way. That is, we suppose that there is a single measure of a man's ends, which can be applied to evaluate the contribution each of the actions possible for him in a situation makes to the overall realization of his ends. A rational man then endeavours to select the action, or one of the actions, which maximizes this contribution.[6]

When a person acts, he brings about one of a number of outcomes each of which is possible in his situation. To deny this is to deny the real possibility of action; it is to take a fatalist view with regard to human behaviour. The outcome actually brought about need not be known to, or intended by, the person acting, but he conceives himself to be acting only in so far as he forms some expectation of the outcome, or of a probability-distribution over possible outcomes, and can distinguish this object of his expectation from other outcomes or probability-distributions over outcomes, which he believes to be also possible in the situation. The object of the person's expectation, whether an outcome or a probability-distribution over outcomes, may be termed the *expected outcome*; thus for example if a coin is tossed to determine how it lands, the expected outcome is a 50% probability of heads and a 50% probability of tails. The act selected, then, is selected to bring about the expected outcome, rather than other possible outcomes, and this expected outcome is the preferred outcome.

Preference in this sense is intentional, manifested in what a person actually takes himself to be doing. His preferences can not necessarily be inferred from the outcomes really possible in his situation, and the outcome actually brought about; it is his conception of the possibilities, and of the expected outcome, and indeed of the action itself, which is decisive. What an individual expects as the outcome of what he takes himself to be doing is what he prefers among the conceived possibilities.

Intentional preference need not correspond to attitudinal preference. A person may favour one outcome over others, yet act consciously and intentionally to realize one of the outcomes not favoured. The problems which arise in accounting for the gap between attitudinal and intentional preference, which are of course similar to those which arise in accounting for *akrasia*, are not of concern here. But the failure of this correspondence indicates a failure of rationality; the rational man acts, or at least intends to act, in accordance with his attitudes. This is not to say that attitudinal preference is more rational than intentional; no standard for the rationality of either intentional preference or attitudinal preference, taken in itself, has yet been introduced. It is only to say that the correspondence of the two is rational, the divergence, irrational.

---

6 This is too direct a statement of the connection between reason and maximization; it applies to what I shall call independent action but not to what I shall distinguish as interdependent action. See V-VII *infra*. Similarly, the discussion of preference must be modified to fit interdependent action; see footnote 16 *infra*.

Reason and Maximization

A person's preferences, whether intentional or attitudinal, may depend on his knowledge and reflection. This dependence provides us with a standard for preferability. One outcome is preferable to another, for a person, if he would prefer it, given full knowledge and reflection. The very real problem of what constitutes fullness of knowledge and reflection is another matter which must be excluded from this essay. And a person is rational, only in so far as his preferences correspond to his subjective judgment of what is preferable—only, then, in so far as what he takes himself to do corresponds to what he judges he would do, and what he favours corresponds to what he judges he would favour, given full knowledge and reflection.

Preferability provides a standard for the rationality of both intentional and attitudinal preference. But this standard is fully compatible with the supposition that the rationality of a person is not determined by the ends he seeks. The rationality of a person, on this view, depends on whether the ends he seeks are those which he judges he would seek under conditions ideal in certain respects. Reason does not assess a man's ends in relation to some standard beyond his passions (in the Humean sense). Rather, reason assesses a man's ends in relation to the standards implicit in the passions themselves, the standards of consistency between intention and attitude, and conformity of both to ideal intention and attitude. Bringing these standards together, a person is a rational agent only if his actions conform to what he supposes he would do and favour, were he sufficiently informed and reflective.

III

Rationality in action is thus more than mere efficiency. But there are further conditions arising from our understanding of preferences. Although reason as instrumental imposes, and can impose, no restraints on the content of particular preferences, it does impose restraints on the relations among the contents of different preferences.[7]

I have said that the rational man acts to bring about that outcome which he prefers, among those which he believes are open to him. Thus he must be able to compare the possible outcomes in any situation, to determine that which he prefers to the others. Let 0_i and 0_j be any two outcomes which logically are alternative possible outcomes for some situation. Then since there is no reason in principle why a person might not be restricted to a choice between these two outcomes, he must be able to determine a preference between them. We require a *connexity* condition: If 0_i, 0_j are any alternative possible outcomes for any situation, then any rational person A must either prefer 0_i to 0_j, or 0_j to 0_i, or be indifferent between them.

---

7 For a fuller discussion of preference and utility, cf. R. D. Luce and H. Raiffa, *Games and Decisions* (New York, 1957), Chap. 2, and works referred to therein.

David Gauthier

This may seem an innocuous requirement, although it assumes a single dimension of comparison among our ends. A second, obviously less innocuous condition, but one equally necessary if one is to select a most preferred outcome in any situation, is that one's preferences not be cyclic. If I prefer apples to pears, pears to peaches, and peaches to apples, and am in a situation in which I must select one of these three fruits, then no selection is most preferred—for any outcome, there is some other outcome which I prefer to it. To avoid this we require a *transitivity* condition: If O_i, O_j, O_k are any alternative possible outcomes for any situation, then if any rational person A does not prefer O_i to O_j, and O_k to O_j, A does not prefer O_k to O_i. (This slightly awkward formulation is required to ensure that transitivity extends to indifference.)

These conditions are sufficient to induce a weak ordering of the possible outcomes in any situation, in terms of an individual's preferences. They do not, however, establish a quantitative measure of preference, which is necessary if rational action is to be identified with maximizing action. Three further conditions are needed to do this.

These further conditions depend on the concept of a *lottery* among outcomes. A lottery is simply a probability distribution over the members of a set of possible outcomes. For example, suppose that I am to receive a fruit, selected at random, from a plate on which there are four apples, two pears, and six peaches. Then there are three possible outcomes—receiving an apple, a pear, a peach—and random selection of a fruit from the plate represents a lottery over these outcomes, with probabilities one-third for apple, one-sixth for pear, and one-half for peach. The conditions then are these:

Substitution: If O_i, O_j are any alternative possible outcomes or lotteries for any situation, and if any rational person A is indifferent between them, then O_i may be substituted for O_j in any lottery or situation without affecting A's preferences.

Unique indifference: If O_i, O_j, O_k are any alternative possible outcomes or lotteries for any situation, and if any rational person A prefers O_i to O_k, and does not prefer O_j to O_i or O_k to O_j, then there is a unique lottery over O_i and O_k which A considers indifferent to O_j.

Positive correlation: If O_i, O_j are any alternative possible outcomes for any situation, and if any rational person A prefers O_i to O_j, then if L_m and L_n are any two lotteries over O_i and O_j, A prefers L_m to L_n if and only if the probability of O_i in L_m is greater than in L_n.

The interpretation of the last two conditions may be assisted by an example. Suppose I prefer apples to pears and pears to peaches. Then the unique indifference conditions requires that there be a single, unique lottery among apples and peaches which I consider indifferent to pears. And the positive correlation condition requires that I prefer a lottery affording me a 50% chance of an apple and a 50% chance of a pear to one affording me a 40% chance of an apple and a 60% chance of a pear.

Reason and Maximization

All of these conditions lack intuitive plausibility in one respect—a respect in which the earlier transitivity condition is also defective. For all require that we have unlimited powers of discrimination in matters of preference. If I prefer apples to pears, then according to the positive correlation condition I must prefer a lottery among apples and pears affording me a 50.00002% chance of an apple to one affording me a 50.00001% chance. But my powers of discrimination do not enable me to detect any practical difference between the two lotteries.

It is not possible to remedy this difficulty within the compass of this essay. We may take our conditions, then, as representing an ideal of reason with respect to preference. A person is rational, in so far as his preferences are concerned, to the extent to which they satisfy these conditions.

We are now able to introduce the measure of a man's ends, which is termed *utility*.[8] To determine such a measure for the members of any set of alternative possible outcomes is to determine a *utility-function* for the members of the set. Let $O_1, \ldots, O_n$ be any set of alternative possible outcomes, ordered so that no member of the sequence is preferred to any preceding member by the person in question, A. If A is indifferent between O_1 and O_n, then he is indifferent among all the possible outcomes, and a utility-function is defined for the members of the set simply by assigning the same number—any number will do—to each. But suppose that A is not indifferent among all the possible outcomes. Let each outcome be replaced by the unique lottery over O_1 and O_n to which it is indifferent for A; for any outcome O_i let this lottery be $(p_iO_1 + (1-p_i)O_n)$. Then U is a utility-function for A over $O_1, \ldots, O_n$ if and only if:

 (i) $U(O_1) = u_1$, where u_1 is any real number;
 (ii) $U(O_n) = u_n$, where u_n is any real number smaller than u_1;
 (iii) $U(O_i) = U(p_iO_1 + (1-p_i)O_n) = p_iU(O_1) + (1-p_i)U(O_n) = p_iu_1 + (1-p_i)u_n = u_i$.

If U is a utility-function for A over the members of any set of outcomes, then any positive linear transform of U, i.e. any function

$$U^* = aU + b \text{ (a greater than 0)}$$

is also a utility-function for A over these outcomes.

A person is a rational agent, then, only if a utility-function can be defined over the alternative possible outcomes in any situation, as a measure of his preference among those outcomes. And so the identification of rationality in action with the aim of individual utility-maximization now seems to be complete. A rational individual, I concluded in II, identifies his intentional

---

8 A more formal treatment would require a proof that the conditions given are necessary and sufficient for the introduction of a utility-function.

David Gauthier

preference, his attitudinal preference, and his supposition of what he would prefer given full knowledge and reflection. For him we may speak simply of preference, referring to all of these. A rational individual, I have now concluded, is one whose preferences can be measured by a utility-function, or in other words, one whose preferences can be replaced functionally by numerical utilities. Bringing these conclusions together, a rational individual is one whose intended actions conform to his numerical utilities, that is, one who acts to bring about an expected outcome with utility at least as great as that of any outcome he considers possible in the situation. Thus the rationality condition established by identifying rational activity with maximizing activity is:

A person acts rationally only if the expected outcome of his action affords him a utility at least as great as that of the expected outcome of any action possible for him in the situation.

This development of rationality from efficiency to utility-maximization is by no means unproblematic. As I have indicated, the argument of II rests on the assumption that there is a single dimension of comparison among our ends, a dimension which I have labelled preference. And the argument of III requires two further assumptions. The first is that preference can be represented as a continuum, rather than, say, a mere ordering. The second is that this continuum has no necessary upper bound, that the formal end, utility, is open. In any particular situation there is a maximum possible utility, but the pursuit of utility is unending. These assumptions are, of course, part of the orthodox conception of economic man, and of the contractarian and utilitarian views which are its alternative elaborations in the realm of morals and politics. But they are not entailed by the conception of reason as instrumental.

IV

Is utility-maximization always possible? If rationality is identified with the aim of individual utility-maximization, and if there are situations in which it is not possible to maximize one's utilities, then there are situations in which it is not possible to act rationally. This is not a conclusion one would willingly accept. Hence a proof of the possibility of utility-maximization, in all situations, is required.

But this task is beyond the compass of this essay. Here, I can consider only three types of situations. The first, and simplest, is that in which the person knows the full circumstances in which he is to act, and the effects of his (intended) action on those circumstances; hence he is able to correlate a determinate outcome with each of his possible actions. This case is unproblematic. The utility of each outcome may be related to the corresponding action, and utility-maximization is achieved by selecting that action, or one of those actions, with greatest utility.

The second case is that in which the person is uncertain about the circumstances, or the effects of his action in those circumstances. To each of his

Reason and Maximization

possible actions he is able to correlate, not a determinate outcome, but only a determinate set, each member of which is the outcome resulting from a particular combination of circumstances and effects possible given the action. If we suppose, however, that he can make some estimate of the probabilities of these various possible circumstances and effects, then he can correlate a unique expected outcome with each possible action, the expected outcome being the appropriate probability-distribution over the set of outcomes.[9] And the utility of this expected outcome (its expected utility)[10] may be determined from the utilities of the outcomes belonging to the set; it is simply the sum of the products of the probabilities and utilities of all the members of the set. This expected utility may then be related to the corresponding action, and utility-maximization is achieved by selecting that action, or one from those actions, with greatest expected utility.

The third, most difficult case is that in which there is more than one person, each rational, and the outcome is the product of their actions in the circumstances.[11] I shall not demonstrate that utility-maximization can be achieved, but only that one problem which arises from the interaction of the persons can be resolved. To illustrate the problem, consider the simplest possibility—two persons, A and B, each able to correlate a determinate outcome with each pair consisting of a possible action for A and a possible action for B. Suppose now that A expects B to perform some one of his actions—or, failing this, assigns a probability to each of B's possible actions, so that he expects, as it were, a probability distribution over B's possible actions. In either case, he can correlate an expected outcome with each of his possible actions, and proceed as before to maximize.

But A must take B's rationality into account. Since B is rational, A must suppose that the action he expects B to perform will maximize B's expected utility, given the action B expects A to perform. A's intended action, then, is utility-maximizing for A against that possible action of B which A expects B to perform, which in turn is conceived by A as utility-maximizing for B against that possible action of A which A expects that B expects A to perform. Now let us make one further, crucial, simplifying assumption. Let us suppose that A assumes that B's expectation is correct. That is, the possible action of A, which A expects that B expects A to perform, is A's intended action. Hence A's action

---

9 I shall not consider the possibility of utility-maximization if the agent is unable to make any estimate of the probabilities of the various circumstances and effects.

10 A person prefers greater utility to less, and is indifferent between equal utilities, whether these utilities are actual or expected. This is assured by the way in which his utility-function is generated from his preferences. Hence the introduction of expected utility makes no difference to the argument; it is in no sense inferior to actual utility.

11 This is the situation analyzed by the mathematical theory of games, to which I owe many of my arguments and concepts.

David Gauthier

is utility-maximizing for A given that action of B which A expects B to perform, which in turn is utility-maximizing for B given A's action. Hence from A's point of view (and also, of course, from B's, which is assumed to be exactly parallel), each action must be utility-maximizing for the agent given the other's action.

It is not obvious that this requirement can always be satisfied. Indeed, it can not be, unless each person is able to select, not only from his possible actions, but also from all probability-distributions over his possible actions, in deciding what to do. To show this, let us consider a simple example. Suppose that A and B find themselves in a situation in which each has but two alternative possible actions. Let these be a_1 and a_2 for A, b_1 and b_2 for B. There are four outcomes, one for each pair of possible actions, which we represent as $0_{11} = a_1 \times b_1$, and similarly 0_{12}, 0_{21} and 0_{22}. Now let there be a utility-function for each person such that the utilities of the outcomes are as shown in this matrix, A's utilities appearing first:

	b_1	b_2
a_1	$0_{11}\,(0\,,3)$	$0_{12}\,(3\,,2)$
a_2	$0_{21}\,(1\,,0)$	$0_{22}\,(2\,,1)$

It is evident by inspection that if A expects B to perform b_1, A should perform a_2, but if B expects A to perform a_2, B should perform b_2. On the other hand, if A expects B to perform b_2, he should perform a_1, but if B expects A to perform a_1, he should perform b_1. There is no pair of actions such that each is utility-maximizing against the other.

However, if we allow probability-distributions over actions, there is such a pair. For if A expects B to randomize on an equal basis between b_1 and b_2, then any of his possible actions is utility-maximizing, and if B expects A to randomize on an equal basis between a_1 and a_2, then any of his possible actions is utility-maximizing. Hence the probability-distributions $(\tfrac{1}{2}a_1 + \tfrac{1}{2}a_2)$ and $(\tfrac{1}{2}b_1 + \tfrac{1}{2}b_2)$ are utility-maximizing against each other.

I shall say that the members of an n-tuple of actions, one for each of the n agents in a situation, are in *mutual equilibrium* if and only if each member of the n-tuple maximizes the respective agent's utility, given the other members of the n-tuple. It has been shown by Nash that, if we include probability-distributions over possible actions as themselves possible actions, then in every situation with finitely many persons, each with a finite range of actions, there is at least one n-tuple of possible actions, such that its members are in mutual equilibrium.[12] Hence one condition which is necessary if each action is to be utility-maximizing can be satisfied.

---

12 J.F. Nash, "Non-cooperative Games," *Annals of Mathematics,* LIV(1951), 286-295.

Reason and Maximization

This completes my argument here for the possibility of utility-maximization. The important conclusion for present purposes is that, in a situation involving several persons in which each assumes the correctness of the others' expectations, each must expect all of the actions to be in mutual equilibrium, if each is to maximize his utilities. If then we suppose that each person can determine correctly the actions of all persons, the identification of rationality with the aim of utility-maximization entails that for rational persons in situations of interaction, all actions must be in mutual equilibrium.[13]

V

Moral philosophers have not been slow to challenge the identification of rationality with individual utility-maximization.[14] To maximize one's utilities is to act prudently, in that extended sense of the term which has become philosophically commonplace, or to act from self-interest, where self-interest is taken to embrace all one's aims, and not only one's self-directed aims. To identify rationality with the aim of utility-maximization is then to identify it with prudence, and in so far as morality is distinct from prudence, to distinguish it from morality. The moral man is not always rational, and the rational man not always moral. To many persons these consequences are unacceptable. Moral philosophers have responded in various ways; the most radical response has been to deny the rationality of utility-maximization.

Not all forms of this denial concern our present argument. But one of the principal objections to the rationality of utility-maximization rests on the insistence that reason and utility are indeed related, but in a way which is deeper than and incompatible with the relationship we have developed. And this type of objection we must consider.

Note first that it is in general not possible for every agent in a situation to achieve his maximum utility. Let us say that an outcome is best if and only if it affords each person in the situation at least as great a utility as that afforded him by any other outcome; then in general no outcome in a situation is best. Hence it would be futile to suppose that we should seek always to bring about best outcomes. However, in every situation there must be at least one outcome, and there may be many outcomes, which afford each person a *maximum compossible utility*, that is, the greatest utility each can receive, given the utilities received by the others. Such outcomes are termed *optimal* or *efficient*; an outcome is optimal if and only if there is no alternative possible outcome affording some person a greater utility and no person a lesser utility. It may

---

13 I shall not consider the possibility of utility-maximization in the case in which not all agents correctly assume that all expectations are correct.

14 Cf. G. E. Moore, *Principia Ethica* (Cambridge, 1903), secs. 58-61; also Richard B. Brandt, *Ethical Theory* (Englewood Cliffs, N.J., 1959), pp. 369-375.

David Gauthier

seem evidently reasonable to require that in any situation, every person should act to bring about an optimal outcome. For if the outcome is not optimal, then some persons might do better, yet no person do worse.

With the conception of optimality established, the first step of the objection is to point out that individual utility-maximization may lead to a non-optimal outcome. The well-known Prisoner's Dilemma is sufficient so show this.[15] The dilemma is found in any situation which can be represented by such a matrix as this:

	b_1	b_2
a_1	0_{11} (1 , 1)	0_{12} (10 , 0)
a_2	0_{21} (0 , 10)	0_{22} (9 , 9)

It is evident on inspection that whatever B does, A maximizes his utility by his action a_1. Similarly, whatever A does, B maximizes his utility by his action b_1. Hence if we identify rationality with utility-maximization, and assume A and B to be rational, they will achieve the outcome 0_{11}, with a utility of 1 to each. But 0_{22} would have afforded each a utility of 9. The actions a_1 and b_1 are in mutual equilibrium, and indeed are the only actions in mutual equilibrium in this situation, but their outcome is not optimal. Hence we have a situation in which the requirement that individual utility-maximizers act in mutual equilibrium is incompatible with the proposal that the outcome of interaction be optimal.

Only in some situations will individual utility-maximization lead to a non-optimal outcome. But since the possibility of these situations can not be ruled out, individual utility-maximizers can not reasonably suppose that in the long run they will do as well for themselves as possible. Whenever they find themselves in an interaction situation in which no equilibrium n-tuple of actions leads to an optimal outcome, they will act to bring about an outcome which denies at least some of them utilities which they might have attained without any utility cost to the others.

But do persons behave irrationally in bringing about a non-optimal state of affairs? This has not yet been argued, so that the objection is incomplete. Consider, then, the following argument, which purports to show that because the policy of individual utility-maximization leads, in some situations, to non-optimal outcomes, it is therefore not rational.

What is rational for one person is rational for every person. Hence what is correctly judged rational for one person must be judged rational for every person, on pain of error. And what one person correctly judges rational, every

15 The Prisoner's Dilemma is attributed to A.W. Tucker.

Reason and Maximization

person must judge rational, on pain of error. Suppose then that some person, A, correctly judges himself rational to maximize his own utility. Then he must judge each person rational to maximize his (that person's) utility. And every person must judge each person rational to maximize his own utility.

What constraint does the identification of rationality with the aim of utility-maximization impose on this judgment? Since there is in general no best outcome, the constraint may not require that every person suppose his own utility maximized by that policy of action he judges rational for each to follow. But the constraint must surely require that every person expect for himself the maximum utility compossible with that received by each other person, from that policy of action he judges rational for each person. Thus, if every person correctly judges each person rational to maximize his own utility, then the policy of individual utility-maximization must afford every person maximum compossible utility, or in other words, individual utility-maximization must yield optimal outcomes, and only optimal outcomes. But we have shown that individual utility-maximization does not always yield optimal outcomes. Therefore every person does not correctly judge each person rational to maximize his own utility. Person A does not correctly judge each person rational to maximize his own utility. And so A does not correctly judge himself rational to maximize his own utility.

This argument captures a way of thinking about the universality of rational judgments which is supposed to rule out the rationality of prudence. But it is a bad argument. It will be recalled that I have presupposed that we ascribe rationality primarily to the individual person. Our concern is with practical reason, and so with the rational *agent*. On the instrumental conception of reason, the rationality of an agent is shown by the relation between the actions he takes himself to perform, and his ends, his basis of action. If we consider this basis of action to enter into his point of view, then we may say that the rationality of an agent is determined by assessing his intended actions in relation to his point of view.

This is not to say that what is rational from one point of view is not or may not be rational from another point of view. What is rational is rational *sans phrase*. But it is the point of view of the agent which determines, from every point of view, whether his actions, and he himself, are rational. If a person A is to assess the rationality of another person B, then it is the relation of B's actions to B's utility, and not the relation of B's actions to A's utility, which is relevant.

The fallacy in the argument just outlined is now easily detected. The fallacious step is the claim that every person must expect for himself the maximum utility compossible with that received by each other person, from that policy of action he judges rational for each person. A's maximum compossible utility is not the relevant criterion for assessing the rationality of the actions of persons other than himself, and hence not the relevant criterion for assessing the rationality of a policy of action in so far as it determines the actions of other persons.

423

David Gauthier

In explicating practical rationality, the argument fails to take seriously the position of the *agent*. The question whether the aim of utility-maximization is rational is the question whether it is rational to *act* in a maximizing manner. It is not the question whether it is rational to act and to *be acted on* in this manner, for this question makes no sense. There is no way of being acted on which is as such either rational or irrational; there is no *rational patient* corresponding to the *rational agent*. There is, of course, the question whether utility-maximization is the most *desirable* way to act and be acted on, and this indeed is the question which is answered negatively by consideration of the Prisoner's Dilemma, for it is in part whether one's utility is maximized, given the utilities received by the other persons, if one acts and is acted on in accordance with the tenets of individual utility-maximization. But the answer to this question does not answer the question how it is rational to act, unless the way in which one acts determines the way in which others act. If in choosing how to act, one chooses how one is to be acted upon, then one's role as patient becomes relevant to one's role as agent. But this is to go beyond the argument we have considered.

VI

Let us then turn to the supposition that the way in which one acts determines the way in which others act, and *vice versa*. So far we have considered only *independent* action, action in a manner which each person selects for himself. But we may contrast this with *interdependent* action, action in a manner on which all agree.[16] Interdependent action is action in *civil society*, by which I understand a common framework of action. Independent action, then, may be termed action in a *state of nature*.

Since reason is the same for all, rational persons must adopt the same manner of action if they share the same condition. But this does not obliterate the distinction between independent and interdependent action. Independent rational persons will each *separately* adopt the same manner of action. Interdependent rational persons will *collectively* adopt a common manner of action. Interdependent persons will act in the same manner, *because* all have agreed so to act; if they are rational, they will act because all have rationally agreed so to act.

---

16 For interdependent action we modify our account of preference in the following way. What the agent takes himself to be doing can be coupled with his beliefs and the agreed manner of action to determine his intentional preference. His attitudinal preference can be coupled with his beliefs and the agreed manner of action to determine a strategy. He is rational only if this strategy corresponds to what he takes himself to be doing. What he supposes he would do, were he sufficiently informed and reflective can then be used to determine intentional preferability; what he supposes he would favour under these ideal conditions can be used to determine a strategy. He is rational only if what he favours and what he would favour determine the same strategy, which corresponds to what he takes himself to be doing and also to what he would do.

Reason and Maximization

What is the rational manner of interdependent, or agreed, action? This question would seem to be equivalent to, on what manner of action is it rational to agree? The identification of rationality with the aim of utility-maximization provides at least a necessary condition for rational agreement.[17] It would not be rational to agree to a way of acting if, should that way of acting be adopted, one would expect a utility less than the maximum compossible in the situation with the utility afforded by the agreement to every other party. And so it is rational for all concerned to agree to a way of acting only if, should it be adopted, each person may expect the maximum utility compossible, in the situation, with that utility which each other person expects. Or in other words, an agreed way of acting is rational only if it leads to an outcome which is optimal so far as the parties to the agreement are concerned.

Individual utility-maximization does not guarantee an optimal outcome. Thus, although in a particular situation, an agreement that each person seek to maximize his own utilities may lead to an optimal outcome, such an agreement will not in general lead to an optimal outcome, and so it is not, in itself, rational. But if it is not rational to agree to individual utility-maximization as such, then individual utility-maximization can not be the rational manner of interdependent action. The argument against the identification of rationality with the aim of utility-maximization, misapplied to independent action, succeeds for interdependent action.

Indeed, it seems that the identification of rationality with the aim of individual utility-maximization leads to a contradiction. Consider any situation, such as that exemplified by the Prisoner's Dilemma, in which there is at least one outcome which affords greater utility to each person than the outcome of rational independent action. Then it is evidently possible to specify at least one agreement such that the outcome of acting on it affords each party to the agreement an expected utility greater than that which he can expect by independent action. Hence if each person in the situation is rational, each must be willing to enter into some agreement. But if one enters an agreement rationally, then one must act rationally in so far as one acts in accordance with the agreement, at least if the circumstances remain as one envisages them in entering the agreement. Hence it must be rational for each person in the situation to act in accordance with some agreement.

Since the outcome of any agreement which each enters rationally must be optimal, the agreed actions of the persons can not be in mutual equilibrium. Thus the agreement must require at least one party to it to act in such a way that the expected outcome does not afford him a utility at least as great as that of the outcome of some other action open to him. But then it can not be rational for him to act in accordance with the agreement. Therefore there is at least one party to the agreement for whom it is both rational and not rational to

---

17 I shall not introduce a sufficient condition in this paper.

David Gauthier

act in accordance with the agreement. This is a contradiction; therefore either it is rational for such a person not to enter the agreement, or it is rational for him to keep the agreement. But the condition established in III, that a person acts rationally only if the expected outcome affords him a utility at least as great as that of the expected outcome of any possible action, is violated in either case. Therefore rationality can not be identified with the aim of individual utility-maximization.

This last argument is again fallacious. A rational person must be willing to enter into an agreement only if entry would afford him a greater expected utility than any alternative action. But since in a situation of the type under consideration, any agreement leading to an optimal outcome would require some person to act irrationally, then, if every person is rational, the agreement must be violated. And so such an agreement must fail to secure its intended outcome. But then the actual expected outcome of entering the agreement need not afford each party a greater utility than the expected outcome of independent action. Since this can be known at the time of making the agreement, it is not the case that each person could rationally expect a greater utility from entry than from non-entry. And so it is not the case that it must be rational for each to enter an agreement. It would be rational for each to enter into an agreement, were it rational for each to keep it, but since it is not rational for each to keep it, it is not rational for each to enter it.

Our reply defends the consistency of identifying rationality with the aim of utility-maximization only at the cost of denying the possibility of rational interdependent action in any form which genuinely differs from rational independent action. A rational agreement can not require any person to perform an action which does not lead to an expected outcome with utility for him at least as great as the utility of the expected outcome of any action possible for him. Agreement, then, can not enable man to escape from Prisoner's Dilemma situations. In such situations any mutually beneficial agreement would require each person to act irrationally, and so no one has reason to make such an agreement.

We seem obliged to conclude, with Hobbes,[18] that man can not escape the state of nature by agreement alone. Of course, if by agreement actions can be made literally interdependent, so that what each party to the agreement does actually depends on what every other party does, then independent violation is impossible, and the agreement may prove effective. Or if by agreement the actions possible for each party may be altered, so that it is no longer possible for each to violate in a utility-maximizing manner, then the agreement may prove effective. Or again, if by agreement the utilities of some of the possible outcomes may be altered, so that the action which one would rationally perform in the absence of agreement no longer leads to an outcome with maximum

18 Cf. Hobbes, *Leviathan*, Chaps. 14, 15, 17.

possible utility, then also the agreement may prove effective. But in each of these cases the effectiveness of the agreement is secured by eliminating any conflict between the action required by the agreement, and the action which leads to an outcome with maximum expected utility for the agent. The agreement will then permit each person to seek to maximize his own utilities, but will impose constraints which ensure that this pursuit of individual utility-maximization will in fact lead to an optimal outcome.

But it would be a counsel of despair to conclude that rational interdependent action is impossible. The straightforward identification of rationality with the aim of individual utility-maximization, although not inconsistent, is nevertheless inadequate, because it denies the possibility of agreements which require one or more of the parties to refrain from the maximization of individual utility, yet secure to each of the parties greater utility than is possible without such agreement. This inadequacy does not, however, show that rationality is not connected with maximizing activity. For it is just because those persons who identify rationality with straightforward individual utility-maximization will not always achieve optimal outcomes, that their conception of rationality is inadequate. I shall, therefore, attempt to formulate more adequately the connection between rationality and maximizing activity, and then demonstrate that this more adequate conception can in fact be derived from an initial acceptance of the view that a person acts rationally only if the utility to him of the expected outcome of his action is as great as possible.

VII

Suppose that we restrict the rationality condition established in III to independent action. Thus it reads: a person acting independently acts rationally only if the expected outcome of his action affords him a utility at least as great as that of the expected outcome of any action possible for him in the situation. And suppose that we formulate a parallel condition for interdependent action, based on the claim that it is rational to agree to a way of acting only if, should that way of acting be adopted, one's expected utility would be the maximum compossible with the expected utility of each other party to the agreement. The condition would be: *a person acting interdependently acts rationally only if the expected outcome of his action affords each person with whom his action is interdependent a utility such that there is no combination of possible actions, one for each person acting interdependently, with an expected outcome which affords each person other than himself at least as great a utility, and himself a greater utility.*

Note that this latter condition in effect implies the former. For to act independently is to act interdependently with oneself alone. Hence by the condition for interdependent action, one acts rationally only if the expected outcome of one's action affords one (as the sole person with whom one is acting

David Gauthier

interdependently) a utility such that one has no possible action with an expected outcome affording one greater utility. And this is equivalent to the condition of independent action.

It is therefore possible to eliminate the phrase 'acting interdependently' from the formulation of the new condition. It is then a general alternative to the unrestricted condition established in III. This new condition requires each person to seek to maximize his utility, not given the *actions* of all other persons in the situation, but rather given the *utilities* of those with whom he acts interdependently, and the actions of any other persons—persons not party to the agreement. This condition does not represent a policy of utility-maximization, as ordinarily understood. Nevertheless, the policy following from this condition is clearly intended to maximize the agent's overall expected utility, by enabling him to participate in agreements intended to secure optimal outcomes, when maximizing actions performed in the absence of agreement would lead to non-optimal outcomes. Hence I propose to term this the condition of agreement-constrained utility-maximization, or for short, the *condition of constrained maximization.* And by constrained maximization, I shall mean that policy, or any policy, which requires individual utility-maximization in the state of nature, and agreed optimization in society.

Agreed optimization, I should note, is not a determinate policy of social action. In most situations there are infinitely many expected outcomes which are optimal; an agreement must single out one such outcome for each situation to which it applies, and require the actions which lead to that outcome. The condition of constrained maximization must be combined with a condition of agreement, to test the rationality of policies of action. We may assume that a rational condition of agreement will require that the expected outcome afford each party to the agreement greater utility than the expected outcome of independent action, for otherwise a rational person will not enter an agreement. But this generally allows considerable opportunity for negotiation, and no test has been provided for the rationality of such negotiation. To provide such a test is to determine the rational distribution of those utilities which are the product of agreement, or, in other words, to determine the rational manner of cooperative activity. This task, which may also be expressed as the task of developing a theory of distributive justice, I have attempted elsewhere.[19]

Leaving aside this question, then, how can we defend constrained maximization? If we identify rationality with the aim of individual utility-maximization, we are led, as I have shown, to the condition of III, which may be termed the *condition of straightforward maximization.* A policy of

---

19 "Rational Cooperation," *Nous,* VIII (1974), 53-65. Cf. also my paper, "Justice and Natural Endowment: Towards a Critique of Rawls' Ideological Framework," forthcoming in *Social Theory and Practice.* Also on this subject cf. R. B. Braithwaite, *Theory of Games as a Tool for the Moral Philosopher* (Cambridge, 1955).

Reason and Maximization

straightforward maximization requires individual utility-maximization under all circumstances, and thus destroys the real possibility of society as a condition in which men act differently than in the state of nature.

We resolve this problem by introducing a new consideration. Suppose a person is to choose his conception of rationality. In such a situation of choice, the several possible actions have, as their outcomes, different possible conceptions of rationality. Hence his action, in choosing, is open to rational assessment. What conception of rationality is it rational for him to choose?

This may seem an impossible question to answer. For, it may be urged, one can only assess the rationality of a choice given some conception of rationality. But if the choice is among such conceptions, by what conception can one make the assessment? It might be suggested that one should assess one's choice by the conception chosen; it is rational to choose a conception of rationality if, given that conception of rationality, it is rational to choose it. This condition, however, seems to be necessary rather than sufficient. If the choice of a certain conception of rationality is not rational, given that conception, then it is surely not a rational choice. But there may be several incompatible conceptions of rationality, each of which is self-supporting in the manner just considered.

Let us return to our point of departure—economic man. The traditional view of his rationality is expressed by the condition of straightforward maximization. We shall assume this condition, and ask what conception of rationality one should choose to afford one the expectation of maximum utility. Is it rational for economic man to choose to be a straightforward maximizer? Or is the form of rationality traditionally ascribed to him not self-supporting?

Our previous arguments make the answers to these questions evident. If we compare the effects of holding the condition of straightforward maximization, with the effects of holding the condition of constrained maximization, we find that in all those situations in which individual utility-maximization leads to an optimal outcome, the expected utility of each is the same, but in those situations in which individual utility-maximization does not lead to an optimal outcome, the expected utility of straightforward maximization is less. In these latter situations, a constrained maximizer, but not a straightforward maximizer, can enter rationally into an agreement to act to bring about an optimal outcome which affords each party to the agreement a utility greater than he would attain acting independently. Now it does not follow from this that such an agreement will come about, for at the very least the status of the other persons in the situation—whether they are straightforward or constrained maximizers, or neither—will be relevant to what happens. And even if an agreement is reached, a constrained maximizer is committed to carrying it out only in the context of mutual expectations on the part of all parties to the agreement that it will be carried out. It would not be rational to carry out an agreement if one supposed that, because of the defections of others, the expected outcome would afford

David Gauthier

one less utility than the outcome one would have expected had no agreement been made. Nevertheless, since the constrained maximizer has in some circumstances some probability of being able to enter into, and carry out, an agreement, whereas the straightforward maximizer has no such probability, the expected utility of the constrained maximizer is greater. Therefore straightforward maximization is not self-supporting; it is not rational for economic man to choose to be a straightforward maximizer.

Is it, then, rational for economic man to choose to be a constrained maximizer? Is there any other conception of rationality, adoption of which would afford him the expectation of greater utility? It is evident that in the context of independent action, either maximizing conception affords one the expectation of the greatest utility possible. In the context of interdependent action, one's expectation of utility will depend on the type of agreement one makes. We have noted that the condition of constrained maximization does not determine this. But the constrained maximizer is committed only to make and carry out agreements which afford him the expectation of greater utility than independent action.

Here then I can argue only that to choose to identify rationality with constrained optimization, in so far as it commits one to seek optimal outcomes, may well afford one an expectation of utility as great as is afforded by the choice of any other conception of rationality, and at least affords one the expectation of greater utility than to choose to identify rationality with straightforward maximization. Hence a rational person who begins by adopting the policy of individual utility-maximization, in accordance with the condition of straightforward maximization, will, following that policy, choose a different conception of rationality, and will prefer a policy which requires agreed optimization whenever possible, to his original policy, and possibly to any alternative policy.

VIII

The supposition that a person chooses, or can choose, his conception of rationality raises many problems which fall outside the scope of this essay. Some may argue that the supposition is unintelligible, insisting that, whatever the status of other norms, the norms of rationality are given and not chosen. Now there is a sense in which this is so from the standpoint of each individual, even on our position. For a person does not and can not begin by selecting a conception of rationality *in vacuo*. Rather, he begins and must begin with a conception which he does not choose, but which affords him the rational basis for a further choice, which may confirm the original conception or may set it aside in favour of a different conception. But the initial conception itself need be given only from the individual's standpoint. Conceptions of rationality are, I should suppose, not fixed in human nature, but rather the products of human

Reason and Maximization

socialization. There seems to me little doubt that the conception of rationality has undergone social change, that neither in classical nor in mediaeval society was rationality identified with maximizing activity. But I have claimed that in our society the received conception, which most persons do accept initially given their socialization, does identify rationality with maximizing activity. And this identification is usually expressed by the condition of straightforward maximization.

Far from supposing that the choice of a conception of rationality is unintelligible, I want to argue that the capacity to make such a choice is itself a necessary part of full rationality. A person who is unable to submit his conception of rationality to critical assessment, indeed to the critical assessment which must arise from the conception itself, is rational in only a restricted and mechanical sense. He is a conscious agent, but not fully a self-conscious agent, for he lacks the freedom to make, not only his situation, but himself in his situation, his practical object. Although we began by agreeing, with Hume, that reason is the slave of the passions, we must agree, with Kant, that in a deeper sense reason is freedom.

In philosophical literature, the classic example of the man who is bound by his conception of reason is Hobbesian man, the self-maintaining engine. The restricted rationality of Hobbesian man becomes evident in Hobbes' insistence that, although men recognize the rational necessity of interdependent action, the necessity, in other words, that each man should covenant with his fellows "to lay down [his] right to all things; and be contented with so much liberty against other men, as he would allow other men against himself,"[20] yet "the Validity of Covenants begins not," and so interdependent action is impossible, "but with the Constitution of a Civill Power, sufficient to compell men to keep them."[21] Men recognize the rationality of entering society, but force, not reason, is required to keep them there.

Hobbesian man is unable to internalize the social requirement that he subordinate his direct pursuit of survival and well-being to the agreed pursuit of optimal outcomes which best ensure the survival and well-being of each person. Thus in our terms Hobbesian man actually remains in the state of nature; the civil power, the Sovereign, can effect only the appearance of civil society, of interdependent action. The real difference between the state of nature and civil society must be a difference in man, and not merely in the external relations of men.

While acknowledging Hobbes' masterful portrayal of the straightforward maximizer, we must offer a different conception of rational man. To the received conception of economic man, we must add Rousseau's recognition that the "passage from the state of nature to civil society produces in man a very

20 Hobbes, *Leviathan*, Chap. 14.

21 *Ibid.*, Chap. 15.

David Gauthier

remarkable change, in substituting justice for instinct in his conduct, and giving his actions the morality which previously they lacked."[22] This passage introduces the last of the concepts we must relate to the identification of rational activity with maximizing activity, the concept of morality. We must conclude by giving economic man a moral dimension.

In our argument, two contexts of action have been distinguished: independent action, in which each person determines his own principle of action, which has been identified with the state of nature, and interdependent action, in which all act on a common principle, which has been identified with civil society. The rational policy of independent action is individual utility-maximization; the rational policy of interdependent action is, or rather involves, agreed optimization. Both of these policies satisfy the condition of constrained maximization, which I have argued best expresses the identification of rational activity with maximizing activity. Only the first of these policies satisfies the more usual condition of straightforward maximization, which I have argued is inadequate because it rules out rational interdependent action. Economic man is usually assumed to accept the condition of straightforward maximization; if we are to continue to identify him with rational man, we must suppose instead that he accepts the condition of constrained maximization.

The policy of individual utility-maximization may be identified with prudence, provided we think of the prudent man as characterized by an exclusive and direct concern with what *he* wants, whatever that may be, and not necessarily by a concern for himself as the object of his wants. The policy of agreed optimization may be identified with morality. For if it be agreed that morality must be rational, or at least not anti-rational, and that morality involves some restraint in the pursuit of one's wants and desires, then agreed optimization is the only candidate. For on the condition of constrained maximization, it is rational to restrain one's pursuit of one's own aims only to fulfil an agreement to seek an optimal outcome unattainable by independent utility-maximization.

Morality may thus be placed within the bounds of the maximizing activity of economic man, given our enlarged conception of economic man, and yet distinguished from prudence, from the direct pursuit of one's wants and desires. The moral man is no less concerned with his own well-being than is the prudent man, but he recognizes that an exclusive attention to that well-being would prevent him from participation in mutually beneficial agreements.

We might then express the relation between prudence and morality accurately, if apparently paradoxically, by saying that the prudent man considers it rational to *become* moral, but not rational to *be* moral. On prudential grounds he can justify the adoption of moral, rather than prudential,

---

22 J-J Rousseau, *Du contrat social*, I, viii. Translation mine. Cf. also Kurt Baier, *The Moral Point of View*, pp. 311-315.

Reason and Max mization

grounds of action, but only if he does adopt moral grounds, and so becomes a moral man, can he justify a moral, rather than a prudential, policy of action.

In this essay I have not attempted to develop an adequate theory of either prudential or moral action. In situations in which men interact independently, rational persons with full knowledge will perform actions in mutual equilibrium, but I have not considered the problem of coordination, which arises in those situations in which there is more than one set of possible actions in mutual equilibrium. In situations in which men interact interdependently, rational persons with full knowledge will perform actions leading to an optimal outcome, but as I have indicated previously, I have not considered the problem of cooperation, or distributive justice, which arises in selecting a particular optimum.

We must not expect that an account of morality, based on agreed optimization, will necessarily resemble our existing conception of morality. There is little reason to suppose that our present conception has developed to correspond to rationality, conceived as identified in any way with utility-maximization. In particular, it is evident that morality, as agreed optimization, can concern only the production and distribution of those benefits which men can secure for themselves only by agreement; it can not concern those benefits which men can or could secure for themselves independently. Our present conception of morality is by no means limited in this respect.

The implications of a rational morality, given the identification of practical rationality with any form of maximization, have not, I think, been adequately understood by our utilitarian and contractarian moral theorists.[23] But these implications are in fact quite straightforward consequences of the conception of man with which this essay began. The morality, and the rationality, with which we have been concerned, are the morality and rationality of economic man, and it is to the adequacy of economic man, as our conception of what it is to be human, that we must turn if rationality as constrained maximization, and morality as agreed optimization, should seem questionable doctrines.

August 1974

---

23 John Rawls and R. M. Hare are two leading examples. For Rawls the identification is quite explicit; cf. *A Theory of Justice* (Cambridge, Mass., 1971), pp. 142-143. For Hare it is more difficult to document, but it is surely implicit; cf. *Freedom and Reason* (Oxford, 1963), Chaps. 6, 7, esp. pp. 92-93, 122-123. My paper "Justice and Natural Endowment, Etc.," referred to in footnote 19 *supra*, attempts to show Rawls failure to grasp the implications of rational morality. To show Hare's failure is certainly not the work of a footnote, but in a phrase, he goes astray because his universal prescriptivism conflates agent and patient; cf. V *supra*.

[11]

THE JOURNAL OF PHILOSOPHY

VOLUME LXXVII, NO. 9, SEPTEMBER 1980

━━━━━━━━━━━━━━━━┿ • ╼┿━━━━━━━━━━━━━━━━

KANTIAN CONSTRUCTIVISM IN MORAL THEORY *

RATIONAL AND FULL AUTONOMY

IN these lectures I examine the notion of a constructivist moral conception, or, more exactly, since there are different kinds of constructivism, one Kantian variant of this notion. The variant I discuss is that of justice as fairness, which is presented in my book *A Theory of Justice*.[1] I have two reasons for doing this: one is that it offers me the opportunity to consider certain aspects of the conception of justice as fairness which I have not previously emphasized and to set out more clearly the Kantian roots of that conception. The other reason is that the Kantian form of constructivism is much less well understood than other familiar traditional moral conceptions, such as utilitarianism, perfectionism, and intuitionism. I believe that this situation impedes the advance of moral theory. Therefore, it may prove useful simply to explain the distinctive features of Kantian constructivism, to say what it is, as illustrated by justice as fairness, without being concerned to defend it. To a degree that it is hard for me to estimate, my discussion assumes some

* Presented as three lectures, on Kantian Constructivism in Moral Theory, given at Columbia University in April, 1980; the first, "Rational and Full Autonomy," on April 14; the second, "Representation of Freedom and Equality," on April 15; the third, "Construction and Objectivity," on April 16. These lectures constitute the fourth series of John Dewey Lectures, which were established in 1967 to honor the late John Dewey, who had been from 1905 to 1930 a professor of philosophy at Columbia.

In revising these lectures for publication I should like to thank Burton Dreben for helpful discussion which has led to numerous improvements and clarifications, and also Joshua Cohen and Samuel Scheffler for valuable criticisms of an earlier version of material included in lectures I and III, originally prepared for the Howison Lecture at Berkeley in May 1979. As always, I am indebted, at many points, to Joshua Rabinowitz.

[1] Cambridge, Mass.: Harvard University Press, 1971. Hereafter referred to as TJ.

0022-362X/80/7709/0515$05.80

acquaintance with *A Theory of Justice*, but I hope that, for the most part, a bare familiarity with its main intuitive ideas will suffice; and what these are I note as we proceed.

I would like to think that John Dewey, in whose honor these lectures are given, would find their topic hospitable to his concerns. We tend to think of him as the founder of a characteristically American and instrumental naturalism and, thus, to lose sight of the fact that Dewey started his philosophical life, as many did in the late nineteenth century, greatly influenced by Hegel; and his genius was to adapt much that is valuable in Hegel's idealism to a form of naturalism congenial to our culture. It was one of Hegel's aims to overcome the many dualisms which he thought disfigured Kant's transcendental idealism, and Dewey shared this emphasis throughout his work, often stressing the continuity between things that Kant had sharply separated. This theme is present particularly in Dewey's early writings, where the historical origins of his thought are more in evidence.[2] In elaborating his moral theory along somewhat Hegelian lines, Dewey opposes Kant, sometimes quite explicitly, and often at the same places at which justice as fairness also departs from Kant. Thus there are a number of affinities between justice as fairness and Dewey's moral theory which are explained by the common aim of overcoming the dualisms in Kant's doctrine.

I

What distinguishes the Kantian form of constructivism is essentially this: it specifies a particular conception of the person as an element in a reasonable procedure of construction, the outcome of which determines the content of the first principles of justice. Expressed another way: this kind of view sets up a certain procedure of construction which answers to certain reasonable requirements, and within this procedure persons characterized as rational agents of construction specify, through their agreements, the first principles of justice. (I use 'reasonable' and 'rational' to express different notions throughout, notions which will be explained below, in section v, 528–530.) The leading idea is to establish a suitable connection between a particular conception of the person and first principles of justice, by means of a procedure of construction. In a Kantian view the conception of the person, the procedure, and the first prin-

---

[2] See, for example, Dewey's *Outlines of a Critical Theory of Ethics* (1891) and *The Study of Ethics: A Syllabus* (1894) reprinted in *John Dewey: The Early Works*, 1882–1898 (Carbondale: Southern Illinois University Press, 1971), in volumes 3 and 4, respectively. From Dewey's critique of Kant in *Outlines*, pp. 290–300, and his statement of his own form of the self-realization doctrine, pp. 300–327, Dewey's debt to idealism is plain enough.

ciples must be related in a certain manner—which, of course, admits of a number of variations. Justice as fairness is not, plainly, Kant's view, strictly speaking; it departs from his text at many points. But the adjective 'Kantian' expresses analogy and not identity; it means roughly that a doctrine sufficiently resembles Kant's in enough fundamental respects so that it is far closer to his view than to the other traditional moral conceptions that are appropriate for use as benchmarks of comparison.

On the Kantian view that I shall present, conditions for justifying a conception of justice hold only when a basis is established for political reasoning and understanding within a public culture. The social role of a conception of justice is to enable all members of society to make mutually acceptable to one another their shared institutions and basic arrangements, by citing what are publicly recognized as sufficient reasons, as identified by that conception. To succeed in doing this, a conception must specify admissible social institutions and their possible arrangements into one system, so that they can be justified to all citizens, whatever their social position or more particular interests. Thus, whenever a sufficient basis for agreement among citizens is not presently known, or recognized, the task of justifying a conception of justice becomes: how can people settle on a conception of justice, to serve this social role, that is (most) reasonable for them in virtue of how they conceive of their persons and construe the general features of social cooperation among persons so regarded?

Pursuing this idea of justification, we take our examination of the Kantian conception of justice as addressed to an impasse in our recent political history; the course of democratic thought over the past two centuries, say, shows that there is no agreement on the way basic social institutions should be arranged if they are to conform to the freedom and equality of citizens as moral persons. The requisite understanding of freedom and equality, which is implicit in the public culture of a democratic society, and the most suitable way to balance the claims of these notions, have not been expressed so as to meet general approval. Now a Kantian conception of justice tries to dispel the conflict between the different understandings of freedom and equality by asking: which traditionally recognized principles of freedom and equality, or which natural variations thereof, would free and equal moral persons themselves agree upon, if they were fairly represented solely as such persons and thought of themselves as citizens living a complete life in an on-going society? Their agreement, assuming an agreement would be reached, is conjectured to single out the most appropriate principles of freedom and equality and, therefore, to specify the principles of justice.

An immediate consequence of taking our inquiry as focused on the apparent conflict between freedom and equality in a democratic society is that we are not trying to find a conception of justice suitable for all societies regardless of their particular social or historical circumstances. We want to settle a fundamental disagreement over the just form of basic institutions within a democratic society under modern conditions. We look to ourselves and to our future, and reflect upon our disputes since, let's say, the Declaration of Independence. How far the conclusions we reach are of interest in a wider context is a separate question.

Hence, we should like to achieve among ourselves a practicable and working understanding on first principles of justice. Our hope is that there is a common desire for agreement, as well as a sufficient sharing of certain underlying notions and implicitly held principles, so that the effort to reach an understanding has some foothold. The aim of political philosophy, when it presents itself in the public culture of a democratic society, is to articulate and to make explicit those shared notions and principles thought to be already latent in common sense; or, as is often the case, if common sense is hesitant and uncertain, and doesn't know what to think, to propose to it certain conceptions and principles congenial to its most essential convictions and historical traditions. To justify a Kantian conception within a democratic society is not merely to reason correctly from given premises, or even from publicly shared and mutually recognized premises. The real task is to discover and formulate the deeper bases of agreement which one hopes are embedded in common sense, or even to originate and fashion starting points for common understanding by expressing in a new form the convictions found in the historical tradition by connecting them with a wide range of people's considered convictions: those which stand up to critical reflection. Now, as I have said, a Kantian doctrine joins the content of justice with a certain conception of the person; and this conception regards persons as both free and equal, as capable of acting both reasonably and rationally, and therefore as capable of taking part in social cooperation among persons so conceived. In addressing the public culture of a democratic society, Kantian constructivism hopes to invoke a conception of the person implicitly affirmed in that culture, or else one that would prove acceptable to citizens once it was properly presented and explained.

I should emphasize that what I have called the "real task" of justifying a conception of justice is not primarily an epistemological problem. The search for reasonable grounds for reaching agreement rooted in our conception of ourselves and in our relation to society replaces the search for moral truth interpreted as fixed by a prior and independent order of objects and relations, whether natural or divine, an order apart and distinct from how we conceive of ourselves. The task is to articulate a public conception of justice that all can live with who regard their person and their relation to society in a certain way. And though doing this may involve settling theoretical difficulties, the practical social task is primary. What justifies a conception of justice is not its being true to an order antecedent to and given to us, but its congruence with our deeper understanding of ourselves and our aspirations, and our realization that, given our history and the traditions embedded in our public life, it is the most reasonable doctrine for us. We can find no better basic charter for our social world. Kantian constructivism holds that moral objectivity is to be understood in terms of a suitably constructed social point of view that all can accept. Apart from the procedure of constructing the principles of justice, there are no moral facts. Whether certain facts are to be recognized as reasons of right and justice, or how much they are to count, can be ascertained only from within the constructive procedure, that is, from the undertakings of rational agents of construction when suitably represented as free and equal moral persons. (The points noted in this paragraph will be discussed in more detail in the third lecture.)

II

These first remarks were introductory and intended merely to suggest the themes of my discussion. To proceed, let's specify more exactly the above-mentioned impasse in our political culture as follows, namely, as a conflict between two traditions of democratic thought, one associated with Locke, the other with Rousseau. Using the distinction drawn by Benjamin Constant between the liberties of the moderns and the liberties of the ancients, the tradition derived from Locke gives pride of place to the former, that is, to the liberties of civic life, especially freedom of thought and conscience, certain basic rights of the person, and of property and association; while the tradition descending from Rousseau assigns priority to the equal political liberties and values of public life, and views the civic liberties as subordinate. Of course, this contrast is in many respects artificial and historically inaccurate; yet it serves to fix ideas and enables us to see that a mere splitting of the difference between these two traditions (even if we should agree on a favored interpretation of each) would be unsatisfactory. Somehow we must find a suitable rendering of freedom and equality, and of their relative priority, rooted in the more fundamental notions of our political life and congenial to our conception of the person.

But how are we to achieve this? Justice as fairness tries to uncover the fundamental ideas (latent in common sense) of freedom and equality, of ideal social cooperation and of the person, by formulating what I shall call "model-conceptions." We then reason within the framework of these conceptions, which need be defined only sharply enough to yield an acceptable public understanding of freedom and equality. Whether the doctrine that eventually results fulfills its purpose is then decided by how it works out: once stated, it must articulate a suitable conception of ourselves and of our relation to society, and connect this conception with workable first principles of justice, so that, after due consideration, we can acknowledge the doctrine proposed.

Now the two basic model-conceptions of justice as fairness are those of a *well-ordered society* and of a *moral person*. Their general purpose is to single out the essential aspects of our conception of ourselves as moral persons and of our relation to society as free and equal citizens. They depict certain general features of what a society would look like if its members publicly viewed themselves and their social ties with one another in a certain way. The *original position* is a third and mediating model-conception: its role is to establish the connection between the model-conception of a moral person and the principles of justice that characterize the relations of citizens in the model-conception of a well-ordered society. It serves this role by modeling the way in which the citizens in a well-ordered society, viewed as moral persons, would ideally select first principles of justice for their society. The constraints imposed on the parties in the original position, and the manner in which the parties are described, are to represent the freedom and equality of moral persons as understood in such a society. If certain principles of justice would indeed be agreed to (or if they would belong to a certain restricted family of principles), then the aim of Kantian constructivism to connect definite principles with a particular conception of the person is achieved.

For the present, however, I am concerned with the parties in the original position only as rationally autonomous agents of construction who (as such agents) represent the aspect of rationality, which is part of the conception of a moral person affirmed by citizens in a well-ordered society. The rational autonomy of the parties in the original position contrasts with the full autonomy of citizens in society. Thus *rational* autonomy is that of the parties as agents of construction: it is a relatively narrow notion, and roughly parallels Kant's notion of hypothetical imperatives (or the notion of rationality found in neo-classical economics); *full* autonomy is that of citizens in everyday life who think of themselves in a certain way and affirm and act from the first principles of justice that would be agreed to. In section v, I shall discuss the constraints imposed on the parties which enable the original position to represent the essential elements of full autonomy.

Let us briefly recall the features of a well-ordered society most relevant here.[3] First, such a society is effectively regulated by a public conception of justice; that is, it is a society in which every one accepts, and knows that others likewise accept, the same first principles of right and justice. It is also the case that the basic structure of society, the arrangement of its main institutions into one social scheme, actually satisfies, and is believed by all on good grounds to satisfy, these principles. Finally, the public principles of justice are themselves founded on reasonable beliefs as established by the society's generally accepted methods of inquiry; and the same is true of the application of these principles to judge social institutions.

Second, the members of a well-ordered society are, and view themselves and one another in their political and social relations (so far as these are relevant to questions of justice) as, free and equal moral persons. Here there are three distinct notions, specified independently: freedom, equality, and moral (as applied to) person. The members of a well-ordered society are moral persons in that, once they have reached the age of reason, each has, and views the others as having, an effective sense of justice, as well as an understanding of a conception of their good. Citizens are equal in that they regard one another as having an equal right to determine, and to assess upon due reflection, the first principles of justice by which the basic structure of their society is to be governed. Finally, the members of a well-ordered society are free in that they think they are entitled to make claims on the design of their common institutions in the name of their own fundamental aims and highest-order interests. At the same time, as free persons, they think of themselves not as inevitably tied to the pursuit of the particular final ends they have

---

[3] These features were not conveniently stated at any one place in TJ. In this and the next lectures I try to give a clearer and more systematic account of this notion and to indicate its basic role as a model-conception.

at any given time, but rather as capable of revising and changing
these ends on reasonable and rational grounds.

There are other features of a well-ordered society, such as its
stability with respect to its sense of justice, its existing under the
circumstances of justice, and so on. But these matters can be left
aside. The essential thing is that, when we formulate the model-
conception of the original position, we must view the parties as
selecting principles of justice which are to serve as effective public
principles of justice in a well-ordered society, and hence for social
cooperation among persons who conceive of themselves as free and
equal moral persons. Although this description of a well-ordered
society is formal, in that its elements taken alone do not imply a
specific content for the principles of justice, the description does
impose various conditions on how the original position can be set
up. In particular, the conception of moral persons as free and
equal, and the distinction between rational and full autonomy,
must be appropriately reflected in its description. Otherwise the
original position cannot fulfill its mediating role to connect a certain conception of the person with definite first principles by means
of a procedure in which the parties, as rationally autonomous agents
of construction, adopt principles of justice, the public affirmation
of which by citizens of a well-ordered society in every-day life enables them to be fully autonomous.

III

Let us descend from these abstractions, at least a bit, and turn to
a summary account of the original position. As I have said, justice
as fairness begins from the idea that the most appropriate conception of justice for the basic structure of a democratic society is one
that its citizens would adopt in a situation that is fair between them
and in which they are represented solely as free and equal moral
persons. This situation is the original position: we conjecture that
the fairness of the circumstances under which agreement is reached
transfers to the principles of justice agreed to; since the original
position situates free and equal moral persons fairly with respect
to one another, any conception of justice they adopt is likewise fair.
Thus the name: 'justice as fairness'.

In order to ensure that the original position is fair between individuals regarded solely as free and equal moral persons, we require
that, when adopting principles for the basic structure, the parties
be deprived of certain information; that is, they are behind what
I shall call a "veil of ignorance." For example, they do not know
their place in society, their class position, or social status, nor do

they know their fortune in the distribution of natural talents and abilities. It is assumed also that they do not know their conception of the good, that is, their particular final ends; nor finally, their own distinctive psychological dispositions and propensities, and the like. Excluding this information is required if no one is to be advantaged or disadvantaged by natural contingencies or social chance in the adoption of principles. Otherwise the parties would have disparate bargaining advantages that would affect the agreement reached. The original position would represent the parties not solely as free and equal moral persons, but instead as persons also affected by social fortune and natural accident. Thus, these and other limitations on information are necessary to establish fairness between the parties as free and equal moral persons and, therefore, to guarantee that it is as such persons that they agree to society's basic principles of justice.

Now the original position, as described, incorporates pure procedural justice at the highest level. This means that whatever principles the parties select from the list of alternative conceptions presented to them are just. Put another way, the outcome of the original position defines, let us say, the appropriate principles of justice. This contrasts with perfect procedural justice, where there is an independent and already given criterion of what is just (or fair) and where a procedure exists to ensure a result that satisfies this standard. This is illustrated by the familiar example of dividing a cake: if equal division is taken as fair, then we simply require the person who cuts it to have the last piece. (I forego the assumptions necessary to make the example airtight.) The essential feature of pure procedural justice, as opposed to perfect procedural justice, is that there exists no independent criterion of justice; what is just is defined by the outcome of the procedure itself.

One reason for describing the original position as incorporating pure procedural justice is that it enables us to explain how the parties, as the rational agents of construction, are also autonomous (as such agents). For the use of pure procedural justice implies that the principles of justice themselves are to be constructed by a process of deliberation, a process visualized as being carried out by the parties in the original position. The appropriate weight of considerations for and against various principles is given by the force of these considerations for the parties, and the force of all reasons on balance is expressed by the agreement made. Pure procedural justice in the original position allows that in their deliberations the parties are not required to apply, nor are they bound by, any antecedently given principles of right and justice. Or, put another way, there exists no standpoint external to the parties' own perspective from which they are constrained by prior and independent principles in questions of justice that arise among them as members of one society.

I call your attention to the following: I have said above that there is no standpoint external to the parties' own perspective from which they are bound in questions of justice that arise between them. Here the phrase 'between them' is significant. It signals the fact that I am leaving aside two important matters: questions of justice between societies (the law of nations), and our relations to the order of nature and to other living things. Both these questions are of first importance and immensely difficult; except in a few special cases, no attempt was made in *A Theory of Justice* to discuss these questions.[4] I shall simply proceed on the idea that we may reasonably begin with the basic structure of one society as a closed and self-sufficient system of cooperation. Should we find a suitable conception for this case, we can then work both inward to principles for associations and practices, and outward to the law of nations and order of nature itself. How far this can be done, and to what extent the conception of justice for the basic structure will have to be revised in the process, cannot be foreseen in advance. Here I merely wish to register these limitations of my discussion.

So far the autonomy of the parties is expressed by their being at liberty to agree to any conception of justice available to them as prompted by their rational assessment of which alternative is most likely to advance their interests. In their deliberations they are not required to apply, or to be guided by, any principles of right and justice, but are to decide as principles of rationality dictate, given their situation. But the propriety of the term 'autonomy' as applied to the parties also depends on what their interests are and on the nature of constraints to which they are subject. So let's review these matters.

IV

Recall that the parties are to adopt principles to serve as the effective public conception of justice for a well-ordered society. Now the citizens of such a society regard themselves as moral persons and as having a conception of the good (an ordered scheme of final ends) for the sake of which they think it proper to make claims on the design of their common institutions. So in the original position we

---

4 See TJ, §58, where several cases of conscientious refusal are considered in connection with the problem of just war. As for our relations with the order of nature, note the last paragraph of §77.

may describe the parties either as the representatives (or trustees) of persons with certain interests or as themselves moved by these interests. It makes no difference either way, although the latter is simpler and I shall usually speak in this vein.

To continue: we take moral persons to be characterized by two moral powers and by two corresponding highest-order interests in realizing and exercising these powers. The first power is the capacity for an effective sense of justice, that is, the capacity to understand, to apply and to act from (and not merely in accordance with) the principles of justice. The second moral power is the capacity to form, to revise, and rationally to pursue a conception of the good. Corresponding to the moral powers, moral persons are said to be moved by two highest-order interests to realize and exercise these powers. By calling these interests "highest-order" interests, I mean that, as the model-conception of a moral person is specified, these interests are supremely regulative as well as effective. This implies that, whenever circumstances are relevant to their fulfillment, these interests govern deliberation and conduct. Since the parties represent moral persons, they are likewise moved by these interests to secure the development and exercise of the moral powers.

In addition, I assume that the parties represent developed moral persons, that is, persons who have, at any given time, a determinate scheme of final ends, a particular conception of the good. Thus the model-conception defines moral persons as also determinate persons, although from the standpoint of the original position, the parties do not know the content of their conception of the good: its final ends. This conception yields a third interest that moves the parties: a higher-order interest in protecting and advancing their conception of the good as best they can, whatever it may be. The reason this is but a higher-order and not a highest-order interest is that, as we shall see later, it is in essential respects subordinate to the highest-order interests.

Now in view of these three regulative interests, the veil of ignorance poses a problem: how are we to set up the original position so that the parties, as representatives of persons with these interests, can make a rational agreement? It is at this point that the account of primary goods is introduced: by stipulating that the parties evaluate conceptions of justice by a preference for these goods, we endow them, as agents of construction, with sufficiently specific desires so that their rational deliberations reach a definite result. We look for social background conditions and general all-purpose means normally necessary for developing and exercising the two moral powers and for effectively pursuing a conception of the good. Thus a very brief explanation of the parties' preference for the primary goods enumerated in *A Theory of Justice* is this: [5]

(i) The basic liberties (freedom of thought and liberty of conscience, etc.) are the background institutions necessary for the development and exercise of the capacity to decide upon and revise, and rationally to pursue, a conception of the good. Similarly, these liberties allow for the development and exercise of the sense of right and justice under social conditions that are free.

(ii) Freedom of movement and free choice of occupation against a background of diverse opportunities are required for the pursuit of final ends, as well as to give effect to a decision to revise and change them, if one so desires.

(iii) Powers and prerogatives of offices and positions of responsibility are needed to give scope to various self-governing and social capacities of the self.

(iv) Income and wealth, understood broadly as they must be, are all-purpose means (having an exchange value) for achieving directly or indirectly almost any of our ends, whatever they happen to be.

(v) The social bases of self-respect are those aspects of basic institutions which are normally essential if individuals are to have a lively sense of their own worth as moral persons and to be able to realize their higher-order interests and advance their ends with zest and self-confidence.

Granted the correctness of these observations, the parties' preference for primary goods is rational. (I shall assume that in this context our intuitive notion of rationality suffices for our purposes here, and so I shan't discuss it until the next section.)

There are many points about primary goods which need to be examined. Here I mention only the leading idea, namely, that primary goods are singled out by asking which things are generally necessary as social conditions and all-purpose means to enable human beings to realize and exercise their moral powers and to pursue their final ends (assumed to lie within certain limits). Here we must look to social requirements and the normal circumstances of human life in a democratic society. Now note that the conception of moral persons as having certain specified highest-order interests selects what is to count as primary goods within the framework of the

---

[5] A fuller discussion can be found in Allen Buchanan, "Revisability and Rational Choice," *Canadian Journal of Philosophy*, v, 3 (November 1975): 395–408. For a more general account of which the use of primary goods is a special case, see T. M. Scanlon, "Preference and Urgency," this JOURNAL, LXXII, 19 (Nov. 6, 1975): 655–669.

model-conceptions. Thus these goods are not to be understood as general means essential for achieving whatever final ends a comprehensive empirical or historical survey might show people usually or normally to have in common under all social conditions. There may be few if any such ends; and those there are may not serve the purpose of constructing a conception of justice reasonable for us. The list of primary goods does not rest on that kind of general fact, although it does rely on general social facts, once the conception of the person and its highest-order interests are fixed. (Here I should comment that, by making the account of primary goods rest upon a particular conception of the person, I am revising the suggestions in *A Theory of Justice*, since there it can seem as if the list of primary goods is regarded as the outcome of a purely psychological, statistical, or historical inquiry.) [6]

What bearing do these remarks about primary goods have on our original question about rational autonomy? We observed that this autonomy surely depends in part upon the interests that move the parties and not solely on their being bound by no prior and independent principles of right. Were the parties moved solely by lower-order impulses, say for food and drink, or by certain particular affections for this or that group of persons, association, or community, we might think of them as heteronomous and not as autonomous. But at the basis of the desire for primary goods are the highest-order interests of moral personality and the need to secure one's conception of the good (whatever it is). Thus the parties are simply trying to guarantee and to advance the requisite conditions for exercising the powers that characterize them as moral persons. Certainly this motivation is neither heteronomous nor self-centered: we expect and indeed want people to care about their liberties and opportunities in order to realize these powers, and we think they show a lack of self-respect and weakness of character in not doing so. Thus the assumption that the parties are mutually disinterested and, hence, concerned to ensure their own highest-order interests (or those of the persons they represent) should not be confused with egoism.

In conclusion, then, the parties as rational agents of construction are described in the original position as autonomous in two re-

6 See, for example, §15, pp. 92 ff, where primary goods are first discussed at some length; and also pp. 142 f, 253, 260, and 433 f. The question whether the account of primary goods is a matter for social theory, or depends essentially on a conception of the person, is not discussed. I am grateful to Joshua Cohen, Joshua Rabinowitz, T. M. Scanlon, and Michael Teitelman for helpful criticism and clarification on this important point.

spects: first, in their deliberations they are not required to apply, or to be guided by, any prior and antecedent principles of right and justice. This is expressed by the use of pure procedural justice. Second, they are said to be moved solely by the highest-order interests in their moral powers and by their concern to advance their determinate but unknown final ends. The account of primary goods and its derivation convey this side of autonomy. Given the veil of ignorance, the parties can be prompted only by these highest-order interests, which they must, in turn, render specific by the preference for primary goods.

v

So much for the notion of rational autonomy of the parties as agents of construction. I now turn to the notion of full autonomy; although this notion is realized only by the citizens of a well-ordered society in the course of their daily lives, the essential features of it must nevertheless be represented in a suitable manner in the original position. For it is by affirming the first principles that would be adopted in this situation and by publicly recognizing the way in which they would be agreed to, as well as by acting from these principles as their sense of justice dictates, that citizens' full autonomy is achieved. We must ask, then, how the original position incorporates the requisite elements of full autonomy.

Now these elements are not expressed by how the parties' deliberations and motivation are described. The parties are merely artificial agents, and are presented not as fully but only as rationally autonomous. To explain full autonomy, let us note two elements of any notion of social cooperation. The first is a conception of the *fair terms of cooperation*, that is, terms each participant may reasonably be expected to accept, provided that everyone else likewise accepts them. Fair terms of cooperation articulate an idea of reciprocity and mutuality: all who cooperate must benefit, or share in common burdens, in some appropriate fashion as judged by a suitable benchmark of comparison. This element in social cooperation I call the *Reasonable*. The other element corresponds to the *Rational:* it expresses a conception of each participant's rational advantage, what, as individuals, they are trying to advance. As we have seen, the rational is interpreted by the original position in reference to the desire of persons to realize and to exercise their moral powers and to secure the advancement of their conception of the good. Given a specification of the parties' highest-order interests, they are rational in their deliberations to the extent that sensible principles of rational choice guide their decisions. Familiar examples of such principles are: the adoption of effective means to ends; the balancing of final ends by their significance for our plan of life as a whole and by the extent to which these ends cohere with and support each other; and finally, the assigning of a greater weight to the more likely consequences; and so on. Although there seems to be no one best interpretation of rationality, the difficulties in explaining Kantian constructivism do not lie here. Thus I ignore these matters, and focus on the more obscure notion of the Reasonable and how it is represented in the original position.

This representing is done essentially by the nature of the constraints within which the parties' deliberations take place and which define their circumstances with respect to one another. The Reasonable is incorporated into the background setup of the original position which frames the discussions of the parties and situates them symmetrically. More specifically, in addition to various familiar formal conditions on first principles, such as generality and universality, ordering and finality, the parties are required to adopt a public conception of justice and must assess its first principles with this condition in mind. (I shall say more about the publicity condition in the next lecture.)

Again, the veil of ignorance implies that persons are represented solely as moral persons and not as persons advantaged or disadvantaged by the contingencies of their social position, the distribution of natural abilities, or by luck and historical accident over the course of their lives. As a result they are situated equally as moral persons, and in this sense fairly. Here I appeal to the idea that, in establishing the truly basic terms of social cooperation, the possession of the minimum adequate powers of moral personality (the powers that equip us to be normally cooperating members of society over a complete life) is the sole relevant characteristic. This presumption, plus the precept that equals in all relevant respects are to be represented equally, ensures that the original position is fair.

The last constraint I shall mention here is this: the stipulation that the first subject of justice is the basic structure of society, that is, the main social institutions and how they cohere together into one system, supports situating the parties equally and restricting their information by the veil of ignorance. For this stipulation requires the parties to assess alternative conceptions as providing first principles of what we may call *background justice:* it is only if the basic structure satisfies the requirements of background justice that a society treats its members as equal moral persons. Otherwise, its fundamental regulative arrangements do not answer to principles its citizens would adopt when fairly represented solely as such persons.

Let us pull together these remarks as follows: the Reasonable presupposes and subordinates the Rational. It defines the fair terms of cooperation acceptable to all within some group of separately identifiable persons, each of whom possesses and can exercise the two moral powers. All have a conception of their good which defines their rational advantage, and everyone has a normally effective sense of justice: a capacity to honor the fair terms of cooperation. The Reasonable presupposes the Rational, because, without conceptions of the good that move members of the group, there is no point to social cooperation nor to notions of right and justice, even though such cooperation realizes values that go beyond what conceptions of the good specify taken alone. The Reasonable subordinates the Rational because its principles limit, and in a Kantian doctrine limit absolutely, the final ends that can be pursued.

Thus, in the original position we view the Reasonable as expressed by the framework of constraints within which the deliberations of the parties (as rationally autonomous agents of construction) take place. Representative of these constraints are the condition of publicity, the veil of ignorance and the symmetry of the parties' situation with respect to one another, and the stipulation that the basic structure is the first subject of justice. Familiar principles of justice are examples of reasonable principles, and familiar principles of rational choice are examples of rational principles. The way the Reasonable is represented in the original position leads to the two principles of justice. These principles are constructed by justice as fairness as the content of the Reasonable for the basic structure of a well-ordered society.

VI

This concludes my account of the distinction between Rational and Full Autonomy and explains how these notions are expressed in the original position. In certain respects, however, the contrast between the Reasonable and the Rational, as drawn in the last two paragraphs, is too stark and may give a misleading impression of how these notions are to be understood. By way of clarification, I consider an objection which parallels the criticism Schopenhauer made against Kant's doctrine of the Categorical Imperative.[7] You will

---

[7] See *On the Basis of Ethics* (1840), Part II, §7, E. F. J. Payne, trans. (New York: Liberal Arts Press, 1965), pp. 89–92. I am indebted to Joshua Cohen for pointing out to me that my previous reply to this criticism misses the force of Schopenhauer's objection. See TJ, pp. 147 f. Thanks to him, I believe the reply in the text is better and connects with the revised account of primary goods. I am indebted also to Stephen Darwall's "A Defense of the Kantian Interpretation," *Ethics*, LXXXVI, 2 (January 1976): 164–170.

recall that Schopenhauer maintained that, in arguing for the duty of mutual aid in situations of distress (the fourth example in the *Grundlegung*), Kant appeals to what rational agents, as finite beings with needs, can consistently will to be universal law. In view of our° need for love and sympathy, on at least some occasions, we cannot will a social world in which others are always indifferent to our pleas in such cases. From this Schopenhauer claimed that Kant's view is at bottom egoistic, from which it follows that it is but a disguised form of heteronomy after all.

Here I am concerned not to defend Kant against this criticism but to point out why the parallel objection to justice as fairness is incorrect. To this end, observe that there are, offhand, two things that prompt Schopenhauer's objection. First, he believes that Kant asks us to test maxims in the light of their general consequences for our natural inclinations and needs, when these maxims are made universal laws, and that these inclinations and needs are viewed egoistically. Second, the rules that define the procedure for testing maxims Schopenhauer interprets as external constraints, imposed so to speak from the outside by the limitations of our situation, which we should like to surmount, and not derived from the essential features of ourselves as moral persons. These two considerations lead Schopenhauer to say that the categorical imperative is a principle of reciprocity which egoism cunningly accepts as a compromise; as such a principle, it may be appropriate for a confederation of nation states but not as a moral principle.

Now consider the parallel criticism of justice as fairness in regard to these two points. Concerning the first, though it is indeed true that the parties in the original position are mutually disinterested and evaluate principles of justice in terms of primary goods, they are moved in the first instance by their highest-order interests in developing and exercising their moral powers; and the list of primary goods, and the index of these goods, is to be explained so far as possible by reference to these interests. Since these interests may be taken to specify their needs as moral persons, the parties' aims are not egoistic, but entirely fitting and proper. It accords with the conception of free personality held in a democratic society that citizens should secure the conditions for realizing and exercising their moral powers, as well as the social bases and means of their self-respect. This contrasts with Schopenhauer's presumption that in Kant's doctrine maxims are tested by their consequences for the fulfillment of the agent's natural inclinations and needs.

Turning to the second point, what I have called "the constraints imposed on the parties in the original position" are indeed external to the parties as rational agents of construction. Nevertheless, these constraints express the Reasonable and, therefore, the formal conditions implicit in the moral powers of the members of a well-ordered society, whom the parties represent. This contrasts with Schopenhauer's second presumption that the constraints of the categorical imperative derive from the limitations of our finite nature, which, prompted by our natural inclinations, we should like to overcome. In justice as fairness, the Reasonable frames the Rational and is derived from a conception of moral persons as free and equal. Once this is understood, the constraints of the original position are no longer external. Thus neither basis for Schopenhauer's objection applies.

Finally, the way in which the Reasonable frames the Rational in the original position represents a feature of the unity of practical reason. In Kant's terms, empirical practical reason is represented by the rational deliberations of the parties; pure practical reason is represented by the constraints within which these deliberations take place. The unity of practical reason is expressed by defining the Reasonable to frame the Rational and to subordinate it absolutely; that is, the principles of justice that are agreed to are lexically prior in their application in a well-ordered society to claims of the good. This means, among other things, that the principles of justice and the rights and liberties they define cannot, in such a society, be overridden by considerations of efficiency and a greater net balance of social well-being. This illustrates one feature of the unity of reason: the Reasonable and the Rational are unified within one scheme of practical reasoning which establishes the strict priority of the Reasonable with respect to the Rational. This priority of the right over the good is characteristic of Kantian constructivism.

Now in a well-ordered society we stipulate that the justification of the principles of justice as the outcome of the original position is publicly understood. So not only do citizens have a highest-order desire, their sense of justice, to act from the principles of justice, but they understand these principles as issuing from a construction in which their conception of themselves as free and equal moral persons who are both reasonable and rational is adequately represented. By acting from these principles, and affirming them in public life, as so derived, they express their full autonomy. The rational autonomy of the parties is merely that of artificial agents who inhabit a construction designed to model this more inclusive conception. It is the inclusive conception which expresses the ideal to be realized in our social world.

It is natural to reply that, all the same, fully autonomous citizens in a well-ordered society act from some desire, and so are still heteronomous, since they are not moved by reason alone.[8] To this the answer is that a Kantian view does not deny that we act from some desire. What is of moment is the kinds of desires from which we act and how they are ordered; that is, how these desires originate within and are related to the self, and the way their structure and priority are determined by principles of justice connected with the conception of the person we affirm. The mediating conception of the original position enables us to connect certain definite principles of justice with a certain conception of free and equal moral persons. Given this connection, an effective sense of justice, the desire to act from the principles of justice, is not a desire on the same footing with natural inclinations; it is an executive and regulative highest-order desire to act from certain principles of justice in view of their connection with a conception of the person as free and equal. And that desire is not heteronomous: for whether a desire is heteronomous is settled by its mode of origin and role within the self and by what it is a desire for. In this case the desire is to be a certain kind of person specified by the conception of fully autonomous citizens of a well-ordered society.

VII

I conclude with a few observations which may help to keep in focus the discussion so far. First, it is important to distingush three points of view: that of the parties in the original position, that of citizens in a well-ordered society, and finally, that of ourselves—you and me who are examining justice as fairness as a basis for a conception of justice that may yield a suitable understanding of freedom and equality.

The first two points of view occur within the doctrine of justice as parts of two of its model-conceptions. Whereas the conceptions of a well-ordered society and of moral persons are fundamental, the original position is the mediating conception once we stipulate that the parties as rational agents of construction are subject to reasonable constraints and are to view themselves as adopting principles to serve as the public conception of justice for a well-ordered society. The intent of justice as fairness is badly misunderstood if the deliberations of the parties and their rational autonomy are confused with full autonomy. Full autonomy is a moral ideal and part of the more comprehensive ideal of a well-ordered society. Rational autonomy is not, as such, an ideal at all, but a device of representa-

---

[8] This seems to be the view of Oliver A. Johnson in his reply to Darwall, see fn 7 above. See *Ethics*, LXXXVII, 3 (April 1977): 251–259, p. 253 f.

tion used to connect the conception of the person with definite principles of justice. (Of course, this is not to deny that rational deliberation, suitably circumscribed, is an aspect of the ideal of full autonomy.)

The third point of view—that of you and me—is that from which justice as fairness, and indeed any other doctrine, is to be assessed. Here the test is that of general and wide reflective equilibrium, that is, how well the view as a whole meshes with and articulates our more firm considered convictions, at all levels of generality, after due examination, once all adjustments and revisions that seem compelling have been made. A doctrine that meets this criterion is the doctrine that, so far as we can now ascertain, is the most reasonable for us.

A final observation: it is also useful to distinguish between the roles of a conception of the person and of a theory of human nature.[9] In justice as fairness these ideas are distinct elements and enter at different places. For one thing, the conception of the person is a companion moral ideal paired with that of a well-ordered society. Like any other ideal, it must be possible for people to honor it sufficiently closely; and hence the feasible ideals of the person are limited by the capacities of human nature and the requirements of social life. To this extent such an ideal presupposes a theory of human nature, and social theory generally, but the task of a moral doctrine is to specify an appropriate conception of the person that general facts about human nature and society allow. Starting from the assumption that full autonomy is a feasible ideal for political life, we represent its various aspects in the original position under the headings of the Reasonable and the Rational. Thus this ideal is mirrored in how this position is set up.

A theory of human nature, by contrast, appears in the general facts available to the parties for them to use in assessing the consequences of the various principles of justice and so in deciding which principles are best able to secure their highest-order interests and to lead to a well-ordered society that is stable with respect to its public conception of justice. When we formulate justice as fairness from the third point of view, we supply the parties with the requisite general facts that we take to be true, or true enough, given the state of public knowledge in our society. The agreement of the parties is relative, then, to these beliefs. There is no other way to proceed, since we must start from where we are. But, leaving this

---

[9] I am indebted to Norman Daniels for clarification of this point.

aside, the point is that a theory of human nature is not part of the framework of the original position, except as such theories limit the feasibility of the ideals of person and society embedded in that framework. Rather, a theory of human nature is an element to be filled in, depending upon the general facts about human beings and the workings of society which we allow to the parties in their deliberations.

In this lecture I have focused on the distinction between rational and full autonomy and have said very little about the notions of the freedom and equality of persons, and even less about how these notions are represented in the original position. These matters I consider in the next lecture.

[12]

CONSTRUCTION AND OBJECTIVITY

IN the preceding lectures I sketched the main idea of Kantian constructivism, which is to establish a connection between the first principles of justice and the conception of moral persons as free and equal. These first principles are used to settle the appropriate understanding of freedom and equality for a modern democratic society. The requisite connection is provided by a procedure of construction in which rationally autonomous agents subject to reasonable conditions agree to public principles of justice. With the sketch of these ideas behind us, I consider in this final lecture how a Kantian doctrine interprets the notion of objectivity in terms of a suitably constructed social point of view that is authoritative with respect to all individual and associational points of view. This rendering of objectivity implies that, rather than think of the principles of justice as true, it is better to say that they are the principles most reasonable for us, given our conception of persons as free and equal, and fully cooperating members of a democratic society. [Here 'reasonable' is used, as explained later (569/70), in contrast with 'true' as understood in rational intuitionism, and not, as previously (528–530), with 'rational', as in the notion of rational autonomy.]

I

To fix ideas, let's look back roughly a hundred years to Henry Sidgwick. *The Methods of Ethics* (first edition 1874) is, I believe, the outstanding achievement in modern moral theory.[1] By "moral theory" I mean the systematic and comparative study of moral conceptions, starting with those which historically and by current estimation seem to be the most important. Moral philosophy includes moral theory, but takes as its main question justification and how it is to be conceived and resolved; for example, whether it is to be conceived as an epistemological problem (as in rational intuitionism) or as a practical problem (as in Kantian constructivism). Sidgwick's *Methods* is the first truly academic work in moral theory,

[1] On Sidgwick now, see the comprehensive work by J. B. Schneewind, *Sidgwick's Ethics and Modern Victorian Moral Philosophy* (New York: Oxford, 1977).

CONSTRUCTION AND OBJECTIVITY   555

modern in both method and spirit. Treating ethics as a discipline
to be studied like any other branch of knowledge, it defines and
carries out in exemplary fashion, if not for the first time, some of
the comprehensive comparisons that constitute moral theory. By
pulling together the work of previous writers, and through its influence on G. E. Moore and others, this work defined much of the
framework of subsequent moral philosophy. Sidgwick's originality
lies in his conception and mode of presentation of the subject and
in his recognition of the significance of moral theory for moral
philosophy.

It is natural, then, that the limitations of *Methods* have been as
important as its merits. Of these limitations I wish to mention two.
First, Sidgwick gives relatively little attention to the conception of
the person and the social role of morality as main parts of a moral
doctrine. He starts with the idea of a method of ethics as a method
specified by certain first principles, principles by which we are to
arrive at a judgment about what we ought to do. He takes for
granted that these methods aim at reaching true judgments that
hold for all rational minds. Of course, he thinks it is best to approach the problem of justification only when a broad understanding of moral theory has been achieved. In the preface of the first
edition of *Methods* he explains that he wants to resist the natural
urgency to discover the true method of ascertaining what it is right
to do. He wishes instead to expound, from a neutral position and
as impartially as possible, the different methods found in the moral
consciousness of humankind and worked into familiar historical
systems.[2] But these detailed expositions—necessary as they are—are
merely preparation for comparing the various methods and evaluating them by criteria that any rational method that aims at truth
must satisfy.

But a consequence of starting with methods of ethics defined as
methods that seek truth is not only that it interprets justification as
an epistemological problem, but also that it is likely to restrict attention to the first principles of moral conceptions and how they can
be known. First principles are however only one element of a moral
conception; of equal importance are its conception of the person and
its view of the social role of morality. Until these other elements
are clearly recognized, the ingredients of a constructivist doctrine
are not at hand. It is characteristic of Sidgwick's *Methods* that the
social role of morality and the conception of the person receive

[2] *The Methods of Ethics* (London: Macmillan 1907), 7th ed., pp. v–vi; parenthetical page references to Sidgwick are to this book, this edition.

little notice. And so the possibility of constructivism was closed to him.

Sidgwick overlooked this possibility because of a second limitation: he failed to recognize that Kant's doctrine (and perfectionism also for that matter) is a distinctive method of ethics. He regarded the categorical imperative as a purely formal principle, or what he called "the principle of equity": whatever is right for one person is right for all similar persons in relevantly similar circumstances. This principle Sidgwick accepts, but, since it is plainly not a sufficient basis for a moral view, Kant's doctrine could not be counted a substantive method (209/10). This formal reading of Kant, together with the dismissal of perfectionism, led Sidgwick to reduce the traditional moral conceptions essentially to three main methods: rational egoism, (pluralistic) intuitionism, and classical utilitarianism. Surely he was right to restrict himself to a few conceptions so that each could be explored in considerable detail. Only in this way can depth of understanding be achieved. But rational egoism, which he accepted as a method of ethics, is really not a moral conception at all, but rather a challenge to all such conceptions, although no less interesting for that. Left with only (pluralistic) intuitionism and classical utilitarianism as methods of ethics in the usual sense, it is no surprise that utilitarianism seemed superior to Sidgwick, given his desire for unity and system in a moral doctrine.

Since Kant's view is the leading historical example of a constructivist doctrine, the result once again is that constructivism finds no place in *Methods*. Nor is the situation altered if we include another leading representative work, F. H. Bradley's *Ethical Studies* (first edition 1876); following Hegel, Bradley likewise regarded Kant's ethics as purely formal and lacking in content and, therefore, to be assigned to an early stage of the dialectic as an inadequate view.[3] The result of these formal interpretations of Kant is that constructivism was not recognized as a moral conception to be studied and assimilated into moral theory. Nor was this lack made good in the first half of this century; for in this period, beginning with Moore's *Principia Ethica* (1903), interest centered mainly on philosophical analysis and its bearing on justification regarded as an epistemological problem and on the question whether its conclusions support or deny the notion of moral truth. During this time, however, utilitarianism and intuitionism made important advances. A proper understanding of Kantian constructivism, on a par with our grasp of these views, is still to be achieved.

[3] See Essay IV: "Duty for Duty's Sake," 2nd ed. (New York: Oxford, 1927).

II

Let us now try to deepen our understanding of Kantian constructivism by contrasting it with what I shall call *rational intuitionism*. This doctrine has, of course, been expressed in various ways; but in one form or another it dominated moral philosophy from Plato and Aristotle onwards until it was challenged by Hobbes and Hume, and, I believe, in a very different way by Kant. To simplify matters, I take rational intuitionism to be the view exemplified in the English tradition by Clarke and Price, Sidgwick and Moore, and formulated in its minimum essentials by W. D. Ross.[4] With qualifications, it was accepted by Leibniz and Wolff in the guise of perfectionism, and Kant knows of it in this form.

For our purposes here, rational intuitionism may be summed up by two theses: first, the basic moral concepts of the right and the good, and the moral worth of persons, are not analyzable in terms of nonmoral concepts (although possibly analyzable in terms of one another); and, second, first principles of morals (whether one or many), when correctly stated, are self-evident propositions about what kinds of considerations are good grounds for applying one of the three basic moral concepts, that is, for asserting that something is (intrinsically) good, or that a certain action is the right thing to do, or that a certain trait of character has moral worth. These two theses imply that the agreement in judgment which is so essential for an effective public conception of justice is founded on the recognition of self-evident truths about good reasons. And what these reasons are is fixed by a moral order that is prior to and independent of our conception of the person and the social role of morality. This order is given by the nature of things and is known, not by sense, but by rational intuition. It is with this idea of moral truth that the idea of first principles as reasonable will be contrasted.

It should be observed that rational intuitionism is compatible with a variety of contents for the first principles of a moral conception. Even classical utilitarianism, which Sidgwick was strongly inclined to favor (although he could not see how to eliminate rational egoism as a rival) was sometimes viewed by him as following from

---

4 See *The Right and the Good* (Oxford: The Clarendon Press, 1930), esp. chs. 1–2. I shall adopt Ross's characterization of rational intuitionism, adjusted to allow for any number of first principles and, thus, as fitting either single-principle or pluralistic intuitionism. I should add that, for my purposes here, I interpret Aristotle's view as combining teleological and metaphysical perfectionism. Although this may not be a sound interpretation in the light of contemporary scholarship, it suits well enough how Aristotle was interpreted up to Kant's time.

three principles each self-evident in its own right.[5] In brief, these three propositions were: the principle of equity so-called: that it cannot be right to treat two different persons differently merely on the ground of their being numerically different individuals; a principle of rational prudence: that mere difference of position in time is not by itself a reasonable ground for giving more regard to well-being at one moment than to well-being at another; and a principle of rational benevolence: the good of one person is of no more importance from the point of view of the universe than the good of any other person. These three principles, when combined with the principle that, as reasonable beings, we are bound to aim at good generally and not at any particular part of it, Sidgwick thought yielded the principle of utility: namely, to maximize the net balance of happiness. And this principle, like those from which it followed, he was tempted to hold as self-evident.

Of all recent versions of rational intuitionism, the appeal to self-evidence is perhaps most striking in Moore's so-called "ideal utilitarianism" in *Principia Ethica* (1903). A consequence of Moore's principle of organic unity is that his view is extremely pluralistic; there are few if any useful first principles, and distinct kinds of cases are to be decided by intuition as they arise. Moore held a kind of Platonic atomism: [6] moral concepts (along with other concepts) are subsisting and independent entities grasped by the mind. That pleasure and beauty are good, and that different combinations of them alone or together with other good things are also good, and to what degree, are truths known by intuition: by seeing with the mind's eye how these separate and distinct objects (universals) are (timelessly) related. This picture is even more vivid in the early philosophy of mathematics of Bertrand Russell, who talks of searching for the indefinable concepts of mathematics with a mental telescope (as one might look for a planet).[7]

Now my aim in recalling these matters is to point out that rational intuitionism, as illustrated by Sidgwick, Moore, and Ross, is sharply opposed to a constructivist conception along Kantian lines. That Kant would have rejected Hume's psychological naturalism as heteronomous is clear.[8] I believe that the contrast with

[5] *Methods*, Book III, ch. 13, pp. 379–389. See Schneewind's discussion, ch. 10, pp. 286–309.

[6] I borrow this expression from Peter Hylton's discussion, *The Origins of Analytic Philosophy*, ch. 3 (Dissertation: Harvard University, 1978).

[7] See *The Principles of Mathematics* (London: Allen & Unwin, 1937), 2nd ed. (1st ed. 1903), pp. xv–xvi. The analogy of the mental telescope is Russell's.

[8] Because it formulates definitions of the basic moral concepts in terms of

CONSTRUCTION AND OBJECTIVITY   559

rational intuitionism, no matter what the content of the view (whether utilitarian, perfectionist, or pluralist) is even more instructive. It is less obvious that for Kant rational intuitionism is also heteronomous. The reason is that from the first thesis of rational intuitionism, the basic moral concepts are conceptually independent of natural concepts, and first principles are independent of the natural world and, as grasped by rational intuition, are regarded as synthetic a priori. This may seem to make these principles not heteronomous. Yet it suffices for heteronomy that these principles obtain in virtue of relations among objects the nature of which is not affected or determined by the conception of the person. Kant's idea of autonomy requires that there exist no such order of given objects determining the first principles of right and justice among free and equal moral persons. Heteronomy obtains not only when first principles are fixed by the special psychological constitution of human nature, as in Hume, but also when they are fixed by an order of universals or concepts grasped by rational intuition, as in Plato's realm of forms or in Leibniz's hierarchy of perfections.[9] Perhaps I should add, to prevent misunderstanding, that a Kantian doctrine of autonomy need not deny that the procedures by which first principles are selected are synthetic a priori. This thesis, however, must be properly interpreted. The essential idea is that such procedures must be suitably founded on practical reason, or, more exactly, on notions which characterize persons as reasonable and rational and which are incorporated into the way in which, as such

nonmoral concepts, this being the mode of identifying those facts which are to count as good reasons in applying the basic moral concepts, naturalism is a form of heteronomy from the Kantian standpoint. The various definitions, presumably arrived at by the analysis of concepts, convert moral judgments into statements about the world on all fours with those of science and common sense. Therefore, these definitions, combined with the natural order itself, now come to constitute the moral order, which is prior to and independent from our conception of ourselves as free and equal moral persons. If time permitted, this could be substantiated by setting out, for example, the details of Hume's view (as often interpreted) and of Bentham's hedonistic utilitarianism, at least once these views are expressed in the requisite naturalistic format. (Rational intuitionism tries to secure a kind of independence of the moral order from the order of nature.)

[9] This fundamental contention is unfortunately obscured by the fact that although in the *Grundlegung* Kant classifies the view of Leibniz and Wolff as a form of heteronomy, his criticism of it is that it is circular and therefore empty. See Academy Edition, p. 443. Much the same happens in the *Second Critique*, Academy Edition, p. 41, where Kant argues that the notion of perfection in practical reasoning means fitness for any given ends and therefore is again empty until these ends are specified independently. These arguments give the erroneous impression that, if perfectionism had sufficient content, it would be compatible with autonomy.

persons, they represent to themselves their free and equal moral personality. Put another way, first principles of justice must issue from a conception of the person through a suitable representation of that conception as illustrated by the procedure of construction in justice as fairness.

Thus in a Kantian doctrine a relatively complex conception of the person plays a central role. By contrast, rational intuitionism requires but a sparse notion of the person, founded on the self as knower. This is because the content of first principles is already fixed, and the only requirements on the self are to be able to know what these principles are and to be moved by this knowledge. A basic assumption is that the recognition of first principles as true and self-evident gives rise, in a being capable of rationally intuiting these principles, to a desire to act from them for their own sake. Moral motivation is defined by reference to desires that have a special kind of cause, namely, the intuitive grasp of first principles.[10] This sparse conception of the person joined with its moral psychology characterizes the rational intuitionism of Sidgwick, Moore, and Ross, although there is nothing that forces rational intuitionism to so thin a notion. The point is rather that, in rational intuitionism in contrast to a Kantian view, since the content of first principles is already given, a more complex conception of the person, of a kind adequate to determine the content of these principles, together with a suitable moral psychology, is simply unnecessary.

III

Having contrasted Kantian constructivism to rational intuitionism with respect to the idea of a moral order that is prior to and independent from our conception of the person, I now consider a second contrast, namely, how each regards the inevitable limitations that constrain our moral deliberations. The constructionist view accepts from the start that a moral conception can establish but a loose framework for deliberation which must rely very considerably on our powers of reflection and judgment. These powers are not fixed once and for all, but are developed by a shared public culture and hence shaped by that culture. In justice as fairness this means that the principles adopted by the parties in the original position are designed by them to achieve a public and workable agreement on matters of social justice which suffices for effective and fair social cooperation. From the standpoint of the parties as agents of construction, the first principles of justice are not thought to represent,

[10] See, for example, *Methods*, pp. 23–28, 34–37, 39 f, read together with the discussion of the self-evident basis of the principle of utility, cited in fn 5 above.

or to be true of, an already given moral order, as rational intuitionism supposes. The essential point is that a conception of justice fulfills its social role provided that citizens equally conscientious and sharing roughly the same beliefs find that, by affirming the framework of deliberation set up by it, they are normally led to a sufficient convergence of opinion. Thus a conception of justice is framed to meet the practical requirements of social life and to yield a public basis in the light of which citizens can justify to one another their common institutions. Such a conception need be only precise enough to achieve this result.

On the constructivist view, the limitations that constrain our moral deliberations affect the requirements of publicity and support the use of priority rules. These limitations also lead us to take the basic structure of a well-ordered society as the first subject of justice and to adopt the primary goods as the basis of interpersonal comparisons. To begin with publicity: at the end of the preceding lecture I mentioned why in a constructivist view first principles are to satisfy the requirements of publicity. The moral conception is to have a wide social role as a part of public culture and is to enable citizens to appreciate and accept the conception of the person as free and equal. Now if it is to play this wide role, a conception's first principles cannot be so complex that they cannot be generally understood and followed in the more important cases. Thus, it is desirable that knowing whether these principles are satisfied, at least with reference to fundamental liberties and basic institutions, should not depend on information difficult to obtain or hard to evaluate. To incorporate these desiderata in a constructivist view, the parties are assumed to take these considerations into account and to prefer (other things equal) principles that are easy to understand and simple to apply. The gain in compliance and willing acceptance by citizens more than makes up for the rough and ready nature of the guiding framework that results and its neglect of certain distinctions and differences. In effect, the parties agree to rule out certain facts as irrelevant in questions of justice concerning the basic structure, even though they recognize that in regard to other cases it may be appropriate to appeal to them. From the standpoint of the original position, eliminating these facts as reasons of social justice sufficiently increases the capacity of the conception to fulfill its social role. Of course, we should keep in mind that the exclusion of such facts as reasons of social justice does not alone entail that they are not reasons in other kinds of situation where different moral notions apply. Indeed, it is not even ruled out that the account of some notions should be constructivist, whereas the account of others is not.

It is evident, then, why a constructivist view such as justice as fairness incorporates into the framework of moral deliberation a number of schematic and practical distinctions as ways that enable us to deal with the inevitable limitations of our moral capacities and the complexity of our social circumstances. The need for such distinctions supports and helps to account for the use of certain priority rules to settle the relative weight of particular kinds of grounds in extremely important cases. Two such rules in justice as fairness are: first, the priority of justice over efficiency (in the sense of Pareto) and the net balance of advantages (summed over all individuals in society), and second, the priority of the principle of equal liberty (understood in terms of certain enumerated basic liberties) over the second principle of justice.[11] These rules are introduced to handle the complexity of the many prima facie reasons we are ready to cite in everyday life; and their plausibility depends in large part on the first principles to which they are adjoined. But although these rules are intended to narrow the scope of judgment in certain fundamental questions of justice, this scope can never be entirely eliminated, and for many other questions sharp and definite conclusions cannot usually be derived. Sharp and definite conclusions are not needed, however, if sufficient agreement is still forthcoming (TJ 44/5).

Similar considerations apply in beginning with the basic structure of a well-ordered society as the first subject of justice and trying to develop a conception of justice for this case alone. The idea is that this structure plays a very special role in society by establishing what we may call *background justice;* and if we can find suitable first principles of background justice, we may be able to exclude enough other considerations as irrelevant for this case, so as to develop a reasonably simple and workable conception of justice for the basic structure. The further complexities of everyday cases that cannot be ignored in a more complete moral conception may be dealt with later in the less general situations that occur within the various associations regulated by the basic structure, and in that sense subordinate to it.[12]

Finally, parallel observations hold in finding a feasible basis for

11 For a statement of these principles and priority rules, see TJ, pp. 60–62, 250, 302/3.
12 See "The Basic Structure as Subject," in A. I. Goldman and Jaegwon Kim, eds., *Values and Morals* (Boston: Reidel, 1978), especially secs. IV–V, pp. 52–57.

interpersonal comparisons of well-being relevant for questions of justice that arise in regard to the basic structure. These comparisons are to be made in terms of primary goods (as defined in the first lecture), which are, so far as possible, certain public features of social institutions and of people's situations with respect to them, such as their rights, liberties, and opportunities, and their income and wealth, broadly understood. This has the consequence that the comparison of citizens' shares in the benefits of social cooperation is greatly simplified and put on a footing less open to dispute.

Thus the reason why a constructivist view uses the schematic or practical distinctions we have just noted is that such distinctions are necessary if a workable conception of justice is to be achieved. These distinctions are incorporated into justice as fairness through the description of the parties as agents of construction and the account of how they are to deliberate. Charged with the task of agreeing to a workable conception of justice designed to achieve a sufficient convergence of opinion, the parties can find no better way in which to carry out this task. They accept the limitations of human life and recognize that at best a conception of justice can establish but a guiding framework for deliberation.

A comparison with classical utilitarianism will highlight what is involved here. On that view, whether stated as a form of rational intuitionism (Sidgwick) or as a form of naturalism (Bentham), every question of right and justice has an answer: whether an institution or action is right depends upon whether it will produce the greatest net balance of satisfaction. We may never be in a position to know the answer, or even to come very near to it, but, granting that a suitable measure of satisfaction exists, there is an answer: a fact of the matter. Of course, utilitarianism recognizes the needs of practice: working precepts and secondary rules are necessary to guide deliberation and coordinate our actions. These norms may be thought of as devised to bring our actions as close as possible to those which would maximize utility, so far as this is feasible. But of course, such rules and precepts are not first principles; they are at best directives that when followed make the results of our conduct approximate to what the principle of utility enjoins. In this sense, our working norms are approximations to something given.

By contrast, justice as fairness, as a constructivist view, holds that not all the moral questions we are prompted to ask in everyday life have answers. Indeed, perhaps only a few of them can be settled by any moral conception that we can understand and apply. Practical limitations impose a more modest aim upon a reasonable conception of justice, namely, to identify the most fundamental questions of justice that can be dealt with, in the hope that, once this is done and just basic institutions established, the remaining conflicts of opinion will not be so deep or widespread that they cannot be compromised. To accept the basic structure as the first subject of justice together with the account of primary goods is a step toward achieving this more modest goal. But in addition, the idea of approximating to moral truth has no place in a constructivist doctrine: the parties in the original position do not recognize any principles of justice as true or correct and so as antecedently given; their aim is simply to select the conception most rational for them, given their circumstances. This conception is not regarded as a workable approximation to the moral facts: there are no such moral facts to which the principles adopted could approximate.

As we have just seen, the differences between constructivism and classical utilitarianism are especially sharp in view of the content of the principle of utility: it always yields an answer that we can at least verbally describe. With the rational (pluralistic) intuitionism of Ross, however, the contrast is less obvious, since Ross's list of self-evident prima facie principles that identify good reasons also specifies but a loose guiding framework of moral deliberation which shares a number of the features of the framework provided by constructivism. But though these resemblances are real, the underlying idea of Ross's view is still essentially different from constructivism. His pluralistic intuitionism rejects utilitarianism (even an ideal utilitarianism) as oversimplifying the given moral facts, especially those concerning the correct weight of special duties and obligations. The complexity of the moral facts in particular kinds of cases is said to force us to recognize that no family of first principles that we can formulate characterizes these facts sufficiently accurately to lead to a definite conclusion. Decision and judgment are almost always to some degree uncertain and must rest with "perception," [13] that is, with our intuitive estimate of where the greatest balance of prima facie reasons lies in each kind of case. And this perception is that of a balance of reasons each of which is given by an independent moral order known by intuition. The essential contrast with constructivism remains.

IV

Having examined several contrasts between Kantian constructivism and rational intuitionism, we are now in a position to take up a

---

[13] See *The Right and the Good*, pp. 41/2. Ross refers to Aristotle's remark: "The decision rests with perception" (*Nicomachean Ethics* 1109 b 23, 1126 b 4).

fundamental point suggested by the discussion so far: an essential feature of a constructivist view, as illustrated by justice as fairness, is that its first principles single out what facts citizens in a well-ordered society are to count as reasons of justice. Apart from the procedure of constructing these principles, there are no reasons of justice. Put in another way, whether certain facts are to count as reasons of justice and what their relative force is to be can be ascertained only on the basis of the principles that result from the construction. This connects with the use of pure procedural justice at the highest level. It is, therefore, up to the parties in the original position to decide how simple or complex the moral facts are to be, that is, to decide on the number and complexity of the principles that identify which facts are to be accepted as reasons of justice by citizens in society (see TJ 45). There is nothing parallel to this in rational intuitionism.

This essential feature of constructivism may be obscured by the fact that in justice as fairness the first principles of justice depend upon those general beliefs about human nature and how society works which are allowed to the parties in the original position. First principles are not, in a constructivist view, independent of such beliefs, nor, as some forms of rational intuitionism hold, true in all possible worlds. In particular, they depend on the rather specific features and limitations of human life that give rise to the circumstances of justice.[14] Now, given the way the original position is set up, we can allow, in theory, that, as the relevant general beliefs change, the beliefs we attribute to the parties likewise change, and conceivably also the first principles that would be agreed to. We can say, if we like that *the* (most reasonable) principles of justice are those which would be adopted if the parties possessed all relevant general information and if they were properly to take account of all the practical desiderata required for a workable public conception of justice. Though these principles have a certain pre-eminence, they are still the outcome of construction. Furthermore, it is important to notice here that no assumptions have been made about a theory of truth. A constructivist view does not require an idealist or a verificationist, as opposed to a realist, account of truth. Whatever the nature of truth in the case of general beliefs about human nature and how society works, a constructivist moral doctrine requires a distinct procedure of construction to identify the first principles of justice. To the extent that Kant's moral doctrine

14 See Lecture II, section I.

depends upon what to some may appear to be a constructivist account of truth in the *First Critique* (I don't mean to imply that such an interpretation is correct), justice as fairness departs from that aspect of Kant's view and seeks to preserve the over-all structure of his moral conception apart from that background.

In the preceding paragraph I said that the way justice as fairness is set up allows the possibility that, as the general beliefs ascribed to the parties in the original position change, the first principles of justice may also change. But I regard this as a mere possibility noted in order to explain the nature of a constructivist view. To elaborate: at the end of the first lecture I distinguished between the roles of a conception of the person and of a theory of human nature, and I remarked that in justice as fairness these are distinct elements and enter at different places. I said that a conception of the person is a companion moral ideal paired with the ideal of a well-ordered society. A theory of human nature and a view of the requirements of social life tell us whether these ideals are feasible, whether it is possible to realize them under normally favorable conditions of human life. Changes in the theory of human nature or in social theory generally which do not affect the feasibility of the ideals of the person and of a well-ordered society do not affect the agreement of the parties in the original position. It is hard to imagine realistically any new knowledge that should convince us that these ideals are not feasible, given what we know about the general nature of the world, as opposed to our particular social and historical circumstances. In fact, the relevant information on these matters must go back a long time and is available to the common sense of any thoughtful and reflective person. Thus such advances in our knowledge of human nature and society as may take place do not affect our moral conception, but rather may be used to implement the application of its first principles of justice and suggest to us institutions and policies better designed to realize them in practice.[15]

In justice as fairness, then, the main ideals of the conception of justice are embedded in the two model-conceptions of the person and of a well-ordered society. And, granting that these ideals are allowed by the theory of human nature and so in that sense feasible, the first principles of justice to which they lead, via the constructivist

[15] Therefore these advances in our knowledge of human psychology and social theory might be relevant at the constitutional, legislative, and judicial stages in the application of the principles of justice, as opposed to the adoption of principles in the original position. For a brief account of these stages, see TJ, §31.

procedure of the original position, determine the long-term aim of social change. These principles are not, as in rational intuitionism, given by a moral order prior to and independent from our conception of the person and the social role of morality; nor are they, as in some naturalist doctrines, to be derived from the truths of science and adjusted in accordance with advances in human psychology and social theory. (These remarks are admittedly too brief, but we must return to the main line of discussion.)

v

The rational intuitionist may object that an essential feature of constructivism—the view that the facts to count as reasons of justice are singled out by the parties in the original position as agents of construction and that, apart from such construction, there are no reasons of justice—is simply incoherent.[16] This view is incompatible not only with the notion of truth as given by a prior and independent moral order, but also with the notions of reasonableness and objectivity, neither of which refer to what can be settled simply by agreement, much less by choice. A constructivist view, the objection continues, depends on the idea of adopting or choosing first principles, and such principles are not the kind of thing concerning which it makes sense to say that their status depends on their being chosen or adopted. We cannot "choose" them; what we can do is choose whether to follow them in our actions or to be guided by them in our reasoning, just as we can choose whether to honor our duties, but not what our duties are.

In reply, one must distinguish the three points of view that we noted at the end of the first lecture (in section vii, 533/4): that of the parties in the original position, that of the citizens in a well-ordered society, and that of you and me who are examining justice as fairness to serve as a basis for a conception that may yield a suitable understanding of freedom and equality. It is, of course, the parties in the original position whose agreement singles out the facts to count as reasons. But their agreement is subject to all the conditions of the original position which represent the Reasonable and the Rational. And the facts singled out by the first principles count as reasons not for the parties, since they are moved by their highest-

16 For this and other objections to what I call "constructivism" in this lecture, see the review of TJ by Marcus Singer, *Philosophy of Science*, xliv, 4 (December 1977): 594–618, pp. 612–615. I am grateful to him for raising this objection, which I here try to meet. Singer's criticism starts from the passage on page 45 of TJ (also referred to above, 564/5). It should not be assumed that Singer's own position is that of rational intuitionism. I simply suppose that a rational intuitionist would make this objection.

order interests, but for the citizens of a well-ordered society in matters of social justice. As citizens in society we are indeed bound by first principles and by what our duties are, and must act in the light of reasons of justice. Constructivism is certain to seem incoherent unless we carefully distinguish these points of view.

The parties in the original position do not agree on what the moral facts are, as if there already were such facts. It is not that, being situated impartially, they have a clear and undistorted view of a prior and independent moral order. Rather (for constructivism), there is no such order, and therefore no such facts apart from the procedure of construction as a whole; the facts are identified by the principles that result. Thus the rational intuitionists' objection, properly expressed, must be that no hypothetical agreement by rationally autonomous agents, no matter how circumscribed by reasonable conditions in a procedure of construction, can determine the reasons that settle what we as citizens should consider just and unjust; right and wrong are not, even in that way, constructed. But this is merely to deny what constructivism asserts. If, on the other hand, such a construction does yield the first principles of a conception of justice that matches more accurately than other views our considered convictions in general and wide reflective equilibrium, then constructivism would seem to provide a suitable basis for objectivity.

The agreement of the parties in the original position is not a so-called "radical" choice: that is, a choice not based on reasons, a choice that simply fixes, by sheer fiat, as it were, the scheme of reasons that we, as citizens, are to recognize, at least until another such choice is made. The notion of radical choice, commonly associated with Nietzsche and the existentialists, finds no place in justice as fairness. The parties in the original position are moved by their preference for primary goods, which preference in turn is rooted in their highest-order interests in developing and exercising their moral powers. Moreover, the agreement of the parties takes place subject to constraints that express reasonable conditions.

In the model-conception of a well-ordered society, citizens affirm their public conception of justice because it matches their considered convictions and coheres with the kind of persons they, on due reflection, want to be. Again, this affirmation is not radical choice. The ideals of the person and of social cooperation embedded in the two model-conceptions mediated by the original position are not ideals that, at some moment in life, citizens are said simply to choose. One is to imagine that, for the most part, they find on examination that they hold these ideals, that they have taken them in part from the culture of their society.

The preceding paragraph ties in with what I said at the beginning of the first lecture, except that there I was talking about us and not about a well-ordered society. Recall that a Kantian view, in addressing the public culture of a democratic society, hopes to bring to awareness a conception of the person and of social cooperation conjectured to be implicit in that culture, or at least congenial to its deepest tendencies when properly expressed and presented. Our society is not well-ordered: the public conception of justice and its understanding of freedom and equality are in dispute. Therefore, for us—you and me—a basis of public justification is still to be achieved. In considering the conception of justice as fairness we have to ask whether the ideals embedded in its model-conceptions are sufficiently congenial to our considered convictions to be affirmed as a practicable basis of public justification. Such an affirmation would not be radical choice (if choice at all); nor should it be confused with the adoption of principles of justice by the parties in the original position. To the contrary, it would be rooted in the fact that this Kantian doctrine as a whole, more fully than other views available to us, organized our considered convictions.

Given the various contrasts between Kantian constructivism and rational intuitionism, it seems better to say that in constructivism first principles are reasonable (or unreasonable) than that they are true (or false)—better still, that they are most reasonable for those who conceive of their person as it is represented in the procedure of construction. And here 'reasonable' is used instead of 'true' not because of some alternative theory of truth, but simply in order to keep to terms that indicate the constructivist standpoint as opposed to rational intuitionism. This usage, however, does not imply that there are no natural uses for the notion of truth in moral reasoning. To the contrary, for example, particular judgments and secondary norms may be considered true when they follow from, or are sound applications of, reasonable first principles. These first principles may be said to be true in the sense that they would be agreed to if the parties in the original position were provided with all the relevant true general beliefs.

Nor does justice as fairness exclude the possibility of there being a fact of the matter as to whether there is a single most reasonable conception. For it seems quite likely that there are only a few viable conceptions of the person both sufficiently general to be part of a moral doctrine and congruent with the ways in which people are to regard themselves in a democratic society. And only one of these conceptions may have a representation in a procedure of construction that issues in acceptable and workable principles, given the relevant general beliefs.[17] Of course, this is conjecture, intended only to indicate that constructivism is compatible with there being, in fact, only one most reasonable conception of justice, and therefore that constructivism is compatible with objectivism in this sense. However, constructivism does not presuppose that this is the case, and it may turn out that, for us, there exists no reasonable and workable conception of justice at all. This would mean that the practical task of political philosophy is doomed to failure.

VI

My account of Kantian constructivism in moral theory (as illustrated by justice as fairness) is now concluded. I should stress, however, that for all I have said it is still open to the rational intuitionist to reply that I have not shown that rational intuitionism is false or that it is not a possible basis for the necessary agreement in our judgments of justice. It has been my intention to describe constructivism by contrast and not to defend it, much less to argue that rational intuitionism is mistaken. In any case, Kantian constructivism, as I would state it, aims to establish only that the rational intuitionist notion of objectivity is unnecessary for objectivity. Of course, it is always possible to say, if we ever do reach general and wide reflective equilibrium, that now at last we intuit the moral truths fixed by a given moral order; but the constructivist will say instead that our conception of justice, by all the criteria we can think of to apply, is now the most reasonable for us.

We have arrived at the idea that objectivity is not given by "the point of view of the universe," to use Sidgwick's phrase. Objectivity is to be understood by reference to a suitably constructed social point of view, an example of which is the framework provided by the procedure of the original position. This point of view is social in several respects. It is the publicly shared point of view of citizens in a well-ordered society, and the principles that issue from it are accepted by them as authoritative with regard to the claims of individuals and associations. Moreover, these principles regulate the basic structure of society within which the activities of individuals and associations take place. Finally, by representing the person as a free and equal citizen of a well-ordered society, the constructivist procedure yields principles that further everyone's highest-order interests and define the fair terms of social cooperation among persons

---

[17] I am indebted to Samuel Scheffler for valuable discussion on this point.

so understood. When citizens invoke these principles they speak as
members of a political community and appeal to its shared point of
view either in their own behalf or in that of others. Thus, the essential agreement in judgments of justice arises not from the recognition of a prior and independent moral order, but from everyone's
affirmation of the same authoritative social perspective.

The central place of the conception of the person in these lectures prompts me to conclude with a note of warning, addressed as
much to me as to anyone else: ever since the notion of the person
assumed a central place in moral philosophy in the latter part of
the eighteenth century, as seen in Rousseau and Kant and the philosophy of idealism, its use has suffered from excessive vagueness
and ambiguity. And so it is essential to devise an approach that
disciplines our thought and suitably limits these defects. I view the
three model-conceptions that underlie justice as fairness as having
this purpose.

To elucidate: suppose we define the concept of a person as that
of a human being capable of taking full part in social cooperation,
honoring its ties and relationships over a complete life. There are
plainly many specifications of this capacity, depending, for example, on how social cooperation or a complete life is understood;
and each such specification yields another conception of the person
falling under the concept. Moreover, such conceptions must be distinguished from specifications of the concept of the self as knower,
used in epistemology and metaphysics, or the concept of the self as
the continuant carrier of psychological states: the self as substance,
or soul. These are prima facie distinct notions, and questions of
identity, say, may well be different for each; for these notions arise
in connection with different problems. This much is perhaps obvious. The consequence is that there are numerous conceptions of
the person as the basic unit of agency and responsibility in social
life, and of its requisite intellectual, moral, and active powers. The
specification of these conceptions by philosophical analysis alone,
apart from any background theoretical structure or general requirements, is likely to prove fruitless. In isolation these notions play no
role that fixes or limits their use, and so their features remain vague
and indeterminate.

One purpose of a model-conception like that of the original position is that, by setting up a definite framework within which a
binding agreement on principles must be made, it serves to fix
ideas. We are faced with a specific problem that must be solved,
and we are forced to describe the parties and their mutual relations

in the process of construction so that appropriate principles of justice result. The context of the problem guides us in removing vagueness and ambiguity in the conception of the person, and tells us how precise we need to be. There is no such thing as absolute clarity or exactness; we have to be only clear or exact enough for the task at hand. Thus the structure defined by the original position may enable us to crystallize our otherwise amorphous notion of the person and to identify with sufficient sharpness the appropriate characterization of free and equal moral personality.

The constructivist view also enables us to exploit the flexibility and power of the idea of rational choice subject to appropriate constraints. The rational deliberations of the parties in the original position serve as a way to select among traditional or other promising conceptions of justice. So understood, the original position is not an axiomatic (or deductive) basis from which principles are derived but a procedure for singling out principles most fitting to the conception of the person most likely to be held, at least implicitly, in a modern democratic society. To exaggerate, we compute via the deliberations of the parties and in this way hope to achieve sufficient rigor and clarity in moral theory. Indeed, it is hard to see how there could be any more direct connection between the conception of free and equal moral persons and first principles of justice than this construction allows. For here persons so conceived and moved by their highest-order interests are themselves, in their rationally autonomous deliberations, the agents who select the principles that are to govern the basic structure of their social life. What connection could be more intimate than this?

Finally, if we ask, what is clarity and exactness enough? the answer is: enough to find an understanding of freedom and equality that achieves workable public agreement on the weight of their respective claims. With this we return to the current impasse in the understanding of freedom and equality which troubles our democratic tradition and from which we started. Finding a way out of this impasse defines the immediate practical task of political philosophy. Having come full circle, I bring these lectures to a close.

JOHN RAWLS

Harvard University

Part V
Are Moral Claims Made True or False by Facts about the Responses of Moral Agents?

[13]

Moral Agent and Impartial Spectator

Gilbert Harman

One important type of ethical theory treats moral properties as analogous in certain respects to "secondary qualities" like colors. According to this sort of theory, whether something is right or wrong depends on how impartial spectators would react to it. In the 18th Century, the Scottish philosophers Francis Hutcheson, David Hume, and Adam Smith explored theories of this type.[1] In the 20th Century this sort of theory has sometimes been discussed under the name "ideal observer theory."[2] Recently, especially in England, there has been renewed interest in this sort of ethical theory and its comparison between moral properties and secondary qualities.[3]

One possible objection to an impartial spectator theory is that it seems to require an overly aesthetic conception of morality to take the primary point of view in ethics to be that of a spectator rather than that of the agent.[4] If the spectator is taken to be primary, then the agent's aim would seem to be to produce something that will or would please the spectator. But that is just wrong. Such an aim is too "outer directed" to count as a moral motive. Morality is more agent-centered than that. It is much more plausible to take the agent's point of view as primary. In the first instance morality is a matter of the moral reasons an agent has to act in one way or another, where these reasons derive from the relevant moral rules rather than from a desire to gain the approval of spectators.

A few years ago, I pressed this objection myself when I discussed the ideal observer theory in a textbook of ethics.[5] But I was too hasty. In reading Adam Smith's *Theory of the Moral Sentiments*, I discovered that Smith explicitly considers this issue and provides a plausible reply to the objection.

Because 20th Century discussions have tended not to consider such "psychological" questions as why agents might be motivated to act in ways that impartial spectators would approve (or, for that matter, why impartial spectators would care about anything), I will in this paper ignore recent discussion and return to the three great versions of the theory that were developed in the 18th Century by Hutcheson, Hume, and Smith, indicating why I think Smith's version of the theory is superior to the others.

Analogy with Secondary Qualities

Hutcheson and Hume each modeled an impartial spectator theory of moral right and wrong after a normal-perceiver theory of secondary

1

qualities like color, taste, sound, etc. The theory of color, for example, takes facts about colors to be facts about the reactions of normal perceivers under ideal lighting conditions. For an object to be red is, in this view, for the object to be such that it would look red to normal observers in good light. Similarly, according to Hutcheson and Hume, for an action to be wrong is for the action to be such that it would displease normal observers under conditions ideal for reacting to actions.

This sort of account explains a property by appeal to the psychological experience of an observer. Redness is explained in terms of an observer's visual experience—how things look to an observer. Wrongness is explained in terms of *moral experience*—how things feel to an observer, what attitude (positive or negative) the observer takes.

The relevant experience does not have to be actual. It is the experience an observer *would* have under certain ideal conditions. In yellow light, an object may look orange to observers but actually be red—if it would look red to normal observers in good white light. An action can seem hateful to actual biased or uninformed observers but really be morally right—if the action would be favored by impartial spectators who knew all the facts.

In fact, this distinction between actual and merely hypothetical reactions was not so clear in the 18th Century. Philosophers who adopted this general approach were apt to worry over the question whether a falling tree makes any sound if no one hears it. The correct answer should have been that the tree does make a loud sound, because, if someone had been there, he or she would have heard something. But philosophers did not always see the possibility of this response. Berkeley thought that the only way to allow for the sound of the falling tree was to have the sound heard by God. Indeed, God was needed even for the tree, since without God's perception, not only would there be no sound, but the tree itself would not be there to fall, according to Berkeley. Hume rejected God as a way of saving the falling tree and its sound and concluded that the unperceived tree was a confused fiction we postulate to give order to our experience of the forest.

But, although 18th Century proponents of theories of this sort do not clearly distinguish between actual and hypothetical reactions of spectators, once the distinction is recognized, it is clear that theories of this sort should refer to hypothetical reactions rather than actual reactions of observers.[6]

Even so there are problems.[7] It seems possible that there might be a red object that would turn green if placed in good light. This red object would look green to normal observers if placed in good light. How can that be, if for the object to be red is for it to be such that it would look red to normal observers if placed in good light? One possible answer is that the object would indeed look red if placed in good light *and* the object were not to change color. (But then what is it in this view for something to change color?)

Similarly, it seems possible that there could be a wrong action that would have been right if only the act had been considered by impartial spectators. Its bad consequences might outweigh its good consequences, but, if it had been considered by impartial spectators as an example, it would have had enough additional good consequences to turn the act into the right thing to do! Then we seem to have a wrong action that would be approved by impartial spectators if they considered it, again violating the claim of this sort of spectator theory. A possible response is to say that an act is wrong if the act would be disapproved of by impartial spectators who considered the act as it actually was, ignoring any features or consequences attaching to the act through its being considered by the spectators. However there are probably other versions of this objection that escape this response.

But let us forget about these (admittedly serious) problems to return to the basic idea behind impartial spectator theories, namely, that the rightness or wrongness of actions is dependent on the actual or hypothetical reactions of impartial spectators in a way that is analogous to the way in which what color something is depends on how it looks or would look to normal observers in good light.

Of course, the analogy can only be partial. One important difference is that an impartial moral spectator does not have to *perceive* the act being judged. It is enough for the "spectator" to be given a sufficiently full description of the act. Indeed, the act itself may well be merely hypothetical. The agent may be considering whether to do it or not. If the act is wrong, let us hope that the agent does not carry it out. In that case, the act does not exist.

The important point of the analogy is that, just as the theory of color takes color judgments to be about the hypothetical reactions of normal perceivers in ideal situations, an impartial spectator theory takes moral judgments to be judgments about the hypothetical reactions of impartial, knowledgeable people. So, in this view, to say that something is morally right is, roughly speaking, to say that impartial spectators are or would be in favor of it. To say that something is wrong is to say that impartial spectators are or would be opposed to it.

3

Key Issues for Impartial Spectator Theories

I now want to consider the following two issues for impartial spectator theories in ethics. First, why should an agent care about the reactions of spectators? Second, why should an impartial spectator care about what an agent does?

The first issue lies behind the objection to impartial spectator theories that I have already mentioned. According to such a theory, the desire to do what is right is the desire to act in a way that spectators will approve. But that is too "outer directed". Such a desire is precisely not a desire to do something simply because it is right.

Impartial spectator theories might try to avoid this objection by arguing that agents are not motivated directly to do what spectators would approve of. A moral agent's intention is not of the form, "Let me do what would gain an impartial spectator's approval." Rather, the agent's intention has the form, "Let me do *D*," where in fact doing *D* will be something that impartial spectators would approve but that fact is not the agent's reason for doing *D*. Now, an adequate impartial spectator theory cannot treat it as a mere coincidence that moral agents are motivated to act in ways that impartial spectators would approve. So this leaves the problem of explaining how moral agents come to act in ways that impartial spectators would approve of without the agents' having the specific intention to act in that way.

The second issue for an impartial spectator theory concerns why the spectator cares about what the agent does. This issue lies behind the question whether the reason an act is right is that impartial spectators favor it or rather the reason that impartial spectators favor the act is that the act is right. In the dialogue *Euthyphro,* Plato has Socrates ask a similar question of the view that something is good if and only if it is beloved by the gods: Are actions good because they are loved by the gods or are the relevant actions loved by the gods because the actions are good? Socrates raises the question in order to insinuate that the correct answer is the second one, good actions are loved by the gods because the actions are good, whereas the theory he is discussing must argue that the correct answer is the first one, good actions are good because they are loved by the gods.

Both answers cannot be right. It cannot be true both (1) that for an action to be good is for it to be loved by the gods and also (2) that what the gods love about the action is that the action is good. For that would imply that what the gods love about the action is that they love it, which is perverse.

4

Similarly, it might be argued against an impartial spectator theory that the second option is the correct one: truly impartial spectators favor actions that are right because the actions are right. Impartial spectator theories are necessarily committed to taking the first option here: acts are right because they would be favored by impartial spectators, who must therefore favor these acts for other reasons than that the actions are right. For it would be perverse to suppose that what impartial spectators would favor in these acts is that the acts would be favored by impartial spectators. This leaves the problem of saying what it is that would lead impartial spectators to favor one or another course of action.

To summarize, any impartial spectator theory in ethics needs to say what explains an agent's moral motivation, what explains a spectator's reaction, and why these two things, agent's motivation and spectator's reaction, should be correlated with each other.

Hutcheson's Theory

Francis Hutcheson (1694–1746) appeals to *benevolence* to answer these questions. In his view, people are innately disposed to like other people's being happy and to dislike others' being unhappy. On the one hand, this tendency motivates agents to act so as to make other people happier. On the other hand, it leads spectators to favor such actions and to oppose actions that have the opposite tendency.

In Hutcheson's view an agent acts morally *in order to make other people happier*. The agent is not motivated to act so as to gain the approval of spectators. To be sure, the agent is motivated to act in a way that spectators would approve. Although this is not an intended aspect of the agent's action, it is also no accident, because the same sort of benevolence that leads the agent to act as he or she does also leads the spectator to approve of so acting.

The agent's act is right because impartial spectators would favor the agent's acting in that way. Spectators would not in the first instance favor the act because the act is right but would favor the act because they want people to be happy and the act makes people happy.

This view yields classical utilitarianism. In Hutcheson's words, "that Action is best, which procures the greatest Happiness for the greatest Numbers; and that, worst, which, in like manner, occasions Misery."[8]

This is an elegant theory, but it faces a serious objection. The account of moral motivation is implausible. Benevolence is too weak a motive to be identified with the motive to do what is right. People are

5

sometimes motivated by benevolence to try to improve the lot of other people, but this motivation is normally quite feeble when compared with ordinary people's aversions to murder, injuring others, stealing, lying, and failing to keep their promises or pay their debts. Generalized benevolence is normally a much weaker motive than self-interest. But the moral motives just mentioned—to avoid killing others, and so forth—are often just as strong as and sometimes stronger than self-interest. Generalized benevolence cannot be the whole story about moral motivation.

Hume's Theory

Impressed by these facts about moral motivation, Hume, like Thomas Hobbes (1588–1679)[9] and Bernard de Mandeville (1670–1733),[10] sees self-interest as an important aspect of the motivation of certain moral acts, namely acts of "justice" such as telling the truth and keeping promises. But, unlike Hobbes and Mandeville and like Hutcheson, Hume argues that benevolence (based on what he calls "sympathy") is another aspect. Self-interest is involved because, if you cannot be trusted to tell the truth, keep your promises or avoid injuring your associates, people will not join up with you in common enterprises and you will lose out in comparison with other people who do tell the truth, keep their promises, and avoid injury to associates. So you have a strong self-interested reason to keep your obligations.

In this view, self-interest leads people to enter into cooperation with others. Over time, cooperation becomes more formalized into a system of cooperation. The overall system of cooperation makes people better off, so benevolent spectators approve of this self-interested motivation. It therefore counts as moral motivation.

Hume allows for benevolent motivation in addition to self-interest. Benevolent feelings in the agent may reinforce self-interested behavior, leading to even stronger motivation. But benevolence by itself is a weak motive. So the motive to be charitable to others is weaker than the motive to keep your obligations. Charity is not in your interest in the way that promise keeping is.

If benevolence plays only a small role in moral motivation, it plays more of a role in explaining the reactions of spectators, in Hume's view. Impartial spectators are (by definition) not personally affected by the agent's act, so self-interest does not favor or oppose the act. Benevolence is therefore the sole source of a spectator's approval or disapproval.

Hume offers an explanation of benevolence in terms of what he calls "sympathy". This contrasts with Hutcheson who simply postulates that God has made us benevolent.

Hume's account of sympathy goes like this. To think of someone else as in pain is to have a painful feeling yourself but located in your image of the other person. To think of another person as pleased is to have a pleasurable feeling located in your image of that person. So, it is pleasant to think that others are happy and unpleasant to think that others are unhappy. That is why impartial spectators prefer agents to do things that tend to make people happier.

For Hume the association of ideas plays an important role in determining what spectators will approve of. When the spectator thinks of the agent acting in a certain way, association of ideas leads the spectator to think of the *typical* effects of such an action. This thought makes the spectator happy to the extent that these envisioned typical effects involve happiness. So, to the extent that Hume's theory is utilitarian, it tends toward rule utilitarianism rather than act utilitarianism.

Roughly speaking, act utilitarianism says that an act is right to the extent that *that very act* makes people happier or less unhappy. Rule utilitarianism says that an act is right to the extent that *acts of that sort* tend to make people happier or less unhappy. Now, any given particular act is of many different sorts of act, so a crucial question for rule utilitarianism is to decide which are the relevant sorts of act for the purposes of moral evaluation. In Hume's version of the theory, this is a psychological question: in thinking about a particular act, a spectator will associate that act with various other acts; this psychological association determines what the relevant sorts of act are for the purposes of moral evaluation.

Hume's theory has little difficulty with the second problem facing an impartial spectator theory, the problem of accounting for the spectator's approval of right actions without supposing the spectator approves of them because they are right. In Hume's view a spectator's approval arises simply from the spectator's sympathetic thought of the pleasures and pains produced by the agent's act and any associated acts, not from any judgment that the act is right. The act is right because it is favored, not favored because it is right.

But Hume's account of moral motivation is still not very plausible. In his view, a moral agent acts largely out of self-interest or out of habits for which there is a self-interested justification. This is an outer-directed motivation—the agent is concerned with the reactions of others because he or she wants them to continue dealing with him or her.

This seems wrong. As Kant objects, a shopkeeper who gives children the correct change because it would be bad for his business if people

7

were to think he or she cheated children is doing the right thing, but not acting from a moral motive. The shopkeeper's act has no particular moral worth.[11]

Hutcheson identifies the moral motive with benevolence. That seems a motive of the right sort to be a moral motive—it is aimed in the right direction—but it is not a strong enough motive. (Kant famously disagrees, holding that benevolent motivation too is of no moral worth. But here Kant's view is counter-intuitive.) People's moral motivation is much stronger than their benevolence. Hume takes the moral motive to be mainly self-interest, which is a strong enough motive, but a motive that does not seem to be aimed in the right direction.

Adam Smith's Theory

Adam Smith (1723–1790) bases his positive theory on an insightful criticism of Hume's account of sympathy. Smith points out that Hume is wrong to suppose that merely knowing what another person feels is sufficient for sympathy with that person. You might very well not sympathize with another person's feelings if you thought those feelings were inappropriate to the situation. Consider someone who is very upset over a minor scratch on his knee from a fall, for example. You can understand perfectly well how upset the person is without at all sympathizing with the person's extreme agitation.

Smith observes, further, that Hume is also wrong in taking sympathy with another person's pain to be always entirely unpleasant. It is more unpleasant to have to have dealings with someone who is inappropriately unhappy, too upset about something the person ought to treat as a trifle, than it is to have dealings with someone who is upset to the same extent but for an appropriate reason. In the first case, you do not sympathize with the person; in the second case you do sympathize with the person. The other person's pain is easier to take if you can sympathize with that person.

Smith thinks Hume is right about the importance of sympathy in ethics but wrong about what sympathy is and why it is important.

For Smith, the key point is that sympathy is desirable. Not only do spectators want to be able to sympathize with agents, but agents also want the sympathy of spectators. This gives agents a motive to try to have reactions of the sort that spectators can sympathize with.

Furthermore, in Smith's view, "Sympathy . . . does not arise so much from the view of the passion, as from that of the situation which excites it."[12] This gives a spectator a standard for judging the other agent. The spectator imagines him or herself in the circumstances of the

8

agent and imagines how he or she would react in those circumstancs. If the agent's reaction is' similar to the reaction the spectator imagines having, the spectator sympathizes with the agent. If the agent's reaction is more extreme than the spectator's imagined reaction, the spectator does not sympathize with the agent.

Spectators approve of reactions they can sympathize with and disapprove of reactions they cannot sympathize with. In Smith's words, "To approve or disapprove . . . of the opinions of others is acknowledged, by every body, to mean no more' than to observe their agreement or disagreement with our own. But this is equally the case with regard to our approbation or disapprobation of the sentiments or passions of others."[13]

Smith's approach leads to a very different conception of the content of ethics. Hutcheson's and Hume's theories imply utilitarianism. The aim is to maximize happiness and minimize unhappiness. Smith's theory has no such implication. Spectators do not just add up pleasures and pains.

Smith's normative theory is more stoical than utilitarian. His approach puts considerable importance on self-control. According to Smith, the feelings an ordinary nonideal spectator imagines having in a given situation are rarely as intense as the feelings the spectator or someone else would have in that situation. What an actual spectator imagines an agent feeling is rarely as intense as what the agent actually is feeling. So, the reaction the spectator imagines having in the agent's circumstances tends not to be as extreme as the agent's actual reaction would be *if* that reaction were not influenced by the thought of how the reaction might appear to spectators. Since a person wants sympathy after stubbing a toe, the person will not for long yell and shout and moan, but will try to restrain his or her feelings so as not to appear ridiculous.

Of course, a more knowledgeable impartial spectator would not underestimate the intensity of an agent's pain. But such a spectator would still favor restraint in the agent's reactions, because the reaction that the spectator (correctly) envisions having in the agent's circumstances would be restrained. The spectator would by now have acquired a habit of restraint in reactions as a way of obtaining the sympathy of people who do underestimate the intensity of pains in others.

In Smith's view, the spectator's reactions are heavily influenced by convention. A spectator tries to imagine how he or she would react in the agent's circumstances. But, if the spectator were in the agent's circumstances, he or she would try to modify an otherwise natural reaction so

9

as to accord with the imagined reactions of other not necessarily ideal spectators. This means that a spectator will be influenced strongly by his or her expectations of how people ordinarily act and react. Conventional ways of acting and reacting serve as evidence about the feelings of other impartial spectators. When a given spectator is imagining how he or she would react, since the spectator will imagine acting in ways that other spectators will sympathize with, what he or she imagines will be skewed in the direction of the conventional reactions. So, Smith's theory is much more conventionalistic than Hutcheson's or even Hume's. Hume takes convention to be important because conventions are useful: people are happier because of what they can accomplish when they adhere to conventions. But for Smith conventions have a more direct effect. The conventions a spectator participates in determine how the spectator will react and so determine what reactions the spectator will sympathize with.

How does Smith handle the problems with which we began? His response to the second problem concerning spectators' reasons for favoring certain actions is the same as the response made by Hutcheson and Hume. The spectators approve or disapprove of actions depending on whether or not they can sympathize with them. Acts are wrong because spectators disapprove of them, i.e. because they do not sympathize with them. It is not that the spectators disapprove of the acts because the acts are wrong.

But what about the first problem concerning the motivation of moral agents? Hutcheson's appeal to benevolence did not work because of the weakness of benevolence. Hume's appeal to self-interest refers to a strong enough motive, but one that is too outer directed if it is involved in the way that Hume thinks it is involved. It may seem that Smith's theory resembles Hume's in this respect. Here again it looks as if the envisioned source of moral motivation is strong enough but too outer directed. Smith seems to be saying that moral motivation is motivation to act so as to obtain the sympathy of spectators. That seems quite wrong.

But in fact, Smith explicitly denies that moral motivation is motivation so as to obtain the sympathy of others. An agent is motivated to be *worthy* of praise.

> The love of praise-worthiness is by no means derived altogether from the love of praise. . . .
> The love and admiration which we naturally conceive for those whose character and conduct we approve of, necessarily dispose us to desire to become ourselves the objects of the like agreeable sentiments,

and to be as amiable and as admirable as those whom we love and admire the most. . . . Emulation, the anxious desire that we ourselves should excel, is originally founded in our admiration of the excellence of others. Neither can we be satisfied with being merely admired for what other people are admired. We must at least believe ourselves to be admirable for what they are admirable. . . . [If others praise us, their] praise necessarily strengthens our own sense of our own praise-worthiness. In this case, so far is the love of praise-worthiness from being derived altogether from that of praise; that the love of praise seems, at least in a great measure, to be derived from that of praise-worthiness.[14]

In order to accommodate this observation, Smith postulates a primitive desire to be worthy of praise.

Nature, when she formed man for society, endowed him with an original desire to please, and an original aversion to offend his brethren. She taught him to feel pleasure in their favourable, and pain in their unfavourable regard. . . .

But this desire of the approbation, and this aversion to the disapprobation of his brethren, would not alone have rendered him fit for that society for which he was made. Nature, accordingly, has endowed him, not only with a desire of being approved of, but with a desire of being what ought to be approved of; or of being what he himself approves of in other men.[15]

This passage is difficult to interpret, since a desire "of being what ought to be approved of" is not quite the same as a desire "of being what [one] approves of in other men." And, simply postulating a desire to be "what ought to be approved of" would not eliminate the difficulty. According to Smith's impartial spectator theory, a desire to be "what ought to be approved of" is precisely a desire to be such that impartial spectators *would* approve of oneself. But, as Smith emphasizes at length, that desire is not yet of the right sort.

A desire to be "what he himself approves of in other men" is more to the point, if it means a desire to be "what he himself would approve of in others from an impartial perspective." But Smith does not really postulate any such desire as a basic unexplained fact about people. Instead, he offers a more complex account of moral motivation that anticipates certain elements of Freud's theory of the super-ego. Smith holds that, at first, a child is motivated to restrain its reactions so as to have the sympathy of parents and other spectators. As an aid in doing this, the child tries to view itself as seen by others. Eventually, it acquires a habit of doing this—a habit of pretending to be an impartial spectator of its own actions and reactions to see which actions it approves and which it disapproves. The child then tries to restrain its reactions so as to

11

be approved by this pretend spectator—the little person within who now serves as a kind of inner conscience.

> When I endeavour to examine my own conduct, when I endeavour to pass sentence upon it, and either to approve or condemn it, it is evident that, in all such cases, I divide myself, as it were, into two persons; and that I, the examiner and judge, represent a different character from that other I, the person whose conduct is examined into and judged of. The first is the spectator, whose sentiments with regard to my own conduct I endeavour to enter into, by placing myself in his situation, and by considering how it would appear to me, when seen from that particular point of view. The second is the agent, the person whom I properly call myself, and of whose conduct, under the character of a spectator, I was endeavouring to form some opinion. The first is the judge; the second the person judged of. But that the judge should, in every respect, be the same with the person judged of, is as impossible as that the cause should, in every respect, be the same with the effect.[16]

This might seem to be even worse than purely outer directed motivation. It may seem that Smith is saying that the agent is motivated to obtain the sympathy and approval of a *pretend* person.[17]

But this is a mistake. Despite the division into what Smith calls "two persons", the "examiner and judge" is not really any different from "the person I call myself." The "examiner and judge" is the agent himself or herself, viewing things from a certain perspective. When the agent pretends to be an impartial spectator, he or she ends up approving and disapproving from an impartial point of view. Viewing things in that way can then influence the agent's motives and feelings, since it is the agent who is doing the viewing and the approving and disapproving and the approval or disapproval is of the agent himself or herself. Consequently, the agent's actual motives will become more moral, because they are in part the result of the agent's looking at things from a moral point of view. To the extent that the agent views things impartially, the agent will genuinely not want to cheat and injure others. What starts as a strategy for knowing what to do to obtain sympathy ends up giving the agent a genuinely moral outlook that can motivate moral behavior.

The truly moral agent does not aim at getting the sympathy of impartial observers. Instead, the moral agent is motivated to act morally by virtue of motives acquired by viewing things from an impartial standpoint. The moral agent cares about the things that an impartial spectator cares about because the agent has in part *become* an impartial spectator.

12

Concluding Summary

Hutcheson, Hume, and Smith all put forward versions of the impartial spectator theory. All three agree that right acts are right because they would be favored by impartial spectators who favor these acts for other reasons than that the acts are right. But they disagree about what explains spectators' reactions and what accounts for moral motivation. They also disagree as to whether the same thing explains agents' motivation and spectators' approval.

Hutcheson and Hume agree that spectators' reactions derive from benevolence. Hutcheson believes that benevolence is also the source of moral motivation. Hume thinks this is too weak a motivation; he thinks moral motivation is also based in self-interest. Where Hutcheson simply treats benevolence as a God given motive, Hume offers an explanation of benevolence in terms of what he calls sympathy.

Smith disagrees with Hume as to what sympathy is. Smith also disagrees with both Hume and Hutcheson about the relevance of benevolence. Smith argues that neither agents nor spectators are much influenced by benevolence, although the desire for sympathy is important. Smith agrees with Hutcheson and disagrees with Hume in holding that moral motivation is of a piece with what it is that leads spectators to approve or disapprove of various actions. What is important, according to Smith, is the taking of an impartial view.

Smith works this theory out with a mass of detail which I cannot try to summarize. I believe that the book in which he works this out, his *Theory of the Moral Sentiments,* is one of the great works of moral philosophy.

I conclude that the Impartial Spectator Theory has an answer to the objection that it offers an overly aesthetic conception of morality, that it overemphasizes the point of view of the spectator over the point of view of the agent, and that it cannot account for the motivation to do what is right.

This is not to say that I am convinced that this is the best theory. One alternative is to try to develop what might be called an ideal agent or ideal practical reasoner theory, as opposed to an ideal observer or impartial spectator theory. This alternative would place primary emphasis on moral reasons for acting, on the viewpoint of the agent. In one version of this theory, the agent has moral principles that the agent intends to follow. The agent's moral reasons typically derive from principles the agent accepts as a member of a group.[18]

I am not sure how to decide between the impartial spectator theory and the ideal reasoner theory.

13

So let me conclude with a couple of further comments on the history of moral philosophy in the 18th Century.

Postscript 1

There is an interesting irony in the way in which Hume's use of the term "sympathy" leads Smith to his own very different theory, a theory that in my view is much better than Hume's at accounting for moral phenomenology. Smith's criticism of Hume's use of the term "sympathy" is not a serious one. It is of no importance whatsoever whether the meaning that Hume gives to the term "sympathy" is the ordinary one and it in no way damages Hume's view for him to acknowledge that his use is nonstandard. Hume can use the term however he wants. If he wants to use it in a special sense in order to develop his own view, there is nothing wrong with that. If someone really objects, the term can be replaced with another. Nothing in Hume's view depends on his having captured the ordinary meaning of the term "sympathy." The irony is that taking Hume's term seriously leads Smith to a more accurate account of morality. A purely verbal point yields a powerful substantive theory.

Postscript 2

Finally, it is perplexing that Adam Smith's ethics should be so relatively unread as compared with Hume's ethics when there is so much of value in Smith. What I have talked about here only scratches the surface. Why should Smith's ethics be so neglected? Is it that Hume also had a metaphysics and an epistemology and that Smith did not? Or is it that Smith was a more important economist than Hume? And why should that matter? I do not know.[19]

NOTES

1. Francis Hutcheson, *An Inquiry concerning Moral Good and Evil* (1725) and *Illustrations upon the Moral Sense (1728).* David Hume, *A Treatise of Human Nature* (London 1739–40) and *Enquiries concerning Human Understanding and the Principles of Morals* (London 1748–1751). Adam Smith, *Theory of the Moral Sentiments,* first edition 1759, sixth edition, 1790. References below are to the Glasgow edition, Oxford 1976, reprinted in paper covers by Liberty Press, Indianapolis, Indiana, 1982.

2. Roderick Firth, "Ethical Absolutism and the Ideal Observer," *Philosophy and Phenomenological Research* 12 (1952). Richard B. Brandt, *Ethical Theory* (Englewood Cliffs, New Jersey; Prentice-Hall: 1959). F. C. Sharp, *Good Will and Ill Will* (Chicago, Chicago University Press: 1950).

3. David Wiggins, John McDowell, and Thomas L. Carson have argued in favor of a view of this sort. David Wiggins, "Truth, Invention, and the Meaning of Life" (British Academy Lecture: 1976); "A Sensible Subjectivism," ms. John McDowell, "Values and Secondary Qualities," in Ted Honderich, *Morality and Objectivity: A Tribute to J. L. Mackie*

14

(London, Routledge and Kegan Paul: 1985), pp. 110–129. Thomas L. Carson, *The Status of Morality* (Dordrecht, Reidel: 1984). Colin McGinn and Simon Blackburn have argued against it. Simon Blackburn, *Spreading the Word* (Oxford, Oxford University Press: 1984), chapter 6; "Errors and the Phenomenology of Value," in Honderich (ed.) *op. cit.*, pp. 1–22. Colin McGinn, *The Subjective View* (Oxford, Oxford University Press: 1983).

4. Stuart Hampshire, "Fallacies in Moral Philosophy," in *Freedom of Mind and Other Essays* (Oxford, Oxford University Press: 1972).

5. *The Nature of Morality: An Introduction to Ethics* (New York, Oxford University Press: 1977).

6. Firth, *op. cit.*

7. Robert Shope notes that problems of this sort arise almost always when philosophers appeal to hypothetical cases in this way. Shope, "The Conditional Fallacy," *Journal of Philosophy* 75 (1978) 397–413.

8. Francis Hutcheson, *An Inquiry concerning Moral Good and Evil*, 2nd edition (London: 1726), III, viii (paragraph 121 in *British Moralists*, edited by L. A. Selby-Bigge (Oxford, Oxford University Press: 1897—paper edition Indianapolis, Indiana; Bobbs-Merrill: 1964)).

9. Thomas Hobbes, *Leviathan, or the Matter, Form and Power of a Commonwealth* (London: 1651).

10. Bernard de Mandeville, *The Fable of the Bees, or Private vices publick benefits* (1714).

11. Immanuel Kant, *Foundations of the Metaphysics of Morals* (1785).

12. Smith, *op. cit.* I,i,1,10.

13. *Ibid.* I,i,3,2.

14. *Ibid.* III.2.2–3. Similar ideas have been recently expressed by John McDowell, *op. cit.*, pp. 117–120 and by David Wiggins, "A Sensible Subjectivism," ms p. 4.

15. *Ibid.* III.2.6–7.

16. *Ibid.* III,1,6.

17. I mistakenly offer this as a criticism of basing morality on the Freudian super-ego in *Harman, op. cit.*, pp. 61–62.

18. Harman, *The Nature of Morality*, Chapter 9.

19. I am indebted to David Levy for getting me interested in this project, to Ralph Lindgren's *Social Philosophy of Adam Smith* (The Hague, Martinus Nijhoff: 1973), which persuaded me that my initial thoughts about Smith were superficial, and to Michael Smith for helpful comments on a prior draft. (This is not to say that any of them agree with what I have said.) Earlier versions of this paper were presented at a Liberty Fund conference on Adam Smith in Washington, as the Selfridge Lecture at Lehigh University in 1984, as the Matchette Lecture at Trinity College (San Antonio, Texas) and at the University of Miami.

15

[14]

DISPOSITIONAL THEORIES OF VALUE

II—David Lewis

Roughly, values are what we are disposed to value. Less roughly, we have this schematic definition: *Something of the appropriate category is a value if and only if we would be disposed, under ideal conditions, to value it.* It raises five questions. (1) What is the favourable attitude of 'valuing'? (2) What is the 'appropriate category' of things? (3) What conditions are 'ideal' for valuing? (4) Who are 'we'? (5) What is the modal status of the equivalence?

By answering these questions, I shall advance a version of the dispositional theory of value. I begin by classifying the theory that is going to emerge. First, it is naturalistic: it advances an analytic definition of value. It is naturalistic in another sense too: it fits into a naturalistic metaphysics. It invokes only such entities and distinctions as we need to believe in anyway, and needs nothing extra before it can deliver the values. It reduces facts about value to facts about our psychology.

The theory is subjective: it analyses value in terms of our attitudes. But it is not subjective in the narrower sense of implying that value is a topic on which whatever we may think is automatically true, or on which there is no truth at all. Nor does it imply that if we had been differently disposed, different things would have been values. Not quite—but it comes too close for comfort.

The theory is internalist: it makes a conceptual connection between value and motivation. But it offers no guarantee that everyone must be motivated to pursue whatever is of value; still less, whatever he judges to be of value. The connection is defeasible, in more ways than one.

The theory is cognitive: it allows us to seek and to gain knowledge about what is valuable. This knowledge is *a posteriori* knowledge of contingent matters of fact. It could in principle be gained by psychological experimentation. But it is more likely to be gained by difficult exercises of imagination, carried out perhaps in a philosopher's or a novelist's armchair.

The theory is conditionally relativist: it does not exclude the possibility that there may be no such thing as value *simpliciter*, just value for this or that population. But it does not imply relativity, not even when taken together with what we know about the diversity of what people actually value. It leaves the question open.

Is it a form of realism about value?—That question is hard. I leave it for the end.

What is 'valuing'? It is some sort of mental state, directed toward that which is valued. It might be a feeling, or a belief, or a desire. (Or a combination of these; or something that is two or three of them at once; or some fourth thing. But let us set these hypotheses aside, and hope to get by with something simpler.[1])

A feeling?—Evidently not, because the feelings we have when we value things are too diverse.

A belief? What belief? You might say that one values something just by believing it to be a value. That is circular. We might hide the circularity by maneuvering between near-synonyms, but it is better to face it at once. If so, we have that being a value is some property such that something has it iff we are disposed, under ideal conditions, to believe that the thing has it. In other words, such that we are disposed, under ideal

---

[1] The most interesting of the hypotheses here set aside is that an attitude of valuing might be a 'besire': a special kind of attitude that is both a belief and a desire and that motivates us, without benefit of other desires, in just the way that ordinary desires do. (Or it might be an attitude that is not identical with, but rather is necessarily connected with, a belief and a desire; or an attitude that is not strictly speaking either a belief or a desire, but is just like each apart from also being like the other.) Valuing X might be the besire that is at once a belief that X is good and a desire for X; where *goodness* just means that property, whatever it may be, such that a belief that X has it may double as a desire for X.

But we should hesitate to believe in besires, because integrating them into the folk psychology of belief and desire turns out to be no easy thing. On the difficulty with instrumental besires, see my 'Desire as Belief' and John Collins, 'Belief, Desire and Revision', *Mind* 97 (1988), pp. 323–342: when a system of attitudes changes under the impact of new information, beliefs evolve in one way and (instrumental) desires in another. A besire, trying to go both ways at once, would be torn apart. Intrinsic besires—a better candidate for the attitude of valuing—face a different difficulty. At least in miniature examples, they turn out to be altogether impervious to change under the impact of experience. Not bad, you might think—why *should* experience change our mind about what's intrinsically good? The trouble is that the result applies not only to perceptual experience but also to experience of moral reflection, 'intuiting', and the like.

conditions, to be right about whether something has it. That is not empty; but it tells us little, since doubtless there are many properties about which we are disposed to be right.

Further, if valuing something just meant having a certain belief about it, then it seems that there would be no conceptual reason why valuing is a *favourable* attitude. We might not have favoured the things we value. We might have opposed them, or been entirely indifferent.

So we turn to desires. But we'd better not say that valuing something is just the same as desiring it.[2] That may do for some of us: those who manage, by strength of will or by good luck, to desire exactly as they desire to desire. But not all of us are so fortunate. The thoughtful addict may desire his euphoric daze, but not value it. Even apart from all the costs and risks, he may hate himself for desiring something he values not at all. It is a desire he wants very much to be rid of.[3] He desires his high, but he does not desire to desire it, and in fact he desires not to desire it. He does not desire an unaltered, mundane state of consciousness, but he does desire to desire it. We conclude that he does not value what he desires, but rather he values what he desires to desire.

Can we do better by climbing the ladder to desires of ever-higher order? What someone desires to desire to desire might conceivably differ from what he does desire to desire. Or. . . . Should we perhaps say that what a person really values is given by his highest order of desire, whatever order that is?—It is hard to tell whether this would really be better, because it is hard to imagine proper test cases.[4] Further, if we go for the highest

---

[2] Often in decision theory and economics, 'value' does just mean a measure of desiredness, and all desires count equally. But it's not the sense we want here.

[3] On desires to desire, see Harry Frankfurt, 'Freedom of the Will and the Concept of a Person', *Journal of Philosophy* 68 (1971), pp. 5–20; and Richard C. Jeffrey, 'Preference Among Preferences', *Journal of Philosophy* 71 (1974), pp. 377–391.

[4] It is comparatively easy to imagine *instrumental* third-order desires. Maybe our addict wishes he could like himself better than he does; and not by doing away with his addiction, which he takes to be impossible, but by becoming reconciled to it and accepting himself as he is. Or maybe he just fears that his second-order desire not to be addicted will someday lead him to suffer the pains of withdrawal. Either way, he wants to be rid of his second-order desire not to be addicted, but he wants it not for itself but as a means to some end. This is irrelevant: presumably it is intrinsic, not instrumental, desiring that is relevant to what someone values.

order, we automatically rule out the case of someone who desires to *value* differently than he does, yet this case is not obviously impossible. I hesitantly conclude we do better to stop on the second rung: valuing is just desiring to desire.

Recall G. E. Moore: 'To take, for instance, one of the more plausible, because one of the more complicated, of such proposed definitions, it may easily be thought, at first sight, that to be good may mean to be that which we desire to desire'.[5] Of course he does not endorse the definition, but at least he does it the honour of choosing it for his target to display the open question argument. I don't say that everything we value is good; but I do echo Moore to this extent. I say that to be *valued* by us means to be that which we desire to desire. Then to be a value—to be good, near enough—means to be that which we are disposed, under ideal conditions, to desire to desire. Still more complicated, still more plausible. It allows, as it should, that under less-than-ideal conditions we may wrongly value what is not really good. As for Moore's open question, we shall face that later.

We have this much of an 'internalist' conceptual connection between value and motivation. If something is a value, and if someone is one of the appropriate 'we', and if he is in ideal conditions, then it follows that he will value it. And if he values it, and if he desires as he desires to desire, then he will desire it. And if he desires it, and if this desire is not outweighed by other conflicting desires, and if he has the instrumental rationality to do what serves his desires according to his beliefs, then he will pursue it. And if the relevant beliefs are near enough true, then he will pursue it as effectively as possible. A conceptual connection between value and motivation, sure enough—but a multifariously iffy connection. Nothing less iffy would be credible. But still less is it credible that there is no connection at all.

In general, to find out whether something is disposed to give response R under conditions C, you can put it in C and find out whether you get R. That is a canonical way to learn whether the disposition is present, though surely not the only possible

---

[5] *Principia Ethica* (Cambridge University Press, 1903) Section 13.

way.[6] If a dispositional theory of value is true, then we have a canonical way to find out whether something is a value. To find out whether we would be disposed, under ideal conditions, to value it, put yourself in ideal conditions, if you can, making sure you can tell when you have succeeded in doing so. Then find out whether you value the thing in question, i.e. whether you desire to desire it. If you do, that confirms that it is a value. (I assume you are one of the appropriate 'we' and you know it.) Now we have this much of an 'internalist' conceptual connection between value judgements and motivation. It is even iffier than the connection between value itself and motivation; and again I say that if it were less iffy, it would be less credible. If someone believes that something is a value, and if he has come to this belief by the canonical method, and if he has remained in ideal conditions afterward or else retained the desire to desire that he had when in ideal conditions, then it follows that he values that thing. And if he desires as he desires to desire, then he desires that thing; and so on as before.

The connection is not with the judgement of value *per se*, but with the canonical way of coming to it. If someone reached the same judgement in some non-canonical way—as he might— that would imply nothing about his valuing or desiring or pursuing.

What is the 'appropriate category'? If values are what we are disposed to desire to desire, then the things that can be values must be among the things that can be desired. Those fall into two classes.

Sometimes, what one desires is that the world should be a

---

[6] It is a fallible way; for it may be that you cannot put the thing in C without making the disposition disappear. Imagine that a surface now has just the molecular structure that disposes things to reflect light; but that exposing it to light would catalyze a swift chemical change and turn it into something unreflective. So long as it's kept in the dark, is it reflective?—I think so; but its reflectivity is what Ian Hunt once called a 'finkish' disposition, one that would vanish if put to the test. (So a simple counterfactual analysis of dispositions fails.) Could a disposition to value, or to disvalue, be finkish? Yes; here is an example due to Michael Tooley. Suppose, as I shall claim, that 'ideal conditions' include imaginative acquaintance; suppose there is no way to imagine direct electrical stimulation of the pleasure centre of the brain except by trying it out; and suppose that one brief trial would enslave you to the electrode and erase all other desires. Then I think you might well have a finkish disposition to disvalue the experience. If, *per impossibile*, you could manage to imagine it without at the same time having your present system of desires erased by the current, you would desire not to desire it.

certain way: that it should realise one of a certain class of (maximally specific, qualitatively delineated) possibilities for the whole world. This class—a 'proposition', in one sense of that word—gives the content of the desire. To desire that the world realise some possibility within the class is to desire that the proposition be true. Call this 'desire *de dicto*'.

But sometimes, what one desires concerns not just the world but oneself: one simply desires to *be* a certain way. For instance, Fred might want to be healthy, or wealthy, or wise. Then what he wants is that he himself should realise one of a certain class of (maximally specific, qualitatively delineated) possibilities for an individual—or better, for an individual-in-a-world-at-a-time. This class—a 'property' in one sense of that word, or an 'egocentric proposition'—gives the content of the desire. To desire to realise some possibility in the class is to desire to have the property, or to desire that the egocentric proposition be true of one. Call this 'desire *de se*', or 'egocentric' or 'essentially indexical' desire.[7]

You might think to reduce desire *de se* to desire *de dicto*, saying that if Arthur desires to be happy, what he desires is that the world be such that Arthur is happy. (You might doubt that such worlds comprise a qualitatively delineated class, so you might consider dropping that requirement.) But no. That is not exactly the same thing, though the difference shows up only when we imagine someone who is wrong or unsure about who in the world he is. Suppose Arthur thinks he is Martha. If Arthur is self-centred he may desire to be happy, desire that the world be one wherein Martha is happy, but not desire that the world is one wherein Arthur is happy. If instead Arthur is selflessly benevolent he may not desire to be happy, yet he may desire that the world be such that Arthur is happy. If Arthur is so befuddled as not to know whether he is Arthur or Martha, but hopes he is Arthur, he does not just desire that the world be such that

[7] See Peter Geach, 'On Beliefs about Oneself', *Analysis* 18 (1957), pp. 23-24; Hector-Neri Castañeda 'On the Logic of Attributions of Self-Knowledge to Others', *Journal of Philosophy* 65 (1968), pp. 439-456; John Perry, 'Frege on Demonstratives', *Philosophical Review* 86 (1977), pp. 474-497, and 'The Problem of the Essential Indexical', *Noûs* 14 (1979), pp. 3-21; my 'Attitudes *De Dicto* and *De Se*', *Philosophical Review* 88 (1979), pp. 513-543; Roderick Chisholm, *The First Person: An Essay on Reference and Intentionality* (Harvester Press, 1981).

DISPOSITIONAL THEORIES OF VALUE 119

Arthur is self-identical! In all these cases, Arthur's desire is, at least in part, irreducibly *de se*.[8, 9]

When we acknowledge desires *de se*, we must distinguish two senses of 'desiring the same thing'. If Jack Sprat and his wife both prefer fat meat, they *desire alike*. They are psychological duplicates, on this matter at least. But they do not *agree* in their desires, because no possible arrangement could satisfy them both. Whereas if Jack prefers the fat and his wife prefers the lean, then they differ psychologically, they do not desire alike. But they do agree, because if he eats no fat and she eats no lean, that would satisfy them both. In general, they desire alike iff they desire *de se* to have exactly the same properties and they desire *de dicto* that exactly the same propositions hold. They agree in desires iff exactly the same world would satisfy the desires of both; and a world that satisfies someone's desires is one wherein he has all the properties that he desires *de se* and wherein all the propositions hold that he desires *de dicto*. Agreement in desire makes for harmony; desiring alike may well make for strife.

As we can desire *de dicto* or *de se*, so we can desire to desire *de dicto* or *de se*. If desiring to desire is valuing, and if values are what we are disposed to value, then we must distinguish values *de dicto* and *de se*. A value *de dicto* is a proposition such that we are disposed to desire to desire *de dicto* that it hold. A value *de se* is a property such that we are disposed to desire to desire *de se* to have it.

It is essential to distinguish. Consider egoism: roughly, the thesis that one's own happiness is the only value. Egoism is meant to be general. It is not the thesis that the happiness of a certain special person, say Thrasymachus, is the only value. Egoism *de dicto* says that for each person X, the proposition that

---

[8] What we can do is to go the other way, subsuming desire *de dicto* under desire *de se*. To desire that the world be a certain way is to desire that one have the property of living in a world that is that way—a property that belongs to all or none of the inhabitants of the world, depending on the way the world is. This subsumption, artificial though it be, is legitimate given a suitably broad notion of property. But for present purposes we need distinction, not unification. So let us henceforth ignore those desires *de se* that are equivalent to desires *de dicto*, and reserve the term '*de se*' for those that are not.

[9] If you like, you can put the egocentricity not in the content of desire itself but in an egocentric mode of presentation of that content. The choice matters little, save to simplicity. See Jeremy Butterfield, 'Content and Context' in Butterfield, ed., *Language Mind and Logic* (Cambridge University Press, 1986).

X is happy is the only value. That is inconsistent, as Moore observed.[10] It says that there are as many different values as there are people, and each of them is the only value. Egoism *de se* says that the property of happiness—in other words, the egocentric proposition that one is happy—is the only value. Moore did not confute that. He ignored it. False and ugly though it be, egoism *de se* is at least a consistent doctrine. What it alleges to be the only value would indeed be just *one* value *de se*, not a multitude of values *de dicto*.[11]

Insofar as values are *de se*, the wholehearted pursuit by everyone of the same genuine value will not necessarily result in harmony. All might value alike, valuing *de se* the same properties and valuing *de dicto* the same propositions. Insofar as they succeed in desiring as they desire to desire, they will desire alike. But that does not ensure that they will agree in desire. If egoism *de se* were true, and if happiness could best be pursued by doing others down and winning extra shares, then the pursuit by all of the very same single value would be the war of all against all.

Because egoism is false and ugly, we might be glad of a theoretical framework that allowed us to confute it *a priori*. And some of us might welcome a framework that promises us harmony, if only we can all manage to pursue the same genuine values. Was it right, then, to make a place for values *de se*? Should we have stipulated, instead, that something we are disposed to desire to desire shall count as a value only when it is a proposition that we are disposed to desire to desire *de dicto*?

No. Probably it is already wrong to reject egoism *a priori* but, be that as it may, there are other doctrines of value *de se*, more plausible and more attractive. Self-improvement and self-sacrifice are no less egocentric than self-aggrandizement and

---

[10] *Principia Ethica*, Section 59.

[11] Someone who said that happiness was the only value might mean something else. which is not a form of egoism at all. He might mean that the proposition that happiness is maximized is the only value—a single value *de dicto*. Or he might mean that for each person X, the proposition that X is happy is a value *de dicto*, and that these many values of parallel form are the only values. Mean what you please—I take these to be legitimate, but derivative, senses in which a property may be called a value. I only say they should not be confused with, or drive out, the sense in which a property may be a value *de se*.

DISPOSITIONAL THEORIES OF VALUE 121

self-indulgence. Surely we should make a place for putative values *de se* of altruism, of honour, and of loyalty to family, friends, and country.[12] We may entertain the substantive thesis that none of these putative values *de se* is genuine, and that all genuine values are *de dicto*. But even if we believed this —myself, I think it wildly unlikely—we should not beg the question in its favour by building it into our theoretical framework.

What conditions are 'ideal'? If someone has little notion what it would be like to live as a free spirit unbound by law, custom, loyalty, or love; or what a world of complete harmony and constant agreement would be like; then whether or not he blindly values these things must have little to do with whether or not they are truly values. What he lacks is imaginative acquaintance. If only he would think harder, and imagine vividly and thoroughly how it would be if these putative values were realised (and perhaps also how it would be if they were not) that would make his valuing a more reliable indicator of genuine value. And if he could gain the fullest imaginative acquaintance that is humanly possible,[13] then, I suggest, his valuing would be an infallible indicator. Something is a value iff we are disposed, under conditions of the fullest possible imaginative acquaintance, to value it.

Compare a version of Intuitionism: by hard thought, one becomes imaginatively well acquainted with X; in consequence, but not as the conclusion of any sort of inference, one intuits that X has a certain unanalysable, non-natural property; and in consequence of that, one comes to value X. My story begins and ends the same. Only the middle is missing. Again, an exercise of imaginative reason plays a crucial role. Again, its relation to what follows is causal, and in no way inferential. But in my story, the consequent valuing is caused more directly, not via the detection of a peculiar property of X.

Can we say that the valuing ensued because X was a value?—Maybe so, but if we do, we are not saying much: it

---

[12] See Andrew Oldenquist, 'Loyalties', *Journal of Philosophy* 79 (1982), pp. 173-193; Michael Slote, 'Morality and Self-Other Asymmetry', *Journal of Philosophy* 81 (1984), pp. 179-192.

[13] Without in the process having his dispositions to value altered—see Footnote 6.

ensues because there is something about imaginative acquaintance with X that causes valuing.[14]

The canonical way to find out whether something is a value
requires a difficult imaginative exercise. And if you are to be
sure of your answer, you need to be sure that you have gained
the fullest imaginative acquaintance that is humanly possible. A
tall order! You had better settle for less. Approximate the
canonical test. Try hard to imagine how it would be if the
putative value were (or were not) realised. Hope that your
acquaintance comes close enough to the fullest possible that
getting closer would not change your response. Then you may
take your valuing as fallible evidence that you were acquainted
with a genuine value, or your indifference as fallible evidence
that you were not. You cannot be perfectly certain of your
answer, but you can take it as sure enough to be going on with,
subject to reconsideration in the light of new evidence. How sure
is that?—Well, as always when we acknowledge fallibility, some
of us will be bolder than others.

New evidence might be a more adequate imaginative exercise
of your own. It might be the testimony of others. It might in
principle be a result of scientific psychology—though it is far
from likely that any such results will come to hand soon!

A trajectory toward fuller imaginative acquaintance with
putative value X is not just a sequence of changes in your
imaginative state. It has a direction to it. And that is so
independently of my claim that it leads, after a point, to ever-
surer knowledge about whether X is a value. For in learning
how to imagine X, you gain abilities; later you have all the
relevant imaginative abilities you had before, and more besides.
And you notice, *a priori*, relationships of coherence or incoherence
between attitudes that might figure in the realisation of X; later
you are aware of all that you had noticed before, and more

---

[14] How does imaginative acquaintance cause valuing, when it does? How does
imagination render values attractive? Does it happen the same way for all values?—For
our purposes, it is enough to say that it happens. We needn't know how. But we may
guess. Maybe imaginative acquaintance shows us how new desires would be seamless
extensions of desires we have already. Or maybe we gravitate toward what we
understand, lest we baffle ourselves—see J. David Velleman, *Practical Reflection*
(Princeton University Press, forthcoming). But that cannot be the whole story, because
some easily understood lives—say a life of lethargy, ruled by a principle of least
action—remain repellent.

besides. And you think of new questions to explore in your imagining—what might the life of the free spirit become, long years after its novelty had worn off?—and later you have in mind all the questions you had thought of before, and more besides. Forgetting is possible, of course. But by and large, the process resists reversal.[15]

Our theory makes a place for truth, and in principle for certain knowledge, and in practice for less-than-certain knowledge, about value. But also it makes a place for ignorance and error, for hesitant opinion and modesty, for trying to learn more and hoping to succeed. That is all to the good. One fault of some subjective and prescriptive theories is that they leave no room for modesty: just decide where you stand, then you may judge of value with the utmost confidence!

There is a long history of theories that analyse value in terms of hypothetical response under ideal conditions, with various suggestions about what conditions are ideal. Imaginative acquaintance often gets a mention. But much else does too. I think imaginative acquaintance is all we need—the rest should be in part subsumed, in part rejected.

First, the responder is often called an ideal *spectator*. That is tantamount to saying that conditions are ideal only when he is observing a sample of the putative value in question (or of its absence). If the putative value is *de se*, a property, then a sample can just be an instance. If it is *de dicto*, a proposition, it is hard to say in general what an observable sample could be. But if it is the proposition that a certain property is instantiated sometimes, or often, or as often as possible, or in all cases of a certain kind, then again a sample can just be an instance of the property. Anyone happy may serve as a sample of the proposition that total happiness is maximised.

Observable samples can sometimes prompt the imagination and thereby help us to advance imaginative acquaintance. But they are of limited use. For one thing, observation does not include mind-reading. Also, it does best with short, dramatic episodes. A lifelong pattern of stagnation, exemplifying the absence of various values, goes on too long to be easily

[15] For a discussion of unidirectionality in aesthetic valuing, see Michael Slote, 'The Rationality of Aesthetic Value Judgements', *Journal of Philosophy* 68 (1971), pp. 821–839.

124   II—DAVID LEWIS

observed. Samples are dispensable as aids to imagination, and
sometimes they are comparatively ineffective. A novel might be
better.

The notion of an ideal spectator is part of a longstanding
attempt to make dispositional theories of value and of colour run
in parallel. But the analogy is none too good, and I doubt that it
improves our understanding either of colour or of value. Drop it,
and I think we have no further reason to say that a disposition to
value is a disposition to respond to observed samples.[16]

Second, the ideal responder is often supposed to be well
informed. If any item of empirical knowledge would affect his
response, he knows it.—But some sorts of knowledge would not
help to make your valuing a more reliable indicator of genuine
value. Instead they would distract. If you knew too well how
costly or how difficult it was to pursue some value, you might
reject the grapes as sour, even when imaginative acquaintance
with the value itself would have caused you to value it. Genuine
values might be unattainable, or unattainable without undue
sacrifice of other values. An ideal *balancer* of values needs
thorough knowledge of the terms of trade. An ideal valuer may
be better off without it. Our present business is not with the
balancing, but with the prior question of what values there are
to balance.[17]

Another unhelpful sort of knowledge is a vivid awareness that
we are small and the cosmos is large; or a vivid awareness of the
mortality of mankind, and of the cosmos itself. If such
knowledge tends to extinguish all desire, and therefore all

[16] If we had demanded samples, we would have had a choice about where to locate the
disposition. Is it within us or without? Is it a disposition in the samples to evoke a response
from spectators?—that is what best fits the supposed parallel with a dispositional theory
of colour. See Robert Pargetter and John Campbell, 'Goodness and Fragility', *American
Philosophical Quarterly* 23 (1986), pp. 155–166, for an analysis of this kind. Or is it a
disposition in the spectators to respond to samples? Or is it a disposition of the sample-
cum-spectator system to respond to having its parts brought together? For us there is no
choice. The propositions and properties that are the values cannot harbour any causal
bases for dispositions. Samples could, but there needn't be any samples. Imaginative
experiences could, but those are within us, and are not themselves samples of values. So
the disposition must reside in us, the responders. Being a value comes out as a
dispositionally analysed property, but not as a disposition of the things that have it.
Values themselves are not disposed to do anything.

[17] Previous theories of hypothetical response may indeed have been concerned as
much with the analysis of right balancing as with value itself. If so, they cannot be faulted
for trying to characterise an ideal balancer. However my present *analysandum* is different.

DISPOSITIONAL THEORIES OF VALUE　　　　125

valuing, it will not help us to value just what is valuable. Likewise it will be unhelpful to dwell too much on the lowly causal origins of things. If some feature of our lives originated by kin selection, or Pavlovian conditioning, or sublimation of infantile sexuality, that is irrelevant to what it is like in itself. Unless he can overcome the illusion of relevance, a valuer will be more reliable if he remains ignorant of such matters.

However, I grant one case—a common one—in which one does need empirical knowledge in order to gain imaginative acquaintance with a given putative value. It may be 'given' in a way that underspecifies it, with the rest of the specification left to be filled in by reference to the actual ways of the world. For instance when I mentioned the life of a free spirit as a putative value, what I meant—and what you surely took me to mean—was the life of a free spirit in a world like ours. In such cases, a valuer must complete the specification by drawing on his knowledge of the world, else he will not know what he is supposed to imagine. To that extent—and only to that extent, I think—being well-informed is indeed a qualification for his job.[18]

Third, it may be said that the ideal responder should not only imagine having (or lacking) a putative value, but also imagine the effect on other people of someone's having (or lacking) it. Thinking what it would be like to live as a free spirit is not enough. You must also think what it would be like to encounter the free spirit and be ill-used.—But again, I think the requirement is misplaced. It is appropriate not to an ideal valuer, but to an ideal balancer who must think through the cost to some values of the realisation of others. In addressing the prior question of what values there are, counting the cost is a distraction to be resisted.

Often, however, realising a putative value *de se* would itself involve imagining the impact of one's conduct on other people. When that is so, imagining realising the value involves

---

[18] Imaginative acquaintance is sometimes thought to consist in the possession of a special kind of 'phenomenal' information. If that is so, of course my own candidate for 'ideal conditions' comes down to a special case of being well-informed. But it is not so—not even in the most favourable case, that of imaginative acquaintance with a kind of sense-experience. See my 'What Experience Teaches' in William Lycan, ed., *Mind and Cognition: A Reader* (Blackwell, 1989).

126   II—DAVID LEWIS

imagining imagining the impact; and that cannot be done
without simply imagining the impact. In such cases, imagining
the impact does fit in; for it is already subsumed as part of
imaginative acquaintance with the value itself.

Fourth, the ideal responder is often said to be dispassionate
and impartial, like a good judge.—Once more, the requirement
is appropriate not to an ideal valuer but to an ideal balancer.
The valuer is not a judge. He is more like an advocate under the
adversarial system. He is a specialist, passionate and partial
perhaps, in some one of all the values there are. On the present
theory, when I say that X is a value iff we are disposed to value X
under ideal conditions, I do not mean conditions that are ideal
simpliciter, but rather conditions that are ideal *for* X. We should
not assume that there is any such thing as a condition of
imaginative acquaintance with all values at once. (Still less, all
putative values.) Imagination involves simulation—getting into
the skin of the part. How many skins can you get into all at once?
Tranquillity and vigorous activity might both be values; but a
full imaginative acquaintance with one might preclude a full
imaginative acquaintance with the other. (The incompatibility
might even be conceptual, not just psychological.) Then if we
value both, as surely many of us do, it is not because of
acquaintance with both at once. It might be a lasting effect of
past imaginative acquaintance at some times with one and at
other times with the other.

A further speculation: it might happen that there were values
that could not even be valued all at once. If so, then conflict of
values would go deeper than is ever seen in hard choices;
because what makes a choice hard is that conflicting values *are*
valued together by the unfortunate chooser. An alarming
prospect!—or exhilarating, to those of us who delight in the rich
variety of life.

Who are 'we'? An *absolute* version of the dispositional theory says
that the 'we' refers to all mankind. To call something a value is
to call it a value *simpliciter*, which means that everyone, always
and everywhere, is disposed under ideal conditions to value it.
Then there are values only insofar as all mankind are alike in
their dispositions.

Maybe all mankind *are* alike. The manifest diversity of

valuing between different cultures—or for that matter within a culture, say between colleagues in the same philosophy department—is no counterevidence. In the first place, people may not be valuing as they would be disposed to value under ideal conditions. In the second place, remember that conditions of imaginative acquaintance are ideal for particular values, not *simpliciter*. So even if all are disposed alike, and all value as they would under ideal conditions, that may mean that some people value X as they would under conditions ideal for X, while others, who are no differently disposed, value Y as they would under conditions ideal for Y. If no conditions are ideal at once for X and for Y (still more if X and Y cannot both be valued at once), there could be diversity of valuing even in a population of psychological clones, if different ones had been led into different imaginative exercises.

We saw that it would be no easy job to find out for sure whether a particular person would be disposed to value something under ideal conditions of imaginative acquaintance with it. It would be harder still to find out all about one person's dispositions. And not just because one hard job would have to be done many times over. It might happen that imaginative acquaintance with X would leave traces, in one's valuing or otherwise, that got in the way of afterward imagining Y. To the extent that there was such interference, each new imaginative experiment would be harder than the ones before.

The fallback, if we are wary of presupposing that all mankind are alike in their dispositions to value, is tacit relativity. A *relative* version says that the 'we' in the analysis is indexical, and refers to a population consisting of the speaker and those somehow like him. If the analysis is indexical, so is the analysandum. Then for speaker S to call something a value is to call it a value for the population of S and those like him; which means that S and those like him are all disposed, under ideal conditions, to value it.

The relative version is not just one version, but a spectrum. What analysis you get depends on how stringent a standard of similarity you apply to the phrase 'the speaker and those somehow like him'. At one end of the spectrum stands the absolute version: common humanity is likeness enough, so whoever speaks, all mankind are 'we'. At the other end, 'we'

means: 'you and I, and I'm none too sure about you'. (Or it
might be 'I, and those who think as I do', which reduces to 'I'.)
In between, 'we' means: 'I, and all those who are of a common
culture with me'. Since mankind even at one moment is not
made up of isolated and homogeneous tribes, and since we should
not limit ourselves to the part of mankind located at one
moment, we may haggle endlessly over how much cultural
affiliation is meant.

(We have a piece of unfinished business: if someone is to find
out about values by the canonical method, he must somehow
know that he is one of the appropriate 'we'. All our versions,
absolute or relative, make this knowledge automatic. Not so for
elitist versions, on which 'we' means 'the best-qualified of us' or
maybe 'the most normal of us'. But elitist versions are pointless.
We're already considering dispositions under extravagantly
ideal conditions; we needn't idealise all over again by being
selective about who counts as one of the 'we'.)

If some relative version were the correct analysis, wouldn't
that be manifest whenever people talk about value? Wouldn't
you hear them saying 'value for me and my mates' or 'value for
the likes of you'? Wouldn't you think they'd stop arguing after
one speaker says X is a value and the other says it isn't?—Not
necessarily. They might always presuppose, with more or less
confidence (well-founded or otherwise), that whatever relativity
there is won't matter in *this* conversation. Even if they accept
in principle that people sometimes just differ in their dispositions to value, they may be very reluctant to think the
present deadlocked conversation is a case of such difference.
However intractable the disagreement may be, they may
go on thinking it really *is* a disagreement: a case in which
two people are disposed alike, but one of them is wrong about
what is a value relative to their shared dispositions, because he is
not valuing as he would under ideal conditions. So long as they
think that—and they might think it very persistently—they can
hold the language of explicit relativity in reserve. It is there as a
last resort, if ever they meet with a proven case of ultimate
difference. But it will not be much heard, since it is a practical
impossibility to prove a case. If the language of absolutism
prevails, that is not strong evidence against relativity.

(Those who have heard of the relativity of simultaneity do not manifest this knowledge all the time. They speak as the ignorant do, and no harm done. They'll resort to the language of relativity when it matters, say in discussing the exploits of the interstellar navy.)

Does the language of absolutism prevail? Not really. With some of us it does. Others of us resort to the language of relativity at the drop of a hat. Yet this too is poor evidence. The eager relativists may have been confused by philosophy. For who can escape it?

So what version should we prefer, absolute or relative?— Neither; instead, I commend a *wait-and-see* version. In making a judgement of value, one makes many claims at once, some stronger than others, some less confidently than others, and waits to see which can be made to stick. I say X is a value; I mean that all mankind are disposed to value X; or anyway all nowadays are; or anyway all nowadays are except maybe some peculiar people on distant islands; or anyway . . . ; or anyway you and I, talking here and now, are; or anyway I am.[19] How much am I claiming?—as much as I can get away with. If my stronger claims were proven false—though how that could be proven is hard to guess—I still mean to stand by the weaker ones. So long as I'm not challenged, there's no need to back down in advance; and there's no need to decide how far I'd back down if pressed. What I mean to commit myself to is *conditionally relative*: relative if need be, but absolute otherwise.

What is the modal status of the equivalence? The equivalence between value and what we are disposed to value is meant to be a piece of philosophical analysis, therefore analytic. But of course it is not obviously analytic; it is not even obviously true.

It is a philosophical problem how there can ever be unobvious analyticity. We need not solve that problem; suffice it to say that it is everybody's problem, and it is not to be solved by denying the phenomenon. There are perfectly clear examples of it: the epsilon-delta analysis of an instantaneous rate of change, for one. Whenever it is analytic that all A's are B's, but not obviously analytic, the Moorean open question—whether all A's are indeed B's—is intelligible. And not only is it intelligible

---

[19] See the discussion of 'anyway' in Frank Jackson, 'On Assertion and Indicative Conditionals', *Philosophical Review* 88 (1979), pp. 565–589.

in the sense that we can parse and interpret it (that much is true
even of the question whether all A's are *A's*) but also in the sense
that it makes sense as something to say in a serious discussion, as
an expression of genuine doubt.

Besides unobvious analyticity, there is equivocal analyticity.
Something may be analytic under one disambiguation but not
another, or under one precisification but not another. Examples
abound. Quine was wrong that analyticity was unintelligible,
right to doubt that we have many clearcut cases of it. If differing
versions of a concept (or, if you like, different but very similar
concepts) are in circulation under the same name, we will get
equivocal analyticity. It is analytic under one disambiguation of
'dog' that all dogs are male; under one disambiguation of 'bitch'
that all bitches are canine. It is analytic under some precisifi-
cations of 'mountain' that no mountain is less than one
kilometre high. When analyticity is equivocal, open questions
make good conversational sense: they are invitations to proceed
under a disambiguation or precisification that makes the answer
to the question not be analytic. By asking whether there are
mountains less than one kilometre high, you invite your
conversational partners to join you in considering the question
under a precisification of 'mountain' broad enough to make it
interesting; yet it was analytic under another precisification that
the answer was 'no'.[20] So even if all is obvious, open questions
show at worst that the alleged analyticity is equivocal.

I suggest that the dispositional theory of value, in the version I
have put forward, is equivocally as well as unobviously analytic.
I do not claim to have captured the one precise sense that the
word 'value' bears in the pure speech, uncorrupted by
philosophy, that is heard on the Clapham omnibus. So far as this
matter goes, I doubt that speakers untouched by philosophy
are found in Clapham or anywhere else. And if they were, I
doubt if they'd have made up their minds exactly what to mean
any more than the rest of us have. I take it, rather, that the word
'value', like many others, exhibits both semantic variation and
semantic indecision. The best I can hope for is that my
dispositional theory lands somewhere near the middle of the

---

[20] See my 'Scorekeeping in a Language Game', *Journal of Philosophical Logic* 8 (1979),
pp. 339–359.

range of variation and indecision—and also gives something that I, and many more besides, could be content to adopt as our official definition of the word 'value', in the unlikely event that we needed an official definition.

I've left some questions less than conclusively settled: the matter of absolute versus relative versus wait-and-see versions, the details of 'ideal conditions', the question of admitting values *de se*, the definition of valuing as second-order versus highest-order intrinsic desiring. It would not surprise or disturb me to think that my answers to those questions are only equivocally analytic—but somewhere fairly central within the range of variation and indecision—and that the same could be said of rival answers. Even if no version of the dispositional theory is unequivocally analytic, still it's fair to hope that some not-too-miscellaneous disjunction of versions comes out analytic under most reasonable resolutions of indeterminacy (under some reasonable precisification of 'most' and 'reasonable'.)

If the dispositional theory is only unobviously and equivocally analytic, why think that it's analytic at all?—Because that hypothesis fits our practice. (The practice of many of us, much of the time.) It does seem that if we try to find out whether something is a genuine value, we do try to follow—or rather, approximate—the canonical method. We gain the best imaginative acquaintance we can, and see if we then desire to desire it. In investigating values by the canonical method, we ignore any alleged possibility that values differ from what we're disposed to value. The dispositional theory explains nicely why we ignore it: no such possibility exists.

Now this should sound an alarm. Phenomenalism, behaviourism, and the like might be supported in exactly the same way: we ignore the possibility that our method of investigation deceives us radically, and the alleged explanation is that no such possibility exists. But in those cases, we know better. We know how systematic hallucination might deceive its victim about the world around him, and how a clever actor might deceive everyone he meets about his inner life (and, in both cases, how it might be that experience or behaviour would remain deceptive throughout the appropriate range of counterfactual suppositions). And it doesn't just strike us that such deception is possible *somehow*. Rather, we can imagine just how it might happen. We

132   II—DAVID LEWIS

can give a story of deception all the detail it takes to make it
convincing. So we must confess that our method of gaining
knowledge of the outer world and the inner lives does consist in
part of ignoring genuine possibilities—possibilities that cannot
credibly be denied.

The case of value is different, because the convincing detail
cannot be supplied. Yes, you might think that perhaps the
genuine values somehow differ from what we are disposed to
value, even under ideal conditions. (Charles Pigden has noted
that a misanthrope might think it because he thinks mankind is
irremediably depraved.) The conjecture is not unthinkable; the
dispositional theory is not *obviously* analytic; counterexamples
are not *obviously* impossible. That is not yet much evidence of
possibility. Better evidence would be a detailed story of just how
it might happen that something—something specific—is after
all a value that we are not disposed to value, or a non-value that
we are disposed to value. But I have no idea how to flesh out the
story. Without 'corroborative detail', insistence that there exist
such possibilities is 'bald and unconvincing'. This time, nothing
outweighs the niceness of explaining the ignoring by denying the
possibilities allegedly ignored.

But is it realism? Psychology is contingent. Our dispositions to
value things might have been otherwise than they actually are.
We might have been disposed, under ideal conditions, to value
seasickness and petty sleaze above all else. Does the dispositional
theory imply that, had we been thus disposed, those things
would have been values? That seems wrong.

No: we can take the reference to our dispositions as rigidified.
Even speaking within the scope of a counterfactual supposition,
the things that count as values are those that we are *actually*
disposed to value, not those we would have valued in the
counterfactual situation. No worries—unless seasickness actually
is a value, it still wouldn't have been a value even if we'd been
disposed to value it.

This is too swift. The trick of rigidifying seems more to hinder
the expression of our worry than to make it go away. It can still
be expressed as follows. We might have been disposed to value
seasickness and petty sleaze, and yet we might have been no
different in how we used the word 'value'. The reference of 'our

actual dispositions' would have been fixed on different dispositions, of course, but our way of fixing the reference would have been no different. In one good sense—though not the only sense—we would have meant by 'value' just what we actually do. And it would have been true for us to say 'seasickness and petty sleaze are values'.

The contingency of value has not gone away after all; and it may well disturb us. I think it is the only disturbing aspect of the dispositional theory. Conditional relativity may well disturb us too, but that is no separate problem. What comfort would it be if all mankind just *happened* to be disposed alike? Say, because some strange course of cultural evolution happened to be cut short by famine, or because some mutation of the brain never took place? Since our dispositions to value are contingent, they certainly vary when we take *all* of mankind into account, all the inhabitants of all the possible worlds. Given the dispositional theory, trans-world relativity is inevitable. The spectre of relativity within our own world is just a vivid reminder of the contingency of value.

If wishes were horses, how would we choose to ride? What would it take to satisfy us? Maybe this new version of the dispositional theory would suit us better: values are what we're *necessarily* disposed to value. Then no contingent 'value' would deserve the name; and there would be no question of something being a value for some people and not for others, since presumably what's necessary is *a fortiori* uniform (unless different dispositions to value are built into different people's individual essences, an unlikely story).

What kind of necessity should it be? Not mere deontic necessity—values are what we're disposed to value on pain of being at fault, where the fault in question turns out to consist in failing to be disposed to value the genuine values. That dispositional theory is empty. Its near relatives are nearly empty. And it won't help to juggle terms; as it might be, by calling it 'rational necessity' and then classifying the disposition to value genuine values as a department of 'rationality'. Probably not nomological necessity either—small comfort to think that we were disposed to disvalue seasickness only because, luckily, our neurons are not subject to a certain fifth force of nature that would distort their workings in just the wrong way. It had better

134   II—DAVID LEWIS

be necessity *simpliciter*, so-called 'metaphysical' necessity.

If we amend the dispositional theory by inserting 'necessarily', we can be much more confident that the 'values' it defines would fully deserve the name—if there were any of them. But it is hard to see how there possibly could be. If a value, strictly speaking, must be something we are necessarily disposed to value, and if our dispositions to value are in fact contingent, then, strictly speaking, there are no values. If Mackie is right that a value (his term is 'objective good') would have to be

> sought by anyone who was acquainted with it, not because of any contingent fact that this person, or every person, is so constituted that he desires this end, but just because the end has to-be-pursuedness somehow built into it;

then he is also right to call values 'queer' and to repudiate the error of believing in them.[21] (Replacing 'sought' by 'valued' would not change that.) If we amend the dispositional theory, requiring values to be all that we might wish them to be, we bring on the error theory. The fire is worse than the frying pan.

Is it, after all, out of the question that our dispositions to value might be necessary? If the theory of mind I favour is true, then the platitudes of folk psychology do have a certain necessity—albeit conditional necessity—to them.[22] There are states that play the functional roles specified in those platitudes, and it is in virtue of doing so that they deserve their folk-psychological names. It is not necessary that there should be any states in us that deserve such names as 'pain', 'belief', or 'desire'. But it is necessary that if any states do deserve those names, then they conform to the platitudes. Or rather, they conform well enough. Now suppose that some of the platitudes of folk psychology specified exactly what we were disposed, under ideal conditions, to desire to desire. And suppose those platitudes were non-negotiable: if a system of states did not satisfy them, that would settle that those states did not conform well enough to folk

---

[21] J. L. Mackie, *Ethics: Inventing Right and Wrong* (Penguin, 1977), p. 40. But note that the queerness Mackie has in mind covers more than just the to-know-it-is-to-love-it queerness described in this passage.

[22] See my 'An Argument for the Identity Theory', *Journal of Philosophy* 63 (1966), pp. 17–25; and D. M. Armstrong, *A Materialist Theory of the Mind* (Routledge and Kegan Paul, 1968).

DISPOSITIONAL THEORIES OF VALUE 135

psychology to deserve the mental names it implicitly defines. Then there would be things we were necessarily disposed to value—on condition that we had mental lives at all!

The suggestion is intelligible and interesting, but too good to be true. For one thing, it only spreads the trouble. Instead of losing the risk that nothing deserves the name of value, we gain the added risk that nothing deserves commonplace folk-psychological names. *Pace* the Churchlands, it's not really credible that there might turn out to be no beliefs, no desires. no pains, . . .[23] For another thing, it proves too much. It denies outright that it's possible for someone to differ from others in his dispositions to value. Yet this does seem possible; and we can flesh out the story with plenty of 'corroborative detail'. This cunning and subtle villain once was as others are; he gained excellent imaginative acquaintance with many values, and valued them accordingly. Now he has gone wrong, and cares not a fig for what he once valued; and yet he has forgotten nothing. (He certainly has not stopped having any mental life deserving of the name.) He hates those who are as he once was, and outwits them all the better because of his superb empathetic uncer-standing of what they hold dear. Could it not happen?—not if the present suggestion were true. So the present suggestion is false. Yet it was the only hope, or the only one I know, for explaining how there might be things we are necessarily disposed to value. The dispositions are contingent, then. And, at least in some tacit way, we know it. If the story of the subtle villain strikes you as a possible story, that knowledge thereby reveals itself.

But if we know better, it is odd that we are disturbed—as I think many of us will be—by a dispositional theory of value, unamended, according to which values are contingent. It feels wrong. Why might that be?—Perhaps because a large and memorable part of our discussion of values consists of browbeating and being browbeaten.[24] The rhetoric would fall flat if we kept in mind, all the while, that it is contingent how we are disposed to value. So a theory which acknowledges that contingency

---

[23] As argued in Frank Jackson and Philip Pettit, 'In Defence of Folk Psychology', forthcoming in *Philosophical Studies*.

[24] See Ian Hinckfuss, *The Moral Society: Its Structure and Effects* (Australian National University Discussion Papers in Environmental Philosophy, 1987).

136   II—DAVID LEWIS

cannot feel quite right. You might say that it is unfaithful to the distinctive phenomenological character of lived evaluative thought. Yet even if it feels not right, it may still be right, or as near right as we can get. It feels not quite right to remember that your friends are big swarms of little particles—it is inadequate to the phenomenology of friendship—but still they are.

I suggested earlier that my version of the dispositional theory of value might be equivocally analytic. So might the amended version, on which values are what we are necessarily disposed to value. Between these two versions, not to mention others, there might be both semantic variation and semantic indecision. If so, it is part of a familiar pattern. One way to create indeterminacy and equivocal analyticity is to define names implicitly in terms of a theory (folk or scientific), and later find out that the theory is wrong enough that nothing perfectly deserves the names so introduced, but right enough that some things, perhaps several rival candidates, deserve the names imperfectly. Nothing perfectly deserves the name 'simultaneity', since nothing quite fits the whole of our old conception. So the name will have to go to some imperfect deserver of it, or to nothing. What it takes to deserve this name, not perfectly but well enough, was never officially settled. One resolution of the indeterminacy makes it analytic that simultaneity must be frame-independent; another, that it must be an equivalence relation; a third, that it must be both at once. The third brings with it an error theory of simultaneity.[25]

I suggest that (for some of us, or some of us sometimes) the amended dispositional theory best captures what it would take for something to perfectly deserve the name 'value'. There are no perfect deservers of the name to be had. But there are plenty of imperfect deservers of the name, and my original version is meant to capture what it takes to be one of the best of them. (But I do not say mine is the only version that can claim to do so. Doubtless there are more dimensions of semantic variation and indeterminacy than just our degree of tolerance for imperfection.) Strictly speaking, nothing shall get the name without deserving it perfectly. Strictly speaking, Mackie is right: genuine values

[25] See Hartry Field, 'Theory Change and the Indeterminacy of Reference', *Journal of Philosophy* 70 (1973), pp. 462-481.

DISPOSITIONAL THEORIES OF VALUE 137

would have to meet an impossible condition, so it is an error to think there are any. Loosely speaking, the name may go to a claimant that deserves it imperfectly. Loosely speaking, common sense is right. There are values, lots of them, and they are what we are disposed *de facto* to value.

Then is my position a form of realism about values?— Irrealism about values strictly speaking, realism about values loosely speaking. The former do not exist. The latter do.

What to make of the situation is mainly a matter of temperament. You can bang the drum about how philosophy has uncovered a terrible secret: there are no values! (Shock horror: no such thing as simultaneity! Nobody ever whistled while he worked!) You can shout it from the housetops— browbeating is oppression, the truth shall make you free.[26] Or you can think it better for public safety to keep quiet and hope people will go on as before. Or you can declare that there are no values, but that nevertheless it is legitimate—and not just expedient—for us to carry on with value-talk, since we can make it all go smoothly if we just give the name of value to claimants that don't quite deserve it. This would be a sort of quasi-realism, not the same as Blackburn's quasi-realism.[27] Or you can think it an empty question whether there are values: say what you please, speak strictly or loosely. When it comes to deserving a name, there's better and worse but who's to say how good is good enough? Or you can think it clear that the imperfect deservers of the name are good enough, but only just, and say that although 'there are values we are still terribly wrong about them. Or you can calmly say that value (like simultaneity) is not quite as some of us sometimes thought. Myself, I prefer the calm and conservative responses. But so far as the analysis of value goes, they're all much of a muchness.

---

[26] See Hinckfuss, *op. cit.*

[27] Simon Blackburn, *Spreading the Word: Groundings in the Philosophy of Language* (Oxford University Press, 1984), Chapter 6.

[15]

DISPOSITIONAL THEORIES OF VALUE

III—Mark Johnston

I

As a recently published letter reveals[1], the same David Hume who seemed to suggest that distinctions of value were mere projections of our sentiments when he wrote[2]

> Vice and virtue therefore may be compared to sounds, colours, heat and cold, which, according to the modern philosophy are not qualities in the object but perceptions in the mind.

also wrote

> Philosophy scarce ever advances a greater paradox in the eyes of the people, than when it affirms that snow is neither cold nor white: fire hot nor red.

Taken together, and without prejudicing the interpretation of Hume, these quotations could serve as the motto of those who have attempted to defend a realism about value by way of an analogy with secondary qualities and with colour in particular. The aim of the analogists has been to undermine the characteristic claim of sentimentalist projectivism about value, namely that value is not a *genuine* feature of persons, acts, states of affairs, etc., but only appears so because we mistake features of our evaluative responses for features of such things. The leading idea of the analogists has been to show that by the same standards of genuineness it would follow that colour is not a genuine feature of surfaces.[3]

---

[1] Letter to Hugh Blair of 4 July, 1762, printed in *Mind*, October, 1986.

[2] *Treatise of Human Nature* edited by Selby-Bigge (Oxford, 1888), p. 469.

[3] See John McDowell 'Non-Cognitivism and Rule-Following' in Holtzman & Leich (eds.) *Wittgenstein: to Follow a Rule* (Routledge, 1981) and 'Values and Secondary Qualities' in Honderich (ed.) *Morality and Objectivity: a Tribute to J. L. Mackie* (Routledge, 1985). Also David Wiggins 'Truth, Invention and the Meaning of Life' and 'A Sensible Subjectivism' both in his *Needs, Values, Truth* (Basil Blackwell, 1987).

The analogy is opposed by Simon Blackburn 'Errors and the Phenomenology of Value' in Honderich (ed.) *op. cit.* and by Colin McGinn *The Subjective View* (Oxford

140   III—MARK JOHNSTON

To fill out the leading idea: the conception of colour which the
analogists typically employ is the so-called dispositional conception; according to which, for example

> *x* is red iff *x* is disposed to look such and so (ostended) way to
> standard perceivers as they actually are under standard
> conditions as they actually are.

Even if this biconditional misrepresents our conception of
colour in general and of redness in particular, as I think it
obviously does,[4] it is probably true that we could have employed
a concept for which something like this was adequate.
Operating with the fiction that such is our concept of redness, it
first would follow that (categorically kosher) predications
involving '*x* is red' have truth conditions and are straightforwardly evaluable as true or false. Secondly, redness would
also be a genuine property: not simply in the sense that the
predicate '*x* is red' and the abstract singular term 'redness'
would have a semantic value, but also in the more interesting
sense that predicating '*x* is red' of things could be part of
straightforward casual/dispositional explanations of why those
things look red to perceivers on *particular* occasions. (This latter
should impress even a Nominalist who spurns the idiom of
property-talk.) Thirdly, thanks to judicious placement of the
rigidifying device 'actually', the biconditional allows that

University Press, 1983), Chapter 8. A sophisticated way of taking the analogy is
presented by Crispin Wright in his 'Moral Values, Projection and Secondary Qualities'
Proceedings of the Aristotelian Society, supp. vol. LXII, 1988.

Of course, the analogy is associated with a long tradition of 'moral sense' and 'ideal
observer' theories. As far as I have been able to make out, it was Anthony Ashley Cooper,
Third Earl of Shaftesbury, who in his *Characteristics of Men, Manner, Opinions, Times*
(1711) first used the term 'moral sense' to denote aspects of our psychology plausibly
taken to be attuned to value. He called the moral sense a 'reflex sense' which when
applied to the objects of our affections gives rise to 'another kind of affection towards
those very affections themselves', *Characteristics*, edited by John H. Robinson, 2 volumes,
(Bobbs-Merrill, 1964) volume 1, p. 251. While it is unclear whether Shaftesbury
intended, in Hume's crucial phrase, 'to derive moral distinctions from a moral sense',
this psychologism was explicit in Francis Hutcheson's *An Inquiry into the Original of our
Ideas of Beauty and Virtue* (London, R. Ware 1753), and in Adam Smith *A Theory of the
Moral Sentiments* (1759) where the ideal observer theory predominates.

A nice article on the tradition is James Ward Smith's 'The British Moralists and the
Fallacy of Psychologism' *Journal of the History of Ideas*, XI, 1950.

[4] This claim is treated in some detail in my 'Objectivity Refigured' in *Realism and
Reason*, John Haldane and Crispin Wright (eds.) (Oxford University Press, forthcoming).

something could have been red even if standard perceivers and standard conditions had been different and even if there were no standard perceivers and no standard conditions.[5] The dispositional view, so spelt out, is not simple subjectivism or idealism about colour. The colours of things are not existentially dependent upon our responses. Rather, colour concepts are conceptually dependent upon the concepts of our responses under certain conditions. (More on this conceptual dependence in section II).

Three kinds of theorists would be confounded if this were the correct account of 'red'. The tables would be turned on colour non-cognitivists, who deny that utterances of the form '*x* is red' are truth-evaluable, instead supposing such utterances to be ejaculations merely prompted or caused by certain colour experiences under certain conditions. Given the dispositional account of 'red', some of the very conditions the non-cognitivist cites as the causal conditions for an ejaculation of the form '*x* is red' turn out to be conditions under which the ejaculation is true.

Related difficulties arise for error theorists about colour, who suppose that while remarks of the form '*x* is red' are or can be genuine assertions they are always in fact false, since nothing in the external world is coloured. The dispositional account shows immediately how external things could be red and indeed how we could get into a canonical condition for telling which things are red.

Finally, the account would expose as unnecessarily arducus the path of those delayed-reaction colour realists who, beginning with the non-cognitivist's starting point, see a problem about how remarks of the form '*x* is red' could be truth-evaluable given their causal origin in our responses, a problem which requires a substantial explanation of how we come to 'earn the right' to express our experiences in terms of judgements about external things. On the dispositional account there is no *earning* the right, we have instead a natural conceptual right. The judgements about the colours of external things are judgements involving conditions on our experiences.

[5] On this use of 'actually' see Martin Davies and Lloyd Humberstone 'Two Notions of Necessity', *Philosophical Studies*, 1981.

142   III—MARK JOHNSTON

Can the analogy between value and secondary qualities plausibly be deployed with corresponding effects against the non-cognitivism of A. J. Ayer, the error theory of J. L. Mackie and the quasi-realism of Simon Blackburn?[6] Everything depends upon just what analogy one has in mind.

Despite the fact that ordinary evaluators can immediately make evaluations on being perceptually confronted with complex situations, values are not in general the object of any perceptual or quasi-perceptual faculty or sense. As the one time currency of talk of the aesthetic sense or aesthetic attitude indicates, the sensuous aesthetic values are *prima facie* candidates for a perceptualist treatment. One can actually perceive the grace of a balletic movement, the satisfying resolution of a dissonance, the vividness of the depictions by the Sienese School. To these we might add sensuous pleasures conceived as the objects of the various ordinary senses.

However, unless we are prepared to presuppose a substantive aestheticism or hedonism about value, we must admit the limitations of any kind of quasi-perceptual acquaintance in discerning the value of such things as truth, justice and the American Way. Cold old correspondence to the facts may leave us unmoved even if we are able somehow to vividly picture an isomorphism of truthbearer and truthmaker. This tells us not that truth is valueless, but that its value is not salient in such ways. Similarly with justice; for if justice involves deviating from equality in the distribution of power, resources or opportunity only when there is good and sufficient *reason* then anything that is like perception in presenting information via a depiction will be too crude an instrument by which to evaluate the justice of some distributional proposal. And of course, if there were such a · thing as *the* American Way, it would be so multifarious in its details and so complex in its internal trade-offs that no depiction, perceptual or imaginative, could begin to discern its value. Any quasi-perceptual medium will thus tend to distort the evaluational message.

[6] See A. J. Ayer *Language, Truth and Logic* (Gollancz, London, 1936). A related non-cognitivist view is taken by C. L. Stevenson in *Ethics and Language* (New Haven, 1941). Mackie's error theory is set out in Chapter 1 of *Ethics: Inventing Right and Wrong* (Penguin, 1977), Simon Blackburn's quasi-realism is well presented in *Spreading the Word: Groundings in the Philosophy of Language* (Oxford University Press, 1984), Chapter 6.

A second and related point about the bruited analogy is that talk about red, colour or secondary qualities, while talk of determinables, is still relatively detailed talk. However, talk about value is talk at a level of almost fantastic abstraction. This remains so when we set to one side all so-called attributive uses of 'good' and talk of *a* good, and concentrate on the predicate '*x* is a value' understood as a universal predicate of favourable assessment applicable to states of affairs. Any nominalization of any sentence has a state of affairs as its semantic value. So states of affairs can be relatively simple or complex, and valuable or not, in a variety of ways (aesthetically, hedonistically, morally, etc.) and for an enormous range of reasons. The only correlative condition of valuers with such enormous generality is the condition of their finding themselves with reason to value the state of affairs in question. That one is moved by a perceptual or quasi-perceptual representation of a state of affairs might indicate, in the absence of defeating considerations, that there is a reason to value it. However, it is incredible that being moved by such perceptions is the only sort of reason to value something or that all relevant reason-giving properly terminates in appeal to such perceptual promptings.

A third disanalogy between dispositional secondary quality concepts and the concept of value concerns the different prospects of an analysis or definitional reduction in the two cases. Colour terms, like terms for other secondary qualities, can be introduced by ostension. For example, we can rely upon the neophyte's quality space and a cannily chosen collection of foils and paradigms to make salient a way things look, going on to introduce the neophyte to a colour concept by saying: 'Something is red just in case it is such as to look the way these paradigms look from here now and not the way those foils look from here now, *but* look that way to standard perceivers under standard conditions'. If, in accord with our fiction that the orthodox dispositional account can be made to work, we could give a substantive specification of standard perceivers and standard conditions without even covertly using the notions of being red or being otherwise coloured, we would here have defined a colour concept ostensively and without relying upon any colour concept as opposed to colour sample.

However, nothing like this will be plausible in the case of the

concept of being a valuable state of affairs. Ostension cannot be
relied upon here because there is no analogue of the perceptual
quality space to secure stable generalizations from any set of foils
and paradigms to the multifarious range of state of affairs which
can be valuable. There is a colour (appearance) solid but no
value (appearance) solid. This is a fundamental weakness in talk
of a moral or evaluational sense. What is a sense without a
quality space?

Fourthly, if, as suggested above, our finding reason to value
something is a response of ours that is relevant to the thing's
being valuable, then our finding *good* reason to value the thing is
at least as relevant in any dispositional account of value.
However the following looks like a trivial analytic connection: if
and only if *x is a good reason* for finding state of affairs *y* valuable is
it the case that if there is no countervailing reason, the state of
affairs of valuing *y* because of *x is valuable*. Given this dependence
of the notion of a good reason on the notion of value it appears
that exploiting the notion of a good reason is giving up the
analytically reductive game with respect to the universal
predicate of favourable assessment of state of affairs. But isn't
this to give up the only game suggested by the analogy between
secondary quality concepts and the concept of value?

II

No, it is not. The most plausible, if highly generalizing, way of
taking the analogy is this: evaluational concepts, like secondary
quality concepts as understood by the analogists, are 'response-
dependent' concepts. Let me explain.

About many areas of discourse philosophers have urged a
qualified realism, asserting both that the discourse in question
serves up genuine candidates for truth and falsity, and that,
nonetheless, the subject matter which makes statements of the
discourse true or false is not wholly independent of the cognitive
or affective responses of the speakers of the discourse. A basic
problem of contemporary philosophy is the problem of explicating the relevant notion of dependence so that the qualified
realism does not turn out to be (empirical) idealism in disguise,
i.e., does not imply that the dependent subject matter would not
exist or be the way it is but for the existence of our responses as
they actually are. Elsewhere I have argued that neither Michael

DISPOSITIONAL THEORIES OF VALUE 145

Dummett's semantic anti-realism nor Hilary Putnam's internal realism are satisfactory solutions to the basic problem.[7] The approach I favour differs from these in not explicating the concept of truth in terms of the concept of our finding warrant to assert things under ideal epistemic conditions. Instead, a different conceptual dependence on concepts of our responses under specified conditions is exploited. The resultant qualified realism can be local and topic-specific, applying to some subject matters and not others, without it following that truth is an equivocal notion across different subject matters. Let us call those concepts which exhibit a conceptual dependence on or interdependence with concepts of our responses in certain specified conditions *response-dependent* concepts. How then are we to demarcate the response-dependent concepts?

If C, the concept associated with the predicate 'is C', is a concept interdependent with or dependent upon concepts of certain subjects' responses under certain conditions then something of the following form will hold *a priori*

> x is C iff In K, Ss are disposed to produce x-directed
> response R
> (or
> > x is such as to produce R in Ss under
> > conditions K.)

Moreover, for the concepts in question such a biconditional will not hold simply in virtue of a reading of K, S or R which makes the biconditional trivial, imposing thereby no constraint on the concept C. Such a trivializing reading would be any reading which overtly or covertly specifies the conditions and subjects as whatever conditions and whatever subjects are required to get it right, or any reading which overtly or covertly specifies R as whatever response is truly C-detecting under the conditions specified. Given a 'whatever-it-takes' reading at any of these three points, the *a priori* truth of the biconditional so read indicates nothing in the way of the conceptual (inter)dependence in which we are interested.

However, when for a given C we have substantial or non-trivializing specifications of K, R and the Ss, and the resultant

---

[7] 'Objectivity Refigured' *op. cit.*

146 III—MARK JOHNSTON

biconditional holds *a priori*, then we have a concept inter-dependent with or dependent upon a concept of subjects' reactions under specified conditions. Such will be a response-dependent concept.[8]

Some concepts wear their response-dependent nature on their face: for example, the correlates of bodily sensation—the nauseating, the dizzying, etc.; the correlates of organ pleasure—the tasty, the titillating, etc.; the correlates of emotion—the shymaking, the embarrassing, etc.; the correlates of desire—the agreeable, the irritating, etc.; the correlates of belief—the plausible, the credible, etc.

The most obvious cases of *response-independent* concepts will be those concepts for which it is very plausible that the correct account of their content will not imply any substantial biconditional of the form above. Examples might be concepts of theoretical science such as the concept of a muon, logical concepts like conjunction, mathematical concepts such as successor. Of course a concept such as successor can be response-independent even if the concept of a subject's employing the concept of successor is response-dependent, being explicated in terms of the subject's dispositions to respond. Only a gross verificationism which confounded the conditions for possessing a concept with the content of the concept possessed would fail to recognize this possibility.

Many pivotal issues in philosophy, for example, issues about linguistic meaning, essence, personal identity, free will and the nature of similarity, can be cast in terms of whether and in what way the central concepts in those areas are response-dependent. So the central issue in the philosophical discussion of colour, the

[8] At least this holds with one proviso having to do with concepts introduced by reference-fixing descriptions and for which we have an *a priori* guarantee that there is some natural similarity underlying the relevant sample. Everyday terms for shapes might provide some examples. On reference-fixing see Saul Kripke *Naming and Necessity* (Harvard, 1980). For a discussion of the issue see 'Objectivity Refigured'. The distinction between response-dependent and response-independent concepts is one which I developed in my seminar on Ethics during the spring of 1986. I was fortunate enough to have Crispin Wright in attendance, and ever since then he and I have talked and corresponded about this and related distinctions. For his purposes he finds a different but related distinction useful. See his talk of 'order of determination' in 'Moral Values, Projection and Secondary Qualities' and his own contribution to the *Realism and Reason* volume. For a comparison of the distinctions see the appendix to my 'Objectivity Refigured'.

DISPOSITIONAL THEORIES OF VALUE 147

issues as between the so-called subjectivists and objectivists, is an issue over the response-dependence of colour concepts.[9] And the place to begin, though not to end, in explicating the primary/secondary quality distinction is with the response-independent, response-dependent distinction.

Notice that nothing in what I have said by way of characterizing response-dependent concepts implies that such concepts admit of a reductive definition or *analysis* in terms of concepts of subjects' responses. Hence the explicit allowance for conceptual interdependence.

The moral of recent philosophy is that many concepts, and most philosophically interesting concepts, have no interesting analysis. How can there fail to be an analysis of a concept C even although a substantial biconditional of the form above holds *a priori* for C? Well, it might be that in specifying the response in question we need to employ the concept C. The relevant x-directed response connected *a priori* to x being C might be the judgement or belief on the part of certain subjects under certain conditions that x is indeed C. Or it might be that in specifying the relevant conditions of response we need to require the stability of x with respect to precisely that range of determinables which includes the concept C. In the case of redness for example, we might want to rule out conditions in which the red thing would change colour if looked at. Or. . . .

That is, it may be that sometimes the biconditional of the relevant form which shows a concept to be response-dependent is strictly speaking circular. Circularity would be a vice if our aim were reductive definition. However our aim is not reductive definition but the exhibition of conceptual connections. In such an endeavour, circularity is a defect only if it implies the triviality of the biconditional. This is not the general case, for circular biconditionals of the relevant form are often sufficiently contentful to be open to *further* objection. (Remember, in the heyday of analysis, the critical papers pointing out that a proposed analysis was not only viciously circular but also subject to six counterexamples. The very nature of the charge indicates

[9] For some difficulties with attempts to characterize the debate between subjectivists and objectivists see the interesting papers by Peter Smith and Gregory McCulloch in the symposium 'Subjectivity and Colour Vision' *Proceedings of the Aristotelian Society supp. vol.*, LXI, 1987.

how a biconditional can be circular and contentful.) Indeed, when it comes to non-reductive explications, circularity can be a benefit and not all a defect, as we shall see. It would not be too strong to say that when it comes to explicating conceptual connections certain kinds of circularity are to be recommended.

Just to sketch the sense in which a response-dependent account of a concept C can be a qualified realism about instances of C, it should be obvious first that the holding of a substantial biconditional of the required form allows for a *realist* as opposed to *irrealist* conception of Cs, i.e., the account can allow that genuine instances of the concept C exist. So also, a response-dependent account of C is compatible with an (empirical) *realist* as opposed to (empirical) *idealist* conception of Cs; i.e. thanks to the dispositional formulation and the right sort of rigidifying on the actual responses under the actual conditions, the account can allow that the instances of C which do exist could still exist and be instances of C even if the relevant conditions and responders had not existed or had been different. So too, a response-dependent account of C can be a *realist* as opposed to an *anti-realist, internal realist or pragmatist* conception of C, i.e., it can deny both (a) that the meaning of statements employing the concept C is to be given in terms of those statements' conditions of warranted assertion, and (b) that the truth predicate applied to such statements is to be analyzed in epistemic terms. This latter is to say that one need not have a response-dependent account of the concept of truth in order to have a response-dependent account of some other concept C. (Indeed, there are reasons to think that any response-dependent account of truth will collapse into empirical idealism.)

In what sense then is a response-dependent realism essentially a *qualified* realism? Precisely in denying the independence of the concept in question from concepts of subjects' responses under specified conditions. Response-dependent realism is, if you like, a conceptual or transcendental idealism. However it implies no such things as noumena. (It may well imply that there must be available response-independent concepts of some things.)

The thesis I wish to explore is this: the notion of value, the all purpose notion of favourable assessment for states of affairs, is a response-dependent notion. The interest for present purposes of such a thesis is largely in the details. I have already indicated that even if one thought that secondary quality concepts like the concept red were response-dependent one might reject the most obvious response-dependent account—the orthodox dispositional view. Similarly, I am not prepared to endorse just any response-dependent account of value. I begin with an elegantly straightforward account of value which, as it happens, is in my terms a response-dependent account. The difficulties for this elegantly straightforward account will lead naturally to my own preferred account.

III

David Lewis claims that

> (L) *x* is a value iff we would be disposed to value *x* under conditions of the fullest imaginative acquaintance with *x*.[10]

We may take the things in the extension of the predicate here being analyzed to be propositions, including egocentric propositions, such as that *I* write a piece for the viola da gamba. We can think of such egocentric propositions in a variety of ways, e.g., as states of affairs under sentential characterizations which are egocentric. (Lewis has his own favoured way of dealing with so-called egocentric propositions. They turn out to be properties self-ascribed. However this difference *should* make no difference in what follows.)

Lewis is what I would call a response-dependent intuitionist about value! He writes

> Compare a version of Intuitionism: by hard thought, one becomes imaginatively well acquainted with x; in consequence, but not as the conclusion of any sort of inference, one intuits that x has a certain unanalyzable, non-natural property; and in consequence of that, one comes to value x. My story beings and ends the same. Only the middle is missing. Again an exercise of imaginative reason plays a crucial role. Again its relation to what follows is causal, and in no way inferential. But in my story, the consequent

[10] See his contribution to the present symposium, p. 113ff.

150   III—MARK JOHNSTON

valuing is caused more directly, not via the detection of a
particular property of x.[11]

Lewis tells us that (L) is not intended to indicate how we are to
balance values but to determine what values there are to
balance. Here, full imaginative acquaintance is the guide,
according to Lewis. However, Lewis holds that there is not
much chance of full imaginative acquaintance with all values at
once. 'Imagination seems to involve simulation—getting into
the skin of the part. How many skins can you get into all at once?
Maybe tranquillity is a value, and so is vigorous activity; but
maybe a full imaginative acquaintance with one precludes a full
imaginative acquaintance with another.'[12]

After the values to be weighed have been determined, the
balancer must, it seems, bring to bear some other technique
besides or along with sheer imagination in order properly to
weigh the values. There may well be a serious difficulty here.
For many propositions, and so substituends for analysis L,
describe evaluatively complex situations. Consider my living
with Brünnhilde—a lively lass to be sure, but then there is that
horse, those heroes and her family! There is no chance of
adequately evaluating the proposition that I live with Brünnhilde
without weighing values and disvalues. If imagination is the
guide to value but not to the weighing of values then it can
only be the guide to the value of evaluatively atomic propositions,
i.e., propositions whose value is not compounded out of the
value of more specific propositions. However this notion of a
proposition being evaluatively atomic is rather obscure. It is not
the notion of the *most* specific propositions. For the best
candidates to be the most specific propositions, e.g., a measure of
a physical parameter at a specific position, do not excite
imaginative desire at all. Worse, whatever was plausible in talk
of aesthetic value as organic unity suggests that it is utterly
implausible to attempt to decompose the value of a painting or a
symphony into a sum or any other function of the values of its
constituent parts. That is, there is something heroic about the
idea that we could build up to the value of a complex
proposition, e.g., about a performance of a symphony, from

---

[11] *Ibid.*, p. 121.
[12] *Ibid.*, p. 126.

evaluatively atomic propositions, e.g. about particular notes.

On the other hand, if imagination were used as the means of balancing, we would not only have Lewis's problem of holding together in mind vivid awareness of conflicting values, but also the problem of biased weighting. When I consider the value of my refusing the bright baubles, fine wine and celestial dishes which have been offered to bribe me, the abstract appeal of justice might well get swamped. As Ogden Nash taught us, duty just does not have the visage of a sweetie or a cutie. Nor is it obvious that duty would acquire such a visage if only we were to more fully imagine it.

This last point may well be unfair to Lewis's intentions. Sometimes the direction 'Imagine more fully what *x* would be like' amounts to a direction to *think* more fully about *x*. Thinking more fully about the injustice of accepting a bribe and about why justice is the first virtue of institutional arrangements may well overcome the appeal of the baubles. And Lewis writes of 'imaginative reason'.[13] However, he imposes a strange constraint if thinking or reasoning to oneself is to be allowed. The relation of imaginative reason to the state of valuing is 'causal and in no way inferential'.[14] Indeed, the analogy with Intuitionism suggests that Lewis mainly thinks of imagination as a quasi-perceptual process. Reasoning and reflection may tell you what aspects of a complex situation to vividly imagine, but imagination, and not reflection in some broad sense, is to be the guide.

Whether or not it is Lewis's idea, the limitations of this idea are worth highlighting; for they point to the connection between value and substantive practical reason, a reflective capacity which subsumes but is not exhausted by *imagination in the narrow sense*—hereafter 'imaginative awareness'.

The fact that vivid imaginative awareness leads us to value something is at most a prima facie reason to consider it valuable. Critical reflection on the deliverances of imagination can and often should overturn patterns of evaluation which even very vivid and complete imaginative awareness prompts. Consider the habitually hopeful but hapless gambler who when he vividly remembers or imagines gambling is particularly moved by the

[13] *Ibid.*, p. 121.
[14] *Ibid.*, p. 121.

winning sequences he vividly recalls or imagines and not so moved by the losing sequences he equally vividly recalls or imagines. Although there is an ominous preponderance of losses, thanks to his optimistic outlook he is more encouraged by a win than discouraged by a loss. So his bookkeeping faculty fails him, and he still ends up valuing being a gambler. Critical reflection, here taking the form of some detailed tallying, is needed to reliably track the values. Nor is it plausible to suppose that as imaginative awareness gets *very* vivid and complete, correct tallying gets somehow built into it.

Moreover, in many cases, vivid and complete imaginative awareness may itself kill off legitimate valuation. Harmlessly frivolous activity, such as dressing up in unexpected costumes for a philosophy seminar, is a value and so legitimately valued. However it is of the nature of the value in the frivolous that it doesn't bear too much thinking upon, and certainly not very complete or vivid imagining. Represent it to yourself too completely or vividly and you may not be able to resist anticipating the embarrassment that would lead you to disvalue the strikingly frivolous. Yet so long as we are restricting ourselves to the harmless, when it comes to the frivolous the more striking, indeed the more surreal, the better. *Mutatis mutandis* for the erotic. Wouldn't one advise certain restrictions on awareness of the details of erotic goings-on? At least the practical wisdom of seduction is full of ways of clouding consciousness and partly masking reality.

Still another range of examples involves concern for others. Even if one is initially benevolent, complete awareness of the suffering of the mass of sentient beings would be horrifically depressing, and hardness of heart rather than valuing their release might well be the causal upshot.[15]

In each of these cases there is a sense of the value of the states of affairs in question which we have and which appears independent of our good guesses merely about the deliverances of vivid or complete imaginative awareness. What is the provenance of these convictions about value? I take it to be a kind of substantive practical reasoning about value. For many values we judge a

[15] For a similar point and some very telling examples and considerations see Alan Gibbard 'A Non-Cognitivistic Analysis of Rationality in Action', *Social Theory and Practice* 9, 1983.

DISPOSITIONAL THEORIES OF VALUE 153

certain degree of awareness to be appropriate just because it is likely to encourage valuing what we independently take to be valuable on the strength of substantive practical reason.

That we rely on such relatively independent standards by which to judge the adequacy of the outputs of imaginative awareness is further shown by considering how Lewis's account stands with respect to the issue of the supervenience of the evaluative upon the descriptive. As Simon Blackburn has reminded us, the supervenience of the evaluative on the descriptive is an *a priori* or conceptual matter. Someone who claimed that he had discovered descriptive duplicates which differed in their evaluational features and not in virtue of extrinsic descriptive differences, such as a history of particularized attachment, would thereby show that he was not fully competent with evaluational terms.[16]

How is this *a priori* supervenience to be secured given L and Lewis's stipulation that the relation between imagination and the output of valuing is a purely causal one? The principle of *similar cause similar effect* is an empirical principle. We possess no *a priori* guarantee here. So we possess no *a priori* guarantee that if two states of affairs descriptively just alike were to produce duplicate feats of imagination in an appropriate subject then the causal output would be the same in each case. So given L and Lewis's stipulation, the *a priori* supervenience of the evaluative on the descriptive simply does not hold. G. E. Moore, who made so much of this supervenience thesis, avoids this problem as a direct result of his response-independent conception of value. His preferred process of intuiting value, like Lewis's, is causally related to valuing. However, for Moore, this causal process is in no way constitutive of the values of things, but is only the characteristic way of detecting those values.

The argument just given actually poses a problem for *any* purely psychologistic account of value. It shows that the *a priori* supervenience of the evaluative will not be secured on any theory which allows that being a value has a sufficient condition stable purely in terms of a pattern of mere psychological causation, since it is conceptually possible that any such pattern can exhibit inconstancy in output for similar description-

---

[16] 'Moral Realism' in John Casey (ed.) *Morality and Moral Reasoning* (Methuen, 1971).

encoding inputs. Evaluative supervenience is instead grounded in a characteristic pattern of evaluative or practical reason-giving, a pattern to which the reason-giving must be answerable if it is to deserve the name of reason-giving. The practical reasoning which justifies adopting various evaluative attitudes towards states of affairs begins by taking into account and making something of the descriptive features of those states of affairs, just as inference to the best explanation begins by taking into account and making something of the observed phenomena. While with both sorts of reasoning different reasoners can make different things of the same material, part of what makes practical reasoning or inference to the best explanation deserve the name of reasoning or inference, as opposed to whim, fancy or imagination, is that the same constraints (as it happens not just deductive constraints) of *good* or correct reasoning or inference apply to all attempting to reason practically or inductively.

So suppose for illustrative simplicity that something like the following biconditional held *a priori*—

> x is a value iff practical reason is on the side of valuing x, i.e., the deliverances of good practical reasoning support the conclusion that x is a value.

Now suppose also that x is a value, and let $D_1, D_2 \ldots$ be all of the descriptive features of x which practical reason would properly make something of in coming out in favour of x. Then any y alike to x in all descriptive features, and hence alike in $D_1, D_2 \ldots$, would be similarly favoured by practical reason. So, if x and y are just alike descriptively then, if x is a value, y is also a value. The corresponding result is likewise derivable if practical reason counts x a disvalue. Nor need we think of practical reason as yielding for any x a single unequivocal result as to its value to derive supervenience in this way. Even if it is indeterminate whether x is a value and to what degree a value, in the sense that practical reason recognizes a number of tenable views on the matter, practical reason will yield the same range of outputs as acceptable or tenable for the same descriptive input.

Thus we derive and explain the *a priori* supervenience of the evaluative on the descriptive. It looks after all as if we can be evaluative realists and also treat the supervenience of the evaluative on the descriptive as importantly unlike the empirically discovered supervenience of colour on primary qualities. What we haven't yet seen is how to be response-dependent evaluative realists and still do this.

The inconstancy of evaluative output from duplicate feats of imaginative awareness is not just a conceptual possibility showing that L lacks the resources to allow for supervenience. It is also an empirical possibility highlighting again the need for a constraint of reasonableness.

Imaginative familiarity with the same initially appealing material can breed contempt. But there is certainly room to ask whether the contempt familiarity breeds is warranted or unwarranted. Contrary to the implications of L, this is not to be decisively answered in terms of whether the later imaginative awareness was more vivid or complete than the earlier. It may be just that independently of variations in completeness or vividness the effect of the same imaginative material on subjects changes with repetition. Think of listening to the same simple and initially appealing piece of music many times over. After a while there need be no change in the degree to which I grasp the musical material. My interest simply wears off. There will then be no non-arbitrary way within the ambit of L to specify which outcomes of which repetitions are value-detecting and which represent the waning of my ability to imaginatively detect value in the material.

What counts as a defective response to value is not merely a matter of whether this or that psychological process occurs with this or that evaluative attitude resulting. What matters is whether the response in question is in accord with the deliverances of substantive practical reason about the subject matter in question.

The need for such a constraint of reasonableness on the actual and counterfactual responses which are to be counted crucial to the values of things points once again to the conceptual autonomy of normative notions, i.e., notions ordinary uses of which thereby express commendation or disapprobation. The concept of value cannot be analyzed or reductively defined by means of notions not themselves normative. Which is to say that there is no analysis of all normative notions. This conceptual autonomy of the normative is the counterpart for the normative

156   III—MARK JOHNSTON

of Brentano's thesis about the conceptual irreducibility of intentional notions.

This pivotal thesis of conceptual autonomy is here intended to cover the so-called 'thin' ethical concepts, i.e., the concepts good, valuable, reasonable, worthy, *etc.*; concepts whose function is *essentially* to commend. Of course, the negative counterparts of these concepts, whose function is *essentially* to censure, are also included. Since I also hold that mortal danger *warrants* fear or that dishonesty *merits* censure it may seem that I should also extend the thesis of conceptual autonomy to the so-called 'thick' ethical concepts. However, I take it that we can say what both mortal danger and dishonesty are without using evaluative notions. More, the fact that dishonesty *merits* censure does not make it essential to the concepts of dishonesty that finding some person or act dishonest involves censure. All that follows is that under ordinary conditions there are substantive reasons on the side of responding to dishonesty with censure. We can imagine extraordinary conditions, e.g. of repressive and invasive political occupation, in which this is not so. We can also imagine ordinary circumstances in which further substantive reasons outweigh the reasons for censuring dishonesty—cases of 'white' lies if you like.

There are 'white' lies but no 'black' values. A full account of the essential connection between the content of the thin concepts and their commendatory function would explain facts like this. Here I offer to defend the claim of essential connection between the concept of value and its commendatory function by showing what this claim explains. The anti-reductive remarks above in connection with supervenience, plus the observations below about the 'So What?' argument, about the iterativity of value and about relativism point to various manifestations of the essential connection.

IV

Speaking now quite generally of accounts of the concept of value, suppose that a theorist proposes that the valuable is what we would value under condition K, where K is not an evaluatively or normatively characterized condition. Someone informed of this putative analysis might now employ the analysans instead of the analysandum. But would they be employable to the same effect? To say that something is valuable is thereby essentially to commend it. To say that something would be valued under condition K is not thereby to commend it, but only to make a descriptive remark about its relation to certain psychological conditions. The commendatory function of the original remark would be recaptured if one said not only that it would be valued under condition K but also that K is the right or a reasonable condition to be in when considering questions of value. This is of course to reimport normative notions. Furthermore, since 'is valuable' is supposed to be the most general term of commendation, and since being right or being reasonable in the context under discussion are ways of being valuable, it looks as though there will be no reductive definition of 'is valuable' available at all. So there will be no reductive response-dependent account of 'is valuable' that is tenable.

Another manifestation of the conceptual autonomy of the normative is the so-called 'So What?' argument. Gilbert Harman, for example, applies the argument against the ideal-observer version of a response-dependent account of value.[17] That version has it that to be a value is to be such as to be valued by a certain kind of observer. Calling the observer 'ideal', although part of the tradition, can be misleading. For 'ideal' is here supposed to be a stand-in for a purely descriptive characterization of the kind of observer in question. Now suppose that I am told that while I value pushpin the 'ideal' observer thinks it worth nothing. I infer that the conditions under which I make my evaluation of pushpin are not the conditions in which the 'ideal' observer makes his evaluations. Notice that I may think this without in any way thinking worse of my evaluation. Upon being told the difference between my evaluation and that of the 'ideal' observer, I may say, without showing any contempt for reason or value, 'So What?'. That is, I may coherently take it that there is no reason to get into the 'ideal' condition and no reason to correct my valuations to accord with my beliefs about the evaluations I or another would make in those conditions.

[17] 'Moral Agent and Moral Spectator', *The Lindley Lecture* (Kansas University Press, 1983).

158 III—MARK JOHNSTON

An ardent defender of the 'ideal' observer analysis might now insist that there is a reason; namely that, as his analysis shows, the 'ideal' conditions are those in which the real values present themselves. Although this is the consistent thing for the ardent defender to say, it is not a very plausible thing to say just because the conditions cited are not normatively or evaluatively loaded. That is, it will not be very plausible just because saying that something would be valued by the 'ideal' observer is not thereby to commend it. If this is the right account of the force of the 'So What?' argument then the argument holds against any reductive account of value.

A third and more novel way of bringing out the conceptual autonomy of the normative begins with the observation that the following principle has an *a priori* status. I mean we know it, but not on the basis of any empirical knowledge.

> Iterativity of Value
> Among the things that are valuable this is:
> to value the valuable.

Now part of the point either of giving an analysis of the concept of value or of giving central play to an *a priori* biconditional of the form

> x is a value iff S would value x under condition K

is to articulate a conceptual connection which is relatively basic or generative in the sense that some of the central *a priori* truths about the relevant subject matter are derivable from it, perhaps in conjunction with other relatively basic *a priori* truths. For the derivation of the iterativity of value to work, something like the following is needed:

> Psychological state K is such that in K one would value valuing what one would value in K.

This claim and the biconditional will yield the iterativity of value. For all I know the claim may be true on certain specific ways of spelling out the psychological state K and the nature of the psychological state of valuing. However any such truth would be true as a matter of empirical psychology. Any derivation employing such a truth would not secure the iterativity of value as an *a priori* matter.

DISPOSITIONAL THEORIES OF VALUE 159

How could such a result be secured? One response is to claim that it cannot be secured and hence that it is nothing against a proposal that it does not generate iterativity. However notice that the following principle also seems *a priori*—the iterativity of what reason supports.

> Among the things reason is on the side of valuing is this: valuing what reason is on the side of valuing.

If we could connect up value with what reason is on the side of valuing, we could derive the iterativity of value. Of course something will remain underived, and one would have to use one's philosophical judgement as to whether the iterativity of value was interestingly derived from the iterativity of reason and the connection between reason and value. Myself I think it is. But for present purposes all we need is that if the iterativity of value is interestingly so derived then one has a further motive for exploring the conceptual connections between the normative notions of value and reason. As to the connection between something being a reason and our taking it to be so, more later.

So far then, we have argued against L on account of the limits of imagination, and against a whole class of analyses like L on account of their conceptually reductive character.

Lewis proposes a conceptual reduction at another point. He suggests that the crucial attitude of valuing is just desiring to desire. Here 'desire' is not to be understood as a state which is coherent only in the believed absence or non-possession of its object. Someone who knows he has a million can desire that million in this sense. The term 'desire' is functioning for Lewis as an all purpose term for any first-order pro-attitude.

I doubt the identification of valuing with desiring to desire, not only because of cases in which one desires to desire without valuing[18], but also because of cases in which one values and yet has reason not to desire, and hence not to desire to desire, reasons which might be thoroughly effective. One case of the latter sort has to do with satisfactions which we might call

---

[18] Discussion of such cases would require examination of Lewis's distinction between instrumental and intrinsic desire and of the extent to which this very distinction is conceptually dependent upon the distinction between instrumental and intrinsic value. See Lewis, footnote 4.

160   III—MARK JOHNSTON

strongly serendipitous, i.e., satisfactions which as a matter of
psychological fact or artificial circumstance come only to those
who are without any prior desire for them. To those who want
such satisfaction they shall not be given. Knowing that some
satisfaction was strongly serendipitous in this sense, I could
reasonably and without doublemindedness value it and
precisely not want to want it. Notice that this kind of point could
be made at any place in the hierarchy of higher-order desires,
throwing into question the identification of valuing with any
order of iterated desire. Such considerations suggest that the
attitude of valuing may be none other than the attitude of
judging valuable. Here we have a further insult to reductionist
sensibilities.

Part of Lewis's motive for the identification of valuing with
desiring to desire is to secure something in the way of
Internalism, i.e., a conceptual connection between value and
motivation. Lewis explains the connection in this way—'If
something is a value, and if someone is one of the appropriate
'we', and if he is in ideal conditions, then it follows that he will
value it. And if he values it, and if he desires as he desires to
desire, then he will desire it.'[19] The connection is not only very iffy,
as Lewis himself points out. It is also a connection whose holding
secures no privileged relation between value and motivation.
For consider the *alcovalues*; where *x* is an alcovalue just in case we
would desire to desire it when plootered, i.e., under conditions of
extreme drunkenness. If something is an alcovalue, and if
someone is one of the appropriate 'we', and if he is in ideal
alcoholic conditions, then it follows that he will desire to desire
it. And if he desires to desires it, and if he desires as he desires to
desire, then he will desire it. Surely however, Internalists meant
to articulate a *privileged* relation between *value* and motivation;
in fact, a relation between judging something valuable and
being motivated to pursue, cherish or maintain it, a relation
supposed to hold whether one made the judgement of value in
canonical conditions for valuing or accepted it on the say-so of
one's spiritual advisor.

The prospects for deriving from any response-dependent
account of value *this* non-contingent and direct relation between

[19] Lewis, p. 117.

DISPOSITIONAL THEORIES OF VALUE 161

judging something valuable and being positively motivated towards it seem to me dim.[20] But this is no objection to a response-dependent account of value. There is a name for not being motivated by what one judges valuable. It is of course 'weakness of will' and, so far as I can see, weakness of will not only can disrupt the expected connection between judging something best and acting to promote it but also can disrupt the expected connection between judging something valuable and desiring it in the extended sense.

As for securing an internal or conceptual connection between value and the will, *this* at least is true: to the extent that one is not weak-willed one will desire (in the extended sense) as one judges valuable. So much is part of the definition of weakness of will. As far as making the connection between judging valuable and desiring (in the extended sense) particularly intelligible, this seems to me achieved by the observation that 'valuable' and 'desire-worthy' are near synonyms. If judging valuable is pretty much judging desire-worthy then it is readily intelligible why judging valuable should lead to desiring. As the 'So What?' argument indicated, the real difficulty is to preserve this ready intelligibility *after* giving a philosophical gloss on the concept of value or desire-worthiness.

V

David Hume also wrote 'Tis not contrary to reason to prefer the destruction of the whole world to the scratching of my finger'[21]; to which an adequate response might be: not contrary to reason in one sense perhaps, but brutally insane, psychopathically callous and demonically indifferent. The widespread appropriation of the terms 'reason' and 'rational' for (i) logical, mathematical and perhaps probabilistic consistency among beliefs, combined with (ii) a tendency to maximise utility in the decision theoretic sense, may be ideologically suspect, but it is probably not bad English. Allowing the appropriation, we should also be mindful of that more substantive reasonableness

---

[20] But see Michael Smith's contribution to this symposium.
[21] *Treatise*, 'On the Influencing Motives of the Will'.

162   III—MARK JOHNSTON

which we look for in both practical and theoretical matters. One
who infers to the best explanation of phenomena, which involves
more than maintaining probabilistic consistency in the face of
the phenomena, is substantively reasonable, as is one who jumps
into a swimming pool to save his drowning father-in-law even
though it will mean getting his pants wet.

Of course, while those who share our form of life share a rich
body of belief about what is substantively reasonable, important
aspects of what is substantively reasonable are essentially
contested. That is just to say that many questions of value are
essentially contested. For what is typically not in question
among the contestants is that

> (1) x is a value iff substantive reason is on the side of valuing
> x.

The concepts of value and of substantive practical reason take
in each other's washing. The point of this Austinian metaphor is
to suggest that (1) may provide no interesting analytic account
of value but only a paraphrase. It is as well however to start by
enshrining acceptable paraphrases, not only because many
putative analyses simply fail to comport with or capture them,
but also for the now familiar reason that analysis may not be a
reasonable aim.

We arrive at something a little more controversial if we add to
(1)—

> (2) y is a substantive reason for/against valuing x iff we are
> disposed stably to take it to be so under conditions of
> increasing information and critical reflection.

Increasing information will come at some point to include the
revelations of imaginative awareness about the relation
between x and y. But it will also include information from other
sources, as well as information about the effect of this relation on
imagination, and the effects of such imagination in its turn.
Critical reflection will then involve attempting to debunk the
beliefs which result from the informational input by examining
the extent to which those beliefs are the result of prejudice,
illusions of salience, self-deception, sour-grapes, false consciousness or other self-protective attitudes which defeat the prima

facie claim of informed belief to be true belief. The undebunked beliefs, still beliefs bearing upon the reasonableness or un-reasonableness of valuing x because of y, are then to be brought into a wider reflective equilibrium with the rest of what we believe.[22]

The requirement that the output of such a process be stable under increasing information will be satisfied just in case (i) there is some state of relevant information about the issue from which critical reflection yields the output, and (ii) any application of critical reflection to *more* inclusive states of information would yield the same output. This slightly round-about formulation is needed to secure the result that although there may be no ideally informed critical condition, the real reasons are those that stand, and would continue to stand, the test of criticism.[23]

Along with (2), we need a clause telling us what the acceptable methods of weighing the various reasons for and against valuing x might be. Clearly, we should allow our beliefs about methods of weighing reasons to be subject to the same potentially mutating influence of critical reflection. Thus, mirroring (2), we have—

> (3) A method for weighing substantive reasons is an acceptable method for determining whether the weight of substantive reason is on the side of valuing x iff we are disposed stably to take it to be so under conditions of increasing information and critical reflection.

Now we say

> (4) Substantive reason is on the side of valuing x iff this is so

[22] On debunking, see Susan Hurley *Natural Reasons* (Oxford University Press, 1989). A crucial type of attempted debunking, relevant to the holding of supervenience, is testing our reactions by the requirement that like cases be treated alike. Thus, critical reflection as characterized here secures the supervenience of the reasonableness of acts of valuing on the descriptive features of those acts. That is, if w and z are like cases, acts of valuing descriptively just alike, then, if y is a reason for w it is also a reason for z. (I am, by the way, indebted to Susan Hurley for extensive discussion of this and many other issues surrounding this paper.)

[23] A fuller discussion of these matters would have to take into account the relationship between J. David Velleman's penetrating critique of Richard Brandt's theories of ideal rationality in his 'Brandt's Definition of the Good', *Philosophical Review* XCVII, 1988 and the present theory of rationality.

164   III—MARK JOHNSTON

according to one and all methods of weighing the
reasons for and against valuing x.

Taking (1) through (4) together, the response-dependent
element in the notion of value will be evident. The notion of
value is conceptually connected to the notion of substantive
reason, as (1) makes clear. The notion of substantive reason is
response-dependent as (2) and (3) indicate. That is, (2) and (3)
together imply that substantive reasonableness is not hyper-
objective or, reworking terminology of Bernard Williams, *hyper-
external*.[24] There are no substantive reasons which we cannot get
to in principle from here, although getting to them may involve
a gradual but thorough reworking of what we take to be
substantive reasons, the appropriate methods of weighing them
and perhaps also the correct styles of critical reflection. If we
think of our present system of substantive reasonableness on the
model of Neurath's ship, not only may the ship require
considerable overhaul but so also may our methods of overhauling
it.

Clause (4) requires some comment. Allowing that there may
be different acceptable ways of weighing reasons seems necessary
given the enormous diversity of value, the controversial nature
of claims about how to weigh evaluative considerations from
disparate domains, and reasonable skepticism about critical
reflection's capacity to dissolve such controversy. So there are
moral considerations, considerations deriving from personal
ideals and loyalties, considerations of utility, aesthetic considerations, and so on. We can only speak non-misleadingly of x,
being a value *simpliciter* if the considerations within and among
these disparate domains tend in the same direction when
subsumed under *any* acceptable method of weighing. Otherwise
we should issue a divided report on the value of x, qualifying our
talk of its value in terms of the various kinds of disparate
considerations and methods of weighing which support or count
against valuing it.

Divided reports will also be necessary whenever the considerations within or across evaluative domains are strongly

----

[24] 'Internal and External Reasons' in B. A. O. Williams *Moral Luck* (Cambridge,
1984). Williams doubts the existence of external reasons even in the sense defended here.

incommensurable, allowing for no acceptable method of weighing.[25] (Hence the rider '*one* and all' in (4). We want to cancel the usual logical implication of the vacuous case.)

Strong incommensurability aside, one only has to think that substantive reason enforces no single method of weighing considerations to regard as conceptually amiss the consequentialist idea of maximizing value *simpliciter*, producing the most valuable or maximally valuable total state of affairs. Divided reports will be too common for this to be a reasonable aim. This suggests that there is more connection between G. E. Moore's response-independent conception of value and his Utilitarianism than is usually recognised. Once one takes a response-dependent view of value, one cannot reasonably hope that the disparate and divided nature of valuation, relatively robust as it is even under conditions of critical reflection, simply testifies to our ignorance of the true values and their true orderings.

Of course, the need for divided reports and the resultant conceptual difficulties with consequentialism would be much lessened if there were a ubiquitous kind of consideration which itself allowed for a privileged commensuration and which trumped other reasons.

The idea that considerations of utility (desire-satisfaction) are of this sort seems to me just a horrible and obvious evaluative error. So I am not the one to give this idea a run for its money. On the other hand, there is the idea, made somewhat plausible by the seriousness of moral considerations, that moral considerations are overriding. At various times and places the social institution of morality has encouraged this pretension by connecting moral reasons with a metaphysical picture of value as unitary and response-independent—as it might be, our true and only end is union with God, and an act is right only to the extent that it makes this more likely. Even Kant's wonderful claim that the only thing in this world or in any other that is good-in-itself is a good, hence autonomous, hence moral, will seems to me to rely upon a response-independent conception of value. For as soon as being good-in-itself is understood in terms

---

[25] On the complex issues surrounding incommensurability and on strong forms of it see Michael Stocker *Plural and Conflicting Values* (Oxford University Press, 1989).

166   III—MARK JOHNSTON

of our finding non-derivative reason to value the thing in question, it becomes clear that more than the moral will qualifies and that the goodness of the moral will need not be overriding on all methods of weighing reasons which we find acceptable.

Hence, on the response-dependent view of value it may be slightly mistaken to ask: how much does morality require of me in the way of sacrificing my personal ideals? Within limits, substantive reason may recognize a range of equally acceptable ways of striking the angels' bargain. Within those limits, the issue may be a matter of invention rather than discovery.

VI

There is an important distinction between allowing the sensible idea of reasonable alternatives within any idealization of our scheme of substantive reason and allowing the probably incoherent idea of reasonable alternatives without. If you like, this is the distinction between Pluralism and Relativism. Relativism can mean the discovery of a surprising relativity in our concepts. In that sense any response-dependent account of value is relativistic. But here I fall in with the tradition of use which appropriates 'Relativism' for a conceptually risky mix of adherence to standards *and* bland tolerance towards those who flout them, so long as the flouters are appropriately alien.

The Relativist begins by pointing to the possibility of the Radically Other—beings who share nothing of our sense of substantive reasonableness though they be perfectly rational in the decision-theoretic sense. Rational crabs perhaps? Despite the exercises of the subtlest philosophy, I see no incoherence in the Relativist's claim that such a radical alternative is possible.[26]

Incoherence threatens however when the Relativist tries to persuade us that there is really nothing to choose between our system of evaluation and the aliens' system of quasi-evaluations. The Relativist's route to this result invariably involves relying upon a neutral viewpoint allegedly incorporating all the information about both patterns of response, their causal histories and analogous roles in the lives of the two communities.

[26] I have in mind Donald Davidson's 'On the Very Idea of a Conceptual Scheme' in his *Inquiries into Truth and Interpretation*. In fact it seems to me that this paper contains the premises for a proof that alternative conceptual schemes *must* be possible.

DISPOSITIONAL THEORIES OF VALUE   167

From this viewpoint, it is claimed, no privilege can be seen to attach to our way of going. Notice that this is not to say that the Relativist requires us to make at the neutral viewpoint a judgement of equivalence of value. That would be straight-forwardly inconsistent, inviting us to value in terms not our own. Instead the Relativist must restrict himself to trying to undermine any preference we would have at the neutral viewpoint, showing it to be arbitrary in the light of the analysis of value and full information about the two ways of going.

Everything depends on what is involved in the neutral viewpoint. One escape route from incoherence is to find in the neutral viewpoint a higher-order evaluative system, realized both in one's own pattern of response and in the aliens' pattern. However this is also an escape route from Relativism to a higher-order Absolutism. To remain Relativistic and make sense of the neutral but *fully informed* viewpoint, the Relativist must, I think, rely upon descriptive reductionism about evaluative and quasi-evaluative judgements, talking as if judgements of each sort could be analyzed in descriptive terms *without evaluative remainder*.

For example, it might be that although about as vulnerable as we are, the aliens are naturally self-destructive in the face of danger. So while it is true that

> x is mortally dangerous iff x is such as to produce the response of mortal fear in us under ordinary conditions.

it is also true that

> x is mortally dangerous iff x is such as to produce the 'in for a penny, in for a pound' response in them under ordinary conditions.

Here we have two opposing and, in one sense, equally natural dispositional patterns of response in the face of mortal danger. For every fact about our underwriting our pattern of response, there is a fact about their underwriting their pattern of response. There is nothing in nature to favour the one pattern of response rather than the other unless we suppose nature somehow gives special value to survival. But the Relativist tells us that all the relevant facts here merely involve our being disposed to desire to desire survival more than they desire to desire it. Taking into account all this information and remaining rational in the formal sense, we will find ourselves without the resources to judge their ways to be worse than ours.

Notice that the Relativist is here trying to invest the illusory capital of the 'So What?' argument. Whereas we earlier employed this argument to show that no reductive account of value is correct, the Relativist employs a reductive account of particular values (or as in the case of mortal danger, disvalues) in order to motivate a viewpoint from which the difference between two patterns of response leaves us with the 'So What?' reaction generalized.

However, once we have abandoned definitional descriptive reductionism about value we can see that the Relativist has indeed omitted some crucial information from the neutral viewpoint, namely that substantive reason is on the side of (improvements of) one pattern of response and not the other. This is not to say that this information is in principle enough to persuade even the aliens that our ways are better. It is to say that, given this information, *we* have decisive and, for us, typically motivating reasons to favour the one pattern of response rather than the other. For, as we saw under the heading of iterativity, substantive reason is on the side of valuing what substantive reason sides with.

So for example, what the Relativist misses in the little story about mortal danger is that it is not just that mortal danger happens to *produce* fear in beings like us. Mortal danger *warrants* fear, i.e., in the ordinary run of things, substantive reason is on the side of feeling fear in the face of mortal danger. What is vulgar in vulgar Relativism is precisely the assumption that such commendations of our patterns of response will get captured or replaced by purely descriptive analyses. A non-reductionist about value can thus hold out against Relativism, even granting the possibility of the merely quasi-evaluating aliens.

For the Relativist's allegedly neutral viewpoint is one from which we are supposed to see any tendency to favour our own way of going on as a failure to analyze that tendency as just another disposition fully characterizable in descriptive terms. As we said, this constant undermining, rather than an attempt to get us to make a global judgement of equal *worth* as between the two ways of going, has to be the Relativist's strategy, otherwise he is simply inconsistent, inviting us to value in terms not our own. But the undermining strategy also fails. For our tendency

DISPOSITIONAL THEORIES OF VALUE   169

to favour our own pattern of response, or rather idealizations of it, is warranted, i.e., supported by substantive reasonableness, and this in its turn is a matter of our finding certain considerations substantively reasonable under conditions of increasing information and critical reflection. These facts are not neutral in the required sense. For our finding certain considerations substantively reasonable warrants our taking those considerations and not others into account. Given such a non-reductive story about our evaluations, the Relativist's viewpoint cannot be both neutral *and* fully informed. Formal rationality augmented with a host of non-commendatory descriptions of our responses falls short of full information about those responses. (Here we individuate information in terms of *a priori* equivalences, as seems independently plausible.)

This discussion of Relativism allows for the possibility of a 'they' disjoint from the 'we' of the present account, because the subtlest philosophy will probably continue to fail to show that there could be no such 'they'. On the other hand, the most informed anthropology is complexly related to the empirical question of the extension of 'we'. For we have no evidence of a 'they' disjoint from us whenever the diversity of valuation is to be explained by false consciousness, ignorance of fact, failure of criticism, or the adoption of divergent mores in reasonable response to divergent histories and contemporary conditions.

Starting with myself and my soulmates, the extension of 'we' in the present response-dependent account is to be determined by including with us all who would stably converge on the same judgements of substantive reasonableness under increasing information and critical reflection.[27] 'We' is in this way ideally inclusive. For all I know it may include some of the more savoury characters of the Marquis de Sade's *Juliette* and a few of Bernard Williams' samurai to boot.[28]

Despite this ideal inclusiveness of 'we', the resultant account is not trivial or empty. For what I (and my soulmates) would take

---

[27] Exactly how much convergence is required? We can leave this vague, in effect offering a cluster of accounts instead of a single one. We want each account within the cluster to provide a reasonable trade-off between the extent of our solidarity and the extent of our agreement. See Lewis's remarks around his footnote 20, and his 'Scorekeeping in a Language Game', *Journal of Philosophical Logic* 8, 1979.

[28] For the samurai see 'The Truth in Relativism' in B. A. O. Williams, *op. cit.*

170   III—MARK JOHNSTON

to be a reason under the ideal conditions is a matter fixed (within a range of indeterminacy) by my psychology and the details of the idealization.

The account may now seem shamelessly self-congratulatory. For it implies that there is a conceptual guarantee that I and my soulmates, or to put the point more bluntly, I, could not be invincibly immune to reason. (After all, just who counts as a soulmate gets determined by empirical facts and the inclusive criterion.) That is, thanks to the response-dependent account of value and the present gloss on 'we', I can know *a priori* that I myself would not fail to track substantive reason under the ideal conditions. However, sad to say, the corresponding truth about you, if it is a truth, is an empirical truth.

This is an objection. But I think that the best that a response-dependent theorist of value can do is the best that can be done. Any residual oddity is testimony to the intuitive residue of a kind of projective or hyper-objectifying error about reason and value.

The best I can do in response to the objection is to point out that you can similarly congratulate yourself. Although there is a strict sense of predicating in which we do not predicate the very same thing of ourselves when we each congratulate ourselves as not invincibly immune to reason or value, there is nonetheless every chance that we will be talking about pretty much the same feature in extension. Value from my point of view may massively overlap with value from your point of view.

VII

The idea that talk of value and reason is unequivocal, quite determinate, and not equivalent to any talk about what we would count valuable or reasonable is entrenched and naturally makes for some residual dissatisfaction with any response-dependent account. But a response-dependent account of value or reason should be offered as a partly revisionary account.

In the *Lecture on Ethics* Ludwig Wittgenstein wrote

> The right road is the road which leads to an arbitrarily predetermined end and it is quite clear to us all that there is no sense in talking about the right road apart from such a predetermined goal.

. . . I think it would have to be the road which *everybody* on seeing it would, *with logical necessity* have to go or feel ashamed for not going.[29]

There is something in the idea that if anything is absolutely and strictly to deserve the name of value it would be a practical demand built into the world in such a way that any merely formally rational being would on pain of inconsistency feel shame if he were not to respect it. This is in effect what John Mackie called the idea of value as 'the objectively prescriptive', an idea which Mackie successfully stigmatized as an error at the heart of our thought about value. Mackie offered a projective metaphor as an account of the provenance of this hyper-objectifying error. According to Mackie, the error arises because we mistake the felt urgency of reasonable response for the pull of a demand thoroughly independent of that tendency to respond. Whatever the origin of the error, the present response-dependent account of value is designed to eliminate precisely this error of supposing that the demands of value or substantive practical reason are thoroughly independent of our tendency to respond to such demands.

If the error is as deeply rooted in our thought about value as Mackie suggests then we should expect recurrent manifestations of the error. Something related to the error is elegantly enshrined in Plato's *Euthyphro*. There Socrates objects to Euthyphro's definition of the pious as what the gods love. Socrates insists that rather than acts being pious because they are loved by the gods, the gods love such acts because they are pious.[30] It simply turns out that, thanks to their natures, the gods are very good detectors of piety which in fact they invariably love. There is, as we might put it, nothing *a priori* about this, as is *shown* by the explanatoriness of the remark 'The gods love pious acts because they are pious' as compared with the lack of explanatoriness of the remark 'The gods love pious acts because they are the acts the gods love'. If *a priori* equivalents can be substituted in explanatory contexts saving explanatoriness, then Euthyphro's account fails, even taken as a mere allegation of *a priori* equivalence.

[29] Published in *The Philosophical Review* LXXIV, 1965.
[30] *Euthyphro*, 10B–11B.

172   III—MARK JOHNSTON

This is precisely the form of argument which highlights the felt independence of value from value-directed responses. It is the characteristic bugbear of response-dependent accounts. Notice however that our kind of response-dependent theory of value will allow many instances of this form of argument as showing that *certain* dependencies are not relevant to the correct account of value. Socrates does indeed have the better of Euthyphro. The fact that the gods love certain acts is not central to the account of piety. Similarly with the ideal observer account of value. Something is valued by the ideal observer because it is valuable, i.e., in accord with substantive practical reason. It is not valuable because it is valued by the ideal observer.

However when it comes to this instance—something is not a reason because we take it to be so, we take it to be so because it is a reason—care must be exercised. Our kind of response-dependent theory can discern an explanatory element in the remark that we take something to be a reason because it is a reason. To use an analogy suggested by Michael Slote, just as we can explain the behaviour of a gas in terms of the way it would behave if it were ideal, we can explain our reason-accepting behaviour in non-ideal conditions in terms of our there approximating what we would accept in ideal conditions.[31]

But now the Socratic objector will take the decisive step, insisting that whatever is a reason is not a reason because we would stably take it to be so as we approach ideal conditions. Rather, in the most fortunate case, we would take it to be a reason under such conditions just because it is a reason. And now our kind of response-dependent theorist must dig in. The hyper-objectifying error has at last been manifested. The objector in effect wants hyper-external reasons, reasons which could in principle outrun any tendency of ours to accept them as reasons, even under conditions of increasing information and critical reflection.

We should now ask the Socratic objector by what consideration he is led to believe that we have ever been in contact with the true hyper-external reasons, or better, by what consideration he

---

[31] Michael Slote 'The Rationality of Aesthetic Value Judgements', *Journal of Philosophy* 68, 1971.

DISPOSITIONAL THEORIES OF VALUE 173

is led to believe that increasing information and critical reflection is a good way of seeking such contact.

For the Socratic objector must regard

> (H) The substantive reasons are to be discovered by taking into account relevant information and critically reflecting on it.

as a contingent empirical hypothesis. But how could such a hypothesis be confirmed? After all we have no independent grip of the idea of the substantively reasonable besides the idea of what is discovered by informed criticism. So there is something essentially bogus about the very idea of finding empirical support for the connection of substantive reasons with such discoveries. At this point, I think the descendants of Euthyphro get the better of the descendants of Socrates.

I cannot expand on these considerations here, but as they stand they may help to locate the present response-dependent account with respect to Simon Blackburn's quasi-realism.[32]

Blackburn himself has provided a battery of persuasive arguments against any analysis of the truth conditions of evaluative judgements in non-normative terms, including versions of the 'So What?' argument and the Euthyphro argument. He has also quite rightly challenged evaluational realists to explain how they propose to generate the *a priori* supervenience of the evaluative upon the descriptive. His own view is that no interesting analysis is available and that the philosophical task in the theory of value as elsewhere is to explain *how*, given the essentially non-cognitive attitudes (sentiments, concerns, etc.) which are expressed in evaluative discourse, we could earn the right to express those attitudes in truth-conditional form.

The non-reductive response-dependent account of value can take on board much of the polemic against reductive accounts of value. But it also implies that there is no need to *earn* the right to the truth-conditional form of expression. Modulo the correction of a hyper-objectifying error, we have a natural conceptual right to this truth-conditional form. Our response-dependent account

---

[32] See Chapter 6 of *Spreading the Word*; 'Morals and Modals' in *Truth, Fact and Value*, Graham Macdonald and Crispin Wright (eds.) (Oxford, 1986); 'How to be an Ethical Anti-Realist' in *Midwest Studies in Philosophy*. Volume XII, Peter French et al. (eds.) (Minnesota, 1988).

174   III—MARK JOHNSTON

of the concept of value does not analyze truth-conditions, it
rather explicates them sufficiently to exhibit the interconnections
with our sensibilities and concerns. Moreover, as we saw, the
response-dependent account has the resources to explain the *a
priori* supervenience of the evaluative on the descriptive.

An appropriate response-dependent account may thus threaten
to make quasi-realism redundant. The quasi-realist programme
is to *somehow* defend our right to employ the truth-conditional
idiom in expressing evaluations. But what kind of truth-
conditional idiom? An idiom whose central concepts are
response-dependent or an idiom whose central concepts are
response-independent? If the former, then quasi-realism might
as well straight-out endorse its preferred response-dependent
account. If the latter, then quasi-realism is not redundant, but it
faces the difficult task of explaining how, given the concern-
expressing point of our evaluational talk, we end up rightfully
employing truth-conditions whose contents appear to transcend
that point. If anything like the present account is correct, the
non-redundant quasi-realist must not only believe in hyper-
external reasons but also defend our right to believe in them
given the quasi-realist conception of the point of evaluative
practice. This is none too easy a pair of things to do.[33]

[33] Special thanks to Paul Boghossian, Susan Hurley, Mark Kalderon, David Lewis,
Denis Robinson and Michael Smith. A version of most of this paper was given as part of a
three-lecture series at New York University in the fall of 1987. I have been much helped
by that occasion. Thanks also the members of the Society for Ethical and Legal
Philosophy (SELF).

[16]

Philosophical Perspectives, 7, Language and Logic, 1993

Circles, Finks, Smells and Biconditionals

Simon Blackburn
University of North Carolina

1. Setting the Scene

The recent interest in 'response-dependent' concepts has generated a large, impressive and increasingly complex literature, although contributors to that literature differ widely in how important they take such concepts to be.[1] Optimists include Philip Pettit who believes in a global form of response-dependence, and others such as Crispin Wright who give it modified but important work to do.[2] They also include Michael Smith, David Lewis, and Mark Johnston, who in their 1989 symposium all present such accounts of evaluative concepts.[3] Pessimists include Huw Price and, under a different hat, Mark Johnston, who thinks that our actual concepts are seldom response dependent, although he is also sympathetic to an error theory of our actual concepts, and a programme of replacing them with hygienic cousins that are so.[4] At least two optimists, Johnston and Wright, have directly expressed the belief that response dependent analyses, for instance of evaluative terms, supersede and sideline expressivist accounts, and others like Lewis clearly sympathize. They thus turn the whirligig of time one more round, since historically expressivist accounts of concepts came in partly because of the failure of the subjectivist analyses to which response dependence is a successor. My aim in this paper is to show that the whirligig should have stayed where it was.

What are the issues? The central idea has been to refurbish a form of analysis of concepts that seem somehow anthropocentric, used and understood only because we have particular sensory or affective systems. The standard examples include concepts of color and other secondary qualities, concepts like being fashionable or chic that centrally reflect the tastes of some identifiable group, or those like being boring or comical, where the application clearly depends somehow on the reactions of people (or some particular people). The

260 / Simon Blackburn

idea rapidly generalizes, and values, intentional concepts, and even causation have been advertised as response-dependent concepts.

The idea of a subjective analysis of some concept is not of course new: those of us brought up on G. E. Moore cut our teeth on refutations of such analyses. But the recent interest has quickened because we have become more sophisticated, or more relaxed, about what a response-dependent 'account' of a concept might involve, and the kinds of argument to which it might succumb. In fact, it is no longer plain to many philosophers that a notion of analysis needs to be put into play at all. Our standards for an 'account' may not involve providing a straight equation, expressing the same concept in other terms. One of my main aims is to pour some cold water on this modern sophistication. But to begin with, it is agreed on all sides is that we can usefully start by thinking in terms of a biconditional whose form we can write as follows:

X is ϕ $\equiv$ [persons] are disposed to [reaction] under [circumstances].

A variation on this equation would be:

X is ϕ $\equiv$ X tends to elicit [reaction] from [persons] under [circumstances]

and for the purposes of this paper the two forms may be taken as equivalent (in case 'tends' worries the reader, it gets modified later). Instances of the basic equation would be:

X is red $\equiv$ normal people would be disposed to judge X red in normal light
X is good $\equiv$ ordinary people would be disposed to choose X when faced with it
X is boring $\equiv$ most people would go to sleep on coming across X

and so on. A common view of such equations is that they work well for some concepts but not others, and that where they work well it is because they have an interesting *a priori* form. Another view is that they work well where they do because they can be read 'right to left'. This means in effect that we can see them as claiming that X is red/good/boring *in virtue of* the dispositions mentioned on the right hand side, and this is suggested by the notion of dependence. These refinements occupy us later.

Complexity obviously arises because the form of the biconditional gives us three different places for fillings, and different choices can be made for each. Amongst the possibilities we have:

[persons]: myself, all of us, those who are normal, the experts, us as we actually are, us as we would be after improving, us as we would be after some specified empirical process...
[reaction]: a non-cognitive reaction, a cognitive reaction, a judgement that something is ϕ, a judgement couched in other terms, an experience,

Circles, Finks, Smells and Biconditionals / 261

a piece of behavior...

[circumstances]: common conditions of acquaintance, standard conditions, conditions appropriate especially to X, conditions of paying appropriate attention to X or having X as an intentional object, ideal conditions, whatever-conditions-it-takes... .

I shall abbreviate these three place-holders as [P], [R] and [C]. When nothing hinges on separating them, I shall lump [P] and [C] together as [P,C]. The many degrees of freedom they introduce are increased when we turn to another choice point. For any equation of this kind might be advanced for different philosophical purposes, and we should keep in mind at least these. There is the purpose of old fashioned analysis. This is to display on the right hand side the very concept from the left, with its structure made visible on the model of 'to be a vixen is to be a female fox'. The biconditionals could therefore be rewritten as straight analyses:

The concept of φ is that of tending to elicit [R] from [P,C]

but the sophistication I have mentioned allows that we do not have to be saying this. The purpose of identifying something about the 'logic' of the concept or 'explicating' it or giving the conditions governing its application may not demand a strict identity. Why will something less than an analysis do? Notably, it has been suggested, a condition on an old fashioned analysis will be non-circularity, whereas for other elucidatory purposes this need not be so. We might presumably learn something about the application conditions of 'boring' by being told that the conditions governing its application are that X is boring ≡ we tend to be bored by X under normal conditions. That this is a substantive claim is proved by its actually being false (normal conditions might be the noisy crowded theatrical milieu hostile to realizing that X is not at all boring, but imaginative and demanding).[5] Adopting a useful term from Richard Holton, we can say that we have an 'echo' proposal when φ reappears on the right hand side.[6] Echoing biconditionals can clearly be true (X is φ ≡ X is φ), and the claim now is that the echo does not disqualify them from doing at least some philosophical work.[7] How much remains to be seen.

A different purpose might be that of giving a substantive truth condition. This can be supposed to be something different from the above, modelled on the 'substantive' identity of water and H_2O or heat of a gas and the kinetic energy of its molecules. But few of those investigating these biconditionals see them as playing this role. Accepting Kripke's account, these scientific identities are necessarily true, but not *a priori*. But the kind of biconditional envisaged for, say, boring or red is usually thought of as *a priori*: part of the interest of the matter is that if true they enable us to know *a priori* that what [P] [react to] under [C] is indeed boring or red.[8]

At this point it is important to keep in mind a distinction. I have laid out

262 / Simon Blackburn

the landscape so far as if our interest is in a kind of *concept* or equivalently a kind of *judgement*, which the right hand side is supposed to illuminate in some way. We need to keep in mind that another focus of interest might be the *property* referred to by the predicate 'ϕ'. For some of us there is not much of a difference here: I myself see properties as the semantic shadows of predicates, not as self-standing objects of investigation. But others see the matter differently: they think of there being a substantive science of identifying the property ϕ which is not the same thing as identifying the concept ϕ, or the role ϕ judgements play in our thought. Thus a popular kind of moral realism ('Cornell realism') searches for natural properties with which to identify the property of being good. Property identity becomes a topic of its own. I shall call this the substantive way of thinking of properties. With it we get a sense/reference distinction for predicates. Two predicates might denote the same property, but in different ways. The judgement that X is good is not the judgement that X creates happiness, even if, on such a philosophy, there is but the one property, creation of happiness, which is also to be seen as goodness, although seeing it this way is doing something extra. We can put this by saying that there is something special about seeing the creation of happiness *under the heading of* being good, and we would not understand ethical *judgement* until we have a sense of what is special about that heading. I return to this point below, but for the moment the topic is its impact on the basic biconditionals.

To make this plain let us focus on a simple example:

(P)   X is poisonous $\equiv$ X tends to elicit illness or death from most of us on being ingested.

This, I hope, sounds about right, and any rough edges are not presently to the point.[9] In fact, it looks like a good old-fashioned analysis of the *concept*, but in any event it affords some elucidation or explication of it. What does it tell us about the property? The substantive way of thinking means that it allows a further hunt for finding what the property of being poisonous actually is. For instance, suppose that all and only things with cyanide molecules are poisonous. Then having cyanide molecules might be the property of being poisonous. This one property can be seen under the one heading-chemically-or the other-medically-and no doubt many others-economically or sociologically.

As I say, I am not myself an advocate of this way of thinking about the semantics of predicates. But at present I am not objecting to it, but pointing out its consequences for the present issues. What it means is that it is quite consistent to hold that (P) tells us everything we need about the *concept* of being poisonous, although it is also true that the *property* of being poisonous is that of containing cyanide molecules. (P) identifies the property under one heading, and this identifies it under another, and each is perfectly acceptable. To take a more interesting example, suppose we have

Circles, Finks, Smells and Biconditionals / 263

(C) X is red ≡ X tends to make normal people see-redly under suitable
conditions of observation

then this is quite compatible with the kind of physicalist hunt for the property of
redness, that hopes to locate some disjunction of physical properties holding of
all and only red things.[10] On the substantive picture, this hunt is not a rival to
an analysis like (C), any more than in the poisonous case, but a supplement to
it.

If (P) is necessary, then things with cyanide molecules would not be
poisonous unless they tended to elicit illness or death from most of us on being
ingested. The right hand side of the biconditional gives us the identifying
condition, or that in virtue of which the property of having cyanide molecules is
that of being poisonous. It explains why having cyanide molecules can be seen
under that heading. Similarly the right hand side of (C) tells us why reflecting
light of 700 nanometers (or...or...) can be seen under the heading of being red.

Here we should notice one cost of the substantive way of thinking. So far
all is well: we have it that containing cyanide molecules is the same property as
being poisonous, and we have the biconditional telling us what it is about the
property that makes it deserve that appellation. But we might reflect that even if
true it seems highly contingent if things of just one or another molecular
structure elicit illness and death, so we seem to be peddling a contingently true
property identity: the property of containing cyanide molecules is the property of
being poisonous, but it might not have been. This is quite compatible with the
substantive way of thinking, but it offends against one strong semantic
intuition, which is that when we turn the predicate 'ϕ' into the noun phrase 'the
property of being ϕ' we end up with a rigid designator of a property. If the
property of being ϕ is the property of being φ, there ought not to be possible
worlds in which they ('they') are not identical. If we want to heed this intuition
we should abandon (thankfully in my view) the substantive way of thinking of
properties, and go back to saying that if the biconditionals give us the property,
then further investigation is simply one of telling us what explains why things
are poisonous or what explains why things are red. We need not then worry
whether these are the only things that *could* have been poisonous or red, as we
have to if rigid reference is in play. But for this paper I am not going to take this
argument as decisive, and shall allow the substantive way of thinking as an
alternative. It is not wholly foreign to everyday ways of thought, and I shall
argue later that it has caused considerable confusion in the area.

2. Dispositions and Finks

Before assessing the work these biconditionals may do, a further point
remains to be made about them. I have deliberately couched them in terms of
dispositions and tendencies. A more ambitious project would remove that

264 / Simon Blackburn

terminology, and substitute conditionals:

$$X \text{ is } \phi \equiv \text{if [P] encounter X in [C] there arises [R].}$$

A subjunctive form might be used instead. Elaborating on the notion of a 'finkish' situation Mark Johnston has been active in generating counterexamples to analyses of this form.[11] In a finkish situation a thing is disposed in some way, but if circumstances apt for manifesting the disposition come about, it will not manifest it. Or conversely, a thing may not be disposed in some way, but if circumstances apt for manifesting the disposition come about, it will do so. This may be because it changes when the antecedent of the conditional is fulfilled. Or it may be because the disposition is what Johnston calls 'masked', or that although the disposition is absent it is mimicked. Examples of finkish situations are: a thing may be brittle, but an angel has decided that if it is dropped she will make it hard; so although it is brittle, if it is dropped it will not break. A thing may be hard, but the same angel has decided that she will render if brittle if it is dropped, and so if it is dropped it will break.

Johnston suggests that these cases and others like them show that we make a distinction between what is 'underwritten by the thing's intrinsic nature and the laws' and what would happen if...In finkish situations a thing's intrinsic nature and the laws make it *such as to* break when dropped, although actually it will not, or vice versa. There are costs in appealing to intrinsic natures, for we may well wonder whether we have any notion at all of a thing's nature and of the laws of nature, that is not itself couched in dispositional terms.[12] But we need not follow Johnston to intrinsic natures as far as these cases go. For we should also notice that insofar as the cases involve supernatural agency this response can hardly be needed: we can just invoke *nature* tout court: a thing is brittle if its breaking when dropped is in accordance with nature and its laws.

It is not so easy to construct finkish cases where we try to put the angel on-board as it were, or in other words imagine a thing being brittle but *naturally* such that when it is dropped its nature transforms into that of something hard. If it continually fails to break, it seems not to be brittle, whatever the underlying evolutions of physical state. This is certainly so for other dispositions. Suppose that I have the 'intrinsic nature' of a capable rock climber: I am strong, agile, fearless, trained, eager. Except that I have one more quirk: the proximity of rock causes me to change (my hands become sweaty), and this temporarily stops me having the same nature as a capable rock climber and I become apt to fall off. The natural description is not that I am a capable rock climber most of the time, but finked when I get on the rock, but that I am a bad rock climber. This is usually what it feels like being a bad rock climber or pianist: it feels as if the circumstances of performance conspire to make your real merit shrink. But this is false consciousness. My rock climber is not a capable rock climber who generates a 'standing illusion' of being worse than he is. The disposition is assessed by the conditional, and *natural* changes in a thing arising on the

Circles, Finks, Smells and Biconditionals / 265

circumstance of manifestation of the conditional do not affect the description.

We can signal this difference between external or supernatural finkish situations, and natural evolutions, by writing the biconditionals:

X is φ ≡ X is naturally such as to elicit [R] from [P] in [C]

where the 'naturally such as to' warns that something might be φ although angels stop it performing as such. But this formula does not allow something to be φ if its own mechanisms trip in to prevent manifestation.

Johnston's further case for invoking intrinsic natures is also supposed to unseat response-dependent analyses of secondary properties such as color. This is the case of the 'shy but intuitive' chameleon. This sits in the dark one color, green, but ready to change to a different color, red, if the light is put on. It is actually green, but by the equation (C) it is red. But although Johnston sees such cases as support for his invocation of an intrinsic nature, the matter is not so simple. After all, in such a story it *is* the intrinsic nature of this chameleon to go into its red mode, so we should expect the parallel result to the rock-climber case, namely that it is always red. Perhaps it is important to distinguish between the thing and its surface, and Johnston's claim will be that the intrinsic nature of the surface is that of a green surface, in the dark, so the right thing to say is that the chameleon's surface, and hence the chameleon is green, in the dark. So suppose instead a light sensitive surface that instantly reacts to bombardment by photons by changing its structure slightly, like photographic paper, only more so. Perhaps my red ruby is like that. It is never ever seen as green, and indeed could not be, although in the dark its surface is physically isomorphic with that of things which, when like that in good light, look green. Is it green in the dark? Johnston's formula gives us no clear guideline. The 'intrinsic nature' of this surface and the laws ensure that when the light goes on it reflects red light. So taken one way we should think of it as red in the dark; on the other hand its physical structure is such that were it to stay as it is when put in the light it would reflect green light.

The case seems to be a 'don't care', hinging on the elasticity of being such as to do something: in some respects the surface of the ruby is such as to appear red, and in other respects it is such as to appear green, because if it stayed with the reflective properties it has in the dark that is how it would appear. We make a verdict on these cases by *imagining* seeing the surface *as it now is*, and retailing the visual experience we imagine ourselves to have. What the case gives us is two ways of looking at how the surface now is, and concentrating on one way we think of ourselves as seeing green, and the other way we think of ourselves as seeing red, (for this surface stays as it now is by clicking into red mode when there is any light).

Here are some other examples of this Berkeleyan genre.

Case 1: the finkish skunk. Suppose skunks with the magic property of sucking all the molecules they emit back in when olfactory systems come near

266 / Simon Blackburn

enough to detect any. Do they emit bad smells? We might think not: you can
safely have one of these as a pet, but you don't want smelly pets. Now suppose
that when an olfactory system is present they retract all the bad molecules and
release Chanel no 5. Are they fragrant —even when they are alone in the forest?
If the purely retractive skunks have no smell, then these have a wonderful smell.
Or, we may, like Hylas, be tempted to say that the skunks emit good or bad
smells depending on the molecules and regardless of the lawlike impossibility of
any smell being perceived. Again, I suggest we have a 'don't care': looked at one
way, the space round the skunks is not a space you would want to be in (keep
the molecules constant, and imagine sniffing). Looked at another, it is fine (keep
the nature of the skunks constant, and imagine sniffing). We can exercise the
imagination either way.

Case 2: The finkish pig. The flesh of these pigs would taste frightful as it is
actually constituted. It contains molecules that have well known bad effects on
taste-buds. But death or dismemberment destroys the molecules, and makes them
taste delicious. Are these pigs delicious as they gambol round the yard, or should
our mouths not water as we look at them? Here there is less temptation to be
even temporarily puzzled, and there is even something off-color and irritating
about the question.[13] But we are surely inclined to give the same answer as for
the rock climber. These pigs are delicious, tout court. (Maybe pigs and pheasants
are actually like this). 'Delicious' may be analyzed by slightly rephrasing our
biconditional:

$$X \text{ is delicious at } t \equiv X \text{ is naturally such that if [C] then [P] give [R]}$$

making it plain that it is what happens in [C] that counts. For pigs, whatever
else it includes, [C] includes being dead. It does not follow that being delicious
cannot be predicated of live pigs, because the left hand side does not include the
qualification 'in [C]'. It could read 'X is delicious always $\equiv$...'. Equally we could
modify both sides with 'at t'. Quite possibly ordinary thought simply does not
care what temporal modifier goes there, and this would explain our irritation
with the question whether the live pig is delicious.[14]

So far we have it that we solve the rock climber and the finkish pig fairly
definitely one way. With the skunk we are more apt to be ambivalent, and I have
suggested that this is a consequence of not having settled what has to stay the
same as we put ourselves in the situation of smelling the skunk. Johnston's
problem with color, I take it, is that he thinks there is a definite verdict going
the other way. The chameleon is supposed to be green, not red, in the dark.
People want to say that colors are categorically present in the dark, and one way
of tightening up that intuition would be to say that we have no freedom to insert
temporal modifications as we wish on the left hand side.

I cannot see this telling us anything deep about color, nor putting an
obstacle in front of a dispositional analysis. For even if we share Johnston's
intuition, the dispositional analysis can accommodate us. Suppose we are

Circles, Finks, Smells and Biconditionals / 267

adamant that the chameleon is green. Then, just as if we are adamant that the lone skunk smells awful, all we need to do is to weight our selection of the feature dominating the 'is naturally such that' clause. Perhaps simple minded faith in colors correlating straightforwardly with physical properties of surfaces encourages this selection, so that we imagine the chameleon's color or the skunk's smell by imagining good circumstance of seeing and smelling but fixing the corrugations of the surface or the distribution of molecules. We then soft-pedal the fact that in good circumstances of seeing and smelling this will not be the set-up any more. Also, if we were attracted to the substantial view of properties, we may have identified the color green with the property of having such and such a corrugated surface, and this will tip our judgement violently that way, and even do the same for the skunk and pig. Otherwise it is hard to see the argument, and I suspect that those who place great importance on objects being colored one way or another in the dark forget that we imagine the colors of reflective surfaces in the dark by imagining the light on.

The upshot is that we can avoid finkish problems by staying with the dispositional suggestions with which I started, and we can sidestep chameleons, skunks, pigs and their ilk by looking out for elasticities in how we think of things as being, or what we think it would be for things to stay the same. We mark this by rephrasing the biconditionals:

$$X \text{ is } \phi \equiv X \text{ (is naturally such as to) tend to elicit [R] from [P] under [C]}$$

where the bracketed phrase reminds us that something may be such as to do this in some respects and not in others, and that these will give rise to wrongly disputed cases.

3. Explanatory Priorities and Analysis

The points already in play enable us to deflect one across-the-board reservation about the success of response-dependent accounts of concepts. Mark Johnston puts it by finding a tension between the *a priori* status the biconditionals have, and the way in which the left hand side functions as an empirical explanation of the right.[15] The 'missing explanation argument' is that frequently it is explanatory to say that it is because X is ϕ that it has or we have the dispositions identified on the right hand side; this being so we cannot see the biconditionals as *a priori* true. Johnston suggests that this argument works at least except for concepts that wear their response dependence on their face (pleasing, shy-making, nauseating). In particular it works for values and it works for secondary properties. He suggests that the argument shows that ordinary concepts are response-independent, although he concedes that this leaves open a programme of reform, suggesting that their response independence is the upshot of something like a projective error.

268 / Simon Blackburn

The argument is a daring one, in the light of all the well-known pragmatic and contextual factors that lead us to allow that one thing is an explanation of another. We can undoubtedly hear ourselves saying that things are disposed to look green to us in favourable circumstances because they are green; seem boring to us because they are boring, and so on. But the superficial linguistic data will not carry the load of this argument, because it is quite compatible with an *a priori* equivalence between explanans and explanandum. As Wright points out, we can equally hear ourselves saying that the figure is a circle because it is the locus of a line equidistant from a point, or that such and such a connective is material implication because it has the truth table TFTT. An a priori status is jeopardized only if the explanation is a contingent one. Johnston recognizes this, and in a response to Wright emphasizes that the explanations in question are contingent, empirical and causal, although he also makes it plain that their causal status is less important than the other two.[16]

As well as showing that the use of the left hand side to explain the right is use of a contingent or empirical or causal connexion, the argument needs extreme care over the explanandum and explanans. The biconditionals may be a priori and indeed analytic, but still we would be able to explain why we found something boring on an occasion or why I find X boring, by saying that X is boring, and such explanations may be contingently true or false. For it may be contingent whether on this occasion I or we were bored because of X being such as to excite boredom from [P,C]. It may be contingent whether the occasion counted as [C], or I or we as [P]. It may be that we were bored because of something quite different: we were out of sorts, or there were roadworks outside the theater. The explanation rules out these possibilities: it works by saying that we were *true-to-form* by being bored. (This point parallels one commonly made about opium and its dormative virtue.)

To put this aside suppose we take the whole population, as we should be doing:

X elicits [R] from [P] in [C] *because* it is φ

can we get a reading which is contingent or empirical or causal, for the appropriate cases, and thereby rules out the a priori equivalence of the two sides? It seems strange that there should be an empirical or causal science of whether it is boring things that bore us, or red things that we see as red. I suspect there are ways of reading such sentences as contingent, and even empirical and causal. But on no way of so reading them does the conclusion follow. These ways are quite compatible with the a priori status of the biconditional. Here are four such possibilities:

(1) [C] or [P] or [R] could be chosen so badly that there is indeed a contingent, causal, and empirical gap between the two sides with the inept substitutions in place. But this is clearly irrelevant to the *a priori* status of the conditional with better judged substitutions. The different question of whether

Circles, Finks, Smells and Biconditionals / 269

any substitutions fit the bill entirely occupies us in the next section.

(2) Even when [C] and [P] and [R] are chosen with care, there may be an empirical investigation in the offing. Suppose we identify some favourable circumstances. The question may still arise why these *are* the favourable circumstances, and contingent and causal factors may enter the answer. But this does not impugn the *a prioricity*. For example, a kite is well designed ≡ it flies well in favourable wind conditions. Which are those? Let us say between force two and six. Why are those the favourable conditions? Because they prevail quite frequently, because we are comfortable in them, because air has the density it does. All of these are contingent, and they underlie the choice of these conditions. But that does not impugn the definitional status of the original biconditional. It simply introduces a new topic of interest.

(3) Perhaps 'because' contexts introduce reference to properties, so the explanation reads in effect that X elicits [R] etc. because of having the *property* φ. Given a substantive theory of properties (see above) this may be contingent, but we saw in section 1 that this contingency is compatible with an analytic status for the biconditional.

Johnston misses this possibility. He cites against Wright the 'Cornell realists' in ethics, who emphasize the propriety of putting ethical predicates into explanatory contexts, and allow, for instance, that it is contingent that we generally approve of things because they are good. But he does not see that the Cornell realists are bad allies at this point. They have a substantive theory of properties, and the properties referred to in the explanation are those natural properties that contingently excite our approval. The contingency of the explanation is perfectly compatible with the a prioricity of the related biconditional (a thing is good ≡ it is such as to excite [R] in [P,C]); this is the point I made above in connexion with the notion of a thing being poisonous. The point is that a prioricity concerns information, or its constituent concepts. Explanation here concerns the relationship between properties. Since properties are here treated as capable of being apprehended in different ways, an a priori proposition can mask a contingent relationship between them. The point was made familiar by Davidson in connexion with events: if something caused φ, then the proposition that the event φ was caused by the cause of φ is a priori, but the events stand in a contingent causal relationship.

(4) Through time a thing may have evolved to be as it is because of the effect that induces: it may be the color that has made the flower successful. This gives us one way of reading the explanatory claim the other way round. But it also gives us a way of reading it as Johnston does. This is easier to see if we use the longer form:

X is naturally such as to elicit [R] from [P] in [C] because it is φ

and here the 'such as to' formula points us to thinking of the same properties as before—the base or underlying properties—now said to be there because of the

270 / Simon Blackburn

redness or whatever that they underlie. Compare: this circuit diminishes the voltage because it has a resistor in it; this circuit has a resistor in it because it diminishes the voltage. Each can be true, and contingent, and each is compatible with there being an analytic equivalence between a component being for diminishing the voltage and its being a resistor.

In these last two cases the substantive view of properties confuses the issue of contingency and makes Johnston's claim look superficially plausible. But as the sense/reference distinction reminds us, it then has no consequences for the a priori status of the biconditionals.

On the other hand, if we eschew the substantive theory of properties, what reading can we give to the explanation? Russell once said it was favoritism to suppose that the things that seem to us red are the things that are red, and I suppose the idea that there might be an empirical and causal investigation of whether this is so in general reflects the same idea. But it does not grip us for long. If it is contingent whether our color vision is adapted for the real color of things then it is very likely contingently false, but what kind of investigation could anybody holding that be envisaging? Might ammonia really have no odor? Has a finkish nature resulted in us being poisoned by things that are not really poisonous? Anybody interested in the dispositional account of secondary properties will reply with justice that part of the point of the analysis is to get away from a general gap between the judgements we are disposed to make and the truth.

The case of values introduces further issues. Once more however it is incredible that a scientific, empirical, causal, investigation is capable of raising a general gap between the right and left hand sides-unless the right hand side is chosen so badly that one of the four options above is in play. What is true is that we can always distinguish in our thought between something being good and it eliciting any reaction in a given population, and we can prosecute that possibility not by a causal empirical investigation, but an ethical one, as we mull over the defects of the population (or their reaction, or the circumstances). But this irreducible normativity waits for the next sections. Meanwhile, the upshot is that the 'missing explanation' argument puts no obstacle in front of an a priori status for the biconditionals.

4. Analyses and Circularity.

With such excavations behind us these biconditionals may seem to be well set to do the work claimed for them, and provide a suitable explication of various concepts. So it is time to concentrate on what seems to me to be a real problem, which is that of circularity. As I have said, it is often claimed that a feature of echo in these biconditionals—the reappearance of ϕ on the right hand side-need not matter, since our goal is explication of a concept rather than analysis. But

Circles, Finks, Smells and Biconditionals / 271

this is at best a half truth: in fact, more like a one tenth truth, and often wholly false. The principle to keep hold of is that if you want some things your biconditional will need to observe some constraints, when if you want others it might not. Suppose, for instance that your concern is with what it is to judge that something is φ. Then you will be disappointed with an echoing biconditional of this kind:

> X is φ ≡ X (is such as to) dispose [P] in [C] to judge it to be φ.

Because it is what these persons are *doing* in judging something to be φ that you wanted explained. For example, if you want to know what it is to judge that something is good, your quest has not been advanced by:

> X is good ≡ X (is such as to) dispose [P] in [C] to judge it to be good.

For even if this is true, you gain no understanding of what the persons are doing (what it has to do with their rationality, or emotions, or standards or social situations, or whatever troubles you).

Obviously a regress arises if we try to make the proposal help with this question by substituting the right hand side into the content of the judgement:

> X is good ≡ X (is such as to) dispose [P] in [C] to judge that X (is such as to) dispose [P] in [C] to judge... .

And this regress is vicious, because either it is never closed, or it leaves the very activity you wanted explained unanalyzed on the clause on which it is closed.

Our goal is frequently to understand judgement that something is φ. Indeed, since we are supposedly investigating the concept of φ, and since concepts and judgements are the same topic, it may be hard to see how we can be doing anything else, in which case insouciance about the echo is entirely unjustified. It is however true that if, surprisingly, understanding judgement had not been your concern, the very same proposal might have had some point. You might feel you understand well enough what people are up to who judge that things are good, but lack any understanding of what could make their judgements *true*, and in the context of that predicament the suggestion could be helpful: what makes it true is that (it is such that) [P] in [C] so judge it. Thus I might feel no philosophical problems about what it is to judge that something is boring (perhaps I have a simple functional story: 'tending to make people fall asleep on contemplating it') and be helped by being told that a thing actually is boring ≡ [P] in [C] judge it boring. So it all depends what we want explaining.

In this context the regress does not arise, because there is no reason to substitute in the content of the judgement. The judging is understood in another way, and the regress sidestepped. But it is essential too to notice that this benefit incurs a cost. For there is a certain lack of harmony between the reaction as specified—tending to fall asleep—and the content that, on this account, that judgement actually has. Naturally I might tend to fall asleep without judging

272 / Simon Blackburn

that [P] in [C] so tend, and I might judge this as it were in an anthropological spirit without myself tending to fall asleep. My own disposition to the reaction will be one thing, but the judgement that X has ϕ (i.e. is such as to elicit [R] from [P,C]) is here quite another. This remains true even if as pure subjectivists we replace [P] with me, since I may tend to fall asleep without judging that I do, and without judging that the conditions are [C]. The lack of harmony is that a prominent semantic anchor for 'X is boring' is that I am absolutely and straightforwardly entitled to voice it on having been bored by X. Whereas I am by no means entitled to voice the left hand side on having been bored by X, unless I can take myself to be representative of [P] and my circumstances to have been in the set [C]. The problems this causes return in the final two sections.

Suppose we stay with the goal of understanding the judgement that X is ϕ. The next problem we meet is not one of regress, but one of navigating between two disasters, that I shall call Scylla and Charybdis. Scylla is that we falsify the kind of judgement 'X is ϕ' actually makes. Charybdis is that we get this right- but at the cost of making (not mentioning, as in the regress problem) the same kind of judgement at some place within the right hand side. It may be no objection that we make the same kind of judgement with the overall right hand side, and indeed it can with justice be urged that this will be the point of the biconditional taken as an analysis. But it can well be objectionable when this is achieved by including the very same kind of judgement within the right hand side.

This structure is familiar in the case of value. Scylla is that we go naturalistic or empirical; Charybdis that we make an ethical judgement on the right hand side. Contrast:

> X is good $\equiv$ X is such as to elicit desires from us as we actually are, when we come across it.
> X is good $\equiv$ X is such as to elicit desires from good people when they come across it.

The first, considered as an attempt to understand ethical judgement, must be deemed to fail, because it only gives us an equation with a natural judgement about X, certifiable by empirical means. Notice that if our interest had been in a substantive theory of ethical properties, this might have been acceptable. We would say, in the spirit of Cornell realism, that this is a candidate for being the property of goodness. This leaves to one side the question of what it is to see this property under the heading of the good, as opposed to seeing it as just another natural property, possibly instanced by very regrettable things. But since we are supposing that our interest is in understanding ethical judgement, seeing it under the special heading is the very topic we are pursuing, and this suggestion has mistaken it. Thus Scylla.

The second proposal fails in the complementary way, since what it has done is equate one ethical judgement with another: it takes not observation but ethical judgement to determine whether something is such as to elicit desires from good people, since you have to judge who are the good people. Of course, in principle an advance *within* ethics could come about this way, since it might be somehow easier to judge who are the good people than it appears to be to judge X's. But this will not be an advance in our understanding of ethical judgement per se. It would be a strictly local advance in first order moral theory.

How wide does Charybdis gape? For a particularly spectacular dive into it consider:

> X is good ≡ X is such as to elicit desires from people under the ideal circumstances, i.e. those under which people desire good things.

Everybody accepts that this is trivial. The running-on-the-spot here is indeed emphasized by the irrelevance of the way the each of [R] and [P] is identified. That is, you might just as well have:

> X is good ≡ X is such as to elicit astonishment from polar bears under the ideal circumstances

if you identify ideal circumstances as those under which polar bears are astonished at good things. Obviously similar equations can be constructed for any judgement at all. But how much ethical can be left in the right hand side? Again, it will depend how much context you bring to it. But so long as the right hand side makes the same *kind* of judgement as the left, it will not serve to elucidate the kind. In the following schema the presence of just one of the curly bracketed terms will disqualify the equation from the task of understanding ethical judgement and color judgement respectively:

> X is good ≡ X {deserves} the judgement that it is {good} from {good/improved/virtuous...} persons under {ideal} conditions
> X is red ≡ X is naturally such as to elicit the judgement that it is {red} from non-{color blind} persons under conditions favourable for {color} discrimination.

The question will be whether the brackets can be removed without stripping the equations of any a priori status they ought to have, and falling into the clutches of Scylla. Putting fig leaves over the bracketed terms only postpones the problem.17

Scylla and Charybdis will flank any attempt to understand judgement of a particular *sui generis* kind by means of these biconditionals. But it may be hard to believe that there is no room to navigate between them. Remembering that the goal is to understand some kind of judgement, we should recall that an increase in understanding may be contextual. For instance

> X is boring ≡ X is such as to elicit sleep dispositions from normal people under circumstances that are good for appreciating X

274 / Simon Blackburn

might look as if it drowns in Charybdis. It will if the best we can say about
circumstances good for appreciating X are: circumstances such that if X is funny,
we laugh; if X is tragic we heave, if X is boring we get bored...(equally we
drown if the best that can be said about normal people is that they are the ones
who laugh at what is funny...and get bored by what is boring). But if we can do
better than that, the equation might be an advance. It will be if we already
understand other kinds of appreciation, and can understand a general notion of
evaluating circumstances of appreciation, and have a general notion of normal
people. We then learn to place the judgement that something is boring within
this family, and that could be the understanding we needed. Once more, this will
be a strictly local advance, placing one of a family of concepts at the table, but
not helping to place the general appreciative table. Again, then, the issue hinges
on the explanatory context.

    All the attempts that I know of to understand value judgements in general
by giving dispositional accounts meet Scylla or drown in Charybdis.

5. Looking at Ourselves?

    Ordinary thought seems to have been rather casual about the identity of [P],
[C], and even [R], if we are to judge by the limited success philosophers have
had in recommending privileged instances. This confirms the evident truth that
to enable a learner to use and communicate regarding smells or colors we do not
have to load them with something like:

> X smells foxy ≡ X is naturally such that it elicits from most normal
> people who do not have colds or other relevant disabilities, in
> circumstances of still air with no other smells (!) present, the judgement
> that X smells like a fox.

On the face of it, using and understanding the concepts here displayed betokens a
much greater conceptual sophistication than knowing how to report that there is
a foxy smell in the garden, which will have been taught by ostension, and by
induction into a fairly flexible practice of subjecting such claims to a certain
amount of critical scrutiny (for which, see more below). Of course, the response-
dependence theorist may reply that he is not trying for an analysis, but as we
saw above this has costs: she is after all trying for some elucidation of the
judgement, and the point is that we have no reason for confidence that the
biconditional shows us how the judgement *works*.

    Connected with this is the point that often these judgements are more like
verdicts than hypotheses about the suspected reactions of some other group under
some putative circumstances. If I am asked whether the picture was beautiful or
the play interesting, I dissemble if I say that it was *because* I hypothesize that
most people find it so, although I personally couldn't stand it. What is expected

Circles, Finks, Smells and Biconditionals / 275

is that I give my own verdict. 'Yes, it was fascinating' expresses how I found it. My verdict can be challenged of course, but the challenge is not itself an hypothesis about [P] and [C], but an attempt to show that my feeling was unwarranted-that I ought not to have found it beautiful or fascinating. Notice too that if I then retreat to say (huffily, as it might be) 'well, *I* thought it was fascinating' I am not retreating to saying that *my* hypothesis was that it was such as to elicit [R] form [P,C]. I am repeating my own verdict or expressing my own reaction.

We here have what I earlier called the lack of harmony between the reaction and the things that make true the biconditional elaborated upon it. The logical space I enter when I make my verdict is not that of an empirical hypothesis about the reactions of some identifiable group of people. As Kant put it for the case of beauty, the judgement of taste does not 'postulate' the agreement of everyone, but 'imputes' it, or 'exacts it from everyone else as necessary'.[18] 'The assertion is not that everyone *will* fall in with our judgement, but that everyone *ought* to agree with it'.[19]

Kant's insight is confirmed by another phenomenon that is prominent in these cases. I may know empirically that X is such as to elicit [R] from [P,C], but because I have no experience of X, I cannot without misrepresentation answer the question 'Is X beautiful/boring/fascinating...?' I can only answer that other people think so, or that I am longing to see it. I cannot say tout court that it was one or the other without giving an overwhelming impression that I have myself been in a position to make a judgement, and have made it. This is highly mysterious on the hypothesis that the judgement functions as a straight descriptions of the reactions of an identified group in identified circumstances.

Of course, a normative element can be overtly included on the right hand side:

X is φ ≡ X is such that [P] in [C] ought to give [R].

And typically this is right enough as far as it goes. A thing is boring ≡ people ought to be bored by it. As Kant saw, the whole question then turns to our right to invoke norms at this point, or in his terms why our judgements do not retain a purely 'subjective validity'.[20] This is the same as the question of how the judgement of taste is as much as possible: how there can be *space* for a genuine judgement here. The quasi-realist project of earning our right to a judgmental form is by no means by-passed but is actually highlighted and center-stage if this is the kind of biconditional on offer. And this is inevitable, given that where value terms are in play the echo is not at all benign, but points us straight at Charybdis. For the right hand side is another example of the kind of judgement we might have been hoping to understand.

276 / Simon Blackburn

6. Secondary Properties Again

Let us return to secondary properties. Even if the biconditionals have lost ground as a device for showing us how evaluation works, might they retain a place here? We have deflected the argument from the missing explanation and from the finkish complexities, so the way might seem relatively clear to relying on them. On the other hand reluctance to take the echoing impredicativity lightly will be difficult to accommodate. For enough work has stressed the impropriety of avoiding the echo by going private and imagining a different property of experience whose presence amounts to the reaction in question. If that route is closed, as I think it is, then the only way of identifying the reaction is as that of someone who judges that something is red, or smells like ammonia, or sounds like concert A. So the form of the offering is now:

$$X \text{ is } \phi \equiv X \text{ is such as to elicit the judgement that it is } \phi \text{ from } [P,C].$$

Does this kind of offering (or the claim that it is *a priori*) help us to understand the way judgement of color or smell or sound works, in spite of the echo? The flexibility in [P] and [C] complicates the issue. But for any substantive fillings something is wrong akin to the misdirection these equations introduce in the case of values. There we do not, as I put it, turn our gaze through 90° and concern ourselves with our reactions. And here too we do not turn our gaze on our population or circumstances. Certainly we do have a sense of our judgements being corrigible, if enough people do not confirm them, or the light turns out to have been deceptive.[21] But we do not wrap this practice of corrigibility, necessary as it is for the purpose of communicating what to expect, into the content for the actual judgement of color. If we did, those of us unfortunate enough not to have a grip on some favoured fillings for [P] and [C] would be unable to judge color.

The point here can be easy to miss. In the context of defending a dispositional account John McDowell once asked rhetorically: 'What would one expect it to be like to experience something's being such as to look red, if not to experience the thing in question (in the right circumstances) as looking, precisely, red?'[22] The answer is straightforward. Imagine anyone able to determine whether something is such as to elicit the judgment that it is red from [P,C] by any means we like: touch, sound when struck, monochromatic contrast with other objects. Just as a chemist might determine that a thing is poisonous by giving himself visual experience of its molecular construction, so any of these methods may certify the disposition of a thing. It will be purely contingent whether there exist such methods for any particular secondary quality. The point is, of course, that anybody arriving at an hypothesis about a secondary quality in such a way is not judging its *color*. She is in the same position as someone who, not having seen the painting, says in the anthropological spirit that it is beautiful because she knows the reactions of those who have. It is the reaction of

Circles, Finks, Smells and Biconditionals / 277

those who are judging the color or the beauty that we need to understand; the fact that an outside could plug into the existence of their reaction, and make the dispositional judgement on her own account, shows that the dispositional judgement is not what was wanted.

McDowell insists that the crucial reaction 'presents itself as perceptual awareness of properties genuinely possessed by the objects that confront one' and in this he may be right. But the perceptual awareness does not typically include in its scope [C] (most people cannot just see for instance whether it is a clear northern light, or one of a different color temperature). Still less does it include [P] and how they would be disposed to react. Similarly, by tasting a substance and being poisoned I may be in a position to guess that others would be so too, but I am certainly not in a position to know that, and still less do I have the content of that judgement presented perceptually. *That* would be something quite different, like a movie of people collapsing.

The crucial residual problem for secondary quality perception is now apparent. Colors are seen, sounds heard, smells smelled. The problem is not that McDowell's remark is true, but of understanding how it can be true. Our reactions *do* present themselves as perceptual awareness, yet we have no stable conception of their *right* to so present themselves.The true situation is probably much more easily understood with smell and taste than with color: we are more easily led by Berkeley to think that the nose or palate tells us nothing about the world than that chromatic vision does not. The problem of right is exactly analogous to Kant's problem with the judgement of beauty, but the solution that we want a normative practice of demanding a similar response from others is not nearly so plausible. Dispositional accounts solve the problem of right, but make colors and the rest essentially imperceptible. Rebounding from that we confront the problem of how the bare subjectivity of response transforms itself into a genuine awareness of a property.[23] Once more then, far from superseding approaches which wrestle with the problem of understanding the emergence of judgement from human response, concentration on the dispositional biconditionals threatens to conceal even the need for just such an understanding.[24]

Notes

1. Volumes substantially devoted to the subject include *Response Dependent Concepts*, (Canberra: Research School of Social Sciences, Australian National University, 1991) and, given the scale of the papers by Mark Johnston and Crispin Wright, *Realism and Reason*, (Oxford: Clarendon Press, 1992). Since this volume is in Press at the time of writing pagination cannot be given in the references.
2. Pettit, 'Realism and Response Dependence', *Mind*, 1991, p. 588. Wright, 'Wittgenstein's rule-following Considerations and the Central Project of Theoretical Linguistics', in *Reflections on Chomsky*, ed. A. George (Oxford: Blackwell, 1989)

278 / Simon Blackburn

3. *Proceedings of the Aristotelian Society, Supplementary Volume* 1989, pp. 89-174.
4. Huw Price 'Two Paths to Pragmatism' in *Response Dependent Concepts,* and Mark Johnston, 'Explanation, Response Dependence and Judgement Dependence' in the same volume, and 'Objectivity Refigured' in *Realism and Reason.* My exploration of this issue owes a great deal to Price's paper.
5. See also Johnston, 'The Dispositional Theory of Value', pp. 147-8.
6. Richard Holton, 'Intentions, Response-Dependence and Immunity from Error' in *Response-Dependent Concepts*
7. Echoing explications are endorsed by, among many others, McGinn, *The Subjective View* (Oxford: Clarendon Press, 1983) and McDowell, 'Values and Secondary Qualities', in *Morality and Objectivity*, ed. Ted Honderich, (London: Routledge & Kegan Paul, 1985). The idea of opening them up is often credited to David Wiggins.
8. The value of *a prioricity* here is stressed by Crispin Wright, 'Moral Values, Projection and Secondary Qualities' *Proceedings of the Aristotelian Society Supplementary Volume* 1988. The difficulty of filling the placeholders so that the biconditionals are not trivial but remain *a priori* is well brought out by Richard Holton, op. cit., and Jim Edwards, 'Secondary Qualities and the A Priori', *Mind* 1992.
9. It is right for foodstuffs, but not for many snakes, which are poisonous although benign when ingested. This shows that [C] may vary with X.
10. Of course, it is known that this disjunction will be hopelessly unwieldy. To repeat, I am not advocating that we think of any such thing as 'being the property of redness', because I do not advocate thinking in these terms at all.
11. Johnston, 'Objectivity Refigured', Appendix 2. I owe the term 'finkish' to David Lewis: Johnston avoids calling his situations finkish, but the term is useful.
12. See my 'Filling in Space', *Analysis*, April 1990
13. We feel quite free with other janus faced dispositions where it is not change that is involved. Many snakes inject several different kinds of venom. Suppose a snake adapted not to poison mammals but only birds, and suppose that only one of its venoms is poisonous in mammals while its second chemical acts as to neutralize the poison. Is it a poisonous snake? It injects a poison, but you can step on it with impunity. We don't much care: in some respects it is such as to poison, and in others not. Do guardian angels guard from danger, or mean that there is no danger?
14. Crispin Wright reacts to the shy but intuitive chameleon by a slightly different modification. He revokes the simple biconditional, and substitutes a 'provisional' equation, of the form 'if [C], then a thing is phi iff [R]'. No verdict is given on the chameleon or the lone skunk or the live pig, because the circumstances of good observation do not hold. This certainly chimes with the irritation we feel with questions like `is he a good rock climber, when there is no rock about?'. My reason for avoiding it is that I believe that the right equation should show us how a dispositional property can be instanced even when not manifested.
15. 'Objectivity Refigured', Appendix 1.
16. Mark Johnston, 'Remarks on Response Dependence' in Haldane & Wright, op. cit.
17. Potential fig leaves: merits, standard, normal, suitable, sees-redly, sees red', has a visual experience as of seeing English pillar boxes... .
18. Immanuel Kant, *The Critique of Judgement*, trans. James Meredith, (Oxford: Clarendon Press, 1952), pp. 52-59.
19. Ibid, p. 84.
20. For aesthetics, many people now probably think in effect that they do.
21. Although the way we actually work this latter is interesting. We do not only say 'it wasn't green: the light was misleading' but also 'funny: it is green in that light'. Our attachment to single colours for objects is quite casual. Metamerism

Circles, Finks, Smells and Biconditionals / 279

is not usually described as things of the same color, which appear different from each other in different lights, but things of the same color in one light, and different color in different lights.

22. John McDowell, 'Values and Secondary Qualities', p. 112.
23. In his excellent paper 'Of Primary and Secondary Qualities' (*Philosophical Review*, 1990) A. D. Smith highlights Descartes saying that 'even bodies are not properly speaking known by the senses or by the faculty of imagination...'. It is one thing to think that Descartes was wrong, but quite another to understand how.
24. The notion of a finkish disposition is due to C. B. Martin, whose paper 'Powers and Conditionals' was read at the Chapel Hill Colloquium in 1968.

Part VI
Are Moral Claims Made True or False by Facts about the Role of Morality in Explanation?

[17]

The Philosophical Review, XCV, No. 2 (April 1986)

MORAL REALISM

Peter Railton

A mong contemporary philosophers, even those who have not found skepticism about empirical science at all compelling have tended to find skepticism about morality irresistible. For various reasons, among them an understandable suspicion of moral absolutism, it has been thought a mark of good sense to explain away any appearance of objectivity in moral discourse. So common has it become in secular intellectual culture to treat morality as subjective or conventional that most of us now have difficulty imagining what it might be like for there to be facts to which moral judgments answer.

Undaunted, some philosophers have attempted to establish the objectivity of morality by arguing that reason, or science, affords a foundation for ethics. The history of such attempts hardly inspires confidence. Although rationalism in ethics has retained adherents long after other rationalisms have been abandoned, the powerful philosophical currents that have worn away at the idea that unaided reason might afford a standpoint from which to derive substantive conclusions show no signs of slackening. And ethical naturalism has yet to find a plausible synthesis of the empirical and the normative: the more it has given itself over to descriptive accounts of the origin of norms, the less has it retained recognizably moral force; the more it has undertaken to provide a recognizable basis for moral criticism or reconstruction, the less has it retained a firm connection with descriptive social or psychological theory.[1]

In what follows, I will present in a programmatic way a form of ethical naturalism that owes much to earlier theorists, but that seeks to effect a more satisfactory linkage of the normative to the empirical. The link cannot, I believe, be effected by proof. It is no more my aim to refute moral skepticism than it is the aim of contemporary epistemic naturalists to refute Cartesian skepticism. The

---

[1]Nineteenth-century evolutionary naturalism affords an example of the former, Dewey—and, on at least one reading, perhaps Mill as well—an example of the latter.

PETER RAILTON

naturalist in either case has more modest aspirations. First, he seeks to provide an analysis of epistemology or ethics that permits us to see how the central evaluative functions of this domain could be carried out within existing (or prospective) empirical theories. Second, he attempts to show how traditional nonnaturalist accounts rely upon assumptions that are in some way incoherent, or that fit ill with existing science. And third, he presents to the skeptic a certain challenge, namely, to show how a skeptical account of our epistemic or moral practices could be as plausible, useful, or interesting as the account the naturalist offers, and how a skeptical reconstruction of such practices—should the skeptic, as often he does, attempt one—could succeed in preserving their distinctive place and function in human affairs. I will primarily be occupied with the first of these three aspirations.

One thing should be said at the outset. Some may be drawn to, or repelled by, moral realism out of a sense that it is the view of ethics that best expresses high moral earnestness. Yet one can be serious about morality, even to a fault, without being a moral realist. Indeed, a possible objection to the sort of moral realism I will defend here is that it may not make morality serious enough.

I. Species of Moral Realism

Such diverse views have claimed to be—or have been accused of being—realist about morality, that an initial characterization of the position I will defend is needed before proceeding further. Claims—and accusations—of moral realism typically extend along some or all of the following dimensions. Roughly put: (1) Cognitivism—Are moral judgments capable of truth and falsity? (2) Theories of truth—If moral judgments do have truth values, in what sense? (3) Objectivity—In what ways, if any, does the existence of moral properties depend upon the actual or possible states of mind of intelligent beings? (4) Reductionism—Are moral properties reducible to, or do they in some weaker sense supervene upon, nonmoral properties? (5) Naturalism—Are moral properties natural properties? (6) Empiricism—Do we come to know moral facts in the same way we come to know the facts of empirical science, or are

MORAL REALISM

they revealed by reason or by some special mode of apprehension? (7) Bivalence—Does the principle of the excluded middle apply to moral judgments? (8) Determinateness—Given whatever procedures we have for assessing moral judgments, how much of morality is likely to be determinable? (9) Categoricity—Do all rational agents necessarily have some reason to obey moral imperatives? (10) Universality—Are moral imperatives applicable to all rational agents, even (should such exist) those who lack a reason to comply with them? (11) Assessment of existing moralities—Are present moral beliefs approximately true, or do prevailing moral intuitions in some other sense constitute privileged data? (12) Relativism—Does the truth or warrant of moral judgments depend directly upon individually- or socially-adopted norms or practices? (13) Pluralism—Is there a uniquely good form of life or a uniquely right moral code, or could different forms of life or moral codes be appropriate in different circumstances?

Here, then, are the approximate coordinates of my own view in this multidimensional conceptual space. I will argue for a form of moral realism which holds that moral judgments can bear truth values in a fundamentally non-epistemic sense of truth; that moral properties are objective, though relational; that moral properties supervene upon natural properties, and may be reducible to them; that moral inquiry is of a piece with empirical inquiry; that it cannot be known *a priori* whether bivalence holds for moral judgments or how determinately such judgments can be assessed; that there is reason to think we know a fair amount about morality, but also reason to think that current moralities are wrong in certain ways and could be wrong in quite general ways; that a rational agent may fail to have a reason for obeying moral imperatives, although they may nonetheless be applicable to him; and that, while there are perfectly general criteria of moral assessment, nonetheless, by the nature of these criteria no one kind of life is likely to be appropriate for all individuals and no one set of norms appropriate for all societies and all times. The position thus described might well be called 'stark, raving moral realism', but for the sake of syntax, I will colorlessly call it 'moral realism'. This usage is not proprietary. Other positions, occupying more or less different coordinates, may have equal claim to either name.

165

PETER RAILTON

II. The Fact/Value Distinction

Any attempt to argue for a naturalistic moral realism runs head-
long into the fact/value distinction. Philosophers have given various accounts of this distinction, and of the arguments for it, but for
present purposes I will focus upon several issues concerning the
epistemic and ontological status of judgments of value as opposed
to judgments of fact.

Perhaps the most frequently heard argument for the fact/value
distinction is epistemic: it is claimed that disputes over questions of
value can persist even after all rational or scientific means of ad-
judication have been deployed, hence, value judgments cannot be
cognitive in the sense that factual or logical judgments are. This
claim is defended in part by appeal to the instrumental (hypothetical) character of reason, which prevents reason from dictating
ultimate values. In principle, the argument runs, two individuals
who differ in ultimate values could, without manifesting any rational defect, hold fast to their conflicting values in the face of any
amount of argumentation or evidence. As Ayer puts it, "we find
that argument is possible on moral questions only if some system of
values is presupposed."[2]

One might attempt to block this conclusion by challenging the
instrumental conception of rationality. But for all its faults and for
all that it needs to be developed, the instrumental conception seems
to me the clearest notion we have of what it is for an agent to have
reasons to act. Moreover, it captures a central normative feature of
reason-giving, since we can readily see the commending force for
an agent of the claim that a given act would advance his ends. It
would be hard to make much sense of someone who sincerely
claimed to have certain ends and yet at the same time insisted that
they could not provide him even *prima facie* grounds for action. (Of
course, he might also believe that he has other, perhaps countervailing, grounds.)

Yet this version of the epistemic argument for the fact/value
distinction is in difficulty even granting the instrumental conception of rationality. From the standpoint of instrumental reason,

---

[2]A. J. Ayer, *Language, Truth, and Logic* (New York: Dover, 1952), p. 111.

MORAL REALISM

belief-formation is but one activity among others: to the extent that
we have reasons for engaging in it, or for doing it one way rather
than another, these are at bottom a matter of its contribution to our
ends.[3] What it would be rational for an individual to believe on the
basis of a given experience will vary not only with respect to his
other beliefs, but also with respect to what he desires.[4] From this it
follows that no amount of mere argumentation or experience
could force one on pain of irrationality to accept even the factual
claims of empirical science. The long-running debate over inductive logic well illustrates that rational choice among competing hypotheses requires much richer and more controversial criteria of
theory choice than can be squeezed from instrumental reason
alone. Unfortunately for the contrast Ayer wished to make, we find
that argument is possible on scientific questions only if some system
of values is presupposed.

However, Hume had much earlier found a way of marking the
distinction between facts and values without appeal to the idea that
induction—or even deduction—could require a rational agent to
adopt certain beliefs rather than others when this would conflict
with his contingent ends.[5] For Hume held the thesis that morality is
practical, by which he meant that if moral facts existed, they would
necessarily provide a reason (although perhaps not an overriding

---

[3]In saying this, I am insisting that questions about what it would be
rational to believe belong to practical rather than theoretical reason. While
results of theoretical reason—for example, conclusions of deductive inferences—are in general relevant to questions about rational belief, they
are not determinative apart from the agent's practical reasons.

[4]Of course, individual belief-formation is not typically governed by explicit means-end reasoning, but rather by habits of belief-formation and
tendencies to invest varying degrees of confidence in particular kinds of
beliefs. If we accept an instrumental account of rationality, then we can call
such habits rational from the standpoint of the individual to the extent that
they fit into a constellation of attitudes and tendencies that promote his
ends. This matter will arise again in Section IV.

[5]Neither these remarks, nor those in subsequent paragraphs, are meant
to be a serious exegesis of Hume's arguments, which admit of interpretations other than the one suggested here. I mean only to capture certain
features of what I take Hume's arguments to be, for example, in Book III,
Part I, Section I of *A Treatise of Human Nature*, edited by L. A. Selby-Bigge
(Oxford: Clarendon, 1973), esp. pp. 465–466, and in Appendix I of *An
Inquiry Concerning the Principles of Morals*, edited by C. W. Hendel (Indianapolis: Bobbs-Merrill, 1957), esp. pp. 111–112.

PETER RAILTON

reason) for moral action to all rational beings, regardless of their particular desires. Given this thesis as a premise, the instrumental conception of rationality can clinch the argument after all, for it excludes the possibility of categorical reasons of this kind. By contrast, Hume did not suppose it to be constitutive of logic or science that the facts revealed by these forms of inquiry have categorical force for rational agents, so the existence of logical and scientific facts, unlike the existence of moral facts, is compatible with the instrumental character of reason.

Yet this way of drawing the fact/value distinction is only as compelling as the claim that morality is essentially practical in Hume's sense.[6] Hume is surely right in claiming there to be an intrinsic connection, no doubt complex, between valuing something and having some sort of positive attitude toward it that provides one with an instrumental reason for action. We simply would disbelieve someone who claimed to value honesty and yet never showed the slightest urge to act honestly when given an easy opportunity. But this is a fact about the connection between the values *embraced by* an individual and his reasons for action, not a fact showing a connection between moral evaluation and rational motivation.

Suppose for example that we accept Hume's characterization of justice as an artificial virtue directed at the general welfare. This is in a recognizable sense an evaluative or normative notion—"a value" in the loose sense in which this term is used in such debates— yet it certainly does not follow from its definition that every rational being, no matter what his desires, who believes that some or other act is just in this sense will have an instrumental reason to perform it. A rational individual may fail to value justice for its own sake, and may have ends contrary to it. In Hume's discussion of our "interested obligation" to be just, he seems to recognize that in the end it may not be possible to show that a "sensible knave" has a reason to be just. Of course, Hume held that the rest of us—whose

------

[6]Philippa Foot has questioned this thesis, although her way of posing and arguing the question differs enough from mine that I cannot judge whether she would be in agreement with the argument that follows. See her *Virtues and Vices* (Berkeley: University of California Press, 1978), especially Essay XI. The presentation of the issues here owes its main inspiration to William K. Frankena's distinction between the rational and the moral points of view.

MORAL REALISM

hearts rebel at Sensible Knave's attitude that he may break his word, cheat, or steal whenever it suits his purposes—have reason to be just, to deem Knave's attitude unjust, and to try to protect ourselves from his predations.[7]

Yet Knave himself could say, perhaps because he accepts Hume's analysis of justice, "Yes, my attitude is unjust." And by Hume's own account of the relation of reason and passion, Knave could add "But what is that to me?" without failing to grasp the content of his previous assertion. Knave, let us suppose, has no doubts about the intelligibility or reality of "the general welfare," and thinks it quite comprehensible that people attach great significance in public life to the associated notion of justice. He also realizes that for the bulk of mankind, whose passions differ from his, being just is a source and a condition of much that is most worthwhile in life. He thus understands that appeals to justice typically have motivating force. Moreover, he himself uses the category of justice in analyzing the social world, and he recognizes—indeed, his knavish calculations take into account—the distinction between those individuals and institutions that truly are just, and those that merely appear just or are commonly regarded as just. Knave does view a number of concepts with wide currency—religious ones, for example—as mere fictions that prey on weak minds, but he does not view justice in this way. Weak minds and moralists have, he thinks, surrounded justice with certain myths—that justice is its own reward, that once one sees what is just one will automatically have a reason to do it, and so on. But then, he thinks that weak minds and moralists have likewise surrounded wealth and power with myths—that the wealthy are not truly happy, that the powerful inevitably ride for a fall, and so on—and he does not on this account doubt whether there are such things as wealth and power. Knave is glad to be free of prevailing myths about wealth, power, and justice; glad, too, that he is free in his own mind to pay as much or as little attention to any of these attributes as his desires and circumstances warrant. He might, for example, find Mae West's advice convincing: diamonds are very much worth acquiring, and "goodness ha[s] nothing to do with it."

---

[7]See the *Inquiry Concerning the Principles of Morals*, Sec. IX, Pt. II, pp. 102–103.

PETER RAILTON

We therefore must distinguish the business of saying what an individual values from the business of saying what it is for him to make measurements against the criteria of a species of evaluation that he recognizes to be genuine.[8]

To deny Hume's thesis of the practicality of moral judgment, and so remove the ground of his contrast between facts and values, is not to deny that morality has an action-guiding character. Morality surely can remain prescriptive within an instrumental framework, and can recommend itself to us in much the same way that, say, epistemology does: various significant and enduring—though perhaps not universal—human ends can be advanced if we apply certain evaluative criteria to our actions. That may be enough to justify to ourselves our abiding concern with the epistemic or moral status of what we do.[9]

By arguing that reason does not compel us to adopt particular beliefs or practices apart from our contingent, and variable, ends, I may seem to have failed to negotiate my way past epistemic relativism, and thus to have wrecked the argument for moral realism before it has even left port. Rationality does go relative when it goes instrumental, but epistemology need not follow. The epistemic

---

[8]The ancient criticism of non-cognitivism that it has difficulty accounting for the difference between moral value and other sorts of desirability (so that Hume can speak in one breath of our approval of a man's "good offices" and his "well-contrived apartment"), gains some vitality in the present context. To account for such differences it is necessary to have a contentful way of characterizing criteria of moral assessment so that moral approval does not reduce to "is valued by the agent." (Such a characterization will be offered in Section IV.) Value *sans phrase* is a generic, and not necessarily moral, notion. One sometimes hears it said that generic value becomes moral in character when we reach that which the agent prizes above all else. But this would invest pets and mementos with moral value, and have the peculiar effect of making amoralism a virtual conceptual impossibility. It seems more plausible to say that not all value is moral value, and that the highest values for an individual need not be, nor need they even seem to him to be, moral values. Once we turn to questions of duty, the situation should be clearer still: moral theorists have proposed quite different relations among the categories of moral rightness, moral goodness, and non-moral goodness, and it seems implausible to say that deeming an act or class of actions morally right is necessarily equivalent to viewing it personally as valuable *sans phrase*.

[9]The character of moral imperatives receives further discussion in Section V.

MORAL REALISM

warrant of an individual's belief may be disentangled from the rationality of his holding it, for epistemic warrant may be tied to an external criterion—as it is for example by causal or reliabilist theories of knowledge.[10] It is part of the naturalistic realism that informs this essay to adopt such a criterion of warrant. We should not confuse the obvious fact that in general our ends are well served by reliable causal mechanisms of belief-formation with an internalist claim to the effect that reason requires us to adopt such means. Reliable mechanisms have costs as well as benefits, and successful pursuit of some ends—Knave would point to religious ones, and to those of certain moralists—may in some respects be incompatible with adoption of reliable means of inquiry.

This rebuttal of the charge of relativism invites the defender of the fact/value distinction to shift to ontological ground. Perhaps facts and values cannot be placed on opposite sides of an epistemological divide marked off by what reason and experience can compel us to accept. Still, the idea of reliable causal mechanisms for moral learning, and of moral facts "in the world" upon which they operate, is arguably so bizarre that I may have done no more than increase my difficulties.

III. VALUE REALISM

The idea of causal interaction with moral reality certainly would be intolerably odd if moral facts were held to be *sui generis;*[11] but there need be nothing odd about causal mechanisms for learning moral facts if these facts are constituted by natural facts, and that is the view under consideration. This response will remain unconvincing, however, until some positive argument for realism about moral facts is given. So let us turn to that task.

What might be called 'the generic stratagem of naturalistic realism' is to postulate a realm of facts in virtue of the contribution they

---

[10]Such theories are suitably externalist when, in characterizing the notions of *reliability* or *warrant-conferring causal process,* they employ an account of truth that does not resolve truth into that which we have reason to believe—for example, a nontrivial correspondence theory.

[11]Or if moral facts were supposed to be things of a kind to provide categorical reasons for action. However, this supposition is simply Hume's thesis of practicality in ontological garb.

171

PETER RAILTON

would make to the *a posteriori* explanation of certain features of our experience. For example, an external world is posited to explain the coherence, stability, and intersubjectivity of sense-experience. A moral realist who would avail himself of this stratagem must show that the postulation of moral facts similarly can have an explanatory function. The stratagem can succeed in either case only if the reality postulated has these two characteristics:

(1) *independence:* it exists and has certain determinate features independent of whether we think it exists or has those features, independent, even, of whether we have good reason to think this;

(2) *feedback:* it is such—and we are such—that we are able to interact with it, and this interaction exerts the relevant sort of shaping influence or control upon our perceptions, thought, and action.

These two characteristics enable the realist's posit to play a role in the explanation of our experience that cannot be replaced without loss by our mere *conception* of ourselves or our world. For although our conceptual scheme mediates even our most basic perceptual experiences, an experience-transcendent reality has ways of making itself felt without the permission of our conceptual scheme—causally. The success or failure of our plans and projects famously is not determined by expectation alone. By resisting or yielding to our worldly efforts in ways not anticipated by our going conceptual scheme, an external reality that is never directly revealed in perception may nonetheless significantly influence the subsequent evolution of that scheme.

The realist's use of an external world to explain sensory experience has often been criticized as no more than a picture. But do we even have a picture of what a realist explanation might look like in the case of values?[12] I will try to sketch one, filling in first a realist

[12]J. L. Mackie, in *Ethics: Inventing Right and Wrong* (Harmondsworth, Middlesex: Penguin, 1977), and Gilbert Harman, in *The Nature of Morality: An Introduction to Ethics* (New York: Oxford University Press, 1977), both challenge moral realism in part by questioning its capacity to explain. Nicholas L. Sturgeon, in "Moral Explanations," David Copp and David Zimmerman, eds., *Morality, Reason and Truth: New Essays in the Foundations of Ethics* (Totowa, N.J.: Rowman and Allanhead, 1984), takes the opposite side, using arguments different from those offered below.

MORAL REALISM

account of non-moral value—the notion of something being desirable for someone, or good for him.[13]

Consider first the notion of someone's *subjective interests*—his wants or desires, conscious or unconscious. Subjective interest can be seen as a secondary quality, akin to taste. For me to take a subjective interest in something is to say that it has a positive *valence* for me, that is, that in ordinary circumstances it excites a positive attitude or inclination (not necessarily conscious) in me. Similarly, for me to say that I find sugar sweet is to say that in ordinary circumstances sugar excites a certain gustatory sensation in me. As secondary qualities, subjective interest and perceived sweetness supervene upon primary qualities of the perceiver, the object (or other phenomenon) perceived, and the surrounding context: the perceiver is so constituted that this sort of object in this sort of context will excite that sort of sensation. Call this complex set of relational, dispositional, primary qualities the *reduction basis* of the secondary quality.

We have in this reduction basis an objective notion that corresponds to, and helps explain, subjective interests. But it is not a plausible foundation for the notion of non-moral goodness, since the subjective interests it grounds have insufficient normative force to capture the idea of desirableness. My subjective interests frequently reflect ignorance, confusion, or lack of consideration, as hindsight attests. The fact that I am now so constituted that I desire something which, had I better knowledge of it, I would wish I had never sought, does not seem to recommend it to me as part of my good.

To remedy this defect, let us introduce the notion of an *objectified subjective interest* for an individual A, as follows.[14] Give to an actual individual A unqualified cognitive and imaginative powers, and full factual and nomological information about his physical and psy-

---

[13]A full-scale theory of value would, I think, show the concept of someone's good to be slightly different from the concept of what is desirable for him. However, this difference will not affect the argument made here.

[14]It was some work by Richard C. Jeffrey on epistemic probability that originally suggested to me the idea of objectifying subjective interests. See note 17. I have since benefited from Richard B. Brandt's work on "rational desire," although I fear that what I will say contains much that he would regard as wrong-headed. See *A Theory of the Good and the Right* (Oxford: Clarendon, 1979), Part I.

PETER RAILTON

chological constitution, capacities, circumstances, history, and so on. A will have become $A+$, who has complete and vivid knowledge of himself and his environment, and whose instrumental rationality is in no way defective. We now ask $A+$ to tell us not what *he* currently wants, but what he would want his non-idealized self A to want—or, more generally, to seek—were he to find himself in the actual condition and circumstances of A.[15] Just as we assumed there to be a reduction basis for an individual A's actual subjective interests, we may assume there to be a reduction basis for his objectified subjective interests, namely, those facts about A and his circumstances that $A+$ would combine with his general knowledge in arriving at his views about what he would want to want were he to step into A's shoes.

For example, Lonnie, a traveler in a foreign country, is feeling miserable. He very much wishes to overcome his malaise and to settle his stomach, and finds he has a craving for the familiar: a tall glass of milk. The milk is desired by Lonnie, but is it also desirable for him? Lonnie-Plus can see that what is wrong with Lonnie, in addition to homesickness, is dehydration, a common affliction of tourists, but one often not detectable from introspective evidence. The effect of drinking hard-to-digest milk would be to further

---

[15] We ask this question of $A+$, rather than what $A+$ wants for himself, because we are seeking the objectified subjective interests of A, and the interests of $A+$ might be quite different owing to the changes involved in the idealization of A. For example, $A+$ presumably does not want any more information for himself—there is no more to be had and he knows this. Yet it might still be true that $A+$ would want to want more knowledge were he to be put in the place of his less well-informed self, A. It may as a psychological matter be impossible for $A+$ to set aside entirely his desires *in his present circumstances* with regard to himself or to A in considering what he would want to want were he to be put *in the place of* his less-than-ideal self. This reveals a measurement problem for objective interests: giving an individual the information and capacities necessary to "objectify" his interests may perturb his psychology in ways that alter the phenomenon we wish to observe. Such difficulties attend even the measurement of subjective interests, since instruments for sampling preferences (indeed, mere acts of reflection upon one's preferences) tend to affect the preferences expressed. For obvious reasons, interference effects come with the territory. Though not in themselves sufficient ground for skepticism about subjective or objective interests, these measurement problems show the need for a "perturbation theory," and for caution about attributions of interests that are inattentive to interference effects.

174

MORAL REALISM

unsettle Lonnie's stomach and worsen his dehydration. By contrast, Lonnie-Plus can see that abundant clear fluids would quickly
improve Lonnie's physical condition—which, incidentally, would
help with his homesickness as well. Lonnie-Plus can also see just
how distasteful Lonnie would find it to drink clear liquids, just
what would happen were Lonnie to continue to suffer dehydration, and so on. As a result of this information, Lonnie-Plus might
then come to desire that were he to assume Lonnie's place, he
would want to drink clear liquids rather than milk, or at least want
to act in such a way that a want of this kind would be satisfied. The
reduction basis of this objectified interest includes facts about
Lonnie's circumstances and constitution, which determine, among
other things, his existing tastes and his ability to acquire certain
new tastes, the consequences of continued dehydration, the effects
and availability of various sorts of liquids, and so on.

Let us say that this reduction basis is the constellation of primary
qualities that make it be the case that the Lonnie has a certain
objective interest.[16] That is, we will say that Lonnie has an objective
interest in drinking clear liquids in virtue of this complex, relational, dispositional set of facts. Put another way, we can say that
the reduction basis, not the fact that Lonnie-Plus would have certain wants, is the truth-maker for the claim that this is an objective
interest of Lonnie's. The objective interest thus explains why there
is a certain objectified interest, not the other way around.[17]

---

[16]'Interest' is not quite the word wanted here, for in ordinary language
we may speak of a want where we would not speak of a corresponding
interest. See Brian Barry, *Political Argument* (London: Routledge and Kegan Paul, 1965), especially Chapter X, for discussion. A more accurate, but
overly cumbersome, expression would be 'positive-valence-making characteristic'.

[17]Suppose for a moment, contrary to what was urged above, that there is
a workable notion of epistemic probability that determines rational degrees of belief independent of the contingent goals of the epistemic agent.
Perhaps then the following analogy will be helpful. Consider a physically
random process, such as alpha-decay. We can ask an individual what subjective probability he would assign to an event consisting in a certain rate of
decay for a given sample of uranium; we can also ask what rational degree
of belief the individual would assign to this event were he to become ideally
informed about the laws of physics and the relevant initial conditions. Call
the latter rational degree of belief the *objectified subjective probability* of the
event, and suppose it to be equal to one fifth. (Compare Richard C.

PETER RAILTON

Let us now say that X is *non-morally good for A* if and only if X would satisfy an objective interest of A.[18] We may think of $A+$'s views about what he would want to want were he in A's place as generating a ranking of potential objective interests of A, a ranking that will reflect what is better or worse for A and will allow us to speak of A's actual wants as better or worse approximations of what is best for him. We may also decompose $A+$'s views into *prima facie* as opposed to "on balance" objective interests of A, the former yielding the notion of '*a* good for A', the latter, of '*the* good for A'.[19]

Jeffrey, *The Logic of Decision* (New York: McGraw-Hill, 1964), pp. 190–196.) But now consider the physical facts that, in conjunction with the laws of quantum mechanics, ground the idealized individual's judgment. Call these the *reduction basis* of that judgment. This reduction basis is a complex set of primary qualities that can be said to bring it about that the event in question has an *objective probability* of one fifth. (It should be said that it is not part of Jeffrey's approach to posit such objective probabilities.) The existence of this objective probability can explain why an ideally informed individual would select an objectified subjective probability equal to one fifth, but the probability judgment of an ideally informed individual cannot explain why the objective probability is one fifth—that is a matter of the laws of physics. Similarly, the existence of an individual's objective interest can explain why his ideally informed self would pick out for his less-informed self a given objectified subjective interest, but not *vice versa*.

[18]More precisely, we may say that X is non-morally good for A at time t if and only if X would satisfy an objective interest of A the reduction basis of which exists at t. Considerations about the evolution of interests over time raise a number of issues that cannot be entered into here.

[19]$A+$, putting himself in A's place, may find several different sets of wants equally appealing, so that several alternatives could be equal-best for A in this sense. This would not make the notion of 'the good for A' problematic, just pluralistic. However, a more serious question looms. Is there sufficient determinacy in the specification of $A+$'s condition, or in the psychology of desire, to make the notion of objective interest definite enough for my purposes? Without trying to say how definite *that* might be, let me suggest two ways in which an answer to the worry about definiteness might begin. (1) It seems that we do think that there are rather definite answers to questions about how an individual A's desires would change were his beliefs to change in certain limited ways. If Lonnie were to learn the consequences of drinking milk, he would no longer want his desire for milk to be effective. But a large change in belief can be accomplished piecemeal, by a sequence of limited changes in belief. Thus, if (admittedly, a big 'if') *order* of change is not in the end significant, then the facts and generalizations that support counterfactuals about limited changes might support an extrapolation all the way to $A+$. (2) Beliefs and desires appear to co-vary systematically. Typically, we find that individuals who differ markedly in their desires—for example, about careers or style of life—

MORAL REALISM

This seems to me an intuitively plausible account of what someone's non-moral good consists in: roughly, what he would want
himself to seek if he knew what he were doing.[20]

Moreover, this account preserves what seems to me an appropriate link between non-moral value and motivation. Suppose that
one desires X, but wonders whether X really is part of one's good.
This puzzlement typically arises because one feels that one knows
too little about X, oneself, or one's world, or because one senses that
one is not being adequately rational or reflective in assessing the
information one has—perhaps one suspects that one has been cap-
tivated by a few salient features of X (or repelled by a few salient
features of its alternatives). If one were to learn that one would still
want oneself to want X in the circumstances were one to view things
with full information and rationality, this presumably would reduce the force of the original worry. By contrast, were one to learn
that when fully informed and rational one would want oneself *not*
to want X in the circumstances, this presumably would add force to
it. Desires being what they are, a reinforced worry might not be
sufficient to remove the desire for X. But if one were to become

---

differ markedly, and characteristically, in their beliefs; as individuals become more similar in their beliefs, they tend to become more similar in
their desires. This suggests that if (another big 'if') the characterization
given of $A+$ fixes the entire content of his beliefs in a definite way (at least,
given a choice of language), then his desires may be quite comprehensively
fixed as well. If we had in hand a general theory of the co-variation of
beliefs and desires, then we could appeal directly to this theory—plus facts
about A—to ground the counterfactuals needed to characterize A's objectified interests, eliminating any essential reference to the imaginary individual $A+$.

[20]The account may, however, yield some counterintuitive results. Depending upon the nature and circumstances of given individuals, they
might have objective interests in things we find wrong or repulsive, and that
do not seem to us part of a good life. We can explain a good deal of our
objection to certain desires—for example, those involving cruelty—by saying that they are not *morally* good; others—for example, those of a philistine
nature—by saying that they are not *aesthetically* valuable; and so on. It seems
to me preferable to express our distaste for certain ends in terms of specific
categories of value, rather than resort to the device of saying that such ends
could under no circumstances be part of anyone's non-moral good. People,
or at least some people, might be put together in a way that makes some not-
very-appetizing things essential to their flourishing, and we do not want to
be guilty of wishful thinking on this score. (There will be wishful thinking
enough before we are through.)

PETER RAILTON

genuinely and vividly convinced that one's desire for X is in this sense not supported by full reflection upon the facts, one presumably would feel this to be a count against acting upon the desire. This adjustment of desire to belief might not in a given case be required by reason or logic; it might be "merely psychological." But it is precisely such psychological phenomena that naturalistic theories of value take as basic.

In what follows, we will need the notion of intrinsic goodness, so let us say that X is *intrinsically non-morally good for A* just in case X is in A's objective interest without reference to any other objective interest of A. We can in an obvious way use the notion of objective intrinsic interest to account for all other objective interests. Since individuals and their environments differ in many respects, we need not assume that everyone has the same objective intrinsic interests. A *fortiori*, we need not assume that they have the same objective instrumental interests. We should, however, expect that when personal and situational similarities exist across individuals—that is, when there are similarities in reduction bases—there will to that extent be corresponding similarities in their interests.

It is now possible to see how the notion of non-moral goodness can have explanatory uses. For a start, it can explain why one's actual desires have certain counterfactual features, for example, why one would have certain hypothetical desires rather than others were one to become fully informed and aware. Yet this sort of explanatory use—following as it does directly from the definition of objective interest—might well be thought unimpressive unless some other explanatory functions can be found.

Consider, then, the difference between Lonnie and Tad, another traveler in the same straits, but one who, unlike Lonnie, wants to drink clear liquids, and proceeds to do so. Tad will perk up while Lonnie remains listless. We can explain this difference by noting that although both Lonnie and Tad acted upon their wants, Tad's wants better reflected his interests. The congruence of Tad's wants with his interests may be fortuitous, or it may be that Tad knows he is dehydrated and knows the standard treatment. In the latter case we would ordinarily say that the explanation of the difference in their condition is that Tad, but not Lonnie, "knew what was good for him."

Generally, we can expect that what A+ would want to want were

MORAL REALISM

he in *A*'s place will correlate well with what would permit *A* to experience physical or psychological well-being or to escape physical or psychological ill-being. Surely our well- or ill-being are among the things that matter to us most, and most reliably, even on reflection.[21] Appeal to degrees of congruence between *A*'s wants and his interests thus will often help to explain facts about how satisfactory he finds his life. Explanation would not be preserved were we to substitute 'believed to be congruent' for 'are (to such-and-such a degree) congruent', since, as cases like Lonnie's show, even if one were to convince oneself that one's wants accurately reflected one's interests, acting on these wants might fail to yield much satisfaction.

In virtue of the correlation to be expected between acting upon motives that congrue with one's interests and achieving a degree of satisfaction or avoiding a degree of distress, one's objective interests may also play an explanatory role in the *evolution* of one's desires. Consider what I will call the *wants/interests mechanism,* which permits individuals to achieve selfconscious and unselfconscious learning about their interests through experience. In the simplest sorts of cases, trial and error leads to the selective retention of wants that are satisfiable and lead to satisfactory results for the agent.

For example, suppose that Lonnie gives in to his craving and

---

[21]To put the matter in more strictly naturalistic terms, we can expect that evolution will have favored organisms so constituted that those behaviors requisite to their survival and flourishing are associated with positive internal states (such as pleasure) and those opposed to survival or flourishing with negative states (such as pain). 'Flourishing' here, even if understood as mere reproductive fitness, is not a narrow notion. In order for beings such as humans to be reproductively successful, they must as phenotypes have lives that are psychologically sustainable, internally motivating, and effectively social; lives, moreover, that normally would engage in a wide range of their peculiarly human capacities. Humankind could hardly have been a success story even at the reproductive level were not pursuit of the sorts of things that characteristically have moved humans to action associated with existences of this kind. However, it must be kept in mind that most human evolution occurred under circumstances different in important ways from the present. It therefore is quite possible that the interaction of evolved human motivational potentials with existing circumstances will produce incongruities between what we tend to aim at, or to be driven by, and what would produce the greatest pleasure for us. That is one reason for doubting hedonism as a theory of motivation.

drinks the milk. Soon afterwards, he feels much worse. Still unable
to identify the source of his malaise and still in the grips of a desire
for the familiar, his attention is caught by a green-and-red sign in
the window of a small shop he is moping past: "7-Up," it says. He
rushes inside and buys a bottle. Although it is lukewarm, he drinks
it eagerly. "Mmm," he thinks, "I'll have another." He buys a second
bottle, and drains it to the bottom. By now he has had his fill of
tepid soda, and carries on. Within a few hours, his mood is improving. When he passes the store again on the way back to his hotel, his
pleasant association with drinking 7-Up leads him to buy some
more and carry it along with him. That night, in the dim solitude of
his room, he finds the soda's reassuringly familiar taste consoling,
and so downs another few bottles before finally finding sleep.
When he wakes up the next morning, he feels very much better. To
make a dull story short: the next time Lonnie is laid low abroad, he
may have some conscious or unconscious, reasoned or super-
stitious, tendency to seek out 7-Up. Unable to find that, he might
seek something quite like it, say, a local lime-flavored soda, or
perhaps even the *agua mineral con gaz* he had previously scorned.
Over time, as Lonnie travels more and suffers similar malaise, he
regularly drinks clearish liquids and regularly feels better, eventually developing an actual desire for such liquids—and an aversion
to other drinks, such as milk—in such circumstances.

Thus have Lonnie's desires evolved through experience to conform more closely to what is good for him, in the naturalistic sense
intended here. The process was not one of an ideally rational response to the receipt of ideal information, but rather of largely
unreflective experimentation, accompanied by positive and negative associations and reinforcements. There is no guarantee that
the desires "learned" through such feedback will accurately or
completely reflect an individual's good. Still less is there any guarantee that, even when an appropriate adjustment in desire occurs,
the agent will comprehend the origin of his new desires or be able
to represent to himself the nature the interests they reflect. But
then, it is a quite general feature of the various means by which we
learn about the world that they may fail to provide accurate or
comprehending representations of it. My ability to perceive and
understand my surroundings coexists with, indeed draws upon the
same mechanisms as, my liability to deception by illusion, expectation, or surface appearance.

MORAL REALISM

There are some broad theoretical grounds for thinking that something like the wants/interests mechanism exists and has an important role in desire-formation. Humans are creatures motivated primarily by wants rather than instincts. If such creatures were unable through experience to conform their wants at all closely to their essential interests—perhaps because they were no more likely to experience positive internal states when their essential interests are met than when they are not—we could not expect long or fruitful futures for them. Thus, if humans in general did not come to want to eat the kinds of food necessary to maintain some degree of physical well-being, or to engage in the sorts of activities or relations necessary to maintain their sanity, we would not be around today to worry whether we can know what is good for us. Since creatures as sophisticated and complex as humans have evolved through encounters with a variety of environments, and indeed have made it their habit to modify their environments, we should expect considerable flexibility in our capacity through experience to adapt our wants to our interests. However, this very flexibility makes the mechanism unreliable: our wants may at any time differ arbitrarily much from our interests; moreover, we may fail to have experiences that would cause us to notice this, or to undergo sufficient feedback to have much chance of developing new wants that more nearly approximate our interests. It is entirely possible, and hardly infrequent, that an individual live out the course of a normal life without ever recognizing or adjusting to some of his most fundamental interests. Individual limitations are partly remedied by cultural want-acquiring mechanisms, which permit learning and even theorizing over multiple lives and life-spans, but these same mechanisms also create a vast potential for the inculcation of wants at variance with interests.

The argument for the wants/interests mechanism has about the same status, and the same breezy plausibility, as the more narrowly biological argument that we should expect the human eye to be capable of detecting objects the size and shape of our predators or prey. It is not necessary to assume anything approaching infallibility, only enough functional success to hold our own in an often inhospitable world.[22]

---

[22]'Functional success' rather than 'representational accuracy' for the following reason. Selection favors organisms that have some-or-other fea-

PETER RAILTON

Thus far the argument has concerned only those objective interests that might be classified as needs, but the wants/interests mechanism can operate with respect to any interest—even interests related to an individual's particular aptitudes or social role—whose frustration is attended even indirectly by consciously or unconsciously unsatisfactory results for him. (To be sure, the more indirect the association the more unlikely that the mechanism will be reliable.) For example, the experience of taking courses in both mathematics and philosophy may lead an undergraduate who thought himself cut out to be a mathematician to come to prefer a career in philosophy, which would in fact better suit his aptitudes and attitudes. And a worker recently promoted to management from the shop floor may find himself less inclined to respond to employee grievances than he had previously wanted managers to be, while his former co-workers may find themselves less inclined to confide in him than before.

If a wants/interests mechanism is postulated, and if what is nonmorally good for someone is a matter of what is in his objective interest, then we can say that objective value is able to play a role in the explanation of subjective value of the sort the naturalistic realist about value needs. These explanations even support some qualified predictions: for example, that, other things equal, individuals will ordinarily be better judges of their own interests than third parties; that knowledge of one's interests will tend to increase with increased experience and general knowledge; that people with similar personal and social characteristics will tend to have similar values; and that there will be greater general consensus upon what is desirable in those areas of life where individuals are most alike in other regards (for example, at the level of basic motives), and where trial-and-error mechanisms can be expected to work well (for example, where esoteric knowledge is not required). I am in no

---

ture that happens in their particular environment to contribute to getting their needs met. Whether that feature will be an accurate representational capacity cannot be settled by an argument of this kind. Of course, it would be a very great coincidence if beings who rely as heavily upon representations as we do were able to construct only grossly inaccurate representations while at the same time managing successfully in a range of environments over a long period of time. But such coincidences cannot be ruled out.

MORAL REALISM

position to pronounce these predictions correct, but it may be to their credit that they accord with widely-held views.

It should perhaps be emphasized that although I speak of the objectivity of value, the value in question is human value, and exists only because humans do. In the sense of old-fashioned theory of value, this is a relational rather than absolute notion of goodness. Although relational, the relevant facts about humans and their world are objective in the same sense that such non-relational entities as stones are: they do not depend for their existence or nature merely upon our conception of them.[23]

Thus understood, objective interests are supervenient upon natural and social facts. Does this mean that they cannot contribute to explanation after all, since it should always be possible in principle to account for any particular fact that they purport to explain by reference to the supervenience basis alone? If mere supervenience were grounds for denying an explanatory role to a given set of concepts, then we would have to say that chemistry, biology, and electrical engineering, which clearly supervene upon physics, lack explanatory power. Indeed, even outright reducibility is no ground for doubting explanatoriness. To establish a relation of reduction between, for example, a chemical phenomenon such as valence and a physical model of the atom does nothing to suggest that there is no such thing as valence, or that generalizations involving valence cannot support explanations. There can be no issue here of ontological economy or eschewing unnecessary entities, as might be the case if valence were held to be something *sui generis,* over and above any constellation of physical properties. The facts described in principles of chemical valence are genuine, and permit a powerful and explanatory systematization of chemical combination; the

---

[23]Although some elements of their reduction basis depend upon our past choices, our objective interests are not therefore subjective in a sense damaging to the present argument. After all, such unproblematically objective facts about us as our weight, income, and spatial location depend in the same way upon past choices. The point is not that our subjective interests have no role in shaping the reduction basis of our objective interests, but rather that they can affect our objective interests only in virtue of their actual (rather than merely desired) effects upon this reduction basis, just as they can affect our weight, income, or spatial location only in virtue of actual (rather than merely desired) effects upon our displacement, employment, or movement.

PETER RAILTON

existence of a successful reduction to atomic physics only bolsters these claims.

We are confident that the notion of chemical valence is explanatory because proffered explanations in terms of chemical valence insert explananda into a distinctive and well-articulated nomic nexus, in an obvious way increasing our understanding of them. But what comparably powerful and illuminating theory exists concerning the notion of objective interest to give us reason to think—whether or not strict reduction is possible—that proffered explanations using this notion are genuinely informative?

I would find the sort of value realism sketched here uninteresting if it seemed to me that no theory of any consequence could be developed using the category of objective value. But in describing the wants/interests mechanism I have already tried to indicate that such a theory may be possible. When we seek to explain why people act as they do, why they have certain values or desires, and why sometimes they are led into conflict and other times into cooperation, it comes naturally to common sense and social science alike to talk in terms of people's interests. Such explanations will be incomplete and superficial if we remain wholly at the level of subjective interests, since these, too, must be accounted for.[24]

IV. NORMATIVE REALISM

Suppose everything said thus far to have been granted generously. Still, I would as yet have no right to speak of *moral* realism,

---

[24]In a similar way, it would be incomplete and superficial to explain why, once large-scale production became possible, the world's consumption of refined sugar underwent such explosive development, by mentioning only the fact that people liked its taste. Why, despite wide differences in traditional diet and acquired tastes, has sugar made such inroads into human consumption? Why haven't the appearance and promotion of other equally cheap foodstuffs produced such remarkable shifts in consumption? Why, even in societies where sugar is recognized as a health hazard, does consumption of sugars, often in concealed forms, continue to climb? Facts about the way we are constituted, about the rather singular ways sugar therefore affects us, and about the ways forms of production and patterns of consumption co-evolved to generate both a growing demand and an expanding supply, must supplement a theory that stops at the level of subjective preferences. See Sidney W. Mintz, *Sweetness and Power: The Place of Sugar in Modern History* (New York: Viking, 1985) for relevant discussion.

MORAL REALISM

for I have done no more than to exhibit the possibility of a kind of realism with regard to non-moral goodness, a notion that perfect moral skeptics can admit. To be entitled to speak of moral realism I would have to show realism to be possible about distinctively moral value, or moral norms. I will concentrate on moral norms—that is, matters of moral rightness and wrongness—although the argument I give may, by extension, be applied to moral value. In part, my reason is that normative realism seems much less plausible intuitively than value realism. It therefore is not surprising that many current proposals for moral realism focus essentially upon value—and sometimes only upon what is in effect non-moral value. Yet on virtually any conception of morality, a moral theory must yield an account of rightness.

Normative moral realism is implausible on various grounds, but within the framework of this essay, the most relevant is that it seems impossible to extend the generic strategy of naturalistic realism to moral norms. Where is the place in explanation for facts about what *ought* to be the case—don't facts about the way things *are* do all the explaining there is to be done? Of course they do. But then, my naturalistic moral realism commits me to the view that facts about what ought to be the case are facts of a special kind about the way things are. As a result, it may be possible for them to have a function within an explanatory theory. To see how this could be, let me first give some examples of explanations outside the realm of morality that involve naturalized norms.

"Why did the roof collapse?—For a house that gets the sort of snow loads that one did, the rafters ought to have been 2×8's at least, not 2×6's." This explanation is quite acceptable, as far as it goes, yet it contains an 'ought'. Of course, we can remove this 'ought' as follows: "If a roof of that design is to withstand the snow load that one bore, then it must be framed with rafters at least 2×8 in cross-section." An architectural 'ought' is replaced by an engineering 'if . . . then . . .'. This is possible because the 'ought' clearly is hypothetical, reflecting the universal architectural goal of making roofs strong enough not to collapse. Because the goal is contextually fixed, and because there are more or less definite answers to the question of how to meet it, and moreover because the explanandum phenomenon is the result of a process that selects against instances that do not attain that goal, the 'ought'-

PETER RAILTON

containing account conveys explanatory information.[25] I will call this sort of explanation *criterial*: we explain why something happened by reference to a relevant criterion, given the existence of a process that in effect selects for (or against) phenomena that more (or less) closely approximate this criterion. Although the criterion is defined naturalistically, it may at the same time be of a kind to have a regulative role in human practice—in this case, in housebuilding.

A more familiar sort of criterial explanation involves norms of individual rationality. Consider the use of an instrumental theory of rationality to explain an individual's behavior in light of his beliefs and desires, or to account for the way an individual's beliefs change with experience.[26] Bobby Shaftoe went to sea because he believed it was the best way to make his fortune, and he wanted above all to make his fortune. Crewmate Reuben Ramsoe came to believe that he wasn't liked by the other deckhands because he saw that they taunted him and greeted his frequent lashings at the hands of the First Mate with unconcealed pleasure. These explanations work because the action or belief in question was quite rational for the agent in the circumstances, and because we correctly suppose both Shaftoe and Ramsoe to have been quite rational.

Facts about degrees of instrumental rationality enter into explanations in other ways as well. First, consider the question why Bobby Shaftoe has had more success than most like-minded individuals in achieving his goals. We may lay his success to the fact that Shaftoe is more instrumentally rational than most—perhaps he has greater-than-average acumen in estimating the probabilities of outcomes, or is more-reliable-than-average at deductive inference, or is more-imaginative-than-average in surveying alternatives.

---

[25]For a discussion of how informally expressed accounts may nonetheless convey explanatory information, see Section II of my "Probability, Explanation, and Information," *Synthese* 48 (1981), pp. 233–256.

[26]Such explanation uses a naturalized criterion when rationality is defined in terms of relative efficiency given the agent's beliefs and desires. A (more or less) rational agent is thus someone disposed to act in (more or less) efficient ways. There is a deep difficulty about calling such explanation naturalistic, for the constraints placed upon attributions of beliefs and desires by a "principle of charity" may compromise the claim that rational-agent explanations are empirical. Although I believe this difficulty can be overcome, this is hardly the place to start *that* argument.

MORAL REALISM

Second, although we are all imperfect deliberators, our behavior may come to embody habits or strategies that enable us to approximate optimal rationality more closely than our deliberative defects would lead one to expect. The mechanism is simple. Patterns of beliefs and behaviors that do not exhibit much instrumental rationality will tend to be to some degree self-defeating, an incentive to change them, whereas patterns that exhibit greater instrumental rationality will tend to be to some degree rewarding, an incentive to continue them. These incentives may affect our beliefs and behaviors even though the drawbacks or advantages of the patterns in question do not receive conscious deliberation. In such cases we may be said to acquire these habits or strategies because they *are* more rational, without the intermediation of any *belief* on our part that they are. Thus, cognitive psychologists have mapped some of the unconscious strategies or heuristics we employ to enable our limited intellects to sift more data and make quicker and more consistent judgments than would be possible using more standard forms of explicit reasoning.[27] We unwittingly come to rely upon heuristics in part because they are selectively reinforced as a result of their instrumental advantages over standard, explicit reasoning, that is, in part because of their greater rationality. Similarly, we may, without realizing it or even being able to admit it to ourselves, develop patterns of behavior that encourage or discourage specific behaviors in others, such as the unconscious means by which we cause those whose company we do not enjoy not to enjoy our company. Finally, as children we may have been virtually incapable of making rational assessments when a distant gain required a proximate loss. Yet somehow over time we managed in largely nondeliberative ways to acquire various interesting habits, such as putting certain vivid thoughts about the immediate future at the periphery of our attention, which enable us as adults to march ourselves off to the dentist without a push from behind. Criterial explanation in terms of individual rationality thus extends to behaviors beyond the realm of deliberate action. And, as with the

---

[27]For a survey of the literature, see Richard Nisbett and Lee Ross, *Human Inference: Strategies and Shortcomings of Social Judgment* (Englewood Cliffs: Prentice-Hall, 1980), where one unsurprisingly finds greater attention paid to drawbacks than advantages.

PETER RAILTON

wants/interests mechanism, it is possible to see in the emergence of such behaviors something we can without distortion call learning.

Indeed, our tendency through experience to develop rational habits and strategies may cooperate with the wants/interests mechanism to provide the basis for an *extended* form of criterial explanation, in which an individual's rationality is assessed not relative to his occurrent beliefs and desires, but relative to his objective interests. The examples considered earlier of the wants/interests mechanism in fact involved elements of this sort of explanation, for they showed not only wants being adjusted to interests, but also behavior being adjusted to newly adjusted wants. Without appropriate alteration of behavior to reflect changing wants, the feedback necessary for learning about wants would not occur. With such alteration, the behavior itself may become more rational in the extended sense. An individual who is instrumentally rational is disposed to adjust means to ends; but one result of his undertaking a means—electing a course of study, or accepting a new job—may be a more informed assessment, and perhaps a reconsideration, of his ends.

The theory of individual rationality—in either its simple or its extended form—thus affords an instance of the sort needed to provide an example of normative realism. Evaluations of degrees of instrumental rationality play a prominent role in our explanations of individual behavior, but they simultaneously have normative force for the agent. Whatever other concerns an agent might have, it surely counts for him as a positive feature of an action that it is efficient relative to his beliefs and desires or, in the extended sense, efficient relative to beliefs and desires that would appropriately reflect his condition and circumstances.

The normative force of these theories of individual rationality does not, however, merely derive from their explanatory use. One can employ a theory of instrumental rationality to explain behavior while rejecting it as a normative theory of reasons, just as one can explain an action as due to irrationality without thereby endorsing unreason.[28] Instead, the connection between the normative and

---

[28]To recall a point from Section II: one may make assessments relative to particular evaluative criteria without thereby valuing that which satisfies them.

MORAL REALISM

explanatory roles of the instrumental conception of rationality is traceable to their common ground: the human motivational system. It is a fact about us that we have ends and have the capacity for both deliberate action relative to our ends and nondeliberate adjustment of behavior to our ends. As a result, we face options among pathways across a landscape of possibilities variously valenced for us. Both when we explain the reasons for people's choices and the causes of their behavior and when we appeal to their intuitions about what it would be rational to decide or to do, we work this territory, for we make what use we can of facts about what does-in-fact or can-in-principle motivate agents.

Thus emerges the possibility of saying that facts exist about what individuals have reason to do, facts that may be substantially independent of, and more normatively compelling than, an agent's occurrent conception of his reasons. The argument for such realism about individual rationality is no stronger than the arguments for the double claim that the relevant conception of instrumental individual rationality has both explanatory power and the sort of commendatory force a theory of *reasons* must possess, but (although I will not discuss them further here) these arguments seem to me quite strong.

*   *   *

Passing now beyond the theory of individual rationality, let us ask what criterial explanations involving distinctively moral norms might look like. To ask this, we need to know what distinguishes moral norms from other criteria of assessment. Moral evaluation seems to be concerned most centrally with the assessment of conduct or character where the interests of more than one individual are at stake. Further, moral evaluation assesses actions or outcomes in a peculiar way: the interests of the strongest or most prestigious party do not always prevail, purely prudential reasons may be subordinated, and so on. More generally, moral resolutions are thought to be determined by criteria of choice that are *non-indexical* and in some sense *comprehensive*. This has led a number of philosophers to seek to capture the special character of moral evaluation by identifying a *moral point of view* that is impartial, but equally concerned with all those potentially affected. Other ethical theo-

189

PETER RAILTON

rists have come to a similar conclusion by investigating the sorts of reasons we characteristically treat as relevant or irrelevant in moral discourse. Let us follow these leads. We thus may say that moral norms reflect a certain kind of rationality, rationality not from the point of view of any particular individual, but from what might be called a social point of view.[29]

By itself, the equation of moral rightness with rationality from a social point of view is not terribly restrictive, for, depending upon what one takes rationality to be, this equation could be made by a utilitarian, a Kantian, or even a non-cognitivist. That is as it should be, for if it is to capture what is distinctive about moral norms, it should be compatible with the broadest possible range of recognized moral theories. However, once one opts for a particular conception of rationality—such as the conception of rationality as efficient pursuit of the non-morally good, or as autonomous and universal self-legislation, or as a noncognitive expression of hypothetical endorsement—this schematic characterization begins to assume particular moral content. Here I have adopted an instrumentalist conception of rationality, and this—along with the account given of non-moral goodness—means that the argument for moral realism given below is an argument that presupposes and purports to defend a particular substantive moral theory.[30]

What is this theory? Let me introduce an idealization of the notion of social rationality by considering what would be rationally approved of were the interests of all potentially affected individuals counted equally under circumstances of full and vivid information.[31] Because of the assumption of full and vivid informa-

---

[29]I realize that it is misleading to call a point of view that is "impartial, but equally concerned with all those potentially affected" a *social* point of view—some of those potentially affected may lie on the other side of an intersocial boundary. This complication will be set aside until Section V.

[30]It also means that the relation of moral criteria to criteria of individual rationality has become problematic, since there can be no guarantee that what would be instrumentally rational from any given individual's point of view will coincide with what would be instrumentally rational from a social point of view.

[31]A rather strong thesis of interpersonal comparison is needed here for purposes of social aggregation. I am not assuming the existence of some single good, such as happiness, underlying such comparisons. Thus the moral theory in question, although consequentialist, aggregative, and

MORAL REALISM

tion, the interests in question will be objective interests. Given the account of goodness proposed in Section III, this idealization is equivalent to what is rational from a social point of view with regard to the realization of intrinsic non-moral goodness. This seems to me to be a recognizable and intuitively plausible—if hardly uncontroversial—criterion of moral rightness. Relative moral rightness is a matter of relative degree of approximation to this criterion.

The question that now arises is whether the notion of degrees of moral rightness could participate in explanations of behavior or in processes of moral learning that parallel explanatory uses of the notion of degrees of individual rationality—especially, in the extended sense. I will try to suggest several ways in which it might.

Just as an individual who significantly discounts some of his interests will be liable to certain sorts of dissatisfaction, so will a social arrangement—for example, a form of production, a social or political hierarchy, etc.—that departs from social rationality by significantly discounting the interests of a particular group have a potential for dissatisfaction and unrest. Whether or not this potential will be realized depends upon a great many circumstances. Owing to socialization, or to other limitations on the experience or knowledge of members of this group, the wants/interests mechanism may not have operated in such a way that the wants of its members reflect their interests. As a result they may experience no direct frustration of their desires despite the discounting of their interests. Or, the group may be too scattered or too weak to mobilize effectively. Or, it may face overawing repression. On the other hand, certain social and historical circumstances favor the realization of this potential for unrest, for example, by providing members of this group with experiences that make them more likely to develop interest-con-

---

maximizing, is not equivalent to classical utilitarianism. I *am* assuming that when a choice is faced between satisfying interest X of A vs. satisfying interest Y of B, answers to the question "All else equal, would it matter more to me if I were A to have X satisfied than if I were B to have Y satisfied?" will be relatively determinate and stable across individuals under conditions of full and vivid information. A similar, though somewhat weaker, form of comparability-across-difference is presupposed when we make choices from among alternative courses of action that would lead us to have different desires in the future.

PETER RAILTON

gruent wants, by weakening the existing repressive apparatus, by giving them new access to resources or new opportunities for mobilization, or merely by dispelling the illusion that change is impossible. In such circumstances, one can expect the potential for unrest to manifest itself.

Just as explanations involving assessments of individual rationality were not always replaceable by explanations involving individual *beliefs about* what would be rational, so, too, explanations involving assessments of social rationality cannot be replaced by explanations involving *beliefs about* what would be morally right. For example, discontent may arise because a society departs from social rationality, but not as a result of a belief that this is the case. Suppose that a given society is believed by all constituents to be just. This belief may help to stabilize it, but if in fact the interests of certain groups are being discounted, there will be a potential for unrest that may manifest itself in various ways—in alienation, loss of morale, decline in the effectiveness of authority, and so on—well before any changes in belief about the society's justness occur, and that will help explain why members of certain groups come to believe it to be unjust, if in fact they do.

In addition to possessing a certain sort of potential for unrest, societies that fail to approximate social rationality may share other features as well: they may exhibit a tendency toward certain religious or ideological doctrines, or toward certain sorts of repressive apparatus; they may be less productive in some ways (for example, by failing to develop certain human resources) and more productive in others (for example, by extracting greater labor from some groups at less cost), and thus may be differentially economically successful depending upon the conditions of production they face, and so on.

If a notion of social rationality is to be a legitimate part of empirical explanations of such phenomena, an informative characterization of the circumstances under which departures from, or approximations to, social rationality could be expected to lead to particular social outcomes—especially, of the conditions under which groups whose interests are sacrificed could be expected to exhibit or mobilize discontent—must be available. Although it cannot be known *a priori* whether an account of this kind is possible, one can see emerging in some recent work in social history and

192

MORAL REALISM

historical sociology various elements of a theory of when, and how, a persisting potential for social discontent due to persistently sacrificed interests comes to be manifested.[32]

An individual whose wants do not reflect his interests or who fails to be instrumentally rational may, I argued, experience feedback of a kind that promotes learning about his good and development of more rational strategies. Similarly, the discontent produced by departures from social rationality may produce feedback that, at a social level, promotes the development of norms that better approximate social rationality. The potential for unrest that exists when the interests of a group are discounted is potential for pressure from that group—and its allies—to accord fuller recognition to their interests in social decision-making and in the socially-instilled norms that govern individual decision-making. It therefore is pressure to push the resolution of conflicts further in the direction required by social rationality, since it is pressure to give fuller weight to the interests of more of those affected. Such pressure may of course be more or less forceful or coherent; it may find the most diverse ideological expression; and it may produce outcomes more or less advantageous in the end to those exerting it.[33]

---

[32]See, for example, Barrington Moore, Jr., *The Social Origins of Dictatorship and Democracy: Lord and Peasant in the Making of the Modern World* (Boston: Beacon, 1966) and *Injustice: The Social Bases of Obedience and Revolt* (White Plains, N.Y.: M. E. Sharpe, 1978); E. P. Thompson, *The Making of the English Working Class* (New York: Pantheon, 1963); William B. Taylor, *Drinking, Homicide, and Rebellion in Colonial Mexican Villages* (Stanford: Stanford University Press, 1979); Charles Tilly, *From Mobilization to Revolution* (Reading, Mass.: Addison-Wesley, 1978); and Charles Tilly, et al., *The Rebellious Century, 1830–1930* (Cambridge: Harvard University Press, 1975).

[33]A common theme in the works cited in note 32 is that much social unrest is re-vindicative rather than revolutionary, since the discontent of long-suffering groups often is galvanized into action only when customary entitlements are threatened or denied. The overt ideologies of such groups thus frequently are particularistic and conservative, even as their unrest contributes to the emergence of new social forms that concede greater weight to previously discounted interests. In a similar way, individuals often fail to notice irrationalities in their customary behavior until they are led by it into uncustomary difficulties, which then arouse a sense that something has gone wrong. For familiar reasons, a typical initial individual response is to attempt to retrieve the *status quo ante*, although genuine change may result from these restorative efforts.

PETER RAILTON

Striking historical examples of the mobilization of excluded groups to promote greater representation of their interests include the rebellions against the system of feudal estates, and more recent social movements against restrictions on religious practices, on suffrage and other civil rights, and on collective bargaining.[34]

Of course, other mechanisms have been at work influencing the evolution of social practices and norms at the same time, some with the reverse effect.[35] Whether mechanisms working on behalf of the inclusion of excluded interests will predominate depends upon a complex array of social and historical factors. It would be silly to think either that the norms of any actual society will at any given stage of history closely approximate social rationality, or that there will be a univocal trend toward greater social rationality. Like the mechanisms of biological evolution or market economics, the mechanisms described here operate in an "open system" alongside other mechanisms, and do not guarantee optimality or even a monotonic approach to equilibrium. Human societies do not appear to have begun at or near equilibrium in the relevant sense, and so the strongest available claim might be that in the long haul, barring certain exogenous effects, one could expect an uneven secular trend toward the inclusion of the interests of (or interests represented by)

---

[34] It should be emphasized that these mechanisms do not presuppose a background of democratic institutions. They have extracted concessions even within societies that remained very hierarchical. See, for example, Taylor, *Drinking, Homicide, and Rebellion.*

[35] Indeed, the mechanism just described may push in several directions at once: toward the inclusion of some previously excluded interests, and toward the exclusion of some previously included interests. To be sure, if interests come to be excluded even though their social and material basis remains more or less intact, a new potential for unrest is created. Some groups present a special problem, owing to their inherent inability to mobilize effectively, for example, children and future generations. To account for the pressures that have been exerted on behalf of these groups it is necessary to see how individuals come to include other individuals within their own interests. (Compare the way in which one's future selves, which can exert no pressure on their own behalf, come to be taken into account by one's present self in virtue of one's identification with them.) Unless one takes account of such processes of incorporation and identification, morality (or even prudence) will appear quite mysterious, but I will have little to say about them here. For some preliminary remarks, see Section IX of my "Alienation, Consequentialism, and the Demands of Morality," *Philosophy and Public Affairs* 13 (1984), pp. 134–171.

MORAL REALISM

social groups that are capable of some degree of mobilization. But under other circumstances, even in the long run, one could expect the opposite. New World plantation slavery, surely one of the most brutally exclusionary social arrangements ever to have existed, emerged late in world history and lasted for hundreds of years. Other brutally exclusionary social arrangements of ancient or recent vintage persist yet.

One need not, therefore, embrace a theory of moral progress in order to see that the feedback mechanism just described can give an explanatory role to the notion of social rationality. Among the most puzzling, yet most common, objections to moral realism is that there has not been uniform historical progress toward worldwide consensus on moral norms. But it has not to my knowledge been advanced as an argument against *scientific* realism that, for example, some contemporary cultures and subcultures do not accept, and do not seem to be moving in the direction of accepting, the scientific world view. Surely realists are in both cases entitled to say that only certain practices in certain circumstances will tend to produce theories more congruent with reality, especially when the subject matter is so complex and so far removed from anything like direct inspection. They need not subscribe to the quaint idea that "the truth will out" come what may. The extended theory of individual rationality, for example, leads us to expect that in societies where there are large conflicts of interest people will develop large normative disagreements, and that, when (as they usually do) these large conflicts of interest parallel large differences in power, the dominant normative views are unlikely to embody social rationality. What is at issue here, and in criterial explanations generally, is the explanation of certain patterns among others, not necessarily the existence of a single overall trend. We may, however, point to the existence of the feedback mechanisms described here as grounds for belief that we can make qualified use of historical experience as something like experimental evidence about what kinds of practices in what ranges of circumstances might better satisfy a criterion of social rationality. That is, we may assign this mechanism a role in a qualified process of moral learning.

The mechanisms of learning about individual rationality, weak or extended, involved similar qualifications. For although we expect that, under favorable circumstances, individuals may become

195

PETER RAILTON

better at acting in an instrumentally rational fashion as their experience grows, we are also painfully aware that there are powerful
mechanisms promoting the opposite result. We certainly do not
think that an individual must display exceptionless rationality, or
even show ever-increasing rationality over his lifetime, in order to
apply reason-giving explanations to many of his actions. Nor do we
think that the inevitable persistence of areas of irrationality in individuals is grounds for denying that they can, through experience,
acquire areas of greater rationality.

The comparison with individual rationality should not, however,
be overdrawn. First, while the inclusion-generating mechanisms
for social rationality operate through the behavior of individuals,
interpersonal dynamics enter ineliminably in such a way that the
criteria selected for are not reducible to those of disaggregated
individual rationality. Both social and biological evolution involve
selection mechanisms that favor behaviors satisfying criteria of relative optimality that are collective (as in prisoner's dilemma cases)
or genotypic (which may also be collective, as in kin selection) as
well as individual or phenotypic. Were this not so, it is hardly
possible that moral norms could ever have emerged or come to
have the hold upon us they do.

Second, there are rather extreme differences of degree between
the individual and the social cases. Most strikingly, the mechanisms
whereby individual wants and behaviors are brought into some
congruence with individual interests and reasons operate in more
direct and reliable ways than comparable mechanisms nudging social practices or norms in the direction of what is socially rational.
Not only are the information demands less formidable in the individual case—that is the least of it, one might say—but the ways in
which feedback is achieved are more likely in the individual case to
serve as a prod for change and less likely to be distorted by social
asymmetries.

Nonetheless, we do have the skeleton of an explanatory theory
that uses the notion of what is more or less rational from a social
point of view and that parallels in an obvious way uses of assessments of rationality from the agent's point of view in explanations
of individual beliefs and behaviors. Like the individual theory, it
suggests prediction- and counterfactual-supporting generalizations
of the following kind: over time, and in some circumstances more

MORAL REALISM

than others, we should expect pressure to be exerted on behalf of practices that more adequately satisfy a criterion of rationality.

Well, if this is a potentially predictive and explanatory theory, how good is it? That is a very large question, one beyond my competence to answer. But let me note briefly three patterns in the evolution of moral norms that seem to me to bear out the predictions of this theory, subject to the sorts of qualifications that the existence of imperfections and competing mechanisms would lead one to expect. I do so with trepidation, however, for although the patterns I will discuss are gross historical trends, it is not essential to the theory that history show such trends, and it certainly is not part of the theory to endorse a set of practices or norms merely because it is a result of them.

Generality. It is a commonplace of anthropology that tribal peoples often have only one word to name both their tribe and "the people" or "humanity." Those beyond the tribe are not deemed full-fledged people, and the sorts of obligations one has toward people do not apply fully with regard to outsiders. Over the span of history, through processes that have involved numerous reversals, people have accumulated into larger social units—from the familial band to the tribe to the "people" to the nation-state—and the scope of moral categories has enlarged to follow these expanding boundaries. Needless to say, this has not been a matter of the contagious spread of enlightenment. Expanding social entities frequently subjugate those incorporated within their new boundaries, and the means by which those thus oppressed have secured greater recognition of their interests have been highly conflictual, and remain—perhaps, will always remain—incomplete. Nonetheless, contemporary moral theory, and to a surprising degree contemporary moral discourse, have come to reject any limitation short of the species.[36]

Humanization. Moral principles have been assigned various origins and natures: as commandments of supernatural origin,

---

[36]Here and elsewhere, I mean by 'contemporary moral theory' to refer to dominant views in the academies, and by 'contemporary moral discourse' to refer to widespread practices of public moral argumentation, in those societies that have achieved the highest levels of development of empirical science generally. Again, the moral realist, like the scientific realist, is not committed to worldwide consensus.

PETER RAILTON

grounded in the will or character of a deity, to be interpreted by a
priesthood; as formalistic demands of a caste-based code of honor;
as cosmic principles of order; as dictates of reason or conscience
that make no appeal to human inclinations or well-being; and so
on. While vestiges of these views survive in contemporary moral
theory, it is typical of almost the entire range of such theory, and of
much of contemporary moral discourse, to make some sort of intrinsic connection between normative principles and effects on
human interests. Indeed, the very emergence of morality as a distinctive subject matter apart from religion is an instance of this
pattern.

Patterns of variation. In addition to seeing patterns that reflect
some pressure toward the approximation of social rationality, we
should expect to see greater approximation in those areas of normative regulation where the mechanisms postulated here work
best, for example, in areas where almost everyone has importantly
similar or mutually satisfiable interests, where almost everyone has
some substantial potential to infringe upon the interests of others,
where the advantages of certain forms of constraint or cooperation
are highly salient even in the dynamics of small groups, and where
individuals can significantly influence the likelihood of norm-fol-
lowing behavior on the part of others by themselves following
norms. The clearest examples have to do with prohibitions of aggression and theft, and of the violation of promises.[37] By contrast,
moral questions that concern matters where there are no solutions
compatible with protecting the most basic interests of all, where
there exist very large asymmetries in the capacity to infringe upon
interests, where the gains or losses from particular forms of cooperation or constraint are difficult to perceive, and where individual
compliance will little affect general compliance, are less likely to
achieve early or stable approximation to social rationality. Clear
examples here have to do with such matters as social hierarchy—
for example, the permissibility of slavery, of authoritarian government, of caste or gender inequalities—and social responsibility—

---

[37]However, such prohibitions historically have shown limitations of
scope that are no longer recognized as valid. The trend against such limitations is an instance of the first sort of pattern, toward increased generality.

MORAL REALISM

for example, what is the nature of our individual or collective obligation to promote the well-being of unrelated others?

Given a suitable characterization of the conditions that prevailed during the processes of normative evolution described by these patterns, the present theory claims not only that these changes could have been expected, but that an essential part of the explanation of their occurrence is a mechanism whereby individuals whose interests are denied are led to form common values and make common cause along lines of shared interests, thereby placing pressure on social practices to approximate more closely to social rationality.

These descriptions and explanations of certain prominent features of the evolution of moral norms will no doubt strike some as naive at best, plainly—perhaps even dangerously—false at worst. I thoroughly understand this. I have given impossibly sketchy, one-sided, simple-minded accounts of a very complex reality.[38] I can only hope that these accounts will seem as believable as one could expect sketchy, one-sided, simple-minded accounts to be, and that this will make the story I have tried to tell about mechanisms and explanation more plausible.

Needless to say, the upshot is not a complacent functionalism or an overall endorsement of current moral practice or norms. Instead, the account of morality sketched here emphasizes conflict rather than equilibrium, and provides means for criticizing certain contemporary moral practices and intuitions by asking about their historical genesis. For example, if we come to think that the expla-

---

[38]Moreover, the accounts are highly general in character, operating at a level of description incapable of discriminating between hypotheses based upon the particular account of moral rightness proposed here and others rather close to it. (Roughly, those characterizing moral rightness in terms of instrumental rationality relative to the non-moral good of those affected, but differing on details regarding instrumental rationality—for example, is it straightforwardly maximizing or partly distributive?—or regarding non-moral goodness—for example, is it reducible to pleasure? For a discussion of not-very-close competitors, see Section VI.) If the method I have employed is to be used to make choices from among close competitors, the empirical analysis must be much more fine-grained. Similar remarks apply to the weak and extended theories of individual rationality appealed to above.

PETER RAILTON

nation of a common moral intuition assigns no significant role to
mechanisms that could be expected to exert pressure toward socially rational outcomes, then this is grounds for questioning the
intuition, however firmly we may hold it. In the spirit of a naturalized moral epistemology, we may ask whether the explanation of
why we make certain moral judgments is an example of a reliable
process for discovering moral facts.

V. LIMITATIONS

Thus far I have spoken of what is morally best as a matter of
what is instrumentally rational from a social point of view. But I
have also characterized a genuinely moral point of view as one
impartial with respect to the interests of all potentially affected,
and that is not a socially-bounded notion. In fact, I have claimed
that a trend away from social specificity is among the patterns
visible in the evolution of moral norms. Part of the explanation of
this pattern—and part, therefore, of the explanatory role of degrees of impartial rationality—is that the mechanisms appealed to
above are not socially-bounded, either. Societies, and individuals
on opposite sides of social boundaries, constrain one another in
various ways, much as groups and individuals constrain one another within societies: they can threaten aggression, mobilize resistance to external control, withhold cooperation, and obstruct
one another's plans; and they are prone to resort to such constraining activities when their interests are denied or at risk. As with
intrasocial morality, so in intersocial morality, the best-established
and most nearly impartially rational elements are those where the
mechanisms we have discussed work most reliably: prohibitions on
aggression are stronger and more widely accepted than principles
of equity or redistribution. Of course, many factors make inter-
societal dynamics unlike intrasocietal ones. . . . But the reader will
for once be spared more armchair social science. Still, what results
is a form of moral realism that is essentially tied to a limited point
of view, an impartial yet human one. Is this too limited for genuine
moral realism?

A teacher of mine once remarked that the question of moral
realism seemed to him to be the question whether the universe
cares what we do. Since we have long since given up believing that

MORAL REALISM

the cosmos pays us any mind, he thought we should long since have given up moral realism. I can only agree that if this were what moral realism involved, it should—with relief rather than sorrow—be let go. However, the account offered here gives us a way of understanding how moral values or imperatives might be objective without being cosmic. They need be grounded in nothing more transcendental than facts about man and his environment, facts about what sorts of things matter to us, and how the ways we live affect these things.

Yet the present account is limited in another way, which may be of greater concern from the standpoint of contemporary moral theory: it does not yield moral imperatives that are categorical in the sense of providing a reason for action to all rational agents regardless of their contingent desires. Although troubling, this limitation is not tantamount to relativism, since on the present account rational motivation is not a precondition of moral obligation. For example, it could truthfully be said that I ought to be more generous even though greater generosity would not help me to promote my existing ends, or even to satisfy my objective interests. This could be so because what it would be morally right for me to do depends upon what is rational from a point of view that includes, but is not exhausted by, my own.

In a similar way, it could be said that I logically ought not to believe both a proposition *p* and a proposition that implies not-*p*. However, it may not be the case that every rational agent will have an instrumental reason to purge all logical contradictions from his thought. It would require vast amounts of cogitation for anyone to test all of his existing beliefs for consistency, and to insure that every newly acquired belief preserves it. Suppose someone to be so fortunate that the only contradictions among his beliefs lie deep in the much-sedimented swamp of factual trivia. Perhaps his memories of two past acquaintances have become confused in such a way that somewhere in the muck there are separate beliefs which, taken together, attribute to one individual logically incompatible properties. Until such a contradiction rears its head in practice, he may have no more reason to lay down his present concerns and wade in after it than he has to leave his home in suburban New Jersey to hunt alligators in the Okefenokee on the off chance that he might one day find himself stranded and unarmed in the backwaters of

PETER RAILTON

southeast Georgia.[39] What an individual rationally ought to do thus may differ from what logic requires of him. Still, we may say that logical evaluation is not subjective or arbitrary, and that good grounds of a perfectly general kind are available for being logical, namely, that logical contradictions are necessarily false and logical inferences are truth-preserving. Since in public discourse and private reflection we are often concerned with whether our thinking is warranted in a sense that is more intimately connected with its truth-conduciveness than with its instrumentality to our peculiar personal goals, it therefore is far from arbitrary that we attach so much importance to logic as a standard of criticism and self-criticism.

By parallel, if we adopt the account of moral rightness proposed above we may say that moral evaluation is not subjective or arbitrary, and that good, general grounds are available for following moral 'ought's', namely, that moral conduct is rational from an impartial point of view. Since in public discourse and private reflection we are often concerned with whether our conduct is justifiable from a general rather than merely personal standpoint, it therefore is far from arbitrary that we attach so much importance to morality as a standard of criticism and self-criticism.

The existence of such phenomena as religion and ideology is evidence for the pervasiveness and seriousness of our concern for impartial justification. Throughout history individuals have sacrificed their interests, even their lives, to meet the demands of religions or ideologies that were compelling for them in part because they purported to express a universal—*the* universal—justificatory standpoint. La Rochefoucauld wrote that hypocrisy is the tribute vice pays to virtue,[40] but 'hypocrisy' suggests cynicism. We might

---

[39] It is of no importance whether we say that he has *no* reason to do this or simply a vanishingly small one. I suppose we could say that a person has a vanishingly small reason to do anything—even to expend enormous effort to purge minor contradictions from his beliefs or to purge alligators from distant swamps—that might *conceivably* turn out to be to his benefit. But then we would have no trouble guaranteeing the existence of vanishingly small reasons for moral conduct. This would allow naturalized moral rightness to satisfy a Humean thesis of practicality after all, but in a way that would rob the thesis of its interest.

[40] François (duc de) la Rochefoucauld, *Reflexions, ou sentences et maximes morales suivi de reflexions diverses*, ed., Jean Lafond (Paris: Gallimard, 1976),

MORAL REALISM

better say that ideology is the respect partisans show to impartiality. Morality, then, is not ideology made sincere and general—ideology is intrinsically given to heart-felt generalization. Morality is ideology that has faced the facts.

I suspect the idea that moral evaluations must have categorical force for rational agents owes some of its support to a fear that were this to be denied, the authority of morality would be lost. That would be so if one held onto the claim that moral imperatives cannot exist for someone who would not have a reason to obey them, for then an individual could escape moral duties by the simple expedient of having knavish desires. But if we give up this claim about the applicability of moral judgment, then variations in personal desires cannot license exemption from moral obligation.[41]

Thus, while it certainly is a limitation of the argument made here that it does not yield a conception of moral imperatives as categorical, that may be a limitation we can live with and still accord morality the scope and dignity it traditionally has enjoyed. Moreover, it may be a limitation we must live with. For how many among us can convince ourselves that reason is other than hypothetical? Need it also be asked: How many of us would find our sense of the significance of morality or the importance of moral conduct enhanced by a demonstration that even a person with the most thoroughly repugnant ends would find that moral conduct advanced them?

---

p. 79. La Rochefoucauld apparently borrowed the phrase from the cleric Du Moulin. I am grateful to a remark of Barrington Moore, Jr. for reminding me of it. See his *Injustice*, p. 508.

[41]Contrast Harman's relativism about 'ought' in *The Nature of Morality*. Harman adopts the first of the two courses just mentioned, preserving the connection between an individual's moral obligations and what he has (instrumental) reason to do. He defends his approach in part by arguing that, if we suppose that Hitler was engaged in rational pursuit of his ends, an "internal" judgment like 'Hitler (morally) ought not to have killed six million Jews' would be "weak" and "odd" compared to an "external" judgment like 'Hitler was evil' (see pp. 107 ff). I would have thought the opposite, namely, that it is too "weak" and "odd" to give an account of morality such that Hitler can be judged to be consummately evil (which Harman claims, without explanation, his brand of relativism *can* do) but in which 'Hitler (morally) ought not to have acted as he did' is false.

PETER RAILTON

One implication of what has been said is that if we want morality
to be taken seriously and to have an important place in people's
lives—and not merely as the result of illusion or the threat of
repression—we should be vitally concerned with the ways in which
social arrangements produce conflicts of interest and asymmetries
of power that affect the nature and size of the gap between what is
individually and socially rational. Rather than attempt to portray
morality as something that it cannot be, as "rationally compelling
no matter what one's ends," we should ask how we might change
the ways we live so that moral conduct would more regularly be
rational given the ends we actually will have.

VI. SUMMARY AND CONCLUSION

I have outlined a form of moral realism, and given some indication of how it might be defended against certain objections. Neither a full characterization of this view, nor full answers to the
many objections it faces, can be given within the present essay.
Perhaps then I should stop trying to say just a bit more, and close
by indicating roughly what I have, and have not, attempted to
show.

I have proposed what are in effect reforming naturalistic definitions of non-moral goodness and moral rightness. It is possible to
respond: "Yes, I can see that such-and-such an end is an objective
interest of the agent in your sense, or that such-and-such a practice
is rational from an impartial point of view, but can't I still ask
whether the end is good for him or the practice right?" Such "open
questions" cannot by their nature be closed, since definitions are
not subject to proof or disproof. But open questions may be more
or less disturbing, for although definitional proposals cannot be
demonstrated, they can fare better or worse at meeting various
desiderata.

I have assumed throughout that the drawing up of definitions is
part of theory-construction, and so is to be assessed by asking
(1) whether the analyses given satisfy appropriate constraints of
intelligibility and function, and (2) whether the terms as analyzed
contribute to the formulation and testing of worthwhile theories.
How do my proposals fit with these criteria?

(1) Beyond constraints of intelligibility, such as clarity and non-

MORAL REALISM

circularity, specifically naturalistic definitions of evaluative terms should satisfy two further analytic constraints arising from their intended function. (a) They should insofar as possible capture the normative force of these terms by providing analyses that permit these terms to play their central evaluative roles. In the present setting, this involves showing that although the definitions proposed may not fit with all of our linguistic or moral intuitions, they nonetheless express recognizable notions of goodness and rightness. Further, it involves showing that the definitions permit plausible connections to be drawn between, on the one hand, what is good or right and, on the other, what characteristically would motivate individuals who are prepared to submit themselves to relevant sorts of scrutiny. (b) The naturalistic definitions should permit the evaluative concepts to participate in their own right in genuinely empirical theories. Part of this consists in showing that we have appropriate epistemic access to these concepts. Part, too, (and a related part) consists in showing that generalizations employing these concepts, among others, can figure in potentially explanatory accounts. I have tried to offer reasonably clear definitions and to show in a preliminary way how they might meet constraints (a) and (b).

(2) However, a good deal more must be done, for it remains to show that the empirical theories constructed with the help of these definitions are reasonably good theories, that is, theories for which we have substantial evidence and which provide plausible explanations. I have tried in the most preliminary way imaginable to suggest this. If I have been wholly unpersuasive on empirical matters, then I can expect that the definitions I have offered will be equally unpersuasive.

It is an attraction for me of naturalism in ethics and epistemology alike that it thus is constrained in several significant dimensions at once. One has such ample opportunities to be shown wrong or found unconvincing if one's account must be responsive to empirical demands as well as normative intuitions. Theorizing in general is more productive when suitably constrained; in ethics especially, constraints are needed if we are to have a clearer idea of how we might make progress toward the resolution of theoretical disputes. Of course, not just any constraints will do. A proposed set of constraints must present itself as both appropriate and useful. Let

205

PETER RAILTON

me say something about (1) the utility of the constraints adopted here, and then a final word about (2) their appropriateness.

(1) Consider three classes of competitors to the substantive moral theory endorsed above, and notice how criticisms of them *naturally* intertwine concerns about normative justification and empirical explanation. *Kantian* conceptions of morality are widely viewed as having captured certain intuitively compelling normative characteristics of such notions as rationality and moral rightness, but it seems they have done so partly at the expense of affording a plausible way of integrating these notions into an empirical account of our reasons and motives in action. Moreover, this descriptive difficulty finds direct expression on the normative side. Not only must any normative 'ought' be within the scope of an empirical 'can', but a normatively compelling 'ought' must—as recent criticisms of Kantianism have stressed—reach to the real springs of human action and concern. *Intuitionist* moral theories also enjoyed some success in capturing normative features of morality, but they have largely been abandoned for want of a credible account of the nature or operation of a faculty of moral intuition. It is too easy for us to give a non-justifying psychological explanation of the existence in certain English gentlemen of something which they identified upon introspection as a faculty of moral insight, an explanation that ties this purported faculty more closely to the rigidity of prevailing social conventions than to anything that looks as if it could be a source of universal truth. *Social choice theories* that take occurrent subjective interests or revealed preferences as given fit more readily than Kantian or intuitionist theories with empirical accounts of behavior, and, unlike them, have found a place in contemporary social science. But they suffer well-known limitations as normative theories, some of which turn out to be bound up with their limitations as explanatory theories: they lack an account of the origin or evolution of preferences, and partly for that reason are unable to capture the ways in which we evaluate purportedly rational or moral conduct by criticizing ends as well as means.

(2) However, the issues at stake when we evaluate competing approaches to morality involve not only this sort of assessment of largish theories, but also questions about which criteria of assessment appropriately apply to definitions and theories in ethics, and about whether definitional systematization and largish theorizing

MORAL REALISM

are even appropriate for ethics. I am drawn to the view that the development of theory in ethics is not an artificial contrivance of philosophers but an organic result of the personal and social uses of moral evaluation: time and again individuals and groups have faced difficult questions to which common sense gave conflicting or otherwise unsatisfactory answers, and so they have pressed their questions further and pursued their inquiry more systematically. The felt need for theory in ethics thus parallels the felt need for theory in natural or social science.[12] It does not follow from this alone that ethical theorizing must run parallel to or be integrable with theorizing in the natural and social sciences. Ethics might be deeply different. Although initially plausible and ultimately irrefutable, the view that ethics stands thus apart is one that in the end I reject. We are natural and social creatures, and I know of nowhere else to look for ethics than in this rich conjunction of facts. I have tried to suggest that we might indeed find it there.[13]

The University of Michigan, Ann Arbor

---

[12]This felt need is also reflected in the codification of laws, and in the development of legal theories. However contrived the law may at times seem, surely the general social conditions and needs that have driven its development are real enough. Indeed, the elaborate artifice of law and its language is in part an indication of how pressing the need to go beyond pretheoretic common sense has been.

[13]I am indebted to a great many people, including Peter Achinstein, Robert Audi, Annette Baier, Michael Bratman, Stephen Darwall, Allan Gibbard, Thomas Nagel, Samuel Scheffler, Rebecca Scott, Nicholas Sturgeon, Nicholas White, and the editors at *The Philosophical Review*, who have kindly provided comments on previous drafts or presentations of this paper.

[18]

The Southern Journal of Philosophy (1986) Vol. XXIV. Supplement

MORAL EXPLANATIONS OF NATURAL FACTS— CAN MORAL CLAIMS BE TESTED AGAINST MORAL REALITY?

Gilbert Harman
Princeton University

Introduction

In the middle of this century it was widely believed that a central question of moral philosophy, perhaps *the* central question, was whether moral claims are subject to empirical testing in the way that scientific hypotheses are. Two seemingly competing answers were given to this question. On the one hand, emotivism and other forms of noncognitivism denied that moral claims are testable to the extent that scientific claims are and traced this difference between moral and scientific claims to a difference in function. Where science was said to aim at description and explanation, morality was said to aim at prescription and evaluation. On the other hand, the impartial spectator (or "ideal observer") theory and other forms of ethical naturalism argued that moral claims are reducible to scientific claims and are therefore as empirically testable as their naturalistic equivalents.

Developments in philosophy since 1950 have made many philosophers sceptical of this approach to moral philosophy. Many philosophers have come to believe that the appearance of a special problem about the testability of moral claims arises from mistakes about the nature of empirical testing. These philosophers see no need to choose between (or even discuss) noncognitivism and reductionism. They believe that moral philosophy should be concerned with moral issues about right and wrong rather than with the epistemological status of moral judgments. They think that ethics should be pursued from inside, by starting with one's present moral views and plausible general moral theories and then adjusting each of these to the other in an attempt to reach a "reflective equilibrium".[1]

I think this is a mistake. I believe that there is a real problem of testability in ethics, a problem that can be formulated without making mistakes about testability in science. Furthermore, I believe that noncognitivism and ethical naturalism are the most plausible responses to the problem. I tried to say what the problem is in the first chapter of a text book in ethics.[2] I will say more in this paper and I will respond to a thoughtful objection Nicholas Sturgeon has raised to my version.[3] But first I want to indicate how certain other ways of formulating the issue rely on false assumptions about scientific testing.

A traditional statement of the issue begins with the assumption that a claim is tested by seeing whether its observational implications are true. It then observes that a moral claim says what *ought* to be the case, whereas a statement of observation says what *is* the case. So normally a moral judgment will have no significant observational implications at all, unless it is reducible to a descriptive naturalistic claim. Given the initial assumption about how a claim is to be empirically tested, this means that there is no way to test moral claims empirically, unless they are reducible to naturalistic claims. Furthermore, if we assume that claims are cognitively meaningful only if they are testable, it follows that, if moral claims are not reducible to naturalistic claims, then either moral judgments are completely meaningless or they have noncognitive meaning, perhaps emotive meaning.

But there are problems with this traditional way of setting out the issue. First, there seem to be two basic ways in which one might try to distinguish the observational implications of a claim from its non-observational implications. One appeals to vocabulary, seeing a distinction between theoretical words and observational words and counting an implication as an observational implication if it contains no theoretical words. The other way counts an implication as an observational implication if everyone in a relevant speech community would reach the same verdict on the truth of the implication if they were to make the same observation in the sense of being exposed to the same sensory stimulation.[4] But neither of these ways is useful in the present context.

First, it is very difficult to divide words into theoretical and observational words. Consider a remark like, "The left particle is larger than the right." Is "larger" an observational word? It seems to matter whether we are talking about visible particles of rock or subatomic particles. But the word "larger" does not have a different meaning depending on the size of what it is used to talk about. So, for example, it makes perfect sense and is even true that a baseball is larger than an electron.

On the other hand, if we suppose that an implication is observational if everyone in the relevant speech community who received the same sensory stimulation would agree about its truth value, then some moral statements will turn out to be observational statements, since in many speech communities there will be moral claims to which everyone would give the same verdict given the same stimulus, for example, "It is wrong for those kids to torture that cat like that!" So, given this second approach, there will be no special problem about testing moral claims, since some moral claims are directly testable in observation.

A second difficulty with the traditional way of putting the issue of testability in ethics is that, even if observational implications could be satisfactorily distinguished from other implications, the problem that was supposed to arise for moral claims would arise just as much for scientific claims too. because scientific claims would not normally have any significant observational consequences by themselves either. In order to derive testable consequences. it would be necessary to add various "auxiliary assumptions" about the conditions of observation. initial conditions, and so forth. And. if we count scientific claims as testable by saying that a claim is testable if it and some further assumptions imply observational consequences, then we must say that any claim is testable, including any moral claim. For example, consider the claim:

(C) It is wrong to cause unnecessary pain to animals.

This claim turns out to be testable if we add certain auxiliary assumptions. for example:

(A1) For Alfred to hit his cat with a stick would be for Albert to cause unnecessary pain to an animal.

(A2) Alfred will not do anything wrong.

The claim (C) and the assumptions (A$_1$) and (A$_2$) jointly imply the negative observational conclusion:

(O) We will not see Alfred hit his cat with a stick.

So. the traditional way of stating the testability problem for ethics does not show that moral claims must be reducible to naturalistic claims if they are to be testable.[5]

Many philosophers have concluded from this that there is no special problem about the observational testing of moral claims, so there is no need to be concerned with metaethical disputes between reductionism and noncognitivism. I want to argue, on the contrary, that there is a real problem about testing moral claims if they are not reducible to naturalistic claims. Let me now try to formulate the problem.

Background

To begin at the beginning, it seems that we ought to distinguish moral claims like, "It is wrong to cause needless pain to animals," from psychological or sociological claims like, "Many Americans are disposed to believe that it is wrong to cause needless pain to animals." I suggest that such psychological and sociological claims are often empirically testable, not because they have "observational implications," but rather because the phenomena in question can have "observational effects." People's beliefs can affect how they act and react, and we can observe and so be influenced by these actions and reactions. We can therefore sometimes support sociological or psychological claims by means of an inference to be best explanation of certain people's behavior. For example, the best explanation of people

59

behaving as they do may be in part that they believe it is wrong to cause needless pain to animals.

Now, are moral claims testable in the same way? Is there some empirical way to test the claim that it is wrong to cause needless pain to animals? Could the wrongness of causing needless pain to animals have an observable effect in the world that could serve as evidence that this is wrong, in the way that people's beliefs about wrongness can have effects that can serve as evidence for the existence of those beliefs? Can there be manifestations of the fact that it is wrong to cause needless pain to animals in the way there can be manifestations of the fact that a particular person believes that this is wrong?

This way of putting the issue does not assume a distinction between observational reports and nonobservational statements. And it does not assume that we test a theory by looking at certain of its logical implications. The key is explanation rather than implication.

But the question is not just whether there are "moral explanations." It is rather whether there are the sorts of moral explanations that would make moral claims empirically testable in all the ways that scientific claims are empirically testable. For example, an emotivist can accept certain moral explanations without supposing that the moral claims involved are empirically testable in the relevant sense. Like anyone else, an emotivist can attempt to develop a general normative theory and such an attempt may involve a kind of inference to the best explanation. The emotivist will try to find a single general principle, or small set of principles, that would account for the rightness or wrongness of particular acts. The principles arrived at represent a normative moral theory that is tested against cases, but it is not clearly being tested against the world. According to the emotivist, the theory is merely being tested against the tester's moral sensibility.

Particular cases that are used to test a moral theory in *this* way do not have to be (and usually are not) actual cases. They are often merely imagined, possible cases. The moral philosopher who develops a normative theory by using the method of reflective equilibrium does "thought experiments", not real experiments. Thought experiments are not confined to ethics, of course. They have been used in physics and other sciences in order to bring out the implications of a theory and to test the theory against a particular scientist's sense of what ought to happen in certain circumstances. But scientific theories can often be tested against the world and not just against a particular scientist's sensibility. That is what makes them empirical theories. The issue I am concerned with is whether moral theories can be tested in this further way, against the world.

Of course, one can study "commonsense physics" by seeing what the average person expects to happen under various circumstances. It might turn out, for example, that the average person expects that, if a car drives off a cliff, it goes straight out for a bit, then plummets straight

60

down, as in movie cartoons. Such a study might be very interesting, but its results would be results in psychology not physics.

A moral philosopher who tries to find general principles to account for judgments about particular cases, hoping eventually to get principles and cases into "reflective equilibrium," is studying common-sense ethics. The results of such a study are results in moral psychology. Just as a study of commonsense physics is not a study in physics, the study of commonsense ethics is not an investigation of right and wrong, *unless* what it is for something to be right and wrong can be identified with facts about moral psychology.

Two physicists with different theories and correspondingly different physical expectations and sensibilities will get different results from their thought experiments. It is not evidence for theory *A* that physicist *A*'s thought experiments accord with that theory. Theorist *A* could not plausibly say, "The evidence for theory *A* is that, when I imagine particles interacting, I imagine them interacting in accordance with the principles of theory *A*." That is not evidence for *A*'s theory, because it is explained by *A*'s holding the theory and having the corresponding physical sensibility, quite apart from whether or not theory *A* is true. To test theory *A* against the world, the theorist needs to find some result in the world that is most plausibly explained by that theory's being true. Such tests are possible in physics, because physical facts can have observable effects on people who do not believe in those facts ahead of time. The issue is whether such tests are possible in ethics. Can the actual rightness or wrongness of a given course of action have observable effects that enable moral claims to be tested against the world in the way that scientific claims can be tested?

Moral Explanations

Nicholas Sturgeon sees no problem here. In his view, there are many clear examples of moral explanations of nonmoral facts. He discusses several examples. A spectator believes that certain children are doing something wrong because he sees them doing something wrong, so the explanation of the spectator's belief is in part that the children are doing something wrong.[6] We believe Hitler was morally depraved because of the things that Hitler did. He did those things because he was morally depraved, so the explanation of our belief is in part that Hitler was morally depraved.[7] The historian Bernard De Voto concluded, "Passed Midshipman Woodworth was just no damned good," because a study of Woodworth's actions revealed that in fact he was just no damned good.[8] A judge's decision not to sentence a particular offender to the maximum prison term the law allows is due to the judge's decency and fairmindedness[9].

These are all cases in which moral aspects of a person or action are appealed to in order to explain certain natural events. But the explanations are clearly not of a sort that would allow us to test moral claims against the world in all the ways in which scientific claims can be tested against the world, as is shown by the fact that an emotivist can agree to all of these explanations without any discomfort.

Consider the following variation of the first example. Jane sees Albert hit his cat with a stick. The cat cries out piteously. Jane believes that Albert's action was wrong. Why does Jane believe this? According to Sturgeon, it may be that Jane believes this because the action *was* in fact wrong. The wrongness of the act can be the best explanation of Jane's belief.

Sturgeon argues that it is a perfectly ordinary empirical matter whether such an explanation is correct. It may be that Jane would think Albert wrong no matter what Albert did. In that case, Jane's belief is not explained by the actual wrongness of what Albert does. But, if Jane would have believed Albert was wrong only if Albert had done something wrong, then the fact that Albert's act was wrong explains why Jane believes it was wrong.

Sturgeon agrees that such explanations could be undermined by further investigation. But he claims they are *prima facie* acceptable and asks what the problem with them is supposed to be.

The problem is that this sort of explanation does not make clear how the actual *wrongness* of Albert's act plays a role in generating Jane's belief. In the absence of a naturalistic reduction of wrongness, Jane's belief can be explained entirely by Jane's moral sensibility plus an observation of Albert's action, whether or not there is anything wrong with causing pain to animals.

Therefore, in the absence of some sort of naturalistic reduction of moral claims, this kind of explanation does not make it possible to test moral claims empirically in all ways in which scientific claims can be empirically tested. For, suppose that another person, Mary, is not convinced that there is anything wrong with causing pain to animals. It is clearly not evidence for Jane's view that Jane believes Albert's act to be wrong. It is no harder for Mary to explain Jane's belief than it is for Jane. There is nothing about this case that should be particularly surprising to Mary, something that is not surprising on the hypothesis that causing pain to animals is wrong. Nor is this a case in which Mary and Jane accept different explanations for something that has occurred, or a case in which Mary lacks an explanation for something that has occurred, while Jane has an explanation for it. Mary and Jane do not really disagree about the explanation of Jane's belief, although they might describe matters differently. The situation is exactly similar to the one involving the two physicists with different theories and physical sensibilities. The fact that the one physicist thinks things will come out as theory *A* predicts is no evidence for theory *A*, only evidence that that physicist accepts theory *A*. In this context, Jane cannot suppose that the explanation of her belief about Albert is that Albert's action was wrong unless she has some further idea of how the wrongness of Albert's action could influence her belief.

This shows that Sturgeon's "counterfactual test" for whether one thing explains another is only appropriate in certain contexts. According to this test, to see whether *H* explains *E*, one must consider whether *E* would have occurred if *H* had not occurred; if *E* would not have occurred in that case, its occurrence is (at least partly) explained by *H*.[10] In the case of Jane's seeing Albert's act of striking his cat with a stick, *E* is "Jane believes that Albert's act is wrong." *H* is, "Albert's act was wrong." To supply Sturgeon's test, we must therefore ask whether Jane would have believed Albert's act was wrong if Albert had not done something wrong. Sturgeon observes that in the circumstances this may be a reasonable thing to suppose.

Well, this counterfactual proposition may well be one it is reasonable to accept in certain circumstances. And it may support a kind of moral explanation that is appropriate in those circumstances. But this does not show that moral claims are empirically testable in the relevant respect, because the explanation in question is not acceptable in the relevant testing context.

A good and conclusive way to see that this sort of explanation is irrelevant to full empirical testing is to notice that a moral epiphenomenalist can accept the relevant counterfactual judgment without having to suppose that moral features of actions ever explain any nonmoral facts. A moral epiphenomenalist takes moral properties to be epiphenomenally supervenient on natural properties in the sense that the possession of moral properties is explained by possession of the relevant natural properties and nothing is influenced or explained by the possession of moral properties.[11] Similarly, an emotivist can accept the relevant counterfactual judgment without at all being committed to abandoning the noncognitivist position and concluding that moral claims are just as empirically testable as scientific claims.[12]

What's needed is some account of *how* the actual wrongness of Albert's action could help to explain Jane's disapproval of it. And we have to be able to believe in this account. We cannot just make something up, saying, for example, that the wrongness of the act affects the quality of the light reflected into Jane's eyes, causing her to react negatively. That would be an example of wrongness manifesting itself in the world in a way that could serve as evidence for and against certain moral claims, but it is not something we can believe in. On the other hand, certain naturalistic reductions of wrongness might enable us to explain how the wrongness of Albert's action could help to explain Jane's disapproval of it. I give some examples later in this paper. My present point is that there is a real issue here.

I can put the point in a slightly different way. We can distinguish between two related propositions: (1) Features of acts that make the acts wrong sometimes explain things that can be observed. (2) The fact that certain features make acts wrong sometimes explains things that can be observed. It is the second of these propositions that has to hold if

moral claims are to be tested against the world in all the ways in which
scientific claims can be tested. The issue is not whether (what are by our
lights) wrong-making features have observable manifestations. It is
whether the wrongness of acts having those features has observable
manifestations. Sturgeon's examples are not examples of (2), they are
examples of (1), and his counter-factual test is only relevant to (1), not
to (2). Therefore, his examples do not help to show that moral claims
can be tested against the world in the relevant sense.

Scepticism

   Sturgeon takes the issue here to be scepticism. He thinks the issue
might still be formulated in terms of his counterfactual test in the
following way: if Albert's action "were one of deliberate, pointless
cruelty, but this *did not make it wrong*, [Jane] would still have thought
it was wrong",[13] although he thinks the antecedent of this conditional is
"puzzling", because he takes it to be "necessarily false." To suppose that
the antecedent is true would be to suppose that Jane is quite wrong
about morality. Sturgeon concedes that if Jane were quite wrong in this
way about morality, she would "still draw exactly the same moral
conclusions" she in fact does. But "we should deny that any sceptical
conclusion follows from this. In particular, we should deny that it
follows that moral facts play no role in explaining our moral
judgments."[14] For he thinks that the situation is just like that in which a
physicist infers from a vapor trail that a proton has gone through a
cloud chamber in a certain way. In this case the "parallel" claim is "that
if there hadn't been a proton there, but there *had* been a vapor trail, the
physicist would still have concluded that a proton was present." So we
can's suppose a skeptical conclusion about morality follows without
supposing that a sceptical conclusion about physics follows. And the
issue is whether there is a contrast between morality and physics.

   But the issue of observational testing is not the same as the issue of
scepticism. Of course, no sceptical conclusion follows from the fact
that, if Jane were quite wrong about cruelty to animals, she would still
draw the same conclusions she does. So, there is at least one parallel
between this example and the vapor trail example. But the issue about
testability is whether there is a further parallel. In the vapor trail
example the physicist thinks he understands how the passage of a
proton through the apparatus might explain a vapor trail such as the
one he sees. That allows the physicist to treat the vapor trail as evidence
for the presence of the proton. But do we think we understand how the
wrongness of Albert's action, i.e. the wrongness of cruelty to animals,
might explain Jane's belief that Albert did something wrong? Moral
claims like Jane's are as empirically testable as scientific claims only if
there is an answer to this sort of question.

Reductionism and Moral Explanations

   As I have said, there are two main responses to the question whether
moral claims are subject to empirical testing in the way that scientific

claims are. On the one hand, noncognitivists argue that moral claims are not subject to empirical testing, because such claims have the nondescriptive functions of stating rules, expressing emotions, and so on. On the other hand, reductionists argue that moral claims are reducible to sociological or psychological claims.

I am inclined to favor a mixed strategy. I believe that reductionism is basically correct, although moral claims have a noncognitive aspect also.

The most plausible varieties of reductionism are impartial spectator theories and theories of practical reasoning. Either variety would allow us to say that the wrongness of Albert's act is part of the explanation of Jane's belief that it is wrong.

According to impartial spectator theories, to say that an action is wrong is to say that it is the sort of action that impartial spectators would disapprove of under conditions that are further specified in various ways in different versions of this sort of theory. Jane believes Albert was wrong, because she finds herself disapproving of his conduct and believes this disapproval is based on a knowledge of the facts and is not the result of some special stake she has in the matter at hand. We can explain Jane's disapproval of Albert's conduct by treating it as an instance of a more general regularity. Jane disapproves of Albert's action because it is the sort of act that spectators tend to disapprove and Jane is the relevant sort of spectator. In other words, the act has certain properties which incline informed impartial spectators to disapprove of the act, and those properties incline Jane to disapprove of the act in much the way they incline other informed impartial spectators to do so. Since the action's wrongness consists in its being of a sort of which spectators in general disapprove, there is a sense in which Jane believes Albert's action is wrong because of the wrongness of that action.

What about Mary who does not feel disapproval of Albert? An impartial spectator theory can allow for at least two possibilities. One is that Mary does not satisfy all the conditions on impartial spectators. She may have a personal stake in the matter. Or she may not have considered vividly enough what it is like for animals to suffer. If so, her failure to disapprove of Albert's action can be accounted for by her failure to satisfy the relevant conditions.

The other possibility is that Mary does satisfy the relevant conditions and still does not feel disapproval of Albert. This means that impartial spectators will not always have the same reactions. If there are only a few areas in which this happens, an impartial spectator theory might rule that an act is wrong only if all impartial spectators would disapprove of it. If disagreement is more widespread, the theory might settle for relativism. A relativistic impartial spectator theory might hold that moral claims make sense only if relativized to a moral outlook. The claim that something is wrong relative to a given moral outlook would then be equated with the claim that any impartial spectator accepting that outlook would disapprove of the act. (A noncognitive aspect to such claims can be allowed for by supposing that such judgments normally presuppose acceptance by speaker and audience of the relevant moral outlook.)

The other main form of reductionism involves a theory of practical reasoning. In this view, for an act to be wrong is for the agent to have sufficient reasons not to do it, where this is equivalent to saying that, if the agent were to reason correctly, the agent would end up deciding not to do the act.

This view too can allow that Jane's belief about Albert is explained in part by the actual wrongness of Albert's action. The act is wrong because there were sufficient reasons for Albert not to do it. If Albert were to have reasoned correctly, he would have ended up deciding not to do it. If Jane was aware of the relevant reasoning and that is why she believes Albert's act was wrong, then her belief is explained in part by the wrongness of Albert's action.

Reductionism Defended

I do not mean to try to resolve this basic issue in ethics. My purpose is only to argue that it is a real issue, one that is not resolved by an appeal to the commonplace examples cited by Sturgeon. In the absence of a way of reducing moral claims to psychological or sociological claims, there is a real problem as to the testability of moral claims, because it is obscure how the rightness or wrongness of an action can manifest itself in the world in a way that can affect the sense organs of people. Apart from such a reduction, to develop a moral theory using the method of reflective equilibrium is to confuse moral psychology with the theory of right and wrong.

Sturgeon disagrees with this. He claims to be an ethical naturalist in the sense that he believes that all moral facts are to be identified with natural physical facts. But he argues "(a) that it is a mistake to require of ethical naturalism that it even promise reductive definitions for moral terms, and . . . (b) that even if such definitions are to be forthcoming it is, at the very least, no special problem for ethical naturalism that we are not *now* in possession of them."[15] He argues further that the best way to find a reduction is to do normative ethics. "If hedonistic act-utilitarianism (and enough of its associated psychology) turns out to be true, for example, then we can define the good as pleasure and the absence of pain, and a right action as one that produces at least as much good as any other, and that will be where the moral facts fit. If, more plausibly, some other moral theory turns out to be correct, we will get a different account and (if the theory takes the right form) different reductive definitions."[16]

But someone who accepts hedonistic utilitarianism cannot plausibly accept the reduction that Sturgeon suggests without further ado, because of something like the old open question argument. Opponents can agree that a certain course of action would maximize the balance of pleasure over pain in the world without agreeing that the given course of action ought to be taken. Something more has to be said in order to account for or explain away the apparent moral issue that remains.

Impartial spectator theories and theories of practical reasoning do better in this respect. It is much more plausible to suppose that moral disagreements are disagreements about what would be acceptable from a knowledgeable impartial point of view or about what practical reasons there are for someone to do something than it is to suppose that they are disagreements about what would maximize the balance of pleasure over pain. Of course, it could turn out that knowledgeable impartial spectators would always end up favoring whatever would maximize the balance of pleasure over pain. In that case, either reduction could be accepted, a reduction to the reactions of impartial spectators or the utilitarian reduction. But the utilitarian reduction would be acceptable only because it coincided with the impartial spectator reduction. That is what I mean when I say that the utilitarian reduction cannot be accepted "without further ado."

On the other hand, a utilitarian might discover that there is no plausible account of moral disagreement compatible with the utilitarian reduction. In that case, noncognitivism might be the best option.[17]

It is certainly not true, as Sturgeon says, that an ethical naturalist need not worry about having a reduction now. I am not sure the ethical naturalist needs to have reductive *definitions*, in Sturgeon's sense, because I am not sure what he means by "definition." But in order to show that moral claims are empirically testable in the relevant sense, the naturalist must say enough about the natural facts with which the moral facts are to be identified to indicate how the moral facts can be manifested in the world in a way that allows the relevant testing. Otherwise, the naturalist has no answer to what seems to me to be the central issue in moral philosophy.

More generally, the options seem to be these: (A) The option of "poisoning the well": deny that scientific claims can be tested in the relevant sense. (B) The math option: claim there is an analogy between ethics and mathematics, deny that mathematics can be tested in the relevant sense, and deny that this is a problem for mathematics. (C) Noncognitivism. (D) Naturalistic reductionism.

As I have said, I favor (D) with a touch of (C). But my aim in this paper has not been to argue for that. Rather, I have argued that there is a real issue here and one or another of these options has to be taken seriously.

NOTES

[1] The term comes from John Rawls. *A Theory of Justice* (Cambridge, Mass.; Harvard University Press: 1971). The method he describes is widely used.

[2] Gilbert Harman, *The Nature of Morality: An Introduction to Ethics* (New York, Oxford University Press: 1977).

67

3 Nicholas Sturgeon, "Moral Explanations," in David Copp and David Zimmerman, eds., *Morality, Reason, and Truth: New Essays on the Foundations of Ethics* (Totowa, New Jersey; Rowman and Allanheld: 1985), pp. 49-78.

4 This is W.V. Quine's notion of "observation sentence" in *Word and Object* (Cambridge, Massachusetts: M.I.T. Press: 1960).

5 This follows the structure of illustrations of the point in Sturgeon, *op. cit.*, pp. 51-52.

6 *Ibid.*, pp. 53, 66-67, objecting to an example I gave in Harman, *op. cit.* p. 4.

7 *Ibid.*, pp. 54, 65, 68.

8 *Ibid.*, p. 63, citing Bernard De Voto, *The Year of Decision: 1846* (Boston, Houghton-Mifflin: 1942), p. 442.

9 Sturgeon, *op. cit.*, p. 64.

10 *Ibid.*, p. 65.

11 In this case the relevant counterfactual works by "backtracking"—if the moral property of wrongness had not been present, then that would have been because Albert had done something else that was not wrong. Sturgeon observes that the counterfactual test is not appropriate where there is the possibility of backtracking and says that his examples are not of that sort. But it begs the question to suppose the examples do not involve backtracking.

12 Of course, the emotivist does have to offer an account of the occurrence of moral terms in the antecedents of counterfactuals and in other similarly embedded contexts. This requires taking moral terms to have something like "wide scope" (or perhaps to function in something like the way in which rigid designators function). For example, a statement containing the word "wrong" as follows, ". . . wrong . . ." (where this is not a context of direct or indirect quotation), might be roughly equated with the following, "Boo!!! to the possession of certain properties F, where it happens that . . . have F . . ." Sturgeon's counterfactual in the present case would then be equated with this: "Boo!!! to the possession of certain properties F, where it happens that Jane would not have believed Albert's act was wrong if Albert had not done something having F."

13 *Ibid.*, p. 69.

14 *Ibid.*, p. 70.

15 *Ibid.*, p. 59.

16 *Ibid.*, p. 61.

17 As in J. J. C. Smart's contribution to Smart and Bernard Williams, *Utilitarianism: For and Against* (Cambridge, Cambridge University Press: 1973) and R. M. Hare, *Moral Thinking: Its Levels, Method and Point* (Oxford, Oxford University Press: 1981).

68

[19]

MIDWEST STUDIES IN PHILOSOPHY, XII

Moral Theory and Explanatory Impotence

GEOFFREY SAYRE-McCORD

1. INTRODUCTION

Among the most enduring and compelling worries about moral theory is that it is disastrously isolated from confirmation. The exact nature of this isolation has been subject to two interpretations. According to one, moral theory is totally insulated from observational consequences and is, therefore, in principle untestable. According to the other, moral theory enjoys the privilege of testability but suffers the embarrassment of failing all the tests. According to both, moral theory is in serious trouble.

After briefly defending moral theory against the charge of in-principle untestability, I defend it against the charge of contingent but unmitigated failure. The worries about untestability are, I suggest, easily met. Yet the very ease with which they are met belies the significance of meeting them; all manner of unacceptable theories are testable. The interesting question is not whether moral theory is testable, but whether moral theory *passes* the relevant tests. Recently, it has become popular to hold that a moral theory passes only if it is explanatorily potent; that is, only if it contributes to our best explanations of our experiences. The problem with moral theory is that it apparently contributes not at all to such explanations.[1] Working out a plausible version of the demand for explanatory potency is surprisingly hard. Even so, once a plausible version is found, I argue, (some) moral theories will in fact satisfy it. Unfortunately, this too is less significant than it might seem, for any argument establishing the *explanatory* potency of moral theory still falls short of establishing its *justificatory* force. (My arguments are no exception.) And, as I will try to make clear, the pressing worries concerning moral theory center on its claim to justificatory force; its explanatory force is largely beside the point. So much the worse for moral theory, one might be inclined to say. If moral theory goes beyond explanation, it goes where the epistemically cautious should fear to tread. Those who demand explanatory potency, however, cannot afford the luxury of dismissing justificatory theory. Indeed, the demand for explanatory potency itself presupposes the legitimacy of justificatory theory, and this presupposition can be turned to the defense of moral theory's justificatory force. Or so I shall argue.

2. OBSERVATIONAL INSULATION

Keeping in mind that observation is theory-laden, one way to put the charge of untestability is to say that moral theory appears not to be appropriately observation-laden; unlike scientific theories, moral theories seem forever insulated from observational implications.

This objection to moral theory emerges naturally from a variation on the empiricist verification principle. Of course, as a criterion of meaning, the verification principle has for good reason been all but abandoned. Still, taken as a criterion of justifiability, rather than as a criterion of meaning, the principle seems to impose a reasonable requirement: If there is no way to verify observationally the claims of a proposed theory, then there is no way to justify the theory (unless all its claims are analytic).[2] Even if moral claims are meaningful, then, they might nonetheless be impossible to justify.

In favor of thinking moral theory untestable is the apparently unbridgeable chasm dividing what is from what ought to be.[3] After all, claims concerning moral obligations cannot be deduced from nonmoral claims ('ought', it is often said, cannot be derived from 'is'), which suggests (to some) that 'ought-claims' are not 'is-claims'. Since observation is always of what is, we may have reason to suspect that observation is irrelevant to what ought to be.

This argument for the is/ought distinction is too strong, though. It mistakenly assumes that definitional reducibility is a prerequisite for putting what ought to be on an ontologically equivalent footing with what is. No matter what we know about the nonmoral facts of the case, the argument emphasizes, we cannot uncontroversially infer the moral facts. Moral assertions are not definitionally reducible to nonmoral assertions. Since nonmoral assertions report what is, and since moral claims are not reducible to these others, then moral claims must not report what is. So the argument goes.

Remarkably, by similar lines of reasoning we would be constrained to admit that the claims made in psychology are not claims about facts; for psychology, no less than morality, resists definitional reduction. No matter what we know of the nonpsychological facts of the case, we cannot uncontroversially infer the psychological facts. Psychological assertions are not definitionally reducible to nonpsychological assertions. Since nonpsychological assertions report what is, and since psychological claims are not definitionally reducible to these others, then (the argument would have it) psychological claims must not report what is. Consequently, if the argument offered in support of the is/ought distinction worked, we would find our-

MORAL THEORY AND EXPLANATORY IMPOTENCE   435

selves stuck with an *is/thought* distinction as well. Psychology, we would have to say, reports not what is but merely what is thought—which is silly.[4]

Yet even if we put aside the is/ought distinction, the claim that moral theory is not properly observation-laden still extracts admirable support from common sense. For if people, or actions, or states of affairs have a worth, or a dignity, or a rightness about them, this is something we seemingly cannot sense directly. And most moral theories recognize this by construing moral properties as not directly observable. This cannot pose a special problem for moral theory's testability, however, since in *this* respect, moral theory is no different from those (obviously testable) scientific theories that postulate unobservable entities.

Moreover, on at least one standard construal of what counts as an observation, some moral claims will actually count as observation reports. Specifically, if one takes an observation to be any belief reached noninferentially as a direct result of perceptual experience, there is no reason to deny that there are moral observations. After all, just as we learn to report noninferentially the presence of chairs in response to sensory stimulation, we also learn to report noninferentially the presence of moral properties in response to sensory stimulation.

On this liberal view of observation, what counts as an observation depends solely on what opinions a person is trained to form immediately in response to sensory stimulation, and not on the content of the opinions.[5] Since such opinions are often heavily theory-laden and are often about the external world rather than about our experiences, the account avoids tying the notion of observation to the impossible ideal of theory neutrality or to the solipsistic reporting of the contents of sensory experience.

Of course, we may be too liberal here in allowing *any* opinion to count as an observation simply because it is reached directly as a result of perception. Surely, one is tempted to argue, we cannot observe what is not there, so that some opinions—no matter that they are directly reached as a result of perception—may fail to be observations because they report what does not exist. As a direct result of perception, I may believe I felt a friend's touch; but in the absence of her touch, my report seems most properly treated as an illusion, not an observation. Taking this into account, it is tempting to distinguish what are merely perceptually stimulated judgments from actual observations, thus reserving 'observation' for those perceptually stimulated judgments that are accurate.

If there were some observation-independent way to determine which judgments are accurate, we might legitimately dismiss a given class of purported observations (say, moral observations) on the grounds that they fail to report the facts accurately. Yet once the prospect of divining some set of basic (and indubitable) empirical statements is abandoned, so too must be the hope of establishing what things exist without appeal (at least indirectly) to observations. If some observations are needed to support the theories we then use to discredit other observations, we need some account of observation that allows us to isolate observations as such without assuming their accuracy has already been shown. Observations (in some onto-

436   GEOFFREY SAYRE-McCORD

logically noncommittal sense) will be needed to legitimize the theories we use to separate veridical from nonveridical observations. It is this ontologically noncommittal
sense of 'observation' that may be characterized simply as any opinion reached as
a direct result of perception; and it is in this sense of 'observation' that we must allow
that there are moral observations. Once moral observations are allowed, the admission that moral theories can be tested against these moral observations will quickly
follow. Just as we test our physical principles against observation, adjusting one or
the other in search of a proper fit, so we can test our moral principles against (moral)
observation, adjusting one or the other in search of a proper fit. (Many have exploited the availability of this sort of observational testing and—unsatisfyingly—
treated it as the sole criterion we have for the acceptability of theories.[6])

So neither the is/ought distinction nor the unobservability of moral properties
seems to support the charge of untestability. In fact, there is reason to think moral
theory passes the testability requirement in the same way any respectable scientific
theory does—even if moral properties count as unobservable. Of course, how scientific theories manage to pass the testability requirement is a notoriously complicated
matter. As Duhem and Quine have emphasized, scientific theories do not pass the
testability requirement by having each of their principles pass independently; many
of the theoretical principles of science have no observational implications when considered in isolation. Observationally testable predictions may be derived from these
scientific principles only when they are combined with appropriate background assumptions.[7]

In the same way, certain moral principles may not be testable in isolation.
Nevertheless, when such principles are combined with appropriate background assumptions, they too will allow the derivation of observationally testable predictions.
To test the view that an action is wrong if and only if there is some alternative action
available that will bring about more happiness, we might combine it with the (plausible) assumption that punishing the innocent is wrong. From these two principles
taken together, we get the testable prediction that there will never be a time when
punishing the innocent brings more happiness than any other action that is available.
Alternatively, consider Plato's contention that 'virtue pays'. If combined with some
account of what virtue is and with the (non-Platonic) view that 'payment' is a matter
of satisfying preferences, we get as a testable consequence the prediction that those
who are virtuous (in whatever sense we settle on) will have more of their preferences
satisfied than if they had not been virtuous. Or again, if a moral theory holds that
a just state does not allow capital punishment, and if we assume some particular state
is just, we get as a testable consequence the claim that this country does not allow
capital punishment.

In each case our moral principles have observationally testable consequences
when combined with appropriate background assumptions. Experience may show
that punishing the innocent does sometimes increase happiness, or that misery often
accompanies virtue, or that the state in question does allow capital punishment.
Upon making such discoveries we must abandon (or amend) our moral principles,

or our background assumptions, or the confidence we place in our discoveries. Something has to give way.[8] Of course, we can often make adjustments in our overall theory in order to save particular moral principles, just as we can adjust scientific theories in order to salvage particular scientific principles. In science and ethics, background assumptions serve as protective buffers between particular principles and observation. Yet those same assumptions also provide the crucial link that allows both moral and scientific theories to pass any reasonable testability requirement. If the testability requirement ruled out relying on background assumptions, it would condemn science as untestable. If it allows such assumptions, and so makes room for the testability of science, it will likewise certify moral theory as testable. Once — but only once — background hypotheses are allowed, both scientific and moral principles will prove testable. Hence, if moral theories are unjustified, it must be for reasons other than that moral theories have no testable consequences.[9]

3. EXPLANATORY IMPOTENCE

Disturbingly, just as moral theory survives any reasonable standard for testability, so too do phlogiston theory, astrology, and even occult theories positing the existence of witches. Like moral theories, each of these theories (when combined with appropriate background assumptions) generates testable consequences, and each makes cognitively packed claims about the world. Still, given what we now know about the world, none of these theories has a claim on our allegiance. Although testable, they fail the test.

Quite reasonably, then, we might wonder whether moral theories likewise fail the empirical tests to which they may admittedly be subjected. Perhaps we ought to think of moral theories as failed theories — as theories betrayed by experience. Perhaps we ought to give up thinking there are moral facts for a moral theory to be about, just as we have abandoned thinking there is such a thing as phlogiston, just as we have abandoned the belief that the heavens control our destiny, and just as we have abandoned the idea that bound women who float are witches.

In our search for an understanding of the world, each of these theories seems to have been left in the dust; every phenomenon we might wish to explain by appeal to these theories can be explained better if they are put aside. Like phlogiston theory, astrology, and theories positing witches, moral theories appear explanatorily impotent.

The problem is that we need suppose neither that our particular moral judgments are accurate nor that our moral principles are true in order to explain why we make the judgments or accept the principles that we do. It seems we make the moral judgments we do because of the theories we happen to embrace, because of the society we live in, because of our individual temperaments, because of our feelings for others, but not because we have some special ability to detect moral facts, not because our moral judgments are accurate, and not because the moral theories we embrace are true. Given our training, temperament, and environment, we would make the moral judgments we do and advance the moral theories we do, regardless of the moral facts (and regardless of whether there are any).

To clarify the challenge facing moral theory, consider two situations (I take these from Gilbert Harman, who has done the most to advance the charge of explanatory impotence.[10]) In one, a person goes around a corner, sees a gang of hoodlums setting a live cat on fire, and exclaims, "There's a bad action!" In the other, a person peers into a cloud chamber, sees a trail, and exclaims, "There's a proton!" In both cases, part of the explanation of why the report was made will appeal to the movements of physical objects, and the effects these movements have initially on light and eventually on the observers' retinas. A more complete explanation would also have to make reference to the observers' psychological states as well as the background theories each accepted. Certainly the scientist would not make the report she did if she were asleep, nor even if awake and attentive, if she did not accept a theory according to which vapor trails in cloud chambers evidence the presence of protons. Had she thought witches left such trails, she might have reported a witch in the chamber instead of a proton. Similarly, the moral judge would not have made the report he did if he were asleep, nor even if awake and attentive, if he did not accept a view according to which burning live animals is wrong.[11] Had he thought cats the embodiments of evil, he might have reported the action as right instead of wrong.

Whatever explanations we give of the reports, one thing is striking: protons will form part of our best explanation of why the proton report was made; in contrast, moral properties seem not to form part of our best explanation of why the moral report was made. We will often explain the scientist's belief that a proton was present by appeal to the fact that one was. But, the argument goes, we will not explain the moral judge's belief that burning the cat is wrong by appeal to the wrongness of the act.

Harman elaborates on the problem with ethics by noting that

> facts about protons can affect what you observe, since a proton passing through a cloud chamber can cause a vapor trail that reflects light to your eye in a way that, given your scientific training and psychological set, leads you to judge that what you see is a proton. But there does not seem to be any way in which the actual rightness or wrongness of a given situation can have any effect on your perceptual apparatus.[12]

This emphasis on affecting (or failing to affect) an observer's perceptual apparatus suggests (mistakenly, I will argue) that the following *Causal Criterion* underlies the explanatory impotence attack on moral theory:

> The only entities and properties we are justified in believing in are those which we are justified in believing have a causal impact on our perceptual apparatus.

Unless moral properties are causally efficacious, and so figure as causes in the explanation of our making the observations that we do, moral theory will fail to meet this criterion's test.

Even though the argument from explanatory impotence turns on a different

MORAL THEORY AND EXPLANATORY IMPOTENCE   **439**

(and more plausible) principle, the Causal Criterion deserves attention because of its intimate ties to the causal theories of knowledge and reference.

4. THE CAUSAL CRITERION, KNOWLEDGE, AND REFERENCE

Any reasonable view of moral theory, and of the language(s) we use to formulate the theory, must (if moral theory is legitimate) be compatible with some account of how we come to *know* about moral properties and how the terms of the language come to *refer* to these properties. Assuming that the causal theories of knowledge and reference are substantially correct, the Causal Criterion is attractive simply because we could neither know about, nor even refer to, any class of properties that failed the Causal Criterion's test.[13] Thus, by requiring that we believe in only those entities and properties with which we believe we can causally interact, the Causal Criterion encapsulates the demands of the causal theories of knowledge and reference.

According to the causal theory of knowledge, we can get evidence only about that to which we bear some appropriate causal connection.[14] All our knowledge arises from the causal interaction of the objects of this knowledge with our bodies; anything outside all causal chains will be epistemically inaccessible.[15] So, if moral properties are causally isolated—if they fail to meet the Causal Criterion—they will be unknowable. More important, if moral properties make absolutely no difference to what we experience, we can never even form reasonable beliefs about what they are like.

The causal theory of reference makes moral theory look all the more hopeless because it suggests that we cannot even successfully refer to, let alone know about, moral properties (if they fail the Causal Criterion). As the causal theory of reference would have it, words in our language refer thanks to their standing at the end of a causal chain linking the speaker's use of the word to the thing to which the word refers. No appropriate chain can be established between speakers of a language (in this case a language containing moral terms) and causally isolated properties. Such properties will lie outside all causal chains, and so outside these causal chains which establish reference.[16]

Moral theory's trouble seems to be that the properties it ascribes to actions, people, and states of affairs, reflect no light, have no texture, give off no odor, have no taste, and make no sound. In fact, they do not causally affect our experience in any way. Were they absent, our experiences would be unchanged. Since we cannot interact with moral properties, there is no way for us to establish a causal chain between ourselves, our use of moral language, and moral properties. Consequently, our moral terms fail to refer.

So put, this criticism of moral theory is much too quick. Even the causal theory of reference allows success in establishing a referential tie between word and world by description as well as by ostension.[17] It is true that ostension works in establishing reference only if the properties (or entities) referred to are causally present (since we can succeed in our ostensions only by locating something in space and time).[18] However, we may still use descriptions to establish a referential link even to that from which we are causally isolated—as long as the appropriate terms of the description succeed in referring. If moral properties fail the Causal Criterion, we will not be able to refer to them by ostension; but we will nonetheless be able to refer to them as long as we can describe the moral properties in nonmoral terms. (Of course, if the description's terms were moral, they would be no help in grounding the requisite referential link.[19]) As a result, the causal theory of reference will serve to undermine ethics only if we cannot refer to moral properties by using nonmoral descriptions, and then only if moral properties are in fact causally isolated.[20] Any argument against moral facts using the causal theory of reference, then, must rely on some independent argument that shows that moral facts (if such there be) are both indescribable in nonmoral terms and causally isolated.

Plainly, our ability to refer to moral properties will be small consolation unless we can also secure evidence about the properties to which we refer. Successful reference may prove epistemically useless. So, even if we can succeed in referring to moral properties, the problems raised by the causal theory of knowledge remain.

Not surprisingly, these problems too are less straightforward than suggested so far. To tell against moral theory, the causal theory of knowledge (like the causal theory of reference) must be supplemented by an argument showing that moral properties are causally isolated (or that they do not exist).

Against theories concerned with abstract entities (like mathematics and Plato's Theory of Forms), the Causal Criterion, and the causal theories of knowledge and reference, apparently meet no resistance. The theories under attack grant right off that the entities in question are causally isolated (because outside space and time). That abstract entities fail the Causal Criterion appears to be a forgone conclusion.[21]

Against moral theories, in contrast, the charge of causal isolation meets with resistance. Unlike abstract entities, moral properties are traditionally thought of as firmly ensconced in the causal nexus: a bad character has notorious effects (at least when backed by power), and fair social institutions evidently affect the happiness of those in society. The ontology of moral theory will not be an unwitting accomplice in the causalist critique of ethics. Of course, moral theory's resistance does not establish that moral properties actually do satisfy the Causal Criterion (and so the causal theories of knowledge and reference); rather, the resistance imposes a barrier over which the causal critique of moral theory must climb. Some argument must be given for thinking moral properties fail to meet the Causal Criterion.

5. THE EXPLANATORY CRITERION

Regardless of whether moral properties satisfy the Causal Criterion, there are good reasons for thinking the criterion itself too strong. To hold tight to the Causal Criterion (and the causal theories of knowledge and reference that support it) is to

MORAL THEORY AND EXPLANATORY IMPOTENCE   441

let go of some of our most impressive epistemological accomplishments; the claims of mathematics, as well as both the empirical generalizations and the laws of the physical sciences, all fail the criterion's test.

We never causally interact with numbers, for instance.[22] So, if causal contact were really a prerequisite to knowledge (and reference), mathematical knowledge and discourse would be an impossibility. For similar reasons, empirical generalizations (like "all emeralds are green"), as well as natural laws (like the first law of thermodynamics), would fall victim to the Causal Criterion. Although these generalizations and laws may help *explain* why we experience what we do as we do, they *cause* none of our experiences. That all emeralds are green does not cause a particular emerald to be green, nor does it cause us to see emeralds as green.[23] These casualties of the Causal Criterion make it clear that we need to replace the Causal Criterion even if we wish to salvage its emphasis on the link between knowledge (or at least justified belief) and experience.[24]

In forging a new criterion, we should concentrate on the reasons that might be given for thinking it reasonable to believe (as I assume it is) in the truth of many mathematical claims, empirical generalizations, and laws of physics. According to one standard line in the philosophy of science (one embraced by Harman, J. L. Mackie, Simon Blackburn, and many other critics of moral theory), the key to the legitimacy of these scientific and mathematical claims is the role they play in the explanations of our experiences. "An observation," Harman argues, "is evidence for what best *explains* it, and since mathematics often figures in the explanations of scientific observations, there is indirect observational evidence for mathematics."[25] Empirical generalizations and physical laws will likewise find their justification by appeal to their role in the best explanations of our experience—"scientific principles can be justified ultimately by their role in explaining observations."[26] The legitimacy of a theory seems to ride on its explanatory role, and not on the causal impact of its ontology. From these points we can extract the *Explanatory Criterion* according to which

> the only hypotheses we are justified in believing are those that figure in the best explanations we have of our making the observations that we do.

Significantly, the Explanatory Criterion retains, even reinforces, the empiricist's demand that epistemology be tied to experience; not only does justification turn on experiential testability, it now requires an *explanatory* link between the truth of our beliefs and our experiences as well. Accordingly, an acceptable theory must do more than have observational consequences; it must also contribute to our explanations of why we make the observations we do.

Two versions of the Explanatory Criterion should be distinguished; the first sets necessary and sufficient conditions for reasonable belief; the second sets only necessary conditions. In its stronger version, the criterion would say:

> A hypothesis should be believed *if and only if* the hypothesis plays a role in the best explanation we have of our making the observations that we do.

In its weaker version the criterion would say instead:

> A hypothesis should be believed *only if* the hypothesis plays a role in the best explanation we have of our making the observations that we do.

Or, in its contrapositive (and more intuitively attractive) form:

> A hypothesis should not be believed if the hypothesis plays no role in the best explanation we have of our making the observations that we do.

Accepting the stronger version of the criterion involves endorsing what has come to be called 'inference to the best explanation'. In this guise, the criterion licenses inferring the truth of a hypothesis from its playing a role in our best explanations of our experiences. To be even remotely plausible, of course, some bottom limit must be set on the quality of the explanations that would be allowed to countenance inferences to the truth of the hypotheses invoked. Despite their being the best we have, our explanations can be so bad that we may be quite sure they are wrong. It would be a mistake to infer the truth of a hypothesis from its being part of our best— but obviously flawed—explanation. Even with a quality constraint, the strong version of the Explanatory Criterion is hopelessly liberal because we have such good grounds for thinking that the best explanations we can come up with, at any given time, are not right.[27] In light of these difficulties, I shall concentrate on the weaker version of the criterion. The weaker version raises all the same difficulties for moral theory without endorsing inferences to the best explanation.

The problem with moral theory is that moral principles and moral properties appear not to play a role in explaining our making the observations we do. All the explanatory work seems to be done by psychology, physiology, and physics.[28] A scientist's observing a proton in a cloud chamber is evidence for her theory because the theory explains the proton's presence and the scientist's observation better than competing theories can. The observation of a proton provides observational evidence for a theory because the truth of that observation is part of the best explanation we have of why the observation was made. A moral 'observation' does not appear to be, in the same sense, observational evidence for or against any moral theory, since (as Harman puts it) the truth or falsity of the "moral observation seems to be completely irrelevant to any reasonable explanation of why that observation was made."[29]

Underlying the Explanatory Criterion is the conviction that confirmation mirrors explanation: theories are confirmed by what they explain. Added to this view of confirmation is the stipulation, motivated by an empiricist epistemology, that we should assume to exist only what we need to explain *our experiences*.

Put generally, some fact confirms whatever principles and hypotheses are part of the best explanation of the fact. So, the fact that some observation was made will

MORAL THEORY AND EXPLANATORY IMPOTENCE 443

confirm whatever is part of the best explanation of its having been made. But the making of the observation will not provide *observational* evidence for a theory unless the observation itself is accurate. And we will have grounds for thinking an observation accurate, on this view, only when its being accurate forms a part of our best explanation of the observation having been made. Thus, embedded within this overarching view of confirmation is a more specific account of observational confirmation. An observation will provide confirming observational evidence for a theory, according to this account, only to the extent that it is reasonable to explain the making of the observation by invoking the theory while also treating the observation as true.[30]

For this reason, moral facts, and moral theory, will be vindicated (in the eyes of the Explanatory Criterion) only if they figure in our best explanations of at least some of the accurate observations we make. Unfortunately, as Harman argues, "you need to make assumptions about certain physical facts to explain the occurrence of observations that support a scientific theory, but you do not seem to need to make assumptions about any moral facts to explain the occurrence of the so-called moral observations."[31] Of course, moral facts would be acceptable, according to the Explanatory Criterion, as long as they were needed to explain the making of some observation or other (regardless of whether it is a moral observation). Just as mathematics is justified by its role in explaining physical (and not mathematical) observations, moral theory might similarly be justified by its role in explaining some nonmoral observations. But the problem with moral theory is that moral facts seem not to help explain the making of *any of our observations*.

Importantly, the problem is not that moral facts explain nothing at all (they may explain other moral facts); the problem is that regardless of whether they explain something, they do not hook up properly with our abilities to detect facts. Even if there are moral facts, and even if some of these facts would help to explain others, none will be epistemically accessible unless some help to explain our making some of the observations we do. No matter how perfect the fit between the content of our moral judgments and a moral theory, no matter how stable and satisfying a reflective equilibrium can be established between them, the theory will not gain observational confirmation unless it enters into the best explanation of why some of our observations are made. We will be justified in accepting a moral theory on the basis of our observations only if we have reason to believe our observations are responsive to the moral facts. And we will have reason to believe this only if moral facts enter into the best explanations of why we make the observations we do. To be legitimized, then, moral facts must explain certain nonmoral facts; specifically, moral facts must explain our making observations.[32]

In order to highlight the problem faced by moral theory, it is a good idea to go back to the (dis)analogy between the scientist's making the observation "there's a proton" and the moral judge's making the observation "there's a bad action." Our best explanation of why the scientist made the observation she did will make reference to her psychology, her scientific theory, the fact that vapor trail appeared in the cloud chamber, and *the fact that a proton left the trail*. Our best explanation of why the moral judge made the observation he did will likewise make reference to his psychology, his moral theory, the fact that a cat was set on fire, and even (when the explanation is more fully elaborated) to the fact that the cat and the kids were composed of protons. Yet our explanation will not make reference to the (purported) fact that burning the cat was wrong: "It seems to be completely irrelevant to our explanation whether [the judge's moral] judgment is true or false."[33] That burning the cat was wrong, if it was wrong, appears completely irrelevant to our explanation of the judge thinking it wrong.[34]

6. EXPLANATORY RELEVANCE AND EXPLANATORY POTENCY

The explanatory critique of moral theory seems to rest on the claim that moral facts are *irrelevant* to explanations of our observations. So, to flesh out the problem, we need some test for explanatory irrelevance. Nicholas Sturgeon proposes the following:

> If a particular assumption is completely irrelevant to the explanation of a certain fact, then the fact would have obtained, and we could have explained it just as well, even if the assumption had been false.[35]

With this in mind, Sturgeon argues that, for those who are not already moral skeptics, moral facts will prove to be explanatorily relevant.

Sturgeon's argument runs as follows. To decide whether the truth of some moral belief is explanatorily relevant to the making of an observation, we must consider a situation in which the belief is false, but which is otherwise as much like the actual situation as possible. Then we must determine whether the observation would still have been made under the new conditions. If so, if the observation would have been made in any case, then the truth of the moral belief is explanatorily irrelevant (the observation would have been made even if it had been false); otherwise its truth is relevant. If a supervenience account of moral properties is right (so that what makes a moral judgment true or false is some combination of physical facts), then for some true judgment to have been false, or some false judgment true, the situation would have had to have been different in some physical respect.[36] Consider the hoodlums' cat-burning. According to Sturgeon,

> If what they are actually doing is wrong, and if moral properties are, as many writers have held, supervenient on natural ones, then in order to imagine them not doing something wrong we are going to have to suppose their action different from the actual one in some of its natural features as well.[37]

Whether we would still judge the action wrong given these changes is a contingent matter that turns on how closely tied our moral judgments are to the morally relevant physical features of the situation. In the case of a curmudgeon, who thinks badly of

MORAL THEORY AND EXPLANATORY IMPOTENCE 445

kids as a matter of principle (averring that "kids are always up to no good"), changing the moral (and so the nonmoral) features of the situation will probably not change his moral judgment. For him, the truth of the judgment is irrelevant to the explanation of his making it. Fortunately, though, many people do not share this bias and are therefore more attuned to the evidence. Such people would have different opinions had the hoodlums found their entertainment in more acceptable ways (say, by petting rather than incinerating the cat). For those to whom the difference would make a difference, part of the explanation of their judgment would be that burning the cat is wrong.[38]

Notice that the same contingency attaches to the scientist's sighting of a proton. Had the proton not been there, whether the scientist would have thought it was depends on how closely tied her scientific judgments are to the relevant features of the situation. If she is a poor researcher, she might well have reported the proton's presence had there really been only a passing reflection. Again fortunately, many scientists are well attuned to the difference between proton trails and passing reflections. At least these scientists would have made different reports concerning the presence of a proton had the proton been absent. For those to whom the difference would make a difference, part of the explanation of their judgment will be that a proton passed.[39]

Sturgeon holds that what separates his own position from Harman's is a differential willingness to rely on a background moral theory in evaluating the question: Would the moral observation have been made even if the observation had been false? Sturgeon assumes the observation to be true (relying as he does on his background moral theory), and believes that for it to be false, some nonmoral features of the situation must be assumed different (because the moral properties supervene upon natural properties). When these nonmoral features are changed, he points out, the moral judgments (along with the explanations of why they were made) will often change as well. Harman, though, does without the background moral theory, so he has no reason to think that if the observation were false, anything else about the situation (including the observer's beliefs) would have been different. Consequently, he holds that the observation would have been made regardless of its truth.

As a result, Sturgeon concludes that Harman's argument is not an independent defense of skepticism concerning moral facts, for its conclusion apparently rests on the assumption that our moral judgments are false (or, more accurately, on the assumption that moral theory cannot be relied on in estimating how the world would have been if it had been morally different).[40]

Unfortunately for moral theory, Sturgeon's argument fails to meet the real challenge. The force of the explanatory attack on moral theory may be reinstated by shifting attention from explanatory *irrelevance* to explanatory *impotence*, where

a particular assumption is explanatorily impotent with respect to a certain fact, if the fact would have obtained and we could have explained it just as well, *even if the assumption had not been invoked in the explanation* (as opposed to: 'even if the assumption had been false').

By charging explanatory impotence, rather than explanatory irrelevance, the explanatory challenge to moral theory survives the admission that we hold our moral theories dear. It also survives the supervenience account's provision of a necessary link between moral and nonmoral properties. For the question becomes: Do we honestly think appealing to moral facts in our explanations of moral judgments strengthens our explanations one bit? Behind this question is the worry that we have been profligate with our theory building (or, perhaps, that we've been unnecessarily and unwholesomely nostalgic about old, and now outdated, theories). The concern is that acknowledging moral facts adds nothing to our ability to explain our experiences. Everything we might reasonably want to explain can, it seems, be explained equally well without appeal to moral facts.[41]

If these worries are well-founded, if moral facts are explanatory 'fifth wheels', and if we accept the Explanatory Criterion for justified belief, then moral facts will become merely unjustified theoretical baggage weighing down our ontology without offering compensation. In the face of this threat, pointing out that we happen to rely on moral facts in explaining people's behavior is not sufficient to justify believing in (even supervenient) moral facts; actual reliance does not establish justified belief.

To see the force of the explanatory challenge, imagine that a belief in witches becomes popular among your friends. Imagine, too, that your friends teach each other, and you, how to give 'witch explanations'. You 'learn' that the reason some bound women float when tossed into ponds, and others do not, is that the floaters are witches, the others not; that the mysterious deaths of newborns should be attributed to the jealous intervention of witches; and so on. No doubt, with enough practice you could become skillful at generating your own witch explanations; so skillful, perhaps, that in your unreflective moments you would find yourself offering such explanations. In order to assuage your philosophical conscience, you might entertain a sort of supervenience account of being a witch. Then you might comfortably maintain that being a witch is explanatorily relevant (in Sturgeon's sense) to your observations. All this might come to pass, and still you would be justified in thinking there are not really any witches—as long as you could explain the floatings, the deaths, and whatever else, just as well without appealing to the existence of witches. Presumably, the availability of such alternative explanations is just the reason we should not now believe in witches.

Certainly, things could turn out otherwise; we might find that witch explanations are actually the best available. We might discover that postulating witches is the only reasonable way to account for all sorts of otherwise inexplicable phenomena. Should that happen, our conversion to a belief in witches would, of course, be quite justified.

The question is, to which witch scenario are our moral explanations more analogous? Are our appeals to moral properties just intellectually sloppy concessions to effective socialization, or do we really strengthen our explanatory abilities by supposing that there are moral properties? This is a substantial challenge, and one not adequately answered by the observation that we often rely on moral properties to explain behavior.

Two points about the explanatory challenge deserve emphasis. First, the challenge recognizes conditions under which a belief in moral facts, or witches, would be legitimate. Specifically, the Explanatory Criterion would take these beliefs to be justified if their truth figured in the best explanation of why we have the experiences we do. Second, the challenge will not be met simply by pointing out that witches, or moral facts, do figure in some of our best explanations of the world. For unless these explanations of the world can be properly linked to *our experiences* of the world, there will be no way for us to justify accepting some of the explanations rather than others. The truth of one or another will make no difference to our experience, and so will be epistemically inaccessible.

7. SUPERVENIENCE AND LENIENCE

The problem with concentrating on explanatory relevance, rather than on explanatory potency, is that it makes a defense of moral properties (and belief in witches) too easy. It permits as justified the introduction of any properties whatsoever, so long as they are construed as supervenient upon admittedly explanatory properties.

The Explanatory Criterion, when interpreted as demanding explanatory potency (rather than mere relevance), promises a stricter standard, which might separate those properties we are justified in believing instantiated from mere pretenders. Yet the criterion must be interpreted in a way that acknowledges as justified belief in two kinds of properties: those which can be reductively identified with explanatorily potent properties and those we have independent reason to think supervene upon, without being strictly reducible to, explanatorily potent properties. These properties demand special attention because, at least initially, they appear explanatorily expendable — despite our belief in them being justified.

For instance, though all the explanatory work of water may be better accomplished by H_2O; all the explanatory work of color, by the wave lengths of light; and all that of psychological states, by neurophysiological states of the brain; we are nonetheless justified in believing that the oceans are filled with water, that roses are red, and that people feel pain and have beliefs. Any criterion of justified belief that would rule these beliefs out as unjustified is simply too stringent. The difficulty (for those attacking moral theory) is to accommodate these legitimate beliefs without so weakening the Explanatory Criterion as to reintroduce excessive leniency.

Of course, some beliefs may plausibly find justification by relying on reductions: because water is H_2O, the justification of our belief in H_2O (by appeal to its explanatory potency) serves equally well as a justification of our belief in water. In cases where identification reductions are available, explanatory potency might well be transitive.[42]

Where identification reductions are not available, however, things become trickier; and it is here that the Explanatory Criterion runs into problems. It seems

448   GEOFFREY SAYRE-McCORD

straightforwardly true that roses are red, for example, but our best explanations of red-rose-reports might well make reference to certain characteristics of roses, facts about light, and facts about the psychological and perceptual apparatus of perceivers—but not to the *redness* of the roses (and not to any particular feature of the roses that can be reductively identified with redness). Despite this, the availability of such explanations expands our understanding of colors; it does not show there are no colors. Similar points hold not just for those properties traditionally characterized as secondary qualities, but for *all* nonreducible properties.[43]

Recognizing this, Harman attempts to make room for nonreducible properties. In discussing colors, he maintains that they satisfy the demand for explanatory potency because

> we will sometimes refer to the actual colors of objects in explaining color perceptions if only for the sake of simplicity. . . . We will continue to believe that objects have colors because we will continue to refer to the actual colors of objects in the explanations that we will in practice give.[44]

Thus, pragmatic tenacity is supposed by Harman to be enough to establish explanatory potency; now the criterion will allow, as explanatorily potent, those properties and entities to which we appeal in our best explanations, plus those that are precisely reducible to properties or entities appealed to in our best explanations, plus those that are pragmatically tenacious.

Relying on such a lenient interpretation of the Explanatory Criterion, Harman is able to treat moral facts as threatened only by resorting to what is patently false: he is forced to argue that moral facts are not "useful even in practice in our explanations of observations."[45] If nothing else, however, moral facts are useful, at least in practice, when explaining our observations. Many very useful, and frequently offered, explanations of events in the world (and so our observations of those events) make reference to moral facts. Mother Teresa's goodness won her a Nobel Prize; Solidarity's popularity is caused by Poland's oppressive political institutions; millions died in Russia as a result of Stalin's inhumanity; people are starving unnecessarily because of the selfishness of others; unrest in Soweto is a response to the injustice of Apartheid. Even if such explanations could eventually be replaced by others that appeal only to psychological, social, and physical factors, without mention of moral facts, the moral explanations would still be useful in just the way talk of colors remains useful even in light of theories of light. If mere pragmatic tenacity is enough to legitimize color properties, it ought to be enough to legitimize moral properties.

If the Explanatory Criterion is to challenge the legitimacy of moral theory, it must require more than pragmatic tenacity for justification. Yet, almost certainly, any stronger requirement that remains plausible will countenance moral properties. For the Explanatory Criterion will be plausible only if it allows belief in those properties needed both to identify and to explain the natural regularities that are otherwise explicable only in a piecemeal fashion as singular events (and not as instances of regularities). Consider Hilary Putnam's example of the peg (square in cross-section)

MORAL THEORY AND EXPLANATORY IMPOTENCE   **449**

that will pass through the square hole in a board, but not through the round hole.[46] To explain a single instance of the peg's going through one hole, we might offer a microstructural description of the peg and the board in terms of the distribution of atoms, and then appeal to particle mechanics. But even if we could eventually work out such an explanation, it would suffer from a serious drawback; it would only explain why the particular peg went through a particular hole at a particular time. The explanation will be of no help when we are faced with another board and peg, or even with the same board and peg a moment later (when the distribution of atoms has changed). The explanation will not extend to new cases. And the properties appealed to in giving an explanation at the level of ultimate constituents will be useless in trying to identify and explain the general fact that pegs of a certain size and shape (whether made of wood, or plastic, or steel) will fail to go through holes of a certain size and shape (whether the holes are in a piece of wood, or plastic, or steel). This general fact will be identifiable and explicable only if we appeal to certain macrostructural features of pegs and holes.

In the same way, certain regularities—for instance, honesty's engendering trust, or justices's commanding allegiance, or kindness' encouraging friendship—are real regularities that are unidentifiable and inexplicable except by appeal to moral properties. Indeed, many moral virtues (such as honesty, justice, kindness) and vices (such as greed, lechery, sadism) figure in this way in our best explanations of many natural regularities. Moral explanations allow us to isolate what it is about a person, or an action, or an institution, that leads to its having the effects it does. And these explanations rely on moral concepts that identify characteristics common to people, actions, and institutions that are uncapturable with finer-grained or differently structured categories.

Of course, even if moral properties do have a role in our best explanations of natural regularities, we might still wonder whether these properties are anything more, anything over and above, psychological properties and dispositions of individuals; and we might wonder to what extent these 'vices' and 'virtues' have any normative authority. For all that has been said so far, we might have no good reason to think the 'virtues' worthy of cultivation and the 'vices' worthy of condemnation. So even if moral properties ultimately satisfy the demands of the Explanatory Criterion (once we get a reasonable interpretation of its requirements), we will at most have established that certain people, actions, and institutions have those properties we label 'moral'. We will not yet have shown that there is any reason to care about the properties, nor that some of the properties are better than others.[47]

As long as we concentrate on which properties satisfy the Explanatory Criterion, and which do not, the distinctive value of moral properties will remain elusive. The structure of a compelling defense of their value will emerge only after we turn our attention to the presuppositions of the Explanatory Criterion itself.

8. THE EVALUATION OF EXPLANATIONS

As the Explanatory Criterion would have it, which hypotheses are justified, and which are not, will depend crucially on our standards of explanation, since it is by figuring in the *best* available explanations that a hypothesis finds justification. No argument that depends on the Explanatory Criterion will get off the ground unless some explanations are better than others. This poses a dilemma for those who suppose that the Explanatory Criterion will support the wholesale rejection of evaluative facts. Either there is a fact of the matter about which explanations are best, or there is not. If there is, then there are at least some evaluative facts (as to which explanations are better than others); if not, then the criterion will never find an application, and so will support no argument against moral theory.

If we say that astronomers, and not astrologers, make the appropriate inferences from what is seen of the constellations, or that evolutionary theorists, and not creationists, have the best explanation of the origin of our species, we will be making value judgments. In trying to legitimize these judgments by appealing to our standards of explanation, a reliance on values becomes inescapable (even if the values appealed to are not themselves mentioned in our explanations).

The obvious response to this point is to embrace some account of explanatory quality in terms, say, of simplicity, generality, elegance, predictive power, and so on. One explanation is better than another, we could then maintain, in virtue of the way it combines these properties.[48]

When offering the list of properties that are taken to be the measures of explanatory quality, however, it is important to avoid the mistake of thinking the list wipes values out of the picture. It is important to avoid thinking of the list as eliminating explanatory quality in favor of some evaluatively neutral properties. If one explanation is better than another in virtue of being simpler, more general, more elegant, and so on, then simplicity, generality, and elegance cannot themselves be evaluatively neutral. Were these properties evaluatively neutral, they could not account for one explanation being better than another.

If we are to use the Explanatory Criterion, we must hold that some explanations really are better than others, and not just that they have some evaluatively neutral properties that others do not. Any attempt to wash evaluative claims out as psychological or sociological reports, for instance, will fail—we will not be saying what we want, that one explanation is *better* than another, but only (for example) that we happen to like one explanation more, or that our society approves of one more. What the Explanatory Criterion presupposes is that there are evaluative facts, at least concerning which explanations are better than others—regardless of whether these facts explain any of our observations.

Even assuming that the Explanatory Criterion presupposes the existence of some *evaluative* facts, the question remains whether we have any good reason for thinking there are moral facts as well. We might be convinced that some explanations really are better than others, but still deny that some actions, or characters, or

MORAL THEORY AND EXPLANATORY IMPOTENCE   451

institutions, are better than others. Significantly, though, once it has been granted that some explanations are better than others, many obstacles to a defense of moral values disappear. In fact, all general objections to the existence of value must be rejected as too strong. Moreover, whatever ontological niche and epistemological credentials we find for explanatory values will presumably serve equally well for moral values.[49]

Without actually making the argument, I shall briefly sketch one of the ways one might defend the view that there are moral values. The aim of such an argument would be to show that some actions, characters, or institutions are better than others—just as some explanations are better than others.

The defense of moral values rests on recognizing and stressing the similarities between the evaluation of actions, and so on, and the evaluation of explanations. The crucial similarity is that in defending our evaluations (whether of actions, institutions, or explanations) we must inevitably rely on a theory that purports to *justify* our standards of evaluation as over against other sets of (moral or explanatory) standards. In both cases, we will be engaged in the process of justifying our judgments, not of explaining our experiences. The analogy to keep in mind here is not that between moral theory and scientific theory, but that between moral theory and scientific epistemology.[50]

Since we must regard certain evaluative claims (those concerning which explanations are better than others) as true, we will be justified in believing those parts of value theory that support our standards of explanatory value. Just as we take the explanatory role of certain hypotheses as grounds for believing the hypotheses, we must, I suggest, take the justificatory role of certain evaluative principles as grounds for believing the principles. If the principles are themselves not reasonably believed, they cannot support our particular evaluations of explanations; and if we can have no grounds for thinking one explanation better than another, the Explanatory Criterion will be toothless.

Thus, if evaluative facts are indispensable (because they are presupposed by the Explanatory Criterion), we can invoke what might be called *inference to the best justification* to argue abstract value claims on the grounds that they justify our lower-level epistemic judgments. And these very same abstract evaluative principles might imply lower-level, distinctly moral principles and particular moral judgments. If so, then in defending moral values we might begin with evaluations of explanations, move up (in generality and abstraction) to principles justifying these evaluations, then move back down, along a different justificatory path, to evaluations of actions, characters, institutions, and so on. That is, to argue for a particular moral judgment (for example, that it is better to be honest than duplicitous), we might show that the judgment is justified by some abstract evaluative principle that is itself justified by its relation to our standards of explanatory quality (which are indispensable to our application of the Explanatory Criterion). In this way, particular moral judgments and more general moral principles might find their legitimacy through their connec-

tion with the indispensable part of value theory that serves to justify our judgments
of explanatory quality.

To take one (optimisitic) example: Imagine that we justify believing in some
property by appeal to its role in our best explanation of some observations, and we
then justify our belief that some explanation is the best available by appeal to our
standards of explanatory quality, and finally, we justify these standards (rather than
some others) by appealing to their ultimate contributions to the maximization of expected utility. Imagine, also, that having justified our standards of explanatory
value, we turn to the justification for cultivating some moral property (for example,
honesty). The justification might plausibly appeal to its contribution to the cohesiveness of one's society, and we might in turn justify cultivating properties conducive
to the cohesiveness of society by appeal to the benefits available only within society.
Finally, we might justify these as benefits by appeal to their maximizing expected
utility. Appeal to the maximization of expected utility would then serve both as the
best justification for certain standards of explanatory value and as the best justification for cultivating particular moral properties. It would justify both our belief that
some particular explanation is better than another and our belief that some moral
properties (for example, honesty) are better than others (for example, duplicity). We
could then deny the justifiability of moral judgments only by denying the justification
of our evaluative judgments of explanations.

So, in pursuing justifications for our standards of evaluation, we might discover that the justificatory principles we embrace have as consequences not only
evaluations of explanations but also recognizably moral evaluations of character, or
behavior, or institutions. Justificatory principles might come most plausibly as a
package deal carrying both explanatory and moral evaluations in tow.

No doubt this picture is overly optimistic. Most likely, the justificatory principles invoked in justifying particular standards of explanatory quality will not be so
neatly tied with the justifications available for having or developing certain (recognizably moral) properties, nor with the justifications available for condemning other
(recognizably immoral) properties. In following out the two lines of justification—
that is, in justifying particular evaluations by appeal to principles, which we in turn
justify by appeal to more general principles—we may never arrive at a single, overarching justificatory principle. Indeed, it is highly unlikely that we will ever get such
a principle either in epistemology or in moral theory.[51] It is even less likely that we
will ever find a single principle that serves for both.

Although inference to the best justification legitimizes both the lower-level
standards of explanatory value (simplicity, generality, and so on) and—more
important—the very process of justification, the substantive principles the process
engenders will probably vary according to what is being justified. When we are
justifying a belief that some property is instantiated, one set of justificatory principles will come into play; when we are justifying the having or cultivating of some
property, a completely different set of justificatory principles may prove relevant.
The two paths of justification might neither coincide nor converge.

MORAL THEORY AND EXPLANATORY IMPOTENCE 453

Yet a failure of convergence would not undermine moral justifications. The legitimacy of moral theory does not require any special link between explanatory and moral justifications. What it does require is that moral properties figure both as properties we are justified in believing exemplifiable and as properties we are justified in cultivating.

In constructing explanatory and justificatory theories, we may discover any of four things: (1) that moral properties are neither possessable nor worth possessing, in which case (I assume) moral theory loses its point; (2) that moral properties (for example, honesty, kindness) are possessed by some but that there is no justification for thinking some better than others, in which case only an unexciting conclusion will have been established—like atomic weights, virtue and value would exist, and claims involving them would have a truth value, but they would be normatively inert; (3) that we have no reason to believe moral properties are exemplified, but we do have reason to cultivate them, in which case a unique version of the is/ought distinction will have been established—there are no instantiated moral properties, even though there ought to be; or finally, (4) that moral properties are actually possessed and (some) are worth possessing, in which case moral theory will have found its strongest defense. Which of these four positions is right can be settled only against the background of an accepted justificatory theory.

Of course, whether we are justified in believing moral properties are both possessable and worth possessing is an open question. Yet it is a legitimate question, a question that can be answered only by engaging in moral theorizing; that is, only by attempting the justifications and seeing where they lead.[52]

Notes

1. For example, see Gilbert Harman's *The Nature of Morality* (New York, 1977) and his "Moral Explanations of Natural Facts—Can Moral Claims be Tested Against Moral Reality?" in *Spindel Conference: Moral Realism, Southern Journal of Philosophy* 24 (1986), Supplement: 57-68; J. L. Mackie's *Ethics: Inventing Right and Wrong* (New York, 1977); Simon Blackburn's *Spreading the Word* (New York, 1984); Francis Snare's "The Empirical Bases of Moral Scepticism," *American Philosophical Quarterly* 21 (1984): 215-25; and David Zimmerman's "Moral Theory and Explanatory Necessity," in *Morality, Reason and Truth*, edited by David Copp and David Zimmerman (Totowa, 1985), 79-103.

2. Although this change in emphasis, from meaning to justification, represents a natural development of the verification principle, it constitutes a significant change. With it comes the rejection of the verifiability principle as grounds for noncognitivism.

3. As Reichenbach notes: "Science tells us what is, but not what should be." *The Rise of Scientific Philosophy* (Berkeley, 1951), 287.

4. Although it is true that what is thought to be is not always so (just as what ought to be is not always so), reports that something is thought to be (or that something ought to be), are still clearly assertions concerning what is the case. Moral theory is as concerned with what is as is psychology. In making claims about what ought to be, moral theory is claiming that what ought to be is such and such. Moral theory characteristically makes assertions such as "Killing humans for entertainment *is* wrong;" "An action *is* made worse if it results in excruciating pain for others"; "The Ku Klux Klan *is* a morally corrupt oganization."

5. Paul Churchland defends this account in *Scientific Realism and the Plasticity of Mind* (Cambridge,

454   GEOFFREY SAYRE-McCORD

1979). See also Norwood Russell Hanson's *Patterns of Discovery* (Cambridge, 1958) and Wilfrid Sellars's *Science, Perception, and Reality* (London, 1963).

6. See as examples John Rawls's *A Theory of Justice* (Cambridge, Mass., 1971), Ronald Dworkin's *Taking Rights Seriously* (Cambridge, Mass., 1977), and Philip Pettit's *Judging Justice* (London, 1980).

7. See Pierre Duhem's *The Aim and Structure of Physical Theory* (Princeton, N.J., 1954) and W. V. O. Quine's "Two Dogmas of Empiricism," in *From a Logical Point of View* (Cambridge, Mass., 1964), 20–46.

8. See Morton White's *What Is and What Ought to Be Done*, (Oxford, 1981), and Nicholas Sturgeon's "Moral Explanations," in *Morality, Reason, and Truth*.

9. The last few paragraphs reiterate points made in my "Logical Positivism and the Demise of 'Moral Science' " in *The Heritage of Logical Positivism*, edited by Nicholas Rescher (Lanham, 1985), 83–92.

10. Harman, *The Nature of Morality*, 6–7.

11. Of course, neither the scientist nor the moral judge need have had a well-worked-out theory in order to make observations. The ability to form opinions (about protons, witches, or morals) as a direct result of perceptual experience is more a matter of effective training than of the conscious application of theory to experience.

12. Harman, *The Nature of Morality*, 8.

13. Actually, the Causal Criterion will be attractive regardless of whether the causal theories are substantially correct, as long as we assume causal contact is a necessary condition for knowledge.

14. Goldman characterizes the appropriate connection in terms of there being a "reliable belief-forming operation." Alvin Goldman, "What Is Justified Belief?" in *Justification and Knowledge*, edited by George Pappas (Dordrecht, 1979), 1–23.

15. Mark Steiner defends mathematical entities from this objection in *Mathematical Knowledge* (Ithaca, N.Y., 1975), 10. See also Penelope Maddy, "Perception and Mathematical Intuition," *Philosophical Review* 89 (1980): 163–96; Paul Benacerraf, "Mathematical Truth," *Journal of Philosophy* 70 (1973): 661–79; Crispin Wright, *Frege's Conception of Numbers as Objects* (Aberdeen, Scot., 1983); and Philip Kitcher, *The Nature of Mathematical Knowledge* (Oxford, 1983).

16. All of this is compatible, of course, with there being a causal story of our use of moral language. Since we do live in a community of moral-language users, we are taught how to use moral words and we stand at the end of a causal (in this case, educational) chain that explains our use of moral terms. Despite there being such a causal story, if moral properties are causally isolated, our language will lack the grounding that would allow it to refer; the linguistic chain would lack an anchor.

17. See Saul Kripke's *Naming and Necessity* (Cambridge, Mass., 1980).

18. Incidentally, one may succeed in referring to an ordinary object, one located in space and time, even if the object does not actually have any causal impact on the referrer. Eyes closed, I may enter a room, point to my left, and declare, "I'll bet that chair is brown." I will have referred to the chair (assuming one is there), and made a bet about its color, despite my neither bumping into it, seeing it, nor in any other way being causally affected by it. At most, successful ostension requires causal *presence* and not causal *impact*.

19. In this paper I shall leave unchallenged the (eminently challengeable) assumption that there is some way to isolate moral from nonmoral language.

20. Note that we need not have naturalistic *definitions* in order to succeed in referring by *description*. Since the Causal Criterion rules out all causally inert properties, while the causal theory of reference allows reference to causally inert properties as long as they are describable, the strictures of the Causal Criterion actually go beyond those of the causal theory of reference.

21. Actually, even when applied to mathematical entities, the game is not quite so easily won. For instance, Kurt Godel maintained that we have a mathematical intuition akin to visual perception that establishes a causal link, of sorts, between numbers and knowers (in "What is Cantor's Continuum Problem?" *American Mathematical Monthly* 54 (1947): 515–25. Penelope Maddy (in "Perception and Mathematical Intuition") has defended this possibility by appeal to recent theories of perception. In the process, she

MORAL THEORY AND EXPLANATORY IMPOTENCE 455

has argued that abstract mathematical entities (e.g., sets) will, contrary to initial appearances, satisfy the Causal Criterion.

22. As Harman notes, "We do not and cannot perceive numbers . . . since we cannot be in causal contact with them" (*The Nature of Morality*, 10).

23. As Harman argues in *Thought* (Princeton, N.J., 1973), 127. Adolf Grunbaum makes the same point in arguing that one scientific law may explain another, even though the first law does not *cause* the second. See "Science and Ideology," *The Scientific Monthly* (July 1954): 13-19.

24. Harman recognizes the shortcomings of the Causal Criterion, and it is in his pointing them out that it becomes clear that he does not accept the criterion. See *Thought*, especially 126-32.

25. Harman, *The Nature of Morality*, 10. My emphasis. There is room, of course, to agree that if the truth of mathematical claims contributes to our best explanations these claims should be believed, while also holding that their truth does not so contribute. This is Hartry Field's position in *Science Without Numbers* (Princeton, N.J., 1980).

26. Harman, *The Nature of Morality*, 9.

27. The one reasonable application of this strong version of the Explanatory Criterion would tie its use to the explanations reached at the ideal limit of inquiry—an explanation *we* will almost surely never get. At this Piercean limit, there is sense to saying we can infer the truth of the hypotheses invoked by the (very) best explanation; for only if there is some such link with epistemology will truth be accessible. So used, though, the principle will never actually countenance any of our inferences.

28. According to Harman, "Moral hypotheses never help explain why we observe anything. So we have no evidence for our moral opinions." *The Nature of Morality*, 13, see also 8.

29. Harman, *The Nature of Morality*, 7.

30. Theories find observational confirmation only from accurate observations, and some particular theory will find observational confirmation from an accurate observation only if the theory also plays a role in explaining the making of that observation. Nonetheless, the making of some observation O' will confirm a theory T' even if the observation is false, as long as T' explains why the false observation was made. Even supposing an observation inaccurate, then, the making of the observation will be confirming evidence (but not *observational* evidence) for whatever theories contribute to the best explanation of the making of that (false) observation. When the report is false, however, it will be the making of the observation, and not its content, that serves to confirm our explanatory theories; and it will be the accurate observation that the false observation was made (and not the false observation itself) that provides observational support for our explanatory theories.

31. Harman, *The Nature of Morality*, 6.

32. Implicit in the Explanatory Criterion, then, is the conviction that legitimate theories must be linked to an acceptable theory of observation. As Putnam argues, "it is an important and extremely useful constraint on our theory itself that our developing theory of the world taken as a whole should include an account of the very activity and process by which we are able to know that a theory is correct." *Reason, Truth and History* (Cambridge, 1981), 132.

33. Harman, *The Nature of Morality*, 7.

34. Of course, that the burning of the cat was wrong might be part of the moral judge's (as opposed to our) best explanation of why he made the observation he did, just as for some people the best explanations they had of their observations made reference to phlogiston.

35. Sturgeon, "Moral Explanations," 65. As Sturgeon recognizes, the test has its limits. It will not be a reliable indicator of explanatory relevance when dealing with two effects of the same cause; neither effect would have occurred without the other (because each would have occurred only if the cause of the other had), even though neither explains the other. And it will not be reliable when using 'that-would-have-had-to-be-because' counterfactuals; it may be that if Reagan had lost the Presidential election, that would have had to be because he failed to get enough votes, even though his being elected is not explanatorily relevant to his getting enough votes. Ibid., 75. For other limitations, see Warren Quinn's "Truth and Explanation in Ethics," *Ethics* 96 (1986): 524-44.

36. At this stage, the relevant feature of a supervenience account of moral properties is that if the

456   GEOFFREY SAYRE-McCORD

moral properties of something are changed, then so must be some nonmoral properties; there is no holding the nonmoral properties fixed while altering the moral properties, as there can be no moral difference without a nonmoral difference.

37. Sturgeon, "Moral Explanations," 66. Which nonmoral facts will have to be altered to change the moral facts is, obviously, open to dispute.

38. As Sturgeon emphasizes, "Hitler's moral depravity – the fact of his really having been morally depraved – forms part of a reasonable explanation of why we believe he was depraved" ("Moral Explanations," 54). Had he not been depraved we very likely would not have thought him depraved; for he would not have done all the despicable things he did, and it is his having done such things that leads us to our condemnation.

39. Our background theories will clearly play a central role in determining explanatory relevance. In the cat-burning case, we will rely on our moral theory in deciding what nonmoral features of the world would have been different had the hoodlums' activities been unobjectionable. Similarly, in the passing proton case, we will rely on our scientific theory in deciding what physical features of the world would have been different had a proton not passed. Such a reliance on background theories will certainly offend a thoroughgoing skeptic. But attacks on moral theory are interesting only if some of our views survive the skeptic's arguments, so I shall assume we may legitimately rely at least sometimes on our background theories

40. Sturgeon, "Moral Explanations," 71. Independently, John McDowell has made essentially the same point concerning skeptical attacks on moral explanations in his "Values and Secondary Qualities," in *Morality and Objectivity*, edited by Ted Honderich (London, 1985), 110–29.

41. Which, of course, is not to say that we can explain everything that we might reasonably want to explain.

42. Yet there is at least some question as to whether the reductive hypothesis itself satisfies the explanatory criterion. What, after all, do we explain with the help of the reductive hypothesis that we could not explain just as well by assuming the reduced claims fail to refer? See Quinn's "Truth and Explanation in Ethics" for more on the tension between the explanatory criterion and reductive hypotheses.

43. There are some significant differences between moral properties and secondary qualities, not least of which is that we can learn to ascribe secondary qualities without having any idea as to what properties they supervene upon, whereas learning to ascribe moral properties requires an awareness of the properties upon which they supervene. This difference will stand in the way of treating moral properties as strictly analogous to secondary properties. But I think it won't underwrite any plausible version of the explanatory criterion that is still strong enough to rule out moral properties. See Quinn's "Truth and Explanation in Ethics."

44. Harman, *The Nature of Morality*, 23.

45. Ibid.

46. Hilary Putnam, "Philosophy and Our Mental Life," in *Mind, Language, and Reality* (Cambridge, 1975), 291–303.

47. Just as reductions of the mental to the physical fail to capture intentionality, reductions of the moral to the mental fail to capture justifiability.

48. For discussions of the (often conflicting) criteria for explanatory value, see Paul Thagard's "The Best Explanation: Criteria for Theory Choice," *Journal of Philosophy* 75 (1978): 76–92, and William Lycan's "Epistemic Value," *Synthese* 64 (1985): 137–64.

49. Of course, this leaves open the possibility that more specific attacks may be leveled at moral values; the point is that once epistemic values are allowed, no general arguments against the existence of values can work.

50. Here I part company with other moral realists (for example, Boyd, Sturgeon, and Railton) who seem to hold that moral theory should be seen as being of a piece with scientific theory. See Richard Boyd's "How To Be A Moral Realist," in *Essays on Moral Realism*, edited by Geoffrey Sayre-McCord (Ithaca, N.Y., forthcoming); Nicholas Sturgeon's "Moral Explanations"; and Peter Railton's "Moral Realism," *Philosophical Review* 95 (1986): 163–207.

MORAL THEORY AND EXPLANATORY IMPOTENCE   457

51. In "Coherence and Models for Moral Theorizing," *Pacific Philosophical Quarterly* 66 (1985): 170–90, I argue that we have good reason for rejecting any proposed unifying fundamental principle we might find.

52. Earlier versions of this paper were delivered at the 1985 Eastern Division meetings of the American Philosophical Association, at the Research Triangle Ethics Circle, and at University of Wisconsin-Madison, University of Notre Dame, Virginia Polytechnic Institute, University of California-Irvine, Duke University, and University of California-San Diego. This paper has benefited considerably from exposure to these audiences, and especially from comments made by Kurt Baier, Douglas Butler, Joseph Camp, Jr., David Gauthier, Joan McCord, Warren Quinn, Michael Resnik, Jay Rosenberg, Robert Shaver, and Gregory Trianosky.

Part VII
How Do we Come by Moral Knowledge?

[20]

SIDGWICK AND REFLECTIVE EQUILIBRIUM*

In his book *A Theory of Justice*, John Rawls introduces and employs the concept of "reflective equilibrium" as a method of testing which of rival moral theories is to be preferred.[1] The introduction of this concept is plainly a significant event for moral philosophy. The criterion by which we decide to reject, say, utilitarianism in favour of a contractual theory of justice (or vice versa) is, if anything, even more fundamental than the choice of theory itself, since our choice of moral theory may well be determined by the criterion we use.

Moral philosophy is an ancient subject. It would be surprising if someone were suddenly to propose a new way of deciding between competing moral theories, implying thereby that all the moral philosophers of the past have been mistaken about the nature of a successful moral theory. Rawls does not see his proposal in this way. Far from being an innovation, the method of reflective equilibrium, he claims, goes back to Aristotle, and can be followed down through the classical writers at least as far as Sidgwick. Rawls quotes from Sidgwick (and from no other classical writer) to show that this is Sidgwick's own method of doing moral philosophy.

I do not intend to examine the moral philosophy of Aristotle, or of any other moral philosopher between Aristotle and Sidgwick. But I shall examine the evidence for the view that Sidgwick uses the method of reflective equilibrium as a test for the validity of moral theories; and, to anticipate the result of this examination, I shall deny that Sidgwick does use this method. I shall then try to say what, for Sidgwick, the ultimate test of a moral theory is. Thus this article

---

* I have greatly benefited from comments on an earlier version from: B. Barry, R. M. Hare, J. L. Mackie, D. Parfit, J. B. Schneewind, and K. Watts. This paper has been read at Johns Hopkins University and Princeton University, and I am grateful to faculty and students there for valuable discussion.

1. John Rawls, *A Theory of Justice* (Oxford: Clarendon Press; Cambridge, Mass.: Harvard University Press, 1972). Hereinafter abbreviated in the text to *ATOJ*.

is in part an attempt to correct Rawls's interpretation of Sidgwick; nevertheless, my concerns are not limited to the desire to refute a few peripheral sentences of *A Theory of Justice*. The issue is important because of the need to decide on the correct method in moral philosophy. Rawls believes that reflective equilibrium is the correct method, and he also thinks it the method of the classical philosophers, including Sidgwick. My own view is that it is not Sidgwick's method, and it is not the correct method either. If it can be shown that Sidgwick uses some other means of testing moral theories, we can ask what that method is, and whether it is preferable to reflective equilibrium. Since Sidgwick is among the clearest and most careful thinkers in the field, and had a profound knowledge of the history of moral philosophy, whatever method he employs is likely to be worth serious consideration.

I

The first question to ask, then, is what this method of reflective equilibrium is. Although Rawls first introduced this idea in his article "Outline of a Decision Procedure for Ethics," [2] I shall use only the more recent account in *A Theory of Justice*.

Rawls begins with our "moral capacity"—that is, the skill we acquire, in normal circumstances, of judging things to be just or unjust, and, presumably, right or wrong, good or bad, as well. He then says:

> Now one may think of moral philosophy at first (and I stress the provisional nature of this view) as the attempt to describe our moral capacity; or, in the present case, one may regard a theory of justice as describing our sense of justice. This enterprise is very difficult. For by such a description is not meant simply a list of the judgments on institutions and actions that we are prepared to render, accompanied with supporting reasons when these are offered. Rather, what is required is a formulation of a set of principles which, when conjoined to our beliefs and knowledge of the circumstances, would lead us to make these judgments with their supporting reasons were we to apply these principles conscientiously and intelligently. A conception of justice characterizes our

---

2. John Rawls, "Outline of a Decision Procedure for Ethics," *The Philosophical Review*, 60 (1951).

moral sensibility when the everyday judgments we do make are in accordance with its principles. [*ATOJ*, p. 46]

At this point Rawls offers an instructive comparison between this method of doing moral philosophy and Chomsky's undertaking of "describing the sense of grammaticalness that we have for the sentences of our native language." The aim here, Rawls tells us, is to formulate principles "which make the same discriminations as the native speaker."

Rawls then adds an important qualification to what has been said so far, by introducing the idea of "considered judgments" which are "those judgments in which our moral capacities are most likely to be displayed without distortion." In other words, we exclude judgments made without real confidence, or under stress, or when we may have been swayed by undue consideration of our own interests. The relevant judgments then, are "those given under conditions favorable for deliberation and judgment in general" (*ATOJ*, p. 48).

We now come to the final statement of reflective equilibrium itself, and it is necessary to quote the central passage in full:

According to the provisional aim of moral philosophy, one might say that justice as fairness is the hypothesis that the principles which would be chosen in the original position are identical with those that match our considered judgments and so these principles describe our sense of justice. But this interpretation is clearly oversimplified. In describing our sense of justice an allowance must be made for the likelihood that considered judgments are no doubt subject to certain irregularities and distortions despite the fact that they are rendered under favorable circumstances. When a person is presented with an intuitively appealing account of his sense of justice (one, say, which embodies various natural and reasonable presumptions), he may well revise his judgments to conform to its principles even though the theory does not fit his existing judgments exactly. He is especially likely to do this if he can find an explanation for the deviations which undermine his confidence in his original judgments, and if the conception presented yields a judgment which he finds he can now accept. From the standpoint of moral philosophy, the best account of a person's sense of justice is not the one which fits his judgments prior to his examining any conception of justice, but rather the one which matches his judgments in reflective equilibrium. As we have seen, this state is one

SIDGWICK AND REFLECTIVE EQUILIBRIUM   493

reached after a person has weighed various proposed conceptions
and he has either revised his judgments to accord with one of them
or held fast to his initial convictions (and the corresponding conception). [*ATOJ*, p. 48]

Thus Rawls's view is that a normative moral theory is like a scientific theory.[3] As in science, the aim of the theory is to explain
all the data; but, also as in science, if a promising theory conflicts
with only one or two observations, the observations may be jettisoned
and the theory retained, rather than the other way around. In science this is achieved by introducing additional hypotheses, or assuming that an instrument was faulty, or some disturbance overlooked; in moral theory, what was previously thought to be a
considered moral judgment may after all have been a result of distorted thinking, and so may be explained away. In both cases,
although there are no "brute" facts, there are facts, and the successful theory is the one that provides a plausible systematization
of them. So Rawls says:

I wish to stress that a theory of justice is precisely that, namely, a
theory. . . . There is a definite if limited class of facts against
which conjectured principles can be checked, namely our considered judgments in reflective equilibrium. [*ATOJ*, p. 51]

These passages may give rise to differing interpretations of the
notion of reflective equilibrium. Most importantly: is the fact that
a moral theory matches a set of considered moral judgments in reflective equilibrium, to be regarded merely as *evidence* of the validity
of the moral theory, or is it then valid *by definition*—in other words,
is the achievement of a stable reflective equilibrium what Rawls
means by "valid", as applied to moral theories, or would he allow
that there is a meaningful sense of "valid" that goes beyond this?
My belief is that Rawls has left no room for any idea of validity
that is independent of achieving reflective equilibrium. The passages I have quoted all point in this direction. Thus we are to start
by thinking of moral philosophy as an attempt to describe our moral
capacity—and there is no sense in which a description can be cor-

3. This analogy was explicit in "Outline of a Decision for Ethics," and
Rawls states that what he now says is in accord with that (p. 46n., 579n.).
He now refers as well to Quine's view of justification, though without ex-
plicitly comparing his own to it (p. 579n.).

rect that is independent of the way it fits what it describes. Admittedly, this starting point is provisional, but I take this to be a reference to the fact that the procedure is not as one-sided as the provisional idea indicates, since our moral capacity may itself alter under the influence of a plausible theory. There is still nothing to suggest room for a notion of validity beyond the conjunction of theory and revised moral capacity. Next, we have the analogy with the attempt to describe the sense of grammaticalness of the native speaker—again, a perfect fit is not merely evidence that the theory of grammar is correct, it is what is meant by a "correct" theory. Finally there is the analogy with science, and in particular with Quine's model of science. This too gives no sense to the idea of a correct theory other than the theory that best fits the data, after that data has been subject to possible revision in the light of plausible theories.

If I am right in attributing this version of the reflective equilibrium idea to Rawls, then Rawls is a subjectivist about morality in the most important sense of this often-misused term.[4] That is, it follows from his views that the validity of a moral theory will vary according to whose considered moral judgments the theory is tested against. There is no sense in which we can speak of a theory being objectively valid, no matter what considered moral judgments people happen to hold. If I live in one society, and accept one set of considered moral judgments, while you live in another society and hold a quite different set, very different moral theories may be "valid" for each of us. There will then be no sense in which one of us is wrong and the other right.[5]

This point is not affected by the question of whether there is one unique reflective equilibrium for all men or not (a question upon which Rawls refuses to speculate). Even if everyone shared the same considered moral judgment, this would only mean that a theory might have intersubjective validity: it would not make for objective

4. R. M. Hare reaches the same conclusion in his "Rawls' Theory of Justice—I," *Philosophical Quarterly*, 23 (1973), pp. 144-47.

5. Perhaps there is room for some doubt about this subjectivist interpretation. Certainly, on pp. 516-17, Rawls appears to claim objectivity for his theory. A careful reading of this passage suggests, however, that it is only the elimination of personal bias, and not real objectivity that Rawls has in mind here.

validity. People might have judged differently, and then a different moral theory would have been "valid".

The second issue of interpretation left unresolved by the passages quoted is whether a moral theory is supposed to match the considered moral judgments of an individual, or of some larger group, such as a society. Rawls, after refusing to discuss whether there is a unique reflective equilibrium for all men, goes on to say: "for the purposes of this book, the opinions of the reader and the author are the only ones that count. The opinions of others are used only to clear our heads" (*ATOJ*, p. 50).

This is a clear statement, but can Rawls really mean it? Throughout the book, some consensus seems to be presupposed. Rawls always writes of "our" judgments, never "mine" or "yours"; this may only be a matter of style, but the assurance with which he assumes that the reader shares his own intuitions can only be based on the assumption that there is a wide consensus about, for example, what is just and what unjust.[6] For the purposes of comparison with Sidgwick, this vacillation need not be forced into one or other interpretation. It needs only to be noted, and will be referred to again after we have examined Sidgwick's own method.

Other points of interpretation will best be dealt with when they come up in the course of the discussion of whether Sidgwick uses the reflective equilibrium method. To this we may now turn.

II

The evidence Rawls himself gives for the claim that Sidgwick does use the method of reflective equilibrium is scanty, though Rawls cannot be blamed for feeling that his book is sufficiently long without adding purely historical digressions. Rawls gives one quotation from Sidgwick, which does look like a description of a procedure similar to Rawls's "reflective equilibrium" idea. Apart from this, he relies on a reference to an article by J. B. Schneewind, entitled "First Principles and Common Sense Morality in Sidgwick's Ethics."[7]

If we follow up the reference to Schneewind's article, we find a clearly written account, backed with numerous quotations, of Sidg-

---

6. Hare, "Rawls' Theory of Justice—I," has pointed out how frequent and deep-rooted the appeal to consensus is for Rawls.

7. *ATOJ*, p. 51n. The full reference for Schneewind's article is *Archiv für Geschichte der Philosophie*, Bd. 45 (1963).

wick's methodology; moreover, it is an account that does support the contention that Sidgwick uses a method rather like reflective equilibrium. Since Schneewind's account is so much fuller than anything Rawls says, and since it merits attention in its own right (and would surely have received more attention had it not appeared in a periodical little read by English-language moral philosophers) I now proceed to a discussion of Schneewind's account of Sidgwick's methodology.

Schneewind sees *The Methods of Ethics* as an elaborate attempt to "prove", in a special sense, the truth of utilitarianism. The argument proceeds, according to Schneewind, in two stages—but in order to understand Schneewind's account, we must first ask in what sense of "proof" Sidgwick is supposed to be trying to prove utilitarianism to be true. As Schneewind points out, Sidgwick, like Mill, is clear that it is impossible to prove a first principle "if by proof we mean a process which exhibits the principle in question as an inference from premises upon which it remains dependent for its certainty; for these premises, and not the inference drawn from them, would then be the real first principles." [8] So what possibilities are left? The following passage is crucial both for an understanding of Schneewind's interpretation of Sidgwick, and for my argument that this interpretation is mistaken:

> Nay, if Utilitarianism is to be *proved* to a man who already holds some other moral principles—whether he be an Intuitional moralist who regards as final the principles of Truth, Justice, Obedience to authority, Purity, etc., or an Egoist who regards his own interest as the ultimately reasonable end of his conduct,—it would seem that the process must be one which establishes a conclusion actually *superior* in validity to the premises from which it starts. For the Utilitarian prescriptions of duty are *prima facie* in conflict, at certain points and under certain circumstances, both with rules which the Intuitionist regards as self-evident, and with the dictates of Rational Egoism; so that Utilitarianism, if accepted at all, must be accepted as overruling Intuitionism and Egoism. At the same time, if the other principles are not throughout taken as valid, the so-

---

8. *The Methods of Ethics*, 7th ed. (London: Macmillan, 1907), p. 419. Hereinafter abbreviated in the text to *ME*. The sixth and seventh editions are practically identical; they differ considerably from the first edition, but the differences are not crucial for present purposes.

SIDGWICK AND REFLECTIVE EQUILIBRIUM   497

called proof does not seem to be addressed to the Intuitionist or Egoist at all. How shall we deal with this dilemma? How is such a process—clearly different from ordinary proof—possible or conceivable? Yet there clearly seems to be a general demand for it. Perhaps we may say that what is needed is a line of argument which on the one hand allows the validity, to a certain extent, of the maxims already accepted, and on the other hand shows them to be not absolutely valid, but needing to be controlled and completed by some more comprehensive principle. [*ME*, pp. 419-20. Italics in original.]

According to Schneewind, Sidgwick is here proposing a two-stage argument. The first part (actually mentioned second in the final sentence of the passage quoted) is an attempt to show that "the principles of Truth, Justice, etc. have only a dependent and subordinate validity"; they require some further principle which is unconditionally and independently valid, to justify exceptions, settle cases on which the subordinate principle is vague or indeterminate, and resolve conflicts between subordinate principles. The second stage, the "systematization argument" is to the effect that the utilitarian principle "affords a principle of synthesis, and a method for binding the unconnected and occasionally conflicting principles of common moral reasoning into a complete and harmonious system" (*ME*, pp. 421, 422). The overall procedure, then, is first to show that our ordinary moral judgments—"the morality of Common Sense," in Sidgwick's terminology—need some further principle for their completion, and then to show that this further principle is none other than the principle of utility.

Now it may seem that since in expounding Schneewind's version of Sidgwick, I have illustrated the exposition with quotations from Sidgwick himself, I can hardly deny that this is in fact the method Sidgwick employs. It is true that these, and many other passages in *The Methods of Ethics* can be cited in support of the Schneewind/ Rawls interpretation. Yet there is something puzzling here, for contrary passages can be quoted with equal ease. For example, on the very first page of the book, Sidgwick says that he prefers to call the subject of ethics a "study" rather than a "Science" because "it is widely thought that a Science must necessarily have some department of actual existence for its subject-matter." Rawls, surely, would say that ethics, like linguistics or other sciences, does have a "department of actual existence" as its subject—namely, our considered moral judgments. So we seem to have contradictory passages in a writer who has the reputation of being one of the most clear-headed and consistent of ethical thinkers.

The contradiction, however, is only a superficial appearance of contradiction, and Sidgwick's reputation can easily be vindicated. Although there are many passages in which Sidgwick uses arguments that look as if they are appealing to our ordinary moral judgments, pruned and refined in various ways, as a test of the validity of moral theories, an examination of the context in which these arguments appear reveals that Sidgwick uses them, not as a criterion of the truth of a theory such as utilitarianism, but as some kind of confirmation of a result independently arrived at, and in particular as an *ad hominem* argument addressed to the supporter of common sense morality. In other words, the appeal to common sense morality is in no way an appeal to a "decision-procedure for ethics". It is, rather, a means by which the utilitarian might win certain kinds of opponents over to his own views.

That the two-stage argument Schneewind describes is one kind of *ad hominem* argument can be seen by recalling the first line of the long passage on how utilitarianism might be proved (quoted above) and by considering the way in which Sidgwick continues after this passage. The first line speaks of proving utilitarianism "to a man who already holds some other moral principles," whether intuitionist or egoist. Then, continuing after the quotation breaks off, Sidgwick refers immediately to a line of argument that might be addressed to an egoist. About this line of argument I shall have more to say later, but for the moment all that needs to be said is that it has nothing at all to do with common sense morality. The upshot of this line of argument, Sidgwick believes, is that "starting with his own principle" the egoist "may be brought to accept Universal happiness or pleasure as that which is absolutely and without qualification Good or Desirable." Only after giving this summary of how the utilitarian might proceed when confronted with an egoist does Sidgwick go on to outline the two-stage argument that a utilitarian might address to an intuitionist (Sidgwick refers to the philosophical representative of common sense morality as an "intuitionist"). Here Sidgwick carefully notes that a different mode of

SIDGWICK AND REFLECTIVE EQUILIBRIUM   499

argument is required because, "as addressed to the Intuitionist," the argument recommended for dealing with the egoist proves only that the utilitarian principle is *one* axiom of morality; it does not prove that it is the sole or supreme moral axiom. The reason for this difference lies in "the premises from which the Intuitionist starts." We must address our argument to what the intuitionist himself already accepts, if we are to win him over to utilitarianism. Commonly, the intuitionist will accept as self-evident independent moral axioms not only the utilitarian principle of rational benevolence, but also principles like Truth, Justice, and so on. Therefore:

> The Utilitarian must, in the first place, endeavour to show to the Intuitionist that the principles of Truth, Justice, etc. have only a dependent and subordinate validity: arguing either that the principle is really only affirmed by Common Sense as a general rule admitting of exceptions and qualifications, as in the case of Truth, and that we require some further principle for systematising these exceptions and qualifications; or that the fundamental notion is vague and needs further determination, as in the case of Justice; and further, that the different rules are liable to conflict with each other, and that we require some higher principle to decide the issue thus raised; and again, that the rules are differently formulated by different persons, and that these differences admit of no Intuitional solution, while they show the vagueness and ambiguity of the common moral notions to which the Intuitionist appeals. [*ME*, p. 421]

This passage could, out of context, be taken as a description of how Sidgwick intends to establish the validity of utilitarianism; as such, it would resemble an application of Rawls's "reflective equilibrium" procedure. In context, however, we can see that Sidgwick regards the argument outlined not as a means of establishing the validity of utilitarianism, but as a means of winning over to utilitarianism one who happens to hold a particular moral position, opposed to utilitarianism—namely, the philosophy of common sense morality, or intuitionism.

Whether the appeal to common sense morality is the ultimate test of the validity of utilitarianism, or an *ad hominem* argument for it, makes a fundamental difference to the nature of ethics as Sidgwick conceived it. Although Schneewind accepts that Sidgwick's

500   PETER SINGER

arguments "are addressed . . . to those who take the morality of common sense to be valid and binding, at least to some extent," [9] Schneewind does not appreciate the significance of this point, for later he writes:

> It [the utilitarian principle] is valid because it is demanded by our actual moral principles (cf. *ME* 420). In a world that was very different from ours, in which very different moral principles were commonly accepted, some other principle might be the independent first principle.[10]

This would be an accurate statement of Sidgwick's method if Sidgwick were using the reflective equilibrium procedure. Yet it is exactly what Sidgwick's appeal to common sense morality does not imply. Nothing whatsoever about the validity of a principle follows from the fact that an *ad hominem* argument may be made against a particular opponent of the principle. Moreover, what Schneewind says here would make nonsense of a point he himself makes about Sidgwick's belief in the objectivity of moral judgments. Schneewind notes that Sidgwick believes moral judgments to be objective, and as evidence cites the reason Sidgwick gives for avoiding the use of the term "moral sense"—because it "suggests a capacity for feelings which may vary from A to B without either being in error, rather than a faculty of cognition: and it appears to me fundamentally important to avoid this suggestion" (*ME*, p. 34).[11] That Sidgwick means by this more than the mere intersubjective sense of truth and falsity that is compatible with a relativistic denial of objectivity between different societies or different worlds is confirmed by the following paragraph, in which he states that "ought", in its ethical sense, applies to "rational beings as such".

This point is worth emphasising. Sidgwick's belief in the objectivity of moral judgments is in itself enough to show that he does not go along with the idea of "reflective equilibrium", because that idea, as we have seen, does imply that if A and B live in very different "worlds" (societies?) they might espouse different ultimate

---

9. "First Principles and Common Sense Morality," p. 140. This is true only of *some* of Sidgwick's arguments—not, of course, of those addressed to the egoist.

10. "First Principles and Common Sense Morality," p. 150.

11. The passage is quoted by Schneewind, "First Principles and Common Sense Morality," p. 150.

SIDGWICK AND REFLECTIVE EQUILIBRIUM   501

ethical principles without either of them being in error: and this is
the very suggestion Sidgwick thinks it "fundamentally important"
to avoid.[12]

On the other hand, to appeal to common sense morality as part
of an *ad hominem* argument is quite compatible with belief in objective truth in morals. Sidgwick is in effect saying to the intuitionist:
"Look, if it is going to be a choice between common sense morality
and utilitarianism, the latter has the advantage of being able to show
that common sense morality requires an independent first principle
like the principle of utility; and furthermore, the utilitarian principle systematizes and makes coherent all the diverse judgments of
common sense morality." To argue in this way is to take common
sense morality as valid for the purpose of the argument, but it does
not commit one to accepting common sense morality in arguments
with those who do not themselves accept it, and it does not debar
one from holding that the principle of utility would be valid even
if it were quite inconsistent with common sense morality. If there
were this inconsistency, it would be much more difficult for a utilitarian to convince a supporter of common sense morality, but it
would not mean that the utilitarian was wrong.

Why do Schneewind and Rawls miss the importance of the *ad
hominem* nature of the argument? The reason may be a general misconception of the intentions of *The Methods of Ethics*—a misconception that appeared in print soon after the book first appeared,
and has survived the intervening century despite an explicit rebuttal
by Sidgwick in his preface to the second edition. This misconception
Sidgwick describes as follows:

> There is, however, one fundamental misunderstanding, on which
> it seems desirable to say a few words. I find that more than one
> critic has overlooked or disregarded the account of the plan of my
> treatise, given in the original preface and in §5 of the introductory
> chapter: and has consequently supposed me to be writing as an
> assailant of two of the methods which I chiefly examine, and a de-
> fender of the third. Thus one of my reviewers seems to regard
> Book iii (on Intuitionism) as containing mere hostile criticism
> from the outside: another has constructed an article on the supposi-
> tion that my principle object is "the suppression of Egoism": a
> third has gone to the length of a pamphlet under the impression

---

12. Rawls seems to accept the fact that reflective equilibrium implies this
kind of relativism. See the reference to Quine mentioned in n. 3, above.

(apparently) that the "main argument" of my treatise is a demonstration of Universalistic Hedonism. I am concerned to have caused so much misdirection of criticism: and I have carefully altered in this edition the passages which I perceive to have contributed to it. [*ME*, p. xx]

Alas, Sidgwick's careful alterations have been in vain. The mistaken impression of the pamphleteer is today the standard view of Sidgwick's book. Schneewind begins his article by a reference to the arguments Sidgwick uses "to establish the utilitarian principle," [13] and Rawls, in his frequent references to Sidgwick, also appears to accept unquestioningly the view the *The Methods of Ethics* is basically an attempt to demonstrate the superiority of utilitarianism over other moral theories. Admittedly, there is no doubt that Sidgwick was a utilitarian (a term he uses interchangeably with "Universalistic Hedonism"). We would know this from his other writings, and from the autobiographical note printed in the preface to the sixth edition of *The Methods of Ethics*, even if it were not apparent from the body of that work. So the standard view is a natural one. Nevertheless, Sidgwick's deliberate intention was "to put aside temporarily the urgent need which we all feel of finding and adopting the true method of determining what we ought to do; and to consider simply what conclusions will be rationally reached if we start with certain ethical premises, and with what degree of certainty and precision" (*ME*, p. vi). This intention explains the title and structure of the book: the three "methods of ethics" Sidgwick discusses are the procedures most commonly used, both by ordinary men and philosophers, for obtaining reasoned convictions about what ought to be done, and the book is a critical exposition of these three methods. Naturally, in the course of this exposition Sidgwick is led "to discuss the considerations which should, in my opinion, be decisive in determining the adoption of ethical first principles," but, as he reiterates, "it is not my primary aim to establish such principles" (*ME*, p. 14).

So *The Methods of Ethics* is an investigatory work. No doubt, Sidgwick hoped that if he impartially examined the major methods one of them would emerge with a superior claim to validity. No

---

13. "First Principles and Common Sense Morality," p. 137; but for Schneewind's present view, see "Sidgwick and Cambridge Philosophy" in this issue of *The Monist*.

doubt, too, Sidgwick expected and hoped that if one method did distinguish itself in this way, it would be the utilitarian method. Nevertheless, to see the whole work as a single-minded attempt to establish utilitarianism is to misunderstand it, and consequently to risk misunderstanding the function of the various arguments that occur in it.

The express primary aim of *The Methods of Ethics*, then, is to define and unfold the methods of ethics implicit in our ordinary moral reasoning, and to point out their relations to each other. The three methods are, of course, Egoistic Hedonism, Intuitionism and Utilitarianism. It should be noted that although there is a reference here to "ordinary moral reasoning", this does not suggest that the validity of a moral theory depends on it being in accordance with these ordinary methods. These methods, being the most popular ones, are merely the ones that Sidgwick chose as the most likely candidates for the position of the correct method. Even if they could all be perfectly harmonized this would not mean that the resulting harmonization was necessarily valid. It might be that all the popular methods are irrational, and some quite esoteric method the only rational one.

A further difference from the reflective equilibrium model is that it is not the *results* of our ordinary moral reasoning, not our particular moral judgments, but the methods we use in reaching these judgments that Sidgwick thinks worth examining. The validity of a method would seem to depend on the self-evidence of the "primary intuition" and the soundness of the reasoning used in its application, not on whether its results match our considered moral judgments.[14]

---

14. It has been suggested to me that if we interpret the reflective equilibrium model so that it is not only our particular judgments that the moral theory is to match, but also our ordinary methods of reasoning, Sidgwick and Rawls are not so far apart after all. Rawls himself appears to be thinking primarily of a match with our particular intuitive judgments (*ATOJ*, pp. 19, 49), and indeed the suggested alteration would cause difficulties for his conception, since our ordinary method of reasoning might itself be a candidate moral theory, and would then be measured up against itself—an unfair advantage, we might well think. In any case, though, the difference pointed out in the previous paragraph still stands, and it is crucial to the nature of the enterprise.

It is, incidentally, the methods of reasoning, and not particular judgments, that are the "primary intuitions" mentioned in the passage from Sidgwick quoted by Rawls, *ATOJ*, p. 51n.

If this is so, it is natural to ask why the book does contain so much discussion of common sense morality—for that it does contain a very detailed, even repetitious, discussion of it is undeniable. Part of the answer to this question has already been given. The discussion in Chapter 3 of Book IV, entitled "The Relation of Utilitarianism to Common Sense" is an *ad hominem* argument by which a Utilitarian might try to prove the superiority of his principle to one committed to common sense morality. The far lengthier discussion which comprises almost the whole of Book III serves a different purpose. This is apparent immediately we reject the idea that Book III is one stage of an argument for utilitarianism. The aim of Book III is to examine a particular method of reaching moral conclusions—the method Sidgwick calls "Intuitionism," which is the view that we can discover what we ought to do simply by consulting our conscience, or, as it used to be called, our "Moral Faculty." The immediate outcome of this method is the set of judgments Sidgwick calls "the morality of Common Sense." So, as Sidgwick says in reviewing his survey of this morality "I wish it to be particularly observed that I have in no case introduced my own views insofar as I am conscious of their being at all peculiar to myself: my sole object has been to make explicit the implied premises of our common moral reasoning" (*ME*, p. 338).

Still, it might be suggested, though not, I think, by those who have, in reading Sidgwick, come to feel an almost personal acquaintance with him, that Sidgwick was being less than candid in his avowals of his aims: alternatively, it might be thought that he was himself deceived about his real intentions. Yet there is evidence that neither of these possibilities was the case. The evidence comes from Sidgwick's discussion of the method of Egoistic Hedonism. As we have seen, Sidgwick's own sympathies are with the utilitarian, or universalistic hedonist method; nevertheless, his examination of the method of egoistic hedonism is not a refutation of that method, nor is it a demonstration of the superiority of utilitarianism. On the contrary, Sidgwick's final verdict in the concluding chapter of the whole book is that the aim of furthering one's own interest stands on just as rational a basis as the aim of furthering the universal interest; and that the two methods lead to incompatible results, except on the hypothesis that there is a Supreme Being who ensures that it is in our own interest to follow the universal interest (Sidg-

wick himself was very doubtful about the truth of this hypothesis).
So, even if we disregard the author's explicit denial, it is impossible
to regard *The Methods of Ethics* as an argument for utilitarianism.
The most that could be said is that it is an argument for both egoistic
and universalistic hedonism against intuitionism. This would be an
odd aim for any book, however, and it is much more plausible to
accept the view that the book is concerned to unfold the implications
of the three methods, rather than to argue for any one (or two!) of
them. If Sidgwick hoped by this unfolding to discover the correct
method, the result is impressive testimony to his fair-mindedness,
for he considers himself unable to establish the rational superiority
of the utilitarian method. The result of unfolding the method happens to be that the method of intuitionism and the method of utilitarianism are shown to be reconcilable, because the judgments of
common sense morality turn out to require the utilitarian principle
to fall back on as an underlying self-evident first principle, and a
means of settling conflicts, resolving vagueness, and so on. On the
other hand, divine interference apart, the opposition between egoism
and utilitarianism leaves an "ultimate and fundamental contradiction in our apparent intuitions of what is Reasonable in conduct"
(*ME*, p. 508).

So Sidgwick's conclusion about egoistic hedonism is independent
evidence of the intentions of his book. At the same time, it is further
evidence of a fairly direct kind against the claim that Sidgwick used
the method of reflective equilibrium to judge between rival theories.
For while Sidgwick thought that utilitarianism coincides with intuitionism, that is, with the philosophical position based on our ordinary
moral judgments, egoism remains the odd man out. Sidgwick clearly
believes that egoism is, at least in some circumstances, incompatible
with both utilitarianism and common sense morality (since he believes that these last two coincide, if egoism is incompatible with one
it must also be incompatible with the other). Thus, Sidgwick sums
up the chapter in which he discusses the compatibility of happiness
and duty by saying:

> although the performance of duties towards others and the exercise
> of social virtue seem to be *generally* the best means to the attain-
> ment of the individual's happiness, and it is easy to exhibit this
> coincidence between Virtue and Happiness rhetorically and popu-
> larly; still when we carefully analyse and estimate the consequences

of Virtue to the virtuous agent, it appears improbable that this coincidence is complete and universal. [*ME*, p. 175. Italics in original.]

This conclusion, as we have seen, is repeated in the concluding chapter (*ME*, pp. 503, 508) and is also brought out clearly in the autobiographical sketch in the preface to the sixth edition.

If Sidgwick were using the reflective equilibrium procedure to test moral theories, the incompatibility of egoism and common sense morality would be a decisive point against egoism. We could argue simply: the test of a moral theory is whether it matches our considered moral judgments in reflective equilibrium; egoistic hedonism is incompatible with at least some of our considered moral judgments and cannot be brought into equilibrium with them; therefore egoistic hedonism is not an acceptable moral theory. But Sidgwick does not argue in this way; indeed, he does not regard the incompatibility between egoism and our considered moral judgments even as a consideration that counts against egoism. Instead he sees the reasonableness of egoism as quite independent of the extent to which it matches our moral judgment—it is based on the plausibility of its starting point, of which Sidgwick says:

> It would be contrary to Common Sense to deny that the distinction between any one individual and any other is real and fundamental, and that consequently "I" am concerned with the quality of my existence as an individual in a sense, fundamentally important, in which I am not concerned with the quality of the existence of other individuals: and this being so, I do not see how it can be proved that this distinction is not to be taken as fundamental in determining the ultimate end of rational action for an individual. [*ME*, p. 498; see also pp. 7, 119-20, 419][15]

_____

15. Schneewind recognizes that "Sidgwick can see no rational way of proving one of these principles [egoistic and universalistic hedonism] to the exclusion of the other" but claims that this shows how little weight Sidgwick is prepared to put on intuition unsupported by considerations like the systematization of our ordinary moral judgments. Schneewind goes on to point out that other philosophers, like Butler and Whewell, were prepared to say that we can simply *see* conscience to be superior in authority to self-love ("First Principles and Common Sense Morality," pp. 155-56). It is true that Sidgwick does not make this move against egoistic hedonism, but that is because, as is evident from the passage just quoted, he thought the "intuition" of the rationality of egoism was as self-evident as any other. What Schneewind fails

SIDGWICK AND REFLECTIVE EQUILIBRIUM   507

I hope that I have now offered sufficient evidence to convince
the reader that Sidgwick does not use the reflective equilibrium procedure to test moral theories. What, then, is the significance of the
coincidence of utilitarianism and common sense morality for Sidgwick, and what is his attitude to common sense morality in general?
A brief discussion of these questions may help to clear up any remaining doubts about the passages that appear to favour the reflective equilibrium interpretation.

On the basis of what has already been said, the significance of
the coincidence of utilitarianism and common sense morality can be
stated briefly. It does not prove the truth of utilitarianism, but it does
mean that utilitarianism is doubly supported. It is supported both on
its own terms—that is, by the initial plausibility of its assumptions
and the absence of any inconsistency or indeterminacy in their unfolding—and it receives the additional support of whatever plausibility is possessed by common sense morality, or more strictly, by
the method of intuitionism. For, according to Sidgwick's account of
intuitionism, any supporter of this method will have to admit that
the only pertinent self-evident intuition, and the one to which all
his more particular intuitions lead him, is the intuition that it is right
to do whatever promotes the greatest happiness for all. Thus he will
be led to become a utilitarian, though on an intuitionist basis.[16]

This is, as I have been saying, an *ad hominem* argument; nevertheless, it must be admitted that for Sidgwick it has a significance
not possessed by any other parallel argument, for instance, that directed against the egoist. Sidgwick had a great deal of respect for
common sense morality. He refers to it as "a marvellous product of
nature, the result of long centuries of growth." At the same time,
Sidgwick was sufficiently skeptical of his own primary method of
testing the truth of moral theories—which was, as we shall see,

---

to address himself to is why, if Sidgwick places great weight on the systematization argument, the superiority of utilitarianism in this respect is not
enough to oust the rival principle. While Sidgwick does, as Schneewind
notes, think that egoism and common sense morality are compatible in many
circumstances, it cannot be denied that he thought that this match breaks
down in a way that the match between utilitarianism and common sense
morality does not—otherwise how would one explain the fact that egoism is
the odd man out in the concluding chapter?

16. On this, see the discussion of Sidgwick's own position, Sec. III, below.

based on the alleged self-evidence of certain ethical axioms—to realize that it was fallible. Accordingly, he looked to common sense morality as a safeguard against error. If an apparently self-evident moral principle has consequences at odds with common sense morality, this should be a warning to us that we may be mistaken in our intuition of self-evidence. Sidgwick stated this view clearly in an article explicitly directed to the question of how first principles are to be established in ethics:

> If we have once learnt, either from personal experience or from the history of thought, that we are liable to be mistaken in the affirmation of apparently self-evident propositions, we may surely retain this general conviction along with the special impression of the self-evidence of any proposition which we may be contemplating; and thus however strong this latter impression may be, we shall still admit our need of some further protection against the possible failure of our faculty of intuition. Such a further guarantee we may reasonably find in "general consent"; for though the protection this gives is not perfect—since there are historical examples of untrue propositions generally accepted as self-evident—it at least excludes all such error as arises from the special weaknesses and biases of individual minds, or of particular sections of the human race. A proposition which presents itself to my mind as self-evident, and is in harmony with all the rest of my intuitions relating to the same subject, and is also accepted by all other minds that have been led to contemplate it *may after all turn out to be false*: but it seems to have as high a degree of certainty as I can hope to attain under existing conditions of human thought.[17]

This passage shows well the similarities and differences between Sidgwick and Rawls. Common sense morality, representing as it does the accumulated experience of mankind, is a useful check on our intuitions of self-evident moral axioms; but even when it is in harmony with our own intuitions we may after all be mistaken. It is this possibility, which I have italicized in the original passage, that marks the distinction between the two authors—for on Rawls's view, one could not even make sense of such a possibility. For Rawls, reaching this kind of harmony is the goal of moral philosophy; it is

---

17. "The Establishment of Ethical First Principles," *Mind*, 4 (1879), p. 108. (The italics are mine.) For a recent statement of a similar position, see R. M. Hare, "The Argument from Received Opinion" in Hare, *Essays on Philosophical Method* (London: Macmillan, 1971).

the definition of "valid" so far as moral theories are concerned: for Sidgwick, it is the best possible insurance against error, but because our target is a moral theory that is true, and not merely in harmony with our intuitions and with common sense morality, we may still be in error.

We may summarize the prominence Sidgwick gives to common sense morality by saying that it plays three different roles: firstly, it is in itself a method of moral reasoning, though one that may be reconciled with utilitarianism; secondly, its reduction to utilitarianism is the foundation on which a utilitarian may construct an *ad hominem* argument in favour of his own principle, which is thereby doubly supported; thirdly, it is an important check on our intuitions of self-evidence about ethical first principles.[18]

III

If Sidgwick did not believe that the truth of a moral theory is shown by its success in systematizing our considered moral judgments, how did he think a moral theory could be shown to be correct?

The short and simple answer is that, as he himself states in the autobiographical sketch already referred to, he is an intuitionist. In this sketch Sidgwick tells how, under the influence first of Kant and then of Butler, he was led to see that:

> The utilitarian method—which I had learnt from Mill—could not, it seemed to me, be made coherent and harmonious without this fundamental intuition . . . the supreme rule of aiming at the general happiness, as I had come to see, must rest on a fundamental intuition, if I was to recognise it as binding at all . . . I was then a Utilitarian again, but on an Intuitional basis. [*ME*, pp. xvi-xx]

There is, however, more to be said than this simple answer reveals. Though from the point of view of what Sidgwick sometimes called "abstract philosophy" he would probably have thought that the self-evidence of the utilitarian principle was the primary

---

18. There is also a fourth role for common sense morality in *ME*, which is less relevant to our purposes: since Sidgwick believes common sense morality to be not only the result of the accumulation of practical wisdom over the centuries, but also, in its essentials, "unconsciously utilitarian", common sense morality can serve the utilitarian as a valuable, though imperfect, guide to the promotion of the general happiness.

reason for accepting it, Sidgwick is not content to stop at abstract philosophy. He is much more interested in the sort of argument that can win over opponents, and in his book he considers various arguments by which a proponent of one of the methods of ethics might try to convince a proponent of another. We have already seen how he thinks a utilitarian might demonstrate the superiority of utilitarianism to a supporter of common sense morality. What, though, would a utilitarian say to someone who had no great respect for our ordinary judgments?

In the short chapter entitled "The Proof of Utilitarianism," before he begins the *ad hominem* argument against the proponent of common sense morality, Sidgwick indicates what a utilitarian might say against a different kind of opponent. What he says there, however, is brief, because many of the points have come up in earlier chapters, to which the reader's attention is directed. The argument needs to be put together from these earlier chapters.

We begin with the search for "real ethical axioms—intuitive propositions of real clearness and certainty" (*ME*, p. 373). This search is in fact the final stage of the unfolding of the intuitionist method, after the intuitions with which we started—those of common sense morality—have been shown to lack the status of self-evident axioms. Putting aside those apparently self-evident principles which turn out, on examination, to be nothing more than tautologies (e.g. "It is right that the lower parts of our nature should be governed by the higher") Sidgwick finds three, and only three, genuine axioms. The first is an axiom of impartiality, in some sense: "whatever action any of us judges to be right for himself, he implicitly judges to be right for all similar persons in similar circumstances" (*ME*, p. 379).[19] The second axiom is an element in the idea of rational self-interest, or prudence: it is the idea of impartial concern for all parts of our conscious life, so that we do not prefer a smaller present good to a greater future good, once any difference in the certainty of gaining the good has been taken into account. This, Sidgwick says, is an axiom about the good for any single indi-

19. Sidgwick takes this axiom from earlier writers, including Clarke and Kant; it also resembles Hare's principle of universalizability: see Hare, *Freedom and Reason* (London: Oxford University Press, 1965), especially Chap. 2.

vidual; but when we consider the notion of universal good, we obtain the "self-evident principle that the good of any one individual is of no more importance, from the point of view (if I may say so) of the Universe, than the good of any other." Here we have more or less reached the third axiom, which is also stated as "it is evident to me that as a rational being I am bound to aim at good generally, . . . not merely at a particular part of it" (*ME*, p. 382).

It is to this third axiom that Sidgwick refers when, in the chapter on the "proof" of utilitarianism, he considers to what extent the principle of utilitarianism might be proved to the egoistic hedonist. Sidgwick's point is that:

> When . . . the Egoist puts forward, implicitly or explicitly, the proposition that his happiness or pleasure is Good, not only *for him* but from the point of view of the Universe . . . it then becomes relevant to point out to him that *his* happiness cannot be a more important part of Good, taken universally, than the equal happiness of any other person. And thus, starting with his own principle, he may be brought to accept Universal happiness or pleasure as that which is absolutely and without qualification Good or Desirable: as an end, therefore, to which the action of a reasonable agent as such ought to be directed. [*ME*, pp. 420-21. Italics in original.]

On the other hand, Sidgwick does not think it possible to prove utilitarianism to an egoist who "confines himself to stating his conviction that he ought to take his own happiness or pleasure as his ultimate end"; under these circumstances "there seems no opening for any line of reasoning to lead him to Universalistic Hedonism as a first principle; it cannot be proved that the difference between his own happiness and another's happiness is not *for him* all-important" (*ME*, p. 420. Italics in original).

This seems to me an important and correct statement. It is analogous with R. M. Hare's mode of argument in *Freedom and Reason*. The analogy may be brought out by putting Sidgwick's point in this way: if a person is concerned only with his own interest, and is not concerned to do what is good in a universal sense, there is no argument we can produce which will force him to concern himself with the interests of others; but if he claims to be aiming at what is morally good, then because of the universalizability inherent in this

claim, we can argue that he cannot, consistently, give greater consideration to his own interests, simply on the ground that they are
his interests, than he gives to the interests of others.[20]

Against the egoistic hedonist, no more can be done, which is
why, in his concluding chapter, Sidgwick recognizes that egoism and
utilitarianism are conflicting fundamental intuitions, and the egoist
can avoid the "proof" of utilitarianism by limiting his concern to
what is the rational ultimate end for himself, thereby disclaiming
any concern for what is good in a universal sense (*ME*, 497-98).

What if the utilitarian's opponent is not even an egoistic hedonist? The universalizing argument just discussed leads to universalistic hedonism (as distinct from some broad utilitarian position that
would include varieties of ideal utilitarianism) only if it is already
admitted that happiness or pleasure is the only thing ultimately good
and desirable. Once this is admitted, the question is merely whether

---

20. In view of this parallel, it is not surprising that Hare should now
acknowledge a much closer connection between his own position and utilitarianism than had previously been recognized: see "Wrongness and Harm"
in *Essays on the Moral Concepts* (London: Macmillan, 1972); cf. *Freedom
and Reason*, Chap. 7. J. L. Mackie has convinced me, however, that Sidgwick's argument is limited to those who try to justify their conduct in terms
of objective *goodness*; it does not hold for those who claim a deontological
justification for their conduct, expressed in terms of the moral "ought". This
is because "Everyone ought to further his or her own interests exclusively,"
held not as a kind of laissez-faire theory for bringing about the universal
good, but as a theory of right conduct, is universalizable. A person who
holds this position is not committed to saying anything about objective goodness at all. He may even deny that it is meaningful to talk of goodness except in the sense of "good for someone".

G. E. Moore attacked Sidgwick's argument on the grounds that no intelligible meaning can be given to the idea of "good for him" which distinguishes it from Universal Good (*Principia Ethica* [Cambridge University
Press, 1903], pp. 96-105); but this is surely a perverse refusal to understand
an expression with a perfectly clear sense. Thomas Nagel's *The Possibility
of Altruism* (Oxford: Clarendon Press, 1970) appears to be based on a
similar denial of the intelligibility of goodness in any subjective sense. As
Nagel says on p. 90: "The principle behind altruism is that values must be
objective, and that any which appear subjective must be associated with
others that are not." The difference between Moore and Nagel, on the one
hand, and Sidgwick, on the other, is that only Sidgwick admits that the use
of the argument against egoism is conditional on the egoist attempting to
justify his position in terms of objective values.

SIDGWICK AND REFLECTIVE EQUILIBRIUM   513

the goal is one's own happiness, or that of every sentient being (no intermediate position having the status of a self-evident axiom). But what if the hedonistic assumption is denied? Can an opponent be brought to admit it?

On this issue Sidgwick refers us back to Book III, Chapter 14, the chapter entitled "Ultimate Good." The argument of this chapter follows on directly from that of the previous chapter, in which the three self-evident ethical axioms were stated. At the conclusion of that chapter, Sidgwick thought, the rigorous demand for really self-evident intuitions had led the intuitionist to a kind of utilitarianism, but only in the broad sense of a principle which judges actions by their tendency to promote "Universal Good" rather than some specific form of universal good, like happiness. Now Sidgwick faces the question whether only happiness is ultimately good in itself. He explicitly rejects the standard utilitarian argument for this conclusion, attributed to Bentham and Mill, which is based on the psychological theory that no one ever does desire anything but happiness. Sidgwick does not think this theory true. What other arguments remain?

The way in which the intuitionist is led from the general notion of universal good to its specific hedonist form illustrates Sidgwick's approach to ultimate questions. The chapter contains both argument and appeals to intuition. The role of the argument is to support the intuition Sidgwick feels to be correct, and in particular to explain why apparently contrary intuitions are not to be taken at face value. In this way the idea that virtue is good in itself, apart from its effects on consciousness, is dismissed, and ultimate good is narrowed down to nothing other than "Desirable Consciousness." This notion still includes more than happiness, since it might be said that knowing the truth, or contemplating beauty or virtue, are desirable forms of consciousness independently of their tendency to promote happiness. Sidgwick does not think this view can be refuted by any decisive argument, but he regards it as a view which, to give his own characteristic phrase, "ought not to commend itself to the sober judgment of reflective persons." To persuade the reader of this he appeals firstly to the reader's own intuitive judgment "after due consideration of the question when fairly placed before it," and secondly to a comparison of the judgments of common sense. In this second appeal, argument again has its place in showing how the superficial aversion common sense sometimes has to regarding happiness as the sole ultimate end of right conduct is compatible with a real acceptance of happiness as the sole end. The appeal to common sense here is, again, not a *test* of the validity of hedonism—if it were, then this appeal alone would be decisive, and the prior appeal to the reader's intuitions would have been superfluous—but is based on the assumption that common sense morality represents the accumulated experience of mankind, and so is worthy of considerable respect.

A final argument for universal hedonism is that if happiness is regarded not as the sole ultimate good, but as only one among ultimate goods, then we need, in practice, to compare and balance these goods with each other, and how we are to go about doing this is a problem to which no one has produced a coherent answer.[21]

Since my present concern is with the method Sidgwick uses for testing the validity of a moral theory, rather than with the arguments for particular theories to be found in his book, I will not discuss the merits of the arguments for utilitarianism. What I have tried to show is that though, for Sidgwick, the ultimate appeal is to the carefully considered intuitive judgment of the reader, this is a very different procedure from one which aims at matching a moral theory with the considered moral judgments either of the reader, or of some widely accepted moral consensus. Even if everyone should agree that the fundamental principle of utilitarianism is a clear and certain rational intuition, this would not, on Sidgwick's view, actually establish the truth of utilitarianism. Agreement, no matter how widespread it may be, is not a criterion for the truth or validity of a normative theory. Sidgwick would admit that, in the end, we have nothing to fall back on other than careful consideration of whether some fundamental principle really is intuitively clear and certain (though we may be able to support our intuitions to some extent by a comparison with common sense morality), but he does not *define* validity for a moral theory in terms of agreement with our ultimate intuitions or in terms of a match with our particular judg-

---

21. This may have been true when Sidgwick wrote, but today it is perhaps the least convincing of his points. Both Rawls in *ATOJ* and Brian Barry in *Political Argument* (London: Routledge & Kegan Paul, 1965), pp. 3-8, have shown how it is possible to deal coherently with values as different from each other as justice and welfare.

ments. Therefore he is not committed to the kind of subjectivism that is consequent upon any such definition of validity for a moral theory.

IV

How are we, as moral philosophers, to, decide between the two ways of doing moral philosophy represented by Sidgwick and Rawls? This question can appear mind-boggling, for it requires us to establish the criteria for the correct choice of criteria for the correct choice of moral theory. Yet I think we can come to a decision by reflection on what it is that we, as moral philosophers, are trying to do.

The historical task of moral philosophy has been to develop theories that serve as guides to conduct. So long as there are grounds for hoping that discussion, argument, and the careful consideration of moral theories can help us to decide how to act, the importance of this historical task cannot be denied. Sidgwick, obviously, was engaged on this task. Can the same be said for Rawls? In a sense, yes. Rawls clearly intends his theory to be a guide to conduct; yet at the same time, his use of the reflective equilibrium idea means that he is on the verge of slipping off into an altogether different activity, that of systematizing the considered moral judgments of some unspecified moral consensus. This latter task, while it may be of some interest, is, like the linguistic and scientific investigations on which it is modelled, a descriptive task from which, without supplementation from other sources, no normative or action-guiding consequences can be derived. We cannot test a normative theory by the extent to which it accords with the moral judgments people ordinarily make. Insofar as Rawls frequently does seem to be testing his own theory in this way, the theory fails to be normative and Rawls cannot be regarded as pursuing the same task as Sidgwick and most other moral philosophers.[22]

Now it is true that Rawls does not really propose that normative theories should be tested by comparison with the moral judgments people ordinarily make. He says, as we have seen, that he appeals directly to the reader's own considered moral judgments. The read-

22. On this point see R. M. Hare, "The Argument From Received Opinion," in Hare, *Essays on Philosophical Method* (London: Macmillan, 1971). See also n. 4, above.

er's own considered moral judgments are relevant for normative
purposes. If the reader simply cannot accept a moral judgment that
follows from a moral theory, he must modify the theory, or else
drop it altogether. Otherwise he is being inconsistent. To this extent
the reflective equilibrium method is sound. But why should the
reader be unable to accept any consequence of a theory that is based
on a fundamental axiom that seems to him clear and undeniable?
This is a question which Rawls never asks, and he never asks it
because from the start he thinks of moral philosophy in the wrong
way. Thus he says: "Now one may think of moral philosophy at
first (and I stress the provisional nature of this view) as the attempt
to describe our moral capacity" (*ATOJ*, p. 46). Even if this is only
provisional, it is a misleading provisional starting point. It leads to
the assumption that we have a certain moral capacity, and that at
least some of the moral judgments we make will, after consideration, remain as fixed points against which theories can be tested.
Why should we not rather make the opposite assumption, that all
the particular moral judgments we intuitively make are likely to derive from discarded religious systems, from warped views of sex and
bodily functions, or from customs necessary for the survival of the
group in social and economic circumstances that now lie in the distant past? In which case, it would be best to forget all about our
particular moral judgments, and start again from as near as we can
get to self-evident moral axioms.

   Rawls could maintain that even this last hypothesis is compatible
with "reflective equilibrium". It is simply the limiting case, in which
there are no moral judgments that survive consideration, and so
there are no considered moral judgments. Again, this is strictly
correct, but it is a result that one is very unlikely to arrive at if one
starts off by thinking about moral philosophy in the way that Rawls
suggests. We are unlikely to arrive at it because we start from a
position in which we are trying to produce a theory that will match
our moral judgments; but there is another reason as well. We have
all been making moral judgments about particular cases for many
years before we begin moral philosophy. Particular views have been
inculcated into us by parents, teachers and society from childhood.
Many of them we act upon every day—telling the truth, not stealing
when we have the opportunity to do so, and so on. These judgments
sink deep, and become habitual. By contrast, when we read Sidg-

SIDGWICK AND REFLECTIVE EQUILIBRIUM   517

wick for the first time we are suddenly called upon to decide whether
certain fundamental moral principles, which we may never have explicitly thought about before, are self-evident. If it is then pointed
out to us that this fundamental moral principle is incompatible with
some of the particular moral judgments we are accustomed to making, and that therefore we must either reject the fundamental principle, or else abandon our particular judgments, surely the odds are
stacked against the fundamental principle. Most of us are familiar
with lingering guilt feelings that occur when we do something that
we are quite certain is right, but which we once thought to be
wrong. These feelings make us reluctant to abandon particular moral
views we hold, but they in no way justify these views.

The reflective equilibrium conception of moral philosophy, then,
by leading us to think of our particular moral judgments as data
against which moral theories are to be tested, is liable to mislead in
two ways: first, it slides easily into the view that moral theories are
to be tested against the moral judgments made by some group or
consensus, and no normative significance can be attached to the judgments of any group; second, even when the "reflective equilibrium"
method says no more than that one cannot consistently accept a
moral theory while holding particular judgments incompatible with
it, it puts this truth in a way that tends to give excessive weight to
our particular moral judgments.

That these dangers are real enough is evidenced by the great
weight placed on particular intuitive judgments, both those of an
assumed consensus and those of the author himself, in *A Theory of
Justice*. It seems preferable to proceed as Sidgwick did: search for
undeniable fundamental axioms; build up a moral theory from them;
and use particular moral judgments as supporting evidence, or as a
basis for *ad hominem* arguments, but never so as to suggest that
the validity of the theory is determined by the extent to which it
matches them.

PETER SINGER

UNIVERSITY COLLEGE, OXFORD
AND NEW YORK UNIVERSITY

[21]

WIDE REFLECTIVE EQUILIBRIUM AND THEORY ACCEPTANCE IN ETHICS *

THERE is a widely held view that a moral theory consists of a set of moral judgments plus a set of principles that account for or generate them. This two-tiered view of moral theories has helped make the problem of theory acceptance or jus-

* I am indebted to Richard Boyd, Arthur Caplan, Christopher Cherniak, C. A. J. Coady, Josh Cohen, Daniel Dennett, Jane English, Paul Horwich, Allan Garfinkel, William Lycan, Miles Morgan, John Rawls, Amelie Rorty, George Smith, and M. B. E. Smith for helpful comments on ideas contained in this paper. The research was supported by an NEH Fellowship for 1977/78.

0022-362X/79/7605/0256$02.00

tification [1] in ethics intractable, unless, that is, one is willing to grant privileged epistemological status to the moral judgments (calling them "intuitions") or to the moral principles (calling them "self-evident" or otherwise a priori). Neither alternative is attractive. Nor, given this view of moral theory, do we get very far with a simple coherence view of justification. To be sure, appeal to elementary coherence (here, consistency) constraints between principles and judgments sometimes allows us to clarify our moral views or to make progress in moral argument. But there must be more to moral justification of both judgments and principles than such simple coherence considerations, especially in the face of the many plausible bases for rejecting moral judgments; e.g., the judgments may only reflect class or cultural background, self-interest, or historical accident.

I shall argue that a version of what John Rawls has called the *method of wide reflective equilibrium* [2] reveals a greater complexity in the structure of moral theories than the traditional view. Consequently, it may render theory acceptance in ethics a more tractable problem. If it does, it may permit us to recast and resolve some traditional worries about objectivity in ethics. To make this suggestion at all plausible, I shall have to defend reflective equilibrium against various charges that it is really a disguised form of moral intuitionism and therefore "subjectivist." First, however, I must explain what wide equilibrium is and show why seeking it may increase our ability to choose among competing moral conceptions.

---

[1] Since the notion of justification is broadly used in philosophy, it is worth forestalling a confusion right at the outset. The problem I address in this paper is strictly analogous to the general and abstract problem of theory acceptance or justification posed in the philosophy of science with regard to nonmoral theories. I am not directly concerned with explaining when a particular individual is justified in, or can be held accountable for, holding a particular moral belief or performing a particular action. So, too, the philosopher of science, interested in how theory acceptance depends on the relation of one theory to another, is not directly concerned to determine whether or not a given individual is justified in believing some feature of one of the theories. Just how relevant my account of theory acceptance is to the question, Is so-and-so justified in believing P or in doing A on evidence E in conditions C, (vary P,A,E)? would require a detailed examination of particular cases. I am indebted to Miles Morgan and John Rawls for discussion of this point.

[2] The distinction between narrow and wide reflective equilibria is implicit in *A Theory of Justice* (Cambridge, Mass.: Harvard, 1971), p. 49, and is explicit in "The Independence of Moral Theory," *Proceedings and Addresses of the American Philosophical Association*, XLVII (1974/75): 5–22, p. 8.

I. WIDE REFLECTIVE EQUILIBRIUM

The method of wide reflective equilibrium is an attempt to produce coherence in an ordered triple of sets of beliefs held by a particular person, namely, (a) a set of considered moral judgments, (b) a set of moral principles, and (c) a set of relevant background theories. We begin by collecting the person's initial moral judgments and filter them to include only those of which he is relatively confident and which have been made under conditions conducive to avoiding errors of judgment. For example, the person is calm and has adequate information about cases being judged.[3] We then propose alternative sets of moral principles that have varying degrees of "fit" with the moral judgments. We do *not* simply settle for the best fit of principles with judgments, however, which would give us only a *narrow* equilibrium.[4] Instead, we advance philosophical arguments intended to bring out the relative strengths and weaknesses of the alternative sets of principles (or competing moral conceptions). These arguments can be construed as inferences from some set of relevant background theories (I use the term loosely). Assume that some particular set of arguments wins and that the moral agent is persuaded that some set of principles is more acceptable than the others (and, perhaps, than the conception that might have emerged in narrow equilibrium). We can imagine the

[3] Though Rawls's earlier formulations of the notion [in his "Outline for a Decision Procedure for Ethics," *Philosophical Review*, LX, 2 (April 1951): 177–197, esp. pp. 182/3] restricts considered judgments to moral judgments about particular cases, his later formulations drop the restriction, so they can be of any level of generality. Cf. Rawls, "Independence of Moral Theory," p. 8. These "ideal" conditions may have drawbacks, as Allan Garfinkel has pointed out to me. Sometimes anger or (moral) indignation may lead to morally better actions and judgments than "calm"; also, the formulation fails to correct for divergence between stated beliefs and beliefs revealed in action.

[4] Narrow reflective equilibrium might be construed as the moral analogue of solving the projection problem for syntactic competence: the principles are the moral analogue of a grammar. This analogy is not extendable to wide equilibrium, as I show in "Some Methods of Ethics and Linguistics," forthcoming in *Philosophical Studies*. Narrow equilibrium leaves us with the traditional two-tiered view of moral theories and is particularly ill suited to provide a basis for a justificational argument. It does not offer a special epistemological claim about the considered moral judgments (other than the rather weak claim that they are filtered to avoid some obvious sources of error), nor are there constraints on the acceptability of moral principles beyond their good "fit" with the initial considered judgments. If we have reason to suspect that the initial judgments are the product of bias, historical accident, or ideology, then these elementary coherence considerations alone give us little basis for comfort, since they provide inadequate pressure to correct for them. Cf. Rawls, *A Theory of Justice*, p. 49.

agent working back and forth, making adjustments to his considered judgments, his moral principles, and his background theories.
In this way he arrives at an equilibrium point that consists of the
ordered triple (a), (b), (c).[5]

We need to find more structure here. The background theories
in (c) should show that the moral principles in (b) are more acceptable than alternative principles on grounds to some degree
independent of (b)'s match with relevant considered moral judgments in (a). If they are not in this way independently supported,
then there seems to be no gain over the support the principles
would have had in a corresponding narrow equilibrium, where
there never was any appeal to (c). Another way to raise this point
is to ask how we can be sure that the moral principles that systematize the considered moral judgments are not just "accidental
generalizations" of the "moral facts," analogous to accidental generalizations which we want to distinguish from real scientific laws.
In science, we have evidence that we are not dealing with accidental generalizations if we can derive the purported laws from a body
of interconnected theories, provided these theories reach, in a diverse and interesting way, beyond the "facts" that the principle
generalizes.

This analogy suggests one way to achieve independent support
for the principles in (b) and to rule out their being mere accidental
generalizations of the considered judgments. We should require
that the background theories in (c) be more than reformulations
of the same set of considered moral judgments involved when the
principles are matched to moral judgments. The background theories should have a scope reaching beyond the range of the considered moral judgments used to "test" the moral principles. Some
interesting, nontrivial portions of the set of considered moral judgments that constrains the background theories and of the set that
constrains the moral principles should be disjoint.

Suppose that some set of considered *moral* judgments (a') plays
a role in constraining the background theories in (c). It is important to note that the acceptability of (c) may thus in part depend
on some *moral* judgments, which means we are not in general assuming that (c) constitutes a reduction of the moral [in (b) and (a)]

---

[5] The fact that I describe wide equilibrium as being built up out of judgments, principles, and relevant background theories does not mean that this
represents an order of epistemic priority or a natural sequence in the genesis
of theories. Arthur Caplan reminded me of this point.

to the nonmoral. Then, our *independence constraint* amounts to
the requirement that (a') and (a) be to some significant degree disjoint.[6] The background theories might, for example, not incorporate the same type of moral notions as are employed by the principles and those considered judgments relevant to "testing" the
principles.

It will help to have an example of a wide equilibrium clearly in
mind. Consider Rawls's theory of justice.[7] We are led by philosophical argument, Rawls believes, to accept the contract and its various
constraints as a reasonable device for selecting between competing
conceptions of justice (or right). These arguments, however, can be
viewed as inferences from a number of relevant background theories, in particular, from a theory of the person, a theory of procedural justice, general social theory, and a theory of the role of
morality in society (including the ideal of a well-ordered society).
These *level* III theories, as I shall call them, are what persuade us
to adopt the contract apparatus, with all its constraints (call it the
level II apparatus). Principles chosen at level II are subject to two
constraints: (i) they must match our considered moral judgments
in (partial) reflective equilibrium; and (ii) they must yield a feasible, stable, well-ordered society. I will call *level* I the *partial* reflective equilibrium that holds between the moral principles and
the relevant set of considered moral judgments. *Level* IV contains
the body of social theory relevant to testing level I principles (and
level III theories) for "feasibility."

The independence constraint previously defined for wide equilibrium in general applies in this way: the considered moral judgments [call them (a')] which may act to constrain level III theory
acceptability must to a significant extent be disjoint from the considered moral judgments [call them (a)] which act to constrain level
I partial equilibrium. I argue elsewhere that Rawls's construction
appears to satisfy this independence constraint, since his central

6 My formulation is not adequate as it stands, since there will even be trivial
truth-functional counterexamples to it unless some specification of 'interesting'
and 'nontrivial' is given, to say nothing of providing a measure for the 'scope"
of a theory. This is a standing problem in philosophy of science [cf. Michael
Friedman's attempt to handle the related question of unifying theories in "Explanation and Scientific Understanding," this JOURNAL, LXXI, 1 (Jan. 17, 1974):
5–19, esp. 15 ff]. I will assume that this difficulty can be overcome, though doing so might require dropping the loose talk about theories. I am indebted to
George Smith for helpful discussion of this point.

7 I draw here on my "Reflective Equilibrium and Archimedean Points," forthcoming in *Canadian Journal of Philosophy*.

level III theories of the person and of the role of morality in society
are probably not just recharacterizations or systematizations of level
I moral judgments.[8] If I am right, then (supposing soundness of
Rawls's arguments!), the detour of deriving the principles from the
contract adds justificatory force to them, justification not found
simply in the level I matching of principles and judgments. Notice
that this advantage is exactly what would be lost if the contract
and its defining conditions were "rigged" just to yield the best level
I equilibrium.[9] The other side 'of this coin is that the level II apparatus will not be acceptable if competing theories of the person
or of the role of morality in society are preferable to the theories
Rawls advances. Rawls's Archimedean point is fixed only against
the acceptability of particular level III theories.

This argument suggests that we abstract from the details of the
Rawlsian example to find quite general features of the structure
of moral theories in wide equilibrium. Alternatives to justice as
fairness are likely to contain some level II device for principle selection other than the contract (say a souped-up impartial spectator). Such variation would reflect variation in the level III theories, especially the presence of alternative theories of the person
or of the role of morality. Finally, developed alternatives to justice
as fairness would still be likely to contain some version of the level
I and level IV constraints, though the details of how these constraints function will reflect the content of component theories at
the different levels.

By revealing this structural complexity, the search for wide equilibrium can benefit moral inquiry in several ways. First, philos-

[8] In particular, Rawls's level III theories rest on no considered moral judgments about rights and entitlements: all such considered judgments are segre-
gated into level I, so that level III theories provide a foundation for our notions
of rights and entitlements without themselves appealing to such notions
(though they appeal to other moral notions, such as fairness and various claims
about persons). Rawls seems attracted to this view of his project [cf. his "Reply
to Alexander and Musgrave," *Quarterly Journal of Economics*, LXXXCII, 4
(November 1974), p. 634]. In contrast, Ronald Dworkin argues that a background right to equal respect is needed at what I call "level III." [Cf. his "The
Original Position," *University of Chicago Law Review*, XL, 3 (Spring 1973):
500–533; reprinted in my anthology, *Reading Rawls* (New York: Basic Books,
1975), pp. 16–53, esp. p. 45, 50 ff.] For an argument that Dworkin is wrong to
posit such a level III right, see my "Reflective Equilibrium and Archimedean
Points."

[9] Rawls leaves himself open to the accusation of "rigging" when he says,
e.g., "We want to define the original position so that we get the desired solution" (*A Theory of Justice*, p. 141). Critics have had a field day using this and
similar remarks to show that the contract can have no justificational role.

ophers have often suggested that many apparently "moral" disagreements rest on other, nonmoral disagreements. Usually these are lumped together as the "facts" of the situation. Wide equilibrium may reveal a more systematic, if complex, structure to these sources of disagreement, and, just as important, to sources of agreement as well.

Second, aside from worries about universalizability and generalizability, philosophers have not helped us to understand what factors *actually do* constrain the considerations people cite as reasons, or treat as "relevant" and "important," in moral reasoning and argument. A likely suggestion is that these features of moral reasoning depend on the *content* of underlying level III theories and level II principle selectors, or on properties of the level I and IV constraints. An adequate moral psychology, in other words, would have to incorporate features of what I am calling "wide equilibrium." Understanding these features of moral argument more clearly might lead to a better grasp of what constitutes evidence for and against moral judgments and principles. This result should not be surprising: as in science, judgments about the plausibility and acceptability of various claims are the complex result of the whole system of interconnected theories already found acceptable. My guess—I cannot undertake to confirm it here—is that the type of coherence constraint that operates in the moral and nonmoral cases functions to produce many similarities: we should find methodological conservatism in both; we will find that "simplicity" judgments in both really depend on determining how little we have to change in the interconnected background theories already accepted (not on more formal measures of simplicity); and we will find in both that apparently "intuitive" judgments about how "interesting," "important," and "relevant" puzzles or facts are, are really guided by underlying theory.[10]

A third possible benefit of wide equilibrium is that level III disagreements about theories may be more tractable than disagreements about moral judgments and principles. Consequently, if the moral disagreements can be traced to disagreements about theory, greater moral agreement may result.

Some examples may perhaps make this claim more plausible.

[10] We know relatively little about these features of theory acceptance in either domain, a fact traceable to the same empiricist and positivist legacy: too narrow an account of the relation between theory and "data," be it laws-plus-observation or principles-plus-judgments.

A traditional form of criticism against utilitarianism consists in deriving unacceptable moral judgments about punishment, desert, or distributive justice from a general utilitarian principle. Some utilitarians then may bite the bullet and reject reliance on these "pretheoretical" intuitions. Rawls has suggested an explanation for the class of examples involving distributive justice. He suggests that the utilitarian has imported into social contexts, where we distribute goods between persons, a principle acceptable only for distributing goods between life-stages of one person. Derek Parfit urges a different explanation: the utilitarian, perhaps supported by evidence from the philosophy of mind, uses a weaker criterion of personal identity than that presupposed by, say, Rawls's account of life plans. Accordingly, he treats interpersonal boundaries as metaphysically less deep and morally less important. The problem between the utilitarian and the contractarian thus becomes the (possibly) more manageable problem of determining the acceptability of competing theories of the person, and only one of many constraints on that task is the connection of the theory of the person to the resulting moral principles.[11]

A second example derives from a suggestion of Bernard Williams.[12] He argues that there may be a large discrepancy between the dictates of utilitarian theory in a particular case and what a person will be inclined to do given that he has been raised to have virtues (e.g., beneficence) that in general optimize his chances of doing utilitarian things. We may generalize Williams's point: suppose any moral conception can be paired with an *optimal* set of virtues, those which make their bearer most likely to do what is right according to the given conception. Moral conceptions may differ significantly in the degree to which acts produced by their optimal virtues tend to differ from acts they deem right. Level III and IV theories of moral psychology and development would be needed to

[11] Compare Derek Parfit, "Later Selves and Moral Principles," in Alan Montefiore, ed., *Philosophy and Personal Relations* (London: Routledge & Kegan Paul, 1973), pp. 149–160. See Rawls's reply in "Independence of Moral Theory," p. 17 ff. The degree to which a theory of the person constrains moral-theory acceptance, and conversely, the degree to which moral theory constrains theories of the person are discussed in my "Moral Theory and the Plasticity of Persons," forthcoming in *The Monist*, LXII, 3 (July 1979). The Marxist worry that there is no non-class-relative notion of the person substantial enough to found a moral theory on thus appears as an argument about level III theory acceptability.

[12] "Utilitarianism and Moral Self-Indulgence" in H. D. Lewis, *Contemporary British Philosophy*, IVth Series (New York: Humanities, 1976), pp. 306–321.

determine the facts here. Since we want to reduce such discrepancies (at least according to some level III and IV theories), we may have an important scale against which to compare moral conceptions.

More, and better developed, examples would be needed to show that the theory construction involved in seeking wide equilibrium increases our ability to choose rationally among competing moral conceptions. But there is a general difficulty that must be faced squarely: level III theories may, I have claimed, depend in part for their acceptability on some considered moral judgments, as in Rawls's level III theories. (If the independence constraint is satisfied, however, these are not primarily the level I considered judgments.) If the source of our disagreement about competing moral conceptions is disagreement on such level III considered judgments, then it is not clear just how much increase in tractability will result. The presence of these judgments clearly poses some disanalogy to scientific-theory acceptance. I take up this worry indirectly, by first considering the charge that reflective equilibrium is warmed-over moral intuitionism.

II. THE REVISABILITY OF CONSIDERED MORAL JUDGMENTS

A number of philosophers, quite diverse in other respects, have argued that the method of reflective equilibrium is really a form of moral intuitionism, indeed of subjective intuitionism.[13] If we take moral intuitionism in its standard forms, then the charge seems unfounded. Intuitionist theories have generally been foundationalist. Some set of moral beliefs is picked out as basic or self-warranting. Theories differ about the nature or basis of the self-warrant. Some claim self-evidence or incorrigibility, others innateness, others some form of causal reliability. A claim of causal reliability might take, for example, the form of a perceptual account which even leaves room for perceptual error. Some intuitionists want to treat principles as basic. Others begin with particular intuitions, and then attempt to find general principles that systematize the intuitions, perhaps revealing and reducing errors among them. Still, and this is the central point, the justification for accepting such moral principles is that they systematize the intuitions, which carry the epistemological privilege.[14]

---

13 The charge is made by R. M. Hare ("Rawls' Theory of Justice," in *Reading Rawls*, p. 82 ff), by Peter Singer ["Sidgwick and Reflective Equilibrium," *Monist*, LVIII, 3 (July 1974): 490–517, p. 494], and by Richard Brandt (*A Theory of the Good and The Right*, Oxford, forthcoming, ch. I).

14 My characterization of intuitionism emphasizes its foundationalism. For an account that deemphasizes its foundationalism, see M. B. E. Smith's excellent

No such foundationalism is part of wide reflective equilibrium as I have described it. Despite the care taken to filter initial judgments to avoid obvious sources of error, no special epistemological priority [15] is granted the considered moral judgments. We are missing the little story that gets told about why we should pay homage ultimately to those judgments and indirectly to the principles that systematize them. Without such a story, however, we have no foundationalism and so no standard form of moral intuitionism.

Nevertheless, it might be thought that reflective equilibrium involves an attempt to give us the *effect* of intuitionism without any fairy tales about epistemic priority. The effect is that a set of principles gets "tested" against a determinate and relatively fixed set of moral judgments. We have, as it were, foundationalism without foundations. Once the foundational claim is removed, however, we have nothing more than a person's moral opinion. It is a "considered" opinion, to be sure, but still only an opinion. Since such opinions are often the result of self-interest, self-deception, historical and cultural accident, hidden class bias, and so on, just systematizing some of them hardly seems a promising way to provide justification for them or for the principles that order them.

This objection really rests on two distinct complaints: (1) that reflective equilibrium merely systematizes some relatively determinate set of moral judgments; and (2) that the considered moral judgments are not a proper foundation for an ethical theory. I will return in section III to consider (2) in a version that abstracts from the issue of the revisability of considered judgments. Here I shall consider objection (1).

"Rawls and Intuitionism," in Kai Nielsen and Roger Shiner, eds., *New Essays on Contract Theory, Canadian Journal of Philosophy*, suppl. vol. III: 163–178. Smith agrees that Rawls's "revisionism" in wide equilibrium is contrary to the spirit of intuitionism. Still, he thinks the intuitionist can accept Rawls's method as a "check" on his own, *provided* it does not lead to strongly counterintuitive revisions. It is unclear to me how much of a "check" one has if such a proviso is imposed. Smith also argues that Rawls's method of wide equilibrium cannot yield principles, such as the principle governing the duty of beneficence. If he is right, then the method not only is not acceptable to the intuitionist who wants "definitive" answers, but also does not meet Rawls's requirements. Though he does not note the point, Smith's argument turns on features of the *contract* and *not* on features of *wide reflective equilibrium* as a method.

[15] The fact that these sources of error have been minimized does give considered judgments *some* modest degree of epistemic priority, as William Lycan has reminded me.

Wide reflection equilibrium does not merely systematize some
determinate set of judgments. Rather, it permits extensive revision
of these moral judgments. There is no set of judgments that is held
more or less fixed as there would be on a foundationalist approach,
even one without foundations. It will be useful to see just how far
from the more traditional view of a moral intuition the considered
moral judgment in wide reflective equilibrium has come.

The difference does not come at the stage at which we filter
initial moral judgments to arrive at *considered* moral judgments.
Sophisticated forms of intuitionism leave room for specifying optimal conditions for avoiding errors of judgment. Nor does the difference come at the stage at which we match principles to judgments, "smooth out" irregularities, and increase the power of the
principles. Again, sophisticated intuitionism is willing to trade
away some slight degree of unrevisability for the reassurance that
errors of judgment are further reduced. It is because *narrow* reflective equilibrium allows no further opportunities for revision than
these two that it is readily assimilated to the model of a sophisticated intuitionism.

But *wide* reflective equilibrium, as I have described it, allows far
more drastic *theory-based* revisions of moral judgments. Consider
the additional ways in which a considered moral judgment is subject to revision in wide equilibrium. Suppose the considered judgment is about what is right or wrong, just or unjust, in particular
situations, or is a maxim that governs such situations. In that
case, it is a judgment relevant to establishing partial reflective equilibrium with general moral principles. Consequently, we must revise it if background theories compel us to revise our general principles or if they lead us to conclude that our moral conception is
not feasible. Suppose, in contrast, the considered moral judgment
plays a role in determining the acceptability of a component level
III theory. Then it is also revisable for several reasons. Feasibility
testing of the background theory may lead us to reject it and therefore to revise the considered judgment. The judgment may be part
of one background theory that is rendered implausible because of
its failure to cohere with other, more plausible background theories, and so the considered judgment may have to be changed.
The considered judgment may be part of a system of background
theories that would lead us to accept principles, and consequently
some other level I considered judgments, which we cannot accept.
If we can trace the source of our difficulty back to a level III con-

sidered judgment that we can give up more easily than we can
accept the new level I judgment, then we would probably revise
the level III judgment.

In seeking wide reflective equilibrium, we are constantly making
plausibility judgments about which of our considered moral judgments we should revise in light of theoretical considerations at all
levels. No one type of considered moral judgment is held immune
to revision. No doubt, we are not inclined to give up certain considered moral judgments unless an overwhelmingly better alternative moral conception is available and substantial dissatisfaction
with our own conception at other points leads us to do so (the
methodological conservatism I referred to earlier). It is in this way
that we provide a sense to the notion of a "provisional fixed point"
among our considered judgments. Since all considered judgments
are revisable, the judgment "It is wrong to inflict pain gratuitously
on another person" is, too. But we can also explain why it is so
hard to imagine not accepting it, so hard that some treat it as a
necessary moral truth. To imagine revising such a provisional fixed
point we must imagine a vastly altered wide reflective equilibrium
that nevertheless is much more acceptable than our own. For example, we might have to imagine persons quite unlike the persons
we know.

Wide reflective equilibrium keeps us from taking considered
moral judgments at face value, however much they may be treated
as starting points in our theory construction.[16] Rather, they are
always subjected to exhaustive review and are "tested," as are the
moral principles, against a relevant body of theory. At every point,
we are forced to assess their acceptability relative to theories that
incorporate them and relative to alternative theories incorporating
different considered moral judgments.[17]

[16] C. F. Delaney suggests quite plausibly that the greater revisability of considered moral judgments in reflective equilibrium in *A Theory of Justice* as
compared to "Outline of a Decision Procedure" corresponds to the shift from
a more positivist view of the relation between facts and theory to a more coherentist, Quinean view. Cf. Delaney's "Rawls on Method," in Nielsen and
Shiner, *op. cit.*, pp. 153–161. The assumption of some critics that Rawls's approach to wide equilibrium is intuitionist may itself derive from their own
latent positivism.

[17] One reason philosophers have thought reflective equilibrium "intuitionist"
is a failure to distinguish narrow and wide equilibria. A more obvious source
lies in Rawls's remark, cited by nearly everyone who makes the charge of intuitionism, that "There is a definite if limited class of facts against which conjectured principles can be checked, namely our considered judgments in reflective equilibrium" (*A Theory of Justice*, p. 51). It is tempting to read the remark

III. COHERENCE AND JUSTIFICATION

A. *No Justification without Credibility.* Consider now the claim
(2) that wide equilibrium uses inappropriate starting points for
the development of moral theory. Here the accusation of neo-intui-
tionism seems to take the opposite tack, suggesting that considered
judgments are not foundational enough. The traditional intuitionist seemed to have more going for him. With some pomp and circumstance, the earlier intuitionist at least outfitted his intuitions
with the regal garb of epistemic priority, even if this later turned
out to be the emperor's clothes. The modern intuitionist, the proponent of reflective equilibrium, allows his naked opinions to
streak their way into our theories without benefit of any cover
story. Richard Brandt has raised this objection in a forceful way
which avoids the mistake about revisability noted earlier.

Brandt characterizes the method of reflective equilibrium as follows. We begin with a set of initial moral judgments or intuitions.
We assign an *initial credence level* (say from 0 to 1 on a scale from
things we believe very little to things we confidently believe). We
filter out judgments with low initial credence levels to form our
set of considered judgments. Then we propose principles and attempt to bring the system of principles plus judgments into equilibrium, allowing modifications wherever they are necessary to produce the system with the highest over-all credence level.[18] But why,
asks Brandt, should we be impressed with the results of such a
process? We should not be, he argues, unless we have some way to
show that "some of the beliefs are initially *credible*—and not
merely initially believed—for some reason other than their coherence" in the set of beliefs we believe the most (*op. cit.*, chapter 1).
For example, in the nonmoral case, Brandt suggests that an initially believed judgment is also an initially credible judgment when
it states (or purports to state) a fact of observation. "In the case
of normative beliefs, no reason has been offered why we should

---

as follows: "to arrive at a reflective equilibrium, treat considered judgments as
a 'definite if limited class of facts' which is to determine the shape and content
of the rest of the theory." R. M. Hare ("Rawls' Theory of Justice," in *Reading
Rawls*, p. 83) and Peter Singer (*op. cit.*, p. 493) read Rawls's remark this way.
But the remark can and should be taken to mean that "the small but definite
class" emerges *only when* reflective equilibrium is reached, and still is revisable
in the light of further theory change.

18 Presumably, we could use fairly standard treatments of degree of belief,
rooted in probability theory, to formalize what is sketched here. This formal-
ization might give particular content to the assumption that persons are rational, imposing certain constraints on revisability and acceptability. I am
indebted to Paul Horwich for discussion of this point.

think that initial credence levels, for a person, correspond to *credibilities.*" [19] The result is that we have no reason to think that increasing the credence level for the system as a whole moves us closer to moral truth rather than away from it. Coherent fictions are still fictions, and we may only be reshuffling our prejudices.[20]

If Brandt's "no credibility" complaint has force, a question I take up shortly, it has such force against wide, and not just narrow, reflective equilibrium. In my reconstruction, considered moral judgments *may* play an ineliminable role constraining the acceptance of background (level III) theories in wide reflective equilibrium. (In general, level III theories do not reduce the moral to the nonmoral, and level IV constraints do not select only one feasible system.) But level III considered moral judgments seem to be as open as level I considered judgments to the objection that they have only initial credence and not initial credibility. At least it would take a special argument to show why worries that initial level I considered judgments about justice lack initial credibility fail to carry weight against initial level III judgments about fair procedures or about which features of persons are morally central or relevant. The problem is that all such initial judgments are still "our" judgments.[21] The fact that wide equilibrium provides support for the principles independent from that provided by level I partial equilibrium does not imply that this support is based on considered judgments that escape the "no credibility" criticism. The criticism does not go away just because wide reflective equilibrium permits an intra-theory gain in justificatory force not provided by narrow equilibrium.

B. *Credibility and Coherence.* Much of the plausibility of the "no credibility" objection derives from the contrast between nonmoral

[19] *Loc. cit.* Brandt's discussion draws on early characterizations of justification by Nelson Goodman ["Sense and Certainty," *Philosophical Review*, LXI, 2 (April 1952): 160–167] and Israel Scheffler ["Justification and Commitment," this JOURNAL, LI, 6 (March 18, 1954): 180–190.] In Scheffler's discussion, the method is described using the notion of "initial credibility," which is not explicated for us. Later in the article we are told that initial credibility is only an indication of our "initial commitment to . . . acceptance" (187). Perhaps Brandt's argument should be construed as the objection to assuming, as Scheffler is willing to do, that initial credibility and initial commitment to acceptance (Brandt's "credence level") correspond in the moral case the way they do in the nonmoral case.

[20] Hare's and Singer's complaints have a similar ring to them, once purged of the mistaken view they share about the unrevisability of considered judgments (see fn 17 above).

[21] Cf. Kai Nielsen, "Our Considered Judgments," *Ratio*, XIX, 1 (June 1977): 39–46.

observation reports and considered moral judgments or "intuitions." A minimal version [22] of the claim that initial credibility attaches to observation reports must do two things. It must allow for the revisability of such reports. It must also treat them as generally reliable unless we have specific reasons to think they are not. Observation reports seem to satisfy these conditions because we can tell some story, perhaps a causal story, that explains why the reports are generally reliable, though still revisable. In contrast, moral judgments are more suspect. We know that even sincerely believed moral judgments made under conditions conducive to avoiding mistakes may still be biased by self-interest, self-deception, or cultural and historical influences.[23] So, if we construe a considered moral judgment as an attempt to report a moral fact, we have no causal story to tell about reliability [24] and many reasons to suspect unreliability.

I would like to suggest three responses to this way of contrasting considered moral judgments and observation reports. First, the assumed analogy between considered moral judgments and observation reports is itself inappropriate. A considered moral judgment, even in a particular case, is in many ways far more like a "theoretical" than an "observation" statement. (I am not assuming a principled dichotomy here, at most a continuum of degree of theory-dependence). Evidence comes from the way in which we support considered moral judgments as compared to observation reports: we readily give reasons for the moral judgments, and our appeal to theoretical considerations to support them is not mainly concerned with the conditions under which the judgments are made. Further evidence for my claim would require that we carry out the programmatic suggestion made earlier: see whether we can explain the features of reason-giving by reference to features of wide equilibrium.

[22] A stronger version can be formulated. It would treat some class of observation reports as self-warranting or even incorrigible. I consider only the more plausible, weaker version above. On the strong version, the criticism of reflective equilibrium is just a foundationalist attack. On the weak version, it is an attempt to show that, foundationalism aside, coherence theories of moral justification face special problems not faced by coherence theories of nonmoral justification.

[23] The contrast is hardly complete, since observation reports may also be affected by various aspects of a person's "set."

[24] Gilbert Harman makes a similar point when he claims that p's obtaining plays no role in explaining my making the moral judgment that p, but q's obtaining does play a role in explaining my nonmoral observation that q. Cf. *The Nature of Morality* (New York: Oxford, 1977), p. 7 ff. I think Harman overdraws the contrast here, but that is a matter for another discussion.

On the other hand, some may cite other evidence to support the analogy between observations and moral judgments. They might point, for example, to language-learning contexts, in which children are taught to identify actions as wrong or unjust much as they are taught to identify nonmoral properties. Or they may point to the fact that we often judge certain acts as right or wrong with great *immediacy*—the "gut reaction," so called. But such evidence is not persuasive. One thing that distinguishes adult from childish moral reasoning is the ready appeal to theoretical considerations.[25] Similarly, we are often impatient with the person who refuses to provide moral reasons or theory to support his immediate moral judgments, much more so than we are with the person who backs up "It is red" with nothing more than "It sure looks red."

Consequently, I conclude, though I have not fully argued the point here, that the comparison of moral judgments to observation reports is misleading. Rightness and wrongness, or justice and injustice, are unlikely to be simple properties of moral situations. Consequently, they are unlikely to play a role analogous to that played by observational properties in the causal-reliability stories we tell ourselves concerning observation reports. But the "no credibility" argument gains its plausibility from the assumption that the analogy to observation reports *should* hold and then denigrates moral judgments when it is pointed out they differ from observation reports. If they *should* and *do* function differently—because they are different kinds of judgments—that is not something we should hold against the moral judgments.

Secondly, the "no credibility" criticism is at best premature. It is plausible to think that only the development of acceptable moral theory in wide reflective equilibrium will enable us to determine what kind of "fact," if any, is involved in a considered moral judgment. In the context of such a theory, and with an answer to our puzzlement about the kind of fact (if any) a moral fact is, we might be able to provide a story about the reliability of initial considered judgments. Indeed, it seems reasonable to impose this burden on the theory that emerges in wide reflective equilibrium. It should

[25] Even the access to theoretical considerations generally found in mature and sophisticated adult moral reasoning will not, of course, be as extensive and developed as what I suggest is involved in wide equilibrium, despite my earlier remark that much more structure may be present than we have recognized. Moreover, how much we expect theory to play a role in adult moral reasoning will depend on our purpose in seeking the particular moral justification. These factors affect the degree to which a coherence theory of justification based on wide equilibrium carries over into a theory of individual justification; see fn 1 above.

help us answer this sort of question. If we can provide a reasonable answer, then we may have a way of distinguishing initially credible from merely initially believed types of moral judgments.

The "no credibility" criticism gains initial plausibility because we *are* able to assign initial credibility to nonmoral observation reports, but not to moral judgments. The credibility assignment, however, draws implicitly on a broadly accepted body of theory which explains why those judgments are credible. Properly understood, the credibility story about nonmoral observation reports is itself only the product of a nonmoral wide reflective equilibrium of relatively recent vintage. In contrast, we lack that level of theory development in the moral case. What follows from this difference is that the "no credibility" argument succeeds in assigning a burden of proof. *Some* answer to the question about the reliability of moral judgments must be forthcoming. But the argument is hardly a demonstration that no plausible story is possible.

Thirdly, a more positive—though still speculative—point can be made in favor of starting from considered moral judgments in our theory construction. It is commonplace, and true, to note that there is variation and disagreement about considered moral judgments among persons and cultures. It is also commonplace, and true, to note that there is much uniformity and agreement on considered moral judgments among persons and cultures. Philosophers of all persuasions cite one or the other commonplace as convenience in argument dictates. But moral philosophy should help us to *explain* *both* facts.

What wide equilibrium shows us about the structure of moral theories may help us explain the extensive agreement we do find. Such agreement on judgments may reflect an underlying agreement on features of the component background theories. Indeed, people may be more in agreement about the nature of persons, the role of morality in society, and so on, than is often assumed. Of course, these other points of agreement might be discounted by pointing to the influence of culture or ideology in shaping level III theories. But it may also be that the agreement is found because some of the background theories are, roughly speaking, true—at least with regard to certain important features. Moreover, widely different people may have come to learn these truths despite their culturally different experiences. The point is that moral *agreement*—at levels III and I—may not be just the result of historical accident, at least not in the way that some moral *disagreements* are. Consequently, it would be shortsighted to deny credibility to considered judgments just because there is widespread disagreement on many of them: there is also agreement on many. Here moral anthropology *is* relevant to answering questions in moral theory.

I conclude that the "no credibility" objection reduces either to a burden-of-proof argument, which is plausible but hardly conclusive, or to a general foundationalist objection to coherence accounts of theory acceptance (or justification). It becomes a burden-of-proof argument as soon as one notices that the credibility we assign to observation reports is itself based on an inference from a nonmoral reflective equilibrium. We do not yet have such an account of credibility for the moral case, but we also have no good reason to think it impossible or improbable that we can develop such an account once we know more about moral theory. On the other hand, the "no credibility" argument becomes a foundationalist objection if it is insisted that observation reports are credible independently of such coherence stories.

My reply to the "no credibility" criticism points again to a strong similarity in the way coherence constraints on theory acceptance (or justification) operate in the two domains, despite the disanalogy between observation reports and considered moral judgments. The accounts of initial credibility we accept for observation reports (say, some causal story about reliable detection) are based on inferences from various component sciences constrained by coherence considerations. Observation reports are neither self-warranting nor unrevisable, and our willingness to grant them initial credibility depends on our acceptance of various other relevant theories and beliefs. Such an account is also owed for some set of moral judgments, but it too will derive from component theories in wide equilibrium. Similarly, in rejecting the view that wide equilibrium merely systematizes a determinate set of moral judgments, and arguing instead for the revisability of these inputs, I suggest that wide equilibrium closely resembles scientific practice. Neither in science nor in ethics do we merely "test" our theories against a predetermined, relatively fixed body of data. Rather, we continually reassess and reevaluate both the plausibility and the relevance of these data against theories we are inclined to accept. The possibility thus arises that these pressures for revision will free considered moral judgments from their vulnerability to many of the *specific* objections about bias and unreliability usually directed against them.

IV. OBJECTIVITY AND CONVERGENCE

I would like to consider what implications, if any, the method of wide equilibrium may have for some traditional worries about objectivity in ethics. Of course, objectivity is a multiply ambiguous notion. Still, two senses stand out as central. First, in a given area of inquiry, claims are thought to be objective if there is some significant degree of intersubjective agreement on them. Second, claims are also said to be objective if they express truths relevant to the area of inquiry. Other important senses of "objectivity" reduce to one or both of the central uses [e.g., "free from bias" (said of methods or claims) and "reliability" or "replicability" (said of methods or procedures of inquiry)]. The two central senses are not unrelated. The typical realist, for example, hopes that methods or procedures of inquiry that tend to produce intersubjective agreement do so because they are methods that give us access to relevant truths. In contrast, there are also eliminative approaches which try to show that one or the other notion of objectivity is either confused, reducible to the other, or irrelevant in a given area of inquiry. Thus some have suggested that knowledge of moral truths is unattainable (perhaps because there are no moral truths) and we should settle for the objectivity of intersubjective agreement (based on rational inquiry) if we can achieve it. Does the method of wide reflective equilibrium commit us to one or another of these approaches to objectivity in ethics?

One traditional worry, that moral judgments are not objective because there is insufficient agreement about them, may be laid to rest by seeking wide equilibrium. I have suggested that seeking wide equilibrium may render problems of theory acceptance in ethics more tractable and may thus produce greater moral agreement. Specifically, it may lead us to understand better the sources of moral agreement and disagreement and the constraints on what we count as relevant and important to the revision of moral judgments. It may allow us to reduce moral disagreements (about principles or judgments) to more resoluble disagreements in the relevant background (level III and IV) theories. None of these possibilities guarantees increased agreement. How much convergence results remains an empirical question. But I think I have made it at least plausible that wide equilibrium could increase agreement and do so in a *nonarbitrary* way. At least, it could provide us with a clearer picture of how much agreement we already have (I return to this point later). And if it does, then there are implications for how objective, at least in the minimal sense of intersubjective agreement, ethics is.

To be sure, many who point to the lack of intersubjective agreement on many moral issues do so to raise a more robust worry about lack of objectivity in ethics. They point to moral disagreement as if it were strong *evidence* for the deeper claim about objectivity, that there are no moral truths for us to agree about. The inference from lack of agreement to the absence of truths to be acquired is generally unpersuasive, however. Sometimes there is the buried assumption that *if* there were such truths, we would probably have enough access to them to produce more agreement than we have. I see no way, however, to formulate this assumption so that it does not rule out the existence of truths in most areas of scientific inquiry, at least at some time in their history. Sometimes there is the qualification that it is not the disagreement about moral claims that is important, but the "fact" that we cannot agree about what would produce resolution of the disagreement. This is likely to be more true in science and less true in ethics than is usually claimed. Still, there is a kernel of truth behind the inference, though it is insufficient to warrant it: agreement, *when it is produced by methods we deem appropriate in a given area of inquiry*, does appear to have some evidential relation to what is agreed on.

What has troubled critics of reflective equilibrium, however, is an opposite worry. Anyone who believes that there *are* objective moral truths will want to leave room for the possibility that there may be consensus on moral falsehoods. The worry is clearly reasonable when we suspect that the factors that led to consensus have little, if anything, to do with rational inquiry (and we need not have in mind anything so drastic as the Inquisition). And if one thought the method of wide equilibrium fell far short of rational inquiry, the worry would again be reasonable. Moreover, it is not obviously unreasonable even if one takes wide equilibrium to be the best method available but wants to acknowledge the possibility that it may lead to justified acceptance of moral falsehoods. The fear here is that intersubjective agreement will be taken as *constitutive* of moral truth or as eliminative of any full-blown (realist) notion of objective moral truth.[26]

The worry might be put this way. Suppose that when diverse

[26] Peter Singer argues that the proponent of reflective equilibrium leaves no room for a notion of the "validity" of moral principles that goes beyond intersubjective agreement. Consequently, the "validity" of moral principles will have to be relativized: it depends on whose considered judgments they are tested against (cf. *op. cit.*, p. 439 ff). I do not see why he thinks so, except that it may be connected to his underestimate of the revisability of considered moral judgments (cf. sec. II above). In any case, Rawls is quite right to deny any straightforward connection between convergence in wide equilibrium and the knowledge of objective moral truths. Cf. Rawls, "Independence of Moral Theory," p. 9.

people are induced to seek the principles they would accept in wide reflective equilibrium, only one shared equilibrium point emerges. Can we still ask, Are these principles objective moral truths? Is the proponent of wide equilibrium committed to the view that such intersubjective agreement *constitutes* the principles and judgments as moral truths? Or is it at best *evidence* that we have discovered objective moral truths? Or is it any evidence at all that we have found some? I shall suggest that though convergence in wide equilibrium is neither a necessary nor a sufficient condition for claiming we have found objective moral truths, such convergence may constitute *evidence* we have found some.

To see that convergence in wide equilibrium is not a sufficient condition for claiming we have found objective moral truths, suppose we actually produced such convergence among diverse persons. Whether or not the principles and judgments they accept would count as such truths would depend on *how* we come to explain the convergence. Suppose, for example, we find that we can *explain* the convergence by pointing to a psychological feature of human beings that plays a *causal* role in producing their agreement. Suppose, to be specific, that, under widespread conditions of child-rearing in diverse cultures, people tend to group others into "in groups" and "out groups" and that the effect of this mechanism is that moral judgments and principles in wide equilibrium turn out to be in-egalitarian in certain ways.[27] Suppose we discover, further, that these child-rearing practices are themselves changeable and not the product of any deep features of human biology and psychology. We might begin to feel that the convergence we had found in wide equilibrium was only a fortuitous result of a provincial feature of human social psychology. Convergence would thus not by itself be sufficient grounds for constituting the principles as moral truths.

We can turn the example around to question the necessity of convergence for constituting the principles as objective moral truths. Suppose we find, after attempting to produce wide equilibria among diverse persons, that there is no actual convergence in wide equilibrium. Different families of equilibria emerge. Suppose also that we can *explain* the failure of convergence by pointing again to a provincial feature of human psychology or biology. But suppose further that we can abstract from this source of divergence. We can construct a modified and *idealized* "agreement" on principles. Such an idealization might, depending on other factors, be

---

27 I think the account is implausible, but cf. Gordon W. Allport, *The Nature of Prejudice* (New York: Addison-Wesley, 1954), chs. III, IV.

a good candidate for containing objective moral truths, even though it is *not* accepted in any actual wide equilibrium.

Which way we should go in either of these cases will have something to do with how fundamental we think the source of divergence or convergence is. But what we count as "fundamental" is itself determined by the view of the nature of moral judgments and principles which emerges in wide equilibrium. For example, if the convergence-producing feature of human psychology turned out to be a central fact about the emotions or motivations, say, some fact about the nature of (Humean) sympathy, which proved invariant to all but the strangest (pathological) child-rearing practices, then we might think we had reached a fundamental fact (related at least to the *feasibility* of moral conceptions). Still, even here, I do not want to assume that metaethical considerations embedded in the background theories would force us to reject a more Kantian stance. To follow up our earlier discussion, we are here concerned with factors that may affect the "credibility" of initial considered judgments, leading us to discount some and favor others; how we weigh these factors will depend on complex features of our background theories.

In short, divergence among wide reflective equilibria does not imply that there are no such things as objective moral truths; [28] nor does convergence imply that we have found them; nor need 'moral truth' be replaced by 'adopted in wide equilibrium'. How we will be motivated, or warranted, in treating the facts of divergence or convergence depends on the kinds of divergence or convergence we encounter and the kinds of explanation we can give for it. This result should not surprise us: wide reflective equilibrium embodies coherence constraints on theory acceptance or justification, not on truth. [29]

Actually, it is necessary to qualify my conclusion that wide reflective equilibrium need not be viewed as constitutive of moral truth. [30] My argument that convergence is neither necessary nor

[28] As Singer seems to think it does; cf. *op. cit.*, p. 494/5; but see also his n. 5, p. 494.

[29] If we construe wide reflective equilibrium as providing us with the basis for a full-blown coherence theory of moral justification, then my argument suggests that it faces the same difficulties and advantages as coherence theories of nonmoral justification. I cannot here defend my view that a coherence theory of justification can be made compatible with a noncoherency account of truth.

[30] There is some evidence that Rawls is attracted to a view resembling the eliminitive view in his portrayal of wide equilibrium as a "constructive" method. Cf. "The Independence of Moral Theory," *op. cit.*, and also a recent unpublished lecture with the same title as the Presidential Address.

sufficient to establish the discovery of moral truths depends on bringing theoretical considerations to bear which seem sufficient to destabilize the actual equilibrium in some way. Suppose we now throw back into the ring these destabilizing considerations and seek a new wide equilibrium. If we can soup up wide equilibrium in this way, so that it adds up to something like "total rational considerations," then perhaps we can revive in a strengthened form the constitutive view. We would have here, perhaps, the analogue of Putnam's "empirical realist" rejection of objective (metaphysical) moral truths.[31] This version of the eliminative view is not open to the most reasonable worries of those who feel simple moral agreement should not be taken to constitute moral truth. In any case, on its form of verificationism, ethics may be no worse off than science!

A more modest way of putting the same objection is this. My reply to the eliminative view is compatible with the following claim: there is a sense in which the question, Do we really have moral truth, given convergence in wide reflective equilibrium? is an *idle* worry in the absence of any *specific* research capable of destabilizing the equilibrium. In the absence of some particular, plausible way to challenge the convergence, the question is tantamount to strong and unfruitful skepticism.

Despite these qualifications, my inclination is not to treat wide reflective equilibrium as constitutive of moral truth (assuming convergence) and to leave room instead for a weaker *evidential* relation holding between agreement in wide equilibrium and moral truth. What we would need to support this possibility is reason to think that the methods of inquiry in ethics that tend to produce convergence do so *because* they bring us close to moral truth. I can offer only a highly qualified and indirect argument to this conclusion.

Consider for a moment a general argument of this form: [32] (1) In a given area of inquiry, the methods used are successful in the sense that they produce convergence and a growth of knowledge; (2) the only plausible account of the success of these methods is that they lead us to better and better approximations to truths of the kind relevant to the inquiry; (3) therefore, we should adopt a realist account of the relevant objects of inquiry. Arguments of this form

31 Cf. Hilary Putnam, *Meaning and the Moral Sciences* (London: Routledge & Kegan Paul, 1978), part IV.

32 I am grateful to Richard Boyd and George Smith for discussion of this argument and of section IV in general.

have been advanced to defend platonism with regard to mathematical objects and realism with regard to the referents of theoretical terms in the empirical sciences. To establish the second premise of such an argument, one must not only show that alternatives to the realist account (say intuitionist accounts in mathematics and verificationist or positivist accounts in science) will not explain the success of the methods used, but that the realist account has some independent plausibility of its own. Otherwise, it may simply seem to be a residual, *ad hoc* account. In mathematics, proponents of platonism, whatever the merits of their refutations of other accounts, have not provided accounts, aside from perceptual metaphors, which make it plausible that we can come to know anything about mathematical objects. In contrast, however, there are some interesting and promising arguments of this form in defense of scientific realism.[33] In these, a version of a causal theory of knowledge and reference is used to satisfy the requirement that we lend plausibility to the realist account of methodology independent of the refutation of alternative accounts.

Suppose a version of such an argument for scientific realism is sound—a supposition I shall not defend here at all. Then we would be justified in claiming that certain central methodological features of science, including its coherence and other theory-laden constraints on theory acceptance (e.g., parsimony, simplicity, etc.), are consensus-producing *because* they are *evidential* and lead us to better approximations to the truth. I have been defending the view that coherence constraints in wide equilibrium function very much like those in science. If I am right, this suggests that we may be able to piggy-back a claim about objectivity in ethics onto the analogous claim we are assuming can be made for science. Suppose then that coherence constraints in wide equilibrium turn out to be consensus-producing. Then, since these constraints are similar to their analogues in science in other respects, they may also be *evi-*

[33] The most persuasive versions of the argument are found in Boyd, "Determinism, Laws and Predictability in Principle," *Philosophy of Science*, XXXIX, 4 (December 1972): 431–450; "Realism, Underdetermination and a Causal Theory of Evidence," *Noûs*, VII, 1 (1973): 1–12; *Realism and Scientific Epistemology* (New York: Cambridge, forthcoming); "What Physicalism Does Not Entail," in Ned Block, ed., *Readings in Philosophy of Psychology* (forthcoming from Harvard University Press); and "Metaphor and Theory Change: What Is 'Metaphor' a Metaphor for?" (unpublished). See also H. C. Byerly and V. A. Luzara, "Realist Foundations of Measurement," *Philosophy of Science*, XL, 1 (1973): 1–27; and the classic K. MacCorquodale and P. E. Meehl, "On a Distinction between Hypothetical Constructs and Intervening Variables," *Psychological Review*, CLV, (1948): 95–107.

dential. That is, we have some reason to think that wide equilibrium involves methods that will lead us to objective moral truths *if there are any.* Notice that this conclusion does not presuppose there are such moral truths, nor does it give an account of what kind of truth such a truth would be.

My suggestion is obviously a highly tentative and programmatic route to an account of objectivity in ethics. Nor can I really defend it here. Some qualifying remarks are definitely in order, however.

(A) Developed versions of the arguments for scientific realism do not simply talk about "convergence," but point to a variety of effects indicative of the cumulative nature or progress of scientific knowledge. For example, they may try to account for "take-off" effects indicative of the maturation of an area of inquiry, or they may point to the absence of "schools" or "sects." My supposition that convergence may emerge in wide equilibrium falls far short of specifying this sort of evidence for growth in moral knowledge. There is a related point: I am not sure we know what to count as evidence for convergence in ethics. For example, we do have moral disagreement on numerous issues; but is the level of disagreement compatible with enough other agreement for it to count as convergence, or not? Does existing disagreement merely represent hard or novel problems at the "frontier"? Or is it the result of special social forces which systematically distort our views in areas of political or religious sensitivity? Some of the difficulty may stem from paucity of work in the history of ethics and in moral anthropology adequate to informing us whether we have experienced moral progress.

(B) The piggy-back argument seems to rest on the assumption that, if a feature of method (a coherence constraint) is similar in one respect (it produces consensus) in two areas of inquiry, then it holds in both areas for the same reason (it leads to relevant truths). I do not think the assumption is obviously or even generally true; that is why my suggestion is only programmatic.

(C) The arguments for scientific realism depend on some causal account of knowledge—e.g., perceptual knowledge depends on reliable detection mechanisms. We are reminded, therefore, of the burden of proof assumed in section III to provide *some* reliability account of moral judgments (at some level). Suppose we could provide no analogue in the moral case to the causal story we may be persuaded of for perceptual knowledge. If we still wanted to talk about "objective moral truths," we might *retreat* to the view that the objects of moral knowledge were "abstract," that is, more like mathematical objects than the things we can know about through the natural sciences. But our moral realism, then, is open to the worry I earlier expressed about mathematical platonism.[34] To be sure, if our causal accounts of knowledge turn out to be unpersuasive, then the argument for scientific realism may be no better off than this in any case.

(D) My account of wide reflective equilibrium has not provided (not explicitly at least) an obvious analogue to the role of experimentation in science. Some story about moral *practice* and what we can learn from it, and not just about moral thought experiments, seems to be needed. That is, we would need to examine the sense in which moral theories guide moral practice and result in social experimentation. But this account must be left for another project.[35]

A final remark is directed not just at my suggestion about the implications of wide equilibrium for objectivity in ethics, but at my account of wide equilibrium itself. The account I have sketched defines a wide equilibrium for a given individual at a given time. The "convergence" I have been discussing is the (at least approximate) sharing of the same wide equilibrium by different persons; the ordered triples of sets of beliefs are the same for these persons. But there would seem to be another approach.

Suppose we begin by admitting into the set of initial considered moral judgments only those judgments on which there is substantial consensus.[36] There seem to be two immediate advantages. First, ethics looks more like science in that the initial considered moral judgments share with observation reports the fact that there is substantial initial agreement on them. The starting point is more "objective," at least in the sense of intersubjective agreement. One *may* gain a slight edge in respect to the problem of initial credibility discussed earlier. (Revisability is, nevertheless, presumed.) Second, the approach makes the wide equilibrium that emerges (if one does)

---

[34] For a similar suggestion, see Jane English, "Ethics and Science," *Proceedings of the XVI Congress of Philosophy*, forthcoming. For some remarks on the analogy between choosing among alternative logics and choosing among moral theories, see my "Some Methods of Ethics and Linguistics," *Philosophical Studies*, forthcoming.

[35] There are some interesting suggestions along these lines in Ruth Anna Putnam, "Rights of Persons and the Liberal Tradition," in Ted Honderich, *Social Ends and Political Means* (London: Routledge & Kegan Paul, 1976).

[36] Just before her tragic death, Jane English reminded me of the importance of this alternative, in comments on an earlier draft of this paper. She argues that ethics should be constructed on such a basis in a brilliant short paper, cited above.

much more a collective or social product from the start than does my approach, which is a quite unnatural idealization in this regard.

Though I think this alternative merits further examination, which I cannot undertake here, I am not persuaded that it offers real advantages. For one thing, it builds into its procedure the assumption that considered judgments *ought* to function like observation reports in science, a question, I have argued, there is good reason to leave open. Its apparent advantage in making ultimate convergence seem more likely might, consequently, be based on the assumption that we ought to have *initial* convergence where there is no good reason to expect it (given all the things that make *initial* considered moral judgments *un*reliable). For another thing, I have assumed that extensive consideration of alternative background theories and sets of principles will produce reasonable pressures to revise and eliminate divergent considered judgments that there are good reasons to eliminate. The alternative method may shift, in too crude a fashion (losing too many possibilities), the intermediate conclusions of my procedure into the position of methodologically warranted starting points. A less important consideration is historical: reflective equilibrium is advanced by Rawls as a model for the process of justification in ethics. Part of what he wanted to capture is a model for how we may make progress in moral argument—where we have to accommodate initial disagreement on some moral judgments. My approach retains this attractive feature, though it sheds some of the other motivations for Rawls's version.[37]

My remarks on objectivity are admittedly quite speculative; indeed, I think it a virtue of the method of reflective equilibrium that it leaves open metaethical considerations of this kind. Still, I think enough has been said about wide equilibrium, these speculations aside, to make its implications for theory acceptance in ethics worthy of closer study.

NORMAN DANIELS

Tufts University

[37] In particular, the analogy to descriptive syntactics (see fn 5).

Part VIII
An Overview of Meta-Ethics

[22]

The Philosophical Review, Vol. 101, No. 1 (January 1992)

Toward *Fin de siècle* Ethics: Some Trends

Stephen Darwall
Allan Gibbard
Peter Railton

1. SETTING THE STAGE

PRINCIPIA'S REVENGE

The *Philosophical Review* is a century old; so too—nearly enough—is a certain controversy in moral philosophy, a controversy initiated by G. E. Moore's *Principia Ethica*.[1] Both centenarians are still full of life. This we celebrate without reserve in the case of the *Review*; should we be equally happy about the continuing vitality of the other?

After all, the controversy began with Moore's charge that previous moral philosophy had been disfigured by a fallacy—the fallacy of defining Good in either naturalistic or metaphysical terms. Yet it has been known for the last fifty years that Moore discovered no *fallacy* at all. Moreover, Moore's accident-prone deployment of his famous "open question argument" in defending his claims made appeal to a now defunct intuitionistic Platonism, and involved assumptions about the transparency of concepts and obviousness of analytic truth that were seen (eventually, by Moore himself) to lead inescapably to the "paradox of analysis." To grant Moore all of the resources he deploys or assumes in his official presentation of the open question argument would suffice to bring the whole enterprise of conceptual analysis to a standstill, and show nothing about Good in particular.[2] One contemporary philosopher concludes

---

[1] Cambridge: Cambridge University Press, 1903.

[2] John Maynard Keynes is said to have thought Moore's *Principia* "better than Plato," but subsequent writers have been more reserved. W. K. Frankena noted Moore's failure to locate a fallacy of any sort, in "The Naturalistic Fallacy," *Mind* 48 (1939): 464–77. Casimir Lewy points out some of Moore's missteps in stating the open question argument—but also tries to

that "as it stands the open question argument is invalid," since it purports to refute all definitional analyses of 'good', but relies upon an arbitrarily narrowed conception of philosophical or scientific definition.[3]

Why, then, isn't Moore's argument a mere period piece? However readily we now reject as antiquated his views in semantics and epistemology, it seems impossible to deny that Moore was on to something.

THE HEYDAY OF ANALYTIC METAETHICS

Moore had discovered not a proof of a fallacy, but rather an argumentive device that implicitly but effectively brings to the fore certain characteristic features of 'good'—and of other normative vocabulary—that seem to stand in the way of our accepting any known naturalistic or metaphysical definition as unquestionably right, as definitions, at least when fully understood, seemingly should be. Dissociated from Moorean thought experiments that call Platonic concepts before the mind's eye, the open question argument can do its job case by case. One asks of any purported account identifying some descriptive property or state P as the meaning of 'good' whether on careful reflection we do not in fact find that we understand the question, "*Is P really good?*" If this question is intelligible—even, it seems, to those who hold that having or being P is a good thing (perhaps the only good thing) and who are moved to give nonlinguistic reasons in defense of a positive answer to the question—then, absent some further story, P could hardly just be what we *mean* by 'good'. If this argumentive device is to succeed conclusively, we must be utterly convinced that

put the argument aright—in "G. E. Moore on the Naturalistic Fallacy," *Proceedings of the British Academy* 50 (1964): 251–62. Pressed by critics later in life to state his criteria of analysis, Moore laid down conditions that left him unable to identify any successful analyses. An open question argument that relies upon these conditions establishes an 'is'/'ought' gap only in the sense that it also establishes a 'brother'/'male sibling' gap. See his "Reply to My Critics," in *The Philosophy of G. E. Moore*, ed. P. A. Schilpp (LaSalle, Ill.: Open Court, 1942), 660–66.

[3]See Gilbert Harman, *The Nature of Morality* (New York: Oxford University Press, 1977), 19–20. He remarks, "There are . . . various kinds of definitions and the open question argument is not relevant to most of them" (19).

TOWARD FIN DE SIECLE ETHICS

the intelligibility of this question does not arise from ignorance of logical implication, or of factual or linguistic information. Here is where the qualification 'absent some futher story' comes into play: How can one claim utter conviction that no logical, factual, or linguistic oversight is involved without simply begging the question?

The best response comes in two parts. First, one should not claim utter conviction, but merely observe that the open question argument *is* compelling for otherwise competent, reflective speakers of English, who appear to have no difficulty imagining what it would be like to dispute whether *P* is good.

Second, one should articulate a philosophical explanation of why this might be so. Here is one such explanation. Attributions of goodness appear to have a conceptual link with the guidance of action, a link exploited whenever we gloss the open question 'Is *P* really good?' as 'Is it clear that, other things equal, we really ought to, or must, devote ourselves to bringing about *P*?' Our confidence that the openness of the open question does not depend upon any error or oversight may stem from our seeming ability to imagine, for any naturalistic property *R*, clear-headed beings who would fail to find appropriate reason or motive to action in the mere fact that *R* obtains (or is seen to be in the offing). Given this imaginative possibility, it has not been *logically* secured that *P* is action-guiding (even if, as a matter of fact, we all do find *R* psychologically compelling).[4] And this absence of a logical or conceptual link to action shows us exactly where there is room to ask, intelligibly, whether *R* really is good.

---

[4]By contrast, Harman claims that if certain tendencies of approval and disapproval were "wired in" in humans, along with associated "automatic" action-tendencies, then "the open question argument fails" (ibid., 29). Noncognitivists have assumed that the connection must be logically rather than nomologically secured—a matter of meaning, not of fact. Such an assumption rests at bottom on the possibility of drawing an interesting analytic/synthetic distinction. As Quine writes:

> My rejection of the analyticity notion just means drawing no line between what goes into the mere understanding of the sentences of a language and what else the community sees eye-to-eye on. ("Epistemology Naturalized," in *Ontological Relativity and Other Essays* [New York: Columbia University Press, 1969], 86)

For more discussion, see below, and section 4.

DARWALL, GIBBARD, RAILTON

This explanation would permit us to see why the open question argument, which has bulked so large in ethics, has had little if any explicitly recognized influence in other areas of philosophy in which reductive naturalistic accounts have been proposed—for these areas have (perhaps wrongly) not been thought to have this conceptual tie to action-guidingness.[5] Moreover, this explanation would permit us to understand how the argument could have come to be seen as convincing against the entire range of reductive naturalisms, not just those considered to date and not just those narrowly definitional. Finally, this explanation would enable us to understand how the argument came to bite the hand that first fed it, and, eventually, to count Intuitionism among its victims. For, it appears no easier to see how an appropriate link to motivation or action could be logically secured if we were to substitute—in the conditional considered in the previous paragraph—'sui generis, simple, nonnatural property Q' for 'naturalistic property R'. The response of Prichard, namely, that seeing the relevant nonnatural property just is seeing a binding obligation to act, with no further explanation or incentive, merely deepens the mystery of the nature of this alleged property and what it would be like to see it clearly or find it normative.[6]

---

[5] This impression may of course be in error. Some recent work has emphasized the normativity of epistemic and semantic concepts. Predictably, this has in turn led to a questioning of the very possibility of naturalistic reductions of these concepts as well. See, for example, Saul Kripke, *Wittgenstein on Rules and Private Language* (Cambridge: Harvard University Press, 1982); Paul Boghossian, "The Rule-Following Considerations," *Mind* 98 (1989): 507–49; and Jaegwon Kim, "What is 'Naturalized Epistemology'?" *Philosophical Perspectives* 2 (1988): 381–405. Whether there is the basis for a nonnaturalistic approach to meaning, say, that avoids the difficulties of Platonism that naturalism was conceived in order to circumvent (compare the discussion of Intuitionism that follows) remains to be seen.

[6] H. A. Prichard, "Does Moral Philosophy Rest On A Mistake?" *Mind* 21 (1912): 21–37. For a similar criticism, see P. H. Nowell-Smith, *Ethics* (London: Penguin, 1954), 41:

> A new world is revealed for our inspection [by "rational intuition" of nonnatural properties] . . . it is mapped and described in elaborate detail. No doubt it is all very interesting. If I happen to have a thirst for knowledge, I shall read on. . . . But what if I am not interested? Why should I do anything about these newly-revealed objects?

Moreover, as Nowell-Smith goes on to claim and as Prichard would agree, even discovering a (mere) *interest* in these properties would not show they could constitute *moral obligations*.

TOWARD FIN DE SIECLE ETHICS

Wittgenstein, for one, could see something else quite clearly—"as it were in a flash of light," he says—namely, that "no description that I can think of would do to describe what I mean by absolute value, [and] I would reject every significant description anybody could suggest, *ab initio*, on the [very] ground of its significance."[7] Description, he concludes, could not be the essential semantic role of a vocabulary with action-guidingness logically built into it.[8]

Yet moral discourse unquestionably has the surface form of a descriptive, property-attributing language. One might at this point be tempted toward the conclusion that moral discourse therefore is systematically misleading. But a potentially more illuminating and less revisionist alternative suggests itself. If we interpret sincere acceptance of a moral judgment as the (noncognitive) expression of an attitude of categorical endorsement, we can dispense with the need to find some indescribable property that moral judgments descry. Categorical endorsement *is* logically tied to the action-tendencies or normative posture of the person making the judgment—categorical endorsement being a *pro-attitude* toward the object of assessment. This account of what is going on in moral judgment thus is not vulnerable to the open question argument as stated above, and, indeed, can take advantage of whatever force this argument may have to help eliminate competitors.

Thus we are led to see noncognitivism as the real historical beneficiary of the open question argument. Of course, it will be able fully to enjoy this benefit only if a noncognitivist reconstruction is possible for the seemingly cognitive aspects of moral discourse, including the phenomena of moral disagreement, and this has proved no easy task. If such reconstruction is possible, then noncognitivism will afford a compact explanation of why such seemingly cognitive disagreement actually proves so resistant (in basic cases) to cognitive—that is, deductive or inductive—resolution.[9]

---

[7] L. Wittgenstein, "Lecture on Ethics," *Philosophical Review* 74 (1965): 11. We are indebted to David Wiggins for drawing our attention to Wittgenstein's "Lecture" as a *locus classicus* for the view of normativity under discussion here, as well as to Casimir Lewy's discussion of Moore, cited in note 2, above.

[8] See also Moore's "Reply to My Critics," 590–91.

[9] Cf. Ayer's defense of emotivism on grounds of the impossibility of resolving basic value conflicts, and also Stevenson's view that it is a condition of any adequate account of goodness that it explain why questions of good and bad cannot be settled by science alone. See A. J. Ayer, *Language,*

DARWALL, GIBBARD, RAILTON

Then too, an appropriately developed noncognitivism could afford considerable insight into the *dynamic social character* of moral discourse.[10] In a social setting we find ourselves with differences in interest and opinion, but also with a need for common principles and practices. Thus we need our subjective expressions on matters of feeling and conduct to have an "objective purport," so that they can be used to apply pressure on others (and even on oneself) to draw toward consensus and compliance even in the presence of conflicting interests.[11]

The capacity of noncognitivism to use the open question argument to its advantage while promising to render morality intelligible and defensible became better understood and more obvious as noncognitivism developed in the 1930s and 1940s. Eventually noncognitivism bested the competition and dominated the scene of analytic metaethics;[12] even Moore found himself half inclined to concede defeat.[13] Stasis—the less charitable would say *rigor mortis*—

Truth, and Logic (London: Gollancz, 1946), chap. 6 and C. L. Stevenson, "The Emotive Meaning of Ethical Terms," *Mind* 46 (1937): 14–31, especially 16–17.

[10]Stevenson in particular demonstrated the potential power of noncognitivism in this connection by stressing the persuasive, rather than merely expressive, role of the invocation of moral terminology. See his *Ethics and Language* (New Haven: Yale University Press, 1944) and *Facts and Values* (New Haven: Yale University Press, 1963).

[11]This objective purport need not be seen simply to be a matter of the (noncognitive) "magnetism" of the moral vocabulary; for it also is manifest in the (cognitive) considerations we take as persuasive in moral discussion, considerations which must be capable of supplying substantive answers to the questions people raise when wondering together about how it makes sense to act. Thus arise both a noncognitivist version of the supervenience of the moral upon the natural—understood as a normative constraint upon admissible moral argumentation rather than as a principle of metaphysics—and also the possibility that some *secondary* descriptive content might accrue to moral terms. In this way noncognitivism would be able to capture for moral discourse not only a conceptual link to action-guidingness, but also its *a priori* supervenience and its descriptive informativeness whenever relatively uncontroversial "standards" or evaluations are in play.

[12]A possible exception was the theory of value, where naturalism had greater staying power. See especially C. I. Lewis, *An Analysis of Knowledge and Valuation* (La Salle, Ill.: Open Court, 1947) and R. B. Perry, *Realms of Value* (Cambridge: Harvard University Press, 1954).

[13]"[I]f you ask me to which of these incompatible views [cognitivism vs. noncognitivism] I have the *stronger* inclination, I can only answer that I

TOWARD FIN DE SIECLE ETHICS

set in. Why, then, do we say that the controversy Moore began is lively today?

THE GREAT EXPANSION

The 1950s witnessed increasing challenges to the adequacy or inevitability of noncognitivism. In England, a number of philosophers urged on broadly Wittgensteinian grounds that we question the picture of language they saw as underlying the noncognitivists' version of the fact/value distinction.[14] Elizabeth Anscombe and Philippa Foot began to force reconsideration of the idea that substantive, even naturalistic, content might be conceptually tied to moral evaluation.[15] At the same time, Peter Geach argued that such linguistic phenomena as embedding moral expressions within conditionals could not be handled by extant noncognitivist accounts, intensifying worries about whether a noncognitivist reconstruction of the cognitive grammar of moral discourse could succeed.[16]

In the United States, W. V. Quine had undermined confidence in the analytic/synthetic distinction, and, with Nelson Goodman, had urged a conception of the task of philosophy in which theory, metatheory, evidence, and inferential norm, or, alternatively, con-

---

simply do not know, whether I am more strongly inclined to take the one than to take the other.—I think this is at least an honest statement of my present attitude," Moore wrote in his "Reply to My Critics" (545).

[14]Such work drew inspiration not from Wittgenstein's "Lecture on Ethics" (first published in 1965) or related work, but from a general approach to meaning and use attributed to the later Wittgenstein, especially in *Philosophical Investigations*, trans. G. E. M. Anscombe (London: Macmillan, 1953). The "Lecture," and perhaps Stevenson's work as well, suggests that there need not be a natural affinity between a Wittgensteinian position and cognitivism. For discussion of the influence of postwar English moral philosophy on the United States, see W. K. Frankena's account of "The Latest Invasion from Britain," in R. M. Chisholm et al., *Philosophy: The Princeton Studies* (Englewood Cliffs, N.J.: Prentice Hall, 1964), 409–15.

[15]See G. E. M. Anscombe, "On Brute Facts," *Analysis* 18 (1958): 69–72, and "Modern Moral Philosophy," *Philosophy* 33 (1958): 1–19 (where Anscombe announces that "the 'naturalistic fallacy' . . . does not impress me, because I do not find accounts of it coherent" [3]); and Philippa Foot, "Moral Arguments," *Mind* 67 (1958): 502–13, and "Moral Beliefs," *Proceedings of the Aristotelian Society* 59 (1958–59): 83–104.

[16]P. T. Geach, "Ascriptivism," *Philosophical Review* 69 (1960): 221–25.

DARWALL, GIBBARD, RAILTON

tent and framework, were not sharply distinguished.[17] This removed some of the pressure to identify either prescriptive or descriptive content as "primary," permitting the relation between them to depend upon general features of our going scheme and circumstances rather than insisting that it be a "conceptual truth" sustained come what may in every corner of logical space. The "ideal observer" and "qualified attitude" theories of Roderick Firth and Richard Brandt explored ways of capturing normativity within a cognitivist account through the *idealization* of dispositions to respond; in a somewhat similar vein, John Rawls suggested a "decision procedure" for ethics.[18] William Frankena identified the centrality of internalism to debates in metaethics, and wondered aloud whether the phenomena of moral discourse and experience really support the sort of internalism that underwrote the move to noncognitivism.[19] Kurt Baier, Stephen Toulmin, and G. H. Von Wright, among others, revived a conception of objectivity in ethics based upon principles of practical reason.[20] Slowly, the landscape of moral philosophy, which had become stark, even dessicated, during the final years of the reign of analytic metaethics, was being populated by a richer variety of views, many of which placed substantive and normative questions at the fore.

---

[17]W. V. Quine, "Two Dogmas of Empiricism," *Philosophical Review* 60 (1951): 20–43 (see also H. Putnam, "The Analytic and the Synthetic," in *Minnesota Studies in the Philosophy of Science*, vol. 3, ed. H. Feigl and G. Maxwell [Minneapolis: University of Minnesota Press, 1962]); N. Goodman, *Fact, Fiction, and Forecast* (Cambridge: Harvard University Press, 1955).

[18]See R. M. Firth, "Ethical Absolutism and the Ideal Observer," *Philosophy and Phenomenological Research* 12 (1952): 317–45; R. B. Brandt, "The Status of Empirical Assertion Theories in Ethics," *Mind* 61 (1952): 458–79, and *Ethical Theory* (Englewood Cliffs, N.J.: Prentice Hall, 1959); and J. Rawls, "Outline of a Decision Procedure for Ethics," *Philosophical Review* 60 (1951): 177–97.

[19]W. K. Frankena, "Obligation and Motivation in Recent Moral Philosophy," in *Essays on Moral Philosophy*, ed. A. I. Melden (Seattle: University of Washington Press, 1958). Frankena also noted a shift in moral philosophy—within metaethics, increasing attention was being paid to the effort to identify morality substantively—in "Recent Conceptions of Morality," in *Morality and the Language of Conduct*, ed. H.-N. Castañeda and G. Nakhnikian (Detroit: Wayne State University Press, 1965).

[20]See K. Baier, *The Moral Point of View* (Ithaca, N.Y.: Cornell University Press, 1958); S. Toulmin, *The Place of Reason in Ethics* (Cambridge: Cambridge University Press, 1961); and G. H. von Wright, *The Varieties of Goodness* (London: Routledge and Kegan Paul, 1963).

122

TOWARD FIN DE SIECLE ETHICS

In the United States in particular, one such view became the reference point for all others, thanks in part to its systematic character and normative attractiveness: John Rawls's *Theory of Justice*, with its method of "reflective equilibrium."[21] The narrowly language-oriented agenda of analytic metaethics was fully displaced, not so much because of a refutation of, say, noncognitivism, but because of an uneasiness about the notions of "meaning" or "analytic truth," and because reflective equilibrium arguments, which tended to set aside metaethical questions, promised to shed much greater light on substantive—and in many cases socially pressing—moral questions. A period that might be called "the Great Expansion" had begun in ethics.

In the Great Expansion a sense of liberation came to ethics. Moral philosophers shed the obsessions of analytic metaethics, and saw—or thought they saw—ways of exploring normative morality as a cognitive domain, without a bad philosophical conscience. The result was an unprecedented pouring of philosophical effort and personnel into ethics, which in turn spread out into the most diverse issues and applications. There is no prospect of summarizing these events here, and no point in trying. What is of chief interest from the standpoint of the present essay is the way that the Great Expansion partly contributed to the contemporary revival of metaethics.

During the Great Expansion, moral intuitions (not Moorean insights into the Forms but substantive moral responses that strike us as compelling) flowed abundantly—occasionally urged on by a bit of pumping. Competing normative theories were "tested" dialectically against these intuitions in a procedure that appeared to be licensed by reflective equilibrium. Over time this reflective equilibrium widened to include a broad range of empirical and philosophical questions.[22] Moral philosophers and their critics grew in-

---

[21]Cambridge: Harvard University Press, 1971.

[22]See, especially, Norman Daniels, "Wide Reflective Equilibrium and Theory Acceptance in Ethics," *Journal of Philosophy* 76 (1979): 256–82 The work of Derek Parfit greatly influenced the broadening of reflective equilibrium by displaying sharply the relevance of metaphysical questions about personal identity. See his "Later Selves and Moral Principles," in *Philosophy and Personal Relations*, ed. A. Montefiore (London: Routledge and Kegan Paul, 1973), and also his *Reasons and Persons* (Oxford: Oxford University Press/Clarendon, 1984).

DARWALL, GIBBARD, RAILTON

creasingly aware that a host of questions about the semantic, epistemic, metaphysical, or practical status of morality arose in full force about new normative methods and theories. Working in somewhat different ways, Gilbert Harman and John Mackie made these questions hard to ignore.[23]

Metaethics has come back to life, though the terms in which its questions can be posed or answered have been changed by the philosophy that has taken place since the heyday of analytic metaethics. New forms of naturalism and nonnaturalism have once again become competitive with noncognitivism, which itself has been significantly refocused, for example, to encompass rationality as well as ethics. And postwar work in game theory and rational choice theory has opened the way to rethinking and sharpening questions of practical justification, bringing them into a prominence they had not enjoyed under analytic metaethics. Finally, as we approach the *fin de siècle*, self-consciousness leaves little untouched; philosophy, including metaethics, has become reflective both about the limitations of the notion of meaning and about the point or prospects of philosophical inquiry itself.

CAVEAT LECTOR

In this way, as we see it, the stage has been set for the contemporary scene in moral philosophy. This scene is remarkably rich and diverse, and our account of it is necessarily selective—emphasis has been placed in order to create coherence. In what follows, we will be concerned largely with (what unblushingly used to be called) metaethical issues, sketching how these issues look, for now, from our three separate but mutually regarding philosophical perspectives.[24,25] We have tried to keep to issues we think important, but

---

[23]G. Harman, *The Nature of Morality*, and J. L. Mackie, *Ethics: Inventing Right and Wrong* (New York: Penguin, 1977).

[24]Among the notable phenomena in contemporary ethics that will receive scant or no attention below are the greatly increased articulation and range of normative ethics, including the emergence of a variety of Kantianisms and virtue theories to challenge consequentialism, as well as the proliferation of more sophisticated forms of consequentialism; the increase in interest and scholarliness in the history of ethics; the dramatic development of applied ethics; feminist critiques of contemporary moral philosophy (but see section 3 for some discussion of the critique of "moral

TOWARD FIN DE SIECLE ETHICS

we could not keep to all important issues. Our sketch is judgmental in other ways as well. Without judgment there would be neither plot nor moral; but judgmental sketches—cartoons are another example—make their points in part by exaggerating and oversimplifying.

2. THE REVIVAL OF METAETHICS

BACK TO BASICS

The method of reflective equilibrium accorded a cognitive and evidential status to moral intuitions or "considered moral judgments," particular and general alike. As the Great Expansion wore on, philosophers increasingly questioned whether this status was deserved.[26] At the same time, partly in response to developments in the philosophy of language, of science, and of mathematics, new conceptions (and new critiques) of objectivity and value were emerging on both sides of the Atlantic. These stirrings induced a widespread philosophical response and ushered in a genuinely new period in twentieth-century ethics, the vigorous revival of metaethics coincidentally with the emergence on several fronts of a criticism of the enterprise of moral theory itself.

Let us postpone discussion of the critique of moral theory for now (see section 3, below), and turn instead to the revival of "metaethics." We use this term broadly, not assuming that one can avoid normative commitments in doing metaethics and not restricting metaethics to the analysis of moral language; we include under "metaethics" studies of the justification and justifiability of ethical

---

theory"); the growing literature on moral emotions and moral psychology generally, including (but not wholly overlapping with) recent phenomenological or "continental" studies in ethics; and approaches to metaethics based on blanket irrealism or antirealism.

[25] Various colleagues have tried—persistently, but with mixed results— to enlarge these perspectives, and we would like to express thanks to them, and to Richard B. Brandt and William K. Frankena in particular, for many and continuing conversations.

[26] Various philosophers, notably Brandt and Hare, had long raised questions of this kind. See R. B. Brandt, *A Theory of the Good and the Right* (New York: Oxford University Press, 1979) and R. M. Hare, *Moral Thinking* (New York: Oxford University Press, 1981). For a forceful expression of this concern, see Gilbert Harman, *The Nature of Morality*.

DARWALL, GIBBARD, RAILTON

claims as well as their meaning, and also the metaphysics and epistemology of morals, and like matters.[27] Indeed, it would be misleading to attempt to draw a clear distinction between the revival of
metaethics in recent years and what broad reflective equilibrium
was becoming during the Great Expansion. For what does broad
reflective equilibrium demand if not that we bring morality into
some congruence with whatever else we hold in our going view of
the world?

But what is our going view of the world? Perhaps most contemporary philosophers would agree that our going view treats empirical science as the paradigm of synthetic knowledge, and that an
acceptable account of ethics must "place" it with respect to this
paradigm, either by effecting some sort of methodological (and
perhaps also substantive) assimilation (which might include a correction of some stereotypes of empirical science), or by establishing
a convincing contrast.[28] Such "placement" would enable us to see
how much of morality remains in order. Without some such placement, one might well ask what business philosophers had in pronouncing or systematizing normative moral judgments as if they
were operating in an area of objective knowledge.[29] Even those
philosophers who have insisted that ethics stands in no need of
underpinnings in order to be an area of objective knowledge have

---

[27] It remains true—and one might well ask how it could be otherwise—
that an approach to the semantic interpretation of moral language typically plays a central role in current discussions of metaphysics and justification.

[28] The term "placing" is due to Simon Blackburn. See his "Errors and the
Phenomenology of Value," in *Morality and Objectivity*, ed. Ted Honderich
(London: Routledge and Kegan Paul, 1985), though we may not be using
it in exactly the sense he intends.

[29] One cannot, of course, assume that 'objective knowledge' has any definite, well-understood and articulated meaning. Especially, one cannot simply assume that it amounts to "knowledge as attained in the empirical
sciences," since that would beg the question straight off (as Thomas Nagel
points out—see *The View From Nowhere* [New York: Oxford University
Press, 1987], especially 144). We use the term 'objective' as an abbreviation
for "of a kind consistent with a respectable resolution of a range of issues—
epistemological, metaphysical, semantic—that in philosophical common
sense are characteristically bundled together in the idea of objectivity."
One of the great hopes one might have for ethical philosophy is that it
would shed some light on this characteristic bundle of issues and ideas.
The development of ethical theory might, for example, permit one to see
the possibility of philosophically respectable conceptions of objectivity

126

TOWARD FIN DE SIECLE ETHICS

tended to *explain* how this could be so by giving a theoretical account of what morality is, and how this compares or contrasts with other areas of thought and practice.

The task set for the revival of metaethics thus has two elements. Put most simply, we can distinguish, first, the need for an account of what existing moral discourse and practice commits us to, and, second, the need for an answer as to how nearly these commitments can be made good. The second question implicitly involves a third, namely, If the commitments can be made good only to an approximation, how good an approximation is needed in order to vindicate moral discourse and practice (or some recognizable successor to them)? To understand the commitments of existing moral discourse and practice, then, is to separate apparent from real commitments (as, for example, the noncognitivist does when he distinguishes the superficially cognitive form of moral discourse from its underlying expressivist character; or, as the externalist does when he denies that "intrinsic reason giving" is a genuine feature of moral experience), and to determine which of the real commitments are most central to the nature and function of morality (as, for example, certain revisionists do when they claim their reforming account permits us to address all the practically significant questions that pre-revised morality was used to pose).

Understanding the commitments of ordinary moral or value discourse and practice would appear to involve accounts of at least the following: the semantics of the language of morals and value; the apparent metaphysical status of moral properties or values; the putative epistemology of morality or value theory; and the relation of morality or values to practical reasoning. These questions are interconnected, since the question of what, for example, values might *be* would appear to be inseparable from the question of how values are supposed to furnish practical reasons or engage us affectively or conatively. No account of the semantics or ontology of moral discourse could vindicate the objectivity of morality without showing either that a suitable relation between moral evaluation and action can be sustained, or that the appearance of such a spe-

---

other than those modeled on mathematics or the empirical sciences. Or, one might find that a notion of objectivity developed for ethics could provide an unorthodox, but superior, understanding of objectivity in mathematics and science.

DARWALL, GIBBARD, RAILTON

cial relation can be explained away without undue revisionism.[30] Similarly, any account of the epistemology of moral understanding and attribution must reckon with the practical character of morality, for example, by showing either that moral knowledge as explicated by the account would not run afoul of constraints against "esoteric morality," or that principled reasons can be given for weakening or rejecting such constraints.

We can distinguish two broad trends in contemporary moral theory depending upon how "the problem of placing ethics" is identified and faced, and the implications drawn. The first starts out from the idea that the "problem" is a product not of ethics, but of the wrong-headed notion of seeking to understand the objectivity of moral judgments on the model of the objectivity of empirical science. This approach depends upon finding some substantial contrast or discontinuity between facts (at least, facts of the paradigm sort treated of in natural science) and norms or values. Perhaps most philosophers find such a contrast *prima facie* plausible; more controversial, and thus the focus of the most urgent dialectical task of this first trend, is the claim that a *bona fide* form of objectivity[31] can be elaborated and defended for the ethical side

---

[30]David Copp has coined the term 'confirmationalism' for the view (which he imputes to some naturalists) that one can rest a case for the objectivity of ethics simply on a showing that the instantiation of properties one identifies as moral can be confirmed by scientific means. See D. Copp, "Explanation and Justification in Ethics," *Ethics* 100 (1990): 237–58. In the end, confirmationalism is not a genuine alternative to the position urged in the text—without a suitable account of the normativity of these purported moral properties, one could not identify them as *moral* properties. Thus, confirmation of their existence as moral properties necessarily involves showing that they satisfy relevant constraints of normativity (whatever these might be). For further discussion, see P. Railton, "Moral Realism," *Philosophical Review* 95 (1986): 163–207, especially 188–89, 204–5.

[31]Compare Blackburn's discussion of "earning truth" in ethics (for example, in *Spreading the Word* [Oxford: Oxford University Press/Clarendon, 1984]). At the heart of these issues is a concern about truth or correctness conditions. Clearly, it would *not* do to explain truth or correctness as a matter of "whatever now happens to strike us as right." What appears to be wanted is a notion of a domain of inquiry which not only *purports* to be apt for truth evaluation, but in which one can also distinguish between *improvement* and *mere change* of opinion, where improvement is suitably represented as in the direction of correctness (as opposed, say, to mere increase in internal coherence). One way of expressing this has been to ask whether the best explanation of our belief that *p* would attribute some

TOWARD FIN DE SIECLE ETHICS

of this contrast. As we will see, philosophers advocating discontinuity have attempted to carry out this task in various ways; perhaps the principal distinction among them turns on whether moral judgment is held to be cognitive (despite the discontinuity with a certain paradigm of factual judgment) or noncognitive (and so objective in some sense that does not involve aptness for—literal—truth evaluation).[32]

The second broad trend in response to "the problem of placing ethics" accepts the challenge of showing that moral judgments are factual in the paradigm sense afforded by empirical or theoretical

---

appropriate role to *p* itself; this would then contrast with a "purely internal" or "merely subjective" explanation of belief that *p*. Part of the source of vagueness here is that there is no agreed upon model of what it would be for *p* to play an appropriate explanatory role. Harman, for example, concludes that

> [t]here does not ever seem to be, even in practice, any point to explaining someone's moral observations by appeal to what is actually right or wrong, just or unjust, good or bad. (*The Nature of Morality*, 22)

(Unless, of course, we could reduce these evaluative terms to some explanatorily efficacious natural property or properties.) This causal-explanatory test has been challenged as too narrow, since we may have good, nonsubjective *reasons* for belief that *p* even in areas where it seems implausible to claim a causal-explanatory role for *p*, for example, in logic and mathematics. (Although some philosophers have thought that mathematics, too, needs a causal-explanatory credential, and have claimed to find it in the alleged "indispensability" of mathematics for science or in the reducibility of those elements of mathematics genuinely needed for science, and the eliminability of the rest. Here we find various parallels to debates in metaethics.)

[32]This distinction can appear to lose its interest under a minimalist conception of truth. For example, if it suffices for a mode of discourse to qualify as truth-evaluable that it bear all the characteristic syntactic features of assertoric discourse, then moral discourse clearly qualifies even before any interesting question of "placing" ethics has been raised, much less settled. Still, though (minimal) truth would not need to be "earned" by ethics, other important contrasts between ethics and, say, empirical science or mathematics might remain. For there will be differences in the kinds of features of the world that figure in the (minimal) *truth conditions* of sentences in various domains, and differences, too, in the *methods* available for establishing (minimal) truth and in the amount of *rational consensus* such methods can bring about. These contrasts might shed a good deal of light on the distinctive nature of ethics. Cf. Crispin Wright, "Realism: The Contemporary Debate—Whither Now?" forthcoming in J. Haldane and C. Wright, *Reality, Representation and Projection* (Oxford: Oxford University Press).

DARWALL, GIBBARD, RAILTON

judgments in the natural sciences.[33] Views in this second broad
trend can also, in principle, be further divided as between cognitivist and noncognitivist. However, despite the readiness with
which it may be admitted that assertoric scientific discourse typically involves some noncognitive elements, few, if any, philosophers seem to occupy the position that "paradigm factual" judgments are primarily noncognitive.[34] The chief dialectical task for
those in this second trend, it would seem, is to show how a paradigm factual area of discourse could have—or could convincingly
provide the appearance of—the peculiar characteristics of the discourse of value or morality, for example, normativity and contestability.

Let us begin our comparative investigation with the first-
mentioned, and by far best-represented, trend: the view that there
is a discontinuity between ethics and science. For brevity, call this
view Discontinuity; its opposite, Continuity.

DISCONTINUITY

Nonnaturalistic intuitionists, such as Moore, famously insisted
that morality is a genuine and objective area of inquiry, but that it

---

[33]This may, but need not, be combined with the view that the scientific
model is the *only* available model of objectivity or factuality. Moreover,
such a position might involve challenging various aspects of orthodox
views of science.

[34]*Noncognitive* here and elsewhere is contrasted not with *realist* but with
cognitivist. Irrealist and antirealist accounts of scientific language that
nonetheless treat such language as apt for literal truth evaluation thus are
placed on the cognitivist side. Instrumentalism, by contrast, is both anti-
realist and a form of noncognitivism about scientific language. But few
instrumentalists have adopted this attitude toward science as a whole, preferring instead to distinguish (allegedly instrumental) theoretical language
from (paradigm factual) observation language. Similarly, those philosophers who have urged that the contrast between "scientific law" and "accidental generalization" be understood along noncognitivist lines (e.g., as
involving a special kind of commitment in the case of laws; cf. A. J. Ayer,
"What is a Law of Nature?" *Revue internationale de philosophie* 36 [1956]),
have characteristically held that (bare) empirical generalizations are to be
interpreted as literally true or false. Thus, examples of continuity founded
on a thoroughly noncognitive interpretation of both scientific and ethical
language are scarce. (Dewey's "instrumentalism" about science, for example, is to be distinguished from logical empiricist varieties, and went along
with a distinctive conception of cognitive inquiry and truth.)

is discontinuous in an important sense with empirical science. On the contemporary scene, the four most active forms of discontinuity are practical reasoning theories (as represented by, e.g., Thomas Nagel, Alan Donagan, Alan Gewirth, Stephen Darwall, and others); constructivism (e.g., John Rawls); noncognitivism (e.g., Simon Blackburn and Allan Gibbard); and (what we will call) sensibility theories (e.g., John McDowell and David Wiggins). Various other forms of discontinuity have their adherents, but we will somewhat arbitrarily confine our discussion to these four groups, discussing them in the order just given. Moreover, some who defend discontinuity *deny*—perhaps partly because of discontinuity—that ethics is in some special sense an area of genuine and objective inquiry; these views, too, will largely be passed over in what follows.[35] While we will discuss some of the particular advantages and disadvantages of various approaches to the question of objectivity, it should be clear in advance that the plausibility of any one of these positions is best assessed comparatively, in light of the philosophical or explanatory power of its competitors. Within the confines of the present project, we can attempt little more than to identify what strike us as areas of comparative strength and weakness, and therefore will say little about overall plausibility.

PRACTICAL REASONING THEORIES

One way of trying to take a broadly cognitivist view of ethics, while stressing discontinuities with science, has been to argue that what is needed in ethics is the idea of a valid reason *for acting*, as opposed to that of a reason for belief as it operates in theoretical disciplines. Unlike the intuitionisms of section 1, the rationalisms that have taken on new life have been those of *practical* reason. Objectivity, for such a view, consists not in accurate representation of an independent metaphysical order, but in universal demands

---

[35] This sort of line is available to those who use noncognitivism as part of an argument that no claims to objective knowledge are part of ethics, or those error theorists who believe that such claims *are* part of ethics, but are systematically mistaken, for example, Mackie, *Ethics: Inventing Right and Wrong.*

DARWALL, GIBBARD, RAILTON

imposed within an agent's practical reasoning. By insisting, on the one hand, that morality must be grounded in practical rather than theoretical reason, these views have stressed a discontinuity with science. It is ethics' intrinsically practical character, its hold on us *as agents*, that explains the open question and, they say, marks ethics off from science.[36] By arguing, on the other hand, that there is such a thing as practical *reason* in which ethics can be grounded, they have tried to assure its objectivity. Recent versions of this approach can be distinguished into those with Hobbesian affinities and those that are broadly Kantian. The first group is typified by Baier and Gauthier, the second by Nagel, Korsgaard, Donagan, Darwall, and Gewirth.

Hobbesian views take the agent's interests or aims as the touch-stone of practical reasons and attempt to argue that the standing of morals can be secured by the fact that moral reasons can be ade-quately based in these. For most recent Hobbesians, the idea is not that moral reasons are a kind of prudential reason. Rather, moral-ity as a system of practical reasoning is in each person's interests; each gains by using it since this is necessary for mutually advanta-geous cooperation.

Recent versions of this view have their roots in ideas advanced by Kurt Baier in the late fifties, and they attempt to address a signifi-cant problem faced by Baier's early view.[37] While it may be in the interest of each that *all* accept interest-trumping, moral reasons, rather than face a mutually disadvantageous war of interests re-sulting from universal unconstrained prudence, it is not clear how this shows that any individual agent should reason morally rather than prudentially.[38] For each agent, *her* acting contrary to moral reasons will still be most in her interest, when morality and self-interest conflict.

One way of dealing with this problem has been to argue, as Baier has recently, that there is an independent constraint of *universal*

---

[36]Thus, Nagel writes that "it is really an unrecognized assumption of internalism that underlies" Moore's open question argument (*The Possibil-ity of Altruism* [Oxford: Oxford University Press/Clarendon, 1970], 8).

[37]Kurt Baier, *The Moral Point of View.*

[38]See, for example, David Gauthier, "Morality and Advantage," *Philo-sophical Review* 76 (1967): 460–75.

TOWARD FIN DE SIECLE ETHICS

acceptability on any theory of practical reasons. No such theory can be correct if the grounds for holding it would be undermined by everyone's accepting it.[39] Since the consequences of everyone's being guided by unconstrained self-interest can hardly be accepted, the theory that practical reasons are exhausted by prudence violates this condition. But what exactly is the argument for thinking that a correct theory of practical reasons cannot be collectively self-defeating?[40]

A second Hobbesian approach, taken by Gauthier, is to hold that collective self-defeat does not rule out a theory of practical reasons, but to insist that individual self-defeat does. Practical reasons consist of whatever considerations inform the practical reasoning of an ideally rational agent, where an agent is ideally rational just in case she reasons in the way likeliest to achieve her interests. So long as agents have enough evidence about each others' motivations, and are unwilling to cooperate with others whom they believe to be disposed not to constrain self-interest when that is necessary for mutual advantage, it will be in the interest of each agent that *she* deliberate with interest-trumping, moral reasons.[41]

Individual or collective self-defeatingness may be grounds for doubting the advisability of acting on or accepting a theory in certain practical contexts, but don't we distinguish between the practical advisability of using or accepting a theory, on the one hand, and the conditions of its epistemic credibility or truth, on the other? Presumably, any cognitivist attempt to defend either of these conditions must show why this distinction, so central in our

---

[39]Baier calls this a principle of *"universalizability"*; without this constraint, he says, "it might not be a good thing if everyone were perfectly rational. But that seems absurd." See Kurt Baier, "The Social Source of Reason," *Proceedings and Addresses of the American Philosophical Association* 51 (1978): 719; see, also, K. Baier, "Moral Reasons and Reasons to be Moral," in *Value and Morals*, ed. A. I. Goldman and J. Kim (Dordrecht, The Netherlands: D. Reidel, 1978).

[40]The term is due to Derek Parfit, who uses it to raise this question in *Reasons and Persons* (Oxford: Oxford University Press/Clarendon, 1984), 87–92.

[41]"Reason and Maximization," *Canadian Journal of Philosophy* 4 (1975): 411–34; and *Morals by Agreement* (Oxford: Oxford University Press/Clarendon, 1986), 157–89.

DARWALL, GIBBARD, RAILTON

thinking about theoretical reason, does not hold when it comes to theories of practical reason.[42] Practical reasoning theorists will insist that this is exactly what one should expect, and that it mirrors the difference between objectivity and knowledge in science and objectivity and knowledge in ethics.

But even if this challenge can be met, both Gauthier's and Baier's theories may face further problems, since they appear to combine a material condition for rationality (connection to the agent's interests) with a formal one (playing the right role in the agent's—or all agents'—deliberation). The rationales for these conditions have different philosophical affinities—Hobbesian versus Kantian, respectively—and perhaps for good reason.[43] And although combining them may suggest a powerful synthetic theory, it also loads rationality with conditions that appear to be, absent some demonstration to the contrary, potentially in conflict. What guarantees that there is available to us any policy for living that will satisfy both conditions at once? If there is none, then perhaps this calls into question one or the other of these conditions as constituents of our notion of rationality, or, then again, perhaps the notion of rationality pulls us in two incompatible directions, and affords morality a shaky foundation.[44]

This brings us to the other major practical reason view: Kantian rationalism. The first steps in this direction in recent years were taken by Nagel in *The Possibility of Altruism*. This work can be (and was) read as having both a modest and a more ambitious agenda. Nagel's more modest goal, suggested by his title, was to show how

---

[42]This relates to the need to show that truth (or objectivity) can be combined with discontinuity. For a brief discussion of this point in connection with Kantian rationalism, see below.

[43]Thus Gauthier originally gave the following rationale for thinking a conception of practical rationality should be (individually) self-supporting: "A person who is unable to submit his conception of rationality to critical assessment, indeed to the critical assessment which must arise from the conception itself, is rational in only a restricted and mechanical sense. . . . [W]e must agree, with Kant, that in a deeper sense, reason is freedom" ("Reason and Maximization," 431).

[44]For further discussion of such worries in connection with Gauthier's views, see Stephen Darwall, "Rational Agent, Rational Act," *Philosophical Topics* 14 (1986): 33–57.

TOWARD FIN DE SIECLE ETHICS

such "objective" (or, as he later called them, "agent-neutral") considerations as "that acting would relieve *someone's* pain" can be genuine reasons to act. A consideration can be rationally motivating, he argued, even if the agent lacks any "unmotivated desire" to explain her acting as the reason recommends. The only implicated present desire may be attributable as a consequence of motivation, and not necessary, therefore, to explain her being motivated by the consideration itself. A person may be moved in this way, he argued, by considering long-term interests. And if motivation at a distance is possible with prudence, there is no reason why it cannot happen with altruism as well. Altruistic (and other agent-neutral) considerations may be no less *rationally* motivating.[45]

Nagel's more ambitious agenda was to show that practical reasoning is subject to a formal constraint which effectively requires that *any* genuine reason to act be agent-neutral. Stressing what he termed the "motivational content" of genuine practical judgments, he argued that a kind of solipsism can be avoided only if an agent is able to make the same practical judgment of himself from an impersonal standpoint as he does from an egocentric point of view. Accepting practical judgments from one's own point of view normally motivates, so, Nagel maintained, making the same judgment of oneself from an impersonal standpoint should normally motivate also. And this can be so only if the reasons that ground the practical judgment are agent-neutral, formulable without a 'free agent variable." It follows that such considerations as that an act will advance *his own* (or *the agent's*) interests cannot be ultimate reasons for acting; at best they are incomplete specifications of some underlying agent-neutral reason, for example, that the act will advance someone's interests.

---

[45]John McDowell later pursued this same line of thought in his critique of Foot's claim that morality can be regarded as a "system of hypothetical imperatives": "Why should the reasons which move people to virtuous behavior not be similar to the reasons which move them to prudent behavior?" ("Are Moral Requirements Hypothetical Imperatives?" *Proceedings of the Aristotelian Society* 52 (suppl.) (1978): 15). If, as Nagel had argued and Foot agreed, prudential considerations can cast a "favorable light" on alternatives that does not derive from an unmotivated present desire, then so might moral considerations. Their recommending force, for the agent, will then apparently be independent of their relation to present desire.

DARWALL, GIBBARD, RAILTON

Were this argument to work it would establish a purely formal conclusion: no ultimate reason for acting can have a free agent variable. By this test, some central moral considerations have the right form to be genuine reasons, while many of those which have been traditionally opposed to morality, for example, self-interest and instrumental rationality, do not. The latter considerations can be reasons only when subsumed under the former. On the other hand, as perhaps became apparent only later, much of common-sense morality is also not of the proper form. Such agent-relative considerations as that an act would keep *one's* promise or provide support for one's child could not be genuine reasons either.[46]

In the end, Nagel rejected the more ambitious agenda as well as the argument designed to secure it. The modest agenda, however, has had a continuing influence.[47] In his more recent writings Nagel has pressed it further, stressing both the phenomenology of moral and deliberative experience, and an autonomous agent's need to endorse her life from perspectives more objective than her own.[48]

Although in some ways Nagel's more ambitious agenda recalled Moorean intrinsic (if not nonnatural) value, it also drew from, and was identified with, the Kantian program in ethics. A number of other philosophers also sought resources in Kant's ideas to mount arguments with similar (some would say "vaulting") ambitions. Like Nagel, each argued that morality can be grounded in *practical* reason—in reason as it is employed in *agency*. Gewirth maintained, for example, that a claim to a right to goods critical to achieving his ends is intrinsic to the rational agent's perspective in *acting*, and that fundamental moral obligations follow from this claim.[49] In

---

[46]Nagel discusses this phenomenon in *The View From Nowhere* (New York: Oxford University Press, 1986), 164–88. It is also discussed in Samuel Scheffler, *The Rejection of Consequentialism* (Oxford: Oxford University Press/Clarendon, 1982); and in Derek Parfit, *Reasons and Persons*.

[47]For example, on Foot and McDowell.

[48]Especially in *The View From Nowhere*, 113–20, 134–37, 149–63.

[49]In *Reason and Morality* (Chicago: University of Chicago Press, 1978). Also, Alan Donagan took the view that, while no argument could establish it, insight into the essence of practical reason reveals that practical reasoning imposes a demand to respect rational agents as ends-in-themselves. If this was a kind of intuitionism, it was a sort different from the variety discussed in section 1; the fundamental moral norm is itself imposed by practical reason, and intuition reveals that fact (Donagan, *The Theory of*

TOWARD FIN DE SIECLE ETHICS

addition to these efforts to bring Kantian rationalistic themes explicitly into contemporary debates, a flourishing scholarly literature on Kant's own writings also contributed substantially to our understanding of the resources available to a rationalism of practical reason.[50]

No doubt the attraction of Kantian theories is that they aim to give some account of the way morality appears to confront agents with objective, categorical demands, which, nonetheless, ultimately issue from deep within the moral agent. As theories of discontinuity, Kantian rationalisms insist that morality's normative grip must be understood practically, as imposed within the practical reasoning of moral agents. And as a version of cognitivism, they aim to ground a notion of validity through the idea of universal norms that practical reason prescribes. However, these twin aims make Kantian rationalism vulnerable from two directions. Noncognitivist discontinuity theorists will agree that any adequate account of morality must stress normative grip, but insist that, just for this reason, cognitivist aims must be abandoned. And cognitivists will second the Kantian rationalist's aim to secure genuine truth and knowledge for morality, but argue that successfully placing it in this way requires continuity, not discontinuity. If Kantian rationalism is attractive because it at least tries to combine these two aspects of a quite common view of morality, it may be unstable precisely because these two aspects resist being combined.

CONSTRUCTIVISM

The views we have been discussing treat morality as a demand of practical rationality as such. Moral reasons are reasons whatever

---

Morality [Chicago: University of Chicago Press, 1977]). Finally, Stephen Darwall argued that the normativity of practical reason is itself best understood through the idea of impartial endorsement of principle (Darwall, *Impartial Reason* (Ithaca, N.Y.: Cornell University Press, 1983]).

[50]See especially Christine Korsgaard, "Morality as Freedom," in *Kant's Practical Philosophy Reconsidered*, ed. Y. Yovel (Dordrecht, The Netherlands: Kluwer Academic Publishers, 1989), 23–48; Henry Allison, "Morality and Freedom: Kant's Reciprocity Thesis," *Philosophical Review* 95 (1986): 393–425; and Thomas E. Hill, Jr., "Kant's Argument for the Rationality of Moral Conduct," *Pacific Philosophical Quarterly* 66 (1985): 3–23.

DARWALL, GIBBARD, RAILTON

one's concerns and desires may be, and this result falls out of a
theory of practical reason that does not presuppose morality—so
these rationalists claim. Recently there has been another trend in
moral theory, also claiming Kantian roots: the family of programs
John Rawls labels "constructivism." Constructivism resembles
Kantian rationalism on a number of counts: It claims a kind of
objectivity for morality, and at the same time holds that this objectivity is sharply different from the objectivity of empirical judgments. It looks to the nature of practical choice as a basis for moral
judgment. Still, in most of its versions, it avoids the daunting rationalist claim that morality is demanded by practical reason independently of even the broadest, deepest contingent features of
one's concerns.

Rawls calls his theory a form of "Kantian constructivism." Like
other broad Kantians, he rejects a picture of reason as discovering
independent moral facts. "Moral objectivity is to be understood in
terms of a suitably constructed social point of view that all can
accept. Apart from the procedure of constructing the principles of
justice, there are no moral facts."[51] He speaks of "the search for
reasonable grounds for reaching agreement rooted in our conception of ourselves and our relation to society." Out goes any "search
for moral truth interpreted as fixed by a prior and independent
order of objects and relations, . . . an order apart and distinct from
how we conceive of ourselves." It is best to endorse moral principles not as true but as "reasonable for us."[52]

Words like these might be read to suggest that as theorists we
must step aside, to await the outcome of a social procedure. In the
meantime we must regard ourselves not as theorists, each able, in
principle, to reach conclusions himself, but as participants in the
social construction of reasonable moral standards. This would be a
sharp departure from the usual conception of moral justification.

Such an interpretation, though, would raise a grave worry, for
social procedures can be horrendous. In that case, principles may
be constructed through an actual social procedure, but we ought
not to accept those principles as a reasonable morality—reasonable

---

[51] John Rawls, "Kantian Constructivism in Moral Theory," *Journal of
Philosophy* 77 (1980): 519.
[52] Ibid.

TOWARD FIN DE SIECLE ETHICS

for us. Reasonable principles must emerge from social procedures that are, in some sense, *suitable*. That gives the moral theorist a job: to say what social procedures would be thus suitable, what procedures count as yielding reasonable principles. And indeed if the theorist can answer that, he may have a further job. We in our society, after all, have never completed a fully suitable procedure. Still, we want to say now what principles of morality are reasonable for us. Perhaps the theorist can settle what principles we would construct if we did engage in a suitable procedure.[53]

It may be in this spirit that Rawls is working, addressing the hypothetical question, How would a suitable procedure for the social construction of moral rules come out? Construction then enters at two points: the theorist constructs a social point of view, a hypothetical circumstance for the choice of moral principles, and hypothetical choosers construct the moral principles that best serve their ends. The hypothetical choosers are "agents of construction" in both senses: the theorist constructs them and they construct principles.

What, then, is constructivism in general? We might read it as another term for what Rawls earlier called "hypothetical contractarianism." Brian Barry proposes a nutshell characterization along these lines, speaking of theories of justice in particular.[54] Constructivism, he says, is "the doctrine that what would be agreed on in some specified kind of situation constitutes justice."[55] This is to treat justice as purely procedural at base. The choice situation is

---

[53]See, also, Rawls, "Justice as Fairness: Political not Metaphysical," *Philosophy and Public Affairs* 14 (1985): 223–51, especially 226–31 and 235–39. Rawls again rejects truth as a goal, and substitutes finding a conception of justice "that can serve as a basis of informed and willing political agreement between citizens viewed as free and equal persons" (230). This might seem to suggest that the only test for proposed principles of justice is an actual procedure eventuating in "informed and willing agreement" to those principles. In this article too, though, Rawls moves to a hypothetical agreement. Appropriate conditions "must situate free and equal citizens fairly" (235).

[54]Rawls himself has mostly confined his theorizing to justice, and in "Justice as Fairness: Political not Metaphysical" he seeks a rationale for principles of justice that will not be dependent on any one comprehensive moral doctrine, but rather can attract an overlapping consensus (246–47).

[55]Brian Barry, *Theories of Justice* (Berkeley: University of California Press, 1989), 268.

DARWALL, GIBBARD, RAILTON

not designed to yield outcomes that are just by some independent
standard—as cutting and choosing leads selfish people to equal
division of a cake. Rather, the very fact that something would be
agreed upon in the specified situation is what makes it constitute
justice. As for the agreement situation itself, it "is specified by a
description of the actors in it (including their knowledge and objectives) and the norms governing their pursuit of their objectives:
what moves are to be legitimate. And the 'emergence' is to be a
particular kind of emergence, namely, the result of the actors in
the situation pursuing their given objectives within the given constraints."[56]

This suggests an even wider reading of the term constructivism:
the constructivist is a hypothetical proceduralist. He endorses some
hypothetical procedure as determining which principles constitute
valid standards of morality. The procedure might be one of coming to agreement on a social contract, or it might be, say, one of
deciding which moral code to support for one's society. A proceduralist, then, maintains there are no moral facts independent of
the finding that a certain hypothetical procedure would have such
and such an upshot.[57]

So understood, constructivism is not a metaethical position in the
old sense. Hypothetical proceduralism does not pronounce on
whether moral thinking is, at base, continuous or discontinuous
with scientific thinking, or what kind of objectivity moral judgments can claim. Rather, it is a family of substantive normative
theories—including hypothetical contractarian theories. A hypothetical contractarian with regard to justice maintains that justice is
whatever would be agreed to in a certain hypothetical position.
This is not a theory of the meaning of moral statements, and it is
not a full theory of their justification. We can ask standard metaethical questions about a contractarian's claims: What do they
mean? What would constitute justifying them? Two contractarians
might embrace different hypothetical situations for agreement.

---

[56]Ibid., 266.
[57]Rawls speaks of "pure procedural justice" as the basis for his theory (*A
Theory of Justice*, 136). We take the term "proceduralism" from David M.
Anderson, "Reconstructing the Justice Dispute in America" (Ph.D. diss.,
University of Michigan, 1990). Anderson gives an extended analysis and
critique of what we are calling hypothetical proceduralism.

TOWARD FIN DE SIECLE ETHICS

What, then, would be at issue between them? The answer might be naturalistic, intuitionistic, noncognitivistic, or reformist. What would it be to justify one claim as opposed to the other? Again, different traditional answers might be given.[58]

Rawls sounds metaethical when he renounces talk of moral truth, but this might be misleading. He says only that there is no moral truth "apart and distinct from how we conceive of ourselves." This would allow for a moral truth somehow dependent on our self-conception.[59] Old-fashioned moral theorists would then want this claim of dependence to be spelled out, and would proceed to ask what this claim means and how it could be justified.

Still, with Rawls's talk of rooting matters "in our conception of ourselves and our relation to society," he moves beyond the bare tenets of hypothetical proceduralism. Consider a hypothetical contractarian: He formulates a particular hypothetical circumstance in which parties are to agree on principles to govern themselves. He needs, though, to justify his choice of this circumstance, to justify the claim that the principles parties would choose in this particular circumstance are valid principles of justice. Constructivism, as Rawls thinks of it, might be a special view of what would constitute this justification. A constructivist theory might explain why some specific form of hypothetical contractarianism is the one that succeeds in identifying what is reasonable for us.[60]

How would it do this? Rawls has not offered detail about how his own form of contractarianism is to be justified, or what it has to do

---

[58]Rawls has his own answer: we seek broad reflective equilibrium (*A Theory of Justice*, 46–53). But that is not part of contractarianism; it is a metaethical position in the old sense.

[59]This would still be a rejection of Platonism in ethics, which says we are equipped to apprehend ethical truths that hold independently of what we ourselves are like. In rejecting ethical Platonism, hypothetical proceduralists would not be alone; ethical Platonism these days has few defenders. (There are still live issues concerning Platonism, to be sure: how far ordinary moral thought is committed to it, how it goes wrong, and how alternatives are to cope with apparently Platonistic aspects of ordinary moral thought—accommodating or rejecting them.)

[60]Indeed, Rawls, in *A Theory of Justice*, suggests that the formulation of his theory in terms of a hypothetical choice is dispensable. The idea "is simply to make vivid to ourselves the restrictions that it seems reasonable to impose on arguments for principles of justice" (18). We could look at the original position as "an expository device" (21).

DARWALL, GIBBARD, RAILTON

with the older frameworks in which the nature of moral judgment was debated. His words suggest, though, that he takes morals and science to have sharply different goals, and hopes that the right insights into the nature of morality will allow us to sidestep traditional metaethics.

Ethics is to be "the search for reasonable grounds for reaching agreement rooted in our conception of ourselves and our relation to society." These words may bear many interpretations. One is both Kantian and conceptually reformist.

Rawls declares himself broadly Kantian; he sees in constructivism a way of elucidating Kant's core insights. Morality is an aspect of practical reason; the search for moral principles consists in reasoning practically, not in tracking independent moral facts. What we validly decide is right or wrong is determined by the nature of our practical reason—in Rawls's case, by what he calls the "rational" and the "reasonable."

How might a construction express this? A constructivist, we might venture, begins with a source of moral concern, a vision of why morality matters to us. In Scanlon's version, it is "the desire to be able to justify one's actions to others on grounds they could not reasonably reject."[61] Rawls himself starts with two ideals: an ideal ("conception") of the person, and an ideal of the social role of morality (a "well-ordered society"). What, he asks, "would free and equal moral persons themselves agree upon, if they were fairly represented solely as such persons and thought of themselves as citizens living a complete life in an on-going society?"[62] Now if we can settle fully on a source of moral concern, perhaps we can find a hypothetical circumstance for agreement that fully speaks to it. Perhaps once we knew what would be agreed to in that circumstance, this knowledge would satisfy all the felt needs that bring us to ethical theory. Then we might no longer care what our moral questions originally meant, or what would have constituted justifying an answer to them. We might have sidestepped traditional metaethics.

---

[61] T. M. Scanlon, "Contractualism and Utilitarianism," in *Utilitarianism and Beyond*, ed. Amartya Sen and Bernard Williams (Cambridge: Cambridge University Press, 1982), 116.
[62] Rawls, "Kantian Constructivism in Moral Theory," 517.

TOWARD FIN DE SIECLE ETHICS

In specifying a source of moral concern, though, a constructivist may face a dilemma. On one horn, he can specify the concern in broad, morally laden language. He can speak of "reasonable" circumstances for agreement, of people "fairly represented solely as free and equal moral beings," of grounds a person "could not reasonably reject." The import of these terms then needs to be specified. It is fine to start with suggestive motivations, but eventually implications must be spelled out, and that can give rise to interpretive problems and disputes. Suppose two people both want to abide by whatever contract they would negotiate in reasonable circumstances—but they fail to agree on which circumstances would be reasonable. Perhaps they simply want different things, and their discord is masked by vague language. Then the theorist can do no more than identify the content of their clashing wants. Perhaps, though, they are in genuine disagreement about what circumstances would be reasonable. If so, old metaethical questions return in new guise. What is at issue in disputes over what is reasonable? What would justify accepting one answer and rejecting another?

On the other horn, the constructivist might stipulate a source of moral concern quite precisely. Concern with justice, he might specify, is concern to abide by the agreement that would be framed in such and such exact circumstances. We listeners, though, may not be at all sure that this concern is precisely the one we have. And if we are told that this, at any rate, is the concern that would constitute a concern with justice, we shall find this claim disputable. It amounts to dogmatically claiming that some specific version of hypothetical contractarianism is correct: that the valid principles of justice are the ones we would have framed in such and such circumstances. Adherents of rival versions of hypothetical contractarianism will dispute this claim, and then, again, old metaethical issues reappear. What is at issue between the disputants, and how would either claim be justified?

A constructivist might sidestep these questions if he could articulate a concern we all found, on consideration, to be all we want from morality. This concern would have to be put in exact terms, and to hold our allegiance even when so put. This is the achievement that might render traditional metaethics obsolete. Or at least it might cause us to find the old metaethical questions less pressing —though we might still ask whether the root concern we found

143

so unproblematic was really justified, and why. In any case, if constructivism is to be metaethically ambitious, its hope must be to find such a specification.

Few constructivists so far would claim any such full success, and it may not be in the offing. Perhaps no constructivist has held such lofty metaethical ambitions. Constructivists have been mostly silent on the old metaethical questions, with not much explanation why. We have explored one possible rationale, but not the only one. Constructivists may simply not think they know what to say on these questions, and think that other questions can fruitfully be pursued in the meantime.[63]

A metaethically modest constructivism would try for important insights into the nature of morality, without claiming to preempt traditional metaethics. The prospects for such a modest constructivism may be brilliant, for anything we have argued. Going versions are so far of limited scope: they tend to deal specifically with social justice, and conceive of the principles of justice as governing a system of mutual benefit. Within this sphere at least, a modest constructivism may hold real promise. It envisions large parts of morality as justified by the social role morality can play, by the mutual appeal of the fruits of moral agreement. It elucidates prime sources of moral concern, and founds morality on the broad social agreement it would be reasonable to make.

NONCOGNITIVISM

If moral theorists cannot long evade questions of meaning, they may find their way back to variants of earlier metaethical theories. Recent years have seen new stirrings of noncognitivism. Noncognitivists claim that moral and scientific meanings differ sharply. Recent noncognitivists, though, have stressed similarities as well as differences. They have sought out aspects of objectivity that they can claim for morality, ways moral judgments mimic strict factual judgments.

A half-century ago, Moore's tests seemed to force anyone to noncognitivism, even kicking and screaming. Subsequent philo-

---

[63]Rawls took a view like this in *A Theory of Justice*; see 51–52.

TOWARD FIN DE SIECLE ETHICS

sophical developments open up better alternatives—or so many philosophers think. Noncognitivists deny this, and so in part their work has been to attack the proffered alternatives. Old problems beset new cognitivisms, they insist.

In addition, though, new problems beset old noncognitivisms, and so noncognitivism has had to develop or die. The new problems come in three clusters. One concerns meaning, objectivity, and the sense in which moral judgments could be noncognitive. A second concerns the state of mind a moral statement expresses. Finally, there is the problem of moral terms in complex grammatical contexts.

First, then, meaning and objectivity: Quine's attacks on a philosophically useful analytic-synthetic distinction, along with new Wittgensteinian treatments of language, not only made alternatives to noncognitivism seem newly eligible; they left it unclear whether noncognitivism itself constitutes a distinct position. Once old theories of cognitive content fall, what is the noncognitivist denying?

Current noncognitivists, then, navigate precariously between two shoals. A classic problem for noncognitivists is that moral judgments have so many earmarks of claims to objective truth. A successful noncognitivism must explain away these earmarks. At the same time, if noncognitivism is to be distinct from cognitivism, it must insist that some judgments are cognitive in contrast with moral judgments. Noncognitivism is threatened not only by hardening values to make them like the hard facts of old; it is threatened by softening facts to make them more like emotive values. Often opponents of noncognitivism work at bridging the fact-value gap from both ends.

Finally, noncognitivists may find themselves losing an exchange with reforming cognitivists. The reformer debunks: he thinks our old concepts are confused, or perhaps even rooted in error. Still, they serve a valuable purpose, he thinks, and a reform will serve that purpose without error or confusion. Now the noncognitivist has a hard time avoiding a stance that is likewise debunking, at least to a degree. Is there nothing to the ordinary sense that right and wrong are properties? If the noncognitivist thinks ordinary thought is confused on this score, he must admit that his too is something of a reform. He then faces a challenge: A naturalistic reformer can retort, "Why not take my reform instead? Mine, after all, gives moral terms a meaning in the usual sense."

DARWALL, GIBBARD, RAILTON

A noncognitivist will then have to argue that his is the better reform. We need a kind of language, he must say, that we come close to having already, but which until now has confused us. The naturalistic reformer, he must claim, beckons us to an overly stark linguistic world. In it we may still have overtly emotive language like "Yea!" and "Boo!" and "Yech!" Moral terms, though, are now like nonmoral terms: thanks to reforming definitions, they now have clear naturalistic criteria. The noncognitivist must say that the old, confused language had virtues this reform loses—virtues that can be preserved in his own reform, and without loss of clarity.

Blackburn argues that if objective-looking emotive predicates did not exist, we would have to invent them. Start with a language with interjections like "Hurrah!" and "Boo!" but no moral predicates like "right" and "wrong." This language does let us express attitudes. But what we need is "an instrument of serious, reflective evaluative practice, able to express concern for improvements, clashes, implications, and coherence of attitudes." To get this, we could "invent a predicate answering to the attitude, and treat commitments as if they were judgements, and then use all the natural devices for debating truth."[64] Blackburn gives this as his cashing out of a Hume-like metaphor, "projecting attitudes onto the world."[65]

Gibbard stresses coordination in a broad game-theoretic sense: narrowly moral judgments, along with normative judgments of other kinds, serve to coordinate actions and feelings. Such coordination is crucial to peaceful and cooperative life together. Appearances of objectivity—the various ways normative judgments mimic judgments of fact—promote this coordination. In evolutionary terms, a coordinating function helps explain why we have the dispositions to normative thought and language that we do. In evaluative terms, the goods that stem from social coordination give us reason to be glad we think and speak in these ways. They give us reason not to reform away the expressive, objective-like aspects of moral language.[66]

---

[64]Simon Blackburn, *Spreading the Word* (Oxford: Oxford University Press/Clarendon, 1984), 195.

[65]Ibid., 170–71, 195.

[66]Allan Gibbard, *Wise Choices, Apt Feelings* (Cambridge: Harvard University Press, 1990), especially 64–80, 293–300.

TOWARD FIN DE SIECLE ETHICS

Current noncognitivists, then, stress the various ways in which a motivation-laden state of mind—an emotive disposition, a universal preference, or the acceptance of a system of norms—might mimic strict factual belief. For convenience, call any such state of mind an "attitude." In the first place, an attitude may be unconditional, applying even to situations where everyone lacks it.[67] In addition, a person's higher-order attitudes may require a given attitude, and require it of everyone.[68] Conversational demands may be made on behalf of an attitude, and other attitudes may sanction those demands.[69]

These features, we might say, "quasi-objectivize" attitudes.[70] A reforming noncognitivist must establish the need for attitudes of some sort that are quasi-objectivized frankly: for motivation-laden states that are not strict factual beliefs, but are treated in many ways as if they were. He claims that what goes on roughly with moral language—and overtly if his reform is accepted—is quasi-objectivizing thought about how to conduct ourselves, and perhaps how to feel about various aspects of life. The noncognitivist will claim that our rough tendencies to do this explain familiar features of moral discourse: the broad action-guidingness of this factual-seeming discourse. It also explains what has been called the "essential contestability" of moral concepts:[71] If a moral term is tied by its very meaning to questions of how to live, any stipulation of a factual property it is to stand for forecloses some questions of how to live—questions we may need to treat quasi-objectively.

---

[67]R. M. Hare, *Moral Thinking*, 208–9; Simon Blackburn, *Spreading the Word*, 11; Gibbard, *Wise Choices*, 164–66.

[68]Harry Frankfurt invokes higher-order desires in "Freedom of the Will and the Concept of a Person," *Journal of Philosophy* 68 (1971): 5–25. Blackburn, in *Spreading the Word*, speaks of how admirable one finds a moral sensibility. Gibbard, in *Wise Choices*, develops a theory of higher-order norms (168–250).

[69]C. L. Stevenson proposed that to call something good is to say, "I like it; do so as well." See "The Emotive Theory of Ethical Terms," *Mind* 46 (1937): 21–25. Gibbard calls this "do so as well" a conversational demand, and develops a theory of norms for conversational demands. See Gibbard, *Wise Choices*, 172–208.

[70]Blackburn speaks of "quasi-realism" (*Spreading the Word*, 171 and elsewhere).

[71]W. B. Gallie, "Essentially Contested Concepts," Proceedings of the Aristotelian Society 56 (1955–56): 167–98.

DARWALL, GIBBARD, RAILTON

All this leaves the question, Is any contrast left between value and fact? Once we are using all the usual devices for debating the truth of moral judgments, does this quasi-truth differ from a real truth we can seriously accept in other realms of language? A "noncognitivist" and a "moral realist" might agree about how moral language works, and disagree only about whether some other kinds of language—scientific language in particular—are descriptive in a way that moral language is not.

This has been one of the most active areas of contention between noncognitivists and those who deny a contrast between moral and "factual" concepts. Those maintaining the contrast claim that on our best, naturalistic view of the universe, factual concepts play an explanatory role that moral concepts do not.[72] Opponents find moral concepts explanatory in the same ways as the concepts used in psychosociological explanation, or they liken moral qualities to secondary quality concepts, factual though not ultimately explanatory.[73] One noncognitivist, Blackburn, argues for another contrast: moral properties are peculiarly supervenient, in a way that is explained if they are quasi-objectivized sentiments.[74] Crispin Wright distinguishes a "thin" truth that moral statements can attain from a substantial truth with various marks of objectivity. To claim substantial truth, one must explain how we have a cognitive capacity to detect the property in question, so that absent any impediment to proper functioning of this capacity, one gets the property right.[75]

Turn now to the second cluster of problems current noncognitivists must sort through: the problem of complex contexts. Most noncognitivists are *expressivists*: they explain moral language as expressing moral judgments, and explain moral judgments as some-

---

[72]Gilbert Harman, *The Nature of Morality*, 6–7; Blackburn, *Spreading the Word*, 164–65, 185–86; Gibbard, *Wise Choices*, 107–25.

[73]Respectively, among others, Nicholas Sturgeon, "Moral Explanations," in *Morality, Reason, and Truth*, ed. David Copp and David Zimmerman (Totowa, N.J.: Rowman and Allanheld, 1985), 49–78; John McDowell, "Values and Secondary Properties," in *Morality and Objectivity*, ed. Ted Honderich (London: Routledge and Kegan Paul, 1985), 110–29.

[74]Blackburn, *Spreading the Word*, 182–89.

[75]A rough gloss of Crispin Wright, "Realism, Antirealism, Irrealism, Quasi-Realism," in *Midwest Studies in Philosophy*, vol. 12, ed. Peter French, Theodore Uehling, and Howard Wettstein (Minneapolis: University of Minnesota Press, 1988), 25–49.

TOWARD FIN DE SIECLE ETHICS

thing other than beliefs.[76] As for what special kind of state of mind a moral judgment is, different expressivists say different things, and each account has its problems.

Emotivists hold that a moral judgment consists in a feeling—or better, in a disposition to have certain feelings. It seems, though, that a person can judge something wrong even if he has lost all disposition to feelings about it. As Ewing and Brandt had suggested decades earlier, moral judgments seem not to be moral sentiments or dispositions to certain moral sentiments, but judgments of what moral sentiments are fitting or justified.[77]

Moreover, if moral judgments are dispositions to feelings, will any old feeling do? What, then, differentiates moral judgments from any other kind of standing like or dislike? Perhaps there are special feelings of moral disapproval, and calling something "wrong," say, expresses such a special feeling—or the corresponding attitude. What, then, is this feeling of moral disapproval? Among theorists of emotion, cognitivists predominate. Emotional "cognitivism" is different from metaethical cognitivism: an emotional cognitivist thinks that having a given emotion, such as anger, involves making some special kind of cognitive judgment. Now in the case of moral disapproval, the only plausible candidate is a cognitive judgment that the thing in question is morally wrong. If so, we need to understand judgments of wrongness before we can understand moral disapproval. We cannot *explain* the judgment that something is wrong as an attitude of moral disapproval.

The sensibility theorists discussed below hold that both directions of explanation are correct: Disapproving something must be explained as feeling that it is wrong, and conversely, to judge something wrong is to judge that it merits disapproval. If this is right,

---

[76]According to Ayer, for instance, moral judgments are emotions; according to Hare, they are universal, overriding preferences. Stevenson stands out among classical noncognitivists as a nonexpressivist: in his analysis of "It is good" as "I like it, do so as well," the noncognitive element is the demand "do so as well." Wright, in "Realism, Antirealism," rejects expressivism. Moral assertions aim to be assertions of truths, not expressions of a state of mind—though the truths are thin.

[77]A. C. Ewing, *The Definition of Good* (New York: Macmillan, 1947), especially 168–69; R. B. Brandt, "Moral Valuation," *Ethics* 56 (1946): 106–21.

DARWALL, GIBBARD, RAILTON

then although moral concepts are to some degree explained in terms of feelings, the explanations are not of the broadly reductive kind an emotivist seeks: they do not explain moral concepts in terms that could be fully understood prior to grasping moral concepts.

Hare sets out to avoid the emotivists' pitfalls. A moral judgment, he says, is a special state of preference—a preference that is "overriding" and "universal." It is a preference all told and not merely one preference tendency among others. It is uninfluenced by who is who in the situation to which it applies.[78] Now one consequence is that a person can never want wrong things done—things he judges wrong, that is. If he thinks it would be wrong for the governor to pardon a murderer, then he must want not to be pardoned himself in the hypothetical case of being the murderer. Hare embraces this consequence; many others find it implausible.[79]

Gibbard rejects emotivism, and adopts a part of Ewing's rival view: moral judgments concern which moral sentiments are warranted or justified. Whereas Ewing was a nonnaturalist about warrant, though, Gibbard remains expressivist: he gives an expressivistic account of judgments of warrant. To call a feeling warranted, he says, is (roughly) to express one's acceptance of norms that permit the feeling. Moral judgments, then, express a state of mind that is not, in the strictest sense, belief in a moral fact. Neither, though, is it a feeling or a disposition to feelings. Rather, it is a complex state of mind that consists in accepting certain norms. His problem, then, is to explain, in psychological terms, what it is to accept norms.[80]

Moral judgments are "normative," everyone agrees, but there is great disagreement among philosophers as to what this normativity consists in. According to Gibbard, it consists in a tie to warrant, and the concept of warrant is *sui generis*. Making a judgment of warrant consists in being in a special, motivation-laden state—namely, accepting a system of norms. Feelings, then, are not treated as nor-

---

[78]See, among other places, R. M. Hare, *Moral Thinking*, 20–24, 107–16.
[79]Hare, *Freedom and Reason* (Oxford: Oxford University Press, 1963), 67–85; *Moral Thinking*, 57–60.
[80]Gibbard, *Wise Choices*, especially 45–80.

TOWARD FIN DE SIECLE ETHICS

mative judgments in themselves. Rather, the special normative judgments that constitute moral convictions consist in accepting norms to govern certain feelings. Norms are motivation-laden, and at the same time, they are crucially discursive and subject to reasoning. They can bear the full weight of quasi-objectivization as discussed above—so Gibbard claims.

Still, like the emotivists, Gibbard holds that moral feelings help explain moral judgments. Moral judgments are judgments about whether guilt and impartial anger are warranted. Gibbard, then, must reject emotional cognitivism. Along with the emotivists, he owes an explanation of specially moral feelings—guilt and impartial anger, in his book—in terms that do not require a prior understanding of moral judgments. Emotional cognitivism has its problems: on the surface, it seems quite possible to feel guilty, say, and yet reject the (purportedly cognitive) claim that one has done wrong. One may think one's guilt irrational. Gibbard surveys lines of psychological explanation of emotions that could fit a Ewing-like theory.[81]

Turn finally to the charge that expressivism fails with "embedded contexts." When a person calls something "wrong," expressivists say, he is not stating a purported fact; he is expressing a special state of mind—a feeling or attitude, say. Now at best, such an account works for simple ascriptions of rightness or wrongness. It does not extend to more elaborate uses of moral language, as in "He did something wrong," or "If taking bribes is wrong, then so is offering them."[82]

Blackburn and Gibbard both take up this problem. Blackburn adopts a strategy of separate explanations for various different grammatical constructions; he works on conjunctions and on conditionals. "If lying is wrong, then so is getting your little brother to lie" expresses rejection of a kind of sensibility: one that condemns lying and yet condones getting little brother to lie.[83] Gibbard attempts a more uniform explanation of normative terms in embed-

---

[81]Gibbard, *Wise Choices*, 129–47.
[82]Peter Geach, "Imperative and Deontic Logic," *Analysis* 18 (1958): 49–56, at 54n.; John Searle, "Meaning and Speech Acts," *Philosophical Review* 71 (1962): 423–32; Geach, "Assertion," *Philosophical Review* 74 (1965): 449–65. Geach attributes the point to Frege.
[83]Blackburn, *Spreading the Word*, 189–96.

DARWALL, GIBBARD, RAILTON

ded contexts: Complex normative judgments are to be explained by their inferential ties to simple normative ascriptions, and to factual judgments. A special class of simple normative ascription—judgments of what is warranted for oneself right now—has a special tie to the world: these judgments tend to motivate. All this makes for a radical modification of expressivism.[84]

Perhaps noncognitivism is obsolete—because it fails with embedded contexts, or because it clings to a bad theory of meaning, or because all refinements that could matter were worked out some time ago. It can seem a theory to beat or fall back on, but not to develop. A handful of authors now see it as full of unrealized possibilities. Some opponents, on the other hand, find the whole list of traditional metaethical possibilities unappetizing, and look for sharply new alternatives. To some of these we now turn.

SENSIBILITY THEORIES

Several of the most influential contemporary writers on the nature of ethics and value, notably John McDowell and David Wiggins, have drawn inspiration from the idea that normative or evaluative judgments might bear some analogy with judgments of secondary qualities, or other judgments essentially tied to the exercise of certain human sensibilities.[85] This analogy holds out the possibility of a cognitivist version of discontinuity, since the judgments tied to the exercise of these sensibilities might be seen as straightforwardly cognitive[86] while yet concerning properties that

---

[84]Gibbard, *Wise Choices*, 92–102.

[85]See especially J. McDowell, "Values and Secondary Qualities," and "Projection and Truth in Ethics," Lindley Lecture (University of Kansas, 1987); and D. Wiggins, "Truth, Invention, and the Meaning of Life," "Truth, and Truth as Predicated of Moral Judgments," and "A Sensible Subjectivism?" reprinted in his *Needs, Values, and Truth: Essays in the Philosophy of Value* (Oxford: Basil Blackwell, 1987). For expository purposes, we will not always distinguish normative (deliberative) and evaluative (value-appreciating) judgments, although sensibility theorists have noticed that they may need different treatment. Wiggins, for example, develops his view for "particular pure valuations," and finds "more questionable" its extension to moral judgments in general ("Truth as Predicated of Moral Judgments," 161).

[86]'Cognitive' both in the sense of "being apt for truth evaluation" and "being the exercise of a cognitive faculty," on analogy, for example, with

TOWARD FIN DE SIECLE ETHICS

are neither part of the fundamental causal/explanatory structure of the world in their own right nor reducible to properties that are. That is, even though such properties would not meet the most ambitious naturalistic strictures, their place in cognition could nonetheless be secure in virtue of their presence to experience and the existence of a fairly well-articulated "space of reasons" regulating their application.[87]

For example, physical science has moved away from color as a significant dimension of similarity in its classification of substances or entities, so that its fundamental explanations are "colorless"; nonetheless, color is a definite feature of our experience, and our attribution of color is an exercise of a perceptual faculty regulated by standards for appraising judgers as better- or worse-situated (e.g., with regard to "standard conditions of viewing") for the detection of color properties, and for appraising judgments as better- or worse-supported by evidence. We clearly recognize greater or lesser degrees of refinement in capacities accurately to discern color, and this possibility of *corrected* judgments and *improved* discernment is manifest in a practice in which we give reasons and make arguments in ways by no means arbitrary or idiosyncratic, but rather capable of yielding considerable interpersonal convergence in judgment. All of this is compatible with the fact that color attribution is, at bottom, dependent upon human subjectivity. So, even though it has turned out that the properties discerned by this

---

perception. Wiggins is careful to distinguish the "cognitive aspiration" of evaluative or normative discourse from success in meeting this aspiration; for both areas of discourse, he appears to hold, a "cognitive underdetermination" exists and helps explain their (claimed) "essential contestability." See his "Truth, Invention, and the Meaning of Life." It should be mentioned here that Wiggins prefers to call his position "subjectivism," whereas McDowell sees his view as a form of "moral realism."

[87]It is somewhat problematic to characterize sensibility theories as versions of "discontinuity," for an advocate of this sort of view can also soften up the "fact" side of the traditional fact/value dichotomy by insisting that in science, too, the notion of truth is *constitutively* tied to the idea of good reasons and arguments, so that we cannot think of Facts of Nature, ready-made, without the help of our going evaluative practices. McDowell appears to be advocating such a softening of the notion of scientific fact in his critical notice of Bernard Williams's *Ethics and the Limits of Philosophy*, in *Mind* 95 (1986): 377–86. However, since the relevant notions of "good reasons and arguments" can be thought of as importantly different in science versus morality, discontinuity can still be upheld.

DARWALL, GIBBARD, RAILTON

practice do not have (what Crispin Wright has called) a "wide cos-
mological role" akin to primary qualities,[88] and that they depend
for their presence in experience upon "rationally optional" sensibilities, this need not undermine their cognitive, even objective,
standing—unless, that is, one presupposes a "scientistic" or "cos-
mological" conception of cognitivity and objectivity.[89]

Thus, sensibility theorists present their approach as a significant
improvement over both noncognitivism and Intuitionism. Noncognitivism has, in their view, rightly stressed the contribution of sentiment to moral judgment, but wrongly forced such judgments into
the mold of expressive projection. Intuitionism has, again in their
view, rightly stressed the cognitive aspects of value judgment, but
wrongly forced such judgments into the mold of detecting a special
realm of independently existing properties. The sensibility theorist
sees neither moral sentiment nor moral properties as able to do
without—or to explain away—the other.[90] As noted earlier, the
resulting view embraces both "directions of explanation," and is
claimed to do greater justice to the cognitive grammar of evaluative
and normative discourse and to the phenomenology of moral experience.

But what of the supposed internal connection between moral
judgment and motivation or will, a connection that has done so
much to account for the appeal of noncognitivism in this century?

---

[88]See Crispin Wright, "Moral Values, Projection, and Secondary Qualities," *Proceedings of the Aristotelian Society* 62 (suppl.) (1988) for related
discussion.

[89]For the dual character of such concepts as objective and subjective, see
Wiggins, "A Sensible Subjectivism?" especially 201–2. There is, of course,
a long tradition of viewing secondary qualities as suspect, and secondary-
quality attributions as erroneous, albeit perhaps cognitive. A sensibility
theorist will argue that this view of secondary qualities is wrong. See Mc-
Dowell, "Values and Secondary Qualities." For discussion of "scientism,"
see McDowell, "Aesthetic Value, Objectivity, and the Fabric of the World,"
in *Pleasure, Preference, and Value: Studies in Philosophical Aesthetics*, ed. Eva
Schaper (Cambridge: Cambridge University Press, 1983), especially 14–
16.

[90]McDowell remarks that "the sentiments [need not] be regarded as
parents of apparent features; it may be pairs of sentiments and features
reciprocally related—siblings rather than parents and children." See "Projection and Truth in Ethics," 12.

TOWARD FIN DE SIECLE ETHICS

McDowell made possible a significant innovation within the contemporary English tradition of nonreductionist cognitivism by showing the availability of an alternative explanation of this connection: the very sensibility that gives individuals the capacity to discern these sensibility-tied properties could, he urged, necessarily involve possession of certain affective or conative propensities.

Humor, for example, is a sense that also is affective; a person with no sense of humor is not someone who discerns the humor in comic situations but simply fails to be amused. Rather, he misses their humorousness altogether. He may, it is said, fully grasp the primary, causal/explanatory qualities of the situations in question; yet there is something about these situations to which he is blind. This blindness stems in part from the absence of a sensibility. This is not akin to the mere absence of a "laugh reflex": it involves a lack of appreciation of reasons for amusement. There may—although this has yet to be shown—be no way of explaining the nature of these reasons, or the nature of the property humorousness, itself, except by depending upon the notion of finding things funny. A circular relation between the sensibility and the property would explain why humorousness seems *sui generis* and unanalyzable, on the one hand, while on the other hand being, for those with a sense of humor, "action-guiding" (so to speak) in a familiar way. If our humorless person were to develop a sense of humor, he would both see the comic features of the world around him (and thus overcome his cognitive lack) and find that they *are* amusing (and thus overcome his affective lack).

Obligation and value might similarly involve a matched pair of sensibility and property.[91] To take the case of obligation: Suppose

---

[91]Once again, a more careful account would attend to relevant differences between obligation and value. For example, the phenomenology of value might be thought to turn on some notion of "attraction," the phenomenology of obligation upon a "must." The general picture suggested by Wiggins in "Truth, Invention, and the Meaning of Life"—in which the relevant "secondary quality" is a kind of attractive highlighting of the landscape of choice brought about by the agent (cf. 137)—is more apt for the former; the picture suggested by McDowell in "Are Moral Requirements Hypothetical Imperatives?"—in which the phenomenology seems to be more than a matter of seeing an option "in a favorable light," since it involves the silencing of various competing considerations—is more apt

DARWALL, GIBBARD, RAILTON

that a child has accidentally become separated from his parents and is wandering down the sidewalk, lost and distressed. A passing individual lacking in moral sensibility might observe this scene and see it as merely curious or annoying, but not as *calling for* intervention. Such a person would not be someone who perceived the *needfulness* of the child's situation but simply failed to feel moved to help. Rather, he would be blind to the needfulness itself.[92] Were the defects in our pedestrian's moral character overcome, he would both see the situation in a way that inherently involves a claim for remedy and find himself motivated to help (or, at least, to feel a certain remorse should he fail to do so).

In this way a sensibility theorist seeks to reconcile cognitivism with the "action-guiding" character of moral judgment that has been thought to tell decisively for noncognitivism: appropriate motivational tendencies are part of the sensibility necessary for the cognitive discernment of certain *sui generis*, but nonetheless genuine, properties. Further, this could contribute to our understanding of the "thickness" of concepts like need, their seemingly inextricable and symmetric fusion of descriptive content and action-guidingness. Speakers who possess authority about the extension of thick concepts to novel cases will be led both by the affective force of their sensibility and by the descriptive features of the world to which this sensibility is attuned.[93]

The sensibility theorist's account would also help explain why (according to a long tradition) moral demands are experienced by those who recognize them as categorical rather than hypothetical.[94] A person with a well-developed moral sensibility will not see the needfulness of the child's situation and then require, as a further condition for rational action, awareness of a desire or interest on

---

for the latter. The distinction between value and obligation are reflected in an older phenomenological tradition, and also, more empirically, in Gestalt psychology. Wiggins and McDowell have attempted to ward off the confusions that have beset recent debates over "moral realism" when the categories of value and obligation are not appropriately distinguished.

[92]Needfulness involves a lack, but not a mere lack: a lack that merits or requires attention. Compare the Pittsburghese idiom, "This needs fixed."

[93]On the idea of a "thick concept," see Bernard Williams, *Ethics and the Limits of Philosophy* (Cambridge: Harvard University Press, 1985), 129, 143–45. In his critical notice of Williams's book, McDowell suggests why, on a view like his, reflection need not emerge as the sort of threat to moral knowledge it does in Williams's account (382–83).

[94]See McDowell, "Are Moral Requirements Hypothetical Imperatives?"

TOWARD FIN DE SIECLE ETHICS

her own part that aiding the child would satisfy. Rather, her very recognition of the needfulness depends upon her being so constituted as to be disposed both to meet it and to find competing *desires* or *interests* inappropriate or overridden or less compelling than they otherwise would have been.[95] (Though, of course, the agent might also recognize—and have to weigh—other *moral* requirements or claims of need.)

However, it is important to emphasize that this account captures only part of what Kant intended by the notion of a categorical imperative, since it does not follow from what has been said that it would be a defect in rationality or autonomy for someone to lack a sensibility that would permit him to descry moral properties. And McDowell apparently does not suppose that such a lack must be a *rational* defect.[96] This is one way one might be led to raise questions about the capacity of sensibility theories to capture the normative force of moral discourse or provide justification or objectivity for morality.

Indeed, for all that we have said thus far, a moral sensibility and a sense of humor are on a par, with perhaps this difference: it appears to be part of a moral sensibility that (at least a subclass of) the properties it enables one to discern have the effect, when recognized, of silencing or outweighing or making less compelling other sorts of reasons or motives in practical deliberation. Could this feature of moral judgments be used to distinguish morality or to justify its special deliberative weight? This seems doubtful since

---

[95]McDowell favors the view that recognition of a moral requirement by a virtuous person silences competing desires:

> If a situation in which a virtue imposes a requirement is genuinely conceived as such, according to this view, then considerations which, in the absence of this requirement, would have constituted reasons for acting otherwise are silenced altogether—not overridden—by the requirement. (Ibid. 26)

Wiggins appears content with the weaker position that the *content* of judgments of moral requirement is categorical—in the sense that it "carries no reference whatever to my inclinations"—though its *motivational force* is simply that of a "good reason," not always a "better reason" than any stemming from my interests. (See his "Reply to Peter Railton," forthcoming in J. Haldane and C. Wright, *Reality, Representation and Projection*.)

[96]"Are Moral Requirements Hypothetical Imperatives?" 13. As mentioned in the previous note, Wiggins departs further from Kant in allowing that other, noncategorical reasons might (rationally) outweigh moral requirements.

DARWALL, GIBBARD, RAILTON

many alternative schemes of normative regulation will support sensibilities that constitutively involve claims of precedence in practical deliberation. Perhaps, for example, only those truly devout really experience the sanctity of certain objects, places, and rites, and for such individuals the sacred *will* call for precedence over appetite or interest. Similarly, *mutatis mutandis*, for those genuinely diabolical, or for the true aesthete. A circular account identifies a structural relationship between a sensibility and its matched property, but since neither is independently characterized, we do not as yet have a way of distinguishing one such sensibility from another[97]—much less of showing one to have a different normative or objective status from another. A peg that fits a round hole has a particular shape; so does a hole that fits a square peg; but what shape in particular do an otherwise unspecified peg and hole have thanks to the fact that they fit each other?

Circular characterizations are not entirely uninformative. For example, if the following circular characterization of *good* is held to be *a priori*:

(1) x is good if and only if x is such as to elicit in us (in "normal circumstances") a sentiment of moral approbation,

then an *a priori* link is being claimed between the property of goodness and a human sentiment, and this might be challenged.[98] Now,

---

[97] For related criticism of circular accounts of color as accounts of content, see Paul A. Boghossian and J. David Velleman, "Colour as a Secondary Quality," *Mind* 98 (1989): 81–103, especially 89–90. Their discussion turns on a more subtle point. A sensibility theorist might urge that we not take over-literally the idea that value or obligation is like redness in being a content of experience, but one can hardly say the same about redness itself. Yet a circular account makes it unclear how redness *could* be a content of experience. To the extent that the sensibility theorist's account of the tie between judgment and motivation does depend upon taking this analogy with the experience of redness seriously (see note 110, below), sensibility theories would inherit this more subtle difficulty as well.

[98] Wiggins writes:

Circularity as such is no objection to it, provided that the offending formulation is also *true*. But what use (I shall be asked) is such a circular formulation? My answer is that, by tracing out such a circle, the subjectivist hopes to elucidate the concept of value by displaying it in its actual involvement with the sentiments. ("A Sensible Subjectivism?" 189)

TOWARD FIN DE SIECLE ETHICS

if the sentiment of moral approbation had a robust and distinctive phenomenology—the way, for example, redness does—then a circular *a priori* equation might simply be a way of saying that the domain of this property is determined by reference to a *sui generis* qualitative state. Thanks to the distinctive character of such a qualitative state, the circular equation would afford a way of *distinguishing* the property (though not of *analyzing* it reductively). But no such robust and distinctive phenomenology exists—or so it seems to us—in the case of moral judgments.[99]

Alternatively, if there were *a priori* ties radiating out from moral approbation—for example, to a *substantively* characterized "space of reasons" that regulates moral approval—then the circular equation would effect a linkage between moral properties and a distinctive class of reasons. These reasons would not need to support anything so strong as an analysis or reduction of moral judgments in order to contribute materially to distinguishing a moral sensibility from others structurally similar, and to open the possibility of a nonreductive "placing" or vindication of morality.[100] However, when McDowell raises the question whether the standing of morality can

---

Of course, one could read (1) in such a way as to make even "involvement with the sentiments" uninformative—if "normal circumstances" were specified to mean "whatever circumstances are necessary in order to guarantee that moral judgments are correct." The interest of (1), then, depends upon avoiding such a trivialization of "normal circumstances" (or, for that matter, of "us").

[99]For example, the convergence of color judgments among ordinary human observers speaking a given language but holding otherwise diverse opinions is a noteworthy difference from the moral case. Moreover, though there may be something to the idea of a "Gestalt" of value or obligatoriness when we experience certain simple and familiar cases, when we face more complex or novel moral questions—for example, questions about distributive justice—where multiple trade-offs and aggregation are involved, it looks as if any experienced "attraction" or "must" will be the result of a complex deliberation, not something that straightforwardly guides judgment. A complex blending of colors still strikes us irresistibly as a color, and close attention to its qualitative character typically guides our classificatory response; the blending of moral considerations may yield a *judgment* that a certain policy or course of action is best, or most just, but not thanks to any irresistible qualitative state to which one can attend closely and that guides judgment (at least, not if the authors' moral experience is typical).

[100]Wiggins might be broaching the idea of such a development of sensibility theory when he notes (in "A Sensible Subjectivism?" 188) that there in fact are *two* elements in a characterization of moral approval, not one:

DARWALL, GIBBARD, RAILTON

be defended against "the idea that there is nothing to ethical thinking but rationally arbitrary subjective stances," he concludes that
"the necessary scrutiny does not involve stepping outside the point
of view constituted by an ethical sensibility."[101] This suggests that
appeal to the "space of reasons" linked to a moral sensibility might
not improve our grip on the content or normative standing of
moral judgments after all.

Perhaps it is misguided to seek a better grip on the content or
standing of moral judgment—explication and justification do have
to come to an end somewhere. Yet it would seem to matter a good
deal where. Many rationally optional "subjective stances" with the
same structure as morality would appear to be candidates for our
allegiance—and some have been in real social competition with
morality. Yet we tend to think something more can be said on
behalf of morality. McDowell rightly points out that the appeal to
internal reasons permits deployment of the full critical resources of
our moral thinking, so that it will not be true that anything goes.[102]
At the same time, however, this will not distinguish or justify the
seeking and following of internal reasons within a moral scheme
from the seeking and following of internal reasons within structurally similar alternative schemes.

Wiggins appears to have taken the question of "objective justification," as he calls it, somewhat further. He asks us to suppose that
our moral practices are "off the ground" already, so there is no
problem of trying to see how they might raise themselves by their
own bootstraps. Then, he urges, we might be objectively justified in
"simple acceptance" of the dictates of our moral sensibility if at
least two further conditions are met: (i) the sensibility and practices
with which moral judgment is bound up are important to our iden-

---

Surely a sentiment of approbation cannot be identified except by its association
[a] with the thought or feeling that x is good (or right or beautiful) and [b] with
the various considerations in which that thought can be grounded, given some
particular item and context, *in situ.*

Care is needed here. Any account of (b) that went as far as stating logically
sufficient "ground[s]" would create the risk of affording epistemic access
to moral facts on the part of those without proper moral character, spoil-
ing the sensibility theorist's account of the tie between judgment and motivation.

[101] McDowell, "Projection and Truth in Ethics," 4–5, 9.
[102] Ibid., 9.

TOWARD FIN DE SIECLE ETHICS

tities as individuals, so that life is "scarcely conceivable without them"; and (ii) these practices are not "manifestly unjust."[103] The first condition will strike some as overly strong on the point of psychic investment; the second, either as an internal condition once again—if, that is, justice is understood by the lights of the sensibility itself—or as a restatement of the problem of objective justification.

It is important to distinguish questions about objective justification from the question whether moral or evaluative discourse, when circularly characterized, is inevitably relativistic. As Wiggins notes, relativism can be avoided if our (circular) characterizations contain an expression that rigidly designates our actual dispositions to respond, following a strategy that does in some respects clearly fit our color discourse.[104] The property of redness is plausibly seen as tied down *a priori* to the features that elicit a red response in humans as they actually are. To imagine humans with a different color sensibility is not to imagine that blood, say, would have had a different color, but only that humans might have seen red things differently. This would, if granted, suffice to rule out a kind of color relativism, and a similar rigidification would rule out certain forms of evaluative or deliberative relativism.

But does rigidification contribute to "objective justification"? It, in effect, guarantees *a priori* that the names 'goodness' and 'rightness', say, belong to properties tracked by *our* sensibilities.[105] Would that tend to show that we are justified in regulating our choices accordingly? Proprietary labeling seems to remove the threat of relativism from our evaluative language without addressing underlying worries about the possible arbitrariness of our evaluative practices,

---

[103]"Reply to Peter Railton." Wiggins also mentions—in a somewhat different connection—the condition that an individual seeking justification not be "on the margins of society . . . [or] systematically disadvantaged by the workings or practices of [the prevailing] morality."

[104]"A Sensible Subjectivism?" 206. For discussion, see the contributions of Michael Smith and Mark Johnston to the symposium "Dispositional Theories of Value," *Proceedings of the Aristotelian Society* 63 (suppl.) (1989). Such a rigidifying strategy was suggested by Martin Davies and Lloyd Humberstone, "Two Notions of Necessity," *Philosophical Studies* 38 (1980): 1–30.

[105]Of course, other societies may have homonyms for 'good' and 'right', linked *a priori* to *their* dispositions. What looks like a disagreement with them over what is good or right might therefore actually be equivocation. See Johnston, "Dispositional Theories," 166–70.

161

DARWALL, GIBBARD, RAILTON

since the feature seized upon to privilege our practices is simply that they *are* our practices. This is not the sort of thing that carries much justificatory weight even within our moral scheme. Not only is it hard to imagine appealing to this feature in an attempted justification aimed at outsiders; it is hard to imagine it succeeding very far in showing nonarbitrariness to ourselves. Thus, we might be led to wonder whether such rigidification does fit a nonrevisionist account of our moral discourse: it might, for example, block expression in that discourse of certain serious, seemingly moral questions.

Sensibility theorists may well be right both about the cognitive character of moral discourse and about the cognitive—even *sui generis*—character of the distinctive sentiments morality engages. The special interest of sensibility theory in morality is that it may afford a way of understand how some form of action-guidingness might—without the demands of a Kantian theory of agency—be "built into" our moral discourse consistently with its possessing cognitivity and objectivity (at least in the sense of intersubjective convergence among "people of a certain culture who have what it takes to understand [the relevant] sort of judgment").[106]

However, sensibility theorists have also noted an important disanalogy between secondary qualities such as color and evaluative properties such as good. Suppose that we accept the following *a priori* equation for *red*, suspending for now any reservations we might have about its circularity:

> (2) *x* is red if and only if *x* is such as to elicit in normal humans as they now are (and in "normal circumstances") the visual impression of redness.

Still, there remains a contrast with *good*. Consider now (a paraphrase of) Wiggins's suggested *a priori* equation for *good*, which involves a revision of (1) that introduces the disanalogy:

---

[106]Wiggins, "Truth as Predicated of Moral Judgments," in *Needs, Values, and Truth*, 160. See, also, McDowell, "Aesthetic Value, Objectivity, and the Fabric of the World," 16n, and Wiggins, "What Would be a Substantial Theory of Truth?" in *Philosophical Subjects: Essays Presented to P. F. Strawson*, ed. Zak van Straaten (Oxford: Oxford University Press/Clarendon, 1980), 218–19.

TOWARD FIN DE SIECLE ETHICS

(3) *x* is good if and only if *x* is such as to make appropriate for
normal humans as they now are (and in "normal circumstances") a sentiment of moral approval.[107]

A noncognitivist would be quick to point out that the analogy with
color (even if it otherwise were sound) breaks down precisely at the
point one would expect were recognition of goodness fundamentally different from experiential knowledge, the point signaled by
the replacement of the perceptual/explanatory expression 'elicit in'
in (2) by the normative expression 'make appropriate for' in (3). Of
course, once we have (2), it is clear why we are entitled to claim that
exposure to normally-red-response-eliciting properties "makes appropriate" a red response (at least, in "normal circumstances" for
normal human observers), and this epistemic certification does not
require any reductive analysis of redness. The difficulty in the case
of good, however, is that we are given nothing like (2) to underwrite the justificatory idiom—we instead are proffered the justificatory idiom itself, namely (3). In the absence both of a robust
phenomenology and of a dispositional grounding on the model of
(2), it becomes harder to say what the distinctive import of the
secondary-quality model is, or whether it can serve to license cognitivism or objectivity about goodness (or rightness).

It is worth asking how much of the insight of sensibility theories
could be preserved if one were to downplay the analogy to secondary qualities[108] and instead try to develop further the idea that

---

[107]"Hume could have said that *x* is good/right/beautiful if and only if *x*
is such as to make a certain sentiment of approbation *appropriate*" (Wiggins,
"A Sensible Subjectivism?" 187; see, also, 189). McDowell makes this contrast with the case of color in "Values and Secondary Qualities," 117–20.

[108]Wiggins at one point remarks that value does not so much appear to
be one other part of the world that impinges upon the individual as it
seems to be an aspect of the world that is *lit up* by the perspective of the
agent. See his "Truth, Invention, and the Meaning of Life," 137. For
would-be value realists, this image may (if it is faithful to the phenomenology of value) be an improvement over Hume's suggestion that the
agent's sensibilities "gild and stain" the world, since the latter seems to
make inevitable a view of values as mere projections. Wiggins's image,
however, also illustrates one other way in which the analogy with secondary qualities breaks down. For secondary qualities are examples *par excellence* of what presents itself in experience as a part of the world that
impinges upon the individual.

DARWALL, GIBBARD, RAILTON

various properties may depend in part on human sensibilities, but nonetheless have conditions of correctness and improvement and, thereby, cognitive (or objective) status.[109] Seen as examples of this general idea, sensibility theories could be very attractive indeed if the worries expressed above could be overcome, or explained away. Such theories would afford a cognitivist interpretation of morality able to supply a version of the internal connection between judgment and motivation that makes expressivism or projectivism attractive.[110] Moreover, they would manage to do so without noncognitivism's complex semantics and purportedly imperfect fit with the phenomenology of moral experience. And sensibility theories could appeal to their diagnosis of an underlying, circular involvement with our sentiments both to explain the often-claimed impossibility of analyzing moral predicates and to locate moral properties within our reach, thus reviving the prospects of a nonreductive moral realism without the dubious epistemology of turn-of-the-century Intuitionism. In these respects, these complex and fascinating theories pose the most important contemporary challenge to the terms of the standard, and perhaps stalemated, dialectic between noncognitivism and naturalistic cognitivism.

The excitement and promise of sensibility theories is that they seek to possess each of two usually-contrasted "directions of expla-

---

[109]Giving a nontrivial account of "correction and improvement" is a crucial part of this task. For related discussion, see Crispin Wright, "Moral Values, Projection, and Secondary Qualities," *Proceedings of the Aristotelian Society* 62 (suppl.) (1988), and Mark Johnston, "Dispositional Theories of Value" and "Objectivity Refigured" (to appear in Haldane and Wright, *Reality, Representation and Projection*, along with a reply by Crispin Wright).

[110]Of course, on sensibility theories the connection is effected by the claim that a properly developed moral sensibility is a precondition for cognitive access to moral or value properties. This view may strike some as too limited—or, alternatively, as genuinely sublime—because it addresses itself so thoroughly to the condition of the virtuous. The view does seem most plausible when cognitive access to moral or value properties is viewed as conforming rather closely to the model of perceptual experience of seemingly ineffable secondary qualities, perhaps along the lines of our discussion above of humorlessness as a kind of "humor-blindness." Further argument would be needed to establish the ineffability of the humorous, the moral, or the evaluative, or to show why one might not be capable of judging correctly—by indirect means, to be sure—that some act *warrants* amusement or moral disapproval even if one oneself lacks the relevant sensibilities.

TOWARD FIN DE SIECLE ETHICS

nation"; their risk, however—like the risk of Aesop's fox, who sought to possess both his bunch of grapes and (what turned out to be) their reflection—is that of genuinely possessing neither.

CONTINUITY

Cognitivism has its attractions, affording by far the most straightforward account of the surface grammar of moral discourse, and promising to avoid revisionism about moral experience and argument. It also has its costs. Sensibility theories seek to provide the attractions at reduced cost, though they may get what they pay for. Perhaps what is needed is a revival of substantive naturalism?[111] Such a revival *is* underway, but surely one is entitled to ask: Must the history of twentieth-century metaethics now be recapitulated?

Perhaps not. The first cycle of criticism of naturalism in this century was directed only at narrowly analytic naturalism; philosophy of language has moved on, and the prospects of naturalisms based on a more expansive view of analyticity, or on views of meaning that do not ask the analytic/synthetic distinction to do much work, are not well known. Thus, the possibility remains that a naturalistic account will emerge able to accommodate all the normative characteristics and uses of moral discourse; or, at least, all such characteristics and uses as survive critical scrutiny.

With this possibility in mind, let us consider three contemporary naturalisms—neo-Aristotelian, postpositivist nonreductionist, and reductionist.[112]

Neo-Aristotelian. Philippa Foot argued, in a series of influential articles,[113] that it would manifest a kind of incompetence with the moral vocabulary to fail to see the inappropriateness of applying

---

[111]For a brief, and hardly unproblematic, characterization of the distinction between substantive and methodological naturalism, see P. Railton, "Naturalism and Prescriptivity," *Social Philosophy and Policy* 7 (1989): 151–74, at 155–57. A noncognitivist—such as Gibbard—can be methodologically naturalistic, but substantively anti- (or non-) naturalistic.

[112]Obviously these categories are not mutually exclusive or jointly exhaustive—they serve here only to organize some competing positions for expository purposes.

[113]See in particular "Moral Arguments," "Moral Beliefs," "Goodness and Choice," and "Morality as a System of Hypothetical Imperatives," all reprinted in *Virtues and Vices.*

DARWALL, GIBBARD, RAILTON

moral terms strictly as a function of pro- or con-attitudes (even when the attitudes have certain "formal" features, such as prescribing universally). For example, suppose there were a community of speakers whose language by and large went smoothly into the English tongue and whose beliefs in general seemed reassuringly familiar, and yet who used a term, 'glim', which in all respects appeared to have the same expressive force as 'morally good' but which they readily applied only to those who demonstrated the physical strength and dexterity to crack a walnut in a bare fist. 'Morally good' would not, it seems, be a happy translation of 'glim' into English—what they are praising, finding admirable, and treating as action-guiding seems to be something other than a person's moral character. One way or another, a connection with certain things—for example, intrinsic concern with effects on human well-being, such as the avoidance of cruelty—seems as intimately a part of our moral usage as, say, universalizability.[114]

This would be a recipe for a potentially unstable "mixed view" of the meaning of moral terms if it combined a claim that possession of certain substantive properties (such as promotion of well-being) is logically sufficient for something to be good with a claim that (correctly) accepting that something is good logically requires endorsing it. For, if Foot is right, there will be no conceptually guaranteed connection between any particular substantive phenomena and such endorsement. Noncognitivists have sought to avoid this instability by insisting that whatever descriptive meaning might accrue to such terms, the prescriptive content is primary.[115] Foot takes the other tack, building the substantive conditions into the meaning of moral terms and ultimately denying that their purported "action-guidingness" is "automatic," claiming instead that it depends hypothetically upon the presence in the population of agents motivated to take the well-being of others seriously.[116] Yet aren't moral requirements categorical?

---

[114]"One way or another...." Indeed; but *which* way, of course, is the crux of the matter. Is it to be interpreted as a matter of *meaning* (analytic) or *doctrine* (synthetic), or are we doubtful about whether there is a fact of the matter? (See section 4, below.)

[115]See, for example, R. M. Hare, *The Language of Morals.*

[116]See, especially, "Morality as a System of Hypothetical Imperatives."

TOWARD FIN DE SIECLE ETHICS

The existence of etiquette shows that norms can be nonhypo-thetical without being categorically motivating: one can sincerely and correctly judge that such requirements apply to oneself (for example) without endorsing compliance or otherwise feeling motivated to comply. Morality, Foot reasoned, could be like that. If morality is more important than etiquette, then the appropriate explanation is that, to us, the promotion of human well-being and the prevention of cruelty are more important than simply giving no offense to conventional expectations. This would dispel the seeming mystery surrounding moral assessment while enabling us to understand how morality might have gotten off the ground—for we can understand how it would be important for a community to evolve and support practices and standards that tend to prevent mutual cruelty and promote mutual well-being, standards that are applied largely independently of (or even in the face of) the particular inclinations of the individuals on whom they are brought to bear by the community, that are reflected at the level of individual moral development in the stringency and priority of moral training, and that are by and large, though not perfectly, internalized.

Such a resolution of the problem of instability seems to do justice to the uncontroversial components of the substantive content of moral expressions in a way that noncognitivism does not. It also might appear to fit better some of the evidence of common sense concerning the somewhat spotty relation between moral evaluation and motivation.[117] Of course, concepts such as cruelty and well-being are not on their face strictly naturalistic. So perhaps the uncontroversiality of the claim that morality is concerned with the prevention of cruelty (for example) trades on a normatively

---

[117]Compare William Frankena's remark that

> the record of human conduct is not such as to make it obvious that human beings always do have some tendency to do what they regard as their duty. The contention that our common moral consciousness supposes that there is no gap [between obligation and motivation] will be met by conflicting evidence. . . . ("Obligation and Motivation in Recent Moral Philosophy," 79)

See, also, his essays "Recent Conceptions of Moral Philosophy" and "Three Questions about Morality," *Monist* 63 (1980): 3–68. Frankena distinguishes the moral point of view in part substantively (as involving, for example, a degree of intrinsic interest in the well-being of others). Over time, however, Frankena's views have become friendlier to internalism.

167

DARWALL, GIBBARD, RAILTON

loaded, prescriptive reading of 'cruelty'. But Foot has argued quite generally that prescriptive readings devoid of primary descriptive content cannot do justice to our linguistic practices, at least in the case of evaluative expressions like 'a good *x*'. And it perhaps is plausible that the notion of well-being contains no normative component other than "a good life for the person who leads it"—in contrast, say, to the imperatival notions of obligation or duty. One might attempt an account of this normative component along Aristotelian lines, although a difficulty would arise: 'good' in its various evaluative uses typically is anchored by attachment to characteristic functions or roles—*a good pitch pipe, a good dentist,* and so on; Aristotelian theory would in principle permit one to carry this functionally anchored use forward into broader-ranging evaluations such as *a good life,* because Aristotle's underlying teleology affords to humans essential functions and roles; but this essentialist teleology is precisely the element of Aristotle's ethics that now seems least likely to be refurbished.[118] The *neo-*Aristotelian can reply that a cosmic teleology would be needed only if one sought to capture the idea of *a cosmically good life.* All that is needed for the idea of *a humanly good life* is the teleology inherent in the psychology of interest and desire, as realized in species-typical human beings. This latter view would nonetheless confront the familiar difficulties attending attempts to capture the normative in terms of the typical.[119]

Postpositivist nonreductionist. Accounts of ethics that are more self-consciously naturalistic have multiplied in recent years, encour-

---

[118]Compare Bernard Williams's comment—in *Ethics and the Limits of Philosophy*—that an Aristotelian ethical objectivism is the only sort that might work, though, in his view, even Aristotle fails to deploy his teleology effectively in securing the objective underwriting needed (44). We are making no claim here that this "functionalist" view of Aristotle's ethics is historically correct or adequate; we simply wish to note that one could be quite comfortable with a function-based naturalism for various evaluative uses of 'good' but still resist extending such an account to *a good human life*—perhaps because one cannot see one's way to a view about what a human life (as opposed to a pitch pipe or even a dentist) is *for.*

[119]See Moore, *Principia,* 44–45. A possible response, though one that might make the neo-Aristotelian position less distinct from a number of recent naturalisms, would be to introduce an idealization of the species-typical in order better to capture normativity, developing an account of *ideal-typical* human desires and interests.

TOWARD FIN DE SIECLE ETHICS

aged in part by work in epistemology, philosophy of science, and philosophy of language.

One important group of continuity theories of this kind starts out from the claim that reflective equilibrium is the method of the sciences as well as ethics.[120] In both cases, use of this method in critically evaluating our beliefs is seen as inevitably involving some appeal both to the evidence of experience and to currently held substantive theory—for example, application of a principle of inference to the best explanation requires recourse to our going theory as well as experience in assessing the plausibility of competing explanatory claims. Thus, the fact that moral epistemology cannot dispense with an appeal to existing moral judgments or "intuitions," and can subject such judgments to criticism and revision only in broadly coherentist ways, does not show a fundamental difference or discontinuity between moral and scientific epistemology. Since, according to such views, we arrive at belief in the reality of moral properties as part of an inference to the best explanation of human conduct and its history, it has become a central issue for them whether so-called "moral explanations" are genuine—and good—explanations.

Harman has denied that *irreducible* moral properties could have a genuine explanatory role, but Nicholas Sturgeon, Richard Boyd, David Brink, and others have pursued analogies with natural and social science to argue that moral properties might be both irreducible and explanatorily efficacious.[121] One might, for example,

---

[120]See Nicholas Sturgeon, "Moral Explanations"; Richard Boyd, 'How to Be a Moral Realist," in *Moral Realism*, ed. G. Sayre-McCord (Ithaca, N.Y.: Cornell University Press, 1988); and David O. Brink, *Moral Realism and the Foundations of Ethics* (Cambridge: Cambridge University Press, 1989).

[121]See Harman, *The Nature of Morality*, chaps. 1 and 2; Sturgeon, "Moral Explanations"; Harman, "Moral Explanations of Natural Facts—Can Moral Claims be Tested against Moral Reality?" and Sturgeon, "Harman on Moral Explanations of Natural Facts" and "What Difference Does It Make Whether Moral Realism Is True?" all in *Moral Realism: Proceedings of the 1985 Spindel Conference*, ed. N. Gillespie, *The Southern Journal of Philosophy*, 4 (suppl.) (1986); Brink, *Moral Realism and the Foundations of Ethics*; and Boyd, "How to Be a Moral Realist." See, also, Richard Miller, "Reason and Commitment in the Social Sciences," *Philosophy and Public Affairs* 8 (1979): 241–66, especially 252–55; and G. Sayre-McCord, "Moral Theory and Explanatory Impotence," in G. Sayre-McCord, ed., *Moral Realism.*

DARWALL, GIBBARD, RAILTON

argue that various chemical or biological "natural kinds"—acid, catalyst, gene, organism—are not obviously type-reducible to the natural kinds of physics, and yet play a role in good scientific explanations.

Moral properties might behave like natural kinds, on this view, because they might effect a theoretical unification of physiochemically and psychosociologically diverse phenomena in ways that would throw into relief common causal-explanatory roles: in light of the diverse physiochemical or psychosociological ways in which cruelty or injustice can be instantiated, there could be an illuminating unifying effect of explanations that successfully attribute various social or behavioral outcomes to cruelty or injustice. Like natural kinds, these moral properties would owe their explanatory capacity in part to their location within a constellation of law-governed—or at least counterfactual-supporting—properties that displays some structural or functional coherence.

For example, the notion of social justice might pick out an array of conditions that enhance the possibility of psychologically self-respecting and attractive individual lives while at the same time promoting social cooperation, stability, and prosperity. Such conditions would, in a sense, be mutually supporting. This would not suffice to secure any very strict form of internalism at the individual level, but it would help to explain how justice, and just social arrangements, might attract and retain public support, leading to the inculcation of norms of justice in individuals. And this in turn would help us to see how justice—or injustice—could have a causal-explanatory role.[122]

Of course, nonreductionists must supply a convincing answer to critics of the application of "inference to the *best* explanation" to the moral case, given the alleged availability of alternative, more minimal, and more obviously naturalistic explanations. It has, for example, been argued that supervenient properties should be ex-

---

[122]Boyd has given the best-developed version of this view, according to which moral properties—like relevant natural kinds in science—pick out "homeostatic clusters." See his "How to Be a Moral Realist." Note that the sort of explanatory role under discussion could not be replaced without loss by explanations in terms of the beliefs about justice of those involved (as has been suggested by Harman, *The Nature of Morality*, 22)—for we can appeal to actual injustice to explain how these beliefs about injustice came about. On this point, see P. Railton, "Moral Realism," 192.

TOWARD FIN DE SIECLE ETHICS.

punged from good explanations, since the "real explanatory work" is being done by the supervenience base. However, this standard of "best explanation" seems unduly restrictive even for natural science, where theory development is not typically a minimalist enterprise and virtues such as depth, unification, and scope are also sought in explanations, and where there may emerge at a supervenient level lawlike regularities that seem genuinely to contribute to explanatory understanding. For example, explanations citing genes and natural selection afford a distinctive and worthwhile insight into the distribution of amino acids over the world's surface, even if this distribution could also be explained in purely physical terms, and even if the biological types are not (neatly) reducible to physical types, but merely supervene upon them. Since no standard account exists of what makes for "the best explanation," even in paradigm natural sciences, it is unlikely that definitive refutation—or vindication—of nonreductive naturalism will come from this quarter.

If moral properties are to be viewed as irreducible natural properties akin to natural kinds, then this sort of naturalism would run afoul of no Moorean argument: no *a priori* analysis is being offered, and full respect is being paid to Moore's Butlerian motto, "Everything is what it is, and not another thing."[123] It would perhaps seem extravagant to admit irreducible moral properties into the domain of natural properties if one did not allow, as the postposi-

---

[123]See the epigram opposite the title page of *Principia*. One question that cannot be entered into in detail here is whether one can overcome various apparent obstacles to application of the semantics of natural kind terms to our evaluative vocabulary. On the view favored by postpositivist nonreductionists, natural kind terms function like proper names, contributing to propositions primarily by serving up a referent rather than providing an essential or identificatory description. According to this account, it is left to the course of science to provide us true descriptions that reveal the essence of the kind in question, and our linguistic usage shows this pattern of deference to theory and expertise, present and future. But our evaluative vocabulary seems to put its putative referents forward under a rather particular mode of presentation (see section 4), and patterns of deference in contemporary evaluative usage are, to say the least, less straightforward. (The normativity of conditions of idealization, discussed below in connection with reductionist accounts, might be one such pattern of deference— we tend to think our current moral or evaluative responses could be misguided in various ways if based upon ignorance, and tend to take our more informed responses as more authoritative, other things equal.)

DARWALL, GIBBARD, RAILTON

tivists do, that moral natural properties supervene (in roughly the sense Moore seems to have had in mind)[124] upon nonmoral natural properties. However, one might wonder whether in this setting supervenience is genuinely distinct from (messy) reducibility. For these accounts operate at the level of properties, not concepts, and advance supervenience as a metaphysical, not normative, doctrine.[125] And supervenience between two seemingly disparate classes of properties is in some respects a quite strong and surprising relation; it is the kind of relation that would appear to call out for explanation. If the postpositivist held that nonmoral properties wholly and exclusively *constitute* moral properties, that would afford some explanation, but it would also make it more difficult to contrast such a view with some species of reductionism.

On the epistemological side, the nonreductionist naturalisms we have been considering must defend the view that reflective equilibrium is the method of natural science as well as ethics, and must explain the sense in which this method, despite its extensive use of intuition and nonconfirmatory desiderata of theory choice such as simplicity and explanatory coherence, genuinely warrants belief in the truth of its conclusions (since the postpositivists under discussion reject coherentism about truth). Now not all postpositivist nonreductionist naturalisms accept reflective equilibrium as an adequate account of justified claims in the sciences or ethics. Richard Miller, for example, insists that justification must involve a nontrivial claim that one's beliefs are the result of a reliable process for detection. Such a claim must itself be justified, on Miller's view, but regress is avoided by bringing such claims to ground in topic-specific principles that are part of the believer's framework, principles whose truth cannot be established by further, topic-neutral justifications. Such a procedure need not be merely self-congratulatory: it could turn out that the actual processes of belief

---

[124]For Moore's view, see his "Reply to My Critics," 588.

[125]Normative theses of supervenience state *commitments concerning the invocation of certain concepts* rather than metaphysical relations among properties. For a noncognitivist, supervenience is a commitment to the effect that nothing can aptly be deemed good except in virtue of some nonnormative features it possesses; thus, if two things are judged different with respect to goodness, one is committed to finding them different in their nonnormative features as well. Theses of supervenience of this ilk carry no special metaphysical implications.

TOWARD FIN DE SIECLE ETHICS

formation that we have employed in morality, say, are not as they would have to be in order to satisfy our fundamental principles concerning moral detection.[126]

Despite their differences, these nonreductionist views do face common opposition from those who question the granting of initial epistemic standing to irreducible moral beliefs, even when they happen to be *our* beliefs. Such criticism is usually countered by noting that theory development in general begins with according *prima facie* standing to some existing beliefs—and indeed there seems to be scant alternative. But critics will reply by citing many differences in the actual *accomplishments* of theory 'development in science as opposed to ethics, differences that might be thought to cast light back on the reasonableness of the original supposition of epistemic standing. Just as, in the case of religion, it has eventually come to count against the reasonableness of taking "religious experience" as possessing *prima facie* epistemic standing that religious theory has proven so persistently controversial and unreliable in its claims about the details of nature and history, so might it be held that the lack of consensus and accomplishment in ethics counts against what would otherwise be a reasonable willingness to assign *prima facie* epistemic weight to moral beliefs. There would of course be little left of ethics, or ethical inquiry, as a cognitive domain were no initial weight given to going moral beliefs; but critics might not find this skeptical result wholly uncongenial.

An effective reply to such critics would involve giving an explanation of moral controversy that competes favorably with the skeptical alternative and, more importantly, would involve developing nonreductionist ethical theory itself, showing it to have (or to make possible) some worthwhile theoretical accomplishments. Accomplishing this task would involve articulating the connections between *sui generis* moral or evaluative properties, on the one hand, and judgment, motivation, behavior, and other elements of social or psychological theory, on the other, in ways adequate both to illustrate the explanatory gains secured by appeal to such proper-

---

[126]See R. Miller, "Ways of Moral Learning," *Philosophical Review* 94 (1985): 507–56, and *Fact and Method: Explanation, Confirmation, and Reality in the Natural and Social Sciences* (Princeton: Princeton University Press, 1987).

DARWALL, GIBBARD, RAILTON

ties and to explicate (and in some suitable sense capture) their normativity.[127]

Reductionist. A more direct, but also riskier, way of attempting to answer a number of the questions raised above—about normativity, about which explanations "do all the work," about epistemic standing, and about supervenience—is to pursue reductionism. Reductionist proposals with regard to moral rightness or nonmoral good have in recent years been broached by, among others, Richard Brandt, Gilbert Harman, Peter Railton, and David Lewis.[128] The reduction might be in the form of a putative analytic truth (of a kind more complex than any envisaged by Moore), a reforming definition, or a synthetic identity statement.[129] By exhibiting which *bona fide* natural properties value discourse can be construed as

---

[127]For example, appeal to homeostatic equilibria will not afford an approach to explanation or normativity for those areas where severe or contentious trade-offs are inevitable. It is open to the postpositivist nonreductionist either to show how some suitable internalist constraint can be met, or to show why internalism is the wrong account of normativity (even while explaining how it has seemed to many philosophers obviously right).

[128]See R. B. Brandt, *A Theory of the Good and the Right*; G. Harman, "Moral Explanations of Natural Facts," 66–67 and *The Nature of Morality*, 125–136; P. Railton, "Moral Realism," "Facts and Values," and "Naturalism and Prescriptivity"; and D. Lewis, "Dispositional Theories of Value," *Proceedings of the Aristotelian Society* 63 (suppl.) (1989). John Rawls, in *A Theory of Justice* (secs. 60–63), offers an account of nonmoral good that shows many affinities with those just mentioned, and he cites a long list of historical and contemporary antecedents. Some of the accounts mentioned above are of moral rightness, others of nonmoral value. For convenience, though at some cost to accuracy and coherence, in what follows we will often speak simply of "value" to cover both.

[129]Reservations expressed above (note 123) about employing a natural kinds semantics for evaluative vocabulary remain in force. For an example of a semantics based upon complex analytic truth, see D. Lewis, "Dispositional Theories of Value." The "putative analytic truth" escapes Moorean refutation by showing that the reduction "scores best" in an overall account of the meaning of the terms, where it is part of the meaning of terms that they apply to whatever fits their associated truisms, or does so near enough. The proposal would identify that which "best deserves" the name 'value', say, and then note that it comes quite close to that which would "perfectly deserve" the name. See also Lewis, "Score-keeping in a Language Game," reprinted in *Philosophical Papers*, vol. 1 (New York: Oxford University Press, 1983). How genuine a difference exists among these three approaches—via putative analytic truth, reforming definition, or synthetic property identity? Functionally, at any rate, they may come to much the same thing when fully developed and suitably hedged.

TOWARD FIN DE SIECLE ETHICS

being about, it is possible to exploit the features of these properties
to answer questions about the motivational or normative force of
evaluation, to give an unmysterious account of the epistemology of
value, and to account for the supervenience of value.[130]

Depending upon the nature of the reduction, it might turn out
that relativism about value or morality is vindicated (Brandt, Harman, Lewis)[131] or not (Railton).[132] Moreover, all of these accounts
are dispositional in the sense that they make matters of value depend upon the affective dispositions of agents. Most, though not
all, seek to capture the component of normativity that consists in
the possibility of criticizing our existing affective dispositions by
providing for some sort of *idealization* of the familiar epistemology
that underwrites so much of our evaluative discourse. The criticism
of our desires and ends typically proceeds by, for example, asking
whether satisfying them would interfere with other ends, or showing that we have misconceived their origins or objects, or convincing us that, if we knew what it would be like to satisfy them, we
would no longer want to be guided by them, and so on. More
generally, we believe that one knows better what one's good is, or
what is right, the more comprehensive or vivid one's awareness of

---

[130]The account of supervenience is not, perhaps, *a priori*, since it may
rely upon a principle such as "same cause, same effect." Critics of reductionist accounts have argued that the supervenience of the moral upon the
nonmoral is a conceptual matter. See, for example, S. Blackburn, *Spreading
the Word* and Mark Johnston, "Dispositional Theories of Value." However,
if we think of value as given by what we are *stably* disposed to want to want,
say, then it will follow *a priori* that nothing could be a value unless the
dispositions exhibited the requisite stability. In any event, it perhaps is in
the normative rather than metaphysical form that supervenience is *a priori*,
and the reductionist is not blocked from viewing supervenience in this
sense as one of the normative commitments that come with *use* of moral
language.

[131]For the moral case, see Brandt, *A Theory of the Good and the Right*, chap.
10; and Harman, "Moral Relativism Defended," *Philosophical Review* 84
(1975): 3–22, "Relativistic Ethics: Morality as Politics," *Midwest Studies in
Philosophy* 3 (1978): 109–21, and "Is There a Single True Morality?" in
Morality, Reason, and Truth. For the case of nonmoral intrinsic value, see
Lewis, "Dispositional Theories of Value."

[132]For the case of intrinsic nonmoral good, the account is relational,
rather than relativistic; see Railton, "Facts and Values," 10ff. Contrast
Lewis's relativistic use of the second-person plural in "Dispositional Theories of Value," 132ff. For an example of nonrelativism about the moral
case, see Railton, "Moral Realism," sec. 4.

DARWALL, GIBBARD, RAILTON

what living out various possibilities would be like for oneself, or for all affected, a view whose ancestry reaches back to Hume on taste, Mill on utility, and, more recently, Firth on the "Ideal Observer."[133] The component of normativity that consists in "action-guidingness" is, in turn, sought by appeal to the motivational force of our affective dispositions (again, perhaps as they are when our circumstances are in certain ways improved or idealized—since motivation when benighted might not be *normative* for us), and including perhaps characteristic desires to see our values or choices as defensible, or to make them part of a coherent and effective life.[134]

These views locate the ultimate ground of normativity in the affective dispositions of agents, and this immediately raises the question whether suitable "objectivity" can be secured for ethics by such reductive naturalisms. If it is essential to the genuineness of value or moral judgments that they not be relational in certain ways—not be tied, for example, to contingent dispositions of creatures like us to be drawn to some things rather than others—then a validation as "objective" would not be forthcoming from the reduction. We will have something better described as "subjectivity objectified" than as objectivity *tout court*. Yet it may be a strength of "idealized response" views that there seems nothing for value to be,

---

[133]D. Hume, "Of the Standard of Taste," reprinted in *Of the Standard of Taste and Other Essays*, ed. J. W. Lenz (Indianapolis: Bobbs-Merrill, 1965); J. S. Mill, *Utilitarianism*, ed. George Sher (Indianapolis: Hackett, 1979), chap. 4; R. Firth, "Ethical Absolutism and the Ideal Observer," *Philosophy and Phenomenological Research* 12 (1952): 317–45.

[134]On the various actual desires engaged by idealized-desire accounts of intrinsic nonmoral value, see Brandt, *A Theory of the Good and the Right*, chap. 8, and Railton, "Facts and Values," 14–17. It is important to notice the diversity of positions available here. Harman, in *The Nature of Morality*, claims that 'ought' judgments cannot sensibly be applied to individuals who are not motivated to comply. The result is a kind of internalism about 'ought' judgments—as distinguished from judgments about what is, from a moral point of view, better or worse. By contrast, Brandt and Railton insist upon a kind of internalism for judgments of intrinsic nonmoral good, and make concessions to the externalist conception of obligation that Harman means to exclude. Harman, in "Moral Relativism Defended" and "Relativistic Ethics: Morality as Politics," seems concerned with actual, nonidealized motivations (though compare his "ideal reasoner" naturalistic account of reasons in *The Nature of Morality*), whereas Brandt is concerned with what moral code one would support in idealized circumstances.

TOWARD FIN DE SIECLE ETHICS

on deepest reflection, wholly apart from what moves, or could move, valuers—agents for whom something can matter. Indeed, one way to defend idealized response views (naturalistic or otherwise) is to observe that there appears to be no alternative in critical discussion of value to a process of asking how things might strike us on reflection. It would, accordingly, be an intolerably reified conception of value or morality to insist that "objective" value must be "absolute" in the sense of possessing independence from all facts about motivation (even, should there be such a thing, "rational motivation").[135]

But even if the specter of absolute value can be laid to rest, and even if such accounts can avoid direct collision with the open question argument in virtue of advancing their claims via reforming definitions, property identities, or non-obvious analytic equivalences, they nonetheless cannot avoid eventual confrontation with something very much like the open question argument. With regard to whatever explication they offer of good in terms of some (possibly complex) property P, it still seems coherent to ask, "Yes, I see that x is P, but isn't there still room for me to wonder whether x is genuinely good, whether I ought to regulate my life accordingly?" This question's intelligibility appears to call for some meaning of 'good' other than the reductionist proposal. Even reductionist proposals set forward as reforming definitions face a similar challenge, since they purport to provide an account of 'good', say, that gives it a clear meaning but also enables us to pose all the significant questions that the pre-reformed term permitted.[136] Yet isn't the question "Yes, I see that x is P, but isn't there still room for me to wonder . . . ?" a significant one? And how could we use the reformed term to state it?

Reductionists will have to convince us better than they have that their proposals make this question less than pressing, at least with

---

[135]Note that there can be "idealized response" views that do not presuppose all moral motivation to be liable to independent characterization such as a reductive naturalist seeks. Such views might be realist, and they would share with the naturalistic view under discussion a criticism of "absolute value" as incoherent. See, for example, Mark Johnston, "Dispositional Theories of Value."

[136]On reforming definitions, see, for example, Brandt, *A Theory of the Good and the Right*, chap. 1.

DARWALL, GIBBARD, RAILTON

respect to, say, a persons's own good. (It need not be the ambition of an account of nonmoral good to tell us *how to lead our lives*, for example, in cases where morality, or friendship, or aesthetics point in ways other than toward promotion of one's own good.)[137] Of course, none of the naturalistic reductionist proposals are free of revisionism, and so none could possibly fit all aspects of English usage. We probably do not suppose that our intuitive notions of value or rightness are free of confusion or ambiguity, and so can hardly expect that any philosophical account of them that is not itself confused and ambiguous will have just the right intuitive "fit."

In this area as in many others, intellectual developments may lead us to a view that differs from common sense, and yet helps us both to understand what common sense does believe, and to correct it in certain ways, consistent with preserving core elements of the function of common sense—whether the area be explanation of the natural world or evaluation of the human world. Even so, the fact that these accounts seem inevitably to be led from some fairly uncontroversial repudiation of reification to some much more controversial account of the conditions of idealization, or of the relation of idealization to actual motivation, indicates the depth of the problems they face—whether they are proposed as linguistic analyses or as reforming definitions.

Questions of revisionism and controversy also inevitably bring us back to the issue of the contestability of questions of morality and value. Reductionist accounts can explain the difficulty in resolving conflicts over these questions in various ways: the intense and inevitable involvement of competing interests; the apparent plurality of values and lack of determinacy about assessment and trade-offs;[138] the inherent complexity of the issues, and the relatively

---

[137]Indeed, even an account of moral rightness need not have the ambition of "deciding for us" what place moral considerations will have in our deliberations. Compare here Mill's distinguishing of the moral, aesthetic, and sympathetic "modes of viewing," in his essay on Bentham, reprinted in J. S. Mill, *Utilitarianism and Other Essays*, ed. M. Warnock (New York: Meridian, 1962), 121f. Mill thought the moral point of view ought to be "paramount," though one can accept his distinctions without—or without always—accepting this further claim.

[138]It need not be an obstacle to realism about value, or to the continuity thesis, that value's boundaries or magnitudes might involve some vague-

TOWARD FIN DE SIECLE ETHICS

underdeveloped state of both of social and psychological theory and of moral theory and theory of value; and so on.[139] But even if such explanations are granted some standing, they may seem to fall well short of taking full measure of the depth of contestability and the issues it raises.

Questions of revisionism and controversy also inevitably bring us back to issues about how a reductionist account might claim to capture the "peculiar connection to action" of morality. Can an account that makes moral motivation other than rationally mandatory yield an adequate explanation—one that is at most tolerably revisionist—of the phenomena of moral experience or of the seeming truisms of commonsense moral thought? Perhaps such features of our ordinary conception of morality as the nonhypothetical scope and content of moral requirements, which the idea of automatic rational authority has been invoked to explain, can be otherwise accommodated, or shown to be less central or indispensible to commonsense moral thought than Kantians have imagined. But reductionists have not gone far in showing any such thing; despite

---

ness or indeterminacy. Consider, for comparison, the question, What is the surface area of Iceland? Do we take the coastline at high or low water, neap or spring tide? How short a "measuring stick" do we use to gauge the coastline's edge? And so on. Iceland's surface area may be indeterminate in these respects, but it also is determinate enough to be clearly greater than Tobago's and less than Great Britain's. The thesis that ethics or value theory is substantively or methodologically continuous with empirical inquiry would hardly be in grave peril if, for example, value turned out to be "no more determinate than the surface area of Iceland." The real difficulty in the case of value is not with vagueness or indeterminacy as such, but with our unhappiness at the idea of resolving vagueness or indeterminacy via any sort of linguistic reform of regimentation. Cartographers may be happy to adopt conventions to resolve indeterminacy about surface area, but merely conventional resolutions seem inappropriate in the case of value: owing to the connection between value and action, such resolutions may strike us as substantive in a way that begs controversial questions about how to live. How we should respond theoretically or practically to this situation is, of course, a central question. One theoretical response would be to show that a purported reduction of value preserves whatever indeterminacy survives critical reflection.

[139]These same considerations suggest that some areas of morality and value should be less controversial than others. A plausible reductionist account should help us to explain which are which. For relevant discussion, see Railton, "Moral Realism," 197–200.

179

DARWALL, GIBBARD, RAILTON

their protestations, they might turn out to be error theorists after all.

3. Modern Morality, Modern Moral Theory

Even the most abbreviated account of recent developments in ethics must record the strenuous criticisms some modern philosophers writing on morality have lodged against modern moral philosophy, and, at times, against modern morality itself.[140]

There surely is a sense in which contemporary "Western" society finds itself without a sufficiently rich shared cosmology or theology, or a sufficiently rich constellation of vigorous, uncontroversial, and unselfconscious collective practices, to be able to escape a certain anxiety about morality, or to be able to articulate crucial moral questions without reaching for a high level of abstraction or generality, a level that seems at times unrelated to the conditions and motivations characteristic of actual lives and their particular sources of interest. Given the diversity of large societies, the tenuousness of many of the connections that bind together their members, the pressures toward rationalization exerted by large and seemingly inevitable institutions, and the universalist aspiration of modern thought in general, there may be little for philosophers out of sympathy with modern morality and modern moral philosophy to do but bemoan this condition. Indeed, discomforted philosophers have typically claimed to find modern philosophy in general to be unhelpful in this predicament—either because, as a child of secular, rationalizing, universalizing impulses itself, it is part of

---

[140]See E. Anscombe, "Modern Moral Philosophy"; P. Foot, "Virtues and Vices"; Alisdair MacIntyre, *After Virtue* (Notre Dame: University of Notre Dame Press, 1981); M. Stocker, "The Schizophrenia of Modern Ethical Theories," and *Plural and Conflicting Values* (New York: Oxford University Press, 1990); B. Williams, *Ethics and the Limits of Philosophy*; A Baier, "Theory and Reflective Practices" and "Doing Without Moral Theory?" reprinted in *Postures of Mind* (Minneapolis: University of Minnesota Press, 1985); James Wallace, *Moral Relevance and Moral Conflict* (Ithaca, N.Y.: Cornell University Press, 1988); and Stanley G. Clarke and Evan Simpson, eds., *Anti-Theory in Ethics and Moral Conservatism* (Albany: State University of New York Press, 1989).

TOWARD FIN DE SIECLE ETHICS

the problem, or because it simply lacks the kind of insight necessary to diagnose the real problems besetting morality and moral philosophy or the kind of power sufficient to affect these problems' real causes.

For the most part, criticisms of morality and moral theory have been set out in bold outline, in somewhat deliberate defiance of the complexities of history, society, and philosophy. So there is no end of possible rejoinders to such critiques of the mincing, "yes, but . . ." form. Certainly this is not the place to present these critiques of morality and moral theory more fully or to ask how much of their force would remain were they made more responsive to the historical record and more nuanced philosophically. However, since we have been up to our necks in moral theory in this essay, it behooves us to make some general sort of reply to these critiques, even if it must be much more schematic than the criticisms themselves.

One can discern at least two aspects of modern moral theory—as opposed to modern morality proper—that have especially been called into question: normative theory (the effort to bring some system or unity to the multiplicity of particular moral assessments and commonsense moral principles by developing—some might say discovering—a highly general set of normative principles or procedures to organize them) and metatheory (understood broadly as the effort to develop—or discover—a systematic understanding of what morality is, or purports to be). Let us take these up in order.

This essay has had little to say about normative theory in its own right.[141] Those who write in a critical vein about normative theory as an enterprise typically find themselves somewhat torn. Existing moral conceptions are, after all, the product of diverse historical forces, and it would be surprising indeed for them to fall into one neat pattern, as perhaps Kantian or utilitarian normative theories might seem to claim. Yet one cannot without qualm call for "fidelity to existing conceptions in all their particularity" as an alternative.

---

[141]Annette Baier has usefully identified the goal of developing a normative theory as the best-defined target for a range of criticisms often leveled at "moral theory" without qualification. See her "Doing Without Moral Theory?"

DARWALL, GIBBARD, RAILTON

Not only are "existing conceptions" in flux, but it would also appear that we owe much of what seems most admirable in modern societies—movements for political democracy and universal suffrage, for the emancipation of slaves and women, for the elimination of racial, ethnic, and religious discrimination, for universal social provision of basic needs, and for international law and human rights—in significant measure to universalizing and generalizing pressures that have precisely gone against the grain of some entrenched (and still powerful) particularistic moral conceptions and individual or group commitments. One might hope for a better reconciliation of universalizing ethics and the particularity of individual lives and communities than either Kantian or utilitarian normative theories have thus far effected. More dramatically, one might insist that this "better reconciliation" will yield something that looks less like a *theory* than either Kantianism or utilitarianism. But pronouncing on this latter question would seem to us premature, given the remarkable development of Kantian and utilitarian theories in recent decades and the fact that some alternative theories, such as hybrid theories and ethics of virtue, have only begun to receive sustained discussion.[142]

About metatheorizing, critics typically manifest a different kind of ambivalence. It is less that they admire the effects of some of its well-known products than that they find themselves hard-working practitioners of the trade. Alisdair MacIntyre, in *After Virtue*, devotes substantial effort to a philosophical investigation of the con-

---

[142]Among the interesting recent works in a broadly Kantian tradition that might have more to say about particularity are Rawls, "Justice as Fairness: Political Not Metaphysical," and Scanlon, "Contractualism and Utilitarianism"; within the utilitarian tradition, recent approaches that may make more room for various sorts of social or individual particularity include David Lyons, "Human Rights and the General Welfare," *Philosophy and Public Affairs* 6 (1977): 113–29, and Michael Slote, *Common-sense Morality and Consequentialism* (London: Routledge and Kegan Paul, 1985). A hybrid theory is discussed in S. Scheffler, *The Rejection of Consequentialism*. See also W. K. Frankena's "mixed deontological theory," in his *Ethics*, 2d. ed. (Englewood Cliffs, N.J.: Prentice-Hall, 1973), 43–54. Some advocates of virtue-based approaches to ethics have seen this as part of a movement against normative theorizing; yet one could very well think that a plausible virtue-based approach will call for a normative theory of the various virtues.

TOWARD FIN DE SIECLE ETHICS

ceptual presuppositions of morality and to a discussion of the adequacy of noncognitivism as a theory of the meaning of moral terms.[143] And Bernard Williams, in *Ethics and the Limits of Philosophy*, defines 'ethical theory' in a way that exempts a systematic attempt to explain what is going on in moral language and thought—including an attempt to "place" ethics with respect to scientific inquiry—if it implies that a given "test" of normative correctness *sometimes* (but not always or never) applies; that is, he defines the term in a way that exempts his own quite interesting metatheorizing.[144] Unable as we are to locate any deep distinction between the sorts of investigations we have been carrying out and those pursued by *les théoriciens malgré eux*, we prefer to see our efforts as animated by a common desire to understand morality, its preconditions, and its prospects, however much our substantive conclusions might differ from theirs.

4. IN LIEU OF A CONCLUSION

Metaethics as revived today differs in a number of ways from metaethics during its analytic heyday, but no difference is more striking than the multiplicity of now active positions and questions. No view currently enjoys the predominance noncognitivism once did, and questions about meaning have been forced to make room for a range of metaphysical, epistemological, and practical questions as well. Such philosophical progress as has been made in metaethics has come not from simplifying the debate or reducing the number of viable alternatives, but from bringing greater sophistication to the discussion of well-known positions and from exploring heretofore disregarded possibilities and interconnections. Indeed, debate has now extended even to the metaphilosophical level, as philosophers have asked with increasing force and urgency whether, or in what ways, theorizing is appropriate to morality. Since there appears to be no immediate danger of things

---

[143]See *After Virtue*, especially chaps. 2–5. Cf. also W. K. Frankena's review essay, "MacIntyre and Modern Morality," *Ethics* 93 (1983): 579–87, especially 582–83.

[144]See *Ethics and the Limits of Philosophy*, 72. Moreover, it may be unclear whether one has a single, relativistic test, or multiple, relative tests.

DARWALL, GIBBARD, RAILTON

returning to a staid consensus, we will end by making a few observations without attempting anything so grand as a conclusion.
Somewhat preversely, perhaps, our observations will be concerned
in part with whether some of the distinctions upon which current
debates have fastened may be of less ultimate significance, or (more
respectfully) of much greater subtlety, than they now appear. Here
follow six examples, not all quite in dead earnest, of areas where
genuine issues exist, but where current debates have exaggerated
contrasts for effect, somewhat masking the issues themselves.

(1) A contemporary noncognitivist, still impressed that the open
question argument reveals something about the meaning of moral
terms, might claim that a naturalistic realism about ethics or value
founded on reforming definitions or property identities should not
be seen as really in competition with his view. The noncognitivist
aims to capture (something roughly equivalent to) the senses expressed by our evaluative terms, made evident by the possibility of
using the words 'good', 'right', to conduct meaningful debate over
competing naturalistic views. The word 'good', for example, is used
to bring something—quite possibly a naturalistic something—
forward in a certain mode of presentation, *as* evaluatively appropriate. The naturalistic realist may by contrast see herself as aiming
to locate those properties that discourse about goodness can—or
could within the limits of tolerable revisionism, or should when we
have cleared away various confusions—be construed as tracking, or
as settling upon as we grow in knowledge and experience. Something like a division of labor between sense and reference might
therefore be in the offing—made possible in part by the fact that
the "sense" which the noncognitivist assigns to the moral vocabulary is expressive, and so *a fortiori* not logically reference-fixing. To
adapt a Moorean distinction: the noncognitivist is seeking the concept "Good" while the naturalistic cognitivist is seeking "good-
making features"; and the latter may stand in a metaphysical, or
nomological, or practical—without insisting upon a logical or conceptual—relation to the attitude 'good' expresses. The noncognitivist thus can say what he wants to say about the peculiar, dynamic
function of evaluative or moral vocabulary, and the naturalist can
say what she wants to say about what makes something good, or
right, and why these are "hard facts."

Those impressed by Quine's critique of analyticity or by the Wittgensteinian dictum that "meaning is use" may find this way of

TOWARD FIN DE SIECLE ETHICS

dividing things up altogether too nice. We might well agree whenever the pattern of use of 'good' or 'right' shows wide consensus on the good- or right-making features. Post-Quine and post-Wittgenstein, the distinction between the concept "Good" and "good-making features," between subject matter and doctrine, may thus be seen to be negotiable, though not in just any way one pleases. To the extent that certain good-making features are truistically so, or certain substantive constraints on dialectical uses of 'good' such that they cannot be violated by speakers without gross anomaly, these features or constraints lay claim to be part of the meaning of 'good' that competent speakers acquire.[145] Where disagreement persists, however, or even seems sensible (as reflected in the possibility of a nongratuitous open question argument), the noncognitivist can plausibly urge that there is a point in trying to capture a distinctive sense of evaluative terms that enables us to understand how the competing accounts could be expressing contending views on something held constant and in common. Presumably, the noncognitivist's claim will be strongest for those terms of most general evaluation—'good', 'right', 'rational'—although all of these appear to have some substance, and so are unlikely to be *purely* expressive. Is anything left? Just the all-important, all-inclusive, almost certainly not substantive, seemingly endlessly contentious, but plainly action-guiding phrase 'the thing to do'.

Of course, our speculation here is over-simple. Suffice it to say that the relation between a noncognitivist and a naturalistic cognitivist could stand some rethinking, perhaps more along the lines of a dynamic oligopoly than over-ambitious efforts toward static monopoly.

(2) Despite the tendency of holders of various views to brand competitors as revisionist, the term cannot be a definitive criticism since virtually every participant in contemporary metaethical debates is willing to entertain some or other degree of revisionism. Noncognitivists try to conserve certain practical aspects of ordinary moral discourse, but perhaps at the expense of semantic revision-

---

[145]Of course, we may for various purposes also find it helpful to distinguish broader versus narrower senses of a term. Compare Stevenson's distinction between "first" and "second pattern" analyses of normative language, in *Ethics and Language*, chap. 4.

DARWALL, GIBBARD, RAILTON

ism and of rejection of the claims of existence internalism.[146] Kantians also try to conserve features of the practical realm, though in a form that may not capture some of the motivational point of judgment internalism. Moreover, their account of reasons for action, though originating in an appeal to commonsense morality, may go beyond anything actually contained in common sense. As a result, they may find themselves facing an unwanted need to reject important elements of commonsense morality in order to insure the required connection to appropriate reasons for action. Naturalists may be prepared to accept some revision in the matter of practicality (at least as neo-Kantian philosophers have conceived it) in order to incur less revision in recognized moral substance. Since we can hardly single out any particular position with the charge of "revisionism of moral common sense," the real issues concern the balances that are struck between revisionism and conservatism, and what purposes a revision can or should serve.

Similarly, the distinction between revisionist accounts and error theories is itself a subtle matter, and may have to do with two little-understood questions: Would the best philosophical clarification of the nature of morality lead us to accept or reject morality so characterized? And, what metaethical relevance does such a "critical reflection" test have?

(3) Although the debate over internalism versus externalism remains central to understanding the divisions in ethical theory, there is no uncontroversial understanding of how much internalism, and what sort of internalism, commonsense or reflective morality requires. Indeed, most views embody internalism at some point, so that all-purpose attacks on "externalism" too often are set pieces. Another set piece debate contrasts corresponding internalist and externalist views with respect to how much they are prepared to leave to contingency. An externalist, for example, typically seeks a contingent or nomological connection between moral

---

[146]For the distinction between *judgment internalism* and *existence internalism*, see S. Darwall, *Impartial Reason*, 54–55. Existence internalism may have been the more important form in shaping the historical evolution of ethics from Hume (and perhaps before) to Kant and Kantianism, although elements of judgment internalism can also be found in Hume. For a related distinction, see D. Brink, *Moral Realism*, on "agent" versus "appraiser internalism" (40).

TOWARD FIN DE SIECLE ETHICS

judgment or moral obligation and motivation, while an internalist insists that the connection is necessary or conceptual. But any appearance that internalists leave less to contingency is misleading. The more conceptual pre-commitments are built into notions such as agency, morality, and reason, the more chancy it becomes whether we humans possess agency, a morality, or reasons.

(4) Now that Platonic ethical intuitionism has lost its following, the distinctions among forms of moral "realism," "constructivism," "quasi-realism," and so on can no longer be understood as turning upon commitment to (or rejection of) a domain of moral facts "independent of human capacities and interests." Moral realists, constructivists, and quasi-realists alike look to the responses and reasons of persons, rather than some self-subsistent realm, to ground moral practice. Such claims are complicated by the fact that "realism" itself bears no agreed-upon significance, that the role or nature of a theory of truth is so much in dispute in philosophy generally, and that "constructivism" as it now stands seems still to embody non-"constructed" normative notions of rationality or reasonableness. It will be some time before these issues are sorted out, and their significance, such as it might be, firmly identified.

(5) There have been, running more or less simultaneously but without notable mutual regard, at least two seemingly independent debates about the justification of morality. The first debate has focused on such matters as the nature of morality, and the objectivity (or lack of it) of the reasons it offers for action. The second debate has focused on the question, Why be moral?, taking the content of morality as given (e.g., by common sense) and requiring that any satisfactory answer show that individuals enjoy advantages for conducting themselves in accord with moral demands. Yet it has become increasingly difficult to see how these two debates might be kept apart, in some measure because the conditions under which the question, Why be moral?, is asked are often restricted or idealized—and not inappropriately, since some otherwise quite impressive ways of making morality advantageous (such as devising a reliable scheme of coercion) are thought to be beside the point. The question of what we are asking for when we seek a rational justification for morality, and what would count as an answer, remains as urgent as ever.

(6) The increasing criticism of ethical theory has itself largely been based upon a theoretical understanding of ethics, or of how

DARWALL, GIBBARD, RAILTON

ethics differs from other areas of inquiry. Often these criticisms therefore seem less to be suggesting how we might content ourselves with less by way of ethical theory, than to be suggesting how ethical theorizing might be improved, either by adding variables or complexity or (theoretically motivated and systematic) relativity at the normative level, or by altering some of our views (again, for theoretically motivated and systematic reasons) about what must be done in order to "place" ethics satisfactorily.

As contemporary metaethics moves ahead and positions gain in sophistication and complexity, victories, or even clear advantages, may become harder to achieve or consolidate. That is a kind of progress, but only if a clearer articulation of the surviving issues emerges as a result.

Finally, in the effervescent discussion of the desirability of moral theory, various camps express agreement that more careful and empirically informed work on the nature or history or function of morality is needed. Perhaps unsurprisingly, very little such work has been done even by some of those who have recommended it most firmly.[147] Too many moral philosophers and commentators on moral philosophy—we do not exempt ourselves—have been

---

[147]There are some exceptions. Empirical psychology plays an important role in Brandt's *Theory of the Good and the Right,* and others have paid significant attention to psychology and social theory in their work; see, for example, Lawrence Blum, *Friendship, Altruism, and Morality* (London: Routledge and Kegan Paul, 1980); Richard Miller, "Ways of Moral Learning"; Owen Flanagan, *Varieties of Moral Personality: Ethics and Psychological Realism* (Cambridge: Harvard University Press, 1991), and some of the essays in Owen Flanagan and Amelie Rorty, eds., *Identity, Character, and Morality: Essays in Moral Psychology* (Cambridge: The MIT Press, Bradford Books, 1990). We should not suppose, however, that there is a well-developed literature in the social sciences simply awaiting philosophical discovery and exploitation. Social psychologists, for example, can be heard to complain that, apart from certain phenomena of moral development, little empirical work has been done on moral deliberation and decision. For examples of some preliminary experiments involving "framing effects" on relatively mature judgments of prudence and fairness—experiments that might be seen as affording philosophers a caution against over-ready reliance on moral intuitions—see A. Tversky and D. Kahneman, "Rational Choice and the Framing of Decisions," and D. Kahneman, J. L. Knetsch, and R. H. Thaler, "Fairness and the Assumptions of Economics," both in *The Journal of Business* 59 (1986): 251–78 and 285–300, respectively. Issues about the role of personality, emotions, identity, and self-concept in deliberation have also begun to receive increasing attention.

TOWARD FIN DE SIECLE ETHICS

content to invent their psychology or anthropology from scratch and do their history on the strength of selective reading of texts rather than more comprehensive research into contexts. Change is underway in this regard, especially, perhaps, in the emergence of less ahistorical approaches to the history of philosophy. But any real revolution in ethics stemming from the infusion of a more empirically informed understanding of psychology, anthropology, or history must hurry if it is to arrive in time to be part of *fin de siècle* ethics.

University of Michigan, Ann Arbor

Name Index